D0216115

THE LIVING LANDSCAPE

THE LIVING LANDSCAPE

AN ECOLOGICAL APPROACH TO LANDSCAPE PLANNING

Frederick Steiner
Arizona State University

SECOND EDITION

McGraw-Hill, Inc.
New York St. Louis San Francisco Auckland Bogotá
Caracas Lisbon London Madrid Mexico City Milan
Montreal New Delhi San Juan Singapore
Sydney Tokyo Toronto

Library of Congress Cataloging-in-Publication Data
Steiner, Frederick R.
The living landscape: an ecological approach to landscape planning / Frederick Steiner.—2nd ed.
p. cm.
Includes bibliographical references.
ISBN 0-07-079398-0
1. Land use—Planning. 2. Land use—Environmental aspects. 3. Landscape architecture. 4. Landscape protection. I. Title.

HD108.6.S74 1999
333.73'17—dc21

99-049557

McGraw-Hill

A Division of The ***McGraw·Hill*** *Companies*

1 2 3 4 5 6 7 8 9 0 DOC/DOC 9 0 5 4 3 2 1 0

ISBN 0-07-079398-0

The sponsoring editor for this book was Wendy Lochner and the production supervisor was Sherri Souffrance. It was set in Optima by North Market Street Graphics.

Printed and bound by R. R. Donnelley & Sons Company.

 This book was printed on acid-free paper.

All photographs by author unless otherwise indicated.

To Anna

CONTENTS

PREFACE TO THE SECOND EDITION

My biggest surprise in connection with the first edition of *The Living Landscape* was its translation into Italian by Maria Cristina Treu and Danilo Palazzo (1994, *Costruire il Paesaggio: Un Approccio Ecologico alla Pianificazione del Territorio*). I had written the book primarily for an American audience. I hoped that it would find Canadian readers too (while acknowledging that many fundamental differences exist between the planning structures of Canada and the United States). Since I had lived in The Netherlands, I thought that some European planners and academics would also find it useful. I have indeed been heartened and enthused by the book's warm reception in Canada, Europe, and Asia.

However, the translation into Italian was especially gratifying. An ecological approach for planning land uses and landscapes is receiving considerable attention in Europe. For example, in 1990 Italian provinces were given the power to design land-use plans. Provinces in Italy are somewhat similar to counties in the United States. A region is roughly analogous in its jurisdictional scope to an American state or a Canadian province. In scale, regions are similar in size to New England states. Italy is divided into 20 regions. Each region, in turn, is comprised of provinces and municipalities. For example, the region of Lombardia has 11 provinces and 1,546 municipalities.

Because of the 1990 Italian law, provinces must prepare land-use plans and, in cooperation with the regions, approve urban plans for municipalities. This law also encourages public participation in the planning process. Another stimulus to the interest in ecological planning by Italians is a 1985 requirement by the European Union that member countries undertake environmental impact assessments. Italy accepted this European Union directive and created its Ministero dell'Ambiente in 1986. Italian law requires environmental impact studies to assess the consequences of government actions.

These Italian initiatives in land use and environmental review are symptomatic of larger trends in Europe, North America, and elsewhere. Globally, there is growing concern about the quality of new urbanization and the loss of environmental values. Increasing populations and expanding settlements have imposed negative consequences on the quality of soils, water, air, and views. Noise pollution has increased, while plant and animal communities have been destroyed.

Advocacy of sustainable development has been one response. The sustainability concept first received widespread public attention as a result of the Brundtland Commission of the United Nations in 1987, headed by Gro Harlem Brundtland, subsequently prime minister of Norway. Even greater prominence was given by the United Nations 1992 Rio Conference on Environment and Development, also known as the Earth Summit. *Sustainability* means maintaining the health and productivity of ecosystems, which provide a variety of benefits over time. *Sustainable development* is that which meets the needs of the present without compromising the ability of future generations to meet their own needs.

We must go beyond sustainability, beyond the maintenance of existing systems. In facing the growing urgency of environmental issues confronting human societies, we must do more than sustain the Earth; we must heal, enhance, and manage the life-sustaining processes of the planet and ensure the integrity and strength of the global environment that connects them. As noted by the American Society of Landscape Architects in their Declaration on Environment and Development, we must "generate design, planning, [and] management strategies and policies from the basis of the cultural context and the ecosystem to which each landscape belongs at the local, regional, and global scale," and, furthermore, we should "actively engage in shaping decisions, attitudes, and values that support human health, environmental protection, and sustainable development."

This regenerative view, as the late John Lyle has called it, is analogous to the philosophies of many Native Americans. The Iroquois, for example, believe that land-use decisions should be guided by their impact on the seventh generation. Thus, a 200-year time frame for planning is established. Such a long view requires an understanding of the ecologies of regions and landscapes.

The first edition of *The Living Landscape* was written mostly while I was on the faculty at Washington State University, and it was completed while at the University of Colorado-Denver. It grew out of teaching landscape planning studios to senior-level landscape architecture and graduate students in planning and environmental science. As a result, many examples in the first edition were from the Pacific Northwest and Colorado.

Since 1989, I have served on the Arizona State University (ASU) faculty as department chair and director of the School of Planning and Landscape Architecture, where I have continued to teach planning studios as well as a course in environmental impact assessment, initiated at Colorado. My work has taken me on an invertent cross-section across the American West, with declining precipitation and increasing population growth rates, in the process. This edition adds my Arizona experience. I have retained examples from the Pacific Northwest and Colorado. As in the first edition, examples from other regions in North America, plus a few from Europe, are also included.

Throughout this edition, I have updated information and expanded sections. For example, I have expanded discussions about regional-level landscape inventories and the takings/givings issue. Scant information about geographic information systems (GIS) was included in the first edition; this edition includes many GIS examples. Two additional techniques for citizen participation, policy Delphi and focus groups, are introduced, while charrettes receive more attention. Other new or expanded topics include urban morphology, remote sensing, design guidelines, floodplain management, wetland and riparian area protection, habitat conservation plans, and historic preservation.

Our knowledge about our environments continues to expand. We have ever-increasing tools for accessing and analyzing information about the environment. Our challenge, then, is not so much in ensuring the availability of sufficient information, but rather in having the will to understand what is available in order to wisely direct our future. The Earth is indeed a "most glorious instrument," as Henry David Thoreau observed. We must be an audience to its strains.

Frederick Steiner
Tempe, Arizona 1999

PREFACE TO THE FIRST EDITION

Two fundamental reasons to plan are to influence equitable sharing among people and to ensure the viability of the future. Because we cannot function by ourselves, each of us is required to share time and space. Sharing is necessary for the well-being of our neighbors and of future generations. This book is about a specific kind of planning; it is about how to share physical space in communities.

The rather abstract notion of human spatial organization manifests itself in the use of land. But the term *land* use oversimplifies the organization of human communities. *Landscape* I find to be a better word. Working with landscapes, planners can begin to understand the connectivity of settlement patterns and functions over time and space. The lines between urban and rural as well as between natural and cultural have become blurred, if indeed such lines were ever clear. With the intermixing of the distinctions between urban/rural and natural/cultural, understanding landscapes from a spatial, functional, and dynamic perspective becomes a key to balancing conflicting uses of land, water, and air.

The landscapes of this planet need help. Conflicts over the use of land and about environmental and social degradation abound. Complex and often seemingly contradictory questions must be addressed: Where should new communities be located? How do new community developers accommodate housing that is affordable? Can new communities be designed that are safe, healthy, and beautiful? How can existing communities be revitalized and restored? Where can new development and open space be located in the existing built-up areas of metropolitan regions? Can we dispose of our hazardous and solid waste in a responsible manner? What about the alternatives of recycling our waste or simply using fewer hazardous products? How do we protect prime agricultural areas in urbanizing regions?

Agriculture and urban uses often conflict, as do many old and new uses—retirement communities and mining, tourism and timber harvesting. Must such old and new uses always conflict? People often move to suburban and rural areas for open space and recreational amenities. In addition to causing problems for existing inhabitants, the new land uses created by the new residents often disrupt wildlife habitats and other environmentally sensitive areas. How do we plan open space that will allow both recreational uses and wildlife habitat? Sometimes new land uses are sited in areas that are susceptible to natural hazards. Can we use our growing knowledge about earthquakes, forest fires, hurricanes, and flooding to direct human uses to the safest locations?

In seeking to address these questions, it is tempting to adopt a global perspective. Certainly many issues that prompt these questions exist internationally. But, because the legal, political, economic, and cultural forces vary widely from nation to nation, I have chosen to focus on planning in the United States. The citizens of the United States share a common boundary and cultural heritage with Canadians. Canada made many advances in environmental planning during the 1980s, when the national leadership in the United States retreated from environmental concerns. Because I have been influenced by Canadian policy and because several Canadian colleagues have read and reviewed portions of this book in its manuscript form, I hope that some Canadians may find it useful for their work. I also hope that my international work filters through the pages that follow. The focus, however, is on the United States.

Americans seem to have an especially difficult time sharing when it comes to the land. We have set aside spectacular natural landscapes, but we despoil other beautiful places with garish signage, trash, and just plain ugly buildings. We Americans produce garbage at an unequaled pace, yet resist the location of waste dumps in our neighborhoods. We seek to live in the countryside but, once we settle in a rural area, try to prevent farmers from continuing their normal, sometimes dirty and smelly, activities. We do not want the government to tell us what to do with our land, but we seek help from the government in times of natural disaster. We want our neighborhoods to be squeaky clean but turn our backs to poor people who live in substandard housing, or in trailers, or on the street.

To more fairly share the bounty of natural resources in the United States, we must ask: Who suffers and who benefits from our decisions? In making and adopting public policy, we must analyze who benefits and who pays for the decisions that elected leaders make. This book presents a framework for presenting information to decision makers. The preparation of the book grew out of my need to explain the planning process to my students. Most of these students have pursued degrees in planning, landscape architecture, and environmental science, but they and I have been enriched by others from geography, architecture, soil science, forestry, civil engineering, business, and sociology. Although written by a teacher, the book is based on my experience as a practitioner and researcher. Through my practical experience and research, I have sought to plan for places that are fit, adaptable, and delightful.

Planning is more than a tool or a technique; it is a philosophy for organizing actions that enable people to predict and visualize the future of any land area. Moreover, planning gives people the ability to link actions on specific parcels of land to larger regional systems. It is up to us to plan with vision. Our responsibility is to retain what we treasure, because we are merely guests on those spaces of the Earth that we inhabit. We should leave good impressions about our visit.

Frederick Steiner
Tempe, Arizona, 1990

ACKNOWLEDGMENTS

There are several colleagues at Washington State University (WSU), the University of Colorado at Denver, and Arizona State University (ASU), who have supported my work and have offered helpful advice and criticism. Those most helpful in the completion of the first edition were Bill Budd, Hamid Shirvani, Paul Rasmussen, Jack Kartez, Mack Roberts, Tom Bartuska, Don Satterlund, Yuk Lee, Lois Brink, Lauri Johnson, Peter Schaeffer, and Ken Struckmeyer. I owe much to my former students in landscape architecture, regional planning, and environmental science at WSU and Colorado. Donna (Hall) Erickson, George Newman, Doug Osterman, and John Theilacker stand out as four to whom I owe the greatest debts for the first edition.

I studied planning at the University of Pennsylvania and was influenced by several of Penn's fine planning and design faculty, especially Ann Strong, John Keene, Jon Berger, Dan Rose, Art Johnson, and Robert Coughlin. Ian McHarg is a wonderful mentor and an enduring inspiration. Lenore Sagan is a constant, steady influence within the Penn community, and I value her sage, maternal guidance through the ivy walks and city streets of Philadelphia.

Several Dutch friends have influenced my thinking about landscape planning, especially Ingrid Duchhart, Hubert van Lier, Meto Vroom, and the late Nico de Jonge of the Dutch Agricultural University, Wageningen. They know much about green fields below dark skies and hope in new worlds.

I benefited greatly from the helpful criticisms by Elizabeth Watson and Sam Stokes on a draft of the manuscript for the first edition. Others who have contributed to my ideas in one way or another include: Mark Lapping, Lloyd Wright, Max Schnepf, Ron Eber, Chuck Little, Bill Toner, Lee Nellis, Warren Zitzmann, Cecily Corcoran Kihn, J. Glenn Eugster, Jean Tarlet, Christine Carlson, Dennis Canty, Larry Larsen, Kip Petersen, and Terri Morrell.

Typing of the manuscript for the first edition was done by various people including Brenda Stevens, Angela Briggs, Gail Rise, Telisa Swan, Nita Thomas, Jane Bower, Doris Birch, and Penn Clerical Services of Philadelphia. The final version of the first edition was typed by Pam Erickson and Kathy Saykally of the School of Architecture and Planning, University of Colorado at Denver. I thank them for preparing that manuscript in its final form.

The first-edition illustrations were completed by a number of people including Lonnie Kennedy, Mark Woods, Gary McMath, Brandon Burch, Clint Keller, Christine Carlson, Doug Osterman, Louis Burwell, Chuck Watson, Brad Nelson, Richard Van De Mark, Brad Pugh, Gary Christensen, Elizabeth Slocum, Joseph Bell, and Gretchen Schalge. I appreciate their diligence and hard work. I also thank the many others who allowed me to use their illustrations and photographs and to quote from their work. Robert Yaro and Chris Reid, then with the Center for Rural Massachusetts; Martin Bierbaum and Michael Neuman, then with the New Jersey Office of State Planning; George Bowechop of the Makah Tribal Council as well as the council's planning consultant, Chuck Warsinske; Annemarie and Hans Bleiker of the Institute for Participatory Management and Planning in Monterey, California; the New Jersey Pinelands Commission; and the late Narendra Juneja were especially generous. Philip Maechling's photographs help portray the essence of the living landscape and made an invaluable contribution to the first edition for which I am grateful.

I would also like to thank the following reviewers for their many helpful comments and suggestions on the manuscript that led to the first edition: Nicholas Dines, University of Massachusetts; Patrick Mooney, The University of British Columbia; and William Shepherd, Virginia Polytechnic Institute and State University.

Four friends have had a substantial influence on the original edition, each in their distinct way, and have made an enduring contribution to this version as well. They are Joanne Barnes Jackson, Jerry Young, Ken Brooks, and Bill Wagner. I am grateful to each of them in many ways. In addition, I am indebted through their published works to the pioneers in ecological planning—Patrick Geddes, Aldo Leopold, Lewis Mumford, Benton MacKaye, Artur Glikson, and G. Angus Hills.

I incurred many debts in writing the original version. I have accumulated many more in the process of revision. Carl Steinitz and the U.S. Environmental Protection Agency were generous in providing permission for the Camp Pendleton study. Professor Steinitz's comments, suggestions, and criticisms were especially insightful. He and Allan Shearer of Harvard University were helpful with the Camp Pendleton maps and illustrations. Kurt Bauer offered excellent recommendations—and a wealth of historical knowledge—about planning in southwestern Wisconsin. The following individuals provided valuable assistance to update information about specific examples (including a few that were edited out because of space limitations): Ron Eber, Rob Ribe, and Ethan Seltzer (Oregon and Portland); Chuck Warsinske (the Makah Reservation); Peter Pollock (Boulder, Colorado); Kip Petersen (Teller County, Colorado); George Newman (Snohomish County, Washington); Ron Shaffer (University of Wisconsin-Extension); Bill Hendrix (Palouse Path); Judith Karinen (West Colfax Avenue, Colorado); and Willie Flucas (Dayton, Ohio).

My ASU students have contributed much, as did their predecessors at my previous universities. Former ASU students who were especially influential for this edition include Jim McCarthy, Michael Collins, Kate Goodrich, Scott Davis, Ross Cromarty, Kim Shetter, Donna Issac, Michael Rushman, Bill Kasson, John Blair, Jeff Schmidt, Susan Jackson, Ginny Coltman, Elisa Corcuera, Joaquin Maruffo, Allyce Hargrove, Scott Pieart, Bill Whitmore, John Leach, and Carlos Licón. Zitao Fang helped compile data for several tables in Chapter 4. Lizi McGeorge, a visiting student from Australia, helped organize the North Sonoran charrette and provided much useful information about charrettes.

At ASU, I am fortunate to be in an interdisciplinary School of Planning and Landscape Architecture in a multidisciplinary College of Architecture and Environmental Design. I benefit greatly working with colleagues from planning, landscape architecture, and environmental resources within the School of Planning and Landscape Architecture.

In particular, I appreciate the ideas of Professor Laurel McSherry with whom I cotaught an environmental planning studio. It is not easy to teach with the school director, because there are many interruptions and distractions. Laurel's good humor made teaching the studio a joy. She also influenced how I view and represent landscapes. David Pijawka was a valued mentor on the subject of sustainability and I enjoy our work together. He is a most generous and valued colleague. I collaborated with several ASU colleagues on a series of studies in northern Phoenix, notably Joe Ewan and Rebecca Fish Ewan. They were generous in providing maps of their wash studies and preserve plans. I especially appreciate the contributions of Jim Burke, Ward Brady, William Miller, Jana Fry, Michael Collins, Nancy Osborne, and Jack Gilcrest to the geographic information systems maps of north Phoenix included in this book. Excellent comments were provided on drafts of this edition by Ramon Arrowsmith, Tony Brazel, John Brock, James Burke, Theresa Cameron, Ash Campbell, Jeffrey Cook, Katherine Crewe, Ron Faas, Joseph Ewan, Rebecca Fish Ewan, Grady Gammage, Douglas Green, Subhro Guhathakurta, John Keane, Mary Kihl, Hubert van Lier, Lynn Miller, Lee Nellis, Jolene Ostler, Ray Quay, Michael Rushman, Max Underwood, and Bob Yaro. Mookesh Patel of the ASU School of Design helped significantly with the consistency of the illustrations. Others who have made contributions in various ways include Dick Eribes, Julie McQuary, Gerald McSheffrey, Alvin Mushkatel, Nan Ellin, Richard Lai, Ignacio San Martin, Ted Cook, Gary Whysong, and Ruth Yabes.

A group of us at ASU joined with colleagues from the city of Phoenix, the State of Arizona, and several firms to form the North Sonoran Collaborative. Since 1994, our informal, interdisciplinary collaborative has produced studies and plans and organized charrettes for the northern Phoenix area. The concept for the collaborative was Ray Quay's, the assistant planning director. Other city leaders of the group include Jim Burke, Jolene Ostler, and Dean Brennan. Urban wildlife specialist Joe Yarkin provided leadership among the state agencies.

I particularly value the mentorship of Dean John Meunier. He provided unwavering encouragement for the multidisciplinary environmental planning mission of our school. I am also grateful to Dean Meunier for his support, as well as that of my colleagues and of Arizona State University, for a sabbatical leave. I spent much of the sabbatical in Rome engaged in preparing this second edition as well as other writing projects. In this regard, I thank the American Academy in Rome and the National Endowment for the Arts. I was fortunate to receive the National Endowment for the Arts Rome Prize Fellowship in Historic Preservation and Conservation which enabled me to be in Italy during my sabbatical. Italy provided an ideal setting for writing this edition. The translators of the Italian edition asked especially probing, thoughtful questions, which influenced my approach to rewriting the book. I am inspired by Maria Cristina Treu's ecological plans for Italian provinces and Danilo Palazzo's comprehensive review of American environmental planning. Ornella Piscopo of the University of Rome was a valued source of knowledge on the carrying capacity concept and its possible implications for planning.

Many individuals provided advice and suggestions on the original edition, which were incorporated into this version. In particular, Donna Erickson, Joan Woodward, and Forster Ndubisi have influenced the ways I approach planning and have made numerous suggestions about how to improve this book. I welcome the reader's criticisms on this edition, because I see it as a living document.

Since 1993, I have been most fortunate to work with Chris Duplissa: a writer could wish for no better word processor. Not only does she not make typing errors, Chris adds a critical understanding to the projects she undertakes, contributing much to the quality in the process. Other staff keep the ASU School of Planning and Landscape Architecture functioning well, for which I am thankful, especially Dena Marson, Stefani Angstadt-Leto, and Sasha Valdez.

I appreciate the support of many McGraw-Hill staff in undertaking this edition, especially Wendy Lochner and Robin Gardner. B. J. Clark and Jean Akers of McGraw-Hill were responsible for the first edition and their contributions were numerous.

My deepest gratitude is for my family. Anna, Halina, and Andrew provide the love and support that makes this work possible.

THE LIVING LANDSCAPE

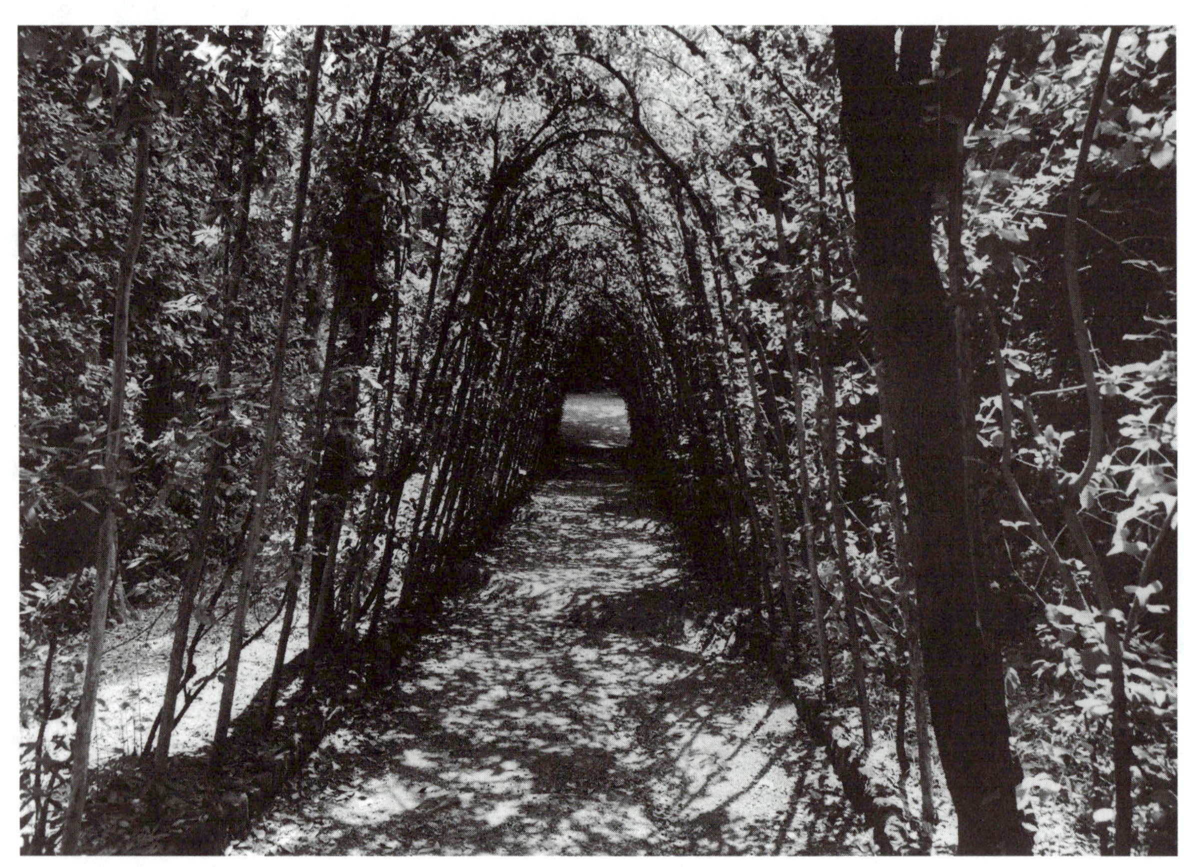

1

INTRODUCTION

Conventionally the planning process is presented as a linear progression of activities. Decision making, like other human behavior, seldom occurs in such a linear, rational manner. Still, it is a logical sequence of activities and presents a convenient organizational framework. The common steps in the process include the identification of problems and opportunities; the establishment of goals; inventory and analysis of the biophysical environment, ideally at several scales; human community inventory and analysis; detailed studies like suitability analysis; the development of concepts and the selection of options; the adoption of a plan; community involvement and education; detailed design; plan implementation; and plan administration. This book is organized around these conventional topics—but with an ecological perspective. The chapters that follow cover most of the steps in the process.

Each chapter includes a "how-to" section for accomplishing the pertinent step, and a few examples where such activities have been successfully undertaken. For many of the chapters, various planning efforts undertaken in northern Phoenix, Arizona, are used to illustrate each step. The author has been involved in the Phoenix planning work for the past decade. Because this work is largely on the suburban fringe, and because ecological planning is also useful for more urban and rural areas, several additional prototypical efforts have been selected to illustrate the principles described and to compare them with the more conventional approaches to planning.

Before discussing each step, it will be helpful to first define a few key terms. It will then be necessary to provide a brief overview of traditional planning in the United States. The ecological planning method, the subject of this book, can then be described and the difference of its approach better understood.

BASIC CONCEPTS

Planning has been defined as the use of scientific, technical, and other organized knowledge to provide options for decision making as well as a process for considering and reaching consensus on a range of choices. As John Friedmann (1973) has succinctly put it, planning links knowledge to action. There is a difference between project planning and comprehensive planning. *Project planning* involves designing a specific object such as a dam, highway, harbor, or an individual building or group of buildings. *Comprehensive planning* involves a broad range of choices relating to all the functions of an area. Resolution of conflicts, often through compromises, is the inherent purpose of comprehensive planning. *Environment* refers to our surroundings. *Environmental planning* is "the initiation and operation of activities to manage the acquisition, transformation, distribution, and disposal of resources in a manner capable of sustaining human activities, with a minimum distribution of physical, ecological, and social processes" (Soesilo and Pijawka 1998, 2072).

Management has been defined as the judicious use of means to accomplish a desired end. It involves working with people to accomplish organizational goals. For practical purposes, many see the distinction between planning and management as largely semantic. The management of resources, such as land, may be a goal of a planning process. Conversely, planning may be a means of management. *Ecosystem management* is the deliberate process of understanding and structuring an entire region with the intention of maintaining sustainability and integrity (Slocome 1998a, 1998b).

Land use is a self-defining term. One can debate whether a harbor involves land use or water use, but "land" generally refers to all parts of the surface of the earth, wet and dry. The same area of that surface may be used for a variety of human activities. A harbor, for instance, may have commercial, industrial, and recreational purposes. A farm field may be used for speculation and recreation as well as for agriculture. All human activity is in one way or another connected with land.

Landscape is related to land use. The composite features of one part of the surface of the earth that distinguish it from another area is a *landscape.* It is, then, a combination of elements—fields, buildings, hills, forests, deserts, water bodies, and settlements. The landscape encompasses the uses of land—housing, transportation, agriculture, recreation, and natural areas—and is a composite of those uses. A landscape is more than a picturesque view; it is the sum of the parts that can be seen, the layers and intersections of time and culture that comprise a place—a natural *and* cultural palimpsest.

The English word *ecology* is derived from the Greek word for house, *oikos.* The expanded definition is the study of the reciprocal relationships of all living things to each other and to their biotic and physical environments (Ricklefs 1973). Obviously, humans are living things and thus are engaged in ecological relationships.

The use of ecological information for planning has been a national policy since late 1969, when the U.S. Congress, through the National Environmental Policy Act (NEPA), required all agencies of the federal government to "initiate and utilize ecological information in the planning and development of resource oriented projects." The act, signed into law by President Richard Nixon on January 1, 1970, is a relatively recent development in American planning. In spite of NEPA and other laws, ecological information has not yet been adequately integrated into the planning process. Although much more work will still be necessary to realize an ecological approach to planning, NEPA represents an important step. To begin to understand its importance, it is useful to quickly review the status of American planning.

THE TRADITIONAL FRAMEWORK OF PLANNING IN THE UNITED STATES

The function of land-use planning in the United States has been the subject of much debate. There are diverse opinions about the purpose of planning; that is, whether it is to achieve a specific physical project, or comprehensive social, economic, or environmental goals. The traditional role of planning in the United States is responsible for many of these divisions. In England, for instance, planning is undertaken as a result of strong statutes. Statutory planning gives English planners considerable authority in the decision-making process. In contrast, American planners generally have more limited statutory power than in England and other European nations.

There are several reasons for the differences between European and American planning. First, land is recognized as a scarce commodity in Europe and in many other parts of the world. In land-hungry Europe over the last century, public officials have been granted increasing planning powers over use of land (and other resources) through the governing process. In Europe, there is much concern about the quality of the environment, both in the older democracies of the European Union and the emerging democracies of Central and Eastern Europe. This concern has resulted in complex systems of planning that

Landscape is the sum of the parts that can be seen with the eye. *(David C. Flaherty, Washington State University College of Engineering and Architecture)*

address a broad range of issues, including housing, recreation, aesthetics, open space, and transportation.

Another reason emerges from the origins of the United States. Thomas Jefferson and the other founding fathers were influenced strongly by John Locke, who viewed the chief end of establishing a government as the preservation of property. Locke, in his *Two Treatises of Government,* defined property as "lives, liberties, and estates" (Laslett 1988). Elsewhere, Locke wrote of the "pursuit of happiness." It was Jefferson who combined Locke's terms, "life, liberty, and the pursuit of happiness." But it has been the view of property as possession, rather than Locke's predominant version—life, liberty, and estate—that has prevailed. The constitution of the Commonwealth of Pennsylvania states in Article 1, Section 1, that "all . . . men have certain inherent and indefeasible rights, among which are those of enjoying and defending life and liberty, of acquiring, possessing and protecting property." And the Fifth Amendment of the U.S. Constitution contains this clause: "No person shall . . . be deprived of life, liberty, or property, without due process of law; nor shall private property be taken for public use without just compensation." To those in the new republic, who had fought against the landed elite of the mother country, property rights were seen as a fundamental freedom.

The Bill of Rights institutionalized the founding fathers' concern about private property rights. Their "Bill of Rights included no fewer than four separate provisions aimed specifically at protecting private interests in property," observes John Humbach (1989, 337). However, Humbach also notes that "private property exists to serve the public good" (1989, 345). The influential British utilitarian philosopher Jeremy Bentham declared that "before laws were made, there was no property; take away laws and property ceases" (1887, 113). As a result, according to Humbach (and other legal scholars), "Property rights are a creation of laws, and the law of property must, like all other law, serve a public purpose" (1989, 345).

The initial public purpose for the new nation was the settlement, or the resettlement by mostly European immigrants, of the American subcontinent (Opie 1998). However, when Jefferson (who had written the Declaration of Independence) and the others who authored the Constitution rode to Philadelphia on horseback or in carriages from their Virginia estates, their Pennsylvania farms, or their New England towns, they traveled through a seemingly endless expanse of woodlands, rich farmlands, and rolling pastures graced by fresh, clear creeks and rivers, abundant game, and pristine coastlines. In Philadelphia they were concerned foremost with protecting human rights and freedoms. Even the most foresighted of the framers of the Constitution could not have envisioned the environmental and social crises that subsequently accompanied the industrialization and urbanization of America.

The U.S. Constitution, however, does give the states and their political subdivisions the power of regulation. Police powers, which provide the basis for state and local regulation, were derived by the states from the Tenth Amendment, which reads: "The powers not delegated to the United States by the Constitution, nor prohibited by it to the States, are reserved to the States respectively, or to the people."

The states, in the use of police powers, must consider the Fifth Amendment because the U.S. Supreme Court has held that the "taking clause" is embodied in the due process clause of the Fourteenth Amendment and hence applies to the states. In addition, state constitutions contain taking clauses, some with rather interesting twists. For instance, Article 1, Section 16 (the Ninth Amendment) of the Washington State Constitution states: "No private property shall be taken *or damaged* for public *or private use* without just compensation having first been made" [emphasis added]. A person's private use of property cannot damage the property of another person in Washington State.

Given this constitutional backdrop, the federal and several state legislatures have slowly but steadily increased statutory authority for planning. In addition, the courts have consistently upheld land-use regulations that do not go "too far" and thus constitute a taking. In addition, courts have supported some restrictions on the use of environmentally sensitive areas, such as wetlands, floodplains, and the habitats of endangered species. However, planning remains a fragmented effort in the United States, undertaken primarily by powerful vested business interests and sometimes by consent. Planning by consent, which depends largely on an individual's persuasive power, has caused several adaptations on the part of American planners. These adaptations can be broken down into two broad categories: *administrative* and *adversary.*

Administrative planners are realists who respond directly to governmental programs either as bureaucrats in a city or regional planning agency or as consultants. Successful administrative planners build political power in the city or metropolitan region where they work. They administer programs for voluntary community organizations and health, education, and welfare associations designed to support the political-economic structure of the nation-state. They may also administer transportation or utility programs deemed necessary by the same structure. By building political power, administrative planners serve the power structure of the city or region. The result is that often the unempowered groups in an area suffer. Poor people suffer the most, bearing the brunt of the social costs, when planners and others administer the programs of the status quo.

Adversary planners are idealists and respond to issues, such as those resulting from social or environmental concerns, often as advocates for a certain position. They usually work outside the power structure, forming new coalitions among the previously unorganized in order to mobilize support for their cause. Often advocacy planners work for veto groups—ad hoc organizations opposed to a controversial project or proposal such as a highway, a high-density housing complex, a factory, or a landfill. Advocacy planners also work for nongovernmental organizations (NGOs), neighborhood planning committees, and community associations.

The rights of people have a deep-seated heritage in American history, from the Declaration of Independence, the Constitution, and the Bill of Rights through the Thirteenth and Nineteenth Amendments and to the labor, civil rights, and women's movements. Human rights have been the important issue for one group of advocacy planners called by various terms including *community organizers, adversary planners,* and *change agents.* In *Reveille for Radicals,* Saul Alinsky (1946) best articulated the philosophy for the latest crest of this movement, which began to ebb when Richard Nixon cut off funding for a variety of programs created during the 1960s. Many of the social programs created during the 1960s were concerned with making basic changes in the urban power structure. The programs were a result of the civil rights movement and the attention brought to the poor living conditions in urban ghettos by the riots that occurred there. The withdrawal of the federal commitment to domestic human rights programs begun by President Nixon continued through most of the 1970s, except during the presidency of Jimmy Carter. During the Ronald Reagan administration, the social programs that had been created during the 1960s were almost completely dismantled. The emphasis on "privatization" and "state and local control" for addressing social issues continued during the 1990s in the United States, as well as in some European nations.

With the passage of the NEPA, the Congress of the United States put into motion the machinery for the protection of the environment by setting forth certain general aims of federal activity in the environmental field, establishing the Council on Environmental Quality (CEQ), and instructing all federal agencies to include an impact statement as part of future reports or recommendations on actions significantly affecting the quality of the human environment. Subsequent regional, state, and federal actions—such as state environmental policy acts, land-use legislation, and the Coastal Zone Management Act (CZMA)—have furthered this commitment.

As with the heritage for human rights, these environmental measures are deeply rooted in the American tradition. Laced throughout the social criticism of Henry David Thoreau, the novels of Mark Twain, the poetry of Walt Whitman, the photography of Ansel Adams, the films of John Ford, the art of Georgia O'Keeffe, and the music of Woody Guthrie is the love for nature.

Even before the recent governmental action, both administrative and adversary planners had been concerned with degradation of the environment. In the nineteenth century, the young Frederick Law Olmsted traveled to England where he witnessed the efforts of reformers to use techniques of the English landscape garden tradition to relieve the pressures of urban blight brought on by the industrial revolution. The resulting public parks were viewed as natural refuges from the evils of the surrounding industrial city. Public parks in English cities were pastoral retreats and escapes from urban congestion and pollution. Olmsted and American reformers adopted the idea. Their first creation was Central Park in New York City, planned and built between 1857 and 1861. Eventually, these efforts led to the City Beautiful Movement, after the World's Columbian Exposition of 1893 in Chicago. The City Beautiful Movement resulted in numerous parks and public facilities being built in the early twentieth century.

During the late nineteenth and early twentieth centuries a great national parks system took form and blossomed under the leadership of President Theodore Roosevelt. Also in the late nineteenth century, the use of river drainage basins or watersheds as the basic geographical unit for planning was initiated. The humanist engineer Arthur Morgan, an advocate of the watershed conservancy idea, helped organize the Miami Conservancy District in and around Dayton, Ohio, and later directed the Tennessee Valley Authority. During the New Deal, greenbelt new towns—new satellite communities surrounded by parks and accessible to cities by automobile—were created by economist Rexford Tugwell and other leaders. Urban parks, national parks, watershed conservancies, greenbelt new towns—each was a response designed to maintain some portion of the natural environment during periods of increased human settlement.

Ian McHarg (1969) is Saul Alinsky's environmentalist counterpart and the author of a manifesto for ecological planning similar to the one Alinsky wrote for community advocacy. Although social activism and environmentalism are separate (and sometimes conflicting) American traditions, they share common problems. Environmental programs were as vulnerable in the 1980s as social programs were a decade earlier. Ronald Reagan chose not to enforce many environmental laws enacted during the 1970s. He appointed people to key positions in environmental and natural resource management agencies who were opposed to the conservation missions of those agencies. Legally established environmental goals will not be achieved unless governmental enforcement is supported by the public. In spite of actions of the Reagan administration, the American public has generally continued to favor the protection of water, air, and land resources. In addition, President Reagan's successor, George Bush, declared himself an environmentalist, and when presenting Ian McHarg with the National Medal of Art in 1992, he stated "It is my hope that the art of the twenty-first century will be devoted to restoring the earth" (McHarg 1997a, 331). Furthermore, Vice President Al Gore is an avowed environmentalist (see Gore 1992). The Clinton-Gore administration established the influential President's Council on Sustainable Development (1996) and generally emphasized more environmentally sensitive policies for the federal government. However, even the Clinton-Gore approach has not been as "green" as those taken by many other nations.

Neither administrative nor advocacy planners have been totally effective. While administrative planners may be able to get things done, unempowered groups often suffer. While advocacy planners may win important civil rights struggles or stop flagrant abuse of the natural environment, overall problems persist and people remain poor—frequently poorer—and environmental degradation continues, too often at a more rapid rate.

A NEW APPROACH

There is a need for a common language, a common method among all those concerned about social equity and ecological parity. This method must be able to transcend disciplinary territorialism and be applicable to all levels of government. And it is imperative that this approach incorporate both social and environmental concerns. As the poet Wendell Berry has observed, "The mentality that destroys a watershed and then panics at the threat of flood is the same mentality that gives institutionalized insult to black people [and] then panics at the prospect of race riots" (1972, 73).

What is needed is an approach that can assist planners in analyzing the problems of a region as they relate to each other, to the landscape, and to the national and local political economic structure. This might be called an *applied human ecology,* or simply *ecological planning.* Each problem is linked to the community in one or more specific ways. Banking is related to real estate which is related to development pressure which is related to schools which is related to a rising tax base which is related to retirees organizing against increasing property taxes. This approach identifies how people are affected by these chain reactions and presents options for the future based on those impacts.

University of Wisconsin wildlife biologist Aldo Leopold was perhaps the first person to advocate an "ecological ethic" for planning, doing so in the 1930s (1933, 1949). He was subsequently joined by such individuals as Lewis Mumford (1944, 1961) and Benton MacKaye (1940). Mumford and MacKaye were strongly influenced by the Scottish biologist and town planner Patrick Geddes and the English garden city advocate Ebenezer Howard. Others who have proposed or developed ecological approaches for planning include the Canadian forester G. Angus Hills (1961); the Israeli architect and town planner Artur Glikson (1971); the American landscape architects Philip Lewis (1969), Ian McHarg (1969, 1996, with Steiner 1998), Anne Spirn (1984), Rob Thayer (1994), and John Lyle (1994); the Canadian landscape architect Michael Hough (1995); the American planners Jon Berger (with Sinton 1985), Randall Arendt (1996), and Tim Beatley (with Manning 1997); the French geographer and planner Jean Tarlet (1985, 1997); the Italian planners Enzo Scandurra and Silvia Macchi (1995); and the American architects Sim Van der Ryn (with Cowan 1996) and Peter Calthorpe (1993). Daniel Smith and Paul Helmund (1993) present a wonderful guide for applying ecology to the planning of greenways, while the Italian planner Danilo Palazzo (1997) provides a comprehensive overview of the development of ecological planning in the United States.

ECOLOGICAL PLANNING METHOD

What is meant by *ecological planning? Planning* is a process that uses scientific and technical information for considering and reaching consensus on a range of choices. *Ecology* is the study of the relationship of all living things, including people, to their biological and physical environments. *Ecological planning* then may be defined as the use of biophysical and sociocultural information to suggest opportunities and constraints for decision making about the use of the landscape. Or, as defined by Ian McHarg, it is the approach "whereby a region is understood as a biophysical and social process comprehensible through the operation of laws and time. This can be reinterpreted as having explicit opportunities and constraints for any particular human use. A survey will reveal the most fit locations and processes" (1997a, 321).

McHarg has summarized a framework for ecological planning in the following way:

> All systems aspire to survival and success. This state can be described as synthropic-fitness-health. Its antithesis is entropic-misfitness-morbidity. To achieve the first state requires systems to find the fittest environment, adapt it and themselves. Fitness of an environment for a system is defined as that requiring the minimum of work and adaptation. Fitness and fitting are indications of health and the process of fitness is health giving. The quest for fitness is entitled adaptation. Of all the instrumentalities available for man for successful adaptation, cultural adaptation in general and planning in particular, appear to be the most direct and efficacious for maintaining and enhancing human health and well-being (1981, 112–113).

Arthur Johnson explained the central principle of this theory in the following way: "The fittest environment for any organism, artifact, natural and social ecosystem, is that environment which provides the [energy] needed to sustain the health or well-being of the organism/artifact/ecosystem. Such an approach is not limited by scale. It may be applied to locating plants within a garden as well as to the development of a nation" (1981, 107).

The ecological planning method is primarily a procedure for studying the biophysical and sociocultural systems of a place to reveal where specific land uses may be best practiced. As Ian McHarg has summarized repeatedly in his writings and in many public presentations: "The method defines the best areas for a potential land use at the convergence of all or most of the factors deemed propitious for the use in the absence of all or most detrimental conditions. Areas meeting this standard are deemed intrinsically suitable for the land use under consideration."

As presented in Figure 1.1, there are 11 interacting steps. An issue or group of related issues is identified by a community—that is, some collection of people—in Step 1. These issues are problematic or present an opportunity to the people or the environment of an area. A goal(s) is then established in Step 2 to address the problem(s). Next, in Steps 3 and 4, inventories and analyses of biophysical and sociocultural processes are conducted, first at a larger level, such as a river drainage basin or an appropriate regional unit of government, and second at a more specific level, such as a small watershed or a local government.

In Step 5, detailed studies are made that link the inventory and analysis information to the problem(s) and goal(s). Suitability analyses are one such type of detailed study. Step 6 involves the development of concepts and options. A landscape plan is then derived from these concepts in Step 7. Throughout the process, a systematic educational and citizen involvement effort occurs. Such involvement is important in each step but especially so in Step 8, when the plan is explained to the affected public. In Step 9, detailed designs are explored that are specific at the individual land-user or site level. These designs and the plan are implemented in Step 10. In Step 11, the plan is administered.

The heavier arrows in Figure 1.1 indicate the flow from Step 1 to Step 11. Smaller arrows between each step suggest a feedback system whereby each step can modify the previous step and, in turn, change from the subsequent step. The smaller indicate other possible modifications through the process. For instance, detailed studies of a planning area (Step 5) may lead to the identification of new problems or opportunities or the amendment of goals (Steps 1 and 2). Design explorations (Step 9) may change the landscape

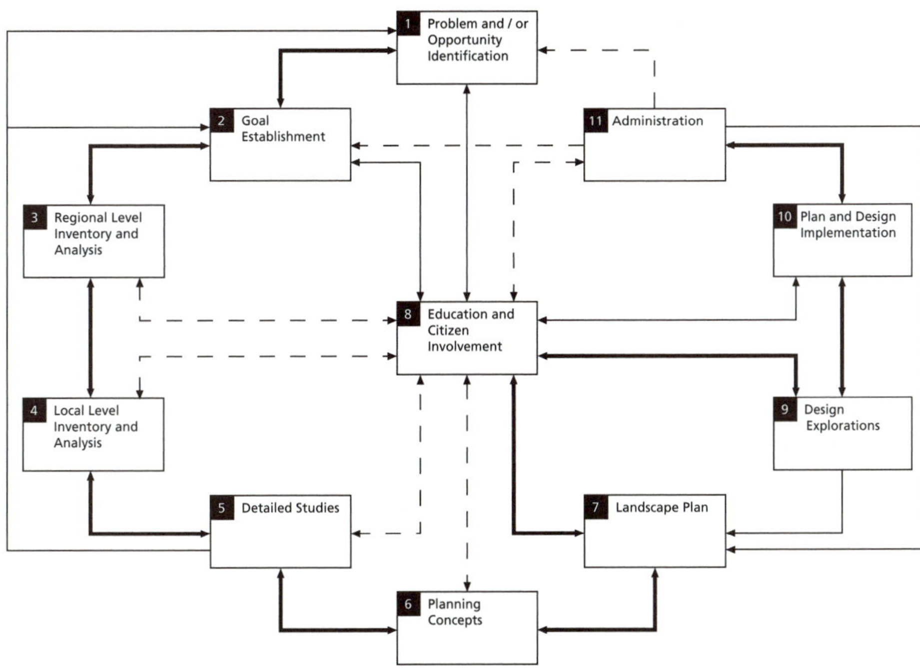

FIGURE 1.1 Ecological planning model.

plan, and so on. Once the process is complete and the plan is being administered and monitored (Step 11), the view of the problems and opportunities facing the region and the goals to address these problems and opportunities may be altered, as is indicated by the dashed lines in Figure 1.1.

This process is adapted from the conventional planning process and its many variations (see, for instance, Hall 1975; Roberts 1979; McDowell 1986; Moore 1988; and Stokes et al. 1989, 1997), as well as those suggested specifically for landscape planning (Lovejoy 1973; Fabos 1979; Zube 1980; Marsh 1983; and Duchhart 1989). Unlike some of these other planning processes, design plays an important role in this method. Each step in the process contributes to and is affected by a plan and implementing measures, which may be the official controls of the planning area. The plan and implementing measures may be viewed as the results of the process, although products may be generated from each step.

The approach to ecological planning developed by Ian McHarg at the University of Pennsylvania differs slightly from the one presented here. The Pennsylvania, or McHarg, model places a greater emphasis on inventory, analysis, and synthesis. This one places more emphasis on the establishment of goals, implementation, administration, and public participation, yet does attempt to do so in an ecologically sound manner.

Ecological planning is fundamental for *sustainable development.* The best-known definition of sustainable development was promulgated by the World Commission on Environment and Development (WCED), known as the Bruntland Commission, as that which "meets the needs of the present without compromising the ability of future generations to meet their own needs" (WCED

1987, 8). A more recent definition was provided by the National Commission on the Environment, which has defined sustainable development as

> a strategy for improving the quality of life while preserving the environmental potential for the future, of living off interest rather than consuming natural capital. Sustainable development mandates that the present generation must not narrow the choices of future generations but must strive to expand them by passing on an environment and an accumulation of resources that will allow its children to live at least as well as, and preferably better than, people today. Sustainable development is premised on living within the Earth's means (National Commission on the Environment 1993, 2).

Enzo Scandurra and Alberto Budoni have stated the underlying premise for sustainability especially well and succinctly: "The planet cannot be considered as a gigantic source of unlimited raw materials, neither, equally, as a gigantic dump where we can dispose of all waste from our activities" (1997, 2). The environment is both a source and a sink, but its capacities to provide resources and to assimilate wastes are not limitless.

Timothy Beatley and Kristy Manning (1997) relate sustainable development to ecological planning. They note that "McHargian-style environmental analysis . . . [has] become a commonplace methodological step in undertaking almost any form of local planning" (Beatley and Manning 1997, 86). They also note, however, that although such analyses are "extremely important, . . . a more comprehensive and holistic approach is required" (Beatley and Manning 1997, 86). The steps that follow attempt to provide a more comprehensive approach.

Step 1: Identification of Planning Problems and Opportunities

Human societies face many social, economic, political, and environmental problems and opportunities. Since a landscape is the interface between social and environmental processes, landscape planning addresses those issues that concern the interrelationship between people and nature. The planet presents many opportunities for people, and there is no shortage of environmental problems.

Problems and opportunities lead to specific planning issues. For instance, suburban development often occurs on prime agricultural land, a circumstance that local officials tend to view as a problem. A number of issues arise involving land-use conflicts between the new suburban residents and the farmers—such as who will pay the costs of public services for the newly developed areas. Another example is an area like an ocean beach or mountain town with the opportunity for new development because of its scenic beauty and recreational amenities. A key challenge would be that of accommodating the new growth while protecting the natural resources that are attracting people to the place.

Step 2: Establishment of Planning Goals

In a democracy, the people of a region establish goals through the political process. Elected representatives will identify a particular issue affecting their region—a steel plant is closing, suburban sprawl threatens agricultural land, or a new power plant is creating a housing boom. After issues have been identified, goals are established to address the problem. Such goals should provide the basis for the planning process.

Goals articulate an idealized future situation. In the context of this method, it is assumed that once goals have been established there will be a commitment by some group to address the problem or opportunity identified in Step 1. Problems and opportunities can be identified at various levels. Local people can recognize a problem or opportunity and then set a goal to address it. As well, issues can be national, international, or

Residents and community leaders can help to identify local environmental issues that require future planning.

global in scope. Problem solving, of which goal setting is a part, may occur at many levels or combinations of levels. Although goal setting is obviously dependent on the cultural-political system, the people affected by a goal should be involved in its establishment.

Goal-oriented planning has long been advocated by many community planners. Such an approach has been summarized by Herbert Gans:

> The basic idea behind goal-oriented planning is simple: that planners must begin with the goals of the community—and of its people—and then develop those programs which constitute the best means for achieving the community's goals, taking care that the consequences of these programs do not result in undesirable behavioral or cost consequences (1968, 53).

There are some good examples of goal-oriented planning, such as Oregon's mandatory land-use law (see, for instance, Pease 1984; Eber 1984; DeGrove 1992; and Kelly 1993). However, although locally generated goals are the ideal, too often goals are established by a higher level of government. Many federal and state laws have mandated planning goals for local government, often resulting in the creation of new administrative regions to respond to a particular federal program. These regional agencies must respond to wide-ranging issues that generate specific goals for water and air quality, resource management, energy conservation, transportation, and housing. No matter at what level of government goals are established, information must be collected to help elected representatives resolve underlying issues. Many goals, those which are the focus of this book, require an understanding of biophysical processes.

Step 3: Landscape Analysis, Regional Level

This step and the next one involve interrelated scale levels. The method addresses three scale levels: region, locality, and specific site (with an emphasis on the local). The use of different scales is consistent with the concept of levels-of-organization used by ecologists. According to this concept, each level of organization has special properties. Novikoff observed, "What were wholes on one level become parts on a higher one" (1945; as quoted by Quinby 1988). Watersheds have been identified as one level of organization to provide boundaries for landscape and ecosystem analysis. Drainage basins and watersheds have often been advocated as useful levels of analysis for landscape planning and natural resource management (Doornkamp 1982; Young et al. 1983; Steiner 1983; Dickert and Olshansky 1986; Easter et al. 1986; Fox 1987; Erickson 1995; Smith et al. 1997; and Golley 1998). Dunne and Leopold provide a useful explanation of watersheds and drainage basins for ecological planning. They state that the term *drainage basin*

> is synonymous with *watershed* in American usage and with *catchment* in most other countries. The boundary of a drainage basin is known as the *drainage divide* in the United States and as the *watershed* in other countries. Thus the term *watershed* can mean an area or a line. The drainage basin can vary in size from that of the Amazon River to one of a few square meters drainage into the head of a gully. Any number of drainage basins can be defined in a landscape . . . depending on the location of the drainage outlet on some watercourse (Dunne and Leopold 1978, 495).

Essentially, drainage basins and watersheds are the same thing (catchment areas), but in practical use, especially in the United States, the term *drainage basin* is generally used to refer to a larger region and the term *watersheds* to a more specific area. Drainage basins cover a river and all of its tributaries, while watersheds generally encompass a single river or stream. Richard Lowrance and his colleagues (1986), who have developed a hierarchial approach for agricultural planning, refer to watersheds as the landscape system, or ecologic level, and the larger unit as the regional system, or macroeconomic level. In the Lowrance et al. hierarchy, the two smallest units are the *farm system,* or *microeconomic level,* and *field system,* or *agronomic level.* The analysis at the regional drainage-basin level provides insight into how the landscape functions at the more specific local scale.

A major aim of landscape analysis is to obtain insight about natural processes. *(A. E. Bye)*

Drainage basins and watersheds, however, are seldom practical boundaries for American planners. Political boundaries frequently do not neatly conform with river catchments, and planners commonly work for political entities. There are certainly many examples of plans that are based on drainage basins, such as water quality and erosion control plans. Several federal agencies, such as the U.S. Forest Service (USFS) and the U.S. Natural Resources Conservation Service (NRCS, formerly known as the Soil Conservation Service or SCS), regularly use watersheds as planning units. Planners who work for cities or counties are less likely to be hydrologically bound.

Step 4: Landscape Analysis, Local Level

During Step 4, processes taking place in the more specific planning area are studied. The major aim of local-level analysis is to obtain insight about the natural processes and human plans and activities. Such processes can be viewed as the elements of a system, with the landscape a visual expression of the system.

This step in the ecological planning process, like the previous one, involves the collection of information concerning the appropriate physical, biological, and social elements that constitute the planning area. Since cost and time are important factors in many planning processes, existing published and mapped information is the easiest and fastest to gather. If budget and time allow, the inventory and analysis step may be best accomplished by an interdisciplinary team collecting new information. In either case, this step is an interdisciplinary collection effort that involves search, accumulation, field checking, and mapping of data.

Ian McHarg and his collaborators have developed a layer-cake model (Figure 1.2) that provides a central group of biophysical elements for the inventory or chorography of the place. Categories include the earth, the surface terrain, groundwater, surface water, soils, climate, vegetation, wildlife, and people (Table 1.1). UNESCO, in its Man and the Biosphere Programme, has developed a more exhaustive list of possible inventory elements (Table 1.2).

Land classification systems are valuable for analysis at this stage because they may allow the planner to aggregate specific information into general groupings. Such systems are based on inventoried data and on needs for analysis. Many government agencies in the United States and elsewhere have developed land classification systems that are helpful. The NRCS, USFS, the U.S.

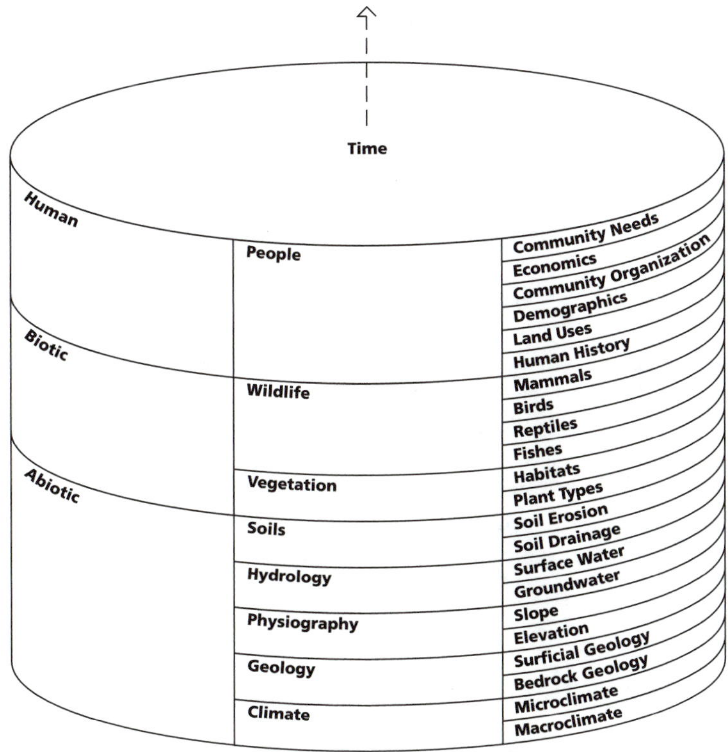

FIGURE 1.2 Layer-cake model. *(Source: Adapted from Ian McHarg and drawn by Mookesh Patel)*

TABLE 1.1
BASELINE NATURAL RESOURCE
Data Necessary for Ecological Planning

The following natural resource factors are likely to be of significance in planning. Clearly the region under study will determine the relevant factors, but many are likely to occur in all studies.

CLIMATE. Temperature, humidity, precipitation, wind velocity, wind direction, wind duration, first and last frosts, snow, frost, fog, inversions, hurricanes, tornadoes, tsunamis, typhoons, Chinook winds

GEOLOGY. Rocks, ages, formations, plans, sections, properties, seismic activity, earthquakes, rock slides, mud slides, subsistence

SURFICIAL GEOLOGY. Kames, kettles, eskers, moraines, drift and till

GROUNDWATER HYDROLOGY. Geological formations interpreted as aquifer with well locations, well logs, water quantity and quality, water table

PHYSIOGRAPHY. Physiographic regions, subregions, features, contours, sections, slopes, aspect, insulation, digital terrain model(s)

SURFICIAL HYDROLOGY. Oceans, lakes, deltas, rivers, streams, creeks, marshes, swamps, wetlands, stream orders, density, discharges, gauges, water quality, floodplains

SOILS. Soil associations, soil series, properties, depth to seasonal high water table, depth to bedrock, shrink-swell, compressive strength, cation and anion exchange, acidity-alkalinity

VEGETATION. Associations, communities, species, composition, distribution, age and conditions, visual quality, species number, rare and endangered species, fire history, successional history

WILDLIFE. Habitats, animal populations, census data, rare and endangered species, scientific and educational value

HUMAN. Ethnographic history, settlement patterns, existing land use, existing infrastructure, economic activities, population characteristics

SOURCE: Adapted from McHarg 1997b.

Fish and Wildlife Service (USFWS), and the U.S. Geological Survey (USGS) are agencies that have been notably active in land classification systems. However, there is not a consistency of data sources even in the United States. In urban areas, a planner may be overwhelmed with data for inventory and analysis. In remote rural areas, on the other hand, even a Natural Resources Conservation Service survey may not exist, or the survey may be old and unusable. An even larger problem is that there is little or no consistency in scale or in the terminology used among various agencies. A recommendation of the National Agricultural Lands Study (1981) was that a statistical protocol for federal agencies concerning land resource information be developed and led by the Office of Federal Statistical Policy and Standards. One helpful system that has been developed for land classification is the USGS Land Use and Land Cover Classification System (Table 1.3).

The ability of the landscape planner and ecosystem manager to inventory biophysical processes may be uneven, but it is far better than their capability to assess human ecosystems. An understanding of human ecology may provide a key to sociocultural inventory and analysis. Since humans are living things, *human ecology* may be thought of as an expansion of ecology—of how humans interact with each other and their environments. Interaction then is used as both a basic concept and an explanatory device. As Gerald Young (1974, 1978, 1983, 1989), who has illustrated the pan-disciplinary scope of human ecology, noted:

> In human ecology, the way people interact with each other and with the environment is definitive of a number of basic relationships. Interaction provides a measure of belonging, it affects identity versus alienation, including alienation from the environment. The system of obligation, responsibility and liability is defined through interaction. The process has become definitive of the public interest as opposed to private interests which prosper in the spirit of independence (1976, 294).

Step 5: Detailed Studies

Detailed studies link the inventory and analysis information to the problem(s) and goal(s). One

TABLE 1.2
UNESCO TOTAL ENVIRONMENTAL CHECKLIST: COMPONENTS AND PROCESSES

Natural Environment—Components	
Soil	Energy resources
Water	Fauna
Atmosphere	Flora
Mineral resources	Microorganisms
Natural Environment—Processes	
Biogeochemical cycles	Fluctuations in animal and plant growth
Irradiation	Changes in soil fertility, salinity, alkalinity
Climatic processes	Host/parasite interactions, and epidemic processes
Photosynthesis	
Animal and plant growth	
Human Population—Demographic Aspects	
Population structure:	Population size
• Age	Population density
• Ethnicity	Fertility and mortality rates
• Economic	Health statistics
• Education	
• Occupation	
Human Activities and the Use of Machines	
Migratory movements	Mining
Daily mobility	Industrial activities
Decision making	Commercial activities
Exercise and distribution of authority	Military activities
Administration	Transportation
Farming, fishing	Recreational activities
	Crime rates
Societal Groupings	
Governmental groupings	Information media
Industrial groupings	Law-keeping media
Commercial groupings	Health services
Political groupings	Community groupings
Religious groupings	Family groupings
Educational groupings	
Products of Labor	
The built-environment:	Food
• Buildings	Pharmaceutical products
• Roads	Machines
• Railways	Other commodities
• Parks	
Culture	
Values	Technology
Beliefs	Literature
Attitudes	Laws
Knowledge	Economic system
Information	

SOURCE: Boyden 1979.

example of such studies is *suitability analysis.* As explained by Ian McHarg (1969), suitability analyses can be used to determine the fitness of a specific place for a variety of land uses based on thorough ecological inventories and on the values of land users. The basic purpose of the detailed studies is to gain an understanding about the complex relationships between human values, environmental opportunities and constraints, and the issues being addressed. To accomplish this, it is crucial to link the studies to the local situation. As a result, a variety of scales may be used to explore linkages.

A simplified suitability analysis process is provided in Figure 1.3. There are several techniques that may be used to accomplish suitability analysis. Again, it was McHarg who popularized the "overlay technique" (1969). This technique involves maps of inventory information superimposed on one another to identify areas that provide, first, opportunities for particular land uses and, second, constraints (Johnson, Berger, and McHarg 1979). Bruce MacDougall (1975) has criticized the accuracy of map overlays and made suggestions on how they may be made more accurate.

Although there has been a general tendency away from hand-drawn overlays, there are still occasions when they may be useful. For instance, they may be helpful for small study sites within a larger region or for certain scales of project planning. It is important to realize the limitations of hand-drawn overlays. As an example, after more than three or four overlays, they

TABLE 1.3
U.S. GEOLOGICAL SURVEY LAND-USE AND LAND-COVER CLASSIFICATION SYSTEM FOR USE WITH REMOTE SENSOR DATA

Level I	Level II
1 Urban or built-up land	11 Residential
	12 Commercial and services
	13 Industrial
	14 Transportation, communications, and services
	15 Industrial and commercial complexes
	16 Mixed urban or built-up land
	17 Other urban or built-up land
2 Agricultural land	21 Cropland and pasture
	22 Orchards, groves, vineyards, nurseries, and ornamental horticultural
	23 Confined feeding operations
	24 Other agricultural land
3 Rangeland	31 Herbaceous rangeland
	32 Shrub and brush rangeland
	33 Mixed rangeland
4 Forestland	41 Deciduous forestland
	42 Evergreen forestland
	43 Mixed forestland
5 Water	51 Streams and canals
	52 Lakes
	53 Reservoirs
	54 Bays and estuaries
6 Wetland	61 Forested wetland
	62 Nonforested wetland
7 Barren land	71 Dry salt flats
	72 Beaches
	73 Sandy areas other than beaches
	74 Bare exposed rocks
	75 Strip mines, quarries, and gravel pits
	76 Transitional areas
	77 Mixed barren land
8 Tundra	81 Shrub and brush tundra
	82 Herbaceous tundra
	83 Bare ground
	84 Mixed tundra
9 Perennial snow ice	91 Perennial snowfields
	92 Glaciers

SOURCE: Anderson et al. 1976.

may become opaque; there are the accuracy problems identified by MacDougall (1975) and others that become especially acute with hand-drawn maps; and there are limitations for weighting various values represented by map units. Computer technology may help to overcome these limitations.

Numerous computer program systems, called *geographic information systems* (GIS), have been developed that replace the technique of hand-drawn overlays. Some of these programs are intended to model only positions of environmental processes or phenomena, while others are designed as comprehensive information storage, retrieval, and evaluation systems. These systems are intended to improve efficiency and economy in information handling, especially for large or complex planning projects.

Step 6: Planning Area Concepts, Options, and Choices

This step involves the development of concepts for the planning area. These concepts can be viewed as options for the future based on the suitabilities for the use(s) that give a general conceptual model or scenario of how problems may be solved. This model should be presented in such a way that the goals will be achieved. Often more than one scenario has to be made. These concepts are based on a logical and imaginative combination of the information gathered through the inventory and analysis steps. The conceptual model shows allocations of uses and actions. The scenarios set possible directions for future management of the area and therefore should be viewed as a basis for discussion where choices are made by the community about its future.

Choices should be based on the goals of the planning effort. For example, if it is the goal to protect agricultural land, yet allow some low-density housing to develop, different organiza-

Step 1 **Map data factors by type**

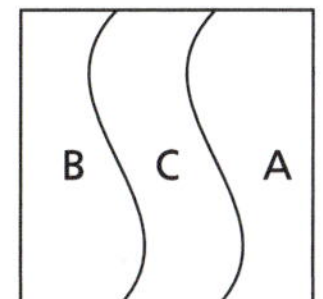

A – 00 – 10 %
B – 10 – 20 %
C – 20 – 40 %

Slope map

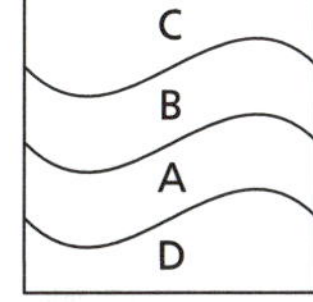

A – Slightly eroded
B – Slight to moderate
C – Moderate
D – Extremely eroded

Erosion map

Step 2 **Rate each type of each factor for each land use**

Factor types

		Agriculture	Housing
Example 1	A	1	1
	B	2	1
	C	3	3
Example 2	A	1	1
	B	2	2
	C	3	2
	D	3	3

1 – Prime suitability
2 – Secondary
3 – Tertiary

Step 3 **Map rating for each and use one set of maps for each land use**

Example 1

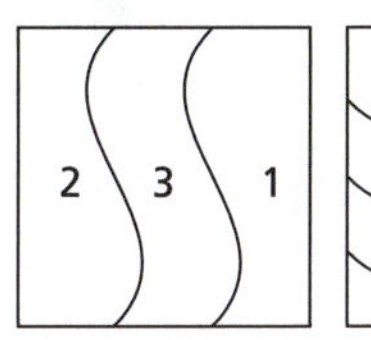

Agriculture

Example 2

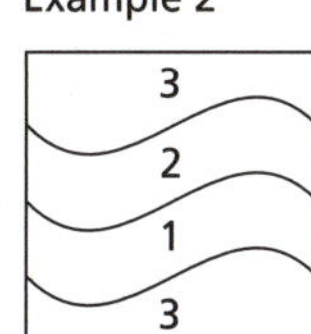

Agriculture

Example 1

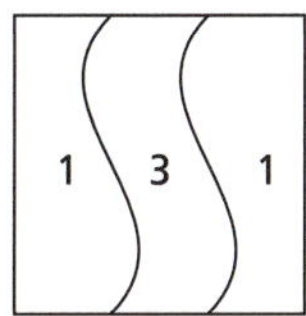

Housing

Example 2

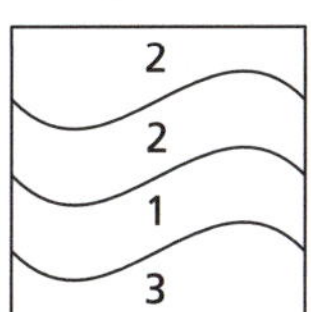

Housing

Step 4 **Overlay single factor suitability maps to obtain composites**
One map for each land use

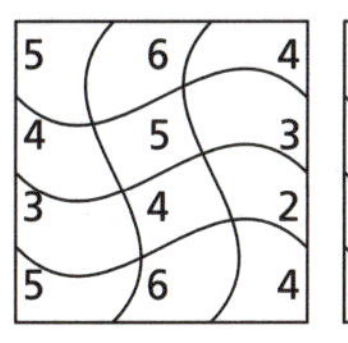

Agriculture

3 5 3
3 5 3
2 4 2
4 6 4

Housing

Lowest numbers are best suited for land use

Highest numbers are least suited for land use

FIGURE 1.3 Suitability analysis procedure.

tions of the environment for those two land uses should be developed. Different schemes for realizing the desired preferences also need to be explored.

The Dutch have devised an interesting approach to developing planning options for their agricultural land reallocation projects. Four land-use options are developed, each with the preferred scheme for a certain point of view. Optional land-use schemes of the area are made for nature and landscape, agriculture, recreation, and urbanization. These schemes are constructed by groups of citizens working with government scientists and planners. To illustrate, for the nature and landscape scheme, landscape architects and ecologists from the *Staatsbosbeheer* (Dutch Forest Service) work with citizen environmental action groups. For agriculture, local extension agents and soil scientists work with farm commodity organizations and farmer cooperatives. Similar coalitions are formed for recreation and urbanization. What John Friedmann (1973) calls a *dialogue process* begins at the point where each of the individual schemes is constructed. The groups come together for mutual learning so that a consensus of opinion can be reached through debate and discussion.

Various options for implementation also need to be explored, which must relate to the goal of the planning effort. If, for example, the planning is being conducted for a jurisdiction trying to protect its agricultural land resources, then it is necessary not only to identify lands that should be protected but also the implementation options that might be employed to achieve the farmland protection goal.

Step 7: Landscape Plan

The preferred concepts and options are brought together in a landscape plan. The plan gives a strategy for development at the local scale. The plan provides flexible guidelines for policymakers, land managers, and land users on how to conserve, rehabilitate, or develop an area. In such a plan, enough freedom should be left so that local officials and land users can adjust their practices to new economic demands or social changes.

This step represents a key decision-making point in the planning process. Responsible officials, such as county commissioners or city council members, are often required by law to adopt a plan. The rules for adoption and forms that the plans may take vary widely. Commonly in the United States, planning commissions recommend a plan for adoption to the legislative body after a series of public hearings. Such plans are called *comprehensive plans* in much of the United States but are referred to as *general plans* in Arizona, California, and Utah. In some states (like Oregon) there are specific, detailed elements that local governments are required to include in such plans. Other states permit much flexibility to local officials for the contents of these plans. On public lands, various federal agencies, including the USFS, the U.S. National Park Service (NPS), and the U.S. Bureau of Land Management (BLM), have specific statutory requirement for land management plans.

The term *landscape plan* is used here to emphasize that such plans should incorporate natural and social considerations. A landscape plan is more than a land-use plan because it addresses the overlap and integration of land uses. A landscape plan may involve the formal recognition of previous elements in the planning process, such as the adoption of policy goals. The plan should include written statements about policies and implementation strategies as well as a map showing the spatial organization of the landscape.

Step 8: Continued Citizen Involvement and Community Education

In Step 8, the plan is explained to the affected public through education and information dissemination. Actually, such interaction occurs throughout the planning process, beginning with the identification of issues. Public involvement is especially crucial as the landscape plan is developed, because it is important to ensure that the goals established by the community will be achieved in the plan.

The success of a plan depends largely on how much people affected by the plan have been involved in its determination. There are numerous examples of both government agencies and private businesses suddenly announcing a plan for a project that will dramatically impact people, without having consulted those individuals first. The result is predictable—the people will rise in opposition against the project. The alternative is to involve people in the planning process, soliciting their ideas and incorporating those ideas into the plan. Doing so may require a longer time to develop a plan, but local citizens will be more likely to support it than to oppose it and will often monitor its execution.

Step 9: Design Explorations

To design is to give form and to arrange elements spatially. By making specific designs based on the landscape plan, planners can help decision makers visualize the consequences of their policies. Carrying policies through to arranging the physical environment gives meaning to the process by actually conceiving change in the spatial organization of a place. Designs represent a synthesis of all the previous planning studies. During the design step, the short-term benefits for the land users or individual citizen have to be combined with the long-term economic and ecological goals for the whole area.

Since the middle 1980s, several architects have called for a return to traditional principles in community design. These "neotraditionals" or "new urbanists" include Peter Calthorpe, Elizabeth Plater-Zyberk, Andres Duany, Elizabeth Moule, and Stefanos Polyzoides. Meanwhile, other architects and landscape architects have advocated more ecological, more sustainable design; these include John Lyle, Robert Thayer, Sim Van der Ryn, Carol Franklin, Colin Franklin, Leslie Jones Sauer, Rolf Sauer, and Pliny Fisk. Michael and Judith Corbett with others helped merge these two strains in the Ahwahnee Principles (Local Government Commission 1991; Calthorpe et al. 1998). (See Table 1.4.)

Ecological design, according to David Orr, is "the capacity to understand the ecological context in which humans live, to recognize limits, and to get the scale of things right" (1994, 2). Or, as Sim Van der Ryn and Stuart Cowan note, ecological design seeks to "make nature visible" (1996, 16). These principles provide clear guidance for ecological design (see also Grant et al. 1996, Beatley and Manning 1997). While some designers and planners might object to the placement of design within the planning process, in an ecological perspective such placement helps to connect design with more comprehensive social actions and policies.

Step 10: Plan and Design Implementation

Implementation is the employment of various strategies, tactics, and procedures to realize the goals and policies adopted in the landscape plan. The Ahwahnee Principles provide guidelines for implementation (Table 1.4). On the local level, several different mechanisms have been developed to control the use of land and other resources. These techniques include voluntary covenants, easements, land purchase, transfer of development rights, zoning, utility extension policies, and performance standards. The preference selected should be appropriate for the region. For instance, in urban areas like King County, Washington, and Suffolk County, New York, traditional zoning has not proved effective for protecting farmland. The citizens of these counties have therefore elected to tax themselves to purchase farmland preservation easements from farmers. In more rural counties like Whitman County, Wash-

TABLE 1.4
THE AHWAHNEE PRINCIPLES

Preamble:
Existing patterns of urban and suburban development seriously impair our quality of life. The symptoms are: more congestion and air pollution resulting from our increased dependence on automobiles, the loss of precious open space, the need for costly improvements to roads and public services, the inequitable distribution of economic resources, and the loss of a sense of community. By drawing upon the best from the past and the present, we can plan communities that will more successfully serve the needs of those who live and work within them. Such planning should adhere to certain fundamental principles.

Community Principles:
1. All planning should be in the form of complete and integrated communities containing housing, shops, work places, schools, parks, and civic facilities essential to the daily life of the residents.
2. Community size should be designed so that housing, jobs, daily needs, and other activities are within easy walking distance of each other.
3. As many activities as possible should be located within easy walking distance of transit stops.
4. A community should contain a diversity of housing types to enable citizens from a wide range of economic levels and age groups to live within its boundaries.
5. Businesses within the community should provide a range of job types for the community's residents.
6. The location and character of the community should be consistent with a larger transit network.
7. The community should have a center focus that combines commercial, civic, cultural, and recreational uses.
8. The community should contain an ample supply of specialized open space in the form of squares, greens, and parks whose frequent use is encouraged through placement and design.
9. Public spaces should be designed to encourage the attention and presence of people at all hours of the day and night.
10. Each community or cluster of communities should have a well defined edge, such as agricultural greenbelts or wildlife corridors, permanently protected from development.
11. Streets, pedestrian paths, and bike paths should contribute to a system of fully-connected and interesting routes to all destinations. Their design should encourage pedestrian and bicycle use by being small and spatially defined by buildings, trees and lighting; and by discouraging high-speed traffic.

Regional Principles:
1. The regional structure should be integrated within a larger transportation network built around transit rather than freeways.
2. Regions should be bounded by and provide a continuous system of greenbelt/wildlife corridors to be determined by natural conditions.
3. Regional institutions and services (government, stadiums, museums, etc.) should be located within the urban core.

Implementation Strategies:
1. The general plan should be updated to incorporate the above principles.
2. Rather than allowing for developer-initiated, piecemeal development, a local government should initiate the planning of new and changing communities within its jurisdiction through an open planning process.
3. Prior to any development, a specific plan should be used to define communities where new growth, infill, or redevelopment would be allowed to occur. With the adoption of specific plans, complying projects can proceed with minimal delay.
4. Plans should be developed through an open process and in the process should be provided illustrated models of the proposed design.

SOURCE: Calthorpe et al. 1998.

ington, and Black Hawk County, Iowa, local leaders have found traditional zoning effective.

One implementation technique especially well-suited for ecological planning is the use of performance standards. Like many other planning implementation measures, *performance standards* is a general term that has been defined and applied in several different ways. Basically, performance standards, or criteria, are established and must be met before a certain use will be permitted. These criteria usually involve a combination of economic, environmental, and social factors. This technique lends itself to ecological planning because criteria for specific land uses can be based on suitability analysis.

Step 11: Administration

In this final step, the plan is administered. *Administration* involves monitoring and evaluating how the plan is implemented on an ongoing basis. Amendments or adjustments to the plan will no doubt be necessary because of changing conditions or new information. To achieve the goals established for the process, planners should pay special attention to the design of regulation review procedures and of the management of the decision-making process.

Administration may be accomplished by a commission comprising citizens with or without the support of a professional staff. Citizens should play an important role in administering local planning through commissions and review boards that oversee local ordinances. To a large degree, the success of citizens' boards and commissions depends on the extent of their involvement in the development of the plans that they manage. Again, Oregon provides an excellent example of the use of citizens to administer a plan. The Land Conservation and Development Commission (LCDC), comprising seven members who are appointed by the governor and supported by its professional staff, is responsible for overseeing the implementation of the state land-use planning law. Another group of citizens, 1000 Friends of Oregon, monitors the administration of the law. The support that the law has received from the public is evidenced by the defeat of several attempts to abolish mandatory statewide land-use planning in Oregon. However, as Department of Land Conservation and Development (DLCD) staff member Ron Eber observes, "It is a myth that planning is easy in Oregon—it is a battle every day!" (personal communication 1999). For example, in the early 1990s, a counterforce to 1000 Friends of Oregon was organized; "Oregonians in Action" is a property-rights group which is opposed to the progressive statewide planning program.

WORKING PLANS

A method is necessary as an organizational framework for landscape planners. Also, a relatively standard method presents the opportunity to compare and analyze case studies. To adequately fulfill responsibilities to protect the public health, safety, and welfare, the actions of planners should be based on a knowledge of what has and has not worked in other settings and situations. A large body of case study results can provide an empirical foundation for planners. A common method is helpful for both practicing planners and scholars who should probe and criticize the nuances of such a method in order to expand and improve its utility.

The following chapters are organized roughly parallel to the method. The identification of planning problems and opportunities is not discussed independently because it is assumed that once an issue has been defined, a process such as the one described here will be triggered. In addition, many of the techniques described in the next chapter can be used to both define issues and establish goals. Also, there are no separate discussions of regional- and local-level ecological inventories (Steps 3 and 4) because the techniques used are similar. Instead, there are separate detailed descriptions of inventories and analyses of the biophysical environment and the human community.

The approach suggested here should be viewed as a working method. The pioneering forester Gifford Pinchot advocated a conservation approach to the planning of the national forests. His approach was both utilitarian and protectionist, and he believed "wise use and preservation of all forest resources were compatible" (Wilkinson and Anderson 1985, 22). To implement this philosophy, Pinchot in his position as chief of the U.S. Forest Service required "working plans." Such plans recognized the dynamic, living nature of forests. In the same vein, the methods used to develop plans should be viewed as a living process. However, this is not meant to imply that there should be no structure to planning methods. Rather, working planning methods should be viewed as something analogous to a jazz composition: not a fixed score but a palette that invites improvisation.

The method offered here has a landscape ecological—specifically human ecological—bias. As noted by the geographer Donald W. Meinig, "Environment sustains us as creatures; landscape displays us as cultures" (1979, 3). As an artifact of culture, landscapes are an appropriate focus of planners faced with land-use and environmental management issues. Ecology provides insight into landscape patterns, processes, and interactions. An understanding of ecology reveals how we interact with each other and our natural and built environments. What we know of such relationships is still relatively limited, but it is expanding all the time. As Ilya Prigogine and Isabelle Stengers have observed, "Nature speaks in a thousand voices, and we have only begun to listen" (1984, 77).

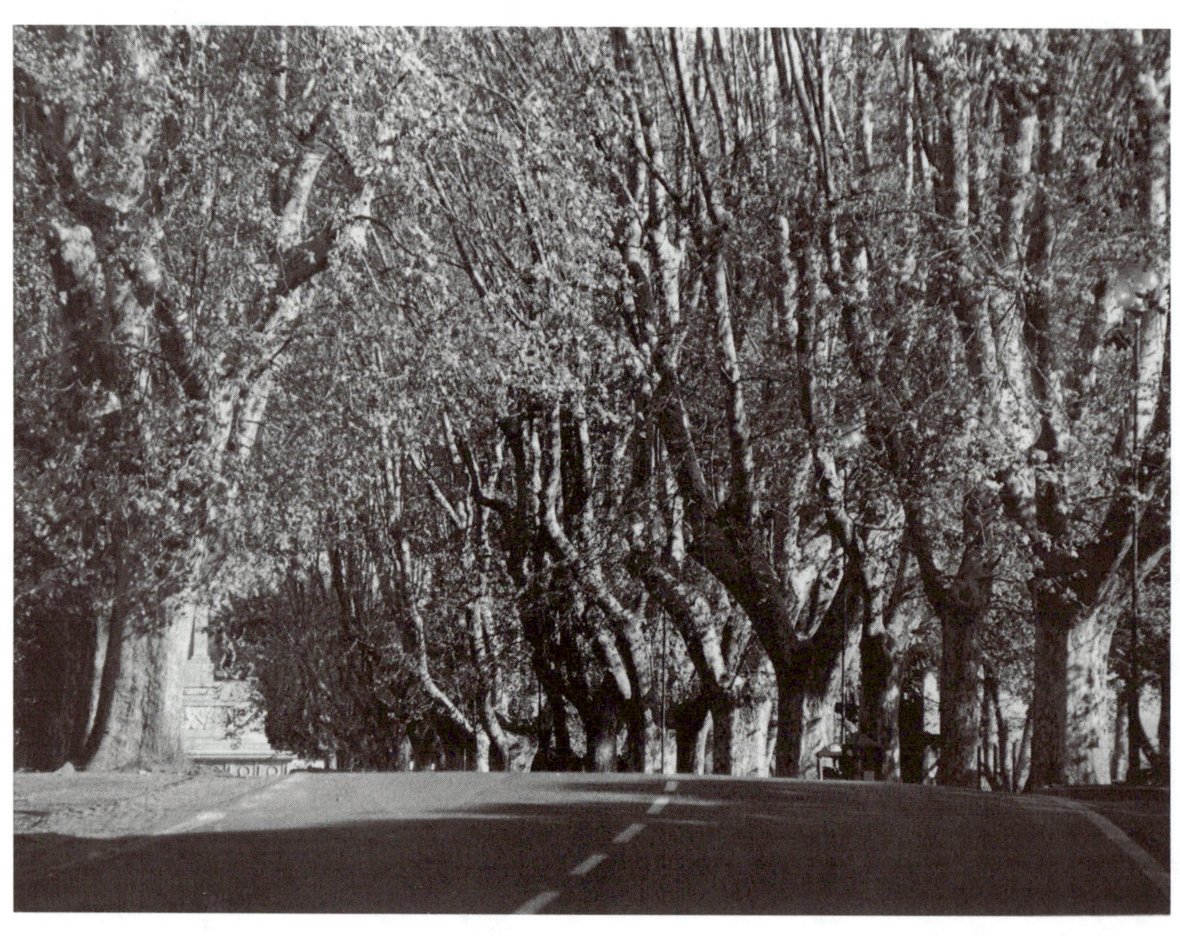

2

IDENTIFYING ISSUES AND ESTABLISHING PLANNING GOALS

Human communities are dynamic where change is inherent and integral. Change is challenging—often presenting an opportunity and a problem simultaneously. For communities, it is important to sort out the important issues associated with change and to develop strategies for coping with the adjustments that may be necessary.

Involving people in decisions about the future is one way to help communities address change. Participation is "the process by which public concerns, needs, and values are incorporated into governmental decision making" (Creighton 1992, 10) and "wherein citizens and government officials jointly plan or implement public policies" (Sarkissian 1994, 11). James Creighton (1992) identifies eight benefits of public participation: (1) improved quality of decisions, (2) the minimization of costs, (3) consensus building, (4) increased ease of implementation, (5) the avoidance of worst-case confrontations, (6) the maintenance of credibility and legitimacy, (7) the anticipation of public concerns and attitudes, and (8) the development of public expertise and creativity. Even though there are many benefits, citizens "will not participate in a . . . planning process unless: there are tangible issues, they consider the issues significant, and they feel their participation has a reasonable chance of making a difference" (Institute for Participatory Management and Planning 1997, III-12).

Wendy Sarkissian observes that the following four components are required for citizen participation:

- Both citizens and government tacitly or explicitly agree to cooperate with each other in the formation of policy.
- An atmosphere of mutual trust and respect must dominate the process, although cooperation need not be complete at all times.
- Both parties have real power to affect public-policy decision-making. Although one side may have more power than the other, the power of neither side may be trivial.
- As a process, rather than as a stable state, participation may evolve or regress. It is possible that cooperation may deepen or there may be a return to conflict (1994, 11).

Strategic planning is a process developed by businesses to set the course of change by linking plans to decision making. The process has also been adopted by NGOs, public agencies, and communities to chart their futures. The strategic planning process begins with an "environmental scan," which helps to identify key issues and the context. The environmental scan has some parallels to the ecological inventory that will be discussed in the next two chapters. After the scan is completed the organization writes a *mission statement,* that is, a brief declaration of the purposes for which the unit exists and functions. The mission statement attempts to clearly delineate the purpose of the unit and its plan. It may be helpful at an early stage in the planning process, for the individuals undertaking the plan to draft a mission statement. This mission should be linked to the key issues to be addressed in the planning process.

Early on, draft goals can be established to direct the process. These goals will be refined through the process and eventually formally adopted (see Chapter 7). The Oregon statewide land-use planning law and the comprehensive management plan for the New Jersey Pinelands are two examples of planning that is goal-oriented and that emphasizes ecological concerns.

TECHNIQUES FOR INVOLVING PEOPLE IN THE IDENTIFICATION OF ISSUES AND THE ESTABLISHMENT OF GOALS

The most straightforward means of arriving at specific planning goals in a democratic society is by voting. However, before goals reach a vote, they must be defined. In addition, many issues do not reach a popular vote and are decided through actions by the legislative and/or the administrative branches of government. As a result, a variety of means have been developed to identify issues, to establish goals, and to assess public opinion about potential issues and goals. Some techniques include the use of task forces, citizens' and technical advisory committees, neighborhood planning councils, group dynamics, nominal-group workshops, focus groups, and Delphi (Gil and Lucchesi 1979). Policy Delphi is a variation on the traditional Delphi technique. Once potential goals are set, politicians and public officials often depend on opinion polls for public reaction. Public opinion polls are also used to survey the problems and opportunities of an area and thereby to identify issues. An alternative to impersonal polling is the noisy, often emotional American tradition of the town meeting, or its stepchild, the public hearing.

Task Forces

A *task force* is an ad hoc agency-sponsored citizen committee with a well-defined problem-solving or specific task and charge relating usually to a single problem or subject (Gil and Lucchesi, 1979). Such a specific task may be establishing goals for a plan. The existence of task forces is temporary. The directed purpose of a task force means membership is limited in number to allow all members to participate actively and effectively. Typical task forces vary in size from 8 to 20 participants. Task forces usually rely on planning agencies for technical assistance and support but sometimes engage outside experts (U.S. Department of Transportation 1976).

For example, a county board of commissioners organizes a task force to explore the feasibility of establishing a goal to protect prime farmland from development. The commissioners must first answer two questions: Who should be appointed to the task force, and what should be the scope of the task force's activities? The county is experiencing considerable growth, so the commissions seek to act as quickly as possible. They select a six-person task force: a soil conservationist, an extension specialist, two farmers (one who already serves on the planning commission, and one who is on the board of the soil and water conservation district), a banker, and a local environmental activist (who is a retired high-school history teacher). The commissioners direct the county planning department and the county attorney to provide staff support for the task force.

The commissioners request that the task force answer a series of questions within a three-month schedule. How serious is the issue of farmland conversion in the county? What are the economic and fiscal consequences of the conversion? What has been the level of past public investment in agriculture in the county? Are some lands better suited for agriculture than others? What state laws and programs encourage agricultural land protection? Are other counties in the state facing the same issue? If so, what actions have those counties undertaken? By focusing on such questions the task force can help the county commissioners assess the farmland conversion issue and determine if a protection goal is warranted.

Citizens' Advisory Committees and Technical Advisory Committees

Citizens' advisory committees are presumed to represent the ideas and attitudes of local groups. Their purpose is to advise some decision-making body such as a planning commission, an agency staff, or a developer (Gil and Lucchesi 1979).

Citizens' advisory committees have become increasingly popular for goal setting and policy-making by legislative bodies (Institute for Participatory Planning 1978). Citizens' advisory committee is a generic term that covers a variety of committees and councils differing in type, membership, and operations. Most, however, share the following characteristics: limited power and authority, large membership (50 to 100 members), agency staff providing technical assistance, a lifespan that is tied to the particular program or project, and infrequent meetings of full membership (U.S. Department of Transportation 1976).

Technical advisory committees are groups that represent bodies of technical or scientific information important to a planning commission, agency, or developer. Often these groups are interdisciplinary or multidisciplinary. Citizens' and technical advisory committees may be organized similar to task forces. However, their role encompasses a broader scope than an individual task. These groups may be involved in identifying issues, setting goals, and later establishing preferences as well as implementing the plan. Sometimes, such committees call themselves "collaboratives" to emphasize their cooperative intentions.

Technical advisory committee is also a generic term. It may be an intraagency committee made up of representatives from various staffs involved with or interested in a specific program or project, or it may be a group outside an agency from universities or consulting companies.

Neighborhood Planning Councils

Neighborhood planning councils are organizations formed by citizens or an outside community organizer that engage in a number of neighborhood programs as well as in advocacy and advice (Gil and Lucchesi 1979). In some cities, these groups are called *village planning committees* or *community planning councils.* Neighborhood planning councils came into wide use during the 1960s as a result of federally funded programs such as urban renewal and model cities. These locally based councils serve as advisory bodies to elected officials and public agencies in identifying neighborhood problems and issues, formulating goals and priorities, and implementing and evaluating plans (U.S. Department of Transportation 1976). Sometimes, they may be used to assist in spending federal or state community development grants. In such cases, spending is linked to neighborhood issues and goals. Neighborhood councils are usually purely advisory in nature and seldom have any decision-making authority.

Organizing neighborhood groups is a complex task. Two approaches familiar to many planners are the *Alinsky approach* and *organization development.* The former was developed by the famous Chicago organizer Saul Alinsky. The steps in the Alinsky (1946) approach include entering the community, sizing it up, making contacts, bringing people together, developing leadership, working with organizations, setting priorities, developing power tactics, building political power, working on self-help strategies, and exiting from the community.

Organization development is a discipline that evolved from group dynamics and field theory, which were established by psychologist Kurt Lewin. Students and followers of Lewin, including Chris Argyris, Warren Bennis, Carl Rogers, Edgar Schein, and other behavioral scientists differ from traditional social scientists in that their role as practitioners, or change agents, occurs in organizations outside the academic environment. Organization development has been used extensively in large corporate structures. Some community planners have adapted these techniques for neighborhood-level organizing. Richard Bolan explains organization development in the following way: "The change agent, together with the client group, analyzes the forces available in support of, and resistant to, change. Such techniques stress awareness of the need for change and levels of change, methods for developing the goals of change, and the overcoming of resistance to change" (1979, 538). Dan Iacofano (1990) identifies citizen participation as an organizational development process for environmental and community planning.

Once organized, neighborhood-level planning councils may assist in the setting of goals for larger communities and provide public participation in other stages of the planning process. Their effectiveness is dependent on the skill with which they are organized and the level of interest in the neighborhood. Pitfalls include the inability of neighborhood groups to connect local issues to the needs of the larger society, and the ephemeral nature of some of these groups.

Group Dynamics

Group dynamics is a generic term for a variety of problem-solving techniques used to clarify goals, encourage group interaction, and resolve conflicts within citizen groups (Gil and Lucchesi 1979). The many techniques vary in their level of sophistication and degree of activity but share some common characteristics, including:

- *Small-group involvement.* Techniques are designed for small groups ranging from 5 to 25 members. If a larger membership is involved, the participants are divided into small groups.
- *Skilled leadership.* Techniques require the direction of a group leader knowledgeable in and comfortable with the use of the particular technique. The role of the leader involves setting the stage for the technique by providing a general introduction and rationale, directing the process and specific activities that may be required, and generally keeping the process going to its conclusion.

- *Structured process.* Each technique involves a controlled, specified activity or series of ordered activities and/or tasks for all members of the group.
- *Timing.* Each technique covers a specific time span ranging from 30 to 90 minutes for completion (U.S. Department of Transportation 1976, 104–105).

Group dynamics can be employed at almost any stage of the planning process, including issue identification and goal setting, in which the public is participating in an advisory committee, a task force, or a neighborhood council. Some strategies employed through group dynamics include empathy, feedback, video-taped group interview, brainstorming, nominal-group workshops, and role playing (U.S. Department of Transportation 1976).

Nominal-Group Workshops

Nominal-group workshops are one form of group dynamics. The Institute for Participatory Management and Planning (formerly the Institute for Participatory Planning) of Monterey, California, explains the concept in the following way: "This technique is built on the premise that any reasonably representative group of people who are concerned with a project [or issue], identify virtually all of the problems associated with a project [or issue] and can make the individual compromises that are necessary for coming up with a single list of priorities or preferences" (1978, V-6).

The nominal-group technique works in the following manner. A large group is brought together and given a balanced presentation of the project or subject being addressed by the workshop. This large group is then divided into nominally small groups of 5 to 12 people. Each person then fills out several blank 3 × 5 cards without consulting others in the group. On each card, the individual writes one major issue and several reasons why this issue is important.

Afterward, each person presents one issue to the small group and why he or she considers it to be important. These issues are listed on a blackboard or on a large sheet of paper. Members of the group take turns presenting issues until all issues are exhausted. The nominal groups' issues are then presented to the whole body. Often only the top 5 or 10 issues from the nominal groups are presented to the larger group. Next a vote is taken. Each person ranks what he or she considers to be the most important issues. Often the top 5 or 10 issues are listed on the ballot. The voting may be done using paper ballots; it is also becoming popular to vote using computers that give an instant tally (Delbecq et al. 1975; Institute for Participatory Planning 1978; Institute for Participatory Management and Planning 1997).

Next, the ballots are counted and ranked. This ranking is followed by general discussion. People lobby for and against issues. Another vote is taken, and the results are listed in priority. If the ranking has drastically changed, then another round of discussion, lobbying, and voting ensues. This continues until a consensus is reached (Delbecq et al. 1975; Institute for Participatory Planning 1978; Institute for Participatory Management and Planning 1997). Nominal-group workshops have been used effectively to first identify problems and opportunities for an area and then to set goals.

Focus Groups

Focus groups were developed by business to elicit opinions and information about new or existing products. Similarly, social scientists and planners use focus groups to assess public opinion about issues and to help set goals (Krueger 1988; Leach 1992). A focus group consists of between 7 and 10 people who are not acquainted with each other but who share similar backgrounds. The focus group participants are brought together, typically for a two-hour session, in a quiet, private room. An experienced facilitator guides and

During the planning process, members of a group present issues identified as important, listing them on large sheets of paper.

focuses discussion by asking open-ended questions of each group member (Leach 1992). Richard Krueger notes that "Focus groups can improve the planning and design of new programs, provide means of evaluating existing programs, and produce insights for developing marketing strategies" (1988, 15).

For example, a planning research team at Arizona State University received a grant from the U.S. Environmental Protection Agency (EPA) for sustainable community design (Ingley 1998). The team selected two sites for the designs: one in central Phoenix and the other on the suburban fringe of Scottsdale. Five focus groups were organized: one each involving neighbors to the two sites; one that included representatives of environmental groups and the environmental sciences; one comprised of developers; and one made up of architects, landscape architects, and planners.

About 20 people attended each of the sustainable development focus group meetings. Each meeting had a facilitator who was responsible for a tightly structured agenda. The structure of the agenda paralleled key sustainable neighborhood design themes, including community facilities; circulation; crime, safety, and security; air and ground pollution; habitat restoration; energy use; building materials; community-oriented growth; neighborhood identity; local employment opportunities; regional context; the sense of community; market feasibility and acceptability; density; implementation obstacles; open space; pedestrian environments; and biodiversity. The design and policy implications for each theme were probed. An important task of the facilitator was to ensure that each participant had an opportunity to contribute and that the meeting was not dominated by a few individuals. The focus group sessions were tape recorded, photographed, and videotaped.

A checklist for the focus group organization identified the following key items:

- Invitations
- Vehicle (set time for departure; riders)
- Video (tapes; operator; equipment; extension cords)
- Refreshments (coolers; ice; food; sodas and water; plates, napkins, and straws)
- Script
- Facilitator
- Transcript
- Themes
- Release forms
- Roster
- Presentation aids (easels; flip charts; site aerial photographs; paper and pencils)

A script for the facilitator included the following:

1. Housekeeping:
   - Introductions.
   - Reminder about sign-in, release, and comments forms.
   - Explanation of video: for record of proceedings and capture of all ideas.
   - Feel free to get up if you need a break, refreshments, or restroom.
   - Please keep comments brief (30 seconds); we want to hear from everyone; record your ideas on notepads.

- As facilitator, I'm not here to share my ideas, rather my role is to direct answers to group; there are no right or wrong answers.
- This is not a debate about specifics. Site is representative of fringe (or infill) development in sensitive desert.

2. Objectives:
   - Capture your visions for development on the suburban fringe (or infill development).
   - What you think are the important elements for neighborhood design that contribute to community well-being?
   - Present your ideas for appropriate, sustainable development on the study site.
3. Discussion questions:
   Tell the group briefly about yourself:
   - Where you live.
   - Your interest in the site, or in fringe development in general.

   How do you think the city is doing in terms of environmentally sensitive development?
   - What are the problems that need to be fixed?
   - What is appropriate with regard to: density; open space; habitat protection; waste generation and disposal; energy consumption; water consumption?

   How does neighborhood design help to create a sense of community? What elements should it contain?

   What are your views regarding "appropriate development" for the site? Use the outline maps in front of you or describe them in a series of statements.

   What needs to be changed in order for your vision to become reality?

Delphi

Delphi, developed in the 1950s by the RAND Corporation, was originally used as a means of technological forecasting and is a technique that relies strongly on experts. The name *Delphi* is taken from the ancient Greek city where travelers went to consult the oracle about the future (Linstone and Turoff 1975; U.S. Department of Transportation 1976; Institute for Participatory Management and Planning 1997). The idea is to conduct consecutive rounds of argument, offering different points of view about a project or issue, until finally reaching a consensus. It is an indirect technique, compared to the direct citizen participation approaches involved in group dynamics.

Delphi works in the following manner. Experts are chosen to form a Delphi panel. The Institute for Participatory Management and Planning suggests this may be done by conducting a survey among people knowledgeable about a particular issue. This can be accomplished, for example, through a bibliographical search of the literature about the issue. From the survey, well-informed individuals are identified. These persons are contacted and asked to nominate others who are also knowledgeable about the subject. They are then contacted and asked to nominate their own list of experts. After a while, the same names keep reappearing. Experts representing different points of view are sought. For instance, if one is trying to establish land-use goals for a reclaimed strip mine, one expert from the mining industry may be identified, while another may be from a nature conservancy, another from agriculture, and so on. The leading experts from the various points of view become a Delphi panel that is never to meet or know who the other members of the panel are (Institute for Participatory Planning 1978; Institute for Participatory Management and Planning 1997).

This panel of 8 to 12 experts is asked to predict the future of the project or issue. These predictions are compiled and distributed to the panel without identifying the authors. The panel reviews the prophesies and each expert is given the opportunity to change his or her own. If the predictions are changed, then a second round is conducted. The process is continued until the panel members reach a consensus or remain firm in their forecasts. The predictions then may be used by a citizens' advisory committee, technical advisory committee, neighborhood council, planning commission, and/or agency staff to establish goals and policy for the project or issue.

Policy Delphi

Policy Delphi is an extension of traditional Delphi techniques. It usually involves a 7- to 15-member Delphi Expert Opinion Panel (Pease and Coughlin 1996; Steiner et al. 1994), although de Loe notes it "can be used to facilitate interaction in groups of up to 50 people" (1995, 53).

Like traditional Delphi, Policy Delphi is a multiple-round, interactive technique. But whereas traditional Delphi is characterized by anonymity, the Delphi Expert Opinion Panel meets and its members interact. The group can consist of public employees with a technical knowledge of the planning focus, representatives of business and industry, and members of public-interest groups and the public.

Needham and de Loe observe that purposes of Policy Delphi include identifying "problems and issues or . . . to generate new information about problems and issues" (1990, 134). Policy Delphi is especially useful early in the planning process, when issues and preliminary goals are being identified. Robert de Loe (1995) argues that Policy Delphi be employed as a precursor to more in-depth workshops or interviews.

De Loe identifies Policy Delphi an "idea-generating strategy." The technique was first proposed by Turoff (1970, 1975) and subsequently refined by de Loe (1995, 1990 with Needham). Policy Delphi design includes the following six steps:

1. *Formulation of the issues.* What is the issue that really should be under consideration? How should it be stated?
2. *Exposing the options.* Given the issue, what are the policy options available?
3. *Determining initial positions on the issues.* Which are the ones everyone already agrees upon and which are the unimportant ones to be discarded? Which are the ones exhibiting disagreement among the respondents?
4. *Exploring and obtaining the reasons for disagreements.* What underlying assumptions, views, or facts are being used by the individuals to support their respective positions?
5. *Evaluating the underlying reasons.* How does the group view the separate arguments used to defend various positions and how do they compare to one another on a relative basis?
6. *Reevaluating the options.* Reevaluation is based upon the views of the underlying "evidence" and the assessment of its relevance to each position taken (adapted from Turoff 1975 by de Loe 1995, 58).

The foregoing techniques are the major ones used for identifying issues and establishing goals. These and others may be used in the subsequent stages of the planning process. The Institute for Participatory Management and Planning has developed a matrix of citizen participation techniques and their relative effectiveness (Figure 2.1). Each planning issue or project should help to determine the appropriate participation technique. An effort should be made to keep people involved in the subsequent steps of the planning process. Sign-up sheets should be collected at all meetings and those lists used to keep people informed over time. Continual communication between the public and the planning agency or consultant can create knowledgeable citizens who will support decisions that result from the process. Some planners have found it helpful to maintain a newspaper article clipping file about public meetings to document public involvement and the planning process. For many planning processes, these direct participation techniques need to be augmented by public opinion polls to ensure that diverse views are recognized.

Public Opinion Polls

Preference surveys, or *public opinion polls* as they are more commonly known, have become a ubiquitous part of American life. Surveys can be conducted through the mail, over the telephone, or by face-to-face interviews. Public opinion polls can be used to identify issues and to set goals. One of the leading practitioners of preference surveying, Don Dillman, a professor of sociology at Washington State University, has suggested that there are three schools of thought concerning public opinion polls. The first is "do not conduct polls." The second view is that surveys are fundamental for community participation. Finally, the third school of thought is that polls can be useful—if done well.

Preference surveys are popular for several reasons. They are convenient for planners and other researchers; a researcher does not have to leave the comforts of her or his office to write a survey or compile the results. Moreover, results are relatively simple to tabulate. In this age of computers it is important that research results can be tabulated for statistical analysis. Finally, polls can be used to demonstrate that the government pays attention to what the people are saying; thus, "because the government is responsive, democracy is working."

The first of the arguments used by people who are pessimistic about the usefulness of polls is that "people are not well enough informed or otherwise capable of stating their real preferences" (Dillman 1977, 31). Dillman questions whether people who never went to high school can effectively assess the needs of higher education, or whether people whose medical experience consists of an annual checkup can accurately determine community health care needs. Land-use and natural resource management issues are equally complicated and may involve technical issues difficult for the average citizen to understand, as, for example, the siting of a nuclear power plant or hazardous waste disposal. Social and environmental issues are also becoming more complex, requiring more specialized knowledge, and may not lend themselves to simple yes, no, maybe, or no-opinion responses.

The second basis of criticism raised by Dillman concerning the use of surveys is the belief that "people's stated preferences are superficial and likely to change; thus, they can provide an inadequate basis for making decisions with long lasting consequences" (1977, 32). A community's perception of a need for a service—a school, hospital, or highway—may be higher than its willingness to pay for the same service. A citizen may want the convenience of cheap electrical power or plastic garbage bags but resist the siting of a power generating plant or chemical factory in her or his community.

The final criticism is a technical one: "The procedures used for assessing people's preferences are inevitably inadequate, leaving a very large gap between survey questions and policy questions they were supposed to address" (Dillman 1977, 32). Dillman (1978) gives several examples. For instance, a survey may ask very general questions, such as, "Do you consider juvenile delinquency to be a serious, moderate, slight, or no problem in this community?" and then attempt to use them to address a specific issue: "Should we increase the parks and recreation budget by 25 percent?"

Dillman presents two models for policy surveys (Figure 2.2). The first, the independent survey, is illustrative of the typical, simplistic one-shot survey. His alternative, the synchronized survey, is one that can be used as an integral part of the entire planning process. In Chapter 4, surveys are discussed as a community inventory technique, while in Chapter 6, the synchronized survey will be presented as a means for the selection of preferences among various choices.

Another form of opinion polling is the community self-survey. In this less scientific approach, the people of an area write and collect a survey themselves instead of utilizing the services of an outsider. The benefit of a self-survey is that it allows and even encourages people to think about the area in which they reside (Littrell 1976). The disadvantages include possible biases in drafting the survey and inaccuracies that may result in tabulating and analyzing the results.

	Techniques' other PROs and CONs												Responsibility					Responsiveness					Effectiveness					
CP Techniques Number…	$ Costs… Expensive: (–)… Cheap: (+)	Time Demanding… Calendar Time	Other Costs	Risk	Difficulty	Flexibility and Adaptability	Creation of Record	Limitations of Written Communications	Limitations of Meetings				1 Establish the legitimacy of your agency and your project	2 Maintain the legitimacy of your agency and your project	3 Establish the legitimacy of your processes	4 Maintain the legitimacy of your processes	5 Establish and maintain the legitimacy of assumptions and earlier decisions	6 Get to know all and potentially affected interests	7 Get to see the project through their eyes	8 Identify all potentially relevant problems	9 Generate solutions	10 Articulate and clarify the key issues	11 Nurture and protect your credibility	12 Have your communications received and understood	13 Receive and understand information that is communicated	14 Search for commonn grounds among polarized PAIs	15 Mediate between polarized interests
1A	– / –	– / –					+ /		– / –	1A	Working meeting	1A	◔	◔	◔	◔	●	◔	◕	●	◑	●	◑	○	○	●	◕
1B	– / –	– / –	/ –	– /	– / –		+ / +		– / –	1B	"Open" meeting	1B	●	●	◕	●	●	◕	◔	◑	○	●	●	◑	◔	⊗	○
1C	– /	– / –					+ / +		– / –	1C	Forum	1C	●	◕	◕	◕	●	●	●	●	◑	●	●	◑	●	◑	◑
1D	/ –	/ –		– / –	– / –				– / –	1D	Public mass meeting	1D	⊗	⊗	⊗	⊗	◑	⊗	◔	◑	⊗	○	◑	◑	○	⊗	⊗
1E	– /	– / –	/ –	– / –	– / –	– / –	+ / +		– / –	1E	Public hearing	1E	●	◕	●	◕	●	◔	○	◔	○	●	●	◔	◔	⊗	⊗
1F	– /	– /		+ /	+ / +	+ / +	+ / +		+ /	1F	Open house	1F	◑	◑	◑	◕	●	●	●	●	◕	◑	●	◕	◕	◑	◕
1G	– /	– / –	/ –	– /	– /		+ /		– / –	1G	Town meeting	1G	◔	◔	◔	◑	●	◑	◑	◕	◑	◑	◕	◕	●	○	○
1H		/ –		– /			+ /		– / –	1H	Samoan Circle	1H	○	○	○	○	◕	◕	◕	◑	◔	⊗	○	○	◑	●	●
1I										1I		1I															
1J										1J		1J															
2A	– /	– / –		– /	– /		+ /		– / –	2A	Popularity-type advice-giving Advisory Committee	2A	◔	◔	◑	◑	◕	◔	◕	◔	◔	◑	◔	◔	◑	●	◕
2B	– /	/ –		– /	– /		+ /		– / –	2B	Content-type advice-giving Advisory Committee	2B	◔	◔	◑	◑	●	◕	◕	●	●	●	●	◔	●	◕	◕
2C	– /	– / –		– /	– / –		+ / +		– /	2C	Blue Ribbon Panel	2C	◑	◑	◑	◑	◕	◔	◑	◕	◑	◕	◑	○	◕	◑	●
2D	– /	– / –	– /	– /	– / –		+ /			2D	Watchdog Advisory Committee	2D	⊗	○	○	○	◑	○	◔	◑	◔	◔	◑	○	◔	○	○
2E	– /	– / –	– / –	– /	– /		+ / +			2E	Constituency-building Advisory Committee	2E	⊗	⊗	○	○	○	○	◔	◕	◑	◑	○	○	○	⊗	○
2F	– /	– / –	– / –	– / –	– / –		+ / +		– / –	2F	Consensus-building Advisory Committee	2F	●	◑	●	◑	●	◕	◑	●	◕	◑	●	◑	◕	●	●
2G	– /	– / –	– / –	– / –	– / –		+ / +		– / –	2G	Referee / third party / negotiating Advisory Committee	2G	○	◑	○	◑	◕	◔	◑	◕	●	●	◑	◔	◕	●	●
2H	– / –	– / –			– / –	+ / +	+ / +			2H	"Go-fors" Advisory Committee	2H	◑	◕	◑	◕	●	●	●	●	●	◕	●	●	●	◕	◔
2I	– /	– /	– / –	– / –	– /		+ /		– / –	2I	"Foxes" Advisory Committee	2I	◑	◑	◕	◑	◕	◔	◑	●	◕	◑	◕	◑	◑	●	◑
2J	/ –	– / –		– /	– / –	+ / +	+ / +			2J	"Beavers" Advisory Committee	2J	●	●	◔	◑	◑	◔	◔	◑	●	◕	◕	◔	◑	○	○
2K										2K		2K															
2L										2L		2L															
2M										2M		2M															
2N										2N		2N															
3		/ –		– /	+ / +	+ /	+ /		+ / +	3	Nominal group workshop	3	○	○	○	○	●	◔	●	●	◕	◑	◔	○	◕	●	◑
4A	+ /					+ /	+ /	– /		4A	Producing and releasing materials to potentially affected interests and the media	4A	●	●	●	●	●	○	○	○	○	●	●	●	◑	◑	◑
4B										4B		4B															
5	– /	– /				+ /	+ /	– /		5	Project or Agency newsletter	5	◔	◑	◕	●	◑	○	○	○	○	◕	◕	●	◔	◔	○
6	+ /	+ /			– /					6	"Napolean's Idiot"	6	○	○	○	○	◑	○	◔	○	○	●	◑	●	◑	◑	◔
7	+ /	/ +			– /	+ /	+ /			7	Educating the potentially affected interests about your PS/DM processes	7	●	●	●	●	●	○	○	○	○	●	◕	◕	◑	◑	◔
8	+ /		– / –	– /			+ /	– /		8	Mapping sociopolitical and environmental data	8	○	○	○	○	◔	○	◑	◕	◕	◑	◔	◑	◔	○	⊗
9A	/ +					+ / +	+ /			9A	Presenting the public the full range of options	9A	○	◑	○	◑	◑	◔	◔	◕	◕	●	◑	◕	◕	◑	◑
9B		– /	+ /		– /	/ +	+ / +			9B	Fishbowl planning	9B	◑	◑	●	●	●	◑	◑	◕	◕	●	●	◕	◕	◕	◕
10	/ +				– / +		+ /			10	Illustrating the final form of a solution in layman's terms	10	○	○	○	○	◑	◔	●	●	◑	◑	◑	●	◑	◔	◔
11	– / +	– / +	+ /		– / +	+ /	+ / +			11	Dealing with the public in the Agency offices	11	◕	◕	◕	◕	○	●	◕	◑	◑	○	◑	○	●	○	◔
12	– / +	– / +	+ /		– / +	+ /	+ / +			12	Ombudsman	12	◑	◑	◑	◑	○	◑	◑	◑	◑	◔	◑	◔	●	◔	◑
13					– /	+ /				13	Facilitating internal communication	13	○	◔	○	◔	●	○	◑	●	●	◑	◔	◔	◔	◔	◔

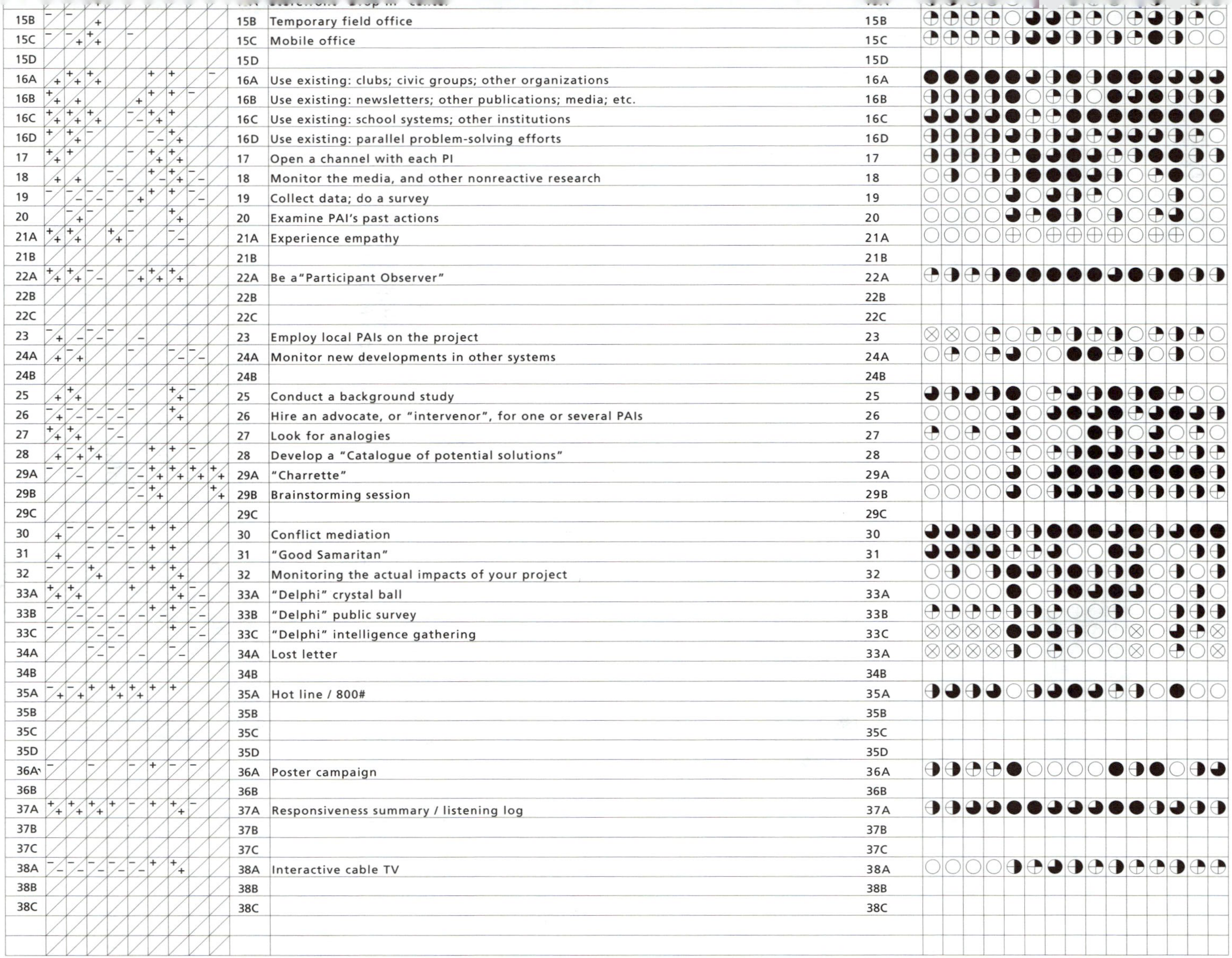

	Technique	
15B	Temporary field office	15B
15C	Mobile office	15C
15D		15D
16A	Use existing: clubs; civic groups; other organizations	16A
16B	Use existing: newsletters; other publications; media; etc.	16B
16C	Use existing: school systems; other institutions	16C
16D	Use existing: parallel problem-solving efforts	16D
17	Open a channel with each PI	17
18	Monitor the media, and other nonreactive research	18
19	Collect data; do a survey	19
20	Examine PAI's past actions	20
21A	Experience empathy	21A
21B		21B
22A	Be a "Participant Observer"	22A
22B		22B
22C		22C
23	Employ local PAIs on the project	23
24A	Monitor new developments in other systems	24A
24B		24B
25	Conduct a background study	25
26	Hire an advocate, or "intervenor", for one or several PAIs	26
27	Look for analogies	27
28	Develop a "Catalogue of potential solutions"	28
29A	"Charrette"	29A
29B	Brainstorming session	29B
29C		29C
30	Conflict mediation	30
31	"Good Samaritan"	31
32	Monitoring the actual impacts of your project	32
33A	"Delphi" crystal ball	33A
33B	"Delphi" public survey	33B
33C	"Delphi" intelligence gathering	33C
34A	Lost letter	33A
34B		34B
35A	Hot line / 800#	35A
35B		35B
35C		35C
35D		35D
36A	Poster campaign	36A
36B		36B
37A	Responsiveness summary / listening log	37A
37B		37B
37C		37C
38A	Interactive cable TV	38A
38B		38B
38C		38C

FIGURE 2.1 Citizen participation techniques and their relative effectiveness. *(Source: Institute for Participatory Management and Planning 1997)*

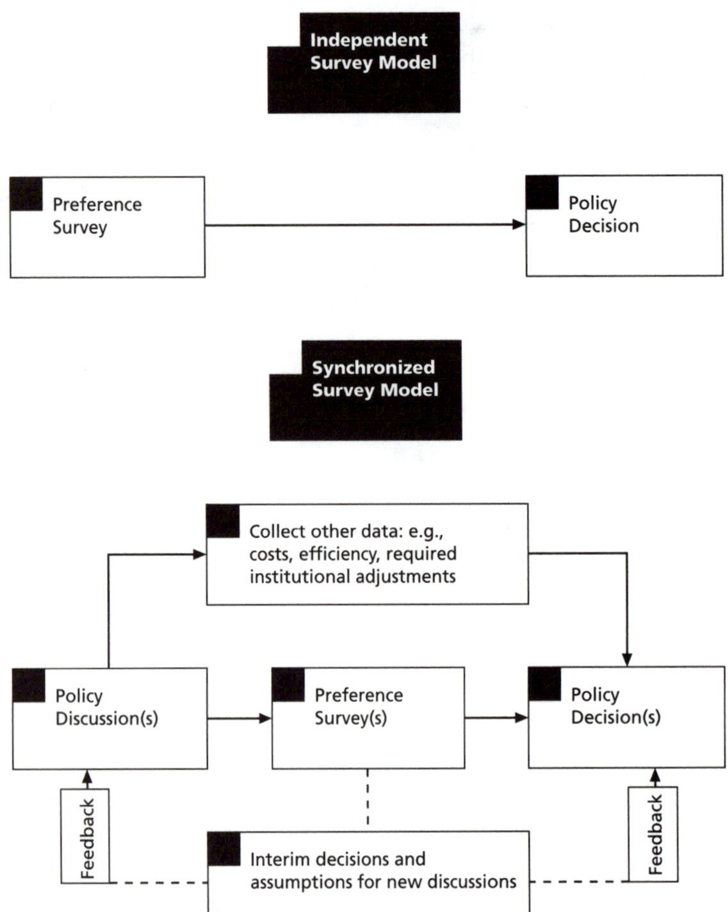

FIGURE 2.2 Two models for bringing stated preferences to bear on policy decisions. *(Source: Dillman 1977)*

Town Meetings and Public Hearings

Whereas citizen participation and public opinion polls may be desirable means to help a community identify issues and establish goals, they are undertaken at the discretion of local officials. Town meetings and public hearings, in contrast, are frequently required by law. The origin of the American tradition of town meetings is in New England. According to planning historian John Reps, in New England "the complete rural-urban settlement was called a town, a word that encompassed not only the nucleated urban-type settlement but the entire community of village lots and farm fields as well" (1970, 147). This form of town continues in New England and has had enduring influence in American politics.

The New England town meeting was an outgrowth of the need to provide defense and to settle agricultural matters. It was strengthened by the religious bond that brought the Puritan settlers from England to the New World and their special political adeptness. The topography and hostile native people reinforced the group consciousness already forged by religious persecution and military fraternity.

While the village became the focus of the New England community, agriculture became its chief occupation. Lots were drawn for house sites in the village, and the surrounding farmland was divided into long strips, also assigned by drawing lots. Reps explains the unique farming structure:

> While the strips themselves were not fenced, it was the usual practice to enclose an entire field by a wooden paling. Each farmer then became responsible for his proportionate share of the fencing. . . . [The group met to determine] what would be grown, when they should be harvested and what land should be left in fallow. Common cultivation was thus carried out (1970, 148).

The Puritans who developed this system of common fields, or proprietor's commons, were not a politically naive group. They had risen in the sixteenth century in the Church of England, demanding greater strictness in religious discipline. During part of the seventeenth century they constituted a powerful political party, ruling England briefly after its bloody civil war. As a result, the New England town meeting was a sophisticated forum where defensive, agricultural, and other political matters were decided after open debate and discussion. Today town meetings continue to be an integral part of local government in New England.

Beginning with President Jimmy Carter, televised town meetings have become increasingly popular with politicians. He and other elected officials have used these broadcasted town meetings "as a tool to stay in touch with the grass roots" (Institute for Participatory Management and Planning 1997, V-15). Town meetings are usually semiformal in their structure. The addition of television cameras adds formality to the gatherings.

Another contemporary heir of the New England town meeting for most of the United States is the *public hearing.* City planners have advocated public hearings as an essential part of good government and comprehensive planning since the beginning of the twentieth century. Hearings are now a part of most municipal and county governments in the United States and are often mandated by federal and state law. Planning commissions as well as the local legislative body—the city council or board of county commissioners—are often required to hold hearings in order to make plans and to amend them. Nowadays, many local issues are debated at public hearings and goals are discussed. A group of citizens may raise an issue at a public hearing, and as a result the planning commission, city council, or county commission may resolve to address the issue.

Diori Kreske observes that public hearings "are normally more formal than public meetings" (1996, 267). Many American states have strict laws that govern the conduct of a hearing. According to Kreske, a "hearing may have (1) a public official who presides over the hearing, (2) ground rules on how the hearing will be conducted, (3) a speaker's microphone and podium, and (4) a court reporter or tape recording of the proceedings, or both" (1996, 267).

Often public hearings can provide the best entertainment in town. Certainly they have more dimensions than the average television fare but to participate one must leave the comfortable confines of one's own home. Many local governments have experimented with broadcasting hearings on cable television public access stations, but such programs seldom dent the Nielsen ratings. The result is that public hearings become dominated by single-issue adversary groups or special interests.

Efraim Gil and Enid Lucchesi explain this situation in the following way:

> Citizen participation is most often stimulated by existing social problems coupled with a lack of con-

> fidence in official solutions—and it varies with economic and social conditions. When citizens feel that officials are making decisions similar to those that they themselves would make, or that these decisions necessitate special knowledge that the official has and the citizens do not have, or when they feel the decision is economically sound, they are not likely to actively participate in government. It is when these criteria of government performance are not being met that citizens lose confidence in government officials and the demand for the active participation arises (1979, 553–554).

Public hearings are a difficult forum in which to involve citizens in goal setting. Because such hearings are often a legal requirement, they may often assume a legal aura, which may intimidate citizens. Some participants have limited time, and goals are often written before such hearings. This means the goals may be composed by a planning staff, perhaps only with the advice of vested interests. Therefore, people must be involved through task forces, advisory committees, or workshops before goals are set.

The role of citizen involvement is much debated. One school of thought holds that citizens are a nuisance and their participation should be avoided. Another viewpoint is that public participation programs are little more than tokenism and are ineffective because citizens are excluded from actual decision making. Many feel there is a gap between government agencies and grass roots community organizations. Ray MacNair (1981) has proposed a model to link agency planning and citizen organizing (Figure 2.3). Town meetings and public hearings can be used at strategic points in this model to improve communication between citizens and planners.

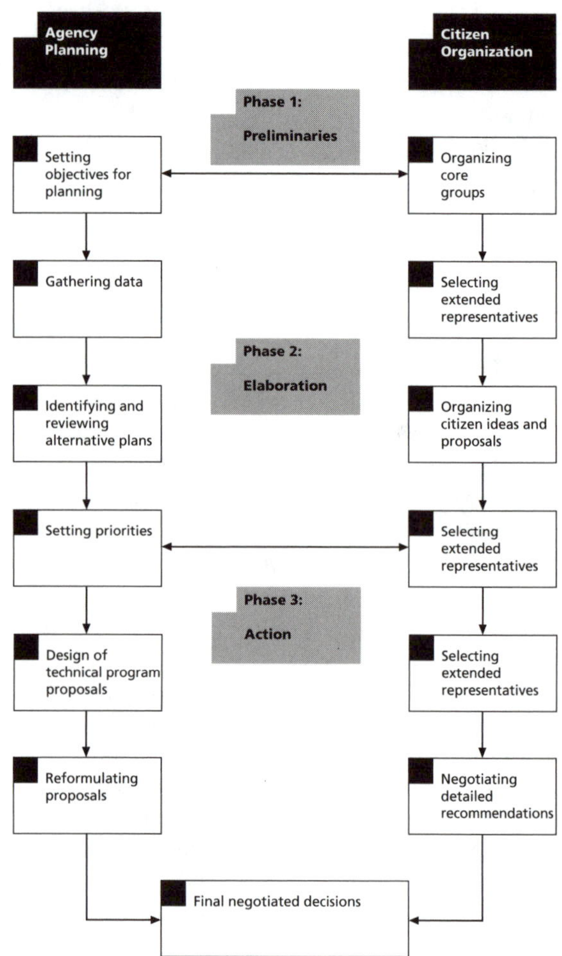

FIGURE 2.3 Coordinated planning and organizing. *(Source: MacNair 1981)*

GOAL SETTING

Often more than one citizen involvement technique will be used by planners to identify issues and to set goals. For example, the local planning commission may believe that rapid growth is causing problems such as linking new public services to new development and raising the funds to pay for those additional public services. Furthermore, members of the planning commission may have observed that the quality of the new development is below existing community standards, creating safety hazards for new residents and negatively impacting the property values of existing homeowners. They may also observe that the siting of some new development is causing environmental damage and creating potential health and safety problems.

The planning commissioners may then request the staff planner or a consultant to study the situation. The staff or consulting planner may conduct a mail survey of the planning area to determine if indeed these perceptions are accurate. If the findings of the survey are affirmative, a task force may be organized to recommend goals for addressing the problems created by the growth. These suggested goals are presented at hearings before the planning commission, which can in turn recommend that goals be established by the county commission or city council. At this step in the planning process, goals should be considered preliminary. Still there should be some agreed-upon goal statement to guide the rest of the process. To address the growth issue, for instance, the goal could be "to provide for planned and orderly development within the planning area, while balancing basic human needs of a changing population and maintaining a healthy environment for future generations."

In an ecological planning process, goals should be approached in an evolutionary manner. At this early step in the planning process, some consensus should be reached about the direction to be taken to address the problems and opportunities facing the area. These aims should be debated and refined throughout the planning process, as suggested by the central position of Step 8 in Figure 1.1. At some point, goals need to be adopted formally. In Chapter 7, it is recommended that goals become part of a landscape plan.

TWO EXAMPLES OF GOAL-ORIENTED PLANNING

Most plans include goals. Few plans link goals to sustained action. Oregon and the New Jersey Pinelands provide examples of planning efforts where goals direct decision making. To borrow from Michael Neuman, these plans "chart collective hope." Neuman argues that "we need to better understand the connection of people to place to plan, if we want to respond to the needs of residents rather than regulations" (1998a, 214).

The Oregon Comprehensive Planning Law

Beginning in the 1960s and continuing to the present, several states adopted ambitious, new land-use planning laws. These new laws often prescribe that local governments adopt specific goals. Among the most far-reaching statewide planning efforts are those of Hawaii, Vermont, Oregon, and Florida (Bosselman and Callies 1971; Bosselman et al. 1973; Callies 1980; DeGrove 1984; Kelly 1993; Nelson and Duncan 1995).

The Oregon comprehensive law provides one of the best examples of statewide goal-oriented planning. The Oregon program began in 1969 with Senate Bill 10 and expanded significantly with the passage of Senate Bill 100 in 1973 (Carson 1998). With Governor Tom McCall and state senators Hector Macpherson and Ted Hallek providing the leadership, Senate Bill 100 was created by the Oregon legislature. The law established the Land Conservation and Development Commission (LCDC), and authorized the governor to appoint citizen members to the LCDC and the LCDC to coordinate planning in Oregon. The Department of Land Conservation and Development (DLCD) was formed to administer the law. Nineteen goals were set as regulations to be followed by city and county governments throughout the state. (Since some goals are specific to coastal counties or those along the Willamette River, the number of goals that local governments must follow varies with their location.) The goals were established in 1975 after a program of 127 citizen workshops that involved 10,000 participants (Pease 1984). Each of these goals reveals much about the problems and opportunities facing Oregon and the policies established to address the planning issues raised by those problems and opportunities.

The 19 statewide goals are printed in a 24-page newsprint tabloid that has been continuously reprinted and distributed throughout the state since 1975. More recently the goals have also become available on DLCD's website (www.lcd.state.or.us). The tabloid and the website offer accessible easy-to-read formats. Definitions of the technical terms are provided. As a result, Oregon's statewide goals are familiar throughout the state. The goals are not a thick technical report that has languished and been forgotten on someone's office bookshelf. Nor are the goals a vapid "vision" statement printed on glossy paper and soon forgotten. A review of several of Oregon's goals helps to illustrate the thrust of the plan. There are three types of goals: process goals (1 and 2); conservation goals (3, 4, 5, 6, 7, 8, and 15); and development goals (9, 10, 11, 12, 13, 14). The coastal goals only apply to jurisdictions bordering the ocean and are not applicable to most jurisdictions, just as goal 15, the Willamette Greenway Goal, only applies to that river corridor. The first goal, a statewide goal, addresses citizen involvement: "To develop a citizen involvement program that [ensures] the opportunity for citizens to be involved in all phases of the planning process" (Land Conservation and Development Commission 1980, 3; Department of Land Conservation and Development 1996).

This goal statement and the ones that follow are accompanied by specific planning and implementation guidelines. The guidelines for the first goal include standards for public involvement, communication, citizen influence, technical information, feedback mechanisms, and financial support (see Chapter 8). Citizens are to be involved throughout the planning process in inventorying, recording, mapping, describing, analyzing, and evaluating the elements necessary for the development of local plans. The public is to participate in the preparation of local plans and the adoption process, plus the implementation, evaluation, and revision of plans.

The second statewide goal addresses land-use planning. It is the second goal of Oregon:

> To establish a land-use planning process and policy framework as a basis for all decisions and actions related to the use of land and to assure an adequate factual base for such decisions and actions. City, county, state, and federal agency and special district plans and actions related to land use shall be consistent with the comprehensive plans of cities and counties and regional plans (Land Conservation and Development Commission 1980, 4; Department of Land Conservation and Development 1996).

The land-use planning goal is accompanied by a statement explaining where exceptions could be made under certain circumstances. An integrated framework is required for the preparation of plans and implementation measures; the conformance of regional, state, and federal plans; the content of the plan; the filing of plans; revisions during the planning process; implementation measures; and the use of the statewide planning goals (Land Conservation and Development Commission 1980) (see Chapter 7).

The LCDC specifies how plans should be done, and it mandates that plans must address the goals and that plans must be based on findings of fact, but what actually goes into the plan is up to the local jurisdiction. Oregon guidelines describe both the factual basis for the plan as well as planning elements. The factual basis of the plan should include data as they relate to the goals. These data address natural resources, human-made structures and utilities, population and economic characteristics, and the roles and responsibilities of governmental units. The elements of the plan include the applicable statewide planning goals, any critical geographic area designated by the Oregon legislature, specific local issues, and time periods of the plan.

These elements are to fit together and relate to one another to form a consistent whole at all times (Department of Land Conservation and Development 1996).

The suggested guidelines for land-use implementation include management measures like ordinances controlling the use and construction on the land, such as building codes, sign ordinances, subdivision regulations, and zoning ordinances. Oregon statutes require that subdivision and zoning ordinances be used to implement the jurisdiction's comprehensive plan. Additional management measures are specific plans for public facilities, capital improvement budgeting, state and federal land-use regulations, and annexations and other governmental boundary reorganizations. Site and specific area implementation measures include building permits, septic tank permits, driveway permits, subdivision review, zone changes, conditional use permits, the construction of public facilities, the provision of land-related public services such as fire and police, the awarding of state and federal grants to local governments to provide these facilities and services, and the leasing of public lands (Land Conservation and Development Commission 1980). Plan implementation measures will be discussed in greater detail in Chapter 10.

Implementation, however, begins with the goals. For example, the third statewide planning goal is to preserve and maintain agricultural lands. This goal states: "Agricultural lands shall be preserved and maintained for farm use, consistent with existing and future needs for agricultural products, forest, and open space and with the state's agricultural land-use policy" (Land Conservation and Development 1996).

Oregon counties authorize farm uses and those nonfarm uses defined by LCDC rule that do not have significant adverse impacts on farm or forest practices. Agricultural zoning implements the goal. Such zoning limits uses which can have significant adverse effects on agricultural and forest land, farm and forest uses, and accepted farming or forest practices. The Land Conservation and Development Commission has directed counties to establish minimum sizes for new lots or parcels in each agricultural zoning designation. These minimum sizes are to be appropriate to sustain the existing commercial agricultural enterprise within the area. The commission authorizes counties to designate certain agricultural land as "marginal" and to allow those uses and divisions on these lands as permitted by law (Department of Land Conservation and Development 1996).

The NRCS land capability classification system is used to define agricultural land in Oregon. In western Oregon, agricultural land is predominantly Class I, II, III, and IV soils, and in eastern Oregon land is predominantly Class I, II, III, IV, V, VI soils (see Chapter 5). Guidelines are established for both the planning and implementation of the agricultural goal. The first planning guideline states that urban growth should be separated from agricultural lands by buffer, or transitional, areas of open space. The second planning guideline states that plans providing for the preservation and maintenance of farmland for agricultural use should consider as a major determinant the carrying capacity of the air, land, and waste resources of the planning area. There are four guidelines for the implementation of the agricultural lands goal. First, nonfarm uses permitted within farm-use zones should be minimized to allow for maximum agricultural productivity. Subsequent to the initial passage of the statewide planning goals, specific rules were adopted regulating nonfarm dwellings in agricultural zones. Second, extension of services, such as sewer and water supplies, into rural areas should be appropriate for the needs of agriculture, farm use, and permitted nonfarm use. Third, to protect the farm-use integrity of the area, special provisions are made for services that need to pass through agricultural lands. Finally, forest and open space uses are to be permitted on farmlands that are set aside for future agricultural development (Land Conservation and Development Commission 1980;

Department of Land Conservation and Development 1996).

The fourth statewide planning goal of Oregon is to conserve forestlands for forest uses. The goal is "to conserve forest lands by maintaining the forest land base and to protect the state's forest economy by making possible economically efficient forest practices that assure the continuous growing and harvesting of forest tree species as the leading use on forest land consistent with sound management of soil, air, water, and fish and wildlife resources and to provide for recreational opportunities and agriculture" (Department of Land Conservation and Development 1996).

Forestlands are defined by the state. Such lands are suitable for commercial forest uses including adjacent or nearby lands which are necessary to permit forest operations or practices as well as other forested lands that maintain soil, air, water, and fish and wildlife resources (Department of Land Conservation and Development 1996). Uses permitted in forest zones include those related to and in support of forest operations. In addition, uses are allowed which conserve soil, water, and air quality and which provide for fish and wildlife habitat as well as agriculture and recreation opportunities in a forest environment. Locally dependent uses and dwellings authorized by Oregon law are permitted too (Department of Land Conservation and Development 1996). Again, there are specific guidelines for the planning and implementation of the forestlands goal.

Goals 5 through 9 address open spaces, scenic and historic areas, and natural resources; air, water, and land resources quality; areas subject to natural disasters and hazards; recreational needs; and the economy of the state. The sixth goal indicates that local governments need to consider the carrying capacity of the air, water, and land when addressing growth in plans (Carson 1998). The tenth goal is "to provide for the housing needs of citizens of the state" (Land Conservation and Development Commission 1980, 10). To achieve this goal, buildable land for homesites is to be identified. Plans are to encourage the development on those lands of "adequate numbers of housing units at price ranges and rent levels which are commensurate with the financial capabilities of Oregon households," and the plans are to "allow for flexibility of housing location, type and density" (Land Conservation and Development Commission 1980, 10; Department of Land Conservation and Development 1996).

The remaining nine goals include:

11. Public facilities and services
12. Transportation
13. Energy conservation
14. Urbanization
15. Willamette River greenway
16. Estuarine resources
17. Coastal shorelines
18. Beaches and dunes
19. Ocean resources

Each of these 19 goals is explained in a succinct statement. Each goal is accompanied by specific suggested guidelines for planning and implementation. Key terms are defined with several of the goal statements and in a glossary on the two final pages of the tabloid. This is the most

Transportation is a focus of Goal 12 in Oregon's statewide planning program.

comprehensive statement of goals ever developed for an American state. The achievement of these goals has required the careful balancing of often-conflicting demands. Because of the difficulty of this task and the success of the Oregon planning effort, it will be used as an example throughout this book, as will the plan for the New Jersey Pinelands.

Oregon's goal-oriented land-use planning has influenced subsequent state-level growth management efforts. This influence provides another reason to continue to probe the Oregon approach. John DeGrove (1998) identifies six common threads in the various state growth management programs, which can primarily be traced to the example set by Oregon's goals: (1) consistency, (2) concurrency, (3) compact urban growth patterns, (4) protection of natural systems, (5) economic development, and (6) affordable housing. Several of these "threads" are self-explanatory and explicit goals in Oregon. Concerning consistency, DeGrove notes, "Beginning with Oregon in 1973, consistency has been one of the common threads among states' systems. It is through the consistency requirement that the roles and responsibilities of state, regional, and local levels are defined" (1998, 86). Oregon's mandate for consistency is absolute. The concurrency "thread" links infrastructure development to its impact. The idea is that planning goals should be concurrent with fiscal policy and construction expenditures. Such concurrency can result in more compact urban growth as well as the protection of natural systems.

The New Jersey Pinelands Comprehensive Management Plan

The New Jersey Pinelands, or Pine Barrens as the region is known by its inhabitants, is a substate, multicounty region (Figure 2.4). The Pinelands is a 935,000-acre (378,000-hectare) forest located in the midst of the most densely populated region in the United States. The New Jersey Pinelands Comprehensive Management Plan was

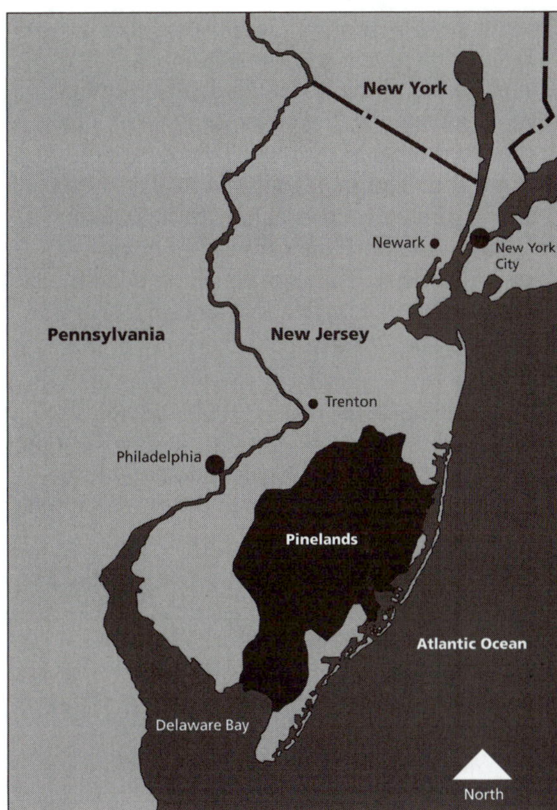

FIGURE 2.4 New Jersey Pinelands location.

a result of both federal and state legislative action. The federal action was the designation by Congress in 1978 of the Pinelands as a national reserve. This legislative mandate was set forth in the National Parks and Recreation Act of 1978, signed by President Jimmy Carter on November 10, 1978. The state action was the 1979 New Jersey Pinelands Protection Act (Pinelands Commission 1980; Lilieholm and Romm 1992; for the most recent planning information, see www.state.nj.us/pinelands).

As a result of these actions, Governor Brendan T. Byrne issued an executive order that established the Pinelands Planning Commission. The commission's composition was prescribed in both the federal and state laws as follows: fifteen members, including one appointed by each of the governing bodies of the seven Pinelands counties, seven appointed by the governor of New Jersey, and one designated by the U.S. Secretary of the Interior. The overriding goals of the acts are to preserve, protect, and enhance the significant values of the land and water resources in the Pinelands. The state act speaks of the need to maintain a contiguous tract of land in its natural state; safeguard the essential character of the Pinelands environment; protect the quality of the surface and groundwater; promote compatible agricultural and recreational uses; and encourage appropriate residential, commercial, and industrial patterns of development (Pinelands Commission 1980).

Based on the state and federal legislation, the Pinelands Commission adopted 5 resource and use goals and 25 policies. The goals and policies were not as comprehensive as those goals and guidelines developed by the LCDC. The resource goals and policies adopted for the Pinelands are in Table 2.1. As can be seen from this table, the Pinelands goals emphasize the protection of natural, historical, cultural, and agricultural resources. Development is to be encouraged in a manner compatible with these resources. The overall goal of the Pinelands plan is to balance resource conservation and development by guiding new growth away from environmentally sensitive areas and into designated growth areas (Lilieholm and Romm 1992). (The plan is discussed further in Chapters 4 and 7.)

During October the Pinelands bogs are flooded to loosen cranberries from their vines, a step in the harvesting of this crop, which yields approximately $23 million a year in sales. *(Norma Martin Milner, New Jersey Pinelands Commission)*

The Pinelands and Oregon cases are two examples of planning goals with a strong emphasis on environmental protection and ecosystem management. These examples have been criticized for not adequately considering local values (for a critique of the Pinelands in this regard, see Berger and Sinton 1985). The effectiveness of the resultant planning programs has also been questioned (regarding Oregon, see, for example, Daniels and Nelson 1986). Nevertheless, both are examples of goals for ecological planning that have been established by state and federal governments. In addition, both plans have resulted in the protection of important lands. For example, all counties in Oregon have adopted exclusive farm-use zones, and "more than 16 million acres [6.5 million hectares] of agricultural land have been protected from development" (American Farmland Trust 1997, 30).

These goals were set because issues were identified and governments responded. The Pinelands region and the State of Oregon face a range of problems and opportunities because of their ecological and scenic resources. In the Pinelands, the threat to these resources was recognized at the state level, which prompted actions by New Jersey and the federal government. The actions set goals for the region and local governments. In Oregon, the environment is highly valued by citi-

TABLE 2.1
PINELANDS GOALS AND POLICIES

Natural Resources Goal	**Preserve, protect, and enhance the overall ecological values of the Pinelands, including its large forested areas, its essential character, and its potential to recover from disturbance.**
Policy 1:	Preserve, protect, and enhance the quality and quantity of surface and groundwater.
Policy 2:	Preserve, protect, and enhance the diversity of plant and animal communities and their habitats.
Policy 3:	Preserve, protect, and enhance existing soil conditions.
Policy 4:	Preserve, protect, and enhance existing topographic features.
Policy 5:	Preserve, protect, and enhance existing air quality.
Policy 6:	Protect natural scenic qualities.
Historic and Cultural Goal	**Maintain and enhance the historic and cultural resources of the Pinelands.**
Policy 1:	Maintain opportunities for traditional lifestyles that are related to and compatible with the overall ecological values of the Pinelands.
Policy 2:	Maintain the social and cultural integrity of traditional Pinelands communities.
Policy 3:	Maintain and enhance historic and archaeological areas and sites of national, state, and local importance.
Agricultural and Horticultural Goal	**Preserve and enhance agricultural and horticultural uses that are compatible with the preservation and protection of the overall ecological values of the Pinelands.**
Policy 1:	Reserve for agricultural purposes prime agricultural soils and soils of statewide significance in or adjacent to established agricultural areas.
Policy 2:	Reserve unique agricultural soils and protect water quality and quantity necessary for cranberry and blueberry cultivation.
Policy 3:	Protect the long-term economic viability of agricultural activities.
Policy 4:	Require the use of recommended management practices in areas of substandard water quality.
Policy 5:	Protect agricultural operations and other private landowners from trespass and vandalism.
Policy 6:	Encourage horticulture of native Pinelands plants.
Development Goal	**Accommodate residential, commercial, and industrial development in a way that is compatible with the preservation and protection of the overall ecological and cultural values of the Pinelands.**
Policy 1:	Permit infill development in existing communities.
Policy 2:	Direct new residential, commercial, and industrial development into environmentally suitable areas in orderly patterns which are with or adjacent to existing developed areas.
Policy 3:	Assure opportunities for housing for all economic groups.
Policy 4:	Allow economic development which supports existing community needs but does not generate new development outside those areas designated for future development by the Comprehensive Management Plan.
Policy 5:	Permit growth-generating capital improvements only within those areas designated for future development.
Recreation Goal	**Protect and enhance outdoor recreational uses and the natural resources on which they depend.**
Policy 1:	Preserve, protect, and enhance those natural resources, including forests, waters, and wildlife habitats, necessary for compatible recreational uses.
Policy 2:	Promote diverse recreational opportunities in a manner that minimizes land-use conflicts.
Policy 3:	Assure that recreational uses in undeveloped areas be of low intensity and compatible with the protection of the natural resources.
Policy 4:	Assure that, insofar as possible, intensive recreational uses be located in or near developed areas.
Policy 5:	Protect and enhance opportunities for proprietary recreational facilities in areas that are suitable for such uses.

SOURCE: Pinelands Commission 1980.

zens throughout the state. Even so, Ethan Seltzer of Portland State University observed,

> The Oregon land use planning program [was initially] primarily an agricultural land preservation program. It grew from the rural parts of the state looking into urban areas, not urban areas looking outward. It had a lot to do with economy of the state, and required strong rural area legislative support. How grassroots it was is open for discussion. Nevertheless, the point is that it wasn't motivated by general concerns for environmental quality and it depended on direct support from the governor and key legislative leaders, rather than a grassroots citizens movement (1998).

However, the environmental leadership and vision provided by Republican Governor Tom McCall is undeniable. In his own words, when opening the 1973 Oregon legislature, Governor McCall warned that "sagebrush subdivisions, coastal condomania, and the ravenous rampage of suburbia in the Willamette Valley all threaten to mock Oregon's status as an environmental model for the nation." And "the interest of Oregon for today and in the future must be protected from the grasping wastrels of the land" (McCall as quoted in Kellington 1998, 3).

This emphasis on ecological values differentiate the Pinelands and Oregon goals from those of conventional planning processes. As compared with conventional programs, the Pinelands and Oregon goals are linked more directly to specific policies and implementation guidelines, which also emphasize environmental protection and natural resource management.

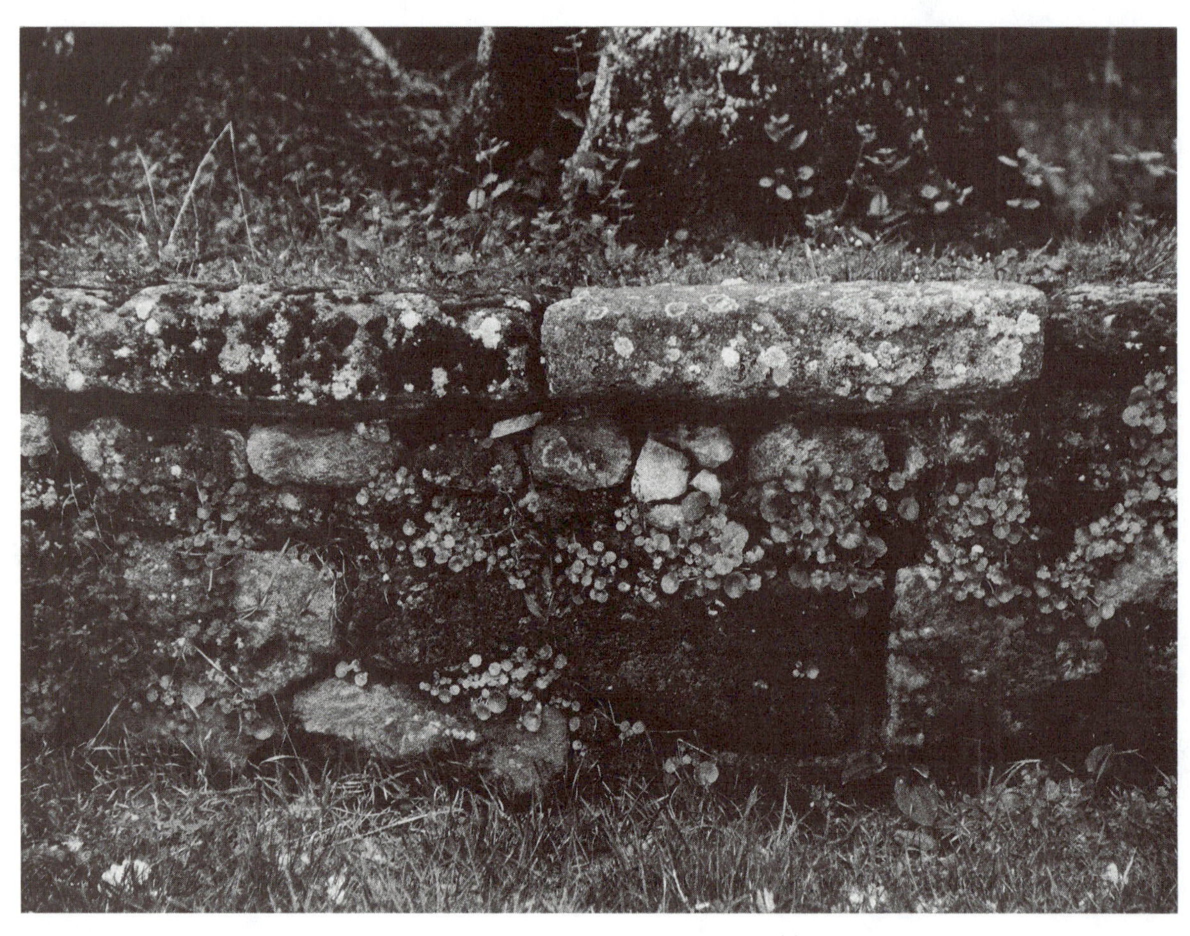

3

INVENTORY AND ANALYSIS OF THE BIOPHYSICAL ENVIRONMENT

After a community has identified the challenges and opportunities that it faces and has reached some consensus concerning its goals to address those issues, then it is necessary to collect the information needed to achieve community goals. An *inventory* is a systematic acquisition of information needed to describe and characterize a place. Inventories provide the basis for ecological analysis. Information about nature has often been used in an ad hoc manner in American planning. Only that information needed to achieve a specific goal is collected—so too often it is disconnected information.

The basic premise of ecology is that everything is connected to everything else. As a result, the ecological approach differs from more traditional methods. For example, a flood frequently prompts community interests in planning, especially when loss of life and property damage has occurred. With a conventional planning response, only the flood-prone areas are identified. Also, this approach focuses primarily on the negative consequences of flooding. Since flooding is recognized by a community as a hazard to human safety, the responsible elected officials adopt a goal to prevent buildings in flood-prone areas. These areas are mapped and building restricted. The goal is one-dimensional. In contrast, in ecological planning the complex matrix of factors related to flooding would be considered. Flooding is the result of the interaction of several natural phenomena—rainfall, bedrock, terrain, soils, temperature, and vegetation, for instance. Since ecological planning rests on an understanding of relationships, broader-range information about the biophysical processes of an area must be collected and analyzed. In addition, an ecological view acknowledges the benefits of natural flooding events, such as the deposition of fertile soils. Moreover, the sequence of collecting this information becomes important.

Older, larger-scale components of the landscape exert a strong influence on more ephemeral elements. Regional climate and geology help to determine soils and water drainage systems of an area, which in turn affect what vegetation and animals will inhabit a place. The challenge for the ecological planner is to think geologically both in space and time. One must think big, because it is likely that the geologic events that occur in a specific planning area or jurisdiction are probably driven by plate tectonic interactions thousands of kilometers away, and climatic events by processes working on a global scale. The temporal scale is also quite large, with the human time scale so much shorter than that of the geologic events within a planning area. As a result, in ecological planning one begins to inventory the older elements and proceeds to the youngest. The systematic survey of information should lead to an understanding of processes, not merely the collection of data.

When conducting such an inventory, it is useful to identify boundaries so that the various biophysical elements can be compared with each other over the same spatial area and at the same scale. Often such a planning area is defined by legislative goals, as, for instance, with the New Jersey Pinelands.

Ideally, several levels of inventories from regional to local are undertaken. As Richard Forman has advised, we should "think globally, plan regionally, and act locally" (1995, 435). A hierarchy of levels is identified so that the planning area may be understood as part of a larger system and specific places may be seen as parts of a whole. The large river drainage basin at the regional level and the smaller stream watershed more locally are ideal units of analysis for ecological planning. A *watershed* is an area drained by a stream or stream system, also called a *catchment area* or, in the United States at a larger river scale, including all the tributaries, a *drainage basin.*

A drainage basin, or watershed, "is the area of land that drains water, sediment, and dissolved materials to a common outlet at some point along a stream channel" (Dunne and Leopold 1978, 495). According to Donald Satterlund and Paul Adams (1992, 51), "A watershed is defined by the stream that drains it." The *drainageway,* meanwhile, "refers to the principal areas of water accumulation (i.e., channels)" (Briggs 1996, 17).

A watershed, or other landscape, may be understood through a *chorography.* In other words, a systematic description and analysis. Ecology can be used to order such a chorography since ecology addresses interrelationships among living things and their environments. The ecologist Eugene Odum has observed the value of using watersheds in planning. Odum noted that "it is the whole drainage basin, not just the body of water, that must be considered as the minimum ecosystem unit when it comes to man's interests. The ecosystem unit for practical management must then include for every square meter or acre of water at least 20 times an area of terrestrial watershed" (Odum 1971, 16).

Peter Quinby (1988) notes that watershed boundaries can be used as ecosystem boundaries. The watershed is a handy unit that contains biological, physical, social, and economic processes. Watersheds have discrete boundaries, yet they can vary in scale. This provides flexibility to adapt to social, economic, and political issues. Watersheds also offer linkages between the elements of regions. One reason they can be considered an ideal is that the flow of water, the linkage, throughout the watershed may be easily visualized.

The use of watersheds for planning is not new. John Wesley Powell, who introduced the term *region* to North America, essentially suggested the use of watersheds in his 1879 plan for the American West. The use of watersheds is also consistent with past efforts of watershed conservancies and river basin commissions, such as the Delaware River Basin Commission, the Columbia River Basin Commission, and the Tennessee Valley Authority, and with programs of the Natural Resources Conservation Service, the Army Corps of Engineers, the National Park Service, and the U.S. Forest Service. But, more often than not, units other than watersheds—political boundaries most frequently—are used. Still the principle of hierarchy can apply to political boundaries, with counties forming the regional scale and cities or towns being used as the unit for local landscape analysis.

In this chapter, a method for the inventory, analysis, and synthesis of the biophysical components of the landscape in the planning process is presented. This approach to data collection can be used at the regional, local, and even site-specific scales. To illustrate this chapter, an example of the Desert View Tri-Villages Area of Phoenix, Arizona, is used. This landscape was formerly named "Planning Areas C & D" by city officials. This biophysical inventory and analysis was conducted as a part of a larger city planning process. The area encompasses approximately 20 percent of the city and was largely undeveloped when ecological inventories were initiated. Two slightly different boundaries appear in the examples that follow because they were drawn from different inventories conducted in the space of three years (Ciekot et al. 1995; Brady et al. 1998). In the intervening years, the city of Phoenix annexed more land, changing the study area boundaries. This chapter presents methods for making base maps, inventorying elements of the landscape, and analyzing and synthesizing this information. Two examples, the New Jersey Pinelands and the region of Camp Pendleton, California, are also used as illustrations. Each example employed an approach similar to the one presented here, but the specific methods were designed by the responsible planning teams.

MAKING A BASE MAP AND A REGIONAL CONTEXT MAP

The starting point for collecting information in a graphic format is the *base map,* a map from which copies are made or derived. The most convenient source for a paper base map in the United States is the USGS 7.5-minute quadrangle maps with a scale of 1:24,000. USGS maps are available for most areas in the United States in paper and, increasingly, digital formats. They give the location of all buildings (except in urban areas), bodies of water, elevations, contour lines, roads, rail lines, political boundaries, and some woodlands. A portion of a quadrangle map or several quadrangle maps pieced together can be photographically reproduced on polyester film. Additional information can be added to the polyester film to form the base map. The most important information includes the map of the study area, a north arrow, a proportional scale, a map title, a legend, the source of the information displayed, the name of the planning area, and the names of the company, university group, and/or agency performing the study.

The same process can be undertaken with the computer with geographic information systems (GIS) technology (Figure 3.1). Planning teams decide how to use the GIS. The data handling and computation process can then be automated. The use of GIS can provide an effective cartographic presentation of the results in addition to creating greater flexibility over paper maps (Xiang 1996, 8).

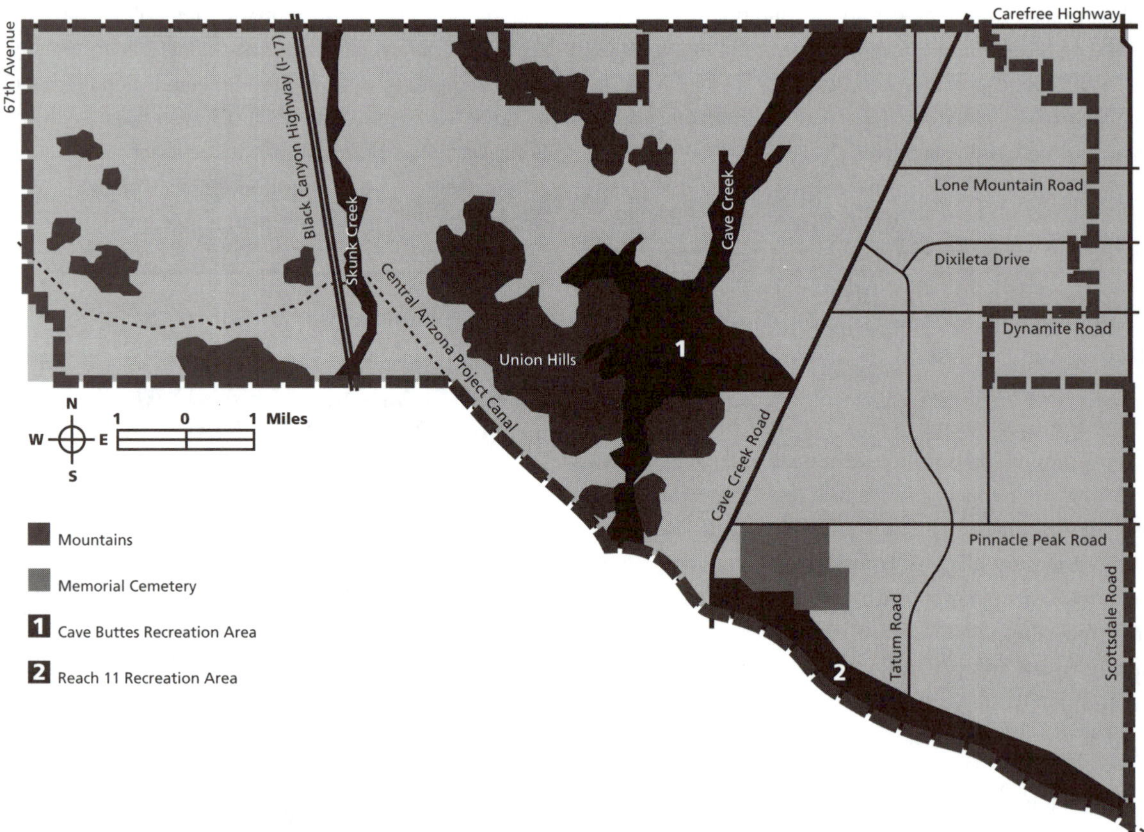

FIGURE 3.1 Desert View Tri-Villages Area base map. *(Source: Adapted from Ciekot et al. 1995)*

When constructing maps, either digitally or manually, one needs to consider the meaning of scale. A 0.5 mm pencil will draw out a 12 m (or driveway-wide) line on the ground if one makes a line with it on a 1:24,000 scale map. Such realization provides some context for map precision. Arguing over centimeters or inches will not be relevant for that usually, but tens to hundreds of meters or feet might be.

In addition to the familiar 7.5-minute quadrangle maps, ortho aerial photographs at the same scale are now available from the USGS for many places. The U.S. Geological Survey also is a source for geology maps, digital elevation model (DEM) data, digital line graph (DLG) data (including transportation, hydrography, jurisdictional boundaries, and public land survey), and hydrological unit data and maps (Peck 1998). Images from satellites provide environmental information on spatial and temporal scales that are not possible through traditional systems (Conway et al. 1997). Satellite images are available from various sources through the Internet (Figure 3.2). According to Sheila Peck, "Recent satellite imagery can be acquired from two private companies, Space Imaging Eosat and SPOT Image Corporation. Space Imaging Eosat carries data from Landsat satellites and India's IRS satellite, while SPOT

FIGURE 3.2 Satellite image of the Desert View Tri-Villages Area. *(Source: Brady et al. 1998)*

Image Corporation features imagery from the French SPOT satellite" (1998, 183). These images are helpful for both performing inventories and displaying information.

A word of caution is necessary. The rectification of imagery and other data, their projection, and then the preparation of overlays of diverse data and derivative maps based upon query of the datasets is a significant undertaking. Such exercises go beyond the basics of cartography. Although much digital data are available, it is important for planning teams to include individuals well-qualified in GIS and cartography.

Next, the study area needs to be placed in a regional context. This is important because people who read a planning report often come from outside the area described. Often it is necessary to place the area in a subregional context, perhaps a county or other governmental jurisdiction, then in a larger regional context, such as the state or multistate region (Figure 3.3).

MAJOR SOURCES OF INFORMATION

1. U.S. Geological Survey
   For maps and related data:
   U.S. Geological Survey
   Reston-ESIC
   507 National Center
   Reston, Virginia 20192
   800-872-6277
   703-648-5548 (fax)
   esicmail@usgs.gov
   http://www.usgs.gov
   For older satellite data:
   U.S. Geological Survey
   EROS Data Center
   Sioux Falls, South Dakota 57198
   605-594-6151
   615-594-6589 (fax)
   custserv@edcmail.cr.usgs.gov
   http://edcwww.cr.usgs.gov
2. Local aerial photography companies
3. Space Imaging Eosat
   4300 Forbes Boulevard
   Landham, Maryland 20706
   800-232-9037 (customer service)
   703-552-3762 (fax)
   http://www.eosat.com
4. SPOT Image Corporation
   1897 Preston White Drive
   Reston, Virginia 20191-4368
   800-ASK-SPOT (customer service)
   703-648-1813 (fax)
   http://www.spot.com

INVENTORY ELEMENTS

Chronology provides a logical framework to organize information about a place. The ecological planner begins with the phenomena that are the major influences on a place: (1) its macroclimatic processes and (2) its geological structure. These phenomena exert influence on subsequent processes such as water flows and soil development. These abiotic features set the stage for life.

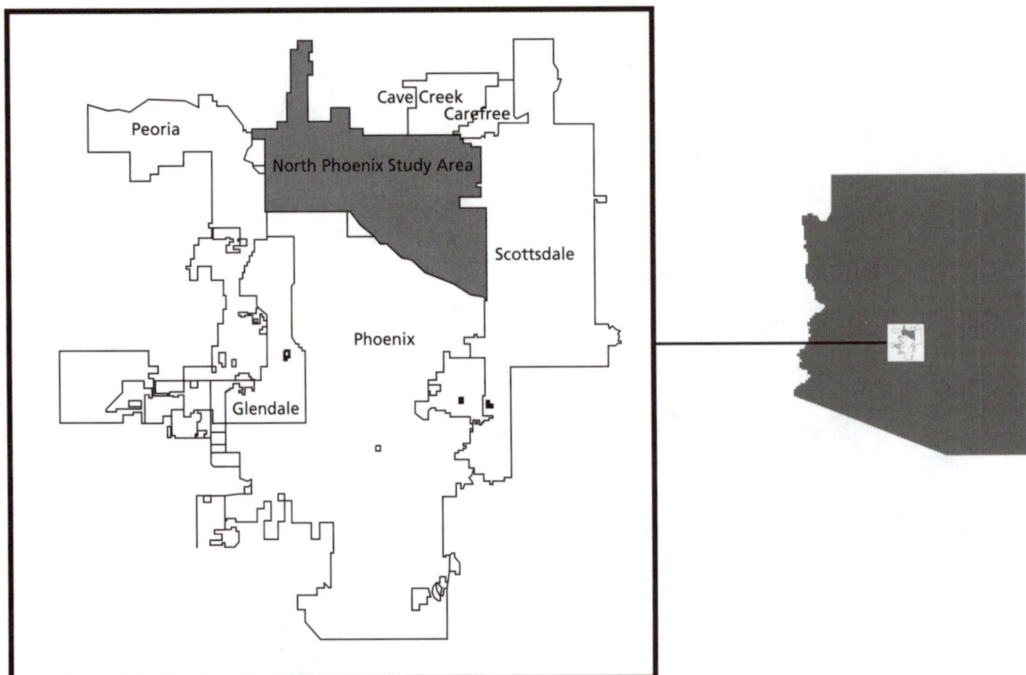

FIGURE 3.3 Regional context of the Desert View Tri-Villages Area. *(Source: Brady et al. 1998)*

Plants, animals, and people inhabit different places according to the varying possibilities of physical geography.

Regional Climate

Climate is the set of meteorological conditions characteristic of an area over a given length of time. It is defined as the study of extremes and long-term means of weather. The regional (or macro) climate is the big picture, the meteorological conditions and patterns over a large area. Macroclimate is affected by physical conditions such as mountains, ocean currents, prevailing winds, and latitude. It in turn affects the formation of the physiographic region through the weathering of the terrain and the amounts of precipitation which fall on the landscape. As observed by R. A. Pielke and R. Avissar (1990), the atmosphere is responsive to the landscape, and landscape ecology will change in response to atmospheric alterations. Changes in land use cause major alterations in both regional and local climate (Pielke and Avissar, 1990).

The study of climate is important in planning for many reasons. As Anthony Brazel notes,

> "the famous 1980 heat wave in the middle of the U.S. was estimated by . . . NOAA [National Oceanic and Atmospheric Administration] . . . to have cost the agricultural and energy sectors some 16 billion dollars; and that one summer event stimulated the entire scientific community to heightened awareness of what a global warming world would portend. Hurricane Andrew, alone, cost society much more than 16 billion [dollars]" (1993, 1).

Hurricanes, tornadoes, and floods result in significant economic costs, as well as causing injury and the loss of life. Global climate change has stimulated considerable interest in the study of weather patterns. Local actions are linked in global and regional weather patterns in numerous ways. Understanding climate, and planning communities accordingly, can result in conserving financial and other resources as well as helping to protect public health and safety.

The Desert View Tri-Villages Area, or the Tri-Villages Area, illustrates the types of climate that should be inventoried in its region. The Tri-Villages Area is located in the Sonoran Desert in the Phoenix metropolitan region (Figure 3.3). The Sonoran Desert covers some 120,000 square miles (310,800 kilometers^2) and comprises much of the states of Sonora (Mexico) and Arizona as well as most of the two states of Baja California (Norte and Sur) and a small portion of California. This desert rings the Gulf of California. In turn, the ocean arcs the desert to the west and to the south, while mountains form an arc to the north and the east. The Sonora, a corruption of Mary's title, *Señora,* is a hot and dry place. If aridity gives the West its character, then the Sonora is among the most western of places.

According to Anthony Brazel,

> Arizona has four "synoptic" or weather systems: (1) the summer thunderstorm or monsoon season of July through September; (2) the late summer-to-fall tropical storm season of August through October; (3) the variable winter low pressure storm season ranging from early storms in November through even April; and (4) spring-to-summer meanderings of the atmosphere that may include late season storms, or the beginning of a very dry spell of early summer, typically from April to late June (1993, 3).

There is no weather station in the Tri-Villages Area. As a result, nearby stations were used to compile climate data (Ciekot et al. 1995; McCarthy et al. 1995). This situation is common. A planning team must frequently use the best available information and interpolate to area studies. The Tri-Villages Area, like much of the Phoenix region, is generally hot and dry. According to the Köppen classification system, the region is a desert. The adjacent town of Carefree (where there is a weather station with the code BW), with monthly average high temperatures ranging from 62.6 to 101.9°F (17 to 38.8°C) and monthly average low temperatures ranging from 37.9 to 75.1°F (3.3 to 23.9°C), is representative of a planning area climate (Sellers et al. 1985). (See Tables 3.1 and 3.2.) These temperatures average 4.0°F (2.2°C) lower than those of central Phoenix.

The Tri-Villages Area has a typical annual rainfall of 8 inches (20.3 centimeters) (Table 3.3). The rainfall in the area to the north that feeds Cave and Skunk Creek washes is approximately 50 percent higher. There are two distinct rainy seasons. Winds from the Gulf of California and the Gulf of Mexico flow into the area from the south to produce dramatic summer thunderstorms from July to September (Figure 3.4). The thunderstorms cover small areas, are brief, and cause significant runoff, and result in the potential for local flooding. Less intense but widespread and steady winter rains associated with cold fronts come from the Pacific Ocean and the north. These rains, which occur from December to March, rarely exceed infiltration capacity of the soil and, therefore, flooding is less common. Because of the sparse rainfall and the lack of perennial streams, the groundwater of the planning area is an important source of drinking water for Phoenix. The biennial rainfall supports a denser vegetation cover than the other deserts of the United States (i.e., the Great Basin, Mojave, and Chihuahuan).

Water and heat are two significant factors to consider in the Phoenix metropolitan area. Climatologists have identified the emergence of a rapidly developing "urban heat island" in the region, which is also being called an "urban heat archipelago." Black asphalt, concrete, and roof surfaces act as solar collectors, emitting heat and

TABLE 3.1

AVERAGE MONTHLY MAXIMUM TEMPERATURE (°F), DESERT VIEW TRI-VILLAGES AREA

Station	Jan	Feb	Mar	Apr	May	Jun	Jul	Aug	Sep	Oct	Nov	Dec	Average
Carefree	62.60	66.70	70.80	78.00	89.60	97.40	101.90	99.00	94.00	84.30	71.40	67.70	81.95
Cave Creek	64.20	66.50	71.60	80.40	89.20	99.30	102.20	99.70	91.20	86.70	73.20	66.60	82.57
Deer Valley	66.50	70.30	74.40	83.20	92.20	102.00	105.20	102.60	98.30	88.20	74.60	66.90	85.37
Phoenix Central	65.70	70.80	75.00	83.90	92.50	102.40	104.90	103.20	99.30	89.30	76.10	68.00	85.93
Phx.-Carefree	3.10	4.10	4.20	5.90	2.90	5.00	3.00	4.20	5.30	5.00	4.70	0.30	3.98

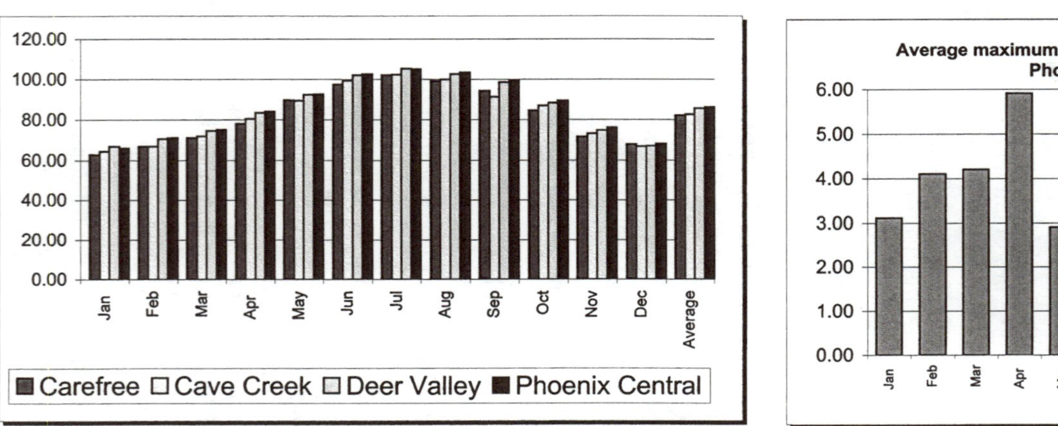

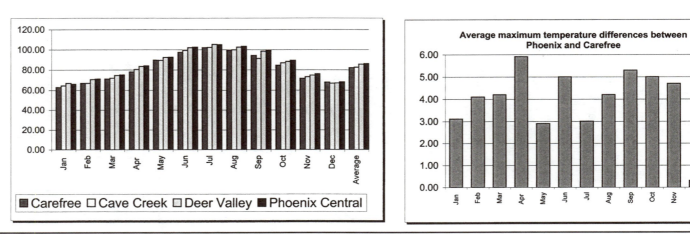

SOURCE: Sellers et al. 1985, adapted from Ciekot et al. 1995.

TABLE 3.2
AVERAGE MONTHLY MINIMUM TEMPERATURE (°F), DESERT VIEW TRI-VILLAGES AREA

Station	Jan	Feb	Mar	Apr	May	Jun	Jul	Aug	Sep	Oct	Nov	Dec	Average
Carefree	37.90	40.90	44.80	48.60	58.40	66.80	75.10	73.70	68.20	58.00	47.50	39.40	54.94
Cave Creek	37.50	38.70	42.40	49.20	56.20	65.90	74.60	72.40	66.20	56.00	43.30	37.80	53.35
Deer Valley	37.20	39.80	43.30	49.20	57.60	66.70	76.30	74.30	67.60	55.50	43.80	37.60	54.08
Phoenix Central	41.60	44.70	48.80	55.80	63.70	72.70	80.00	78.20	72.40	61.20	48.60	42.40	59.18
Phx.-Carefree	3.70	3.80	4.00	7.20	5.30	5.90	4.90	4.50	4.20	3.20	1.10	3.00	4.24

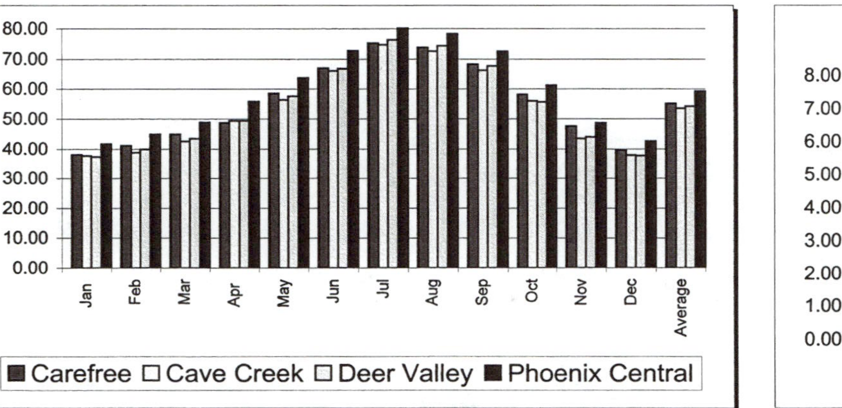

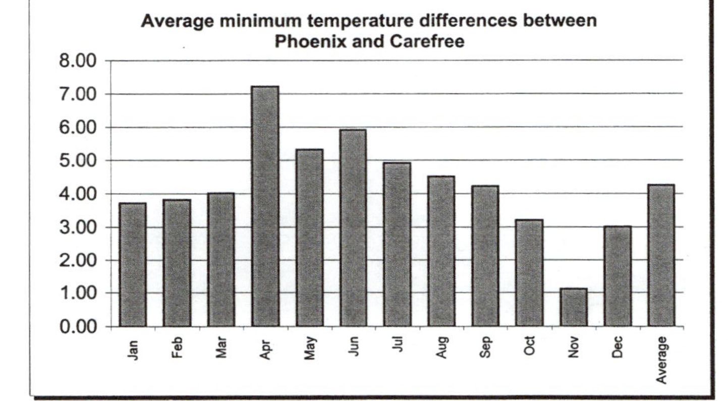

SOURCE: Sellers et al. 1985, adapted from Ciekot et al 1995.

TABLE 3.3
AVERAGE MONTHLY AND ANNUAL PRECIPITATION IN INCHES (°F), DESERT VIEW TRI-VILLAGES AREA

Station	Jan	Feb	Mar	Apr	May	Jun	Jul	Aug	Sep	Oct	Nov	Dec	Total
Carefree	0.89	1.05	1.57	0.42	0.20	0.19	1.23	1.65	1.16	0.98	1.16	1.75	12.25
Cave Creek	1.03	0.80	0.78	0.43	0.10	0.27	0.87	1.52	0.59	0.70	0.72	1.26	9.07
Deer Valley	0.96	0.74	0.95	0.25	0.16	0.13	0.69	1.32	0.52	0.71	0.66	0.93	8.02
Phoenix Central	0.88	0.66	0.86	0.32	0.17	0.11	0.68	1.20	0.56	0.71	0.53	0.83	7.51
Carefree-Phx.	0.01	0.39	0.71	0.10	0.03	0.08	0.55	0.45	0.60	0.27	0.63	0.92	4.74

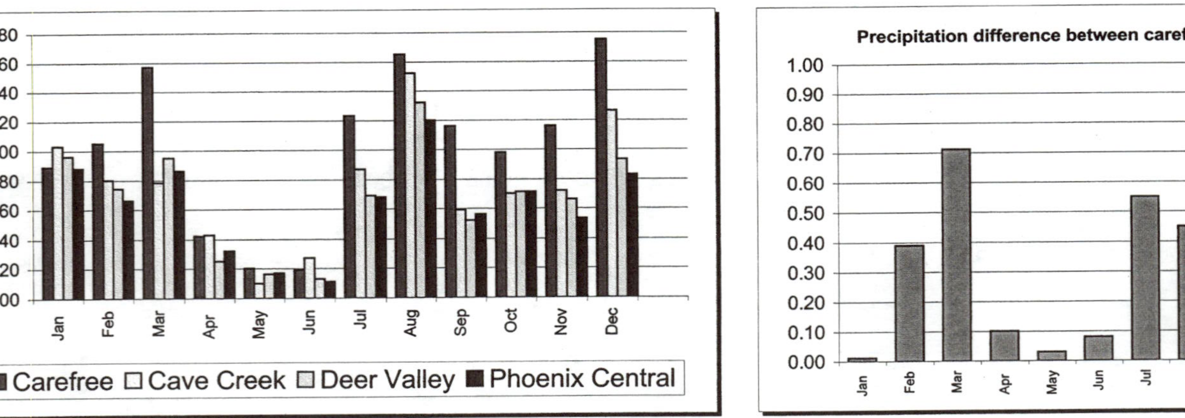

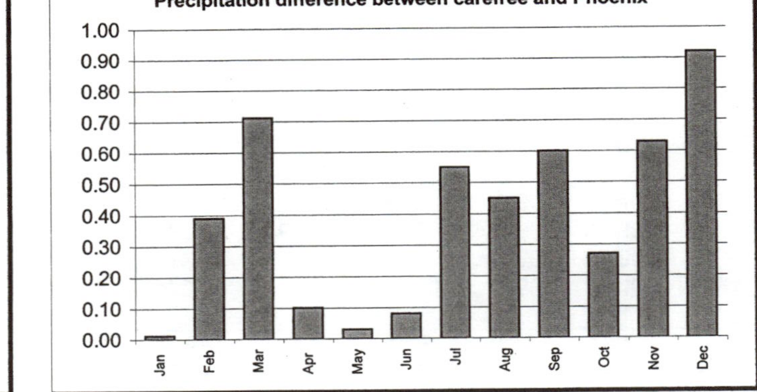

SOURCE: Sellers et al. 1985, adapted from Ciekot et al. 1995.

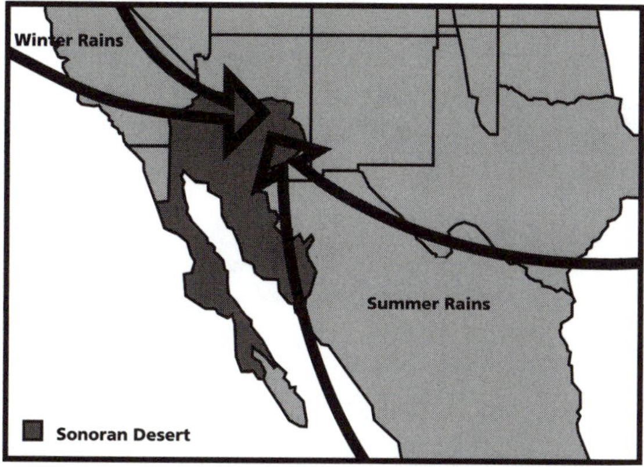

FIGURE 3.4 Macroclimate influences on the Desert View Tri-Villages. *(Source: Adapted from Ciekot et al. 1995)*

increasing urban air temperatures (Botkin and Beveridge 1997). Cities and towns in the Phoenix metropolitan region are spread out, resulting in many patches of more intense development. As a result, heat islands are spread out, too, but connected by corridors of development. According to Robert Balling and Sandra Brazel, since 1970 "the summer nighttime temperatures have increased 3.9°F (2.2°C) while afternoon temperatures have risen by approximately 1.1°F (0.6°C)" (1987, 75). The heat island effect has been identified in several other American cities, including Los Angeles (Botkin and Beveridge 1997).

Not all land uses or land covers contribute equally to this warming. Figure 3.5 is a Landsat image of the Phoenix metropolitan region, enhanced for heat reflectivity. The darker areas are cooler, while the lighter areas are warmer. Ray Lougeay and his colleagues used Landsat thermal remotely sensed data to analyze surface temperatures for various land uses. They found that radiative surface temperatures do indeed vary by land-use surface type (Lougeay et al. 1996) (Table 3.4). Irrigated agricultural and residential areas had among the relatively cooler surface temperatures, while desert and barren lands were hotter.

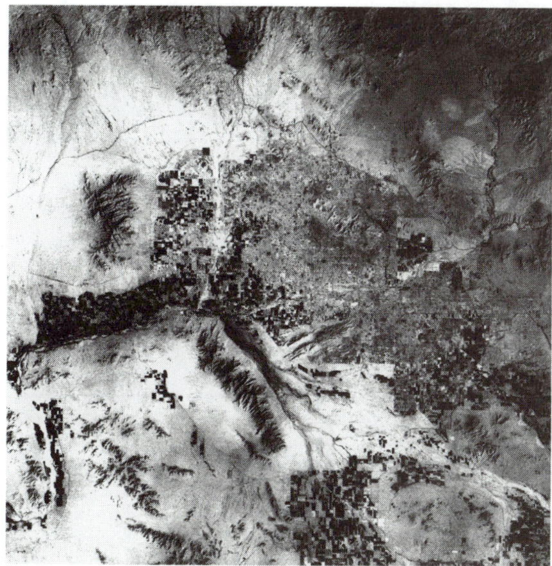

FIGURE 3.5 Landsat image of the Phoenix metropolitan region. *(Source: City of Scottsdale)*

They noted that "spatial temperature patterns of the metropolitan region were strongly correlated with the presence of open water or biomass which provide an evapotranspirative heat sink" (Lougeay et al. 1996, 79).

Some understanding about the regional climate of a place can be gained by asking a series of questions and by getting the answers (Steiner and McSherry 2000), such as:

- What is the regional climate of the planning area?
- How has the regional climate of the planning area determined where and how people live?
    - How has it determined the types and methods of construction?
    - The size of homes?
    - The layout of ranches and/or farm fields?
- How does climate influence who lives in the planning area?
- What is the relationship between climate and sense of place for the planning area?

TABLE 3.4
RADIATIVE SURFACE TEMPERATURES (10:00 A.M.) AND AREAL COVERAGE (PHOENIX, ARIZONA JUNE 24, 1992)

Surface Type	Surface Temp Deg. c*	Min. Temp Deg. c*	Max. Temp Deg. c*	Standard Dev. Deg. c*	Area km^2	% of scene**
Water	30.07	22	35	1.58	6	0.2
Irrigated Ag.	31.54	26	36	1.43	210	5
Irrigated Res.	37.9	35	40	1.35	331	7
Dry Res.	43.64	42	45	0.89	468	11
Commercial	44.41	41	47	1.72	935	21
Desert	47.18	33	53	2.20	595	13
Barren	45.41	42	48	1.26	140	3
Unclassified (masked mountain slopes)	—	—	—	—	1760	40

* Surface temperatures (adjusted for emissivity) extracted from Landsat Thematic mapper band 6.
** Total imaged area of metropolitan Phoenix equals 4446 square kilometers.
SOURCE: Lougeay et al. 1997, 85.

How are these characteristics reflected in the location and character of the built landscape?
How do these characteristics compare with other regions in the state or elsewhere?

- What is the quality of the air in the planning area?

SUMMARY OF REGIONAL CLIMATE INVENTORY ELEMENTS

1. Köppen classification
2. Average temperatures
3. Average precipitation
4. Prevailing winds; wind velocity and duration
5. Relative humidity

MAJOR SOURCES OF INFORMATION

1. National Weather Service
2. National Oceanic and Atmospheric Administration (NOAA)
   The best source for climate information is:
   National Climatic Data Center
   National Oceanic and Atmospheric Administration
   Federal Building
   151 Patton Avenue, Room 120
   Asheville, North Carolina 28801-5001
   704-271-4800
   704-271-4876 (fax)
   orders@ncdc.noaa.gov
   http://www.ncdc.noaa.gov
   Regional information is available concerning monthly precipitation, temperature, and wind data from
3. Federal Aviation Administration (FAA)
4. State climatologists
5. Local weather stations and/or airports
6. College or university libraries
7. Farmers

Earth

Geology is the study of the earth. This study involves both what has happened in the past, or geological history, and what is happening on and in the earth today. The inventory of a place requires an understanding of the geological history and processes of the region. Such understanding can begin with a *geological map,* which is "a graphic representation of the rock units and geological features that are exposed on the surface of the Earth. . . . In addition to showing different types and ages of rocks, most geological maps depict geologic features, such as faults, folds, and volcanoes" (Reynolds no date, 1). The relative timing of events can usually be determined from a geologic map, usually by the application of these principles: superposition (younger layers are above older ones); original horizontality (layers formed from deposition of sediment were originally flat); cross-cutting relationships (younger features cross-cut older ones; a fault will be younger than the layers or contacts it cuts); and inclusions (a rock unit is younger than the layers from which the inclusions it contains came).

According to geologist Stephen Reynolds, geologic maps have four useful purposes: "(1) to discover mineral and energy resources; (2) to assess the potential for natural hazards, such as earthquakes and volcanoes; (3) to evaluate the suitability of an area as a construction site; and (4) to convey information about the geologic history of an area" (No date, 1). Furthermore, he notes that: "areas that contain recent volcanic rock (less than several million years old) are more likely to have volcanic eruptions than regions that lack such rocks. Likewise, earthquakes are more likely to occur in areas where faults displace recent rocks or deposits, such as river gravels. High concentrations of radon gas are commonly associated with volcanic rocks, such as particular types of granite, that have an anomalously high uranium content" (Reynolds no date, 2). As a result, knowledge of geology is valuable for protecting the health and safety of residents. Geologic information is also invaluable for the construction of roads, bridges, buildings, and other elements of developments.

As epitomized by the Grand Canyon, much of Arizona's famous scenery is geologic. As in other places, an understanding of geological processes is important for community and economic development in Arizona. The state has three geological provinces: the Colorado Plateau, the Transition Zone, and the Basin and Range Province (Nations and Stump 1981). Figure 3.6 provides a columnar section for the Transition Zone, the province north of the Desert View Tri-Villages Area. Figure 3.7 indicates the symbols commonly used to show kinds of rocks in columnar sections and geologic cross sections.

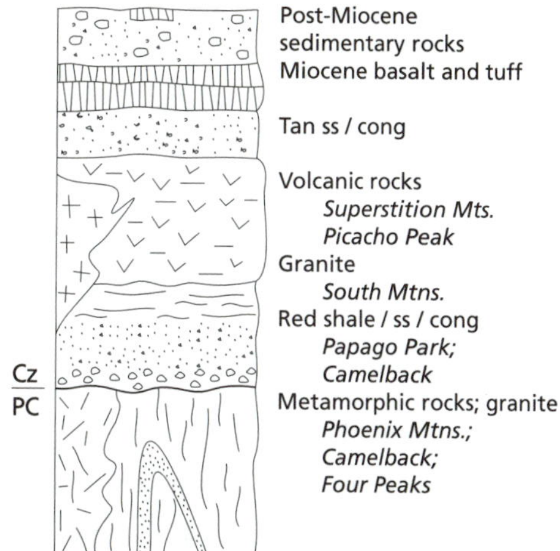

FIGURE 3.6 Stratigraphic section of the transition zone. *(Source: Adapted from Reynolds, no date)*

"Basin and Range" is the name of the geologic province where the Arizona portion of the Sonoran Desert is located. The name neatly describes the area: broad alluvial valleys surrounded by northwest-southeast trending, elongated mountain ranges (Nations and Stump 1981). To the northeast of the Sonoran Desert, a giant escarpment called the Mogollon Rim rises above the desert dividing it from the Colorado Plateau. The Baja portion of the desert was once connected to present-day Arizona and Sonora but was separated, and the Gulf of California created in the process, by tectonic activity that continues in California (Nations and Stump 1981). Most of the desert lies below 3048 feet (1000 meters) in elevation. In general, the whole region tilts toward the sea.

The Tri-Villages Area is located in the Basin and Range Province. The planning area is characterized by three major landforms: granite and metamorphic mountain masses, alluvial fans, and

Symbol	Description
18	Strike and dip of strata
90	Strike of vertical strata; tops of strata are on side marked with angle of dip
⊕	Structure of horizontal strata; no strike, dip = 0
43	Strike and dip of foliation in metamorphic rocks
	Strike of vertical foliation
	Anticline; arrows show direction of dip away from axis
	Syncline; arrows show directions of dip toward axis
21	Anticline, showing direction and angle of plunge
15	Syncline, showing direction and angle of dip
	Normal fault; hachures on downthrown side
	Reverse fault; arrow shows direction of dip, hachures on downthrown side
21 U D	Dip of fault surface; D, downthrown side; U, upthrown side
	Directions of relative horizontal movement along a fault
43	Low-angle thrust fault; barbs on upper block

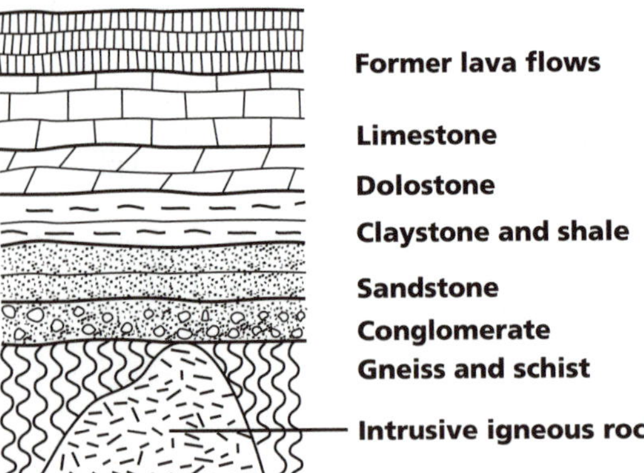

FIGURE 3.7 Common geologic symbols. *(Source: Adapted from Flint and Skinner 1974)*

relatively flat alluvial plains (Little 1975) (Figure 3.8). Many intermittent washes cross the area, along with several major drainageways, most notably Cave Creek and Skunk Creek (Figure 3.9). The landscape is a dramatic mixture of higher gaunt hills and broad alluvial plains (Figure 3.10).

Six major types of rock comprise the Desert View Tri-Villages Area: basalt, granite, metavolcanic, volcanic, older surficial deposits, and surficial deposits (Chronic 1983; Jagillo 1987; Ciekot et al. 1995; Brady et al. 1998). Alluvial fans are an especially important surficial feature. Thornbury notes that these fans are formed when "a heavily loaded stream emerges from hills or mountains onto a lowland" where "there is a marked change in gradient with resulting deposition of alluvium, apexing at the point of emergence and spreading out in a fan-like form onto the lowland" (1969, 173). When a series of alluvial fans coalesce, a *bajada* is formed (Thornbury 1969).

Philip Pearthree observed that the "piedmonts of Arizona are complex mosaics composed of alluvial fans and stream terraces" (1991, 1). According to Pearthree, these alluvial fans, including those in the Desert View Tri-Villages Areas, "are cone-shaped depositional landforms that emanate from a discrete source and increases in width downslope" (1991, 1). The stream terraces are described by Pearthree as "steplike landforms that are typically inset below adjacent fan surfaces. They represent former floors of stream valleys that were abandoned as the streams downcut even further" (1991, 1).

Rock is a natural mixture or aggregate of materials and can be classified into three general types on the basis of origin: (1) igneous rocks, which have solidified from magma; (2) sedimentary rocks, which are derived from preexisting rock or rock materials by surficial geological processes of weathering, transportation, and deposition or as a result of chemical and biological processes; and (3) metamorphic rocks, which form from existing rocks as a result of heat or pressure changes in the crust of the earth. A columnar section can be

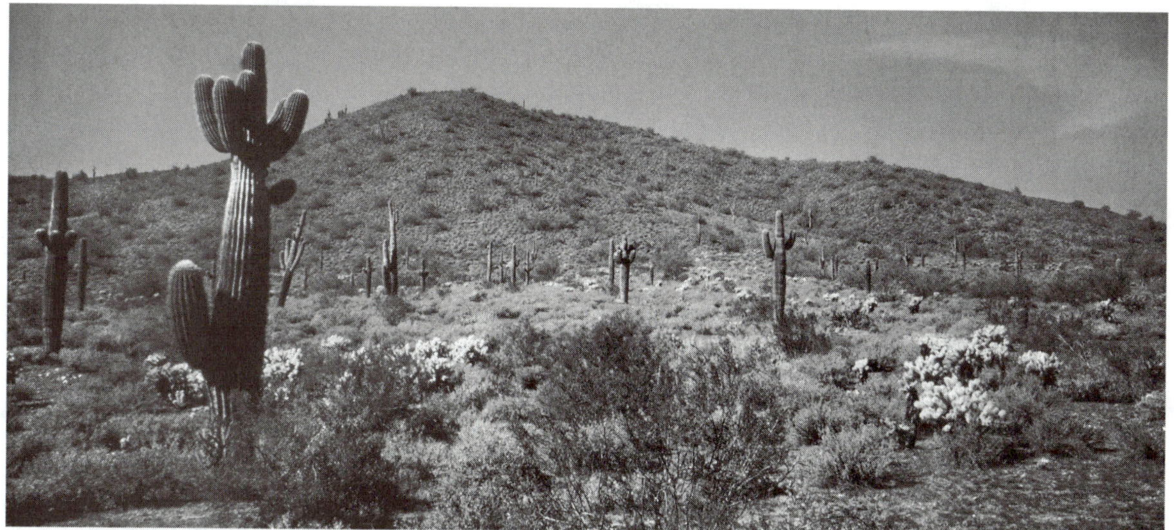

A typical Sonoran Desert landscape. *(Jane Heller Ploeser)*

accompanied by a geologic history that explains the origin of rock units.

In some regions, it is helpful to produce separate maps for bedrock and surficial deposits or regolith. A bedrock geology map shows the continuous solid rock of the continental crust, while the surficial geology map illustrates the distribution of deposits on the surface of the landscape. In the Tri-Villages demonstration area, these two maps were combined. In many places, it is important to map geologic hazards, such as radon-prone deposits and active fault zones. Such information may be included on the geology map or a separate hazards map.

The bedrock and surficial geology of a place can be understood by asking a series of questions and seeking answers, such as:

Bedrock Geology

- What is the regional geology of the area?
- How has the regional geology influenced landforms?
- What are the ages of the rocks in the area?
- Do the rocks possess any mineral or energy value?
- Do the geologic processes pose any threat to human health or safety?
- Are some areas easier and more economical to build on then others?
- What is the depth to bedrock?

Surficial Geology

- Have large areas been deposited by air or water?
- What is the relationship between surficial deposits and the deeper bedrock structure?

SUMMARY OF GEOLOGIC INVENTORY ELEMENTS

1. Regional geographic history
2. Depth to bedrock
3. Outcrops
4. Bedrock types and characteristics
5. Cross sections, columnar sections
6. Surficial deposits (regolith): kames, kettles, eskers, moraines, drift and till
7. Mineral resources
8. Major fault lines, earthquake zones, and seismic activity
9. Rock slides and mud slides

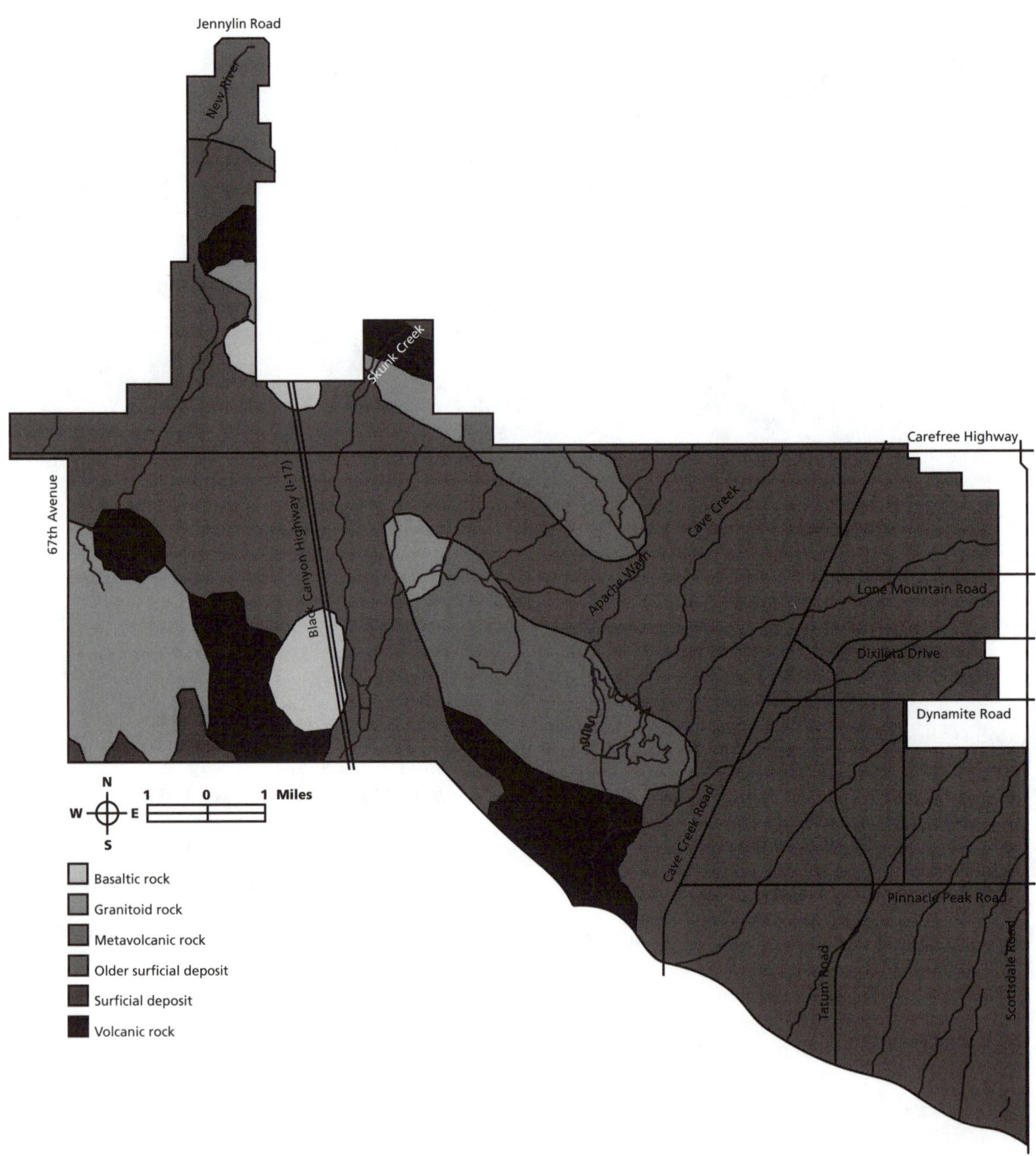

FIGURE 3.8 Geology, Desert View Tri-Villages Area. *(Source: Brady et al. 1998)*

FIGURE 3.9 Primary drainages of the Desert View Tri-Villages Area. *(Source: Adapted from Ciekot et al. 1995)*

MAJOR SOURCES OF INFORMATION

1. USGS. The best source for obtaining information is the circular titled *A Guide to Obtaining Information from the USGS* (Geological Survey Circular 900). It is available from:
   Branch of Distribution
   U.S. Geological Survey
   Box 25286, Federal Center
   Denver, CO 80225
   http://greenwood.cr.usgs.gov/circular.html
2. *Bibliography of Geology.* Published annually and compiled every 10 years by the USGS.
3. State departments of natural resources, mining, and ecology
4. College or university libraries

Terrain

The world is a myriad of peaks and depressions, ridges and valleys, rolling hills and flat areas, small bumps and slight slumps; it is uneven, varied. *Physiography* deals with the physical conditions of the surface of the land. The broad physiography of an area can be determined by the knowledge of the physiographic region in which it lies. For instance, as previously noted, the Desert View Tri-Villages Area lies in the Basin and Range Province of Arizona. This region is characterized by northwest-to-southeast trending mountain ranges with wide valleys in between. Two helpful resources for determining physiographic regions

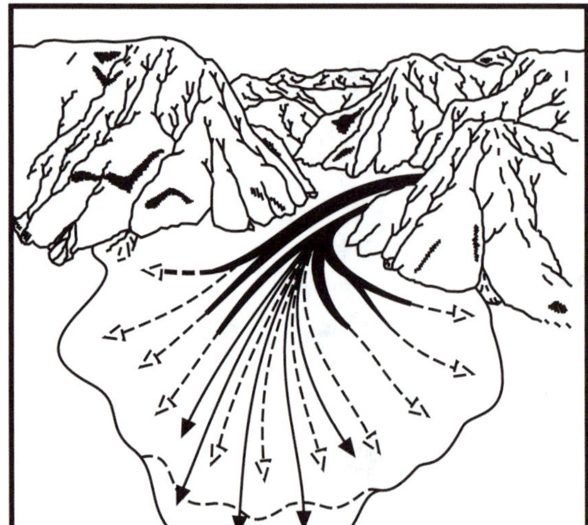

FIGURE 3.10 Alluvial fan building. *(Source: Adapted from Ciekot et al. 1995)*

are Charles B. Hunt's *Physiography of the United States* (1967) and William L. Graf's *Geomorphic Systems of North America* (1987).

The important aspects of physiography are elevation and slope. Slope, soils, geology, hydrology, microclimate, plants, and animals may be strongly related to elevation. This means that elevation is an important feature in analyzing landscapes. William Marsh of the University of Michigan identifies the two major planning problems related to the misuse of slopes. First, structures and facilities can be placed on slopes "that are already unstable or potentially unstable" (Marsh 1998, 76). Second, stable slopes can be disturbed, "resulting in failure, accelerated erosion, and/or ecological deterioration of the slope environment" (Marsh 1998, 76). The causes of disturbance include the mechanical cut and fill of slopes, deforestation, and drainage alteration (Marsh 1998).

Elevation maps are easily constructed by selecting intervals from the base maps. Altitudes can be represented by coloring spaces between topographic intervals. Elevation changes are depicted in shades of browns, yellows, or grays with felt markers, colored pencils, crayons, or through the use of computer technology, becoming lighter or darker as elevation increases (Figure 3.11). For some study areas, it may be useful to build a physical model of the elevation.

The Tri-Villages Area slopes downward to the southwest, with elevations ranging from 2200 feet (671 meters) above sea level in the far northeastern corner of the planning area to 1500 feet (457 meters) in the southwestern area. The mountain uplands, which form a backdrop to the north of the Tri-Villages Area, rise out of the basin floor and reach 4890 feet (1491 meters) (McCarthy et al. 1995).

A slope analysis was conducted for a portion of the Tri-Villages planning area, using GIS technology (Figure 3.12). For this analysis, three categories were used 0 to 5 percent; 6 to 10 percent; and 11 percent and higher. Slope maps can be constructed manually through GIS. Marsh explains the manual construction of a slope map as follows:

1. *Definition of the minimum size mapping unit.* This is the smallest area of land that will be mapped, and it is usually fixed according to the base map scale, the contour interval, and the scale of the land uses involved. For 7.5 minute U.S. Geological Survey quadrangles (1:24,000), units should not be set much smaller than 10 acres (4.05 hectares), or 660 feet square (61.3 meters^2).
2. *Construction of a graduated scale* on the edge of a sheet of paper, representing the spacing of the contours for each slope class. For example, on the 7.5 minute quadrangle where 1 inch represents 2000 feet (2.54 centimeters = 609.6 meters) and the contour interval is 10 feet (3.048 meters), a 10 percent slope would be marked by a contour every $\frac{1}{20}$ inch (0.127 centimeter).
3. *Next, the scale should be placed on the map* in a position perpendicular to the contours to delineate the areas of various slope classes.
4. *Finally,* each of the areas should be coded or symbolized according to some cartographic scheme (Marsh 1998, 79–80).

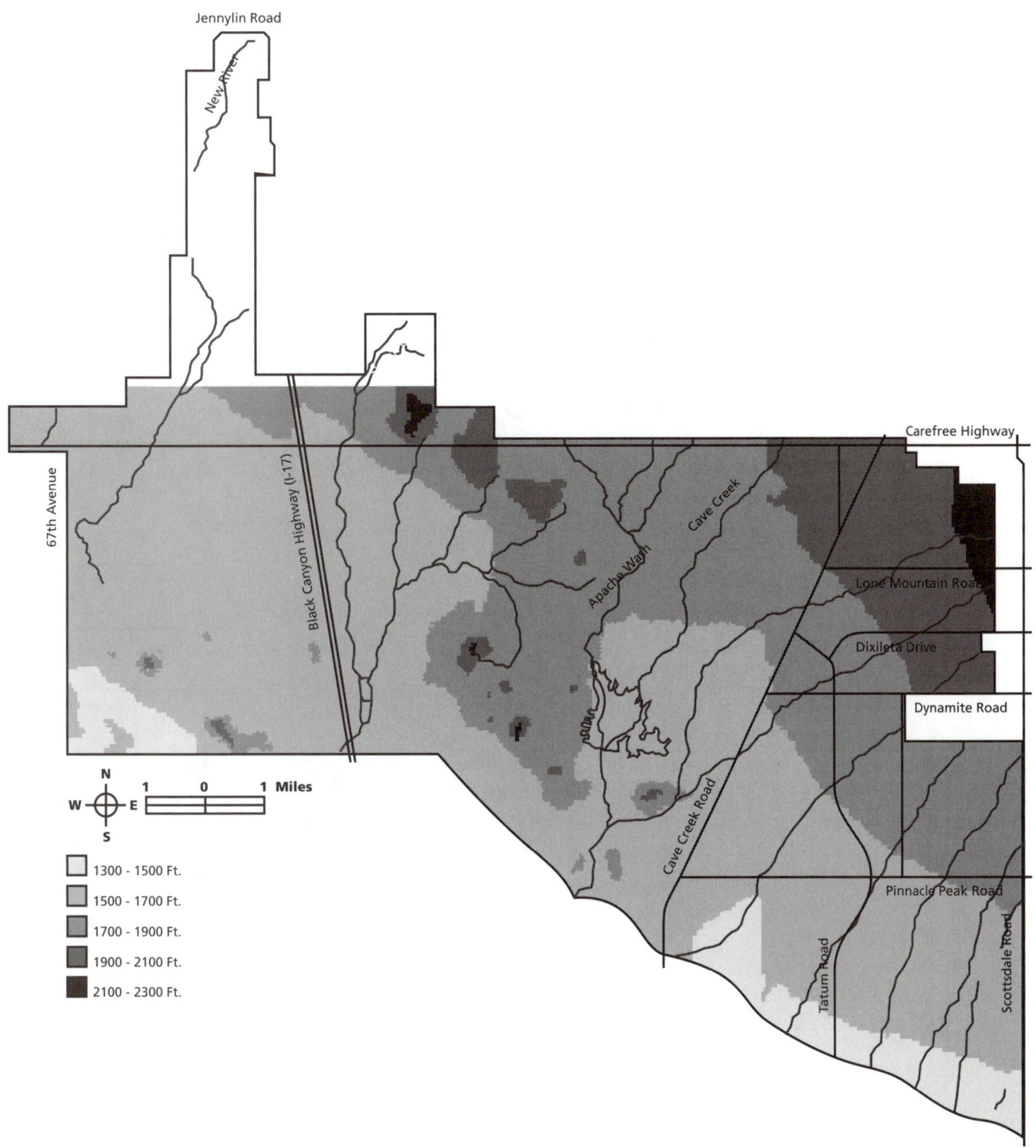

FIGURE 3.11 Elevation, Desert View Tri-Villages Area. *(Source: Brady et al. 1998)*

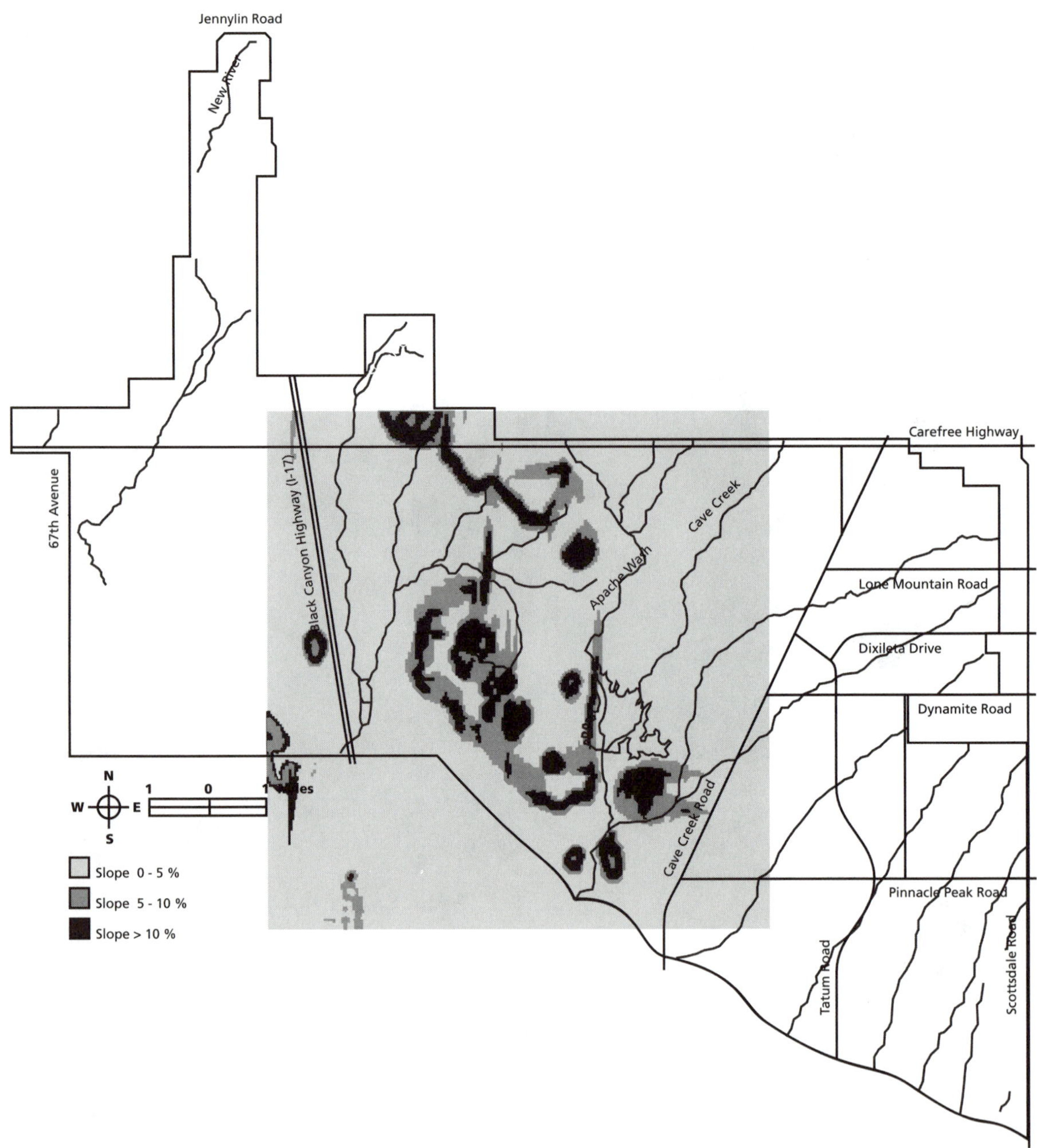

FIGURE 3.12 Slope, central portion of the Desert View Tri-Villages Area. *(Source: Brady et al. 1998)*

Slopes may be subdivided according to steepness and direction. Slope direction is referred to as *aspect,* or orientation. Steepness may be important for such activities as agriculture or the construction of buildings, while the direction of slopes is an important factor for such activities as siting housing for solar energy collection. Slope composition and related *lithology* needs to be determined. Lithology is "the soil and rock material that comprise a slope" (Marsh 1998, 80) or the physical characteristics of sedimentary materials. As with the elevation map, the division of slope categories will depend on the study. In the Desert View Tri-Villages Area, three categories were useful for the scale and issues addressed in the study. In another area or for more specific studies or after the identification of additional issues, the changes in topography may require different slope categories.

Computer technology presents many opportunities to analyze the physiography of a planning area. For example, a Landsat image was superimposed over a portion of the Tri-Villages Area (Figure 3.13). A topographic model was first constructed in the computer, and then the Landsat image was combined with it in three dimensions (Figure 3.14) (Brady et al. 1998). In addition, digital terrain, or digital elevation models, can be built (Figure 3.15) (Burke and Ewan 1998a).

In urban locations, buildings can be considered a physiographic feature. For such places, figure-ground analyses are helpful. In a figure-ground map, buildings are usually represented in black, while the ground is white, but this pattern can be reversed (Trancik 1986). The field of *urban morphology* may also be helpful in understanding the physiography of a developed planning area. Urban morphology is "the study of the city as human habitat" (Moudon 1997, 3). The field was pioneered in England by M. R. G. Conzen (Whitehand 1981; Slater 1990) and in Italy by Saverio Muratori (1959; Muratori et al. 1963). Two aspects of the Conzenian urban morphological approach, which may be applied in conjunction to physiography, are building form analysis and ground plan or town plan analysis. For example, a team of environmental planning graduate students at ASU constructed an urban morphological cross section of central Phoenix (Figure 3.16). The cross section relates to building and ground elevations, exaggerating both to emphasize variations (Andres et al. 1998). We will return to the topic of urban morphology in the land-use portions of this chapter and the next.

Answers to a few key questions can help with the understanding of the planning area, including:

- What are the key features of the planning area, including place names and major geographic features?
- What are the highest and lowest places in the area?
- Where are the other high spots and low spots?
- Where are the steeper areas?
- Why are some places steeper than others?
- In what directions do the slopes face?

SUMMARY OF PHYSIOGRAPHY INVENTORY ELEMENTS:

1. Physiographic region
2. Elevation
3. Slope: steepness and direction
4. Lithology
5. Digital terrain model
6. Figure-ground analysis

MAJOR SOURCES OF INFORMATION

1. U.S. Geological Survey
2. College or university libraries
3. *Physiography of the United States* (Hunt 1967) and/or *Geomorphic Systems of North America* (Graf 1987)

Water

Water is essential for all forms of life. It is also a finite resource. Most water in the hydrosphere is salt water (97.20 percent). Water in the polar ice-

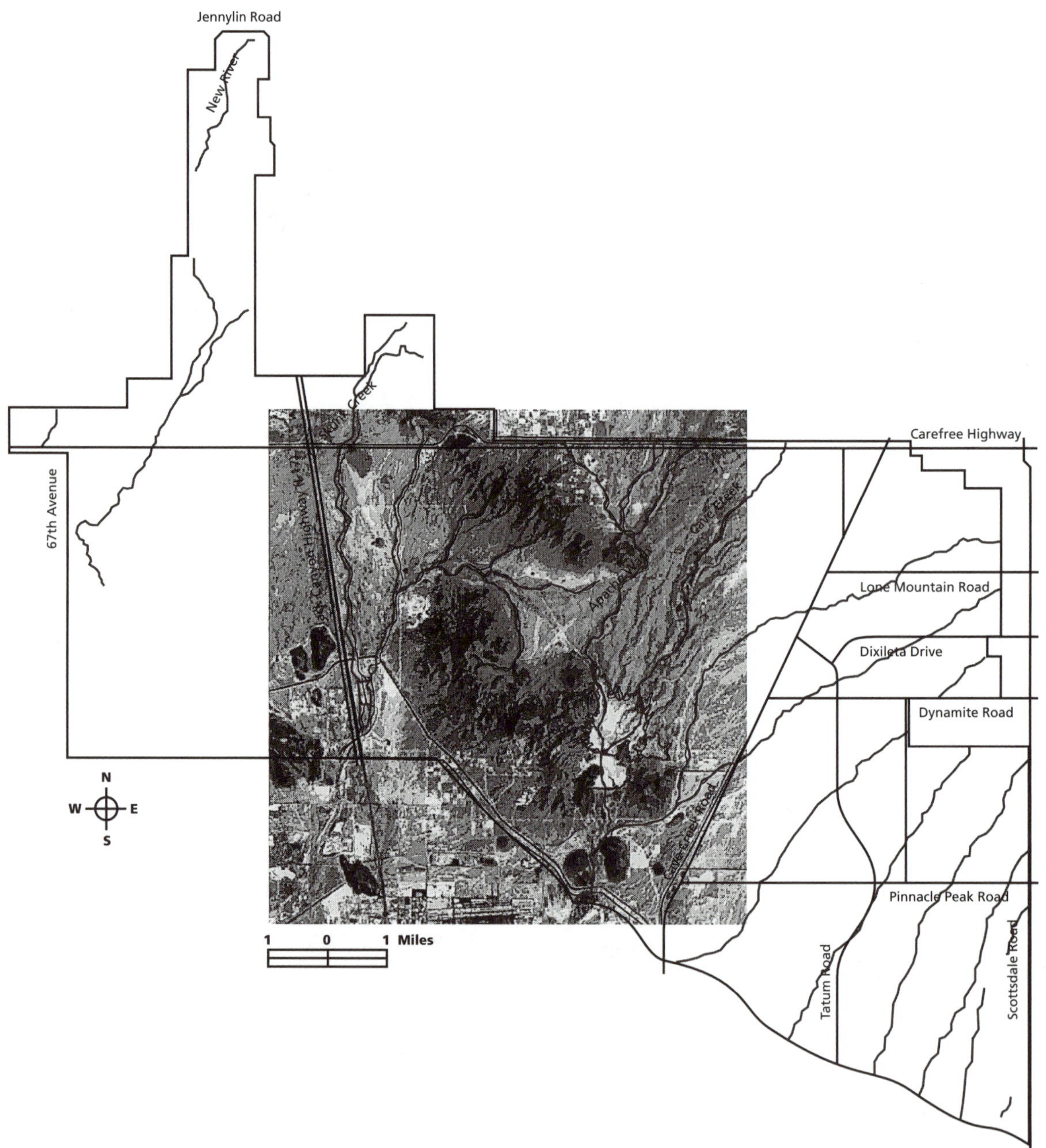

FIGURE 3.13 Landsat image superimposed over a portion of the Desert View Tri-Villages Area. *(Source: Brady et al. 1998)*

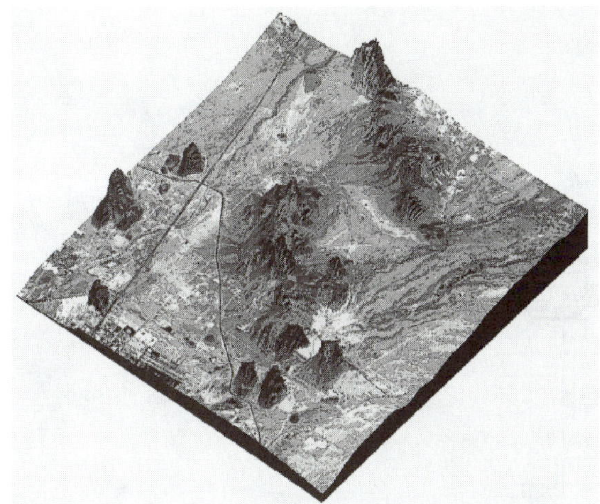

FIGURE 3.14 Landsat image and physiography. *(Source: Brady et al. 1998)*

caps and other frozen areas accounts for 2.15 percent of the resource. This means only 0.65 percent of the water in the world is fresh, and its distribution and quality is uneven (Tarjuelo and de Juan, 1999). As a result, water is an essential factor to consider in planning.

Bernard Palissy first explained in the sixteenth century that springs originate from and are fed by rain alone. He showed how this happens: seawater evaporates and is condensed to form rain, which falls, percolates into the ground, and emerges later as springs and rivers that return the water to the sea. This is the *hydrologic cycle* (Figure 3.17). The hydrologic cycle expresses the balance of water in its various forms in the air, on land, and in the sea (Morisawa, 1968, 12).

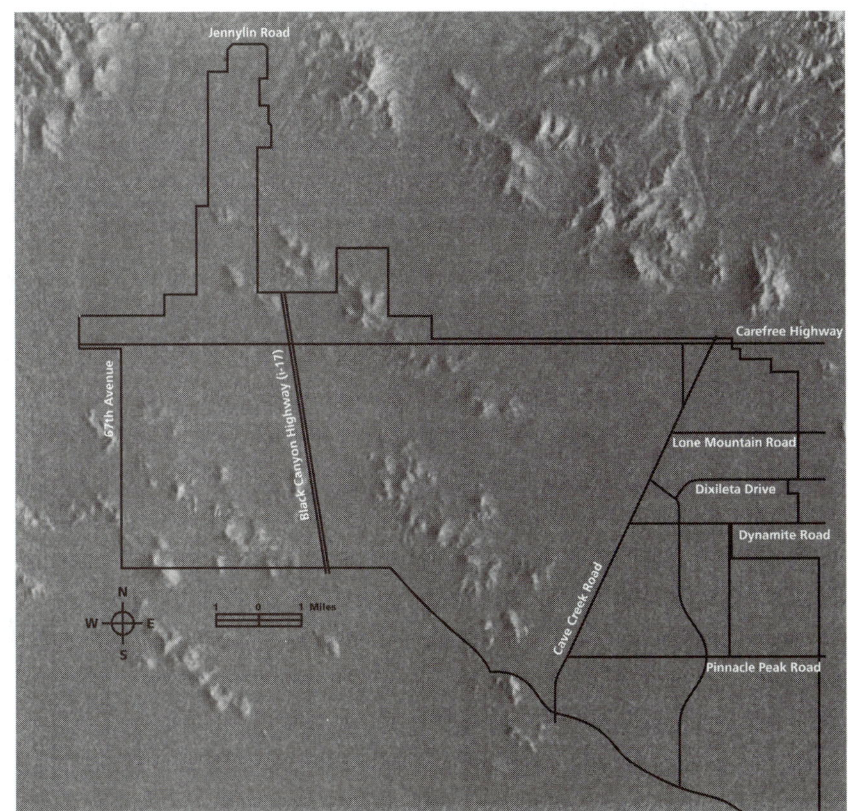

FIGURE 3.15 Digital elevation model. *(Source: City of Phoenix Parks, Recreation and Library Department 1998)*

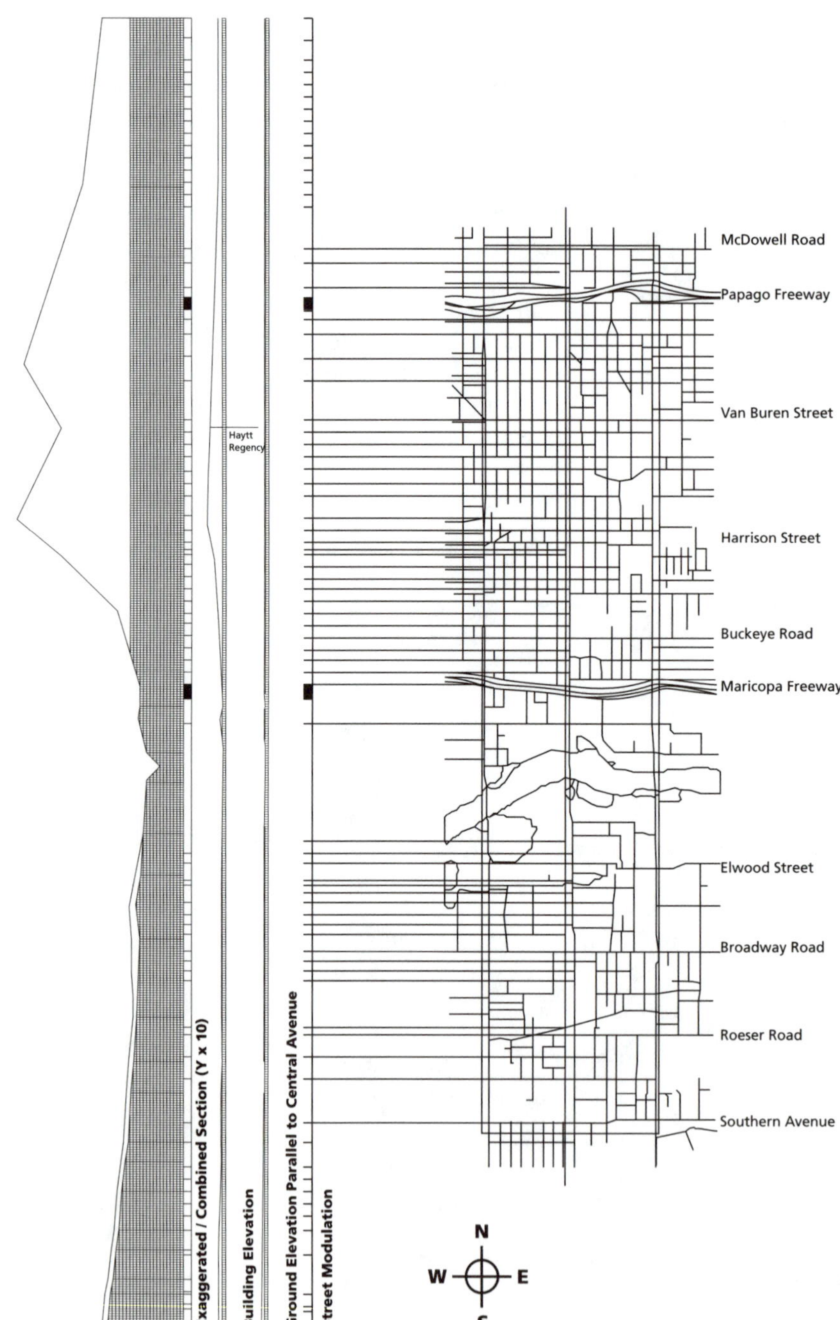

FIGURE 3.16
Morphological cross section of central Phoenix. *(Source: Adapted from Andres et al. 1998, originally drawn by Matt Jennings)*

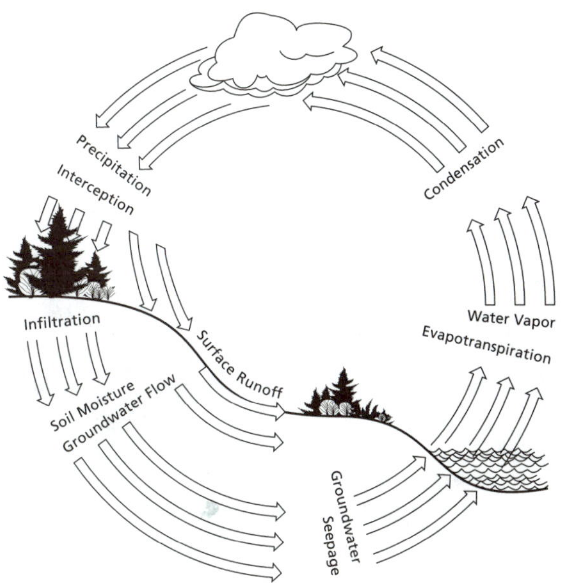

FIGURE 3.17 Hydrologic cycle.

As the hydrologic cycle and water budget illustrate, *hydrology* deals with the movement of water through the landscape both on the surface and in the ground. *Groundwater* is water that fills all the unblocked pores of materials lying beneath the surface. *Surface water* is water that flows above the ground. Depth to water table, water quality, aquifer yields, direction of movement, and the location of wells are important groundwater factors. Data concerning these factors can be obtained from various sources including the U.S. Environmental Protection Agency (EPA), the USGS, the NRCS, various state agencies, and individual well owners. From the geology map, the location of aquifers can be determined. An *aquifer* is a water-bearing layer of permeable rock, sand, or gravel. The process of water filtering through the surface to an aquifer is known to *infiltration.* Vegetation, soil permeability, slope, and soil saturation are the factors controlling infiltration rates (Easterbrook 1999).

A water budget can be constructed for an average year, which represents the inflow and outflow through the hydrologic cycle. Figure 3.18 illustrates the water budget for Pullman, Washington. As can be seen, there is a water surplus early in the year, followed by a period when moisture in the soil is being utilized. Then through the summer and early autumn there is a period of water deficiency, and finally moisture is recharged in the soil.

Water is an especially important resource in the desert. The Phoenix metropolitan region receives its water from two sources. First, the winter rains and snows in the nearby mountains are especially important, as is the relationship between the ranges and basins. Moisture is captured in the higher elevations as it moves in from the seas to the east. Often the moisture falls to the ground as snow and is stored in the mountains until it melts and flows into the basins below. The higher the range, the greater the precipitation. The greater the distance from the mountains and from the sea, the drier the desert and the less the frequency of surface water flow. The orientation and steepness of the slopes also has a strong impact on water flow and plant growth.

The second source is groundwater. Much water seeps from the higher elevations into the ground. The water then reemerges at lower elevations, so much so that one derivation of the name of Arizona is from the "place of small springs." The Phoenix metropolitan region is located over a large groundwater aquifer. The aquifer capacity is significant, with a depth of bedrock of over 1000 feet (300 meters) near the Salt River, south of the Tri-Villages Area (U.S. Army Corps 1976; Ciekot et al. 1995). The Tri-Villages Area is at the northern edge of this large aquifer, so it is important for regional recharge (Figure 3.19). In the planning area, the water table depth varies from approximately 200 to 800 feet (60 to 240 meters) (Ciekot et al. 1995).

Aspects of groundwater use in Arizona are strictly regulated as a result of the Groundwater

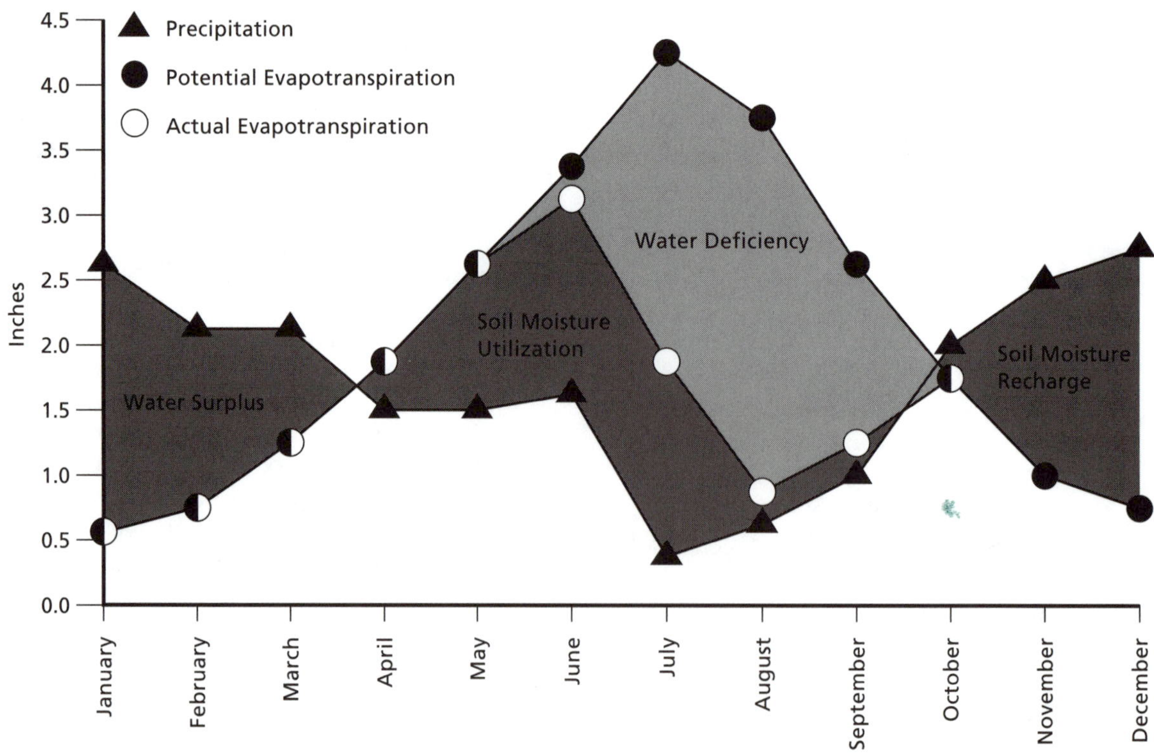

FIGURE 3.18 Water budget for Pullman, Washington.

Management Act (GMA) of 1980. This act essentially discourages new, large-scale irrigation in the Tri-Villages Area. Active management areas (AMAs) were also established by the act. The Tri-Villages Area is assigned to the Phoenix AMA. Within the Phoenix AMA, there is a goal to balance future groundwater pumping with groundwater recharge by 2025. The wells in the Tri-Villages Area are "among the most productive in Phoenix" (Ciekot et al. 1995, 5-4).

Another provision of the GMA is that a 100-year-assured water supply must be guaranteed before development within an AMA can proceed. In addition to groundwater, there are two surface water sources that assure such a 100-year supply for the Tri-Villages. The first is water from the Salt River drainage basin—which has been the traditional source for the region. The second is from the more controversial Central Arizona Project (CAP). Controversy exists due to CAP's use of much electricity as well as its negative environmental impacts. The CAP was constructed mainly for agricultural use and the city of Tucson to the south. Agriculture has declined, making more CAP water available. For several years, the CAP canal formed the northern border of the city of Phoenix. The canal presented an obstacle for infrastructure development. It is the southern edge of the Tri-Villages Area.

The planning area is part of the Salt River drainage basin, which in turn is part of the Gila River basin. The Gila River drains into the Colorado River. Drainage systems in deserts differ

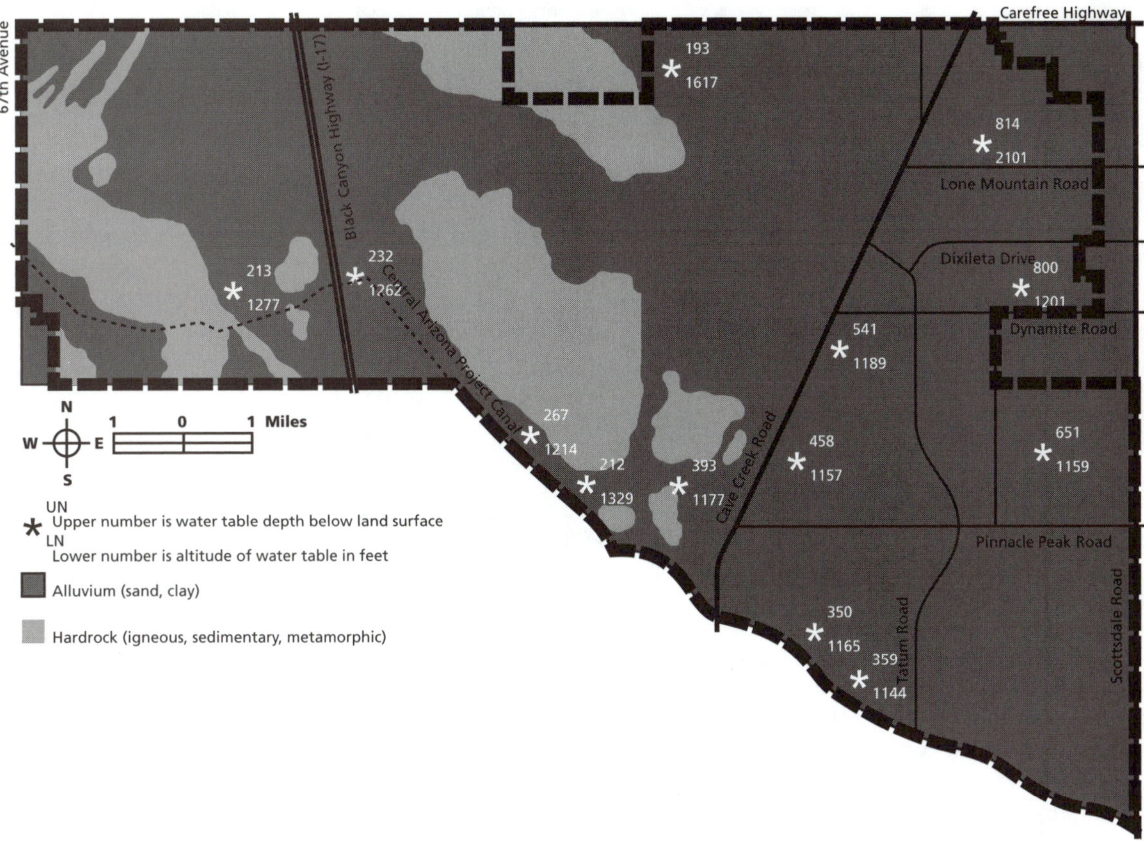

FIGURE 3.19 Groundwater, Desert View Tri-Villages Area. *(Source: Adapted from Ciekot et al. 1995)*

from those in more humid regions. Since water is scarce, fewer free-flowing streams and rivers exist. The primary drainageways are ephemeral *washes,* or *arroyos,* as they are known in Spanish.

The two primary drainageways in the Desert View Tri-Villages Area are the Cave Creek Wash and the Skunk Creek Wash (Figure 3.9). They both flow in a southerly direction into the more developed portions of the city. The headwaters of Cave Creek are in the Tonto National Forest to the north of the planning area. Cave Creek drops approximately 51 ft/mi (9.7 m/per kilometer) through the Tri-Villages Area (Ciekot et al. 1995). Its natural flow is interrupted at Cave Buttes Dam, which, in conjunction with two dikes, retains the flow to reduce flooding in central Phoenix.

The second primary drainage is Skunk Creek. Its headwaters are near the western edge of the Tonto National Forest. Skunk Creek drops approximately 14 ft/mi (2.7 meters per kilometer) in the Tri-Villages Area (Ciekot et al. 1995). Many smaller tributaries feed the Skunk and Cave Creeks. As Stephanie Ciekot et al. observed, the system of washes with the adjacent floodplains and riparian vegetation, "provide flood water distribution, groundwater recharge, moisture for vegetation, wildlife habitat, and scenic beauty" (1995, 5-8) (Figure 3.20).

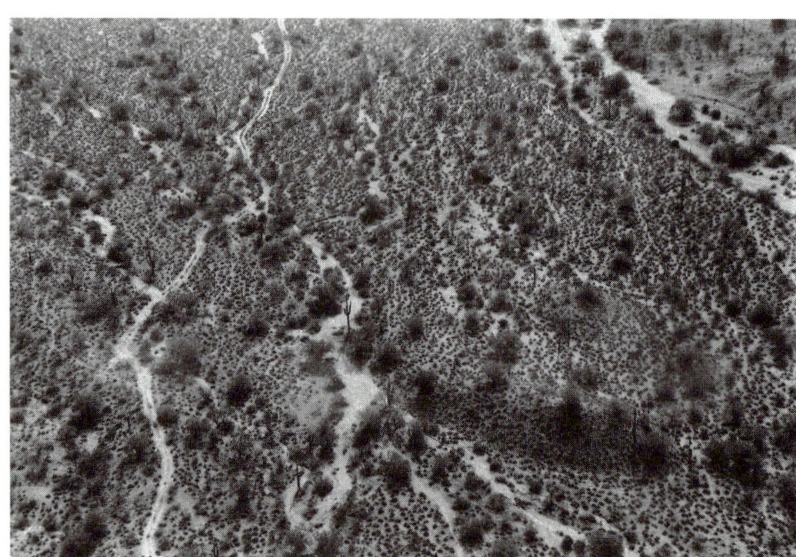

Aerial view of small Sonoran Desert washes.

For nondesert regions, several methods have been suggested for stream ordering. The method proposed by A. N. Strahler (1957) is the most straightforward. According to his system, stream orders are designated as first, second, third, and so on. *First-order streams* are primary drainageways; they are fingertip tributaries at the head of the stream system. *Second-order streams* are formed by the confluence of two first-order streams, and *third-order streams* are formed by the confluence of two second-order streams, and so on (Figure 3.21).

First-order streams are usually at higher elevations and travel a shorter distance over a steeper grade than do second-order streams. Second-order streams are at higher elevations and travel a shorter distance over a steeper grade than do third-order streams, and so on. Gravity causes this manner of stream movement toward a steady state. This can be expressed graphically by plotting elevation versus stream length for the streams in the study area (Figure 3.21). Average stream length can also be plotted against stream order. Streams develop along a location determined by a balance between available energy and resistance. Thus, the patterns of stream drainage in the landscape are determined by the regional geologic structure. Common types of drainage patterns are also shown in Figure 3.21.

In desert and semiarid regions, the natural hierarchy of drainage systems is reversed in the canal system. Larger canals are found at the headwater point. Flows in canals become progressively smaller as water is used for agricultural, industrial, and residential purposes.

Flooding is the general and temporary condition of a partial or complete inundation of normally dry land areas either from the overflow of streams, rivers, and other inland water or from abnormally high tidal water or rising coastal water resulting from severe storms, hurricanes, or tsunamis. Flooding is also any relatively high flow as measured by either gauge height or discharge quantity (Waananen et al., 1977). *Floodplains* "are lowlands adjacent to rivers, streams, oceans, lakes, or other water bodies that have been or may be inundated with water" (Morris 1997, 11).

FIGURE 3.20 Floodplains and washes, Desert View Tri-Villages Area. *(Source: Brady et al. 1998)*

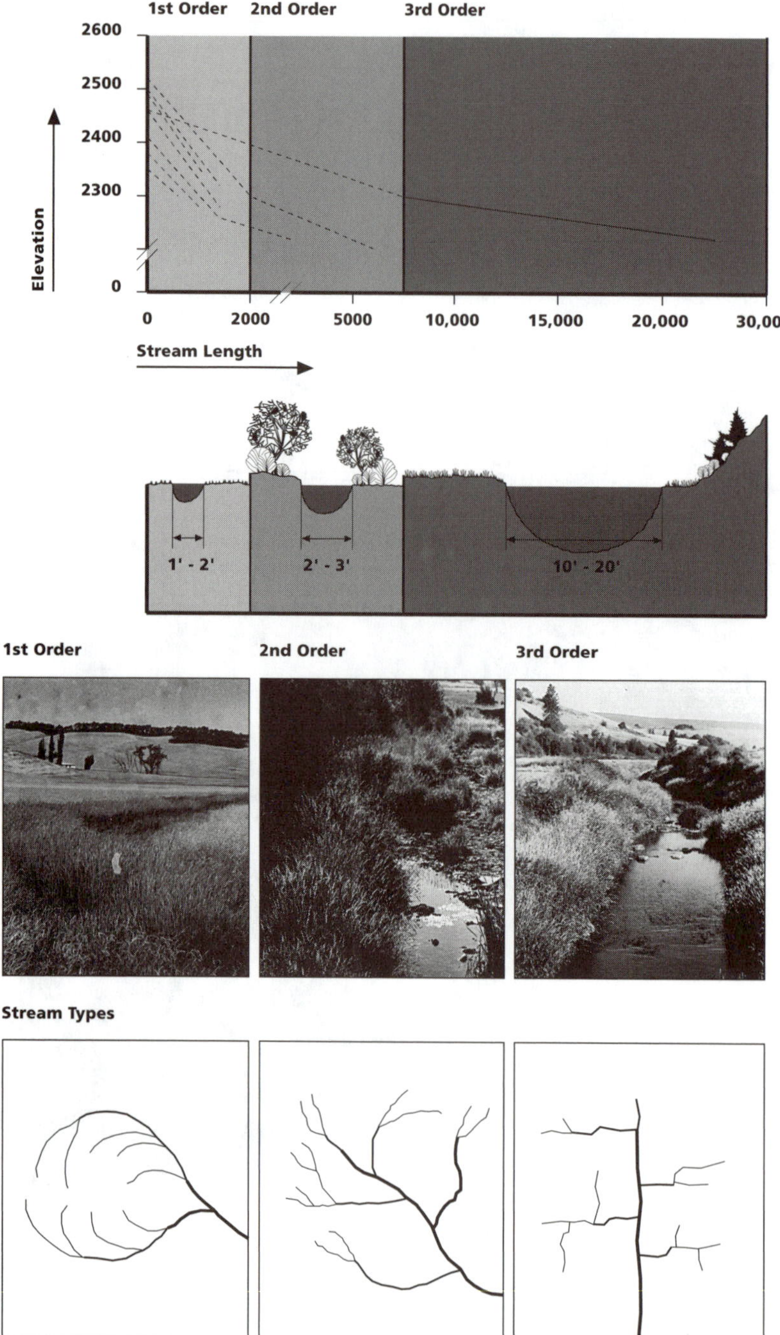

FIGURE 3.21 Elevation versus stream length, stream orders, and common drainage patterns stream orders.

Canal near Valladolid, Spain.

Floodplains include the channel of the drainageway, its floodway, and the flood fringe (Figure 3.22). For urban areas in the United States, maps indicating 100-year and 500-year floodplains are available from the Federal Emergency Management Agency (FEMA).

As can be seen in Figure 3.20, much of the Tri-Villages Area is in a floodplain. Flooding is a serious problem in the Phoenix region. By definition, desert environments, the Sonoran included, experience little precipitation. However, rains do fall in deserts, and in the Sonoran Desert the intensity and amount can be significant. Human settlement affects where the water flows once it reaches the earth. Paved streets and buildings can prevent the infiltration of water (Botkin and Beveridge 1997). Increased urbanization results in greater runoff at higher velocities. In the desert, this runoff is frequently dramatic. Sometimes the consequence is destructive flash floods. In response, city officials in Arizona have adopted measures to encourage and sometimes to require that storm water be retained on site. For example, the City of Tempe has an ordinance requiring property owners and developers "to provide storage of sufficient volume to hold the total runoff from the . . . storm falling on that

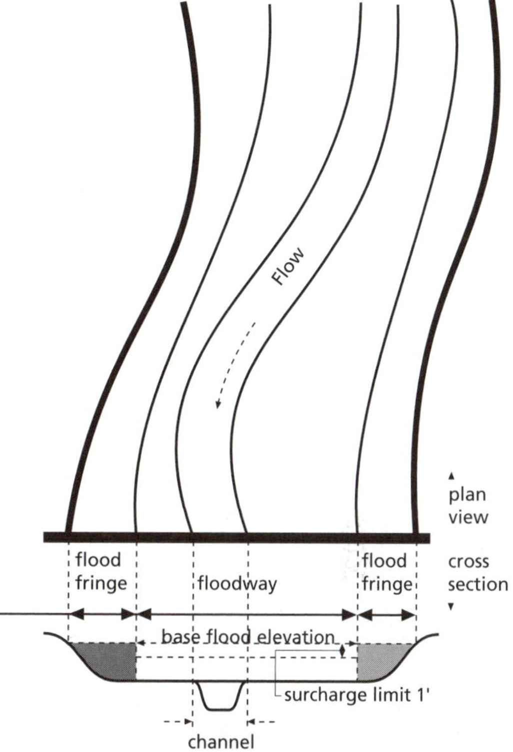

FIGURE 3.22 Elements of the 100-year floodplain. *(Source: Morris 1997)*

[property]." In addition, there is increased attention on protecting wash corridors. Many communities are adopting measures to reduce the hazards of floods. (For an excellent primer on the subject, see Morris 1997.) In the Tri-Villages Area, flooding erodes the banks of the washes and results in some sedimentation problems. Flooding also is an important mechanism for bank building through deposition and is an agent for sediment routing.

While water quantity is an important consideration for planning—we need enough water to support our communities, but too much may pose a hazard—water quality is equally essential. The quality of the groundwater in the Tri-Villages Area is good and "does not contain the nitrates, chromium, and organics found in other Phoenix groundwater" (Ciekot et al. 1995, 5-4).

Limnology is the study of fresh waters in all their physical, chemical, geological, and biological aspects (Odum, 1971). There are two broad types of freshwater habitats: standing-water habitats (lakes, ponds, swamps, or bogs) and running-water habitats (springs, streams, or rivers). For purposes of hydrological inventory and analysis, the chemical and biological aspects of aquatic ecosystems and the types of freshwater habitats are important.

In coastal areas, a hydrologic inventory may be replaced or supplemented by an analysis of oceanography and/or estuarine ecology. *Oceanography* is the study of the sea in all its physical, chemical, geological, and biological aspects (Odum, 1971). For purposes of inventory and analysis of hydrology, the chemical and biological aspects of oceanography are important, while the physical and geological aspects may be covered in other inventory steps. Effective management of coastal zones and their related ocean environment is important for many reasons, including the recent dramatic decline in fisheries. According to Carl Safina (1998), the giant bluefin tuna population has declined by 90 percent off the Atlantic coast since the early 1980s. Meanwhile, Pacific salmon have disappeared from about 40 percent of their breeding range in Washington, Oregon, Idaho, and California (Safina 1998).

Eugene Odum defines an estuary as "a semi-enclosed coastal body of water which has a free connection with the open sea; it is thus strongly affected by tidal action, and within it sea water is mixed (and usually measurably diluted) with fresh water from land drainage" (1971, 352). Again the chemical and biological aspects of this environment are the most important ones for hydrological inventory and analysis, while the physical and geologic aspects may be covered in other inventory elements.

The U.S. Fish and Wildlife Service has developed a useful classification system of wetlands and deepwater habitats of the United States (Cowardin et al., 1979). This classification system was especially designed to be used for biophysical inventories. It describes ecological taxa, arranges them in a system useful for resource managers and planners, furnishes units for mapping, and provides uniformity of concepts and terms. Five systems form the highest level of classification hierarchy, including marine, estuarine, riverine, lacustrine, and palustrine. These systems are further subdivided into subsystems and classes. Figure 3.23 summarizes these systems, subsystems, and classes.

Wetlands are generally perceived to be swamps, marshes, estuaries, and similar areas. Some forested areas can also technically be termed wetlands. *Riparian areas* are those ecosystems within or adjacent to drainageways and/or their floodplains and are characterized by species and/or life-forms different from the immediately surrounding upland (Lowe 1964). Riparian areas are variously considered by scientists to be a type of wetland (Brown et al. 1978) or to be physiographically distinct from wetlands (Odum 1978). Wetlands and riparian areas are considered as two physiographically (but not functionally) distinct ecosystems for federal and state regulatory purposes.

The changing public perception of the importance of wetlands has to do with their many positive ecological functions and the values that people place on these functions. According to M. Williams, "it is difficult to say where a function becomes a value and there is much imprecision about these terms . . . the word benefit [can] be used where we cannot clearly separate a function from a value" (1990, 13).

The functions, values, and benefits of wetlands and riparian areas are perceived to be similar: groundwater recharge and discharge, sediment stabilization, flood flow attenuation, water quality maintenance, fish and wildlife habitat, climate moderation, shoreline protection, food production, and recreation (Cooper et al. 1990; Meeks and Runyon 1990; Kusler and Opheim 1996). Sixty-six percent of commercially harvested fish depend on

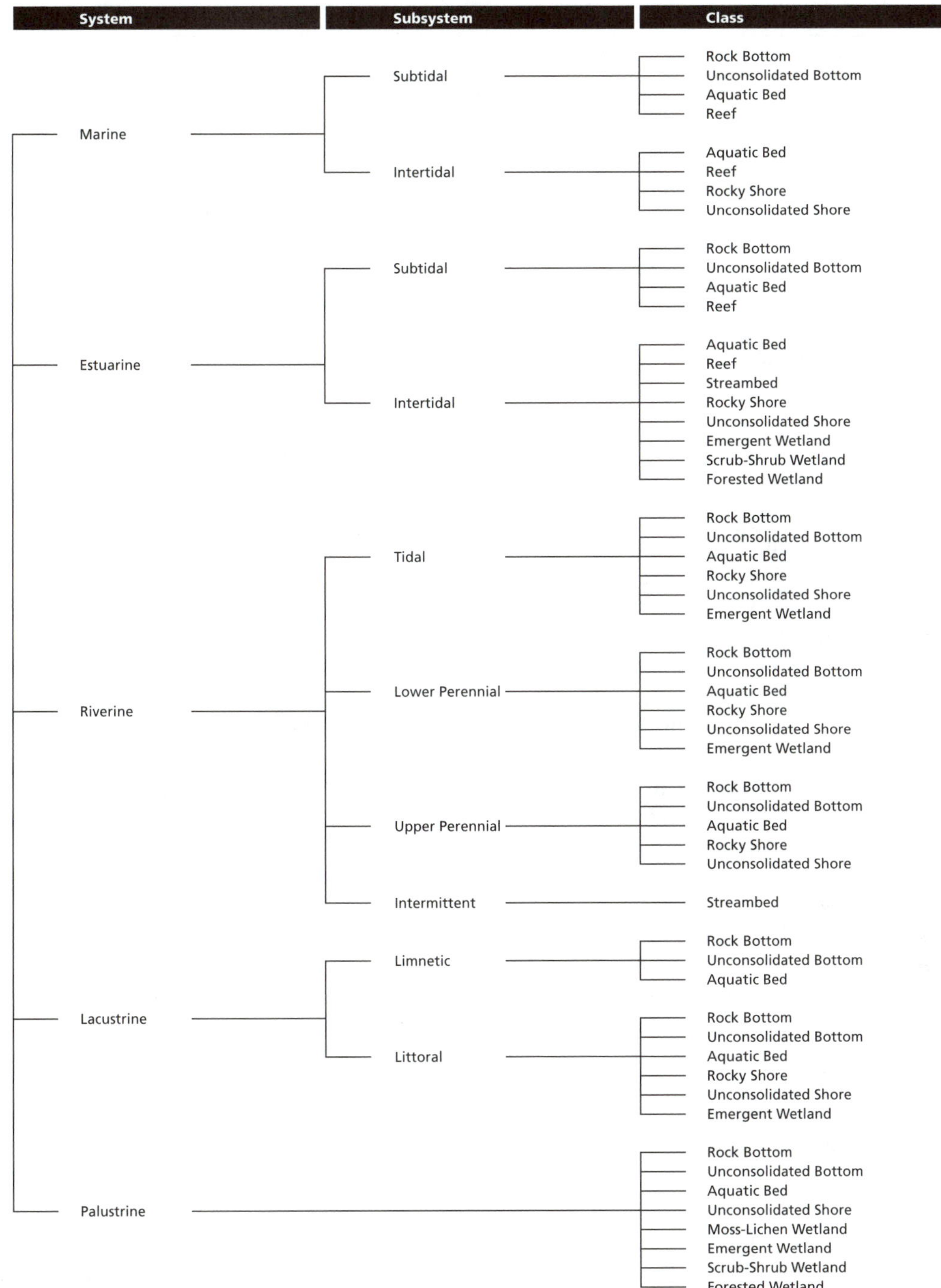

FIGURE 3.23 Classification hierarchy of wetlands and deepwater habitats, showing systems, subsystems, and classes. The Palustrine system does not include deep-water habitats. *(Source: Cowardin et al. 1979, courtesy of U.S. Fish and Wildlife Service)*

wetlands for food or reproduction (Blumm and Zaleha 1989). Riparian areas support 75 percent of the nation's breeding birds, 50 percent of the mammals, and more than 100 endangered species (McCormick 1978; Steiner et al. 1994).

Several approaches have been developed to classify functions, values, and benefits of wetlands. R. W. Tiner (1984) suggests three categories: (1) fish and wildlife values, (2) environmental quality values, and (3) socioeconomic values. Williams (1990) employs four broad groups: (1) physical/hydrological, (2) chemical, (3) biological, and (4) socioeconomic. Williams notes that "none of these categories is exclusive and each can have a profound effect on the other" (1990, 13). Williams (1990) classified flood mitigation, coastal protection, aquifer recharge, and sediment trapping as the major physical/hydrological functions. The chemical functions of wetlands include: pollution trapping, removal of toxic residues, and waste processing (Williams 1990). Williams considers productivity and habitats to be the biological functions. The major socioeconomic qualities are consumptive values for farming, fishing, hunting, fuel, and fiber, plus nonconsumptive benefits for views, recreation, education, science, and history (Williams 1990).

An estimated 53 percent of wetlands in the coterminous United States have been lost from the 1780s to the 1980s. In the 1980s, wetlands constituted an estimated 5 percent of the land surface of the lower 48 states (Dahl 1990). Alaska and Hawaii have also experienced wetland losses. Wetlands continue to decline nationwide, but estimates of decline vary (Leslie and Clark 1990). It is estimated that some 80 percent of the remaining wetlands are privately owned (*Environmental Reporter* 1990). The causes of wetland conversions from the mid-1950s to mid-1970s were as follows: agriculture, 87 percent; urban development, 8 percent; and other development, 5 percent (U.S. Department of Interior 1988).

Wetlands have been lost and degraded both as a result of human action and natural causes. Human actions include: drainage, dredging and stream channelization, deposition of fill material, diking and damming, tilling for crop production, grazing by domesticated animals, discharge of pollutants, mining, and alteration of hydrology (U.S. Environmental Protection Agency 1988; Kusler and Opheim 1996). Natural causes include erosion, subsidence, sea level rise, droughts, hurricanes and other storms, and overgrazing by wildlife (U.S. Environmental Protection Agency 1988).

There has been no comprehensive national or regional analysis of the loss or alteration of riparian areas. It has been estimated, however, that 70 to 90 percent of riparian ecosystems have been altered, and that natural riparian communities now comprise less than 2 percent of the land area in the United States (Brinson et al. 1981; Ohmart and Anderson 1986). Riparian areas are especially important in the American West, where they are estimated to constitute 0.5 percent of the landscape (Ohmart and Anderson 1986; Monroe 1991). Estimated losses for states in the Intermountain West (parts of Nebraska, Kansas, South and North Dakota, Washington, Oregon, California, Arizona, New Mexico, Texas, and Oklahoma) can be found in Cooper et al. (1990).

The implications of the trend toward increasing wetland and riparian area losses are significant. Flooding cycles have been altered, resulting in flood damage and associated costs for repair or prevention (Gosselink and Maltby 1990). Human safety and property are put at risk by floods. Long-term food supplies, genetic diversity, and wildlife reserves can also be negatively impacted by flooding (Gosselink and Maltby 1990). J. G. Gosselink and E. Maltby (1990, 32) observe: "Wetlands are important elements in the global cycles of nitrogen and sulphur. . . . Inevitably the continuing loss of wetlands . . . must have significant impacts on these cycles, impacts whose repercussions we do not at present clearly understand." They also note negative consequences for the carbon cycle (Steiner et al. 1994).

The hydrology of a landscape can be studied by asking questions and seeking answers to those questions (Steiner and McSherry 2000), such as:

- How is water, *or the lack of water,* expressed within the planning area?
- Is there a regional connection?
- What is the visual connection to water?
- Is this visual connection limited to particular places within the area?
- How has the presence of water determined the location of land development, ranching, and farming?
- What is the relationship between water and sense of place in the planning area?
- Relative to the expression of water in the planning area:
  Does water express itself through built form?
  Through the location of houses?
  Schools?
  Farms or ranches?
  Roadways?
- What are the functions, values, and benefits of wetlands and riparian areas?
- How does the spatial pattern of development reflect water as either an abundant or a limited resource?

SUMMARY OF HYDROLOGIC INVENTORY ELEMENTS:

A. Groundwater systems
   1. Aquifer recharge areas
   2. Consolidated and unconsolidated aquifer location and yield
   3. Well locations and yields
   4. Water quantity and quality
   5. Water table, artesian supplies
   6. Seasonally high water table
   7. Water-bearing characteristics of geologic units
   8. Infiltration rates

B. Surface water systems
   1. Watershed and drainage basins
   2. Stream, lake, estuary, coastline, and wetland locations
   3. Stream volumes
   4. Lake levels, tides
   5. Floodplains, flood-hazard areas
   6. Physical water-quality characteristics (sediment loads and temperature)
   7. Chemical water-quality characteristics (such as pH, nitrogen, phosphorus, chlorine, boron, and electrical conductivity)
   8. Bacteriological water-quality characteristics
   9. Freshwater or marine flora and fauna (may also be included in the vegetation and wildlife parts of the inventory and analysis process)
   10. Eutrophication
   11. Water supply systems
   12. Sewage treatment systems
   13. Existing industrial disposal and discharge points
   14. Existing solid-waste disposal sites affecting water quality
   15. Existing storm sewer systems and discharge points
   16. Algal bloom problems
   17. Aquatic weed problem areas
   18. Fish hatcheries and stocking areas (may also be included in the land-use portion of the inventory and analysis process)

MAJOR SOURCES OF INFORMATION

1. U.S. Geological Survey (USGS)
National Wetland Inventory
National Cartographic Information Center
507 National Center
Reston, Virginia 22092
http://water.usgs.gov

2. U.S. Fish and Wildlife Service (USFWS)
National Wetland Inventory
9720 Executive Center Drive
Suite 101 Monroe Building
St. Petersburg, Florida 33702

3. Federal Emergency Management Agency (FEMA)
Map Service Center
6730 Santa Barbara Court
Baltimore, Maryland 21227-5623
Phone 1-800-358-9616
Fax 1-800-358-9620

4. U.S. Natural Resources Conservation Service (NRCS)

5. Agricultural Stabilization and Conservation Service (ASCS)
6. U.S. Army Corps of Engineers
7. U.S. Department of Housing and Urban Development (National Flood Insurance Program)
8. U.S. Forest Service (USFS)
9. Environmental Protection Agency (EPA)
10. National Marine Fisheries Service (U.S. Department of Commerce)
11. Office of Coastal Zone Management (NOAA, U.S. Department of Commerce)
12. Federal Aviation Administration (FAA)
13. U.S. Coast Guard
14. State departments of fisheries and coastal management
15. State sea-grant universities
16. College and university libraries
17. River basin commissions
18. State departments of natural resources, mining, and ecology
19. Individual well owners

Soils

Soils occupy a unique position in the lithosphere and atmosphere. They are a transition zone that links the biotic and abiotic environments. *Soil* is a natural three-dimensional body on the surface of the earth that is capable of supporting plants. Its properties result from the integrated effect of climate and living matter acting upon parent material, as conditioned by relief over periods of time. Many processes are linked within the soil zone, so soils often can reveal more about an area than any other natural factor.

Soils scientist William Broderson has noted, "Much of our life's activities and pursuits are related and influenced by the behavior of the soil around our houses, roads, septic and sewage disposal systems, airports, parks, recreation sites, farms, forests, schools, and shopping centers. What is put on the land should be guided by the soil that is beneath it" (1994, 1).

Fortunately, many dedicated conservationists have mapped soil information for most of the United States. These conservationists, working for the U.S. Natural Resources Conservation Service, an agency of the U.S. Department of Agriculture (USDA), have compiled map information in soil surveys for much of the nation. The soil survey includes the information necessary:

- To determine the important characteristics of soils
- To classify soils into defined types and other classificational units
- To establish and to plot on maps the boundaries among kinds of soils
- To correlate and to predict the adaptability of soils to various crops, grasses, and trees, their behavior and productivity under different management systems, and the yields of adapted crops under defined sets of management practices

The principal purposes of the soil survey are:

- To make available all the specific information about each kind of soil that is significant to its use and behavior to those who must decide how to manage it
- To provide descriptions of the mapping units so the survey can be interpreted for land uses that require the fundamental facts about soil

According to Broderson:

> "A soil survey generally contains soils data for one county, parish, or other geographic area, such as a major land resource area [MLRA]. During a soil survey, soil scientists walk over the landscapes, bore holes with soil augers, and examine cross sections of soil profiles. They determine the texture, color, structure, and reaction of the soil and the relationship and thickness of the different soil horizons. Some soils are sampled and tested at soil survey laboratories for certain soil property determinations, such as cation-exchange capacity and bulk density" (1994, 1).

Soil surveys describe some of what is known about the soil science, or *pedology,* of the area and include information about soil associations, catenas, series, phases, capability classes, profiles, erosion, and drainage. A landscape has a distinctive characteristic pattern of soils. Such a pattern is called an *association.* It normally consists of one or more major soils and at least one minor soil and is named for the major soil or soils. A related but different grouping is a *catena,* a sequence of soils of about the same age, derived from similar parent material, and occurring under similar climate conditions but having different characteristics due to variation in relief and drainage.

A *soil series* is a group of soils having soil horizons similar in characteristics and arrangement in the soil profile, except for the texture of the soil, and developed from a particular type of parent material. Each soil series generally is named for a town or other geographic feature near the place where a soil of that series was first observed and mapped. Soils of the same series name are essentially alike in those characteristics that affect their behavior in the undisturbed landscape.

Soils of one series can differ in texture from the surface layer and in slope, stoniness, or some other characteristic that affects human use of the soil. On the basis of such differences, a soil series is divided into *phases.* The name of a soil phase indicates a feature that affects management. For example, in the Desert View Tri-Villages Area, the Gilman series is divided into nine soil phases, such as, Gilman fine sandy loam and Gilman loam, 1 to 3 percent slopes (Hartman 1977) (Figure 3.24). A *mapping unit* is usually equivalent to a phase. A phase is a division of the series divided by properties that are important to soil use, such as texture and slope (Broderson 1994). In a soil survey, these units are numbered.

Soil capability classification is a general way of showing the suitability of soils for agricultural purposes. Soils are grouped according to their limitations, the risk of erosion under use, and the way they respond to treatment. Capability classification will be described further in Chapter 5.

The *soil profile* is an important part of the description of each soil series and is defined as the sequence of layers (*horizons*) from the surface downward to rock or other underlying material (Figure 3.25). These layers, or horizons, include:

O—Organic horizons (litter derived from dead plants and animals)

A—Mineral horizons of maximum biological activity

E—Eluvial horizons (mineral horizons that lie at or near surface and are characterized as zones of maximum leaching)

B—Illuvial horizons (the layers of accumulation into which the above minerals are washed)

C—Unconsolidated material under A and B layers

R—Bedrock

Soil erosion is the searing away of the land surface by running water, wind, ice, or other geologic agents and by processes such as gravity. Erosion hazard may be considered the susceptibility of soils to these factors. The factors affecting erosion can be expressed in the following equation:

$$E = f(C, S, T, SS, M)$$

where

E = erosion,
f = function of (),
C = climate,
S = soil properties,
T = topography,
SS = soil surface conditions, and
M = human activities (Renard and Foster 1983; Renard et al. 1997).

Soil scientists developed an equation to express the functional relationship among these factors. As early as the 1930s, erosion prediction equations were developed which came together as the *uni-*

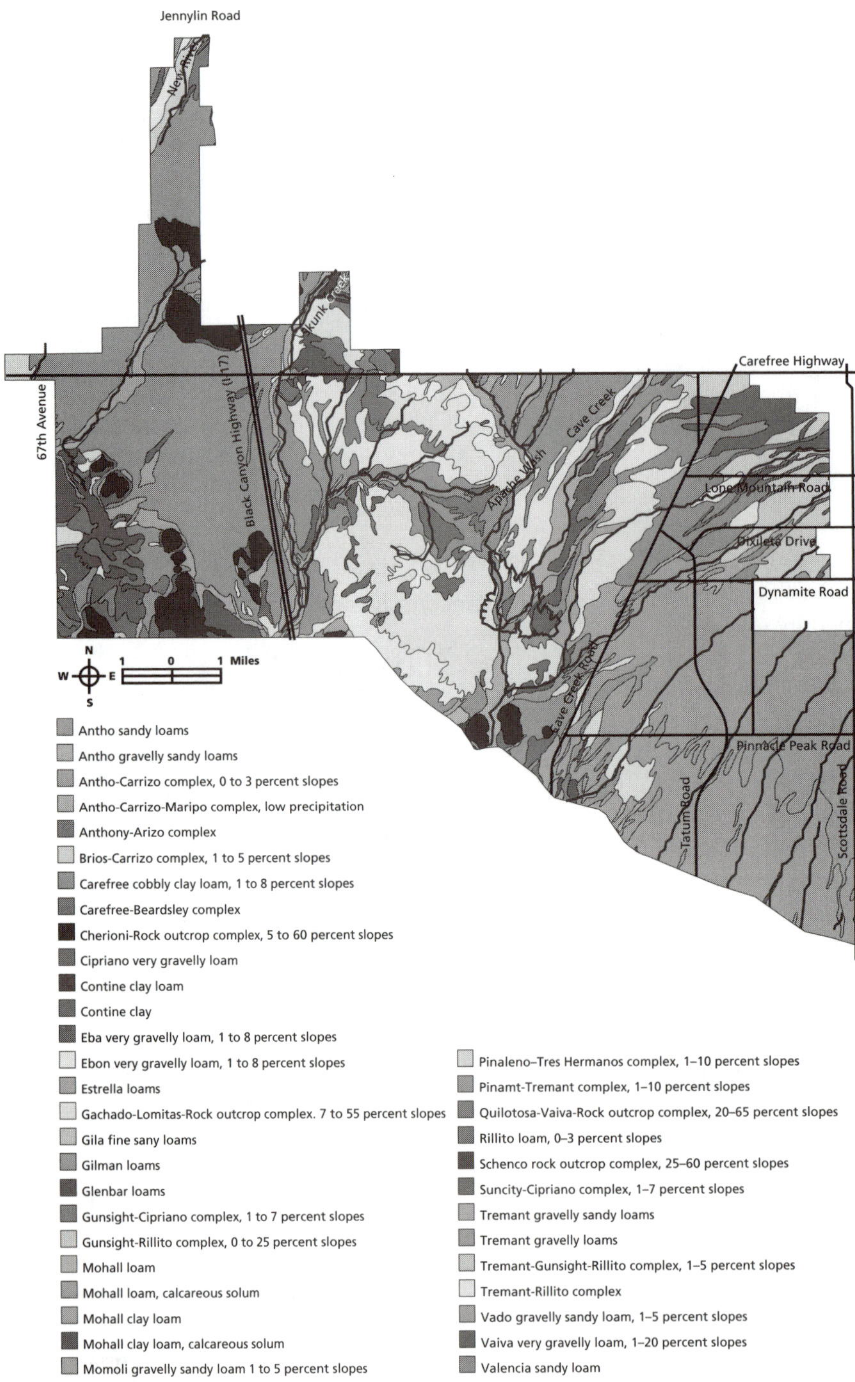
Jennylin Road
Carefree Highway
67th Avenue
Black Canyon Highway (I-17)
Cave Creek
Apache Wash
Lone Mountain Road
Dixileta Drive
Dynamite Road
Cave Creek Road
Pinnacle Peak Road
Tatum Road
Scottsdale Road
N
W
E
S
1 0 1 Miles
Antho sandy loams
Antho gravelly sandy loams
Antho-Carrizo complex, 0 to 3 percent slopes
Antho-Carrizo-Maripo complex, low precipitation
Anthony-Arizo complex
Brios-Carrizo complex, 1 to 5 percent slopes
Carefree cobbly clay loam, 1 to 8 percent slopes
Carefree-Beardsley complex
Cherioni-Rock outcrop complex, 5 to 60 percent slopes
Cipriano very gravelly loam
Contine clay loam
Contine clay
Eba very gravelly loam, 1 to 8 percent slopes
Ebon very gravelly loam, 1 to 8 percent slopes
Estrella loams
Gachado-Lomitas-Rock outcrop complex. 7 to 55 percent slopes
Gila fine sany loams
Gilman loams
Glenbar loams
Gunsight-Cipriano complex, 1 to 7 percent slopes
Gunsight-Rillito complex, 0 to 25 percent slopes
Mohall loam
Mohall loam, calcareous solum
Mohall clay loam
Mohall clay loam, calcareous solum
Momoli gravelly sandy loam 1 to 5 percent slopes
Pinaleno–Tres Hermanos complex, 1–10 percent slopes
Pinamt-Tremant complex, 1–10 percent slopes
Quilotosa-Vaiva-Rock outcrop complex, 20–65 percent slopes
Rillito loam, 0–3 percent slopes
Schenco rock outcrop complex, 25–60 percent slopes
Suncity-Cipriano complex, 1–7 percent slopes
Tremant gravelly sandy loams
Tremant gravelly loams
Tremant-Gunsight-Rillito complex, 1–5 percent slopes
Tremant-Rillito complex
Vado gravelly sandy loam, 1–5 percent slopes
Vaiva very gravelly loam, 1–20 percent slopes
Valencia sandy loam

FIGURE 3.24 Soils, Desert View Tri-Villages Area. *(Source: Brady et al. 1998)*

	Horizon	Description
Organic Horizons	Oi	Slightly decomposed organic matter.
	Oe	Intermediately decomposed organic matter.
	Oa	Highly decomposed organic matter.
Mineral Horizons of Maximum Biological Activity	A	Surface mineral horizon that has an accumulation of well-decomposed organic matter that coats the mineral particles and darkens the soil mass. With plowing or other disturbances the Ap notation is used.
Horizons of Eluviation (removal of materials dissolved or suspended in water)	E	Subsurface horizon that has lost organic matter, clay, iron, or aluminum through eluviation with concentration of resistant sand and silt-sized particles.
	AB, EB	Transitional from A or E to the B but more like A or E horizon.
	BA, BE	Transitional from A or E to the B but more like B than the A or E horizon.
Mineral Horizons of Illuviation (accumulation of dissolved or suspended material from above and/or alteration of the parent material)	B (Bh, Bs, Bo, Bk, Bt, Bc, Bg, By, Bw)	Mineral horizon that is characterized by one or more of the following: 1. Illuvial accumulation of clay (Bt), organic matter (Bh), carbonates (Bk), silica (Bq), gypsum (By), iron and aluminum oxides (Bs); 2. Residual concentration of iron and aluminum oxides (Bo); 3. Development of surface and/or coatings of iron and aluminum oxides that give darker, stronger, or redder colors (Bw); and 4. Evidence of carbonate removal.
	BC	Transitional from B to C but more like the B horizon.
	CB	Transitional from B to C but more like the C horizon.
Mineral Horizon (excluding bedrock, which is little affected by soil forming processes)	C (Cg, Ck, Cz, Cy)	Mineral horizon, other than bedrock, that may or may not be similar to presumed parent material. Has been little affected by soil-forming processes but may be otherwise weathered. Numerical prefixes are used to designate C horizons unlike presumed parent material as 2C, 3C, etc. This designation also is used with other horizons. Cg = C horizon with intense gleying or reduction of iron compounds. Ck = C horizon with accumulation of carbonates such as CaCo3. Cy = C horizon with acculul ation of gypsum. Cz = C horizon with accumulation of soluble salt.
Hard Bedrock	R	Underlying consolidated bedrock.

FIGURE 3.25 Horizons that could occur in a soil profile. *(Source: Hendricks 1985)*

versal soil loss equation (USLE) originally in the late 1950s and the early 1960s (Wischmeier and Smith 1965, 1978). Erosion prediction equations are improved constantly which has resulted in the *revised universal soil loss equation* (RUSLE). Both USLE and RUSLE compute the average annual erosion expected on field slopes as

$$A = R \cdot K \cdot L \cdot S \cdot C \cdot P$$

where

A = computed spatial average soil loss and temporal average soil loss per unit of area, expressed in the units selected for K and for the period selected for R. In practice, these are usually selected so that A is expressed in ton · $\text{acre}^{-1} \cdot \text{yr}^{-1}$, but other units can be selected (that is, $\text{t} \cdot \text{ha}^{-1} \cdot \text{yr}^{-1}$).

R = rainfall-runoff erosivity factor—the rainfall erosion index plus a factor for any significant runoff from snowmelt.

K = soil erodibility factor—the soil-loss rate per erosion index unit for a specified soil as measured on a standard plot, which is defined as a 72.6-ft (22.1-m) length of uniform 9 percent slope in continuous clean-tilled fallow.

L = slope length factor—the ratio of soil loss from the field slope length to soil loss from a 72.6-ft length under identical conditions.

S = slope steepness factor—the ratio of soil loss from the field slope gradient to soil loss from a 9 percent slope under otherwise identical conditions.

C = cover-management factor—the ratio of soil loss from an area with specified cover and management to soil loss from an identical area in tilled continuous fallow.

P = support practice factor—the ratio of soil loss with a support practice like contouring, stripcropping, or terracing to soil loss with straight-row farming up and down the slope (Renard et al. 1997).

There are also wind-erosion equations that consider similar factors for wind erosion (see Skidmore 1994, for example). Some soil erosion occurs naturally, so the question can be raised: What rate is tolerable? *Tolerable soil loss* can be defined as the maximum rate of annual soil erosion that will permit a high level of crop productivity to be sustained economically and indefinitely. These T values vary from soil to soil, depending on how fast new topsoil can be formed to replace the soil lost to erosion. Typically the universal soil-loss equation and the universal wind-erosion equation are used to determine what cropping and tillage practices are necessary to keep soil loss within a tolerable level.

Soil drainage may be defined as the relative rapidity and the extent of the removal of water from the surface and from within the soil under natural conditions. Soil series in a soil survey will include a description of drainage. Some of this soil survey information will be explored further, using the Desert View Tri-Villages Area as an example.

The soils map (Figure 3.24) shows the mapping units in the Desert View Tri-Villages Area. The soils of the area vary in texture. Sands, silts, and clays are present. Figure 3.26 shows the soil textural classes, while Table 3.5 illustrates the various particle sizes and the corresponding nomenclature. There are four basic texture groups—sands, silts, clays, and loams—that can be subdivided further to reflect various mixtures (for instance, loamy sands and sandy loams). *Sand* is coarse-textured and comprises loose, single-particle grains that can be easily seen or felt. *Silts* have a medium texture, while *clays* are fine-textured and comprised of the smallest particles. *Loams* have a

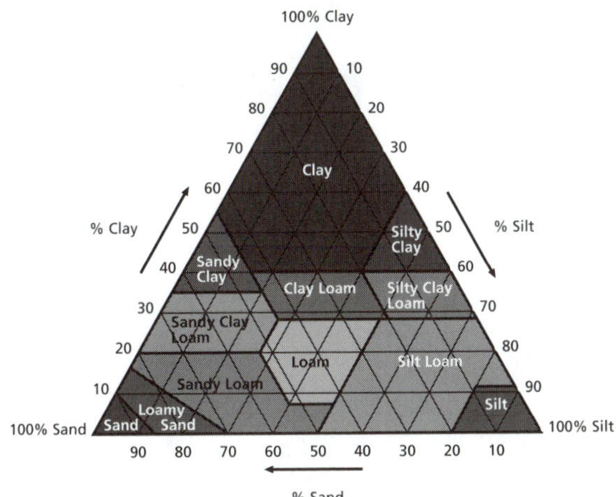

FIGURE 3.26 Soil textural classes.

mixture of different sand, silt, and clay particles (Rogers, Golden, and Halpern, 1986).

The soils in the Tri-Villages Area can be grouped into three broad categories based on their *parent material.* Parent material refers to a great variety of unconsolidated organic (such as fresh peat) and mineral material in which soil formation begins (Broderson 1994). According to Stephanie Ciekot and her colleagues (1995), the three categories are: soils formed from recent alluvium, soils formed from old alluvium, and soils derived from mountains and buttes (Figure 3.27).

The soils from recent alluvium occur on nearly level to gently sloping areas. They are found along the primary washes, such as Cave Creek and Skunk Creek and on the valley plains in the south-

TABLE 3.5
PARTICLE DIAMETER

Texture	mm	Inch (approximate)
Clay	<0.002	$<8 \times 10^{-5}$
Silt	0.002–0.050	8×10^{-5} to 20×10^{-5}
Sand	0.050–2.000	20×10^{-5} to 0.080

SOURCE: adapted from Brady 1974; Brady and Weil 1996.

eastern portion of the Tri-Villages Area, just north of the Central Arizona Project canal (Ciekot et al. 1995). Gilman is an example of these soils. Its profile reveals a yellowish-brown, loam surface layer about 5 inches (12.7 centimeters) thick. According to the soil survey, the underlying material is light yellowish-brown loam and very fine sandy loam to a depth of 64 inches (162.6 centimeters). Gilman is "moderately alkaline throughout and is weakly effervescent to strongly effervescent" (Hartman 1977, 27) (Figure 3.28).

Soils from old alluvium consist of nearly level to moderately steep slopes on alluvial fans, *bajadas,* and valley plains. The most common soils in the Tri-Villages Area are derived from a wide mixture of basalts, granite, granite-gneiss, schist, rhyolite, andesite, and quartzite (Ciekot et al. 1995; Hartman 1977; Camp 1986). Ebon is an example. Its profile reveals a brown, gravely loam surface layer about 2 inches (5.1 centimeters) thick. According to the soil survey for the central part of Maricopa County, the subsoil extends to a depth of 60 inches (152.4 centimeters). The upper 11 inches (27.9 centimeters) of this subsoil are reddish-brown very cobbly clay loam, the next 25 inches (63.5 centimeters) are yellowish-red and reddish-brown very cobbly clay, and the lower 22 inches (55.9 centimeters) are light reddish-brown very cobbly sandy clay loam (Hartman 1977). Ebon soils are moderately alkaline throughout and noneffervescent in the upper 23 inches (58.4 centimeters) (Hartman 1977).

The soils formed on the mountain and butte areas are poorly developed and thin. As they start to develop, these soils are eroded into the valleys (Ciekot et al. 1995). The Cherioni soils are an example. The Cherioni series has a white, silicaline-cemented hardpan. The soil above the hardpan is a very gravely, yellowish brown surface loam about 1-inch (2.5-centimeter) thick and a 5-inch (13-centimeter) thick layer of yellowish brown to very pale brown loam (Camp 1986; Hartman 1977).

The soils series name is like a plant or animal common name. For a broader exchange of infor-

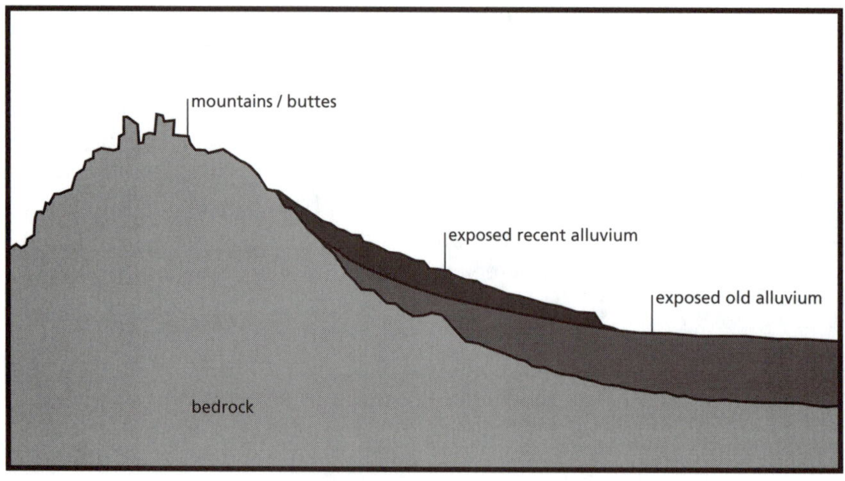

FIGURE 3.27 Components of the characteristic desert profile. *(Source: Adapted from Ciekot et al. 1995)*

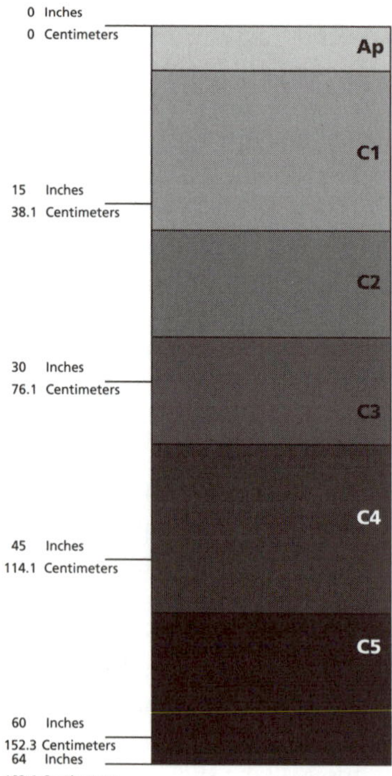

Taxonomy

Order	:	**Entisols**
Subgroup	:	**Typic Torrifluvents**
Family	:	**Coarse-loamy, mixed (Calcareous), hyperthermic (Alluvial)**

0 to 5 inches (12.7 centimeters), yellowish-brown (10 YR 5/4) loam, dark brown (7.5 YR 4/4) when moist; massive; slightly hard when dry, friable when moist; sticky and plastic when wet; common fine roots; many fine interstitial pores; strongly effervescent; moderately alkaline; abrupt, smooth boundary.

5 to 18 inches (12.7 to 45.7 centimeters), light yellowish-brown (10 YR 6/4) loam, dark brown (7.5 TR 4/4) when moist; massive; hard when dry, friable when moist; sticky and plastic when wet; few medium and common fine roots; few fine and medium and many very fine tubular pores; strongly effervescent; few, fine, faint, white (10 YR 8/2) filaments of lime; moderately alkaline; clear, smooth boundary.

18 to 27 inches (45.7 to 68.5 centimeters), light yellowish-brown (10 YR 6/4) loam, dark yellowish-brown (10 YR 4/4) when moist; massive; slightly hard when dry, very friable when moist; slightly sticky and plastic when wet; many fine roots; many fine and very fine and few medium tubular pores; strongly effervescent; few, fine faint, pinkish-white (7.5 YR 6/4) filaments of lime; moderately alkaline; gradual, smooth boundary.

27 to 37 inches (68.5 to 93.9 centimeters), light yellowish-brown (10 YR 6/4) loam, dark brown (10 YR 4/3) when moist; massive; slightly hard when dry, very friable when moist; slightly sticky and slightly plastic when wet; common fine roots; few fine and very fine tubular pores; slightly effervescent; moderately alkaline; gradual, smooth boundary.

37 to 51 inches (93.9 to 129.4 centimeters), light yellowish-brown (10 YR 6/4) very fine sandy loam, dark brown (10 YR 4/3) when moist; massive; slightly hard when dry, very friable when moist; slightly sticky and non-plastic when wet; common fine and medium and few coarse roots; many fine interstitial pores; strongly effervescent; moderately alkaline; gradual, smooth boundary.

51 to 64 inches (129.4 to 162.4 centimeters), light yellowish-brown (10 YR 6/4) very fine sandy loam, dark yellowish-brown (10 YR 4/4) when moist; massive; slightly hard when dry, very friable when moist.

FIGURE 3.28 Gilman soil profile. *(Source: Adapted from Hartman 1977)*

mation it is probably better to use a soils great group name. All soil surveys have a table relating soil series name to the soils classified, or scientific name. For example, alluvial soils along the washes of the Tri-Villages Area by Phoenix are classified as *Torrifluvents.* The *ents* syllable in the name means that the soil has no developed horizons. The process forming this soil is soil movement by running water, indicated by the *fluv* syllable, an abbreviation for *fluvial.* The *torri* syllable denotes a climate with torrid temperatures. Thus, the great group name provides considerably more information than stating the soil is of the Ebon series.

David Hendricks (1985) identifies *Torrifluvents* as one of 64 soil associations in seven temperature-precipitation units in Arizona. Torrifluvents are a hyperthermic arid soil, according to Hendricks' classification (Figure 3.29). Hendricks (1985) applied the USDA soil taxonomy system for his classification of Arizona soils. This soil taxonomy consists of a hierarchy, with soil series the narrowest category (Figure 3.30). More than 14,000 soil series have been identified in the United States (Hendricks 1985). In contrast, the most general category is the orders (Table 3.6).

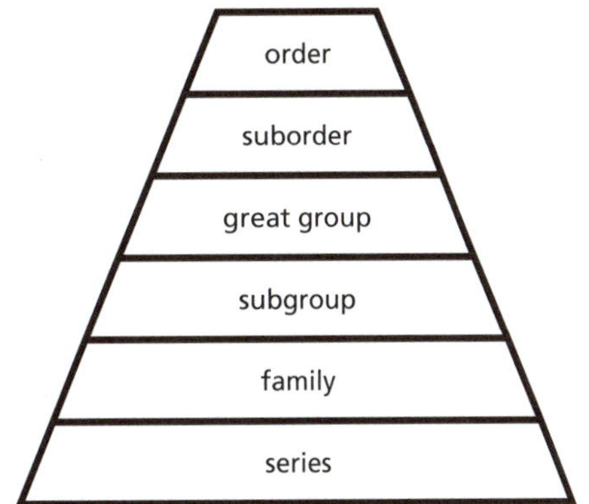

FIGURE 3.30 Hierarchical soil classification. *(Source: Hendricks 1985)*

Soil survey information can be interpreted to produce maps that show processes in the planning area. For example, Figure 3.31 illustrates erosion potential. Soil surveys also frequently include helpful drawings, such as Figure 3.32 of soils formed in recent alluvium. The drawing shows

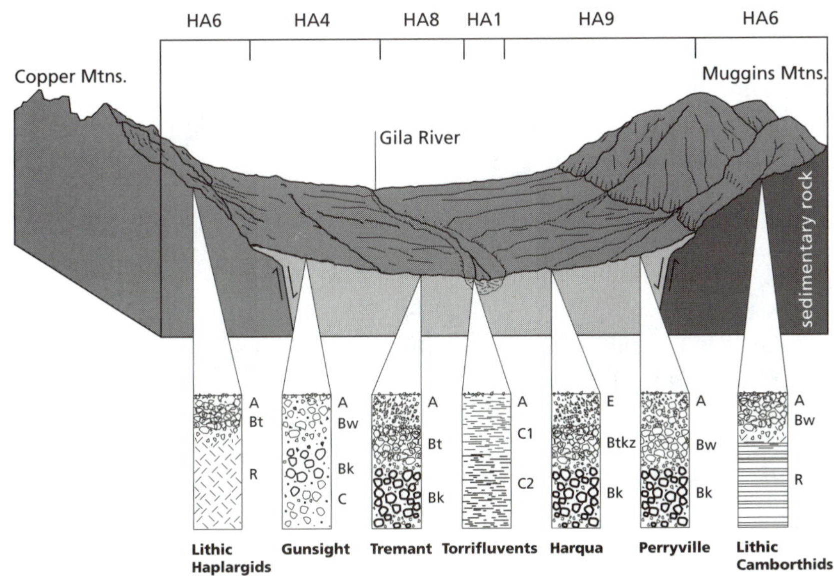

FIGURE 3.29 Representative soils and profiles. *(Source: Hendricks 1985)*

TABLE 3.6
NAMES AND IMPORTANT PROPERTIES OF THE ORDERS

Name	Important Properties
Alfisols	Mineral soils relatively low in organic matter, with relatively high base saturation. Contains horizon of illuvial clay. Moisture is available to mature a crop.
Aridisols	Mineral soils relatively low in organic matter. Contain developed soil horizons. Moisture is inadequate to mature a crop without irrigation in most years.
Entisols	Mineral soils lacking developed soil horizons. Moisture content varies.
Histosols	Soils composed mostly of organic matter. Moisture content varies.
Inceptisols	Mineral soils containing some developed horizons other than one of illuvial clay. Moisture is available to mature a crop.
Mollisols	Mineral soils with thick, dark surface horizons relatively high in organic matter and with high base saturation.
Oxisols	Mineral soils with no weatherable minerals. High in iron and aluminum oxides. Contain no illuvial horizons.
Spodosols	Soils that contain an illuvial horizon of amorphous aluminum and organic matter, with or without amorphous iron. Usually moist or well leached.
Ultisols	Mineral soils with an illuvial clay horizon. Has low base saturation. Generally found in humid climates.
Vertisols	Clayey soils with deep wide cracks at some time in most years. Moisture content varies.

SOURCE: Hendricks 1985.

three associations. According to the soil survey, this "group of associations consists of nearly level to gently sloping soils formed in recent alluvium on alluvial fans at the base of mountains, in stream channels, on low stream terraces, and on valley plans" (Hartman 1977, 3).

Hardpans, or *caliche,* are common in the Sonoran Desert. Desert soils are affected by the precipitation of salts produced by the weathering of rock-forming minerals. Because seepage from rainfall is frequently not sufficient to carry these salts down to the water table, they accumulate in the soil as the water evaporates. Alluvial deposits are then cemented by calcium carbonate to form the sometimes concrete-like caliche (Ciekot et al. 1995).

During the inventory process, questions can be asked about soils. The answers to these questions can assist in the understanding of the place, such as:

- Why are some soils different in color from others?
- Do some places seem to erode more than others?
- What areas drain most rapidly? Most slowly?
- Do crops grow better in some places than in others? Why?
- What crops were grown in the past?

SUMMARY OF SOILS INVENTORY ELEMENTS:

1. Soil series
2. Permeability
3. Texture
4. Profiles
5. Erosion potential
6. Drainage potential
7. Soil associations and catenas
8. Cation and anion exchange
9. Acidity-alkalinity

FIGURE 3.31 Soil erosion potential, Desert View Tri-Villages Area. *(Source: Adapted from Ciekot et al. 1995)*

MAJOR SOURCES OF INFORMATION:

1. U.S. Natural Resources Conservation Service (NRCS)
   Soil survey information located at county offices. Additional information available at the NRCS website: http://www.nrcs.usda.gov
2. Agricultural Stabilization and Conservation Service (ASCS)
3. Soil Science Society of America
4. Soil and Water Conservation Society
5. College or university libraries
6. County extension agents

Microclimate

Meteorological elements change vertically and horizontally within short distances. Small-scale variations are brought about by changes in slope and orientation of the ground surface; soil type and moisture; variations in rock, vegetation type and height; and human-made features. These different climates found within a small space are grouped together under the general description of *microclimate*. The term *topoclimate* is used when the effects of topographic variations of the land on the microclimate are considered. Generally,

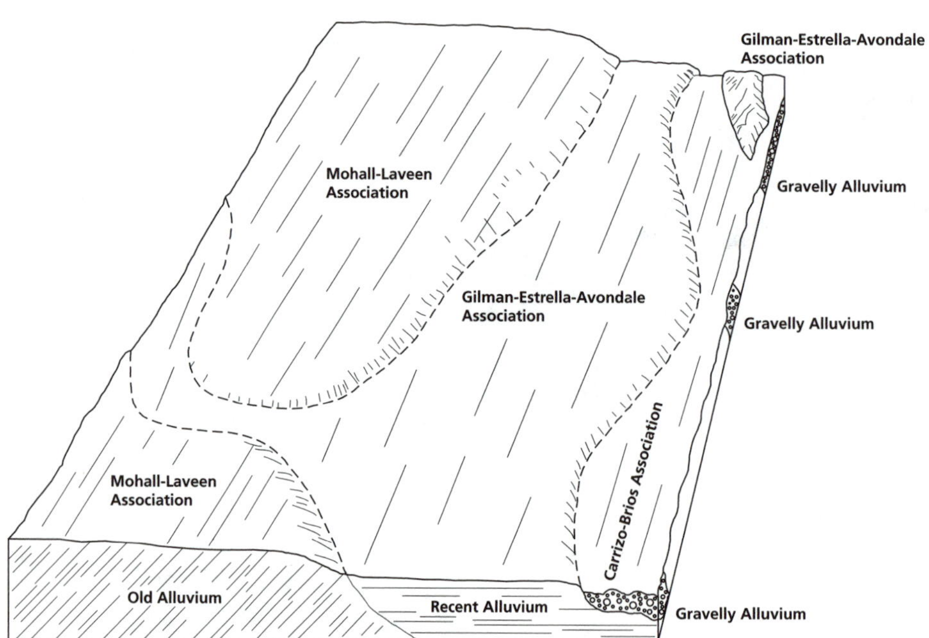

FIGURE 3.32 Soils formed in alluvium. *(Source: Adapted from Hartman 1977)*

topoclimate is an extension of microclimate into the higher layers of the atmosphere and over landscapes, depending on the relief of the land. Therefore, topoclimate can be considered to occupy an intermediate level between macroclimate and microclimate. It is important to understand microclimate and topoclimate for many of the same reasons that macro, or regional, climate is important. These finer layers, however, relate more directly to building and open space design. Some important microclimate elements to consider are ventilation, fog and frost, solar and terrestrial radiation, and vegetative changes.

Ventilation is the circulation of fresh air across the landscape and is largely dependent on landforms and wind direction. The calculation of ventilation is "important in determining local climate; furthermore, wind pressure and eddy formation largely depend on the degree of landform relief" (University of Pennsylvania, 1985, B1.4). Ventilation is greatest in those areas where the terrain is aligned with the prevailing wind. Rudolf Geiger, a German scientist who studied the effects of topography on climate, developed the formula in Figure 3.33 to determine the relative values of ventilation. The formula relates wind direction to landform. The *d* in the formula is determined by the direction of seasonal regional winds; thus different ventilation calculations may be necessary for the various seasons. It has been noted that, in general: "The greater or more pronounced the relief [then] the greater the wind pressure on the slopes perpendicular and facing the wind (windward) and the greater the formation of eddies on the lee side. These factors influence temperature and humidity and, therefore, have important influence on local microclimate" (University of Pennsylvania, 1985, B1.4).

Subtle topographic changes and their relative elevation greatly affect temperature near the ground surface. These changes in temperature, in

Wind Direction

$$D = \frac{d^2}{d + b} \cdot \frac{1}{t} \text{ where:}$$

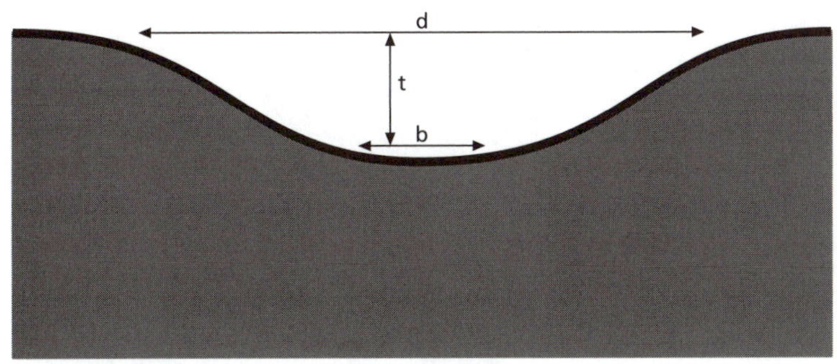

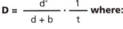

FIGURE 3.33 Geiger ventilation formula. *(Source: Adapted from Geiger 1965, via the University of Pennsylvania 1985)*

turn, influence the susceptibility of an area to fog and frost (Figure 3.34).

Solar radiation is influenced by slope steepness and direction. Donald Satterlund and Joseph Means (1979) have observed that solar radiation is the primary variable in energy exchange processes that determine ecosystem distribution, composition, and productivity. In addition, radiation melts snow, powers the hydrologic cycle, and significantly influences agricultural productivity.

Vegetation influences and results from microclimate in a variety of ways. Ventilation, fog and frost, and solar radiation all are modified by changes in vegetation. Figure 3.35 illustrates some of the ways vegetation influences microclimate.

Anthony Brazel of the Arizona State University Office of Climatology and the Department of Geography has studied the influence of various surface conditions (such as asphalt, irrigated agriculture, and natural desert) on microclimate. Surfaces respond differently to daytime solar load and nighttime cooling processes. *Albedo,* which is the

FIGURE 3.34 Fog and frost susceptibility.

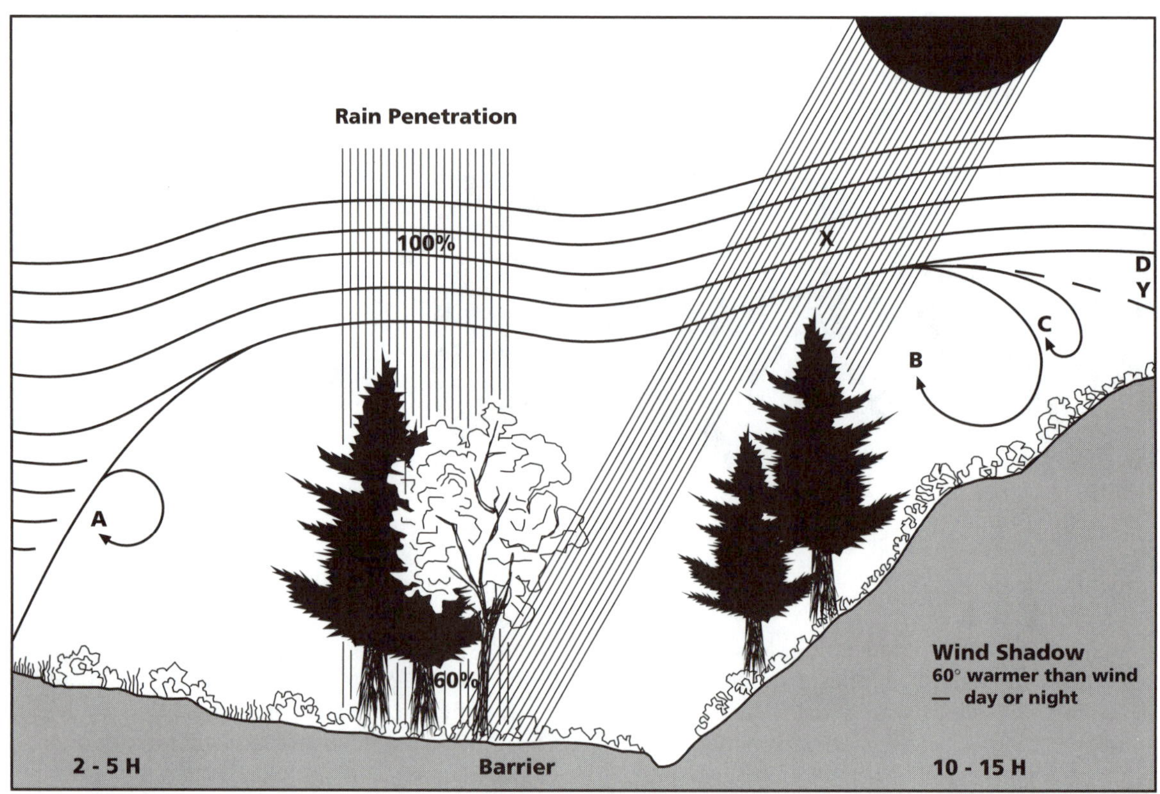

H — Height of barrier
A — Pressure eddy
B — Suction eddy
C — Turbulent wake motion characterized by large eddies
D — Motion with relatively small turbulence superimposed on mean flow, but occasional large eddies from **C** may break through
XY — Subsidiary boundary separating wind shadow from rest of turbulence

FIGURE 3.35 Vegetation influences on microclimate. *(Source: Adapted from Higashi et al. 1978)*

ratio of light reflectivity to incoming light, is typically employed to assess the absorption and subsequent heating of different surface materials. *Thermal admittance* is another surface characteristic that determines net heat storage and resultant energy flow over a surface. In a study of various surfaces in Scottsdale, Arizona (near the Desert View Tri-Villages Area), Brazel (1998) found that surfaces with lower albedos and high thermal admittances, like black asphalt, were warmer than those with higher albedos, if not mitigated by other microclimatic factors like evaporation. Understanding microclimate is important for ecological planning and design. For example, in his work for Scottsdale, Brazel (1998) recommended to city planners that new asphalt surfaces be minimized to help sustain climate, and that existing asphalt areas be shaded or lightened to ameliorate heat islands. In addition, he suggested the preservation of parks and green spaces for cooling.

The topo- and microclimate of a specific environment can be understood by asking questions and seeking answers (Steiner and McSherry 2000), like:

Topoclimate

- What is the relation between the sun and the location/type of development in the planning area?
- Identify the orientation of specific slopes.
  - How does slope orientation influence microclimate, and thus vegetation patterns?
  - How does slope orientation influence microclimate, and thus the pattern of development?
  - How does this orientation influence the style of architecture?
  - How does this affect the pattern of development?
- Has urbanization, suburbanization, or rural development affected the climate of the planning area? If so, how?
- Identify the places where it is warmer or cooler.
  - How does this determine the location of the development of public amenities, such as farms, ranches, wells, roads, schools, and markets?
  - When are the first and last frosts?
  - Where are fog and frost likely to occur?
- How is air quality related to soils, vegetation, land use, and traffic?

Microclimates

- What are the sheltering effects of building edges?
- What influence does shading (and climate) have upon land use, both built and temporal?
- How does the light level change through the day?
- Do colors appear different in the morning, at midday, and at sundown?
- What are the albedos for various surfaces?

SUMMARY OF MICROCLIMATE INVENTORY ELEMENTS:

1. Ventilation
2. Fog and frost frequency and location
3. First and last frosts
4. Solar radiation
5. Surface condition albedos and temperatures
6. Vegetation changes

MAJOR SOURCES OF INFORMATION:

1. National Weather Service
2. National Oceanic and Atmospheric Administration (NOAA)
3. Federal Aviation Administration (FAA)
4. Environmental Protection Agency (EPA)
5. State environmental quality agencies
6. State climatologists
7. Local weather stations and/or airports
8. College or university libraries
9. County extension agents
10. Farmers

Vegetation

The ecologist Robert E. Ricklefs observed that "life is an extension of the physical world" (1973, 81). This observation is reinforced by J. E. Lovelock's Gaia hypothesis, which suggests "the biosphere is a self-regulating entity with the capacity to keep our planet healthy by controlling the chemical and physical environment" (1979, xii). Living things are a result of the physical processes that have been discussed thus far plus their interaction with other life-forms. Vegetation refers to plant life—trees, shrubs, cacti, herbs, and grasses. Because of the omnipresence of vegetation, it would seem that plants would be simple to inventory. This, however, is not the case. For various reasons, naturally occurring vegetation has not been inventoried to the extent that the earth, water, soils, or climate have. As a result, plants are too often ignored in the planning process in the United States.[1]

1. An exception is that work done by the U.S. Forest Service or state agencies responsible for forestry and range programs. In this case, vegetation is viewed as an economic resource.

Plants are important to study for many reasons. They may have economic and medicinal value. They provide habitat for wildlife. They have significant influence on natural events like fires and floods and may reduce the human consequences of such events. Plants are beautiful and contribute to the scenic quality of landscapes. Plants are the source of oxygen, which humans need to survive.

In addition, native plant species are in decline worldwide. According to a 1998 international study, one in eight known plant species on earth is either threatened or nearly extinct (Suplee 1998). Curt Suplee reports that the "results of a 20-year joint effort among 16 organizations show that habitat destruction and introduction of non-native species have caused approximately 34,000 species to become so rare that they could easily disappear. That amounts to 12.5 percent of the 270,000 fern, conifer, and flowering species known worldwide" (1998, 1).

There are several ways to classify land cover. One helpful system is the USGS Land-Use and Land-Cover Classification System that was developed for use with remote sensor data (Anderson et al. 1976) (see Table 1.2). Once a system is selected, it is necessary to identify the specific units. The most straightforward method is to use aerial or satellite images to identify the homogeneous areas, then field-check the units. Ward Brady developed a potential natural vegetation map (Figure 3.36) and a more detailed land cover classification map (Figure 3.37) for the Desert View Tri-Villages Area. The latter was derived from Landsat imagery. Brady's maps were influenced in part by detailed wash vegetation studies led by Joseph Ewan and Rebecca Fish Ewan (Ewan et al. 1996). A relatively abundant and specialized plant community has evolved, especially in the northeastern section of the Tri-Villages Area. Because of the higher altitude and greater rainfall, the plant community is abundant in density and diversity when compared to other areas of the Phoenix metropolitan region.

In two detailed studies led by Professors Rebecca Fish Ewan and Joseph Ewan of the ASU School of Planning and Landscape Architecture for the City of Phoenix, five vegetation types have been identified in the Desert View Tri-Villages Area (Ewan et al. 1996, 1998). *Wash vegetation* is the first type and includes "the sandy, rocky, open channel and sand bars and is characterized by annuals, big leaf bursage (*Ambrosia ambrosioides*), desert broom (*Baccharis sarothroides*), and seep willow (*Baccharis salicifolia*) (Ewan et al. 1998, x). Along the edges of the washes are the richest concentrations of vegetation. Ewan and his colleagues note that blue palo verde (*Cercidium floridum*) and ironwood (*Olneya tesota*) "are characteristic trees that grow along the wash edges" (1998, x).

Creosote bush-bursage flats are the second type and are "dominated by creosote bush (*Larrea tridentata*) and triangle-leaf bursage (*Ambrosia deltoidea*)" (Ewan et al. 1998, x). This vegetation, according to Ewan and his colleagues, is the most widespread in the area "because it can tolerate saline caliche soil and hot arid conditions of the desert flats" (1998, x).

The third vegetation type in the Tri-Villages is found on hillsides and slopes. Foothill palo verde (*Cercidium microphyllum*), triangle-leaf bursage, creosote, teddy bear cholla (*Opuntia bigelovii*), buckthorn cholla (*Opuntia acanthocarpa*), and the magnificent saguaro cacti (*Carnegiea gigantea*) are the characteristic vegetation of the hillside type (Ewan et al. 1998).

Tanks are cowboy watering holes and form the fourth vegetation type. These artificial detention areas support dense communities of mesquite (*Prosopis velutina*) (Ewan et al. 1998). The final type occurs in damaged areas. The main causes of the damage are fire and cattle grazing (Ewan et al. 1998).

After the vegetation units are identified and mapped, it is often helpful to list the individual species in the area. (A comprehensive vegetation list for the Desert View Tri-Villages Area is located

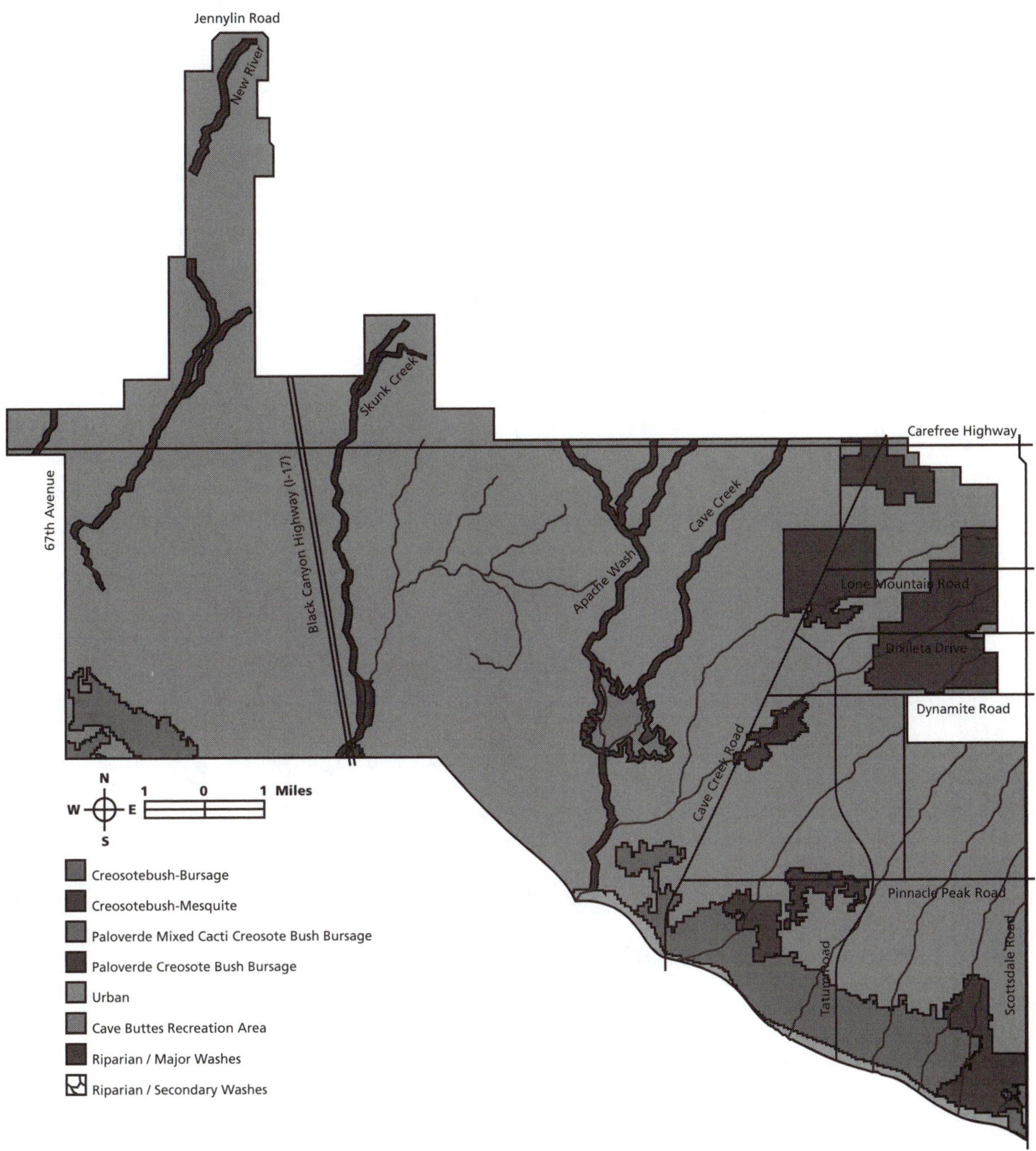

FIGURE 3.36 Potential natural vegetation, Desert View Tri-Villages Area. *(Source: Brady et al. 1998)*

FIGURE 3.37 Land cover classification, Desert View Tri-Villages Area. *(Source: Brady et al. 1998)*

in Appendix A.) *Physiognomic profiles* show plant communities in three dimensions (Figure 3.38). Peter Skaller has noted that "besides revealing a great deal about ecosystem processes, physiognomy affords a quick look at the structural components of wildlife habitat" (in Berger et al. 1977, 101). Between the vegetation units are boundaries (Figure 3.38) whose edges form ecotones. *Ecotones* are transitional areas between ecological communities and are generally of greater richness and equitability than the communities they separate.

In urban areas, vegetation is identified frequently either as ornamental or as weedy. Ornamental decorates a home or a business. A weed is a plant out of place. What commonly may be called a weed, ecologists term a *ruderal* or a *disturbance adaptive plant.* Again, we can ask questions about the plants we see, such as:

- Which plants are native and which have been introduced?
- Which ones are rare, endangered, or threatened?
- What are the tallest plants?
- What species are present near water?
- When do blooms occur?
- Which trees drop their leaves?
- What species seem to grow together?
- How does vegetation change throughout the year?
- Where does the vegetation grow?
- Where has native vegetation been disturbed by human uses, such as grazing, mining, logging, dumping, and development?

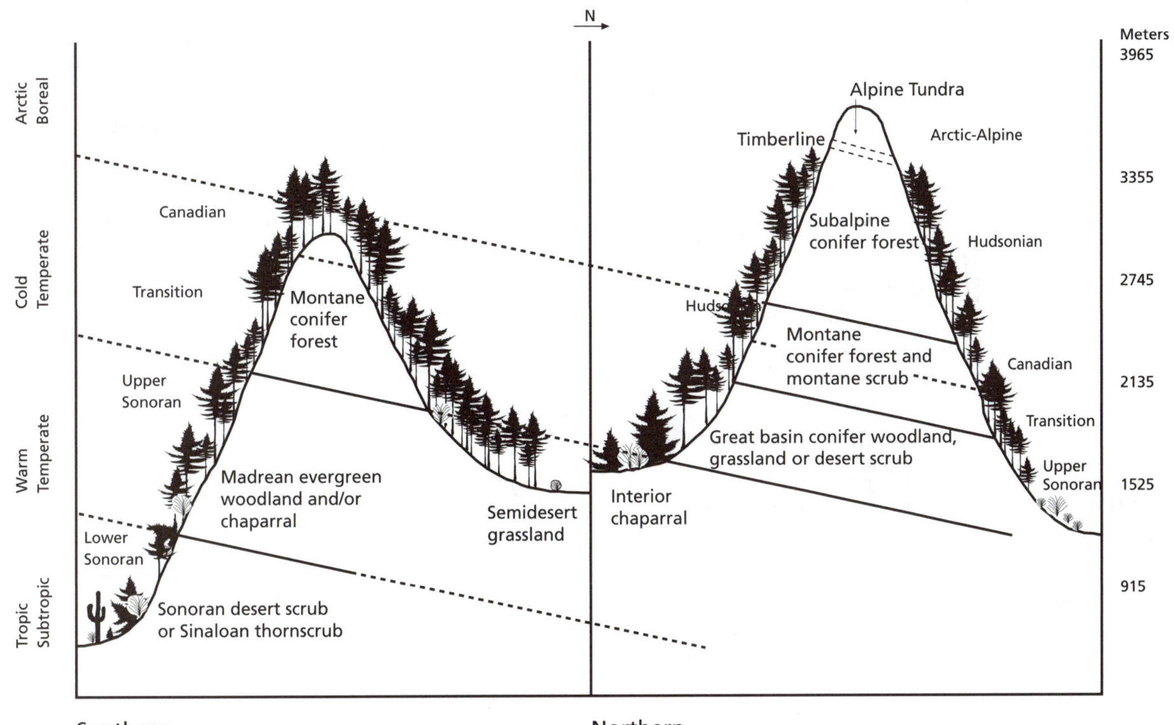

FIGURE 3.38 Vertical climatic zonation. *(Source: Lowe and Brown 1994)*

SUMMARY OF VEGETATION INVENTORY ELEMENTS:

1. Plant associations and communities
2. Vegetative units
3. Species list
4. Species composition and distribution
5. Physiognomic profiles
6. Ecotone and edge profiles
7. Rare, endangered, and threatened species
8. Fire history

MAJOR SOURCES OF INFORMATION:

1. U.S. Geological Survey (USGS)
2. U.S. Natural Resources Conservation Service (NRCS)
3. U.S. Forest Service (USFS)
4. Botanical gardens
5. Native plant societies
6. Nurseries and seed companies
7. National, state, and local conservation and environmental groups
8. College or university libraries

Wildlife

Broadly, *wildlife* is considered to be animals that are neither human nor domesticated. Insects, fish, amphibians, birds, and mammals are more mobile than plants. While closely linked to vegetative units for food and shelter, wildlife often use different areas to reproduce, eat, and sleep. Like vegetation, wildlife has not been extensively inventoried except where the animals have some commercial value. Because animals are mobile, they are even more difficult to inventory than vegetation.

Planners are paying increased attention to wildlife (Beatley 1994a; Duerksen et al. 1997; Peck 1998). Christopher Duerksen and his colleagues note that most "people realize that the presence and protection of wildlife improves their lives" (1997, 1). They observe that in addition to enhancing the quality of life, wildlife protection is important for ethical and moral reasons, for recreational benefits, and for economic and tourist values (Duerksen et al. 1997).

A starting point is to compile a list of species in the area (Table 3.7). State departments of game are useful sources of information for hunted or fished species. Some state game departments conduct research on some nongame species as well, but this is still the exception rather than the rule. Conservation groups and academic facilities are usually the best resources for nongame species.

Once such a list is compiled (which can be a substantial task in itself), it is important to analyze where the species live. One helpful tool is a matrix. Figure 3.39 is a matrix for the Pullman, Washington, area. Species were listed with both their common and scientific names. The individual species were then matched with the vegetative units they use for breeding, living, and eating. It was noted whether each species was common, uncommon, or rare, and what its seasonal occurrence was. Additional remarks for each species were also included. For example, the northwestern whitetail deer (*Odocoileus virginianus*) is a common resident of the area. This species uses a variety of habitats year-round and is a vegetarian. Figure 3.40 is a similar matrix developed for a regional plan in Valladolid, Spain, by Juan Luis de las Rivas and his colleagues.

The dense plant life of the Tri-Villages Area gives it a distinctive visual identity and forms the habitat for the resident animal life. The palo verde, cacti, and mixed scrubs support a rich bird life, with a variety ranging from several species of hawks (e.g., *Buteo jamaicensis*) to hummingbirds (Brown 1982). Various doves, including the white-winged, mourning, and Inca are found, as are several varieties of quail. Numerous colorful birds such as cardinals, Gila woodpeckers, and flickers are also found. Birds such as the cactus wren, the curved-bill thrasher, the northern mockingbird, and quails and doves are notable because of the distinctive sound patterns that they produce, which are as much a part of the desert environment as the visual experience. Although not seen as often, several species of owls are an important part of the biological balance of the area (McCarthy et al. 1995; Steiner et al. 1999).

TABLE 3.7
LIST OF WILDLIFE FOUND IN THE DESERT VIEW TRI-VILLAGES AREA

Mammals		
Antelope Jack Rabbit *Lepus alleni*	Desert Kangaroo Rat *Dipodomys deserti*	Ringtail *Bassariscus astutus*
Arizona Pocket Mouse *Perognathus amplus*	Desert Pocket Mouse *Perognathus penicillatus*	Rock Squirrel *Spermophilus variegatus*
Badger *Taxidea taxus*	Gray Fox *Urocyon cinereoargenteus*	Round-tailed Ground Squirrel *Spermophilus tereticaudus*
Blacktailed Jack Rabbit *Lepus californicus*	Harris Antelope Squirrel *Ammospermophilus barrisii*	Sanborn's Long-nosed Bat *Leptonycteris sanborni*
Bobcat *Felis rufus*	Kit Fox *Vulpus macrotis*	Spotted Ground Squirrel *Spermophilus spilosoma*
Brazilian Free-tailed Bat *Tadarida brasiliensis*	Merriam's Kangaroo Rat *Dipodomys merriami*	Striped Skunk *Mephitis mephitis*
Collard Peccary (Javelina) *Dicotyles tajacu*	Mule Deer *Odocoiileus hemionus*	Western Mastif Bat *Eumops perotis*
Coyote *Canis latrans*	Pallid Bat *Antrozus pallidus*	Western Pipistrelle *Pipistrellus hesperus*
Deer Mouse *Peromyscus maniculatus*	Pocket Gopher *Thomomys bottae*	White-throated Woodrat *Neotoma albigula*
Desert Cottontail *Sylvilagus audubonii*	Raccoon *Procyon lotor*	Yuma Myotis *Myotis velifer*

SOURCE: adapted from Ciekot et al. 1995.

Among the most commonly observed mammals in the area are several rabbit species, including the desert cottontail rabbit and blacktail jackrabbit. Several species of squirrels, including the Harris antelope, the rock, and the roundtailed ground squirrel, are present. Several species of pocket gophers, wood rats, and kangaroo rats, along with the desert pocket mouse, are also found. Large mammals include the coyote and, less often, bobcat, collared peccary (javelina), gray fox, and mule deer (McCarthy et al. 1995).

The night reveals the presence of mammalian species that are not normally seen in the day. Because of the numerous rock formations in the region and the available insect life, there is a significant variety of bats in the planning area. These include the Brazilian free-tailed, the pallid, the western mastif, the big brown, and the Sanborn's long-nosed bat. (The latter species is rare and endangered.) Ground-based nocturnal mammals include the ringtail and raccoon. Several skunks, including the striped skunk and the less common spotted skunk, are resident (McCarthy et al. 1995).

There is a significant variety of reptiles in the planning area, including the desert tortoise, which, although not technically endangered, is rare and sensitive to disturbance. The Gila monster occurs in the area and has an endangered standing similar to that of the desert tortoise. The area harbors various species of poisonous and nonpoisonous snakes. Three species of rattlesnakes are resident, including the western diamondback, the tiger, and the blacktail. Nonpoisonous snakes include the western coachwhip, patch-nose, common king, ground, lyre, western blind, Arizona glossy, blackhead, and

Species	Animal Habitat			Occurrence					Comments
	Breeding	Living	Eating	Common	Uncommon	Rare	Migrant	Resident	
American Robin *Turdus migratorius*	W	W	G S	●			●	●	
Barn Owl *Tyto alba*	W	W	W S	●				●	
Mourning Dove *Zenaida macroura*	G S	G S	G S C	●				●	
Red-tailed hawk *Buteo jamaicensis*	W	W	G W S C R		●			●	
Porcupine *Erethizon dorsatum*	W	W	W			●		●	
Norway rat *Rattus norvegicus*	G S	G S	G S C	●				●	
Beaver *Castor canadensis*	W R	R	W R		●			●	
White-tailed deer *Odocoileus virginianus*	W	W S	W S G C	●				●	

G — Grass **S** — Shrub **W** — Woods **C** — Crop **R** — River

FIGURE 3.39 Species-habitat matrix for the Palouse region of eastern Washington and northern Idaho.

gopher snake. Chuckwallas, horned lizards, geckos, and various other species of lizards reside in the planning area. At least five species of toads are found there, as well as the uncommon canyon tree frog (McCarthy et al. 1995).

It is important to rate the habitats for their relative value (Figure 3.41). This can be done through a series of interviews with game officials, conservation club representatives, landowners, and wildlife ecologists. Again, this task can be as complex as the planning issue requires. In many areas, there is some debate between farmers and state game officials about the value of various habitats. Although many farmers enjoy hunting, they may also view some game birds and deer as pests. Game officials argue that habitats need to be preserved for these species. The value of inventorying wildlife lies in gaining an understanding of the ecosystem of an area. Food webs (Figure 3.42) are useful illustrations that help show people of an area how the living things use the region.

Questions that might be asked when conducting a wildlife inventory are:

- Which birds are residents or migrants?
- Which species are native and which ones were introduced?
- What are the dominant large mammals, small mammals, birds of prey, song birds, amphibians, fish, and insects?
- What species are hunted and fished?
- What are the urban pests? Who are their predators?
- What species are rare, endangered, or threatened?

Familia	Especie	Pisuerga	Cega	Valderaduey	
Centrarchidae	*Lepomis gibbosus*	●			
Ciprinidae	*Barbus bocagei*	●	●	●	
Familia	***Especie***	**Presencia segura**		**Presencia probable**	**Hábitat principal**
Salamandridae	*Salamandra salamandra*			●	CC / RB
	Triturus marmoratus			●	RB
	Triturus boscai	●			RB
	Pleurodeles waltl	●			RB
Discoglossidae	*Discoglossus galganoi*	●			RB
	Alytes obstetricans	●			RB / EM
Bufonidae	*Bufo bufo*	●			RB / CC / MH
	Bufo calamita	●			RB / CC / MH
Amphisbaenidae	*Blanus cinereus*	●			PA / CC
Scincidae	*Chalcides chalcides*	●			CC
Lacertidae	*Podarcis hispanica*	●			MR / MH
	Podarcis bocagei			●	EM
	Lacerta lepida	●			EM
	Psammodromus algirus	●			EM
	Psammodromus hispanicus				PA
Familia	***Especie***	**Especie protegida**		**Hábitat principal**	**Estatus**
Accipitridae	*Circus aeruginosus*	●		CC	R
Accipitridae	*Circus pygargus*	●		CC	E
Accipitridae	*Cyrcus cyaneus*	●		CC	I
Familia	***Especie***	**Protegida**		**Presencia probable**	**Ligada al Medio acuático**
Felidae	*Felis sylvestris*	●		●	EM
Viverridae	*Genetta genetta*	●		●	EM

FIGURE 3.40 Valladolid species matrix. *(Source: Courtesy of Juan Luis de las Rivas, Universidad de Valladolid)*

SUMMARY OF WILDLIFE INVENTORY ELEMENTS:

1. Species list
2. Species-habitat matrix
3. Animal populations
4. Habitat value map
5. Habitat of rare, endangered and threatened species

MAJOR SOURCES OF INFORMATION

1. State departments of game and/or fisheries
2. U.S. Fish and Wildlife Service (USFWS)
3. U.S. Forest Service (USFS)
4. U.S. Natural Resources Conservation Service (NRCS)
5. National, state, and local conservation and environmental groups
6. College or university libraries

Existing Land Use and Land Users

Existing land use refers to the physical arrangement of space utilized by humans. Almost all the land on the planet—from the wilderness areas of Alaska to the alleyways of Philadelphia—is used by people in some way. The human ecology, that

● Valuable
◐ Moderately valuable
○ Not valuable

	Grassland and pasture	Shrubland	Cropland	Woodland
Game officials	◐	◐	●	◐
Conservationists	◐	●	●	◐
Biologists	◐	●	●	◐
Hunters	◐	◐	●	◐
Land owners	◐	◐	◐	●

FIGURE 3.41 Habitat value matrix. *(Source: Adapted from Brunton et al. 1977)*

is, the living network of an area, is much more complex than how land is used. However, land and other resource utilization is a significant component of human ecology. Human impact on the environment is great. So it is important when inventorying and analyzing an area to recognize how people are using the land, as well as to distinguish land use from land users.

Land use is fairly simple to define, but it is not necessarily easy to understand. A particular area of land is either used for agriculture or it is not. However, different users may view that area of land with different perspectives. For instance, farmland may be used for a variety of crops or for pasture; or it may be used for hunting or other forms of recreation. Its owners also may see it primarily as an investment.

Land use is only the beginning in the establishment of user groups. A particular person in a given location may use many parcels of land. Part of the land used by an individual will be called *home* (residential); another part will be called *work* (commercial or industrial); many parts may be labeled *play* and be tennis courts, restaurants, the homes of friends, or roads for either driving or jogging (recreation, commercial, residential, transportation).

A helpful starting point for identifying existing land use and land users is the history of an area. Information about the history of a place can be gathered from various sources, including interviews with older residents and research in community libraries. The first people settled the Tri-Villages Area in approximately A.D. 450. The Hohokam people established a sprawling culture in what is now the Phoenix metropolitan area. They developed a sophisticated irrigation network to support agriculture. The Hohokam established villages along Cave Creek, where they grew crops. These "ancient ones" (as their name means in the Pima language) thrived, until they suddenly "disappeared" around A.D. 1400 (Carlson 1988; Ciekot et al. 1995).

After the Hohokam, the Tonto Apaches used the area for hunting. The Apache were ferocious warriors who discouraged Spanish exploration and settlement of the area. Americans opened the Butterfield Stage Route across Arizona in 1850 to deliver mail to Californians. When gold was discovered in Arizona in 1858, many prospectors moved into the territory, which prompted understandable hostility from the Apache. In response, the U.S. Army established Fort McDowell to subdue the Apache (Ciekot et al. 1995).

In the 1870s the town of Cave Creek was established along a wagon road and stage line because of the availability of nearby water. Mining and ranching would dominate the area for most of the next 90 years. Extensive irrigation, which began in the early twentieth century and which was to transform most of the Phoenix metropolitan area, first into agriculture, then into expansive post-World War II development, occurred to the south of the Desert View Tri-Villages Area. Grazing dominated the landscape into the 1950s, but tourists were beginning to be attracted to the area because of its great scenic appeal. Since the 1980s rapid development has occurred in the Tri-Villages Area, and today it is the focus of considerable specula-

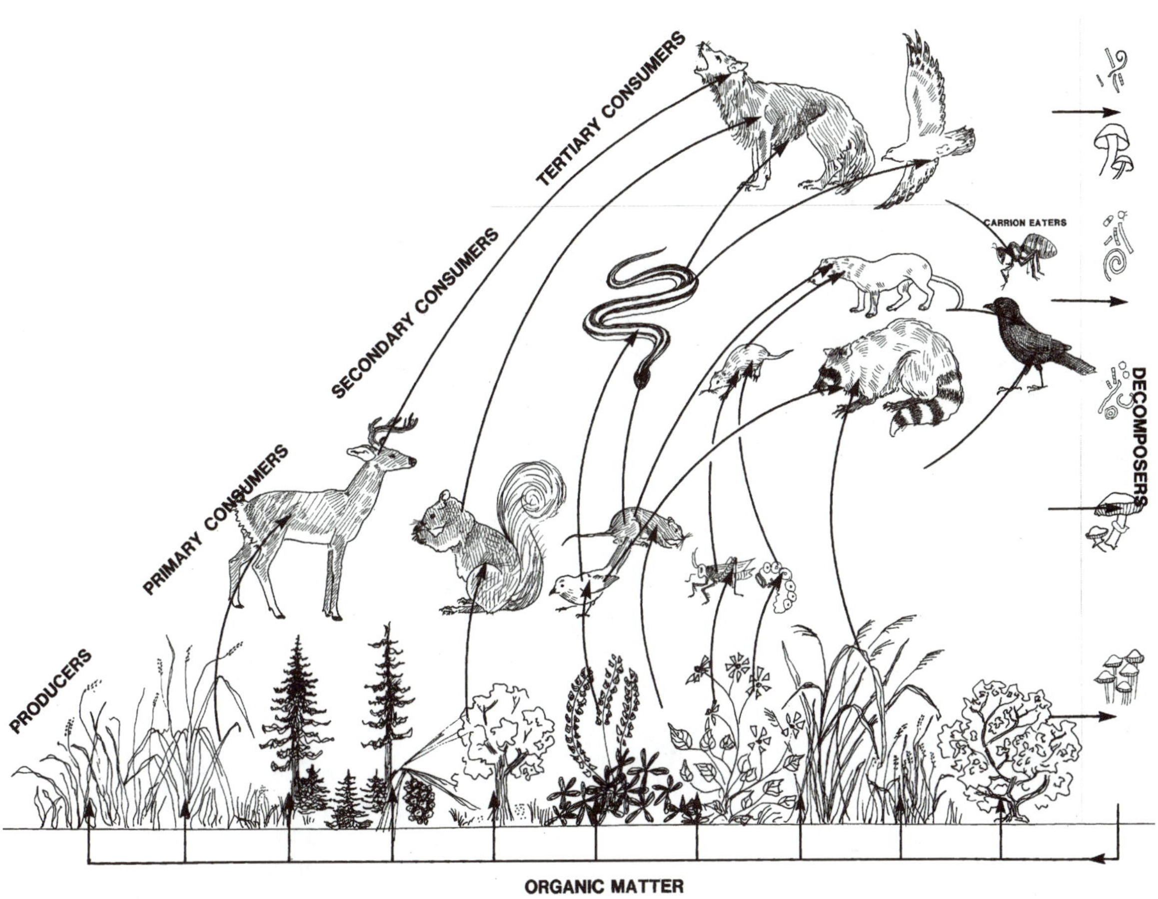

FIGURE 3.42 Food web.

tion, much controversy, and ongoing planning. A time line can be a helpful way to summarize the land-use history of an area (Table 3.8).

The next step is to determine land-use categories. As with the vegetation inventory, the USGS Land-Use and Land-Cover Classification System provides helpful standard categories (Anderson et al. 1976). Again aerial photographs and field checking are useful to compile a land-use map (Figure 3.43). For many planning processes, this is just the beginning of analyzing land use—property ownership, housing condition, and farm management maps also may be required (Figure 3.44). Much of the Tri-Villages Area consists of State Trust Lands, managed by the Arizona State Lands Department. According to the state constitution, these lands must be sold for the "highest and best" use to benefit state schools and other agencies. Much land ownership and land management information can be gathered from the local tax assessor and the county NRCS office. For other information, fieldwork will be necessary.

TABLE 3.8
DESERT VIEW TRI-VILLAGES HISTORY TIMELINE

450 A.D.	Hohokam culture evidence, especially along Cave Creek
1450	Grazing and gathering lands for Apache tribes
1540	Spanish prospectors, probably first Europeans to explore area
1850	Butterfield stage route across Arizona enacted by Congress
1860	U.S. Army influence prevalent while Native Americans are subdued and confined to reservations
1870	Homesteaders and miners begin to infiltrate region
1880	Mining boom, first post office established
1890	Cattle and sheep ranches expand, school district established, Rio Verde Canal Company proposals initiated
1900	Tubercular cabins common as Arizona climate attracts many people with lung diseases; Tonto National Forest established
1910	Recreational outings in area expanding, stage coach line to Phoenix operates
1920	Long drought climaxes as many ranchers give up; Paradise Verde Irrigation District begins competition with Salt River Water Users Association
1930	U.S. Department of the Interior rules in favor of Salt River Water Users due to population explosion of Phoenix; Bartlett Dam constructed on Verde River
1940	Electricity begins to replace candles and kerosene lanterns in buildings of region; Horseshoe Dam constructed
1950	Phone service relay system begun; real estate developers "discover" area
1960	Residential and resort popularity of area increases as more people seek "quiet lifestyles and retreats"
1970	Region along Bell and Scottsdale Roads becomes center of Arabian horse breeding and training in United States
1980	Town of Cave Creek incorporates
1990	Marketing the "High Sonoran Lifestyle"; acres of pristine desert are converted for development
1995	North Area Charrette organized by the City of Phoenix Planning Department and the Arizona State University College of Architecture and Environmental Design
1995	Detailed ecological inventory conducted by Master of Environmental Planning students from the Arizona State University School of Planning and Landscape Architecture
1996	General plan for the eastern portion of the area adopted by the Phoenix city council to emphasize desert preservation and development character types
1998	Sonoran Preserve Plan adopted by city council, protecting much of the area from development

SOURCE: adapted and updated from Ciekot et al. 1995.

Although reviewing census information is a good starting point for understanding who uses the land, an even better method is to go out into the community and talk to people. By talking with people in their homes or places of work and by taking photographs or making sketches, an idea of settlement patterns (Figures 3.45, 3.46, and 3.47) can be realized. (See Hart 1998 for information about rural settlement patterns.) Also, by meeting with people in their community, the researchers can become acquainted with their concerns and issues. As Allan Jacobs of the University of California at Berkeley has observed, "Planners tend to be more careful in deciding on policies and actions when they associate real people's faces and images of places with the decisions" (1985, 8).

One of Stephanie Ciekot's colleagues, Carlos Licón, did three settlement pattern sketches and

FIGURE 3.43 Land use, Desert View Tri-Villages Area. *(Source: Adapted from Ciekot et al. 1995)*

related them to where they are located in the Tri-Villages Area (Ciekot et al. 1995). The first (Figure 3.45) is for rural residential settlement. This type of settlement varies considerably in density, but in the northeastern portion of the planning area the density is 1 house per acre (2.5 houses per hectare) or less (Ciekot et al. 1995). Many residents own horses and like living in the desert because of the equestrian opportunities in the area. The homes in this settlement type are mostly surrounded by desert vegetation, except where horses have removed much of the understory (Ciekot et al. 1995).

The second settlement pattern (Figure 3.46) is single-family residential. This settlement type is located in two main areas in the eastern portion but is expanding. These areas have a density of about 5 houses per acre (12 per hectare), and little or no desert vegetation remains, except in a few natural washes (Ciekot et al. 1995). The third settlement pattern (Figure 3.47) is townhouse residential. At the time of the Ciekot et al. study in

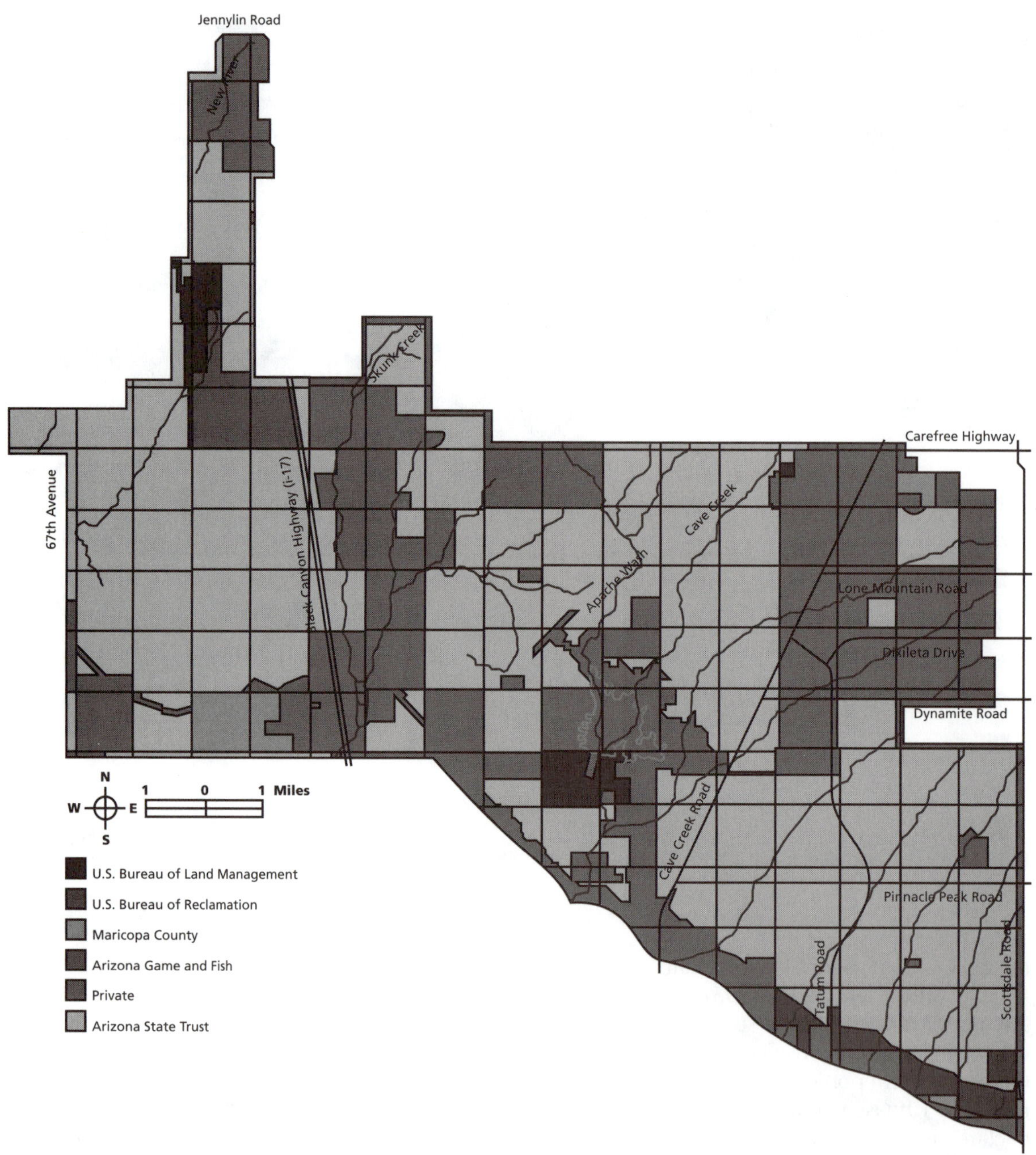

FIGURE 3.44 Land ownership, Desert View Tri-Villages Area. *(Source: Brady et al. 1998)*

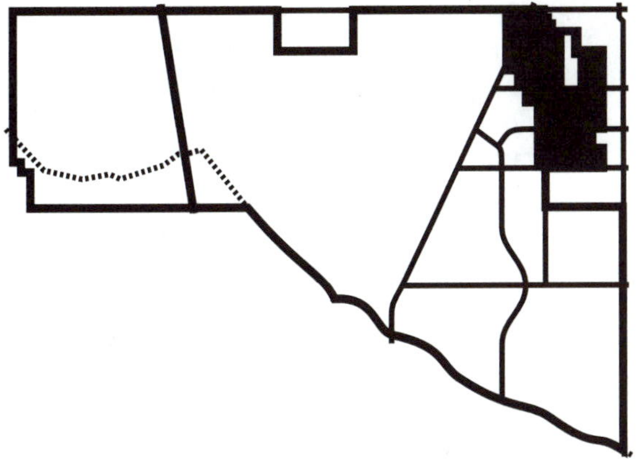

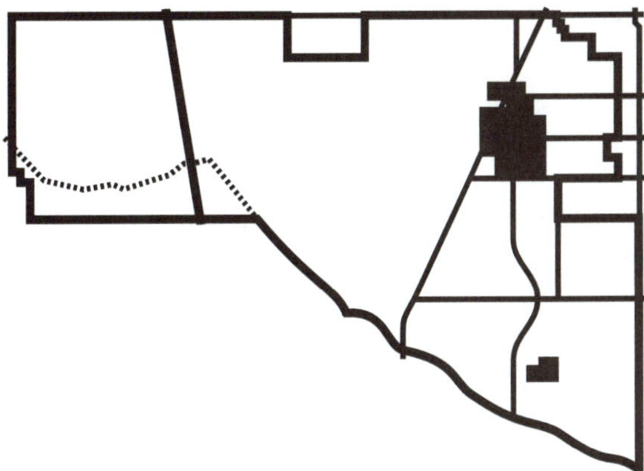

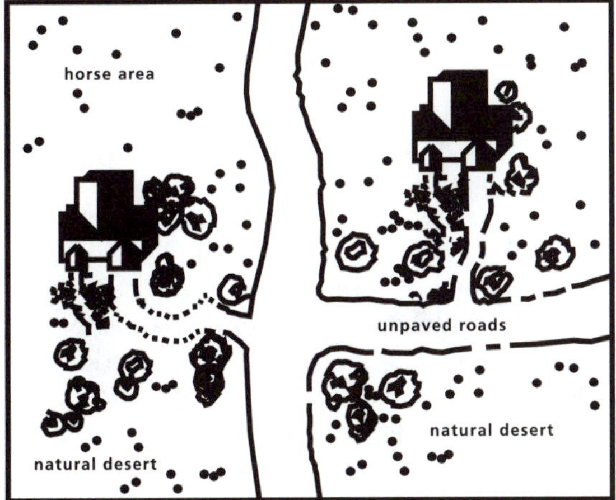

FIGURE 3.45 Settlement patterns, rural horse properties, Desert View Tri-Villages Area. *(Source: Adapted from Ciekot et al. 1995, drawn originally by Carlos Licón)*

FIGURE 3.46 Settlement patterns, lower density suburban housing, Desert View Tri-Villages Area. *(Source: Adapted from Ciekot et al. 1995, drawn originally by Carlos Licón)*

1995, only one townhouse settlement existed in the Tri-Villages Area. It had 108 houses on 28.69 acres (11.6 hectares), for a gross density of 3.76 houses per acre (1.5 houses per hectare). The houses are clustered, leaving much of the site in open space (Ciekot et al. 1995).

In his comprehensive study of human settlement in the Sierra Nevada Mountain region, Timothy Duane (1996) identified five exurban development patterns: (1) compact small towns of 100 to 10,000 people; (2) contiguous subdivisions at suburban densities; (3) stand-alone "gated" communities at suburban densities; (4) large, single-family lots with private on-site infrastructure; and (5) rural agriculture, natural resource, and open-space lands. Duane's exurban settlement patterns are typical for other regions of the American West. The compact small towns are remnants from the nineteenth century, the traditional American settlement form in the region. Duane de-

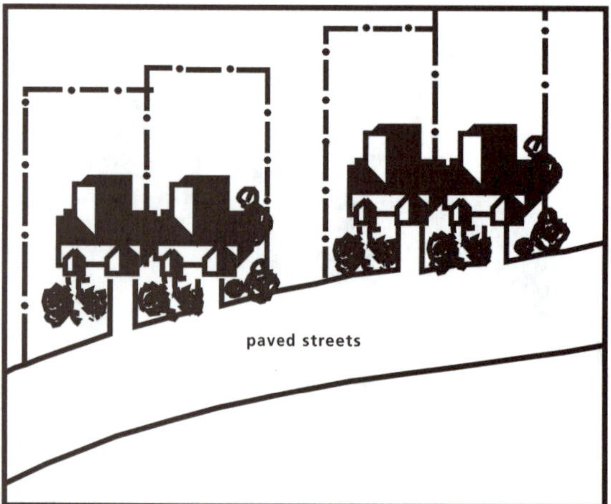

FIGURE 3.47 Settlement patterns, clustered suburban housing, Desert View Tri-Villages Area. *(Source: Adapted from Ciekot et al. 1995, drawn originally by Carlos Licón)*

scribes them as walkable and compact because they "were built before the automobile had been invented . . . around mining or other commodity extractive industries" (1996, 276).

Duane's "contiguous exurban subdivisions" in the Sierra Nevada were built after the Second World War, usually adjacent to the older small towns. They are connected by water and sewer systems to the small towns with densities similar to those of suburban communities in metropolitan regions. Roads consume 20 percent of the land in these communities (Duane 1996). The wide streets are lined mostly with single-family houses with large yards.

The stand-alone gated communities are neither "physically contiguous to nor socially integrated with the small towns" in the Sierra Nevada, according to Duane (1996, 277). These communities are "private" and "homogeneous in ethnic (white), social (well-educated exurbanites), demographic (more retirees), economic (wealthy relative to the rest of the region) and political (conservative) characteristics" (Duane, 1996, 277). These bedroom communities "are often built around significant recreational amenities (e.g., lakes and golf courses), and they generally have larger lots and more expensive homes" than their neighbors (Duane 1996, 277).

Duane dubbed his fourth Sierra Nevada settlement pattern "large single-family lots with private on-site infrastructure" (1996, 277). The size of lots for this pattern is, according to Duane, "primarily a function of the public health need to separate on-site water supplies from on-site sewage disposal through septic tank and leach field systems" (1996, 278). This settlement pattern is very attractive to many Americans who seek to be close to nature and as far away from urban areas as possible.

The final settlement pattern that Duane identified in the Sierra Nevada relates to rural agriculture, natural resource, or open-space lands. People who live in such settlements are directly involved in agriculture, commodity extraction, or recreation. The specific structure of these settlements varies with the industry (i.e., agriculture or forestry) as well as with the location in the landscape (i.e., river valley or mountain land). Settlement typologies, such as that developed by Duane (1996), can be helpful to understand the structure and function of places.

Such settlement pattern analysis may be considered a type of urban morphology, or perhaps in the case of the Tri-Village Area, suburban or rural morphology. Anne Moudon states that morphological analysis is based on three principles:

1. Urban form is defined by three fundamental physical elements: buildings and their related open spaces, plots or lots, and streets.
2. Urban form can be understood at different levels of resolution. Commonly, four are recognized, corresponding to the building/lot, the street/block, the city, and the region.
3. Urban form can only be understood historically since the elements of [which] it is comprised undergo continuous transformation and replacement (1997, 7).

Moudon notes then that "*form, resolution,* and *time* constitute the three fundamental components of urban morphological research" (1997, 7). We can ask questions about the land-use and settlement forms of an area as well as about who lives there (Duane 1996; Steiner and McSherry 2000), such as:

- Who are the people who live in the planning area?
- Where did they and/or their ancestors come from?
- How is the land used?
- Are there areas of multiple use?
- Are there land-use conflicts?
- What characteristics contribute to its uniqueness?
- Are they traditional? Are they contemporary? Natural? Built?
- How has this place changed over time?
- What influences (physical, economic, and political) have caused the changes?
- What are the resulting changes?
- What role does history play in the land-use issues facing the planning area?
- What were the historical patterns of human settlement?
- What is the relationship between settlement patterns and land-use designations and policies in local plans and zoning ordinances?
- What are the ecological, social, and economic consequences of human settlement patterns?

By identifying land use and land users and analyzing who uses what, an elementary understanding of the social organization of an area can be gained. How these groups are linked to resources and issues is more complex, but this understanding is crucial to planning. These relationships will be explored in Chapter 4.

SUMMARY OF EXISTING LAND-USE AND LAND-USER ELEMENTS:

1. Historical development
2. Existing land use
3. Settlement patterns
4. Land-user groups
5. Settlement pattern-groups matrix
6. Groups-issues matrix
7. Building and open space types
8. Plot, lot, and street arrangement

MAJOR SOURCES OF INFORMATION[2]

1. Individual interviews
2. Interviews with groups and associations
3. Local newspapers and libraries
4. Tax assessors
5. U.S. Bureau of the Census
6. U.S. Natural Resources Conservation Service (NRCS)
7. U.S. Geological Survey (USGS)
8. College and university libraries

ANALYSIS AND SYNTHESIS OF INVENTORY INFORMATION

When collecting information about a place, the ecological planner notes the emergence of certain relationships that form patterns on the landscape. The amount of rainfall changes up a mountain slope and the rain turns to snow. Flora respond to these changes, and so one finds different plant

2. Refer to Table 4.1 for a more complete list.

communities on the higher elevations than in lower places. Several techniques enable the ecological planner to synthesize the collected information and to analyze process and pattern; these include bivariate relationship analysis, the compilation of "layer cakes," and the Holdridge life-zone system.

Bivariate Relationships

If it is true that everything is connected to everything else, then to be helpful for planning, those connections need to be made explicit. Synthesis helps the planner connect the many elements that comprise a landscape into a whole. As Paul Smith, Jr., observed, "We experience the natural environment not merely as discrete physical objects, but as a multidimensional gestalt which is in a state of continual synthesis" (1992, 1). A useful first step in making synthetic connections in that "multidimensional gestalt" is to analyze how the inventory elements relate to each other. A useful guide is to identify bivariate relationships between all possible pairs of landscape elements (Figure 3.48).

	Geology	Physiography	Climate	Soils	Groundwater	Surface water	Vegetation	Wildlife	Land use
Geology		1	2	3	4	5	6	7	8
Physiography			9	10	11	12	13	14	15
Climate				16	17	18	19	20	21
Soils					22	23	24	25	26
Groundwater						27	28	29	30
Surface water							31	32	33
Vegetation								34	35
Wildlife									36
Land use									

FIGURE 3.48 Bivariate relationships.

In the Desert View Tri-Villages, as in most regions, geology influences elevation and slope (bivariate relationship 1 in Figure 3.48) in several ways. The physiography of the Tri-Villages Area is an interplay between small mountains and alluvial wash valleys (Ciekot et al. 1995). These kinds of relationships between geology and physiography are almost always an important factor in analyzing the broad physical pattern of a region. The effect of geology on elevation and slope can be quite striking, as with the Front Range of the Colorado Rocky Mountains, or obvious, as with the New Jersey Coastal Plain, or more subtle, as in the Great Plains.

Locally in the Tri-Villages Area, geology influences microclimate (relationship 2). The microclimate is affected by both the small mountains and the alluvial wash valleys. The north sides of the hills are cooler than the south sides. The Tri-Villages' higher altitude in relationship to most of the rest of the Phoenix metropolitan region results in a lower average temperature (Ciekot et al. 1995). This situation has attracted tourists and is increasingly desirable to individuals seeking to escape the Phoenix heat island. In other regions, agriculture, forestry, tourism, or shipping may be affected by how geology and climate are related.

Geologic parent material is an important ingredient to the soil-forming process (relationship 3). The granites of the Tri-Villages Area are large-grained and decompose readily. Stephanie Ciekot and her colleagues (1995) observed evidence of such decomposition in the *bajadas.* The alluvial parent material in the washes includes large rocks carried into the valleys and finer grained deposits. The parent material in the Tri-Villages has not produced soils that are productive for agriculture.

Certain rock formations make better aquifers and aquicludes than others (relationship 4). The alluviums present in the valleys between the small mountains of the Tri-Villages Area are the primary locations of groundwater. The underlying bedrock creates the basin for the aquifer. The alluvial soils help prevent water from evaporating before it percolates down to the aquifer. The granite-derived soils are highly permeable, which also facilitates the percolation of water to the groundwater basin (Ciekot et al. 1995). The interrelationships between geology and hydrology are important for determining available water supplies and understanding stream flows.

Geology influences vegetation and wildlife (relationships 6 and 7) through its effect on physiography, climate, and soils. Rocks affect soil type and moisture distribution. The alluvial soils in the washes are more fertile than the rest of the Tri-Villages Area. As a result, the number and diversity of plant species is greater in the washes than elsewhere in the area.

The rocks and surficial deposits are particularly critical for reptiles. Snakes and lizards use rocks for shelter and shade. The rock formations are also important for burrowing species, such as the kangaroo rat. The walls along the washes, especially Cave Creek Wash, are important for bats, owls, and other cliff inhabitants (Ciekot et al. 1995; Ewan et al. 1996; Burke and Ewan 1998a).

Land use is influenced in several ways by geology (relationship 8). The rocky, mountainous portions of the Tri-Villages Area pose difficulties for construction, and generally, development has not occurred there. The alluvial valleys have fewer constraints and have been used for grazing and scattered rural (and increasingly suburban) housing. In some regions, geologic conditions can cause hazards to human settlement, as in the case of earthquakes and volcanoes, and thus can be important when determining the location of various land uses.

Physiography is the surface expression of geology. As a result, the influence of physiography on climate (relationship 9) is similar to that of geology. In the Tri-Villages Area, rainstorms frequently originate in the nearby mountains to the north and east. These storms move into the area, resulting in somewhat more rainfall than other portions of the metropolitan region (Ciekot et al. 1995). Physiography influences soils (relationship 10) in several ways. In the Tri-Villages Area, the amounts and types of soil are closely related to slope. In the small mountains, soils are shallow or there are only rocky surfaces. As slope angles decrease, the soils become deeper, because less soil is washed away and more is deposited (Ciekot et al. 1995). In even steeper regions of the United States, like the Rocky Mountains, such relationships will be more dramatic. In flat regions, such as the New Jersey Coastal Plain, physiography will exert a more subtle influence.

Physiography is related to groundwater through recharge (relationship 11) especially in relationship to steepness. Groundwater has accumulated in the valley basins of the Tri-Villages Area. Surface water flows at different levels in relationship to elevation and slopes (relationship 12). Essentially, water runs downhill, and it flows faster on steeper slopes than in flatter areas. The floodplains along the washes are an especially important feature of the physiography-surface water relationship. In the Tri-Villages Area, the water flows ephemerally, except where it has been dammed by the Central Arizona Project. In such places, small water pools exist along the CAP canal bank (Ewan et al. 1998). Because the water flows infrequently but very dramatically, multiple braided courses are formed.

Physiography influences plant community development (relationship 13). Elevation exerts a significant influence on vegetation because of its relationship to water flows in the Desert View Tri-Villages Area. Plant types, density, and canopy change in response to elevation. In their wash studies, Joseph Ewan, Rebecca Fish Ewan, and their colleagues identified four plant communities related to the terrain of the Tri-Villages Area. Their wash vegetation type occurs in the lowest elevations, that is in the wash bottoms and along the edges. Both the hillside-slope and the creosote bush-bursage flat types are defined mostly by where they occur in the landscape. Tanks are found at lower places, where they collect water (Ewan et al. 1996, 1998).

Since physiography influences vegetation, it also influences wildlife (relationship 14), since animals depend on plants for their habitat and food supply. The physiography-land use (relationship 15) relationships are similar to those of geology and land use. Development and grazing has occurred more in the flat portions of the Tri-Villages Area than steeper areas. In other regions of the country the influence of terrain on land use is also evident, as, for example, in the San Francisco Bay area. Too often in the United States land use has been poorly adapted to physiography.

Climate plays a strong role in soil development through a number of processes (relationship 16). Weathering impacts soil formation through the processes of deposition and erosion. Most of the soils in the Tri-Villages Area have been deposited and eroded by water processes. However, especially in the small mountains, some of the clay constituent of the soils is deposited by wind (Ciekot et al. 1995). Wind also erodes the surface of the Tri-Villages and contributes to particulate pollution.

Rainfall determines the moisture content of the soil, which, in turn, influences the rate and manner of its development. In addition, moisture affects leaching characteristics, which is important for the formation of the caliche in the area. Infrequent wetting and rapid drying result. There are some secondary clay deposits in the soils of the desert floor. These argillic horizons are the results of wet and dry cycles which transport clay colloids in the soil. The hot dry temperature is an important factor for desert soil development. The high temperatures accelerate the rate of drying as well as the rate of chemical reactions. As Stephanie Ciekot and her colleagues observe, "Consequently, the small amount of organic material that is generated degrades very rapidly and is quickly lost" (1995, 9-8).

There are obvious relationships between climate and hydrology (relationships 17 and 18). The frequency and intensity of rains, when combined with the high temperature, affect the groundwater level and surface water flows. The dryness of the Tri-Villages Area means that water evaporates rapidly, limiting both its percolation into the ground and its surface flow. In the Sonoran Desert, flash floods and dramatic sheet flows occur during rainstorms. Conversely, long periods of dry weather mean that perennial flows do not occur in the Tri-Villages Area (Ciekot et al. 1995).

Vegetation is also greatly affected by climate (relationship 19). Water and solar radiation are the key influences on plant development. The hot temperature and paucity of precipitation in the Tri-Villages Area are the major determinants of its desert vegetation. The region's two rainy seasons mean that it is a more lush desert than most others (Ciekot et al. 1995). Every 10 to 15 years the desert experiences a wildflower display during El Niño events. Frosts do occur in the area, and the more frost-sensitive and drought-tolerant plants appear in the lower elevations (Ciekot et al. 1995). The plants are marvelously adapted to the desert climate. Small shrubs and trees such as creosote bush (*Larrea tridentata*) and foothills or little-leaf palo verde (*Cercidium microphyllum*) grow close to the ground, with small, thin leaves. Many plants, like the palo verde (which means green stem) have green bark to aid with photosynthesis. Of course there are cacti too, including the magnificent saguaro (*Carnegiea gigantea*). The saguaro's ribs are vertical, and the plant expands like an accordion when water is available. During storm seasons, the saguaro grows roots quickly to capture every available drop.

Similarly, climate influences wildlife (relationship 20) through precipitation and solar radiation. Reproduction, migration, hibernation, and feeding are all influenced by the variation in climate through the seasons. Many mammals in the Tri-Villages "have adapted to high diurnal temperatures by altering their behavior such as spending much of the day underground or aestivating" (Ciekot et al. 1995, 9-9). People are about the only animals who live in the desert aboveground and during the day. Most desert creatures are nocturnal; many bite and sting, and several are venomous. With scarce resources, desert animals are master recyclers and adapters. The pack rat, as its name indicates, will collect and store about anything. The pack rat binds its nest with "urine cement," which is capable of preserving its junk pile for centuries. The kangaroo rat, which is neither a kangaroo relative nor a rat, never drinks water and eats its own excrement.

The major land uses in the Tri-Villages Area, and in fact throughout the metropolitan region, are dependent on climate (relationship 21). Until the introduction of refrigeration and air-conditioning, the Phoenix region was much more sparsely inhabited by people. As refrigeration and air-conditioning contributed to significant population growth since World War Two, past lessons about how to build more appropriately in the desert were abandoned. An understanding of climate in planning and design can help to conserve energy and water resources. In the southwestern United States, such relationships are especially dramatic, but land use is affected by climate everywhere.

Soils influence the amount of water that flows through the ground to feed aquifers (relationship 22). The sandy alluvium facilitates the flow of water into the groundwater in the Tri-Villages Area. In addition the permeability of the sandy soils contributes to the recharge of the aquifers (Ciekot et al. 1995). Water flowing across the land surface is a major factor in erosion and drainage (relationship 23). Water also deposits material that develops into alluvial soils, called *fluvents.*

Soil characteristics such as texture, pH level, and cation exchange capacity are interrelated with vegetation (relationship 24). Some plants have adapted to the alkaline soils in the area, while the shallow caliche limits the root growth of other plants (Ciekot et al. 1995). Wildlife species use soil as a habitat (relationship 25). Again, it is hard to separate the influence of soil on vegetation from wildlife.

The soils have impacted past uses of the land in the Desert View Tri-Villages Area (relationship 26). Because of the poor quality of the soils, agriculture crops were not grown there. Many soils in the area are suitable for septic tanks, so scattered rural development has occurred.

Groundwater recharge influences stream flow (relationship 27). Surface flow is abundant after a rainstorm; then it disappears. It also provides the supply of water available for vegetation, wildlife, and humans (relationships 28 to 30). Most existing rural settlements in the area use well water, while newer developments are using both well water and water from remote surface sources. Except in low-lying areas along the washes, vegetation in the Tri-Villages is largely independent of groundwater (phreatic water). Instead, it is dependent on soil moisture (radose water). Rebecca Fish Ewan, Joseph Ewan, and their colleagues note strong relationships between water and vegetation. For example, the wash beds are subject to scouring during floods, "which inhibits growth of large trees and dense patches of shrubs, and maintains a dynamic vegetation composition in which forbs are dominant" (Ewan et al. 1998, x).

Surface water is related again to water supply for animals and people (relationships 31 to 33), as well as providing a habitat for certain types of plant and animal life. Surface water is of concern to grazing in the Tri-Villages because of erosion, and to other land uses because of flooding. In other regions, irrigation or land drainage will be important.

The interrelationship between vegetation and wildlife is strong (relationship 34). Vegetation provides food and shelter for animals. The saguaros have been called "desert condominiums" because of the number of bird species they house. Animals, in turn, may affect the reproduction and growth of plants. For example, long-nosed bats pollinate saguaro cacti. Kangeroo rats cache seeds of plants for food that can germinate before being eaten. Energy-flow and food-web diagrams are good ways to visualize these relationships. Plants and animals influence how land is used by people (relationships 35 and 36). Vegetation can provide energy-efficient homesites that make pleasant places for people to live. Certain wildlife species conflict with suburban development. That is, coyotes will eat kittens, while cats eat native bird species. Animals relate to land use and users both as pests and as sources of recreation.

By reviewing bivariate relationships in such a manner, linkages between different elements of the landscape can be made more explicit. One can also start to view each element as it relates to other elements. This perspective should be helpful when contemplating options in the use of resources.

Layer-Cake Relationships

One useful tool that helps to show how these elements interrelate across the landscape is layer-cake relationships (Figure 1.2). Each element is considered one "layer" in the landscape as a whole. Stephanie Ciekot and her colleagues produced three layer-cake diagrams of the Desert View Tri-Villages Area. Figure 3.49 shows the location of the three diagrams (Figures 3.50 through 3.52), which were constructed by using the same set of points overlaid on each of the inventory maps. The collected information was then stacked to form a "layer cake."

This layer cake helps to illuminate bivarite relationships and aids in analyzing multiple interrelationships between elements across the landscape. For instance, the relationships between the elevation and vegetation types as well as between vegetation and water availability are readily apparent.

Depending on the study area, several such layer-cake diagrams should be constructed to analyze how the different elements interrelate at different places in the landscape. In addition to being a useful analytical device, layer-cake diagrams can help an ecological planner explain complex relationships to elected officials and to the public.

The Holdridge Life-Zone System

L. R. Holdridge (1967) of the Tropical Science Center in Costa Rica devised a system for classifying life, or bioclimatic, zones. His goal was to develop a means of determining the basic natural units for ecology. Holdridge observed that: "Among plant ecologists, the usual definition of association has restricted the unit to a given set of plant species.

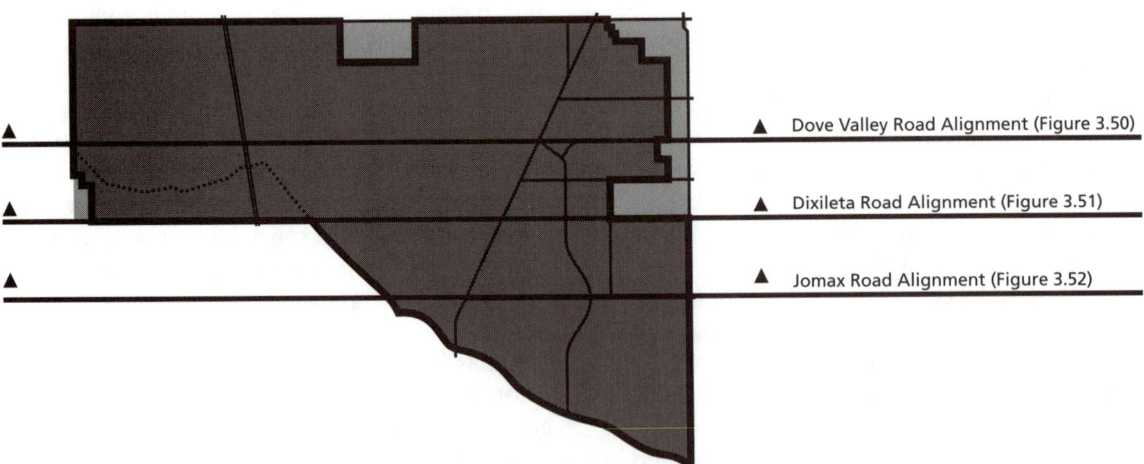

FIGURE 3.49 Location of layer-cake diagrams, Desert View Tri-Villages Area. *(Source: Adapted from Ciekot et al. 1995)*

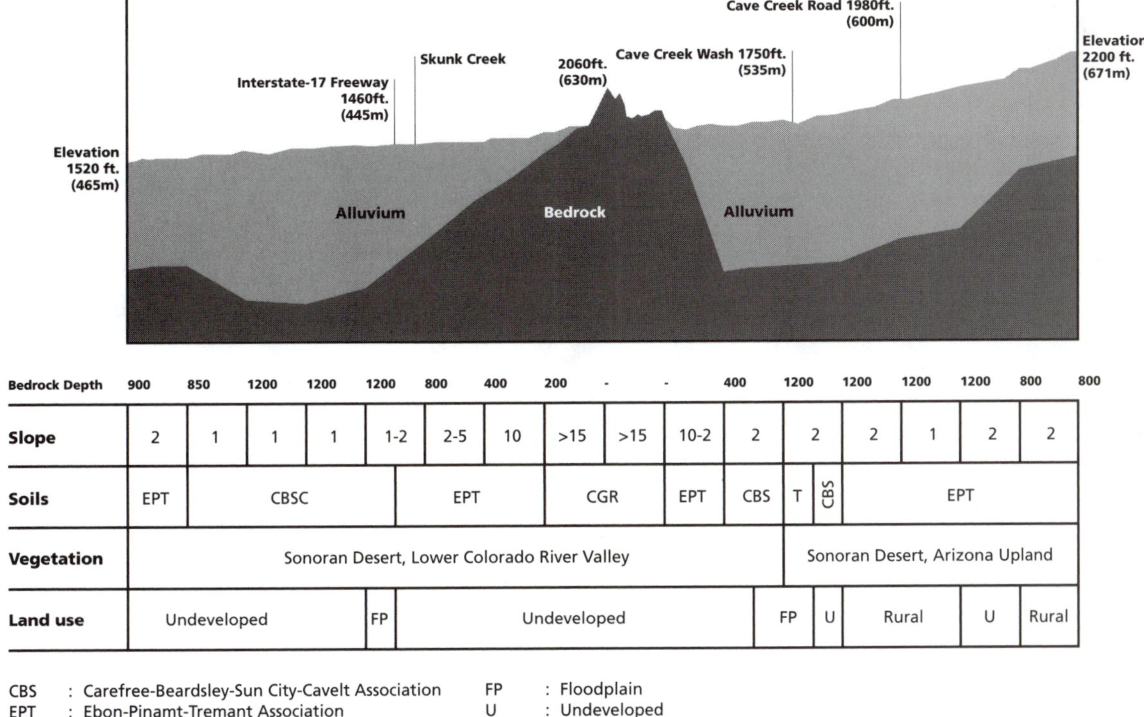

Bedrock Depth 900 850 1200 1200 1200 800 400 200 - - 400 1200 1200 1200 1200 800 800

Slope	2	1	1	1	1-2	2-5	10	>15	>15	10-2	2	2	2	1	2	2
Soils	EPT	CBSC			EPT			CGR		EPT	CBS	T / CBS	EPT			
Vegetation	Sonoran Desert, Lower Colorado River Valley											Sonoran Desert, Arizona Upland				
Land use	Undeveloped				FP	Undeveloped					FP	U	Rural		U	Rural

CBS : Carefree-Beardsley-Sun City-Cavelt Association
EPT : Ebon-Pinamt-Tremant Association
CGR : Cherioni-Gachado Rock Outcrop Association
T : Torrifluvents
FP : Floodplain
U : Undeveloped
R : Rural

FIGURE 3.50 Layer-cake diagram, Desert View Tri-Villages Area. *(Source: Adapted from Ciekot et al. 1995)*

Such a definition not only places complete emphasis on vegetation alone, but renders difficult the mapping of associations" (1967, 7). Holdridge took a broader view, contending that: "The association must be thought of as a natural unit in which the vegetation, the animal activities, the climate, the land physiography, geological formation and the soil are all interrelated in a unique recognizable combination which has a distinct aspect or physiognomy" (1967, 7). The system he developed is helpful for analysis and synthesis in planning because of this wider perspective.

Holdridge based his life zones on equivalently weighted divisions of three major climatic factors: heat, precipitation, and moisture. Based on his work in the Caribbean region, he developed the chart shown in Figure 3.53. According to Holdridge: "The life zone permits the groupings into natural units of several hundred or perhaps well over one thousand associations of the earth. The life zone chart, considered as a three-dimensional representation, separates 120 distinct life zones, provided that the subunits of the Subtropical region and Premontane belt are counted life zones" (1967, 14).

Life zones, then, are defined by Holdridge as a group of associations related through the effects of heat, precipitation, and moisture. His system is applied in the following manner. By constructing a triangle (Figure 3.53), using the three parameters of temperature, precipitation, and evapotranspiration as the three axes, any spot on earth with climatic records can be placed in one of the

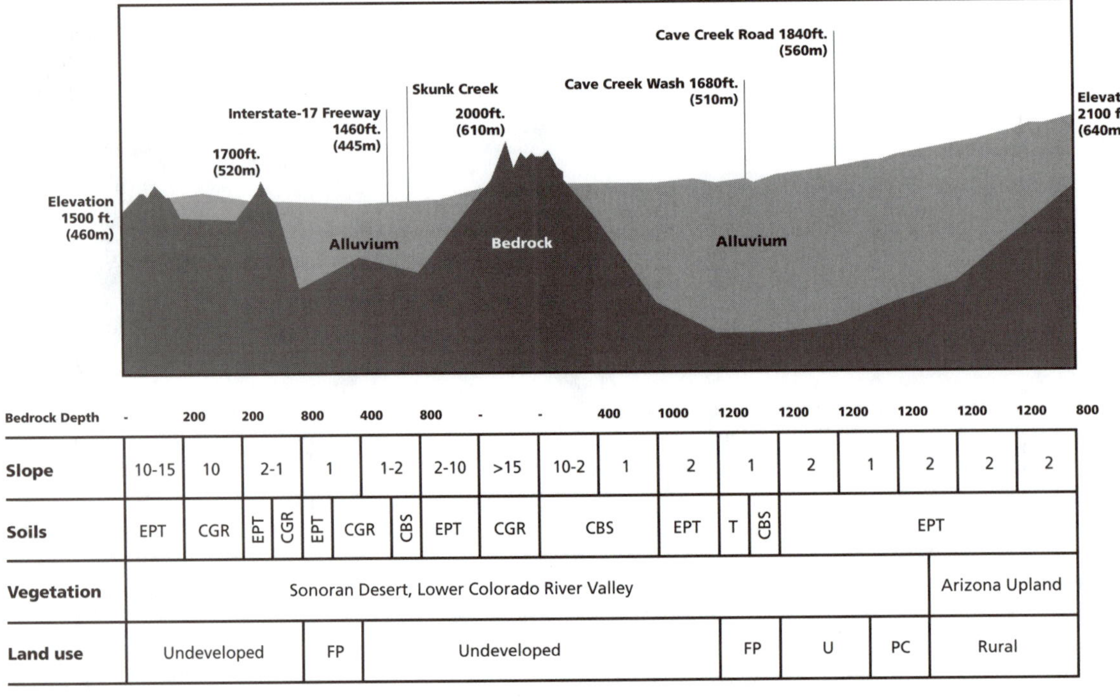

CBS : Carefree-Beardsley-Sun City-Cavelt Association
EPT : Ebon-Pinamt-Tremant Association
CGR : Cherioni-Gachado Rock Outcrop Association
T : Torrifluvents
FP : Floodplain
U : Undeveloped
PC : Planned Community (Tatum Ranch)

FIGURE 3.51 Layer-cake diagram, Desert View Tri-Villages Area. *(Source: Adapted from Ciekot et al. 1995)*

Holdridge life zones. The life-zone designations are those of the "climatic association" characteristics of the zone, that is, the normal climatic vegetation. This can be much modified by edaphic soil factors so that many plant associations are possible within each life zone, but there should be only one type of climax vegetation.

The life zone of the Tri-Villages Area can be determined by locating its average maximum temperature [82.57°F (28.1°C)] and average annual precipitation [8 inches (20.3 centimeters)]. According to Holdridge's chart, the Tri-Villages Area is in the Desert Scrub zone. The life-zone system may be especially helpful in larger, more complex planning areas. For instance, the system was used for an inventory and analysis of a large county in southeastern Washington state (Beach et al. 1978). The layer-cake models in Figure 3.54 illustrate how the life zones related to other inventory elements.

TWO EXAMPLES OF BIOPHYSICAL INVENTORY AND ANALYSIS

The inventories of the New Jersey Pinelands and the Camp Pendleton region were based on an understanding of landscape ecology. The ecological planners who undertook these inventories and analyses sought to reveal the complexities of these places. The best available science was used

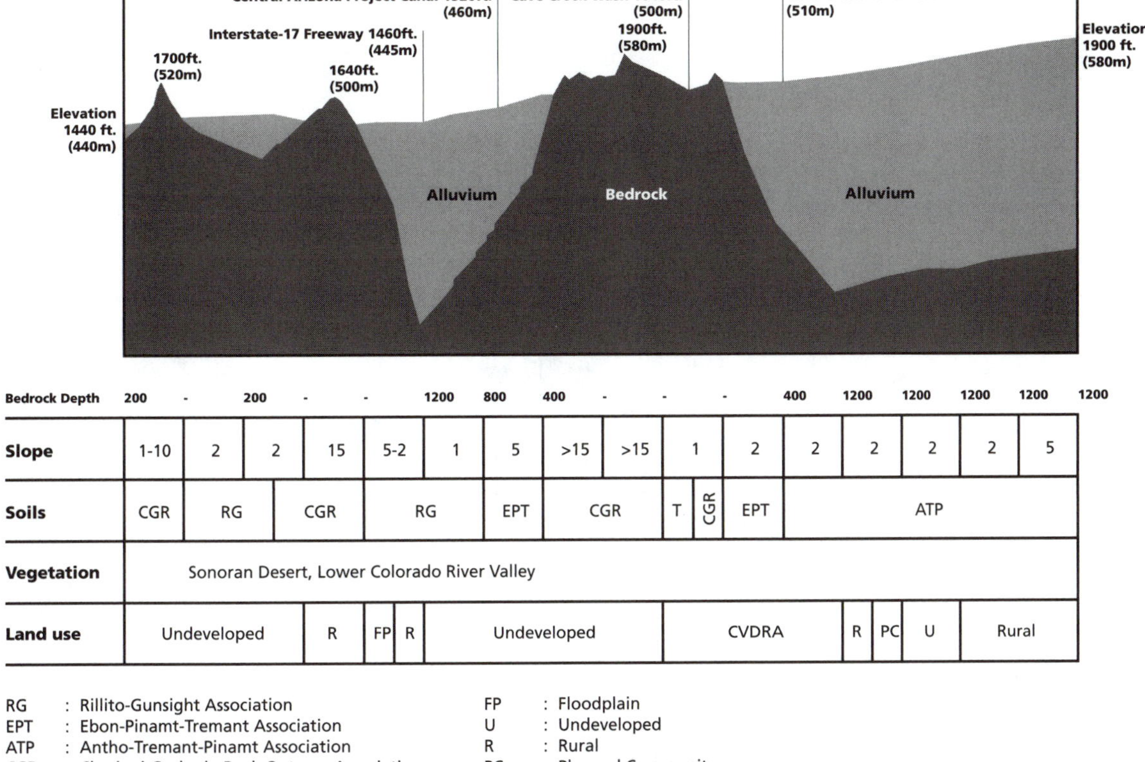

FIGURE 3.52 Layer-cake diagram, Desert View Tri-Villages Area. *(Source: Adapted from Ciekot et al. 1995)*

in each case. The planners and landscape architects created syntheses of this information to help the public and decision makers understand how elements and processes are connected.

The New Jersey Pinelands Comprehensive Management Plan

New Jersey is one of the most densely populated states in America. Yet, after 300 years of settlement by Europeans, African-Americans, and their descendants as well as by more recent immigrants, natural areas still remain in the state. The Pinelands is the largest of such areas. "The Pinelands is a patchwork of oak forests, tea-colored streams and rivers, spacious farms, crossroad hamlets, and small towns stretched across southern New Jersey" (New Jersey Pinelands Commission 1998). The basis for the New Jersey Pinelands Comprehensive Management Plan was a natural resource inventory.

This inventory summarizes reports by several consulting firms, state agencies, and environmental organizations. The Pinelands Commission's work, including the reports that constituted the biophysical inventory, was supported with state and federal funds in addition to grants from private organizations. For instance, the Geraldine R. Dodge Foundation contributed $200,000 to the effort (Pinelands Commission, 1980).

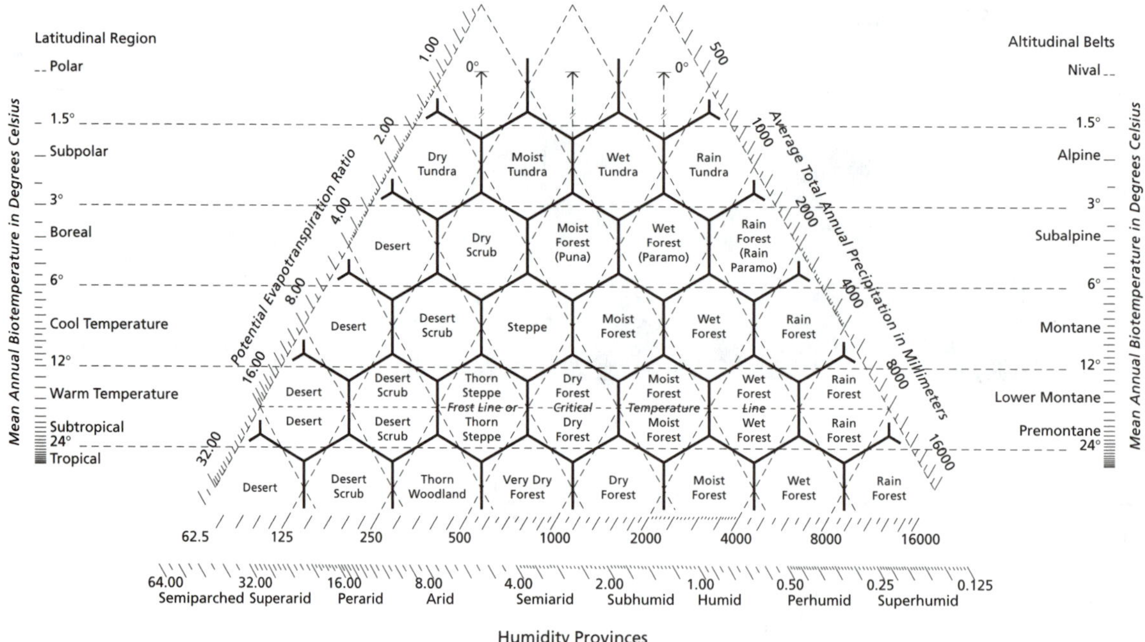

FIGURE 3.53 The world life-zone system of ecological classification by L. R. Holdridge. *(Source: Adapted from Holdridge 1967)*

The biophysical inventory and analysis sections in the management plan included a discussion of the evolution of the Pinelands ecosystem and a review of geology, hydrogeology, surface hydrology, soils, vegetation, aquatic communities, wildlife, climate, and air quality. The evolution of the Pinelands ecosystem was a broad review from the early geologic processes and the Pleistocene ice age through 10,000 years ago and the time of European colonization to the present. A summary of human influences was also included. Land users were included in the human inventory and analyses sections and will be discussed in Chapter 4.

The Pinelands is located in the Atlantic Coastal Plain formation. Much of the description of the Coastal Plain in the management plan was based on the work of the geologist E. C. Rhodehamel. The Coastal Plain has developed over the past 170 to 200 million years as a result of deposition and erosion. The region is characterized by a gently rolling terrain with sandy, droughty soils with no rock outcrops, steep slopes, or mountain peaks. The geology of the Coastal Plain comprises a wedged-shaped series of unconsolidated layers of sands, clays, and marls on a gently southeastward-dipping bedrock (80 to 100 feet per mile), that is, 1300 to 6000 feet (397 to 1830 meters) below the surface. These layers extend seaward into the submerged continental shelf (Pinelands Commission, 1980). A thorough description of the geological components of the Coastal Plain was included in the plan with a foldout map of the surficial geology and a foldout geologic cross section.

The hydrogeology of the Coastal Plain is characterized by extensive sand aquifers. According to the comprehensive management plan (1980), this groundwater supports 89 percent of the flow in the Pinelands streams, discharging primarily through the many swamps and marshes in the region. The aquifers are replenished solely by pre-

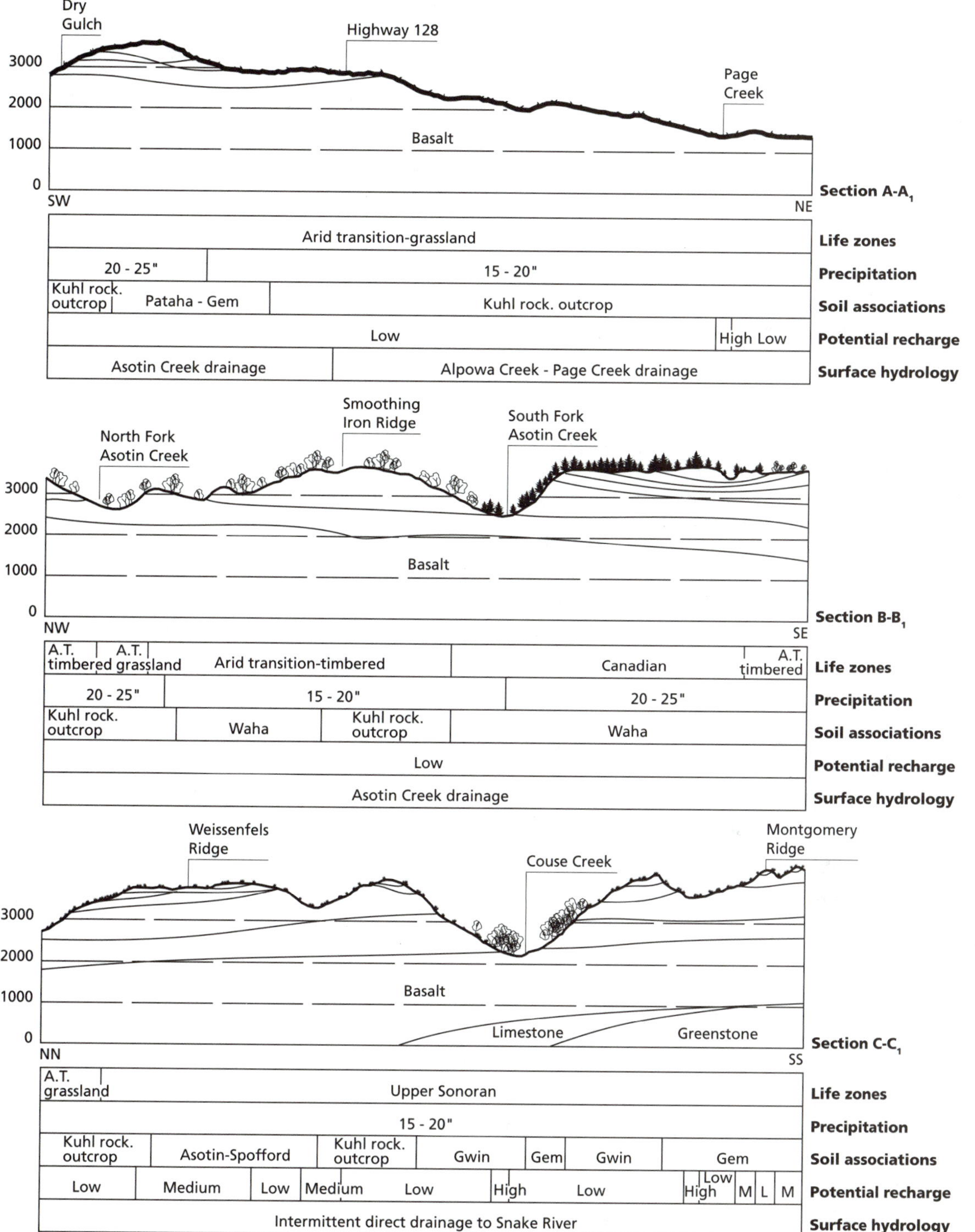

FIGURE 3.54 Layer-cake diagrams related to life zones. *(Source: Beach et al. 1978)*

cipitation, of which about 44 percent of the annual total percolates through the sandy surface. The major Coastal Plain groundwater systems are the Potomac-Raritan-Magothy, the Englishtown formation, the Wenonah formation, and Cohansey-Kirkwood. These systems and their relative importance to the Pinelands are described, as are hydraulic flows (Figure 3.55), groundwater quality, and groundwater contamination.

Surface water is a distinctive character of the Pinelands. The Pinelands streams are typically slow-moving and shallow because of the flat topography. The components of surface hydrology considered by Pinelands planners include drainage basins, a hydrologic budget, surface water quality, and drainage basin water quality. This information is discussed and summarized in tables and maps in the management plan.

The soils have developed from a parent material of the sandy geologic deposits. These soils are unusually porous and acidic. Pinelands planners analyzed information about soil classification, development and mineralogy, characteristics and interpretations, depth to water table, hydrologic soil groups, factors that limit use for septic tank absorption fields, and waste treatment information. Chemical aspects such as nitrogen, phosphorus, pH, and organic matter were considered as well to gain an understanding about the potential soil productivity. Soil survey information from the then Soil Conservation Service (now U.S. Natural Resources Conservation Service) was used for mapping and description. The Pinelands Commission also utilized the then SCS (now NRCS) important farmland system to describe prime, unique, and statewide important farmlands (Pinelands Commission, 1980).

The Pinelands contains one of the largest natural areas in the northeastern United States. The authors of the Pinelands management plan characterize it as "low, dense forests of pine and oak, ribbons of cedar and hardwood swamp bordering drainage courses, pitch pine lowlands, bogs and marshes" (1980, 58). There are two distinct floristic complexes in the Pinelands, the uplands and the lowlands. Pine-oak and oak-pine forests are characteristic of the uplands complex, while cedar and hardwood swamps and pitch pine lowland forests dominate the lowland complex (Pinelands Commission, 1980).

The Pinelands are a unique "pygmy forest," with trees only 2 to 5 ft (.61 to 1.5 m) in height. Of the 580 native species in the Pinelands, 71 have been classified as rare, endangered, threatened, or undetermined (Mason 1986). Fifty-four plant species are in danger of disappearing entirely from the state (New Jersey Pinelands Commission 1998). The management plan included analyses of

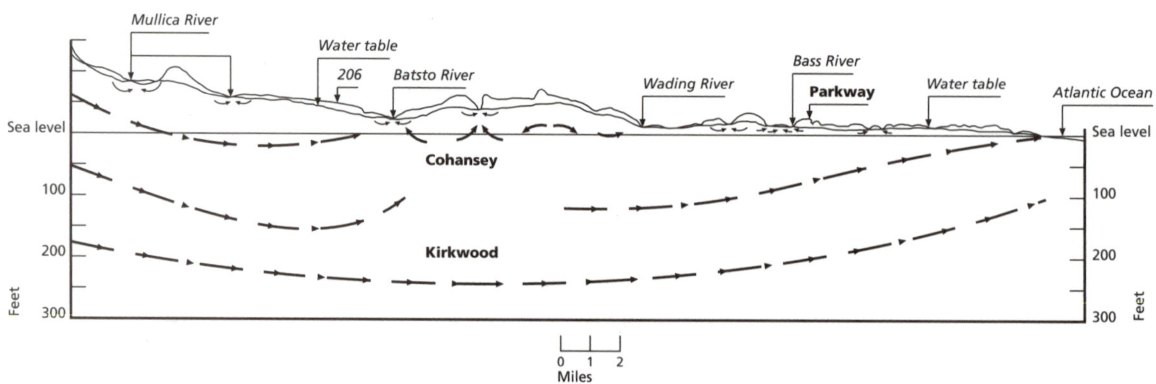

FIGURE 3.55 Hydrological flows of the Cohansey-Kirkwood aquifer system. *(Source: Pinelands Commission 1980)*

The largest known population of the rare Pine Barrens Treefrog—bright green with a lavender and white side stripe—thrives in its boggy southern white cedar habitat in the New Jersey Pinelands. *(Norma Martin Milner, New Jersey Pinelands Commission)*

vegetation trends and patterns, the value of wetlands, endangered and threatened plants, forest fire management, and forestry.

The general aquatic habitat types in the Pinelands include streams, lakes and ponds, and bogs. The components of these aquatic habitats discussed in the management plan include algae, macrophytes, macroinvertebrates, and fish. Factors influencing Pinelands aquatic communities, human influences, and a watershed inventory were also included (Pinelands Commission, 1980). The different types of Pinelands wetlands, such as cedar swamps and pitch pine lowlands "help reduce pollution, prevent flooding, and serve as the home for many of the region's rare plants and animals" (New Jersey Pinelands Commission 1998).

Several wildlife studies were summarized in the management plan. Table 3.9 lists the mammals of the Pinelands and their habitats, while Table 3.10 lists the total number of Pinelands mammals associated with each habitat. Similar species lists and habitat relationships were developed for birds, reptiles, and amphibians. There were also discussions about arthropods, wildlife, and fisheries resources and management practices (Pinelands Commission, 1980). The Pinelands contains 39 species (30 birds, 5 reptiles, and 4 amphibians) considered threatened or endangered (New Jersey Pinelands Commission 1998).

Regional climate characteristics were analyzed by planners for the 1980 plan, including information about temperature, precipitation, and winds. The brief description of climate was followed by a review of air quality. Chemical air pollutants—particulates, lead, sulfur dioxide, carbon monoxide, ozone, and nitrogen dioxide—were reviewed, as were point, area, and line sources of air pollution (Pinelands Commission, 1980).

TABLE 3.9
MAMMALS OF THE PINELANDS AND THEIR HABITATS

		Habitats													
Species	**Status***	**Pine-oak**	**Oak-pine**	**Pitch pine lowland**	**Cedar swamp**	**Hardwood swamp**	**Water**	**Bog**	**Marsh**	**Nonpine barrens**	**Agricultural**	**Urban**	**Nonforested**	**Borrow pit**	**Old fields**
Opossum, *Didelphis virginiana*	C	•	•	•	•	•		•	•	•	•	•			•
Raccoon, *Procyon lotor*	C	•	•	•	•	•		•	•	•	•	•			•
Long-tailed weasel, *Mustela frenata*	C	•	•	•	•	•		•	•	•	•				•
Mink, *Mustela vison*	C	•	•	•	•	•		•	•	•	•				•
River otter, *Lutra canadensis*	C			•	•		•	•	•					•	
Striped skunk, *Mephitis mephitis*	C	•	•	•	•	•		•	•	•	•	•			•
Red fox, *Vulpes fulva*	C	•	•			•				•	•				•
Gray fox, *Urocyon cinereoargenteus*	A	•	•	•		•									•
Black bear**, *Ursus americanus*	Ex	•	•	•		•					•				•
Bobcat**, *Lynx rufus*	Ex	•	•	•		•				•					
Eastern coyote, *Canis latrans*	P/UC	•	•	•		•				•	•	•			•
Gray squirrel, *Sciurus carolinensis*	C		•			•					•	•			
Red squirrel, *Tamiasciurus hudsonicus*	A	•	•												
Woodchuck, *Marmota monax*	UC					•				•	•				•
Beaver, *Castor canadensis*	C			•	•	•	•	•			•				
Muskrat, *Ondatra zibethica*	C			•	•		•	•	•		•				
Eastern cottontail, *Sylvilagus floridanus*	C	•	•	•						•	•				•
White-tailed deer, *Odocoileus virginianus*	C	•	•	•	•					•	•	•			•
Masked shrew, *Sorex cinerus*	UC	•	•			•		•			•				•
Short-tailed shrew, *Blarina brevicauda*	UC	•	•	•		•		•							•

Least shrew, *Cryptotis parva*	UD							•	•						•
Eastern mole, *Scalopus aquaticus*	C							•			•	•			•
Starnosed mole, *Condylura cristata*	UC			•	•	•		•	•		•				
Little brown bat, *Myotis lucifugus*	UD	•	•	•	•	•	•	•	•	•	•	•	•	•	•
Eastern pipistrelle, *Pipistrellus subflavus*	UD	•	•	•	•	•	•	•	•	•	•	•	•	•	•
Big brown bat, *Eptesicus fuscus*	UD	•	•	•	•	•	•	•	•	•	•	•	•	•	•
Eastern chipmunk, *Tamias striatus*	C	•	•	•		•				•	•	•			•
Flying squirrel, *Glaucomys volans*	C	•	•	•		•					•				
Rice rat, *Oryzomys palustris*	UD								•						
White-footed mouse, *Peromyscus leucopus*	C	•	•			•					•				•
Red-backed vole, *Clethrinonomys gapperi*	C	•	•	•	•	•									
Meadow vole, *Microtus pennsylvanicus*	C			•	•	•		•			•				
Pine vole, *Pitymys pinetorum*	C	•	•	•	•	•		•							
Southern bog lemming, *Synaptomys cooperi*	UD				•	•		•							
Norway rat, *Rattus norvegicus*	C										•	•			•
House mouse, *Mus musculus*	C										•	•			•
Meadow jumping mouse, *Zapus hudsonius*	UD			•	•	•		•							•

* Explanation of status codes:

Abundant (A)—The species reaches its highest population densities in the Pinelands when compared to other areas of New Jersey.

Common (C)—The species population is at a level consistent with the habitat available in the Pinelands, but the density here is exceeded in other areas of New Jersey.

Uncommon (UC)—The species population level is below the level which the Pinelands is capable of supporting, or the species is rarely encountered because of a scarcity of habitat.

Undetermined (UD)—A species about which there is not enough information available to determine status.

Extirpated (Ex)—A species that occurred in the Pinelands within the last 300 years but no longer exists within the region.

Peripheral (P)—The species reaches the limits of its distribution in the Pinelands. It may be uncommon to abundant. This designation will be used along with another status.

** Potential habitats exist for these extirpated species.

SOURCE: Pinelands Commission 1980.

TABLE 3.10
TOTAL NUMBER OF PINELANDS MAMMALS ASSOCIATED WITH EACH HABITAT

Habitat	Number of species
Pine-oak forest	23
Oak-pine forest	24
Pitch pine lowland	25
Cedar swamp	18
Hardwood swamp	27
Water	6
Bog	20
Marsh (inland and coastal)	13
Non-pine barrens forest	15
Agricultural	26
Urban	13
Nonforested	3
Borrow pits	4
Old fields	24

SOURCE: Pinelands Commission 1980.

The Pinelands Commission relied on a series of consultants to develop studies incorporated into their management plan (see, for instance, Berger and Sinton, 1985; and Mason 1986). These consultants utilized both existing data and fieldwork. This information was presented in such a way as to illustrate the interrelationships between the biophysical components of the Pinelands.

The Biodiversity Plan for the Camp Pendleton Region, California

The landscape study for the Camp Pendleton region explores how urban growth and change in rapidly growing southern California might impact biodiversity. The focus of the two-year study (1994 to 1996) was the U.S. Marine Corps base north of San Diego. The study was sponsored by the U.S. Department of Defense, the U.S. Department of Energy, and the U.S. Environmental Protection Agency. It was undertaken by an interdisciplinary team of researchers from Harvard University, Utah State University, the National Biological Service, the U.S. Forest Service, The Nature Conservancy, and the Biodiversity Research Consortium. The research team cooperated with the Marines as well as two regional planning agencies—the San Diego Association of Governments and the Southern California Association of Governments. The team included leading landscape planners such as Carl Steinitz and Stephen Ervin, landscape ecologists Richard Forman and Michael Binford, and landscape architects Craig Johnson and Dick Toth, among others.[3] The study combined the latest geographic information systems technology with new concepts about landscape ecology in one of the fastest growing regions in the nation.

The study area was a 49.7 by 83.2 mile (80 by 134 kilometer) rectangle between San Diego and Los Angeles, California (Figure 3.56). According to the research team, their strategy was "based on the hypothesis that the major stressors causing biodiversity change are related to urbanization" (Steinitz et al. 1996, ii). This hypothesis helped determine what inventory elements were used to describe the region. Geographic information systems technology was used to collect, store, and analyze the data. Several GIS software programs were used, with the Arc/Info GRID analysis package from the Environmental Systems Research Institute of Redlands, California, forming the core for the analytical models of the database. A multiscale approach was employed, which consisted of the region as a whole, a third-order watershed, a subdivision, and several specific restoration projects (Steinitz et al. 1996).

The landscape process was organized and reported as follows:

- Terrain
- Soils

3. The other team members included Paul Cote, Harvard University; Thomas Edwards, Jr., National Biological Service; Ross Kiester, U.S. Forest Service; David Mouat, U.S. Environmental Protection Agency; Douglas Olson, Harvard University; Allan Shearer, Harvard University; Robin Wills, The Nature Conservancy; plus landscape architecture graduate students from Harvard University and Utah State University.

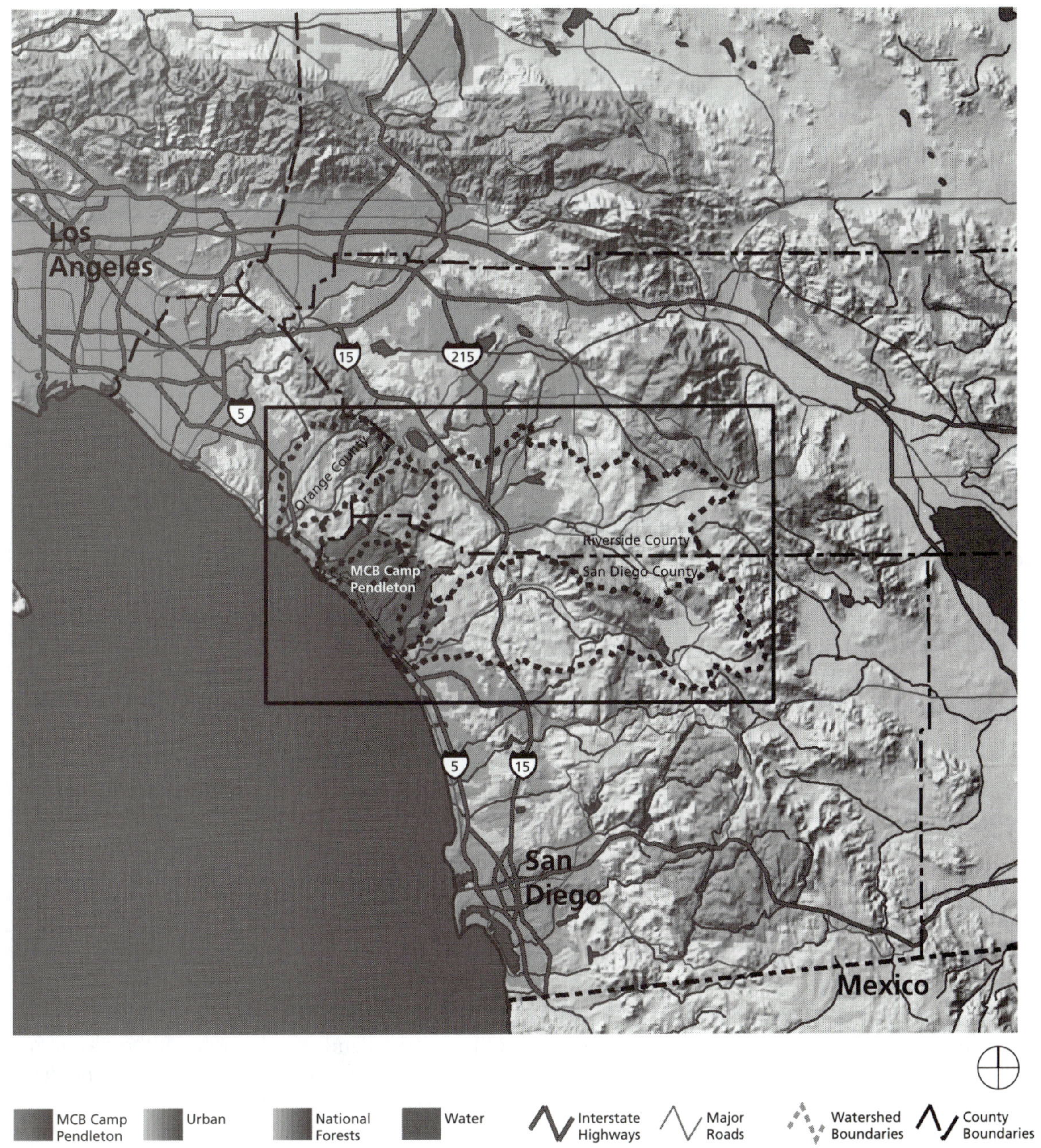

FIGURE 3.56 Camp Pendleton region, California. *(Source: Steinitz et al. 1996)*

- Hydrology
- Fire
- Vegetation
- Landscape ecological pattern
- Single species potential habitat
    - Arroyo southwest toad
    - Orange-throated whiptail lizard
    - Coastal cactus wren
    - Least bell's vireo
    - California gnat catcher
    - Western bluebird
    - Brown headed cowbird
    - Gray fox
    - Mule deer
    - California cougar
- Species richness
- Visual preference (Steinitz et al. 1996).

These elements were used to address how the landscape operated as a process (Figure 3.57) (Steinitz et al. 1996, also see Steinitz 1990, 1993a). As examples, the descriptive aspects of the terrain, soils, hydrology, and vegetation will be summarized. Then, the operational aspects of the landscape ecological pattern and one of the single-species potential habitat analyses will be summarized.

The Pendleton research team employed GIS to analyze different slope models and to calculate the amount of land in each category (Figure 3.58). After mapping soil types from NRCS data, prime agricultural soils were located (Figure 3.59). For hydrology, the team simulated "the relationships between land cover and the hydrological regime" (Binford in Steinitz et al. 1996, 32). The diagram in Figure 3.60 illustrates the procedures used for "simulating both long-term hydrological and single-even regimes" (Steinitz et al. 1996, 32). A drainage subbasin map (Figure 3.61) was constructed showing the seven river basins that are located on or adjacent to Camp Pendleton. The vegetation map (Figure 3.62) was developed with digital vegetation-type data, classified by the California Natural Diversity Database/Holland Code (Holland 1986).

One type of synthesis used by Steinitz and his colleagues was the development of a landscape ecological pattern. The elements that comprised this pattern were:

- *Contiguous natural vegetation:* Areas larger than 500 hectares (1235 acres) which currently form the pattern matrix and the principal source of biodiversity
- *Isolated natural vegetation:* Areas less than 500 hectares (1235 acres) which form natural patches and stepping stones surrounded by disturbed or built landscape
- *Natural edges:* A 90 meter (295.3 feet) wide band that extends into the contiguous and isolated natural vegetation from disturbed areas
- *Stream corridors:* Linear features up to 90 meters (295.3 feet) across which can connect patch elements
- *Disturbed landscape:* Primarily agriculture and military impact zones, which have repeatedly disturbed vegetation
- *Built landscapes:* All urban land and roads
- *Water* (Steinitz et al. 1996, 50).

These elements were identified following Forman and Godron (1986) and mapped with GIS technology (Figure 3.63). The research team observed that the Camp Pendleton landscape "still remains a set of natural patches and smaller 'stepping stones,' connected by stream and riparian vegetation corridors" (Steinitz et al. 1996, 52).

As part of their process and evaluation models of the Camp Pendleton landscape, the research team studied the specific habitats of 10 species. The Habitat Suitability Index (HSI) models of the U.S. Fish and Wildlife Service was used (USFWS 1981). According to Craig Johnson, "HSI models focus on spatially explicit habitat data, which include vegetation type, stand age, stand density, percent cover, vertical and horizontal structure,

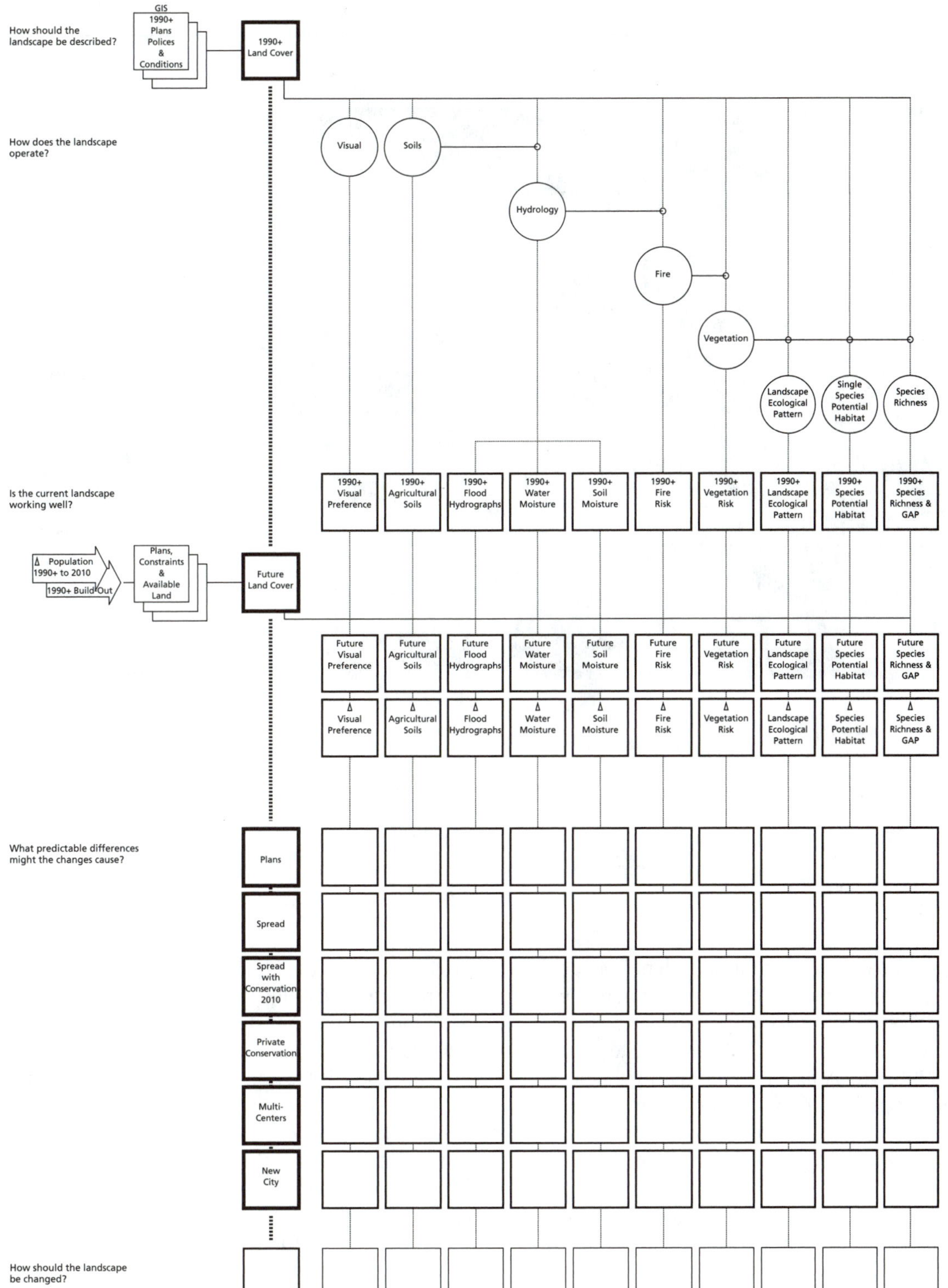

FIGURE 3.57 Steinitz landscape planning process. *(Source: Steinitz et al. 1996)*

FIGURE 3.58 Slope in percent rise, Camp Pendleton study area. *(Source: Steinitz et al. 1996)*

patch size, patch configuration, edge, juxtaposition of plant community types, disturbance, elevation, aspect, soil, special features and other spatially explicit factors" (Johnson in Steinitz et al. 1996, 56). A list of possible animal species was developed, then the 10 wildlife specific species selected to ensure that all the major plant community types were included in the analysis.

The California cougar (*Felis concolor californicus*) was one of the ten species selected. It is the top carnivore remaining in the Camp Pendleton region and requires large contiguous areas of habitat (Steinitz et al. 1996). The Camp Pendleton research team modeled and mapped the cougar's 1990 home range, its "stepping stones" or connecting areas, and the residual areas (Figure 3.64). The team used 1990 because that was the oldest data in the model.

The inventory of ecological processes for planning is a relatively new art. The Pinelands example was published in 1980, and the Camp Pendleton study a decade and a half later. The major advances of the latter study were the use of GIS technology, the development of a set of models about landscape processes interacting with

FIGURE 3.59 Prime agricultural soils, Camp Pendleton study area. *(Source: Steinitz et al. 1996)*

policy, and the application of theory from landscape ecology. This theory is apparent in the multiscale approach used by the Camp Pendleton researchers. Both examples differ from conventional planning processes in the scope of biophysical information collected and analyzed. In both cases, a slice of time was taken of the interacting elements of the place. This slice represents a momentary glimpse of a continuous process where natural factors and human society are in constant change. The landscape changes accordingly. This concept is illustrated in Figure 3.65. Since the landscape is constantly changing, inventories should be viewed as a continuing activity that includes periodic updating and reassessment of information as new data become available.

The landscape is a result of the interaction of natural factors and human activities. The natural factors include physical, or *abiotic,* elements such as climate, geology, hydrology, and soils as well as the *biotic* elements of plants and animals (Vroom et al., 1980). As noted by the Pinelands Commission: "The present Pinelands landscape and ecosystem have been shaped by natural processes which began millions of years ago and, more recently, by the influence of man. A knowledge of these events is necessary to fully appreciate the region's significance and to plan for its continuing maintenance" (1980, 1).

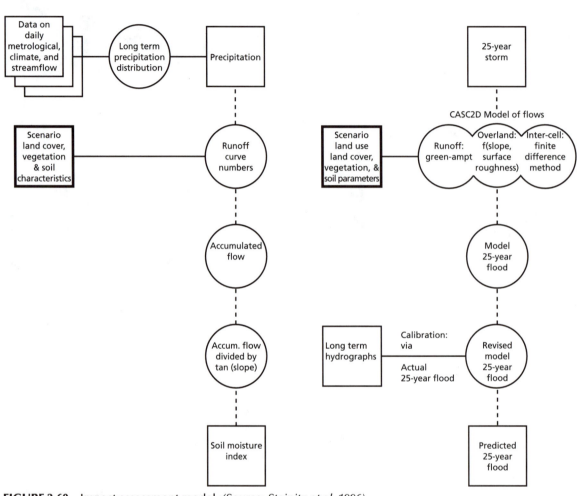

FIGURE 3.60 Impact assessment model. *(Source: Steinitz et al. 1996)*

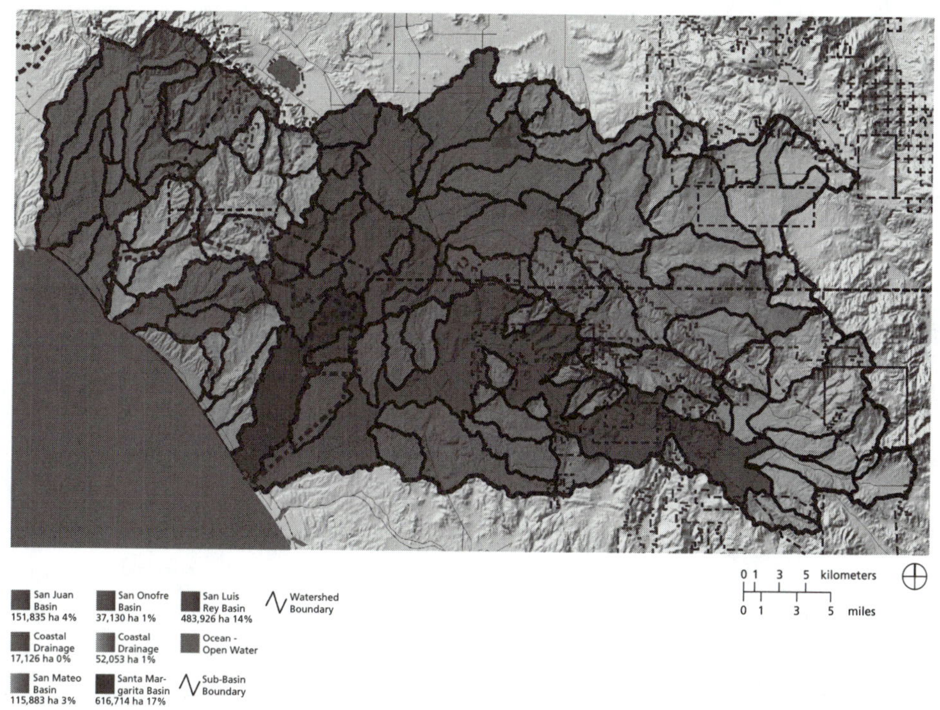

FIGURE 3.61 Drainage subbasin, Camp Pendleton study area. *(Source: Steinitz et al. 1996)*

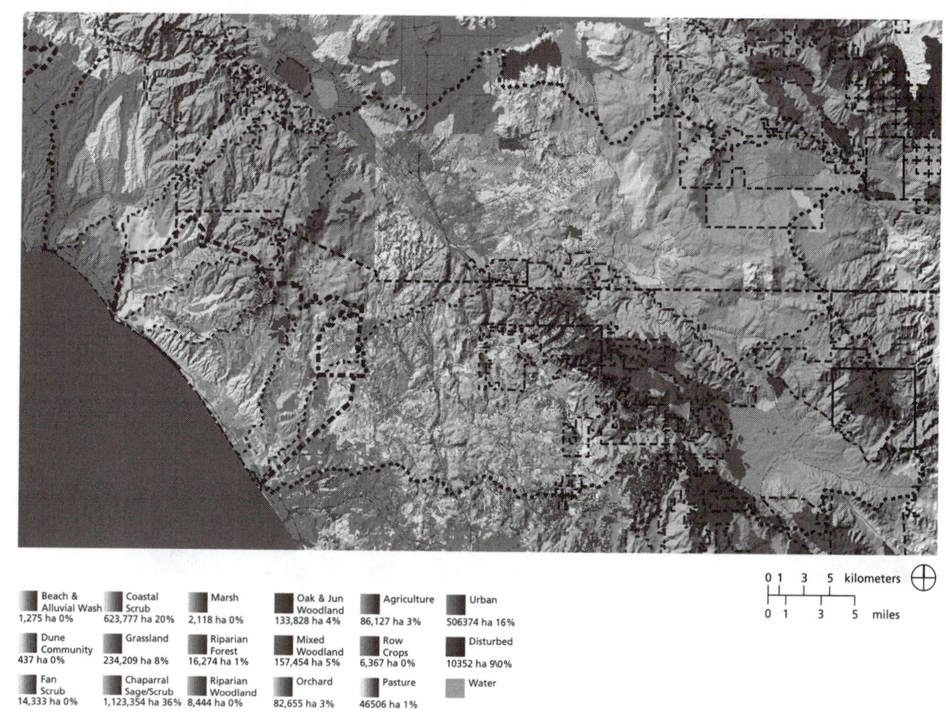

FIGURE 3.62 Vegetation, Camp Pendleton study area. *(Source: Steinitz et al. 1996)*

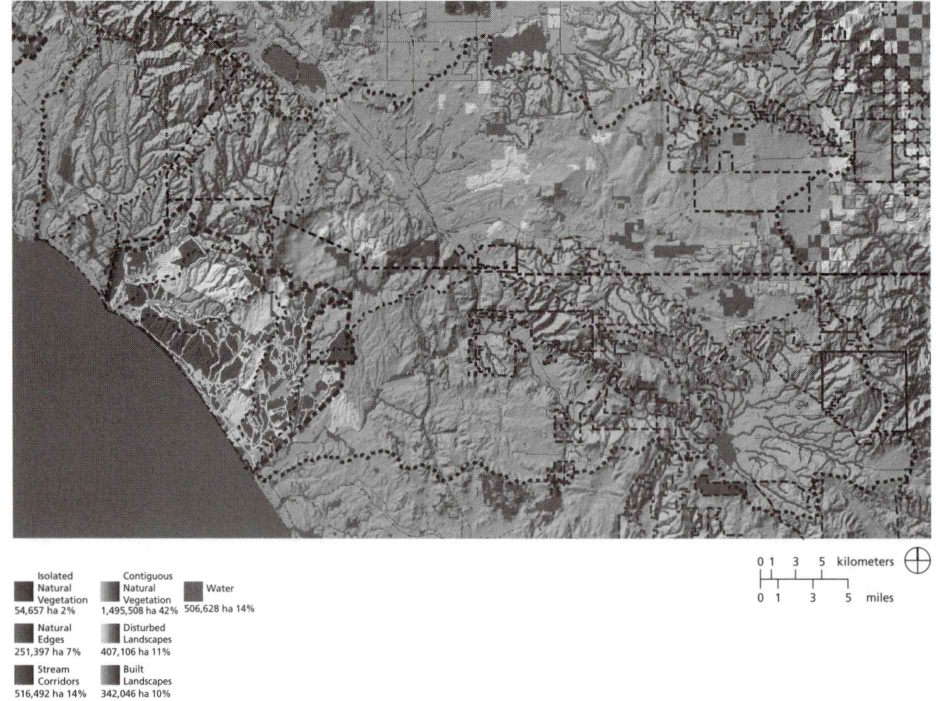

FIGURE 3.63 Landscape ecological patterns, Camp Pendleton study area. *(Source: Steinitz et al. 1996)*

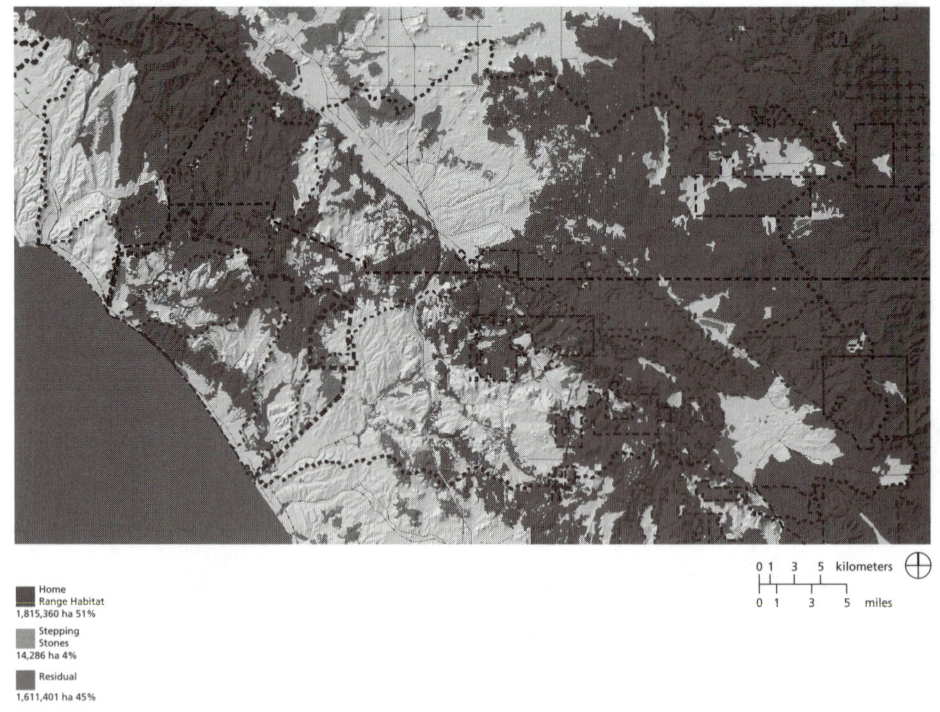

FIGURE 3.64 Cougar home range. *(Source: Steinitz et al. 1996)*

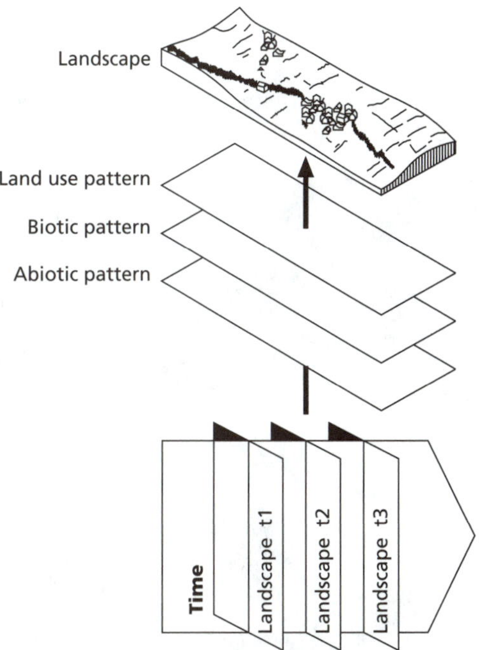

FIGURE 3.65 Landscape in a slice of time. *(Source: Vroom et al. 1980)*

In the Pinelands and in Camp Pendleton such knowledge was directly incorporated into the rest of the planning process. Whereas a more conventional process may have included simple maps or descriptions of selected natural factors, in the Pinelands and in Camp Pendleton a more holistic perspective was taken. In both cases, the relationship of people with nature was carefully considered.

Jon Berger and John Sinton (1985) provide descriptions of how the people of the Pine Barrens are linked to natural factors. Human interaction with these factors is more complex than simply the use of the land. The next chapter explores the elements that need to be collected to understand the human ecology of a place.

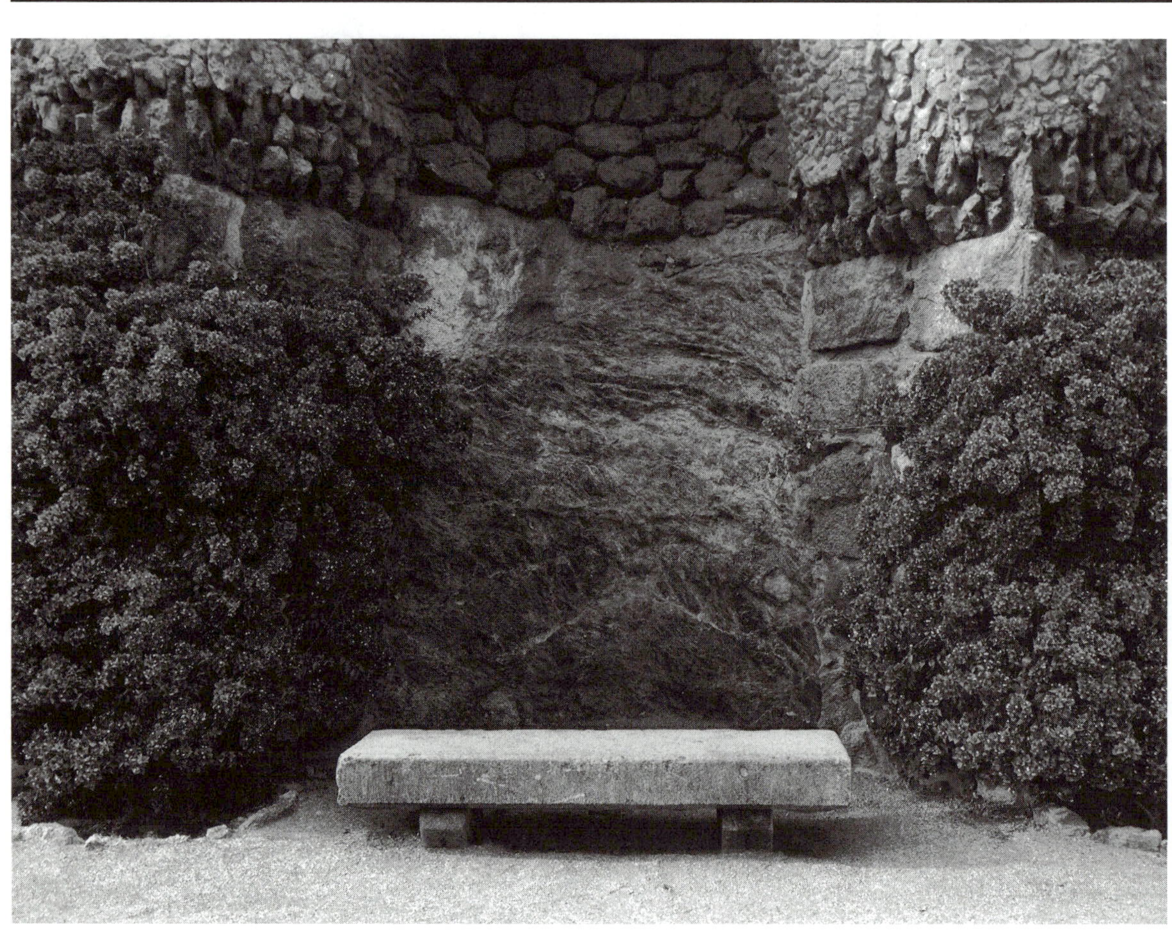

4

HUMAN COMMUNITY INVENTORY AND ANALYSIS

Conventional approaches to planning incorporate surveys of socioeconomic information. However, connecting such studies to landscape ecological analysis for planning is relatively new. In this chapter, those population and economic studies familiar to planners will be reviewed. In addition, a framework for integrating information about people and nature will be presented. Planners use a variety of types of social information, and, basically, these materials fall into three categories: *existing data, new information from existing data,* and *original information.* These data include *quantitative* information—such as the number of people living in an area, as counted by a census. Data also may be more *qualitative*—such as the perceptions of people about the visual impacts of a new roadway or dam.

Different planning projects and programs require different types of social information. For example, a growth management plan requires an estimate of future population, economic, and development trends. This information can be derived from existing sources and is quantitative. Conversely, for the placement of a new electric transmission line, planners need to collect original, qualitative information about perceptions and reactions through interviews with affected residents. Because of the wide variety of planning projects and programs that are possible, a blanket prescription cannot be given for the specific social inventories that should be conducted. The issues that have stimulated the planning process as well as the goals that have been identified to resolve those problems and opportunities will determine the types of data to be collected and analyzed.

An understanding of current and possible future population trends and characteristics will probably be essential for a community to achieve many of its goals. In Oregon, for instance, local governments are required to address specific goals concerning agriculture and housing. As a result, planners must inventory and analyze information concerning trends in farm population (e.g., is it growing or declining?) and characteristics of the agricultural community (e.g., what is the average age of farmers?). Planners must also analyze population trends and characteristics and forecast future possibilities to make recommendations about housing needs.

To accomplish such tasks, planners need to understand local economies. For agriculture, the percentage that farming contributes to the economic base of a community is important to know, as are the most important commodities and their markets. Through an analysis of the local agricultural economy, planners can determine how healthy it is, whether it is worth protecting, and whether intervention is necessary to improve local farming systems. Understanding the economic base of a locality helps planners analyze community needs. If the economic base comprises primary industries (such as farming, fishing, mining, and logging) rather than those of the tertiary sector (such as retail, wholesale, and services), then demands for housing, for instance, will be different. Where primary industries are involved, it may be necessary for dwellings to be relatively close to farmland, the ocean, the mountains, or forests. With tertiary industries, the linkage between home and workplace may be less spatially dependent.

Conventional planning processes have considered and incorporated population and economic studies. But in conventional planning the social characteristics are not always related to the landscape—and this marks a major distinction between conventional approaches and ecologically based planning. In an ecological approach, social processes are connected to landscape features. For instance, agriculture can be related to specific combinations of biophysical elements that vary with crops. Raising wheat requires different climate, water, and soil characteristics than does raising cranberries. Rural housing units have different needs than do high-rise apartments. Different users of the land—cranberry farmers or high-rise apartment dwellers—place different demands on the landscape.

Each human community must be viewed as having unique characteristics. In a major Texas city (Dallas, for instance), a population growth of 1500 people per year may not be dramatic or even a source of concern. But in a rural west-Texas county, the same number of new residents may be quite significant and have consequences for several land uses, especially agriculture and housing. Ranching may have great symbolic value in Dallas, but the number of real cowboys there may be few, while in a west-Texas county, people actively engaged in ranching may constitute the most important economic sector. Certainly, the biophysical processes are different in Dallas than in west Texas. As a result, each place, whether in Texas, Oregon, or New Jersey, must be inventoried and analyzed for its special qualities.

Planners can use many existing sources of information to conduct social inventories. These sources are summarized in the next several paragraphs, and a discussion will follow about how such existing data can be used to generate new information about population, future development, and land users. Some planning efforts may require the generation of original information. Three ways of collecting new information are through surveys, interviews, and participant observation.

Once information has been collected, there is a need to analyze it. Ecological frameworks for analysis include identifying landscape patterns, social interactions, and relationships between people and nature. The inventory and analysis should lead to an assessment of community needs. This chapter presents examples of social inventories and analyses from the New Jersey Pinelands and the Camp Pendleton Region Biodiversity Plan in California.

SOURCES OF EXISTING INFORMATION

Before discussing inventory and analysis methods, the major sources of social information must be identified. Major information sources include maps, histories, census data, newspapers, phone books, community organizations, universities, and public agencies (Table 4.1). Maps are one way to summarize social and economic information. Various maps of social characteristics are now frequently available in both paper and digital formats. Many organizations and agencies maintain websites with current information.

Land-Use Maps and Settlement Pattern Diagrams

Land-use, land-user, and settlement pattern maps were introduced in Chapter 3. Land use and land users are elements of both the biophysical and the sociocultural environments. The best sources include interviews with individuals and associations; observations; the U.S. Natural Resources Conservation Service; city, county, and regional planning agencies; and city and county property tax assessors. School districts; public libraries;

Settlement patterns and land uses vary from place to place. Cracow, Poland.

TABLE 4.1
SUMMARY OF SOURCES OF INFORMATION FOR HUMAN COMMUNITY INVENTORY, ANALYSIS, AND SYNTHESIS

Land-Use Maps and Settlement Pattern Diagrams
1. Interviews with individuals and associations
2. Observation
3. NRCS, USGS
4. City, county, and regional planning agencies
5. City and county tax assessors
6. School districts
7. Public libraries
8. Engineering, landscape architecture, architecture, and planning consulting firms
9. Gas stations
10. The Library of Congress
11. Election boards
12. State departments of commerce and finance
13. Real estate agents
14. Chambers of commerce

Histories
1. Fire insurance maps
2. Public libraries
3. Interviews
4. Local and state historical societies
5. College and university libraries
6. Community college, college, and university departments of history, folklore, geography, and anthropology
7. The Library of Congress
8. Local used bookshops
9. Genealogical societies

Census Data
1. U.S. Bureau of the Census, U.S. Department of Commerce
   ACSD Customer Service
   Washington, D.C. 20233
   301-457-1128
   301-457-3842 (fax)
   http://www.census.gov
2. Agricultural Census, U.S. Department of Agriculture
3. Public utilities
4. Telephone companies
5. Hospital and newspaper birth and death records
6. College and university departments of geography and sociology

Newspapers and Periodicals
1. Local newspapers
2. City, regional, or state magazines and periodicals (for example, *Philadelphia, Boston, New York, Cincinnati, Sunset, Southern Living, Washington, California, High Country News*)
3. Public libraries

Phone Books
The numerous private-advertising phone directories

Community Clubs and Organizations
1. Chambers of commerce
2. League of Women Voters
3. Service clubs
4. Educational organizations
5. Garden clubs
6. Political parties
7. Community or neighborhood associations
8. Fraternal organizations
9. Labor unions and guilds
10. Business and professional associations
11. Scouts and other youth groups
12. Arts associations
13. Churches and synagogues
14. Farmers organizations (for example, the Grange, the Farm Bureau, commodity groups)
15. Nature and conservancy groups
16. Sports clubs
17. Volunteer firemen
18. United Way and Community Chest

Colleges and Universities

Government and Public Agencies
1. City, township, county, and regional agencies
   a. Planning commissions and/or staffs
   b. Councils of government
   c. School boards and administrators
   d. County extension agents
   e. Utility companies
   f. Special-use districts

TABLE 4.1
(Continued)

Government and Public Agencies *(Continued)*

- g. County offices that record land tenure, titles, sales, marriages, divorces, deaths, criminal offenses, and employment
- h. Hospital registers and files
- i. Fire department and emergency services
- j. Police and sheriff offices
- k. Welfare agencies
- l. Health departments
- m. Water and sewer departments, departments of public works
- n. Juvenile delinquency centers
- o. Park and recreation departments
- p. Drug and alcohol counseling centers
- q. Councils on aging
- r. City and/or county prosecutors
- s. Public transit authorities
- t. Recycling centers

2. State (or provincial) agencies
   - a. Elected officials and their staffs
   - b. Departments of planning, education, health, safety, welfare, and natural resources
3. Federal (or national) agencies
   - a. Elected officials and their staffs
   - b. U.S. Department of Housing and Urban Development
   - c. U.S. Department of Energy
   - d. U.S. Department of Education
   - e. U.S. Department of Health and Human Services
   - f. U.S. Department of Commerce
   - g. U.S. Department of Agriculture
   - h. U.S. Department of Transportation
   - i. Environmental Protection Agency
   - j. The Library of Congress
4. International organizations. The United Nations has several programs that may provide helpful information which might be used to put local communities into a global perspective.

private engineering, landscape architecture, and planning consulting firms; gas stations; the Library of Congress; election boards; state departments of state and finance; and real estate agents may all be mapping sources. Aerial photographs constitute another good source; these may be obtained from the NRCS, U.S. Geological Survey, private pilots and air survey companies, and state highway departments.

Histories

A sense of history is vital to the understanding of a community or region. Fire insurance maps, notably those from the Sanborn Map Company, are an especially rich source of information about the historical land use of American communities. Sanborn maps comprise over 300,000 maps of more than 3500 cities and towns in the United States. Sanborn maps were created for the fire insurance industry for risk assessment purposes and date from the early twentieth century to the 1990s. The maps include many land-use details, including street widths, land elevations, water pipes under streets, fire hydrants, open waterways, parks, and railroad tracks.

Many communities have at least one unofficial historian who has compiled an account of past events. Local histories can be gathered through interviews and discussions. Public libraries and local historical societies frequently keep unpublished manuscripts about local events in their archives. As oral histories become more popular, often these may be stored in local libraries or historical societies. State libraries, college and university libraries, and the Library of Congress are also good sources, as are community college, college, and university departments of history, folklore, geography, American studies, and anthropology.

Landscape ecological histories are especially helpful. For example, the San Francisco Estuary Institute spent four years (1994 to 1998) compiling a historical view of the San Francisco Bay circa 1800, as well as a current view (Figure 4.1). This historical view of wetlands and other surface waters is based upon eighteenth, nineteenth, and

FIGURE 4.1 1800 view (left) and current view (right) of San Francisco Bay. *(Source: San Francisco Estuary Institute)*

Napa
Fairfield
Petaluma
Novato
San Rafael
Concord
Richmond
Oakland
San Francisco
Hayward
San Mateo
Fremont
Redwood City
San Jose
Deep Bay/Channel
Shallow Bay/Channel
Tidal Flat
Tidal Marsh
Tidal Marsh Pan
Lagoon
Agricultural Bayland
Diked Wetland
Salt Pond
Storage or Treatment Pond
Undeveloped Bay Fill
Developed Bay Fill
Riparian Forest/Willow Grove
Moist Grassland
Grassland/Vernal Pool Complex
River or Creek
SCALE 1:465,000
0 2 4 6 8 Miles
0 4 8 Kilometers
Bay Area EcoAtlas ©1999 SFEI

twentieth-century maps, sketches, paintings, photographs, engineering reports, oral histories, explorers' journals, missionary texts, hunting magazines, interviews with living elders, and other sources (Grossinger et al. 1998).

A similar approach has been taken by Paola Falini in Italy (Falini et al. 1980; Falini 1997). She has adapted the urban morphological approach of Saverio Muratori for landscapes and produced historical maps documenting Italian cities from the times of the Romans through the Renaissance and Industrial Revolution to the present. Such landscape histories can help illustrate how humans have modified places through time.

Census Data

The Bureau of the Census, administered by the U.S. Department of Commerce, is the finest single source of demographic information in the United States. A national census is undertaken the first year of every decade. These censuses include vital information about age and sex composition, birth and death statistics, ethnic composition, rural/urban distribution, migration, general population characteristics, housing, and general economic characteristics, such as employment and income. There is more thorough information available for metropolitan statistical areas (MSAs) than for rural regions. Census information is available in published reports and over the Internet.

A review of specialized census information, *Census Catalog and Guide,* is published annually by the Bureau of the Census. The Census Bureau also provides computerized geographical data. These TIGER line files include information about streets, rivers, railroads, jurisdictional boundaries, and census tracts (Peck 1998). Geographically census information is organized by blocks, block groups, and tracts. Additional socioeconomic information may be obtained from the agricultural census of the U.S. Department of Agriculture. State and regional agencies as well as colleges and universities act as clearinghouses or storage centers for census data. The use of census data will be discussed later in this chapter.

Newspapers and Periodicals

Local newspapers and regional magazines can reveal much about a community or region. Both daily and weekly newspapers can be rich sources of information about local happenings. Some of the information that can be found in local newspapers includes different perspectives on local issues, employment opportunities, the availability of real estate, and the activities of voluntary organizations and civic groups. By reading past newspaper articles and keeping an ongoing clipping file, a planner can track opinions about issues and learn something about trends in employment and real estate.

An ever-growing number of magazines may help to establish the vernacular character of regions. Some of these magazines, such as *Philadelphia, New York, Boston,* and *Cincinnati,* focus on an individual city. Others, like *California, Washington, Sunset, Southern Living, New West,* and *Rocky Mountain,* address a state or broader region. A wonderful biweekly newspaper focusing on western environmental issues is *High Country News* of Paonia, Colorado. If a planner is new to a region or is a consultant from some other place, then this type of periodical can provide some information about the character of the planning area.

Phone Books

The yellow, white, and blue pages of phone books each contain much information about the communities they serve. The yellow pages provide an index of industry, commerce, and services in the area. The white pages provide a source for family names, which may reveal some information about ethnic heritage. The locations of ethnic neighborhoods may also be identified. The blue pages, which include government listings, often include a map of the area served by the phone book and a brief history of the area. In addition, local place and street names can be learned from phone books.

Community Organizations and Clubs

Many people join organizations or clubs to associate with people of similar interests. They may also attend a particular church, synagogue, mosque, or temple. Thus the social and religious clubs and organizations found in a community reveal much about how the people there spend their leisure time, what their political and religious beliefs are, and what the nature of their employment is. In addition to the phone book, good sources of lists of community organizations and clubs are usually the local chamber of commerce, the League of Women Voters, and religious institutions. A list of community organizations and clubs with names and addresses may be useful if the planner is developing a mailing list to send newsletters or other information about the planning program. Such a list can offer information about the scope of community activities in the planning area. For some planning programs and projects, it may be necessary to interview representatives from these groups, which is discussed later in this chapter.

Colleges and Universities

The two main sources of cultural information in colleges and universities are their libraries and individual faculty members. Faculty in departments of sociology, anthropology, economics, planning, geography, business, African-American studies, ethnic studies, education, home economics, history, political science, landscape architecture, and law should be able to provide information about the sociocultural characteristics of an area. Other members of academic communities, such as librarians and registrars, may be helpful additional information sources. The extension services of land-grant and sea-grant universities often publish bulletins with socioeconomic profiles of counties and cities.

Government and Public Agencies

Government and public agencies collect and store a wealth of material about communities. Usually, however, there is a lack of coordination between the various agencies, which means that information must be collected, analyzed, and put into a format with meaning for the particular studies. All levels of government—local, regional, state, and national—are good sources. International organizations may be a useful resource for some planning studies.

Synopsis of Information Sources

Paper and digital maps, histories, census data, newspapers and periodicals, phone books, community organizations and clubs, colleges and universities, and government agencies can yield much information for inventories of human communities. Maps are important for understanding the spatial organization of the planning area. Planners also may need maps to study the relationship of social systems to natural patterns. Histories inform the planner about the past of the place—when it was settled and why. Newspapers and periodicals can help the planner to confirm or deny the issues that have been identified as well as to learn what individuals or groups have an interest in the issue. Phone books reveal much about who lives and works in the area. Community and government organizations represent the official social structure of the planning area. Universities and colleges provide a bank of information about the place—its history, its social organization, and its culture.

USE OF EXISTING DATA TO GENERATE NEW INFORMATION

The identification of existing sources of information is just the beginning of a social inventory and analysis. These existing data form the basis for the generation of new information about the people and economy of a community. Information that is widely available includes population data, development projections, economic analyses, and land-use classification which suggests who are using the land.

Population Trends, Characteristics, and Projections

Three types of population studies are important in planning for the future: *trends, characteristics,* and *projections.* Population trends include changes in numbers, location, and components of people. Population characteristics include age and gender composition, birth statistics, death statistics, ethnic composition, distribution, migration, and population pyramids. Generally, this information is available from the U.S. Census. Other sources may also need to be studied; these include the records of county and city governments, hospitals, newspapers, phone companies, public utilities, councils of government, and state agencies. Projection techniques include the cohort-survival model, geometric interpolation, and simulation models. In this section, the Desert View Tri-Villages will be used as an example of population studies that were conducted as part of a planning process.

Trends. Planners study population trends to learn how the planning area has changed over time. Whether the population has been growing or declining will be important to know in many planning programs and projects. If a goal of the planning effort is to encourage economic development, then the planner will want to know whether the area is growing or declining, in order to devise business recruitment strategies. If growth management is a goal, then trends give an indication of how many people have moved to the area and when. If the development of new facilities is involved (schools and parks, for instance), then population trends reveal past demand for these services.

Phoenix is located in Maricopa County, Arizona, one of the fastest-growing regions in the United States. At the end of the Second World War, Phoenix had 100,000 residents; now it has well over a million and is the sixth-largest city in the nation. From 1980 to 1997, the population of Phoenix increased from 798,704 to 1,205,285, a 53 percent increase. In the 1940s Maricopa County was home to 186,193 residents; by 1995 over 2.4 million people lived there. Table 4.2 illustrates population trends in Maricopa County from 1940 to 1990, as interpreted from the 1990 census. This table includes the city of Phoenix and the three census tracts that comprise the Desert View Tri-Villages Area. Comparisons with neighboring jurisdictions, in this case nearby cities and towns, and with a larger entity, in this case the city of Phoenix, help to show how the planning area relates to other places. The table shows a slower growth for the Tri-Villages than other areas of the metropolitan regions, but this situation has changed dramatically since 1990 and will continue to change into the future.

Population trends may also show shifts in the location of people from urban to rural or from rural to urban areas. These changes have been dramatic since the Second World War. As demographers and planners have noted, continued suburbanization, regional redistribution, and rural repopulation are the three major trends shaping population settlement in the United States and other developed nations (Nelson 1992; Long 1981; Wardwell and Gilchrist 1980). For example, whereas Maricopa County grew by 41 percent between 1980 and 1990 (and another 22.7 percent between 1990 and 1997, according to Gober 1998), rural population growth was only seven percent, while urban areas grew by 42 percent (Table 4.3). Globally, the redistribution of people in nonmetropolitan areas has a dramatic impact on energy use, the conversion of important farmland, coastal management, and the protection of environmentally sensitive areas. In Maricopa County, the dramatic population growth

TABLE 4.2
MARICOPA COUNTY POPULATION BY DECADE

	1940	1950	Change	1960	Change	1970	Change	1980	Change	1990	Change
Maricopa County	186,193	331,770	78.2	663,510	100.0	971,228	45.8	1,509,175	56.0	2,122,101	40.61
% of state population	37.29	44.26	156.09	50.95	135.69	54.70	127.22	55.55	104.67	57.90	4.22
Phoenix	65,414	106,818	63.3	439,170	311.1	584,303	32.4	789,704	35.8	983403	24.53
% of county population	35.13	32.20	80.95	66.19	311.10	60.16	70.74	52.33	63.93	46.34	-11.44
Desert View Tri-Villages						7,658		16,057	109.7	19,472	21.27
Census Tract 303.33						7,658		6,137		7,350	19.77
Census Tract 303.42								9,920		8,014	
Census Tract 303.43										4,108	
Carefree						1,285		964		1,666	72.82
Cave Creek								1,712		2,925	70.85
Fountain Hills								2,771		10,030	261.96
Glendale	4,855	8,179	68.5	15,686	91.9	36,228	127.9	97,172	168.2	148134	52.45
Scottsdale		2,032		10,026	393.4	67,823	576.5	88,412	30.4	130,069	47.12
Pima County	72,838	141,216	93.9	265,660	88.1	351,667	32.4	531,443	51.5	666,880	25.48
Pinal County	28,841	43,191	49.8	62,673	45.1	68,579	8.4	90,918	33.9	116,379	28.00
State	499,261	749,587	50.1	1,302,161	73.7	1,775,399	36.0	2,716,546	53.5	3,665,228	34.92

SOURCES: U.S. Bureau of Census 1950, 1960, 1970, 1980, and 1990; Arizona Department of Commerce, Community Profile 1998.

Note: Fountain Hills is a planned, family-oriented community established in 1970. Before 1970, the area was a cattle ranch and part of one of the largest cattle holdings in Arizona. Therefore, we record the data beginning from 1980.

From 1940 to 1970 the census tracts 303.33, 303,42, and 303.43 all merge into one census tract 303. However the aforementioned three census tracts occupy more than about 80% of the tract 303 area. Plus tract 303 is north of the Bell Road and had a very low population density in 1970. We apply the whole tract 303's population to represent the Desert View Tri-Village Area.

TABLE 4.3
URBAN AND RURAL POPULATION, 1950–1990

	Maricopa County			Pima County			Pinal County			State		
	Total	Urban	Rural	Total	Urban	Rural	Total	Urban	Rural	Total	Urban	Rural
1950	331,770	237,983	93,787	141,216	78,307	62,909	43,191	12,067	31,124	749,587	416,000	333,587
% of total	100.00	71.73	28.27	100.00	55.45	44.55	100.00	27.94	72.06	100.00	55.50	44.50
1960	663,510	574,204	89,306	265,660	234,482	31,178	62,673	27,599	35,074	1,302,161	970,616	331,545
% change	99.99	141.28	-4.78	88.12	199.44	-50.44	45.11	128.71	12.69	73.72	133.32	-0.61
% of total	100.00	86.54	13.46	100.00	88.26	11.74	100.00	44.04	55.96	100.00	74.54	25.46
1970	967,522	903,797	63,725	351,667	300,065	51,602	67,916	32,704	35,212	1,770,900	1,408,864	362,036
% change	45.82	57.40	-28.64	32.37	27.97	65.51	8.37	18.50	0.39	36.00	45.15	9.20
% of total	100.00	93.41	6.59	100.00	85.33	14.67	100.00	48.15	51.85	100.00	79.56	20.44
1980	1,509,052	1,437,392	71,660	531,443	468,810	62,663	90,918	54,077	36,841	2,718,215	2,278,728	439,487
% change	55.97	59.04	12.45	51.12	56.24	21.44	33.87	65.35	4.63	53.49	61.74	21.39
% of total	100.00	95.25	4.75	100.00	88.21	11.79	100.00	59.48	40.52	100.00	83.83	16.17
1990	2,122,101	2,045,271	76,830	666,880	616,367	50,513	116,379	68,903	47,476	3,665,228	3,206,973	458,255
% change	40.62	42.29	7.21	25.48	31.47	-19.39	28.00	27.42	28.87	34.84	40.74	4.27
% of total	100.00	96.38	3.62	100.00	92.43	7.57	100.00	59.21	40.79	100.00	87.50	12.50

SOURCE: U.S. Bureau of Census 1990.

has come mostly at the expense of irrigated farmlands and increasingly fragile desert areas.

Another element of population trends is the components of change. Components of change include changing birth, death, and migration rates. Birth and death rates are natural trends, while migration rates are due to factors such as changes in employment opportunities. Table 4.4 shows components of change in Maricopa County from 1950 to 1990.

Characteristics. Planners study population characteristics to learn about who is living in the planning area. If the planning issue involves economic development, then the planner will want to know about the labor force. If growth management is a goal of the process, then population density becomes important. Age distribution is crucial to know if the planning issue relates to schools or parks.

Density, population distribution, dependency ratios, and labor force participation are important in Maricopa County planning. Density is one characteristic of population, and is determined by dividing the total population by the total area. Table 4.5 compares the density of Maricopa County with that of Pima and Pinal Counties. The Maricopa County population density of 230.6 persons per square mile (88.8 per square kilometer) can be contrasted to that of the Netherlands (1,086 people per square mile, or 419 per square kilometer) or Alaska (1.0 people per square mile, or 0.4 per square kilometer).

Population densities need to be considered for the specific issue being addressed by a plan. For example, when only the urban portions of Maricopa County are considered, the density increases to 669 persons per square mile (258.3 per square kilometer). For some situations, the densities of an entire jurisdiction may be necessary to consider. In other cases, either the urban area or the rural area only may be important.

Age and gender distribution are characteristics of population. A popular method of displaying this information is the population pyramid, such as Figure 4.2. Because of the number of retirees in the Phoenix region, Maricopa County exhibits an increase in older cohorts whereas in most parts of the United States there is a decline. Also note on Figure 4.2 the number of women in the highest age bracket, reflecting their longevity compared to males.

Racial and ethnic distribution are those characteristics that reveal how many and where minority people live. Special care should be taken to get an accurate count of minorities, since they have been traditionally undercounted in the U.S. Census. Some racial and minority categories used by the Bureau of the Census and planners include *white* (*excluding Spanish surname*), *white* (*Spanish surname*), *black, American Indian, Asian, mixed ethnic background,* and *other.*

Dependency ratios refer to those portions of the population outside the wage-earning range group. Such ratios are determined by dividing the sum of those in the 0 through 19 age group and those over 65 years old by those from 20 through 64. Table 4.6 illustrates dependency ratios for Maricopa, Pima, and Pinal counties and for the state of Arizona.

Another characteristic of population that is useful is the labor force participation rate (Table 4.7). This is determined by dividing the number of people in the labor force by the total population. As can be seen from Table 4.7, the participation rate in the labor force of Cave Creek, near the Desert View Tri-Villages Area, is higher than the state average. It may also help to show age and sex distributions in the work force (Table 4.8). Men and women in the 25 to 54 year age group comprise the majority of the Maricopa County labor force.

Projections. Planners make projections to forecast who will be living in the area. As an employee of a municipal, county, or state agency, the planner may be responsible for making the projections. Planning consultants may rely on these projections or, depending on the project or

TABLE 4.4
COMPONENTS OF POPULATION CHANGE IN MARICOPA COUNTY, 1950–1990

		Net Population Change		Components of Change			
	Population	Number	%	Natural Increase*	Rate⁺	Net Migration	Rate⁺
1950	331,770						
1960	663,510	331,740	99.99	96,049	28.95	235,691	71.04
1970	971,228	307,718	46.38	111,790	16.85	195,928	29.53
1980	1,509,175	537,947	55.39	117,813	12.13	420,134	43.26
1990	2,122,101	612,926	40.61	200,290	13.27	412,636	27.34

Net Migration = Net Population Change Number – Natural Increase
Natural increase* = births – deaths
⁺Rate per 1,000
SOURCES: U.S. Bureau of Census 1950, 1960, 1970, 1980a, 1990; The University of Arizona, Arizona Statistical Abstract 1990; Arizona Department of Health Service, Arizona Health Status and Vital Statistics 1996.

program, make new forecasts. If there is an economic development goal, then it is crucial to know whether new people are likely to move into the planning area. Growth management involves allocating places for new residents to live. The number of new people will determine how many new schools and parks are necessary. Conversely, if population projections indicate decline, then different economic development and facility planning strategies will be called for.

There are several methods for projecting population. Those methods most familiar to planners include the *cohort-survival* model, *multiple regression* model, and *simulation* model (Kaiser et al. 1995; Chapin and Kaiser 1979; Hightower 1968). The assumptions that planners make in

TABLE 4.5
POPULATION DENSITY, 1990

		Total Land Area		Density	
	Population	Mi^2	Km^2	Persons/mi^2	Persons/km^2
Maricopa	2,122,101	9,204.0	23,838.5	230.6	89.0
Pima	666,880	9,187.0	23,794.3	72.6	28.0
Pinal	116,379	5,370.0	13,908.3	21.7	8.4
STATE	3,665,228	113,642.2	294,333.4	32.3	12.5

Note: Density is computed using land area.
SOURCE: U.S. Bureau of the Census 1990.

Age group	Total of all persons	Male	%	Female	%
75+	108,630	41,728	1.97	66,902	3.15
70 - 74	71,088	31,309	1.48	39,779	1.87
65 - 69	85,539	38,025	1.79	47,514	2.24
60 - 64	81,617	37,494	1.77	44,123	2.08
55 - 59	80,724	38,815	1.83	41,909	1.97
50 - 54	89,632	43,528	2.05	46,104	2.17
45 - 49	114,248	56,273	2.65	57,975	2.73
40 - 44	147,121	73,033	3.44	74,088	3.49
35 - 39	167,557	84,088	3.96	83,469	3.93
30 - 34	193,788	98,235	4.63	95,553	4.50
25 - 29	199,380	101,593	4.79	97,787	4.61
20 - 24	164,561	84,886	4.00	79,675	3.75
15 - 19	144,889	74,632	3.52	70,257	3.31
10 - 14	143,550	73,486	3.46	70,064	3.30
5 - 9	159,595	81,589	3.84	78,006	3.68
Under 5 years	170,182	87,064	4.10	83,118	3.92
Total	2,122,101	1,045,778	49.28	1,076,323	50.72

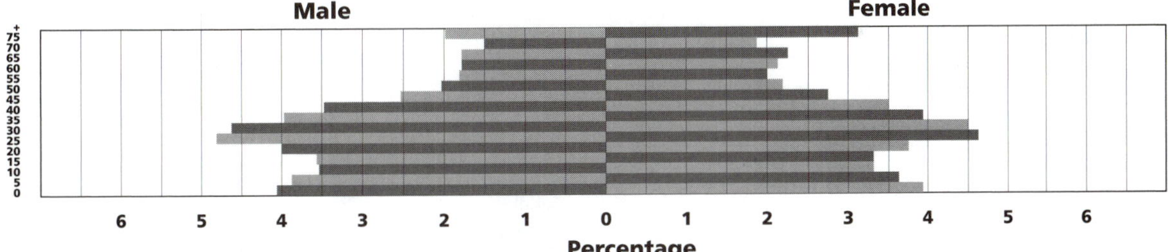

FIGURE 4.2 Maricopa County population distribution by age and gender. *(Source: Adapted from U.S. Census information)*

making projections (for example, future household size) constitute a critical factor in all of the methods.

Three main components are considered when using the cohort-survival model: (1) fertility, (2) mortality, and (3) net migration (Figure 4.3). The natural-increase segment of cohort survival determines the projected number of births by applying fertility rates to the female population of childbearing age. Each population group is then "sur-

TABLE 4.6
DEPENDENCY RATIOS, 1990

	Dependency Ratios*
Maricopa County	**0.473**
Pima County	**0.500**
Pinal County	**0.566**
STATE	**0.504**

*Dependency ratios = population of 9 to 19 age group + population of those over 64 years divided by population of 20 to 64 age group.
SOURCE: U.S. Bureau of the Census 1990.

TABLE 4.7
POPULATION IN THE LABOR FORCE (16 YEARS AND OLDER) BY CENSUS COUNTY DIVISIONS, 1990

Census County Divisions	Labor Force	Population Over 16	Labor Force Participation Rate
Maricopa County	1,079,401	1,623,198	66.50
Buckeye division	5,496	8,506	64.61
Chandler division	48,009	68,663	69.92
Deer Valley division	18,495	29,119	63.52
Gila Bend division	2,334	3,531	66.10
Phoenix division	995,611	1,480,861	67.23
St. Johns division	749	1,766	42.41
Salt River division	1,896	3,749	50.57
Tonto division	536	1,272	42.14
Wickenburg division	6,275	25,615	24.50
Cave Creek	1,586	2,349	67.52
Phoenix	517,387	743,781	69.56
Pima County	320,208	518,088	61.81
Pinal County	44,467	85,246	52.16
STATE	1,753,478	2,785,730	62.95

SOURCE: U.S. Bureau of the Census 1990.
Note: The labor force includes all persons classified in the civilian labor force (employed and unemployed) plus members of the U.S. Armed Forces.

TABLE 4.8
PERCENTAGE IN LABOR FORCE BY SEX AND AGE, 1990

	Maricopa		Pima		Pinal		Arizona	
Age group	Number in labor force	%	Number in labor force	%	Number in labor force	%	Number in labor force	%
Male:								
16-19 years	35,059	3.25	9,750	3.04	1,618	3.64	57,823	3.30
20-24	70,825	6.56	21,480	6.71	2,788	6.27	115,629	6.59
25-54	425,302	39.40	122,703	38.32	17,968	40.41	686,581	39.16
55-64	49,691	4.60	15,002	4.69	2,756	6.20	84,814	4.84
65+	15,784	1.46	4,686	1.46	607	1.37	26,499	1.51
Female:								
16-19 years	30,154	2.79	9,869	3.08	1,101	2.48	50,272	2.87
20-24	58,735	5.44	18,327	5.72	1,734	3.90	94,034	5.36
25-54	346,160	32.07	102,770	32.09	13,554	30.48	555,968	31.71
55-64	36,932	3.42	11,972	3.74	1,776	3.99	63,047	3.60
65+	10,759	1.00	3,649	1.14	565	1.27	18,811	1.07
Total	1,079,401	100.00	320,208	100.00	44,467	100.00	1,753,478	100.00

SOURCE: U.S. Bureau of the Census 1990.

vived"; that is, an appropriate mortality rate is applied to each five-year period. These steps provide an estimate of future population if it were to grow by natural increase alone, with no in-or-out migration. The net migration rate is then considered, usually based on past trends. Multiple regression has been used primarily as a supplement to cohort-survival models. Statistical simulation models involve the use of a sample to project larger trends.

Depending on the project or program, a planning team may make its own projections, or it may use existing projections from various sources. As its name indicates, the Tri-Villages Area is divided by the city into three parts (Figure 4.4). The city has used estimates from the Maricopa Association of Governments (MAG), which derives its data from traffic analysis zones (TAZ). Table 4.9 displays the estimates for the three areas.

In collecting information about population trends, characteristics, and projections, one can ask several questions, including (adapted, in part, from Duane 1996):

- What were the historical patterns of population growth or decline?
- What were the primary factors driving population growth or decline over the past quarter-century?

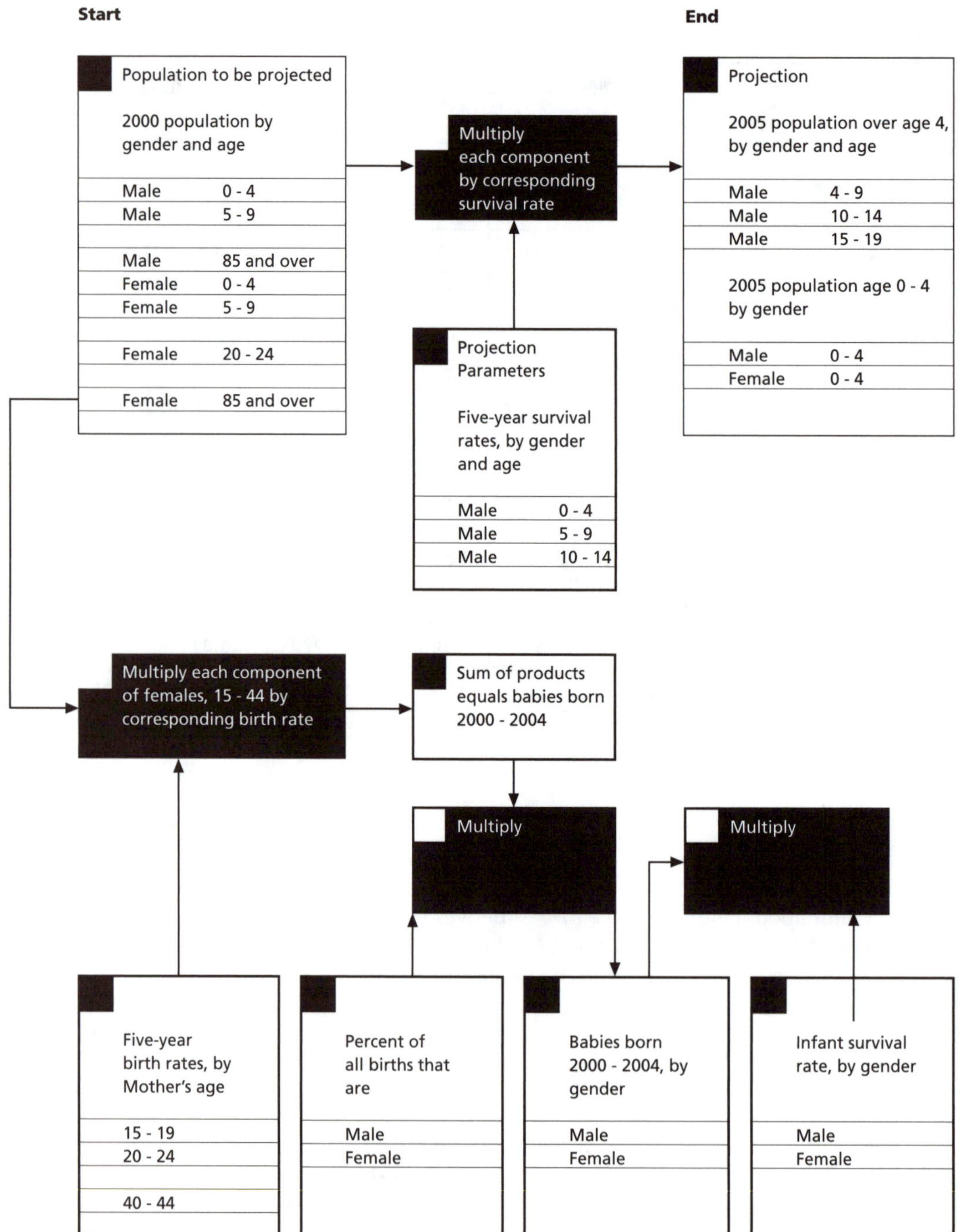

FIGURE 4.3 Procedure used for the cohort-survival model. *(Source: Adapted from Hightower 1968)*

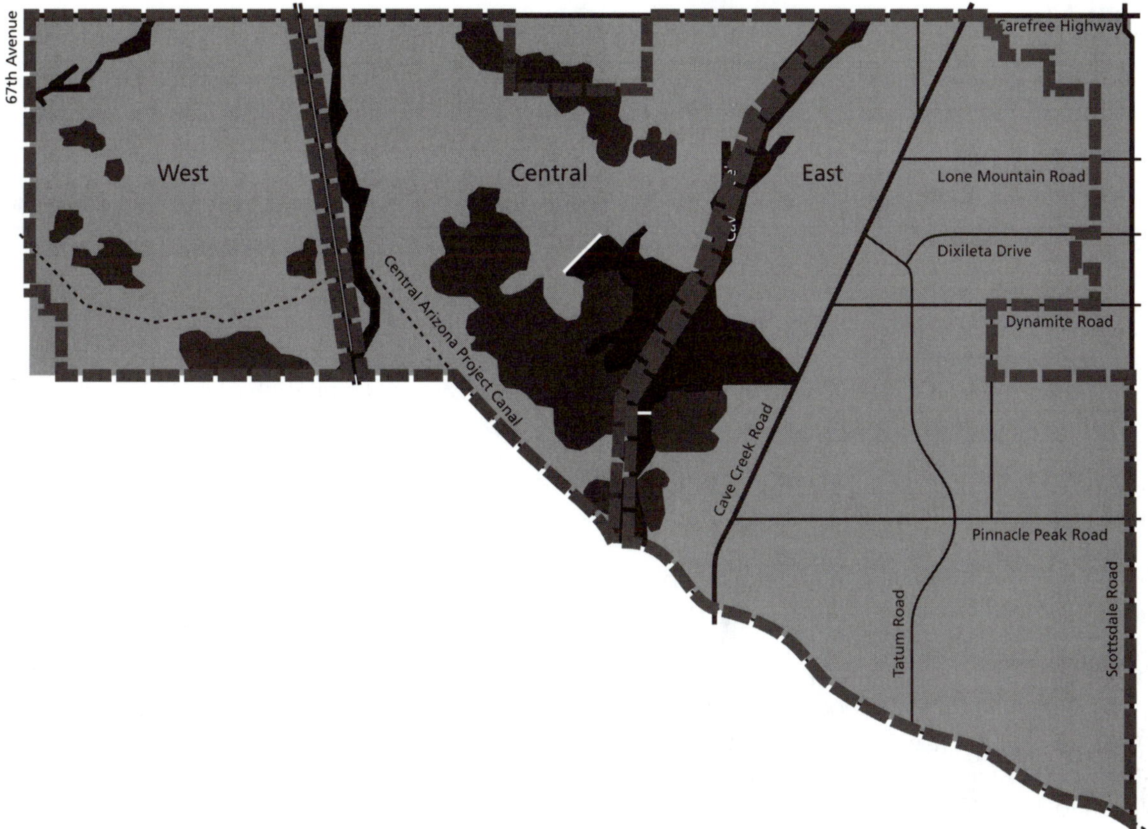

FIGURE 4.4 West, Central, and East Villages of the Desert View Tri-Villages Area. *(Source: Adapted from Ciekot et al. 1995)*

- What are the ecological, social, and economic consequences of projected population growth or decline?
- What is the current spatial pattern of population distribution and housing density by density class?
- What are the relationships between development densities and other census variables?

Development Projections

For many situations, it is necessary for planners to make development projections based on population studies. If a community is preparing a growth management plan, for instance, then local officials will want to know how much new housing and commercial building will be needed to accommodate the new people. Projections can be made for future development needs based on the relationship between population increase and residential building permits.

For example, according to the records of a county for the past 10 years, the population increase for each building permit issued has remained between two and four people per permit. To project the number of additional building permits in future years, a ratio of three people to each permit may be chosen. An

TABLE 4.9
POPULATION AND POPULATION PROJECTIONS

Year	1990	1995	2000	2005	2010	2015	2020	2025	2030	2035	2040	2045	2050
West	139	150	239	1471	6773	12892	19874	27829	36354	43100	48148	53659	60407
Central	182	354	1884	3718	3851	6762	7621	12798	19060	25375	32158	39014	46214
East	2230	7444	13550	34206	59290	81880	100735	116837	135108	153796	169081	179134	182988
Total	**2551**	**7948**	**15673**	**39394**	**69914**	**101534**	**128230**	**157464**	**190522**	**222271**	**249287**	**271807**	**289609**

SOURCE: City of Phoenix 1995, adapted from Ciekot et al. 1995.

assumption is made that the additional building permits correspond with the number of additional housing units. The ratio of three people per building permit then can be divided by the population increase projected from one period to the next.

City of Phoenix planners have estimated the future numbers of dwelling units (Table 4.10) and the future nonresidential square footage (Table 4.11) for the three subareas of the Tri-Villages. In 1987, a build-out population for the area was estimated to be between 335,000 and 350,000, with 80,000 to 90,000 new jobs (City of Phoenix 1987). A subsequent estimate lowered the population to 290,000 (City of Phoenix 1995). Overall the Phoenix metropolitan region is adding about 63,000 residents a year, who require about 23,000 new housing units (McCarthy et al. 1995).

Table 4.10 illustrates the dwelling unit projections for the Tri-Villages Area (Ciekot et al. 1995). The city has assumed the density in the area to be from less than 1 dwelling per acre (2.5 DU/hectare) to 15 DU/acre (37.5 DU/hectare), with an average of 4 DU/acre (10 DU/hectare) and 2.5 persons per dwelling (Ciekot et al. 1995, based on City of Phoenix data). As a result, 15,700 acres (6,280 hectares) of land will be consumed by residential land use according to these projections. This is the equivalent to 25 square miles (64.72 kilometers^2) or 23 percent of the Tri-Villages Area as it existed in 1995 (Ciekot et al. 1995). The city has also estimated the amount of land needed for public facilities, parks, libraries, fire and police stations, community centers, and schools, based on the estimates in Table 4.9.

Land is only one resource to consider when making development projections. Especially in the western United States, water availability is also a crucial consideration. There may be enough suitable land available for new development, but not enough water to supply to new residents. Arizona state law requires a guaranteed 100-year water supply before new development can be permitted. Even though Phoenix is located in an arid region, there is ample water to support new development in the Desert View Tri-Villages Area. However, the projected amounts of water necessary vary, depending on the amount used per household. For example, the amount of water necessary for an irrigated lawn is much higher than one with desert plants. In addition, the water supply does not account for off-site environmental impacts of its use.

In some areas limitations in other public services, such as sewer capacity or road budgets, might constrain development. Like land and water, the levels necessary will vary depending on assumptions about future use. For example, different road widths can be used to estimate a range of projected costs. The topics of environmental and fiscal impact assessment will be addressed in Chapter 11.

Development projections can lead to several questions about a planning area, such as (adapted, in part, from Duane 1996):

TABLE 4.10
DWELLING UNITS AND DWELLING UNIT PROJECTIONS

Year	1990	1995	2000	2005	2010	2015	2020	2025	2030	2035	2040	2045	2050
West	56	60	96	588	2709	5157	7950	14344	16981	19001	21205	23802	26612
Central	73	142	754	1487	1540	2705	3048	5119	7624	10150	12863	15606	18486
East	892	2978	5420	13682	23716	32752	40294	46735	54043	61518	67632	71654	73195
Total	**1021**	**3180**	**6270**	**15757**	**27965**	**40614**	**51292**	**66198**	**78648**	**90675**	**101700**	**111062**	**118293**

SOURCE: City of Phoenix 1995, adapted from Ciekot et al. 1995.

TABLE 4.11
NONRESIDENTIAL SQUARE FOOTAGE PROJECTIONS IN 1000s

Year	1990	1995	2000	2005	2010	2015	2020	2025	2030	2035	2040	2045	2050
West	3	3	3	3	33	393	208	353	1123	1915	2965	4245	4930
East	0	5	5	105	110	410	930	1120	2320	2900	3380	4385	5030
Central	0	3	248	800	1400	2560	5250	5865	7820	8623	9597	9892	10187
Total	**3**	**11**	**259**	**908**	**1543**	**3063**	**6388**	**7338**	**11263**	**13438**	**15942**	**18522**	**20147**

SOURCE: City of Phoenix 1995, adapted from Ciekot et al. 1995.

- What is the likely spatial distribution of future population growth or decline?
- What are the relationships between development patterns and infrastructure access and costs?
- What are the relationships between development patterns and environmentally sensitive areas?
- What are the infrastructure needs and available financing mechanisms to support future development?

Economic Analyses

The first step in an economic study is to determine the economic base of the planning area. Some of the common sources of economic information are listed in Table 4.12. An economic base survey may be necessary where such data are not described in existing sources. A survey may be a preferred source if published information is out of date or if more detailed data are needed. If a new economic survey is conducted, then existing information will provide the initial data base. Lay Gibson suggested the following outline for conducting an economic base survey:

1. *The base area.* Determine the base area. For a planning study this would follow the boundaries for the established planning area.
2. *The measure of magnitude.* Use existing employment figures to show where the area's economy is based. Dollar value of sales, income, or some other measure may also be used.
3. *The labor force.* All public and private sector employers should be surveyed. Additionally, it is probably wise to interview at least the largest employers outside the study area if they provide substantial employment opportunities for residents of the planning area. It may be assumed that they are, functionally if not physically, part of the local economic base.

TABLE 4.12
COMMON SOURCES OF ECONOMIC INFORMATION

U.S. Government

Bureau of the Census
- Census of Population (printed copies and summary tape files)
- Current Population Report
- Census of Housing
- Annual Housing Survey
- Census of Retail Trade (years ending on 2 and 7)
- Census of Manufactures (years ending on 2 and 7)
- Census of Wholesale Trade (years ending on 2 and 7)
- Census of Service Industries (years ending on 2 and 7)
- Census of Mineral Industries (years ending on 2 and 7)
- Census of Transportation (years ending on 2 and 7)
- Census of Construction Industries (years ending on 2 and 7)
- Survey of Minority-Owned Businesses
- Survey of Women-Owned Businesses
- Census of Governments
- County Business Pattern
- Bureau of Census Catalog (annual: describes all reports and data files issued during the year)

Internal Revenue Service
- Statistics of income: Individual income tax returns

Bureau of Economic Analysis (BEA)
- *Survey of Current Business* (Magazine containing information about national income, federal deficit, and other economic news. Periodic changes in how national income is defined are also published in this magazine.)
- BEA Regional Projections
- Local Area Personal Income

National Center for Health Statistics
- Vital and Health Statistics

Social Security Administration
- Earnings Distribution in the United States

National Institute of Education
- Tax Wealth in Fifty States

Energy Information Administration
- Monthly Energy Review
- Annual Energy Review

Office for Civil Rights
- Directory of Elementary and Secondary School Districts, and Schools in Selected School Districts

U.S. Department of Labor
- Monthly Labor Review
- Survey of Consumer Expenditures

USDA

Federal Bureau of Investigation

Federal Reserve Board

Immigration and Naturalization Service

Federal Trade Commission

Nongovernmental Sources

American Bus Association

American Public Transit Association

Association of American Railroads

Dun and Bradstreet, Inc.

Motor Vehicle Manufacturers Association

National Education Association (teachers' salaries)

Transportation Association of America

Editor and Publisher Company, Inc.
- Market Guide

International Council of Shopping Centers

Communication Channels, Inc.
- Shopping Center World (monthly)

Lebhar-Friedman, Inc.
- Chain Store Age Executive (monthly)

Urban Land Institute
- Dollars and Cents of Shopping Centers (updated periodically)
- Various development handbooks (such as the *Industrial Development Handbook*)

The National Research Bureau, Inc., Chicago
- Directory of Shopping Centers in the United States (annually)

National Retail Merchants Association
- Stores (monthly)
- Sales and Marketing Management (Annual survey of buying power)

Northeast-Midwest Institute, Washington, D.C.
- The YEAR Guide to Government Resources for Economic Development

SOURCE: Adapted from unpublished class handout of Peter Schaeffer, Program in Urban and Regional Planning, University of Colorado at Denver.

4. *The questionnaire.* Questions must be designed (a) to produce a full-time equivalent employment figure—one that is a standard expression of employment magnitude—and (b) to determine the local and nonlocal sales. For an economic base survey, it is enough to determine the portion of total sales made to local and nonlocal customers (adapted from Gibson, 1975, 4–6).

After existing or new information is collected, it is often useful to divide the local economy into sectors, that is, to classify employment into different industry types. A general breakdown is:

1. *Primary sector:* Industries that use raw materials (i.e., extractive industries such as farming, fishing, mining, and logging).
2. *Secondary sector:* Industries that assemble products or parts of products from raw materials. These can range from steel mills to clothing manufacturers to makers of calculators. The sector may also be defined to include such local types of manufacture as bakeries (which sometimes causes confusion).
3. *Tertiary sector:* Industries and services that primarily survive on the needs of the resident population. These are internally linked activities that rest on the base of primary- and secondary-sector income: retail, wholesale, and trade; financial services such as banks, real estate, and insurance firms; business services such as lawyers and accountants; repair services; personal services such as barbers and dry cleaners; and recreation and entertainment.

The U.S. government classifies industries according to the Standard Industrial Classification (SIC) code. The SIC is based on the primary product or service produced by the business. The broadest level of industry divides economic activities into ten groups, known as sectors or industry divisions, which are:

- Agriculture
- Mining
- Construction
- Manufacturing
- Transportation, communication, and public utilities
- Retail trade
- Wholesale trade
- Finance, insurance, and real estate
- Services
- Public administration (or governments) (McLean and Voyteck 1992).

The second level of detail is called "major industry groups" and is based on two-digit SIC codes. According to Mary McLean and Kenneth Voyteck, there are "83 major industry groups currently identified" (1992, 23). Three-digit SIC codes identify "industry groups," and four-digit SIC codes are based on product lines (McLean and Voyteck 1992).

Economic information may be summarized in tables and figures. As with population data, it may be helpful to compare and contrast the planning area with similar areas and place it in a larger context. Table 4.13 summarizes occupation and selected industries for the three census tracts in the Desert View Tri-Villages Area as well as for the Phoenix metropolitan statistical area. The percentage that each occupation and industry comprises in the region is also displayed. As can be noted, employed persons in the Tri-Villages Area comprised 0.98 percent of the total regional work force in 1990. Table 4.14 illustrates the labor force status, that is, how many individuals are in the labor force, employed, unemployed, or not in the labor force.

Next it is important to provide a measure of the impact of new economic growth (such as new jobs) on the planning areas. Two common methods include *economic base analysis* and *input-output analysis. Economic-base analysis* is a generic term covering several techniques, such as location quotient, shift-and-share analysis, and minimum-requirement analysis. Each builds on

TABLE 4.13
OCCUPATION AND SELECTED INDUSTRIES, DESERT VIEW TRI-VILLAGES AREA

	Phoenix MSA	Tract 303.33	Tract 303.42	Tract 303.43	Sum	Sum/MSA
Employed persons 16 years and over	1005925	3727	3883	2224	9834	0.98%
Executive, administrative, and managerial occupations	137453	639	620	444	1703	1.24%
Professional specialty occupations	143084	495	510	308	1313	0.92%
Technicians and related support occupations	42049	196	202	104	502	1.19%
Sales occupations	132040	674	419	418	1511	1.14%
Administrative support occupations	175072	591	795	353	1739	0.99%
Private household occupations	3710	17	12	7	36	0.97%
Protective service occupations	17599	89	156	22	267	1.52%
Service occupations	112959	277	282	131	690	0.61%
Farming, forestry, and fishing occupations	18888	60	21	110	191	1.01%
Precision production, craft, and repair occupations	110418	315	522	194	1031	0.93%
Machine operators, assemblers, and inspectors	45878	108	141	31	280	0.61%
Transportation and material moving occupations	32864	147	124	54	325	0.99%
Handlers, equipment cleaners, helpers, and laborers	33951	119	79	48	246	0.72%
Construction	64475	139	275	217	631	0.98%
Manufacturing	151425	544	636	228	1408	0.93%
Transportation, communications, and other utilities	78498	250	443	231	924	1.18%
Wholesale and retail trade	221601	887	697	368	1952	0.88%
Finance, insurance, and real estate	90255	533	599	343	1475	1.63%
Business and repair services	61954	271	190	145	606	0.98%
Professional and related services	213758	684	653	398	1735	0.81%

SOURCE: U.S. Bureau of Census 1990, adapted from Ciekot et al. 1995.

TABLE 4.14
LABOR FORCE STATUS, DESERT VIEW TRI-VILLAGES AREA

	Phoenix MSA	Tract 303.33	Tract 303.42	Tract 303.43	Sum	Sum/MSA
Persons 16 years and older	1623198	5757	5756	3233	14746	0.91%
In labor force	1079401	3901	4052	2329	10282	0.95%
Percent of persons 16 years and older	66.50%	67.76%	70.40%	72.04%	69.73%	
Civilian labor force	1070667	3883	4052	2328	10263	0.96%
Employed	1005925	3727	3883	2224	9834	0.98%
Percent of civilian labor force	94%	96%	96%	96%	96%	
Unemployed	64742	156	169	104	429	0.66%
Percent of civilian labor force	6.05%	4.02%	4.17%	4.47%	4.18%	
Not in labor force	543797	1856	1704	905	4465	0.82%

SOURCE: Adapted from Ciekot et al. 1995.

data that may be collected from a survey or census. Jack Kartez (1981) has summarized these techniques, showing how they may be used, the data requirements, and the level of detail that may be expected (Table 4.15).

User Groups

A planning area will probably be used by a variety of people. Identifying user groups is often important in order to clarify who will be impacted by a project or program. Sometimes a goal of the planning effort is to protect what already exists—the status quo. For instance, a community may be seeking to preserve wetlands, an historic building, or prime farmland. In such cases, it will be crucial to know who uses these places. On the other hand, an economic development plan may involve enticing new users into a locality. In such cases, it may be helpful to identify current users to ensure that efforts are made to protect their interests while new users are being invited to the area.

Preliminary user-group categories may be based on land use. The Land-Use and Land-Cover Classification System devised by the USGS for remote sensing (see Table 1.3) provides standard categories. But land use is only the beginning in the establishment of user groups. *Land-use* classification is relatively straightforward in comparison to *land-user* classification. User-group identification is much more difficult, especially for those users whose livelihoods are not directly related to the landscape.

People can use the same place in various ways. Central Park, New York City.

User activities are actions performed in the landscape-specific categories of people engaged in certain types of activities in particular places. These diverse actions may be triggered by seasonal cycles and are likely to be affected by population and economic trends. Land uses occur spatially and are organized around specific resources. Any person who passes through a region is a consumer of that place's resources.

In early stages of an inventory, land-use and land-user classifications may be general. At the beginning, it may be possible only to identify those users who are most directly associated with the land (such as farmers). It may be helpful to regard land users in a fashion similar to that used by ecologists in their community studies (see Ricklefs 1973, 589–775, for instance). It is not difficult to see how the concept of food chains can be expanded to form land chains, and the explanation of primary production can be used as the basis to explain primary land users.

As the inventory and analysis proceeds and user groups are identified, their recognized view of the landscape and adaptive strategies will become apparent as will the linkages between user groups. Tables 4.16 and 4.17 were developed for the Kennett region of southeastern Pennsylvania to show user groups there. It must be pointed out that the class, religious, and ethnic distinctions were those that the people of the area used to describe themselves and each other. They were not imposed by the planning team.

The unfortunate thing is that humans do make distinctions concerning the groups with which they identify based on skin color, class and occupation, ethnicity or nationality, and religious or political beliefs. The question that must be asked is: Do planners meet the needs of all people by recognizing these distinctions or by pretending they do not exist?

TABLE 4.15
SUMMARY OF TECHNIQUES FOR ECONOMIC-BASE ANALYSIS AND INPUT-OUTPUT ANALYSIS

Technique	Use	Data Needs	Detail
Location Quotient	Identifies those local sectors or activities that have "comparative advantage" when compared to the same activities in a larger economy (state, region).	Employment data can be collected from the Decennial Census or elsewhere.	Very general. Only a *descriptive* tool. Identifies "basic" industry only vaguely.
Shift-and-Share Analysis	Identifies how local economic change compares to change by sector or industry in a larger economy. Helps summarize employment data in a format that reveals how employment change locally may have been due to either (1) the fact that the locality has a large percentage of employment in nationally growing or declining industries, or (2) because the locality had particularly low or high growth in an industry compared to a larger economy.	As above. Secondary data.	Only descriptive. Useful in understanding trends in employment data. Can help identify "basic" activities.
Minimum-Requirements Analysis	Identifies that portion of employment for each industry type which is believed to be "basic" when compared to areas of similar size. Somewhat better basis than location quotients in that it explains why a percentage of employment is defined as being *basic* employment for a particular industry in a particular size range of communities.	Again, secondary data can be collected from the Census.	Provides a method of determining overall multipliers for basic activity in a locality. Cannot determine industry-specific data.
Input-Output Analysis	Provides a very detailed economic accounting of the linkages between each type of industry or activity. Provides the basis for developing industry-specific multipliers. This means that it provides an accurate basis for tracing the probable changes in other industries' employment or sales due to an initial change in another industry type in the local economy.	Requires that original data be collected from individual firms in the area.	Provides highly accurate information on how a change in employment affects other types of activities.

SOURCE: Kartez 1981.

TABLE 4.16
KENNETT, PENNSYLVANIA, USER GROUP LOCATION

Groups			Farmstead/ Estate Tenant	Farmstead/ Estate Tenant	Cross-roads	Strip Development			Subdivision			Mushroom	
Class*	Religion	Ethnicity	Dispersed	Contiguous	Town	High	Moderate	Low	High	Moderate	Low	Complex	Borough
UC	Epis.	Anglo		X									
UC	Quaker	Anglo		X									
UC	Cath.	Ital.		X			X		X				
UMC	Epis.	Anglo		X			X						
UMC	Quaker	Anglo	X	X				X				X	
UMC	Cath.	Ital.		X				X				X	X
MC	Quaker	Anglo	X	X	X	X	X					X	
MC	Pres.	Anglo	X	X	X	X	X		X				X
MC	Meth.	Anglo	X	X	X	X	X		X				X
MC	Bapt.	Anglo	X	X	X		X						X
MC	Jewish	Jewish											X
MC	Cath.	Ital.			X			X			X		X
MC	AME	Black			X								X
WC	Pres.	Anglo	X	X	X		X	X			X		X
WC	Meth.	Anglo	X	X	X		X	X			X		X
WC	Bapt.	Anglo	X	X	X		X	X			X		X
WC	Cath.	Ital.		X	X		X	X				X	X
WC	Bapt.	South						X			X	X	
WC	AME	Black	X		X			X					X
WC	Cath.	Hispanic										X	

* UC, upper class; UMC, upper middle class; MC, middle class; WC, working class.
SOURCES: Rose, Steiner, and Jackson 1978/1979; Jackson and Steiner 1985.

GENERATION OF NEW INFORMATION

Often planners will need to conduct original research to understand the community where they are working. Sometimes existing information may reveal opinions or attitudes about the issues being addressed by the planning effort, but at other times more information will be necessary. For example, what do people think about new housing development? Newspaper articles may indicate that local residents support new housing. If they do indeed favor it, then are they willing to pay the taxes for the necessary services to support the new housing? What do people feel about new industrial development? If they are opposed, then are they aware of the possible implications for the tax base of the community? How is the community organized—formally and informally? Who are the community leaders? Such questions can be posed through mail and telephone surveys, face-to-face interviews, and participant observation.

Mail and Telephone Surveys

In Chapter 2, surveys were introduced as a means to help establish community goals. Surveys can also be used to inventory community characteristics and as a basis for analysis of the attitudes of citizens. The major ways to conduct surveys are by mail and telephone, although interactive television may also be an option. No one needs to respond to yet another bad survey. Before intruding on people's privacy, planners should ask if the

TABLE 4.17
DISTRIBUTION OF USERS IN THE CONTROLLING INSTITUTIONS OF THE KENNETT, PENNSYLVANIA, REGION

			Agriculture							Commerce and Industry		Land Development		Government			
Class	Religion	Ethnicity	Horse	Dairy	Hort.	Mush.	Beef	Extraction (Quarry)	Finance (Banking)	Retail	Textiles/ Electronics	Real Estate	Developer/ Builder	Twp.	Co.	St.	Fed.
UC	Epis.	Anglo	O/W				O		O	O	O		O		A		A
UC	Quak.	Ango	O/W	O/W		O	O		O	O	O		O	E	A	E	
UC	Cath.	Ital.	O/W			O											
UMC	Epis.	Anglo	W			O				O	E	O	A				
UMC	Quak.	Anglo		O/W	O/W	O	W									E	
UMC	Cath.	Ital.				O							O			E	
MC	Quak.	Anglo			O/W	O								E	A	A	
MC	Pres.	Anglo			W	W	W/O			W/O					E		
MC	Meth.	Anglo				W	W/O		W	W/O		O	O	E			
MC	Bapt.	Anglo			W	W			W	W/O		W/O		E			
MC	Jewish	Jewish				O			W	W/O			O	A			
MC	Cath.	Ital.		W		O/W		O	W	W/O		W	W/O	E			
MC	AME	Black							W	W/O	W			A			
WC	Pres.	Anglo	W		W	W				W/O	W		W				
WC	Meth.	Anglo	W		W	W				W/O	W		W				
WC	Bapt.	Anglo	W		W	W				W/O	W		W				
WC	Cath.	Ital.		W		O/W				W/O	W						
WC	Bapt.	South			W	O/W	W/O				W/O		W				
WC	AME	Black	W		W	W		O/W		W/O	W		W				
WC	Cath.	Hisp.			W	W				W/O							

O, owner; W, worker; E, elected; A, appointed.
SOURCES: Rose, Steiner, and Jackson 1978/1979; Jackson and Steiner 1985.

information is truly necessary for the planning effort. If a survey is indeed called for, then it should be written by someone practiced in the art and science of preparing questionnaires. A sociologist should be retained through a consulting company or university, or, if the budget and scope of the project is appropriate, a social scientist with survey experience should be included on the planning team. If the budget or the scope of the project is more limited, then the planning team should obtain a copy of a standard survey text such as Dillman (1978); Sudman and Bradburn (1983); Fowler (1993); DeVellis (1991); and Le Compte and Preissle (1993).

Don Dillman's total design method (TDM) has two parts. First, he suggests that each aspect of the survey process that may affect the quality or quantity of the response be identified. Each aspect should then be designed in such a way that "the best possible responses are obtained" (Dillman 1978, 12). Second, Dillman suggests an administrative plan "guided by a theoretical view about why people respond to questionnaires. It provides the rationale for deciding how each aspect, even the seemingly minute ones, should be shaped" (1978, 12). The purpose of the administrative plan is "to ensure implementation of the survey in accordance with design intentions" (Dillman 1978, 12). According to Dillman, the essence of the administrative plan is to:

- Identify all the tasks to be accomplished.
- Determine how each task is dependent on the others.
- Determine in what order the tasks must be performed.
- Decide the means by which each task is to be accomplished (1978, 20).

Dillman provides clear guidelines and suggestions for realizing these principles. He also reports a high response rate to surveys which use the TDM. Essentially, there are eight steps in conducting a survey:

1. Define the purpose of the survey.
2. Choose the study design.
3. Select the sample.
4. Construct and pretest the questionnaire.
5. Implement the questionnaire by mail, over the telephone, or in person (mail surveys may require a follow-up step).
6. Code the interviews.
7. Tabulate and analyze the results.
8. Write a report (steps adapted from Survey Research Center 1976).

The Survey Research Center of the University of Michigan's Institute for Social Research has prepared a manual to follow these eight steps for interviews (Survey Research Center 1976). A good questionnaire is dependent on the quality of the questions asked. The text by Seymour Sudman and Norman Bradburn (1983) provides especially helpful suggestions about how to ask questions. Together, the Dillman, Sudman and Bradburn, and Survey Research Center books provide much guidance for the preparation of surveys.

When designing a survey to provide inventory information, it is useful to remember other steps of the planning process. Synchronized surveys, introduced in Chapter 2 and discussed again in Chapter 6, may be used throughout the process to integrate the steps. Integrated, synchronized surveys can assist planners to identify issues, establish goals, collect information, and select options for realizing planning goals.

Face-to-Face Interviews

Face-to-face interviews are a personal alternative to the mail and telephone. Through personal interviews, the planner "can enter the mental world of the individual, to glimpse the categories and the logic by which he or she sees the world" so that the planner can see "into the life world of the individual, to see the content and pattern of daily experience" (McCracken 1988, 9). Face-to-face interviews may be conducted at random, or individuals may be preselected, depending on the nature of the planning project or program. For random interviews, it will be important to select representative neighborhoods of the planning area. Interviews should be conducted in a variety of settlement types and with people of various income levels and ethnic backgrounds. At a minimum the planner should record the date, time, and place of the interview and ask questions about the age of the resident; the size of the family; the occupations of the husband, wife, and children; the place of work; and the length of residence in the planning area (Berger et al. 1977). Planners should explain the purpose of the interview and, if appropriate, ensure confidentiality.

If interviewees are selected at random, then there is the possibility that the person may not be a resident. In such cases, it is important to ask why the individual is visiting the planning area. For planning efforts with tourism and recreation issues involved, visitors may be targeted for interviews. Planners may interview people at rest stops or gas stations to learn more about why visitors are attracted to the area.

Interviews can also be conducted with what ethnographers call *key informants.* Carl Patton and David Sawicki (1993) call this approach the *elite or intensive interviewing process.* A list of organizations and clubs can be compiled (see Table 4.1). Officers of these associations can then be contacted and interviewed. In addition to recording the date, time, and place of the meeting, the planner should note the name of the organization and of the person being interviewed. The planner should try to obtain an official statement of the purpose of the group, an organizational chart, and a written biography of the association. The planner should try to learn about the committee structure, scheduled meetings, membership, and dues and funds.

The specific questions asked during the interview will depend on the planning effort. Face-to-face interviews with association officers should yield information about community leadership, how issues are perceived in the planning area, and the use of natural resources by various groups of people.

Participant Observation

Participant observation involves actually living in a community, becoming involved in its activities, and carefully recording events. Many agency staff planners live in the community where they work and are participants in its affairs; however this technique for generating new information about a community goes beyond living in a place. Participant observation is used by ethnographers in their fieldwork. The technique involves active listening, supplemented by taking careful field notes. A journal can be used to record observations. Such observations should be carefully recorded and include the date and the places and people involved.

If a team of planners is involved, then they will meet to discuss their observations. One approach is to place individual planning team members in areas and homes of representative individuals from various segments of the community. For instance, one planner may live in a neighborhood with a high-income family; another with a middle-income family; and a third with a low-income family. One person could live in a neighborhood of an ethnic minority, another in a majority neighborhood. In this way a cross section of observations can be compiled.

Allan Jacobs (1985) suggests a framework for organizing observations about the built environment. He recommends that the planner first walk the entire planning area. A checklist can be prepared prior to such a walk to help with note taking and observation. The checklist should include spaces for visit-specific information such as the date, time of day, and weather, as well as detailed information about streets, sidewalks, curbs, street trees, maintenance, building arrangement, and topography (Morrell 1989). A map that can be written on should also be taken so that the planner can record the route and mark points of interest. Sketches can also be made during the first visit, but a camera should be left in the office. Sketching encourages looking closely, whereas when taking pictures details may be overlooked.

A second site visit can then be made with a camera, photographing the area and verifying initial observations (Jacobs 1985; Morrell 1989). A third visit can then be made with a local expert, a key informant in ethnographic terms. The observations from these visits can be recorded in the journal and compared with published information about the study area. During such observation, Jacobs urges planners "to constantly question what one sees as well as the conclusions one comes to" (1985, 28). Because planners bring their own cultural values to any observation, it is, according to Jacobs, "necessary to constantly question and refine one's definition of what is really being seen" (1985, 28; see also Jacobs 1993).

Reading the landscape is an art. Planners can learn to look for visual clues that can reveal much about a human community. For instance, the date that some buildings were constructed may be displayed on their facades. By looking at a place a planner can start to understand something about the history of the community and the people who dwell there. Participant observation can yield rich, personal insights about communities that cannot be gained by reading existing information or by collecting new data through surveys and interviews.

The observation of the built environment is only part of what a planner should study. Planners should also attend meetings of community organizations and clubs to learn more about the people who live in the planning area. These meetings may be with the same associations whose officers have been interviewed. Agenda and membership lists should be collected. In this way, active members of the community can be identified and issues confirmed and denied as being important to local citizens. A mailing list can be compiled, which can assist planners in forming a network to distribute information about the planning process.

ANALYSIS AND SYNTHESIS OF SOCIAL INFORMATION

After new and existing information has been collected, it is then necessary to pull it together and determine what it reveals about the area. By combining this information with the information about biophysical processes, planners can identify patterns that occur on the landscape. Planners can also determine interactions and relationships that occur among groups of people and between social and biophysical processes.

Establish Visual and Landscape Patterns

Ecological processes tend to reveal themselves in certain visual and landscape patterns. Landscape ecologists have explored the spatial arrangement of communities and are studying landscape patterns and functions (Forman and Godron 1986). The use of ecological concepts such as patches, corridors, matrices, and networks can help planners understand the patterns of human interaction that occur in the landscape. Rachel Kaplan and her colleagues from the University of Michigan suggest the use of patterns to understand relationships between "aspects of the environment and how people experience or react to them" (Kaplan et al. 1998). What we see largely determines our experience and reactions (see Tuan 1974).

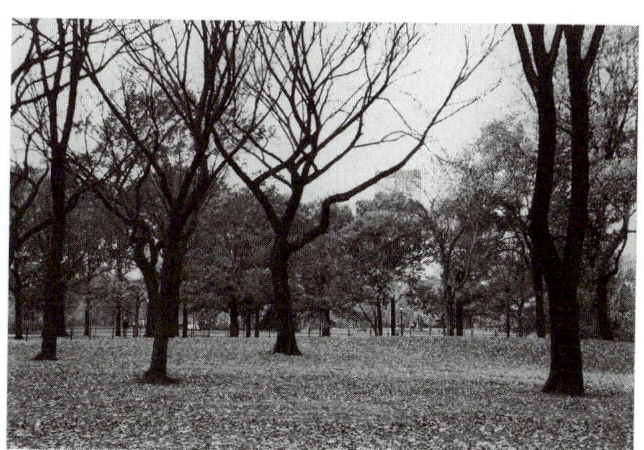

Ecological and cultural processes combine to form visual patterns. Central Park, New York City.

Visual analysis is a complex art. The National Environmental Policy Act required that "presently unquantified environmental amenities and values" be considered in decision making and that "the environmental design arts" be used when assessing the impacts of projects and programs (U.S. Congress 1969).

In response, landscape architects have developed several approaches for incorporating visual considerations into decision making (Kaplan et al. 1998; Schauman 1986, 1988a, 1988b). R. Burton Litton, then a University of California, Berkeley, landscape architecture professor, worked closely with the USFS and was especially influential (Litton 1968; U.S. Forest Service 1973, 1974). Litton's work was influenced by others who had proposed ways of reading the landscape, including Donald Appleyard and Kevin Lynch. Many planning projects and programs will require a detailed visual analysis. In such cases, a landscape architect who specializes in visual resource assessment should be included in the planning team. Landscape architects, who have experience assessing visual characteristics, are included on many U.S. Forest Service, National Park Service, and U.S. Bureau of Land Management planning teams.

According to Ervin Zube and his colleagues (1982) there are four primary "paradigms" of visual assessment:

- *The expert paradigm,* which involves evaluation of visual quality by a trained expert incorporating knowledge from design, ecology, or resource management
- *The psychophysical paradigm,* which focuses on a population's preference for specific landscape qualities based primarily on physical characteristics in the landscape
- *The cognitive paradigm,* which emphasizes human meaning associated with landscape properties based on past experience, future

expectation, and sociocultural conditioning of the observer

- *The experiential paradigm,* which considers landscape values based on interaction of people with the landscape (as adapted by Whitmore et al. 1995, 29)

In the context of human community analysis, some of the techniques developed for visual resource assessment can be adapted to help identify landscape patterns. Many of these approaches to assess the visual attributes of a place have been developed from the perspective of an outsider, an expert, according to the classification system developed by Zube and his colleagues (1982). Viewing the landscape from the road, areas are mapped and evaluated. Such an approach can be helpful in the determination of visual sensitivity to change. (See Tables 10.4 and 10.15 for examples of how this type of information can be used in classifying environmentally sensitive areas.)

The view-from-the-road approach is an outgrowth of windshield surveys. These surveys are undertaken by systematically driving throughout the planning area. The planning researcher takes photographs, draws sketches, and writes notes about her or his observations. Another general approach to visual analysis is to try to learn the insider, or land user, view of the landscape. Several techniques have been developed to attempt to gain such a perspective. Photographs are a common tool. One option is to give cameras to land users in the planning area and ask them to take pictures of things that they like and do not like about their landscape. These photographs are then collected, compared, and analyzed. Another option is for the researcher to take photographs. These photographs can then be used to conduct preference surveys. Preferences can be determined by showing the photographs at public meetings, through one-on-one interviews, or by mail surveys. Visual surveys from either the expert or user perspective can be integrated with the participant-observation efforts.

The visual and participant-observation findings should enable the planner or the planning team to identify visual patterns that reflect cultural values. Such patterns can be identified using rather simple land-use terms (e.g., *agricultural, commercial, residential, industrial, natural*). Ideally, however, the patterns should reveal more complex relationships between biophysical and sociocultural processes that are visually apparent and that are specific to the area (e.g., *rolling wheatland, old town center, lakeshore suburb, old stream-bank industry, valley conifer woodland*).

The "language of landscape," as suggested by Anne Spirn (1998), includes a vocabulary to describe both the visual patterns and the ecology of places. For instance, where Kevin Lynch (1960) used *node, path,* and *district,* Forman and Godron (1986) use *patch, corridor,* and *matrix* (Hirschman, 1988, after Steinitz, 1988). Such terms are helpful for describing the visual and cultural patterns observed in a place.

Several methods, paralleling roughly the Zube et al. classification, were employed by a team of planners in the planning of the Verde Valley greenway in Arizona (Cook et al. 1991, Whitmore et al. 1995). The team determined that three methods of visual assessment would be used in the study, with a goal to involve the public in the visual assessment. First, an expert evaluation method involved trained observers, in this case landscape architects and planners, without public interaction. Second, a public valuation method incorporated images selected by the same experts, which were then reviewed at public meetings. (This method followed procedures developed by Ricki McKenzie for the New Jersey Pinelands, discussed later in this chapter.) Third, a public nomination method was used that was completely dependent on the scenic preferences of local residents (Cook et al. 1991, Whitmore et al. 1995).

The public valuation method was especially helpful in the identification of landscape patterns for planning purposes. This method involved a field landscape inventory, following procedures described in the previous chapter. Comprehensive photo documentation of the Verde River corridor was undertaken to identify, describe, and map visual landscape types (Whitmore 1993). The team identified landscape types, initially in the field, then refined through detailed analysis of hundreds of photographs. After the team identified 29 landscape types, seven workshops were conducted in the Verde Valley where these types were rated for preference. The ratings revealed close relationships between visual preferences and natural features such as geologic structures, riparian forests, and emergent marsh edges (Whitmore et al. 1995). Furthermore, cultural features played a significant role in the preference ratings, from Native American cliff dwellings to mill tailings (Whitmore et al. 1995). The planning team found that, in addition to assisting the state park agency plan the greenway, the visual preference process helped the planners engage local residents in discussions about their landscapes.

Urban Morphology

Urban morphology is another way to help reveal human settlement patterns. Anne Vernez Moudon (1997) has provided a helpful summary of this "emerging interdisciplinary field." Moudon notes that as a result, "*form, resolution,* and *time* constitute the three fundamental components of urban morphological research" (1997, 7).

Michael Schmandt explains Conzen's trifold classification as follows:

> Building form pertains to the physical characteristics of the structure—features such as color, height, and architectural style. . . . Ground plan, termed "town plan" by Conzen, is the spatial location and interaction of streets, parcels and buildings. Conzen divided the ground plan into three components: streets and their street network, parcels and their aggregation into blocks, and the orientation of buildings within the streets and parcels. When these forms are overlaid, attention shifts from the individual entities to the association between these forms. . . . The third part of Conzen's classification is land use, defined . . . as the activity or function of a parcel or parcel section (1995, 13).

Schmandt used the Conzen classification to read the landscapes of three western American downtowns (Phoenix, San Antonio, and San Diego). He sought to assess the impact of the "postmodern" on the urban landscapes. Schmandt found that land uses "depict a tendency towards mixture and gentrification" with greater attention "paid to historic detail, traditional uses, and to the integration . . . within the existing urban fabric" (1995, ii). Schmandt's study helps illustrate the utility of the Conzen classification to contemporary urban landscape morphology.

Identification of Interactions and Relationships

Building on the visual, landscape, and urban morphological patterns, overlay and computer maps, matrices, and systems diagrams can be used to identify interactions and relationships. The specific technique chosen will be determined, in large measure, by the issues that have been identified and the goals established for the planning effort. Matrices will be used here to illustrate how sociocultural interactions can be analyzed.

Although biophysical and sociocultural factors must be viewed together, it may be useful to consider them separately before putting them together in a synthesis chart. Figure 4.5 demonstrates a way to establish biophysical factor interaction that builds on the bivariate diagram discussed in Chapter 3. Symbols, letters, or numbers can be used in the boxes to indicate if a relationship exists and the relative importance of that relationship. Written descriptions can be used to elaborate and explain the relationships.

In a matrix, land users can be classified in at least two ways, that is, either by their use of the land or by the terms the local people use to clas-

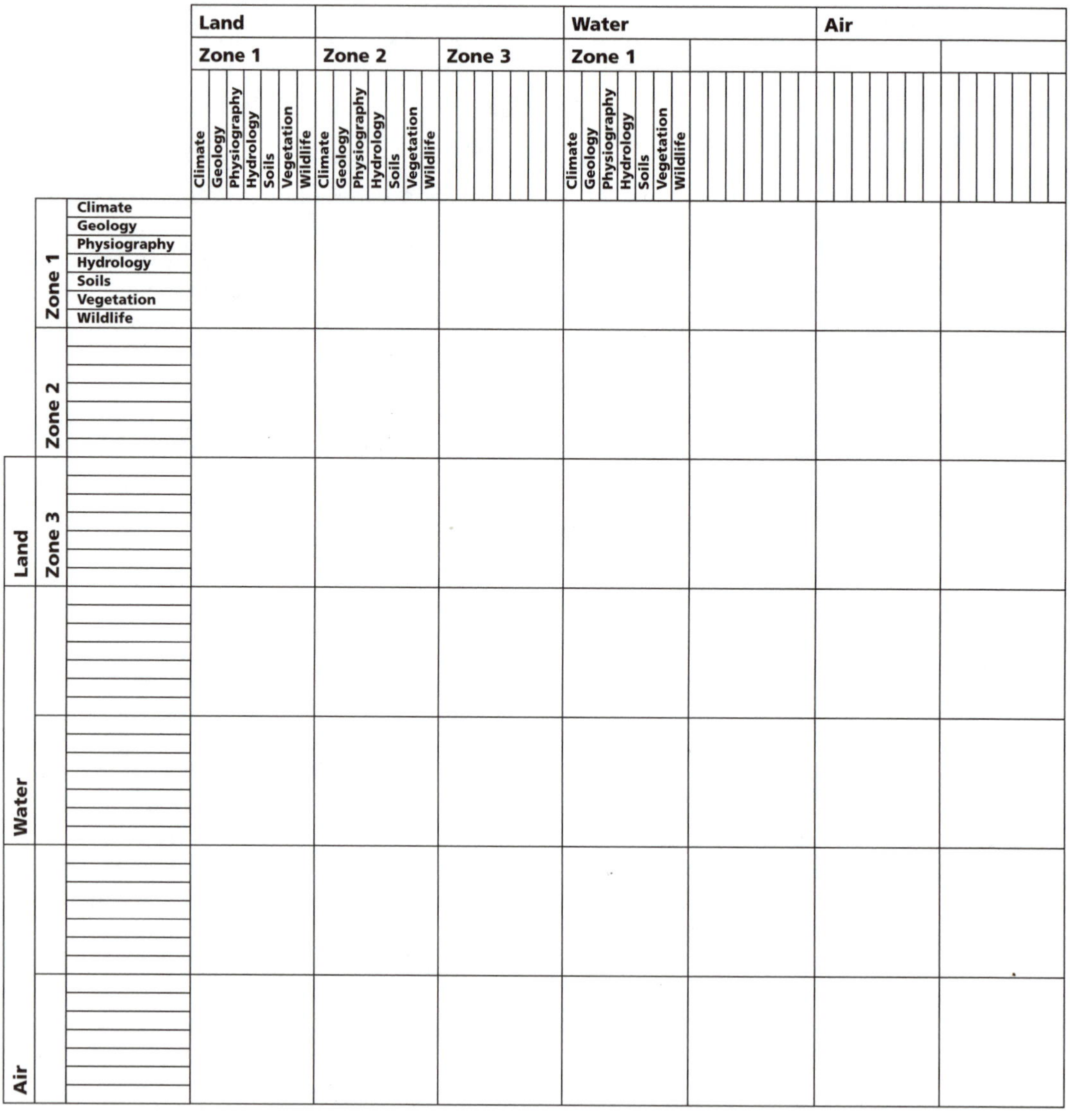

	Land			Water		Air	
	Zone 1	Zone 2	Zone 3	Zone 1			
	Climate, Geology, Physiography, Hydrology, Soils, Vegetation, Wildlife	Climate, Geology, Physiography, Hydrology, Soils, Vegetation, Wildlife		Climate, Geology, Physiography, Hydrology, Soils, Vegetation, Wildlife			
Zone 1: Climate, Geology, Physiography, Hydrology, Soils, Vegetation, Wildlife							
Zone 2							
Land — Zone 3							
Water							
Air							

FIGURE 4.5 Biophysical factor interaction. *(Source: Adapted from Jackson and Steiner 1985)*

sify themselves and each other. As with biophysical factors (see Figure 4.6), a numbered matrix can be constructed so that relationships can be explained in writing. (In Figure 4.6 simple land-use designations—such as *industrial*—are used for illustration. Certainly, more descriptive visual and cultural landscape patterns—like *old stream bank, corridor industry,* or *industrial node*—can be used as well.)

After classifying land users, it is possible to examine user-group demands. Some of these demands are quite basic: skiers need snow,

	Residential	Commercial	Industrial	Transportation	Recreation	Agriculture	Extraction
Residential							
Commercial							
Industrial							
Transportation							
Recreation							
Agriculture							
Extraction							

FIGURE 4.6 User-group interaction. *(Source: Adapted from Jackson and Steiner 1985)*

	Residential	Commercial	Industrial	Transportation	Recreation	Agriculture	Extraction
Climate							
Geology							
Physiography							
Hydrology							
Soils							
Vegetation							
Wildlife							

FIGURE 4.7 User demands. *(Source: Adapted from Jackson and Steiner 1985)*

foresters need timber, farmers need productive soil and ample water, and hunters need game. The relationship between user-group demands and biophysical factors can be illustrated and summarized in a matrix (Figure 4.7) (Jackson and Steiner 1985).

Community Needs Assessment

The preceding inventory and analysis of population and economic characteristics as well as the synthesis of human community information should lead to an assessment of needs. These needs should relate to the issues and goals being addressed by the planning effort. These studies, however, may reveal the necessity to amend or establish new goals and may raise new issues. Take, for instance, once again, three of the Oregon statewide planning goals: agriculture, housing, and urbanization. The agricultural goal is to preserve and maintain agricultural lands, while the housing goal is to provide for housing needs of the citizens of the state (Land Conservation and Development Commission 1980). According to Wendie Kellington, "The Oregon land-use planning program contemplates a balance between resource preservation and the provision of adequate land supply for housing" (1998, 3). Meanwhile, the urbanization goal is to provide for an orderly and efficient transition from rural to urban land use (Department of Land Conservation and Development 1996).

What are the social, economic, and political needs for agriculture in a planning area? And how do those needs relate to the biophysical environment? The answers for the first question should lie in the studies described in this chapter. Through an ecological analysis, linkages should start to be made between the human community and the biophysical environment. Population and economic studies should reveal trends in the agricultural sector and what the needs are to continue to support farming in the planning area. These needs can be quantified. For instance, one can determine the number of cows, farmers, and land needed to support a milk-processing plant. These numbers may vary if the cows graze on the farm or if feed is imported. They may also vary if technology, such as milking machines or the cost of energy, changes the labor required to maintain a dairy.

As outlined in the Oregon statewide planning goal, housing needs may be affected by (1) the amount of buildable land; (2) the distribution of existing population by income compared with the distribution of available housing units by costs; (3) a determination of vacancy rates, both overall and at varying rent ranges and cost levels; (4) a determination of expected housing demands at varying rent ranges and cost levels; (5) an analysis of a variety of densities and types of residences; and (6) the amount of sound housing units capable of being rehabilitated (Land Conservation and Development Commission 1980). Some obvious conflicts exist between the needs for agriculture and housing. Oregon's urbanization goal attempts to address these conflicts. Preference in Oregon is given to agricultural land protection. Consequently, jurisdictions need to justify how much land should be contained within the urban growth boundary and how much of the rural land is either unsuited for resource use or already too developed or too fragmented to be returned to farm use. As a result, in Oregon, the challenge is not in estimating how much agriculture there should be, but in determining how much of everything else there would be in the plan. Oregon's emphasis on farmland protection is unique. Elsewhere in the United States, it is common to decide on every possible other use first, and then dedicating what is left over to farm use. Chapter 5 will address how to determine the potential allocation of land uses.

TWO EXAMPLES OF HUMAN COMMUNITY INVENTORY AND ANALYSIS

Collecting information about people is not new, but connecting such data to natural systems and to planning the future of places is a relatively new art. Planners in the New Jersey Pinelands and at Camp Pendleton, California, have sought to make such connections.

New Jersey Pinelands Comprehensive Management Plan

The human community inventory and analysis of the Pinelands were accomplished in the same manner as the biophysical studies (see Chapter 3), that is, through the use of consultants. The management plan first reviewed prehistorical, historical, and cultural resources and then land use. The Pinelands has been inhabited and used by humans for approximately 10,000 years. The management plan provides a synopsis of what is known about the prehistory of the region. There is an inventory of sites of archaeological significance and an historical review, beginning with the people who called themselves the "Lenni-Lenape" who inhabited the area at the time of the initial European contact. The historic activities of Europeans and their American descendants are described in the plan. These include forestry; shipbuilding and seafaring; hunting, gathering, trapping, and fishing; agriculture; iron production; glassmaking; and tourism and recreation (Pinelands Commission 1980).

Jon Berger and John Sinton interviewed 300 Pineland residents and analyzed the cultural resources and attitudes about the Pinelands. They found settlement of the Pinelands taking place in three general patterns, and they grouped these into three major cultural regions: forest, agricultural and rural suburban, and coastal. Then they identified a number of distinct cultural and ethnic groups, including baymen, blacks, Germans, Italians, Jews, mixed urbanizing, Puerto Ricans, Quakers, rural residents, and Russians. Based on this work, a number of culturally significant areas were identified (Pinelands Commission 1980; Berger and Sinton 1985). These areas contributed to the development of the plan for the Pinelands (see Chapter 7).

Based on the sociocultural study, varied perceptions of the future were drawn, and potential land-use conflicts for the area were foreseen. These conflicts are listed in Table 4.18. This analysis was followed by a description of land use that was linked to the ethnic and cultural groups of the area. Current land uses occur in national reserve, forest and wetland, agricultural land, and built-up land (Table 4.19). This information was linked with future and current demands for agriculture (Table 4.20), sewage systems and wastewater disposal, water supply and water use, solid waste generation and disposal, transportation, government facilities, resource extraction, and recreation.

In addition to the work of Berger and Sinton, other landscape planners led by Ricki L. McKenzie of the U.S. Department of Interior analyzed scenic resources. They identified 53 visual types (Figure 4.8), which they divided into 27 natural types, "landscapes that are mostly green with few human structures," and 26 cultural types, "landscapes dominated by buildings and paving" (McKenzie 1979, 5). Three types (one woodland and two farmland) were included in both sets, so there are actually only 50 types.

Each visual type was illustrated with a transparent color photograph that was projected at nine public meetings involving about 155 people to collect preference votes. The 50 visual types were scored and ranked for preference (Figure 4.9). Certain patterns (e.g., the forested lake type) were clearly liked by the people who participated in the meetings. Other images, such as the nuclear power plant, were "actively disliked" (McKenzie 1979; Pinelands Commission 1980).

The management plan then put the Pinelands into a regional perspective, using population and economic studies. The population of the Pinelands study area was 394,154 and growing steadily (Table 4.21). The economic activities in the management plan included development activity and land transactions that were reviewed for the region as a whole and for each county in the Pinelands. Development regions and trends were determined. Two development phenomena in New Jersey especially impact the Pinelands: the proliferation of retirement communities and the advent of casino gambling in nearby Atlantic City. From these studies, population and housing demand projections were made for each county to the year 2000 (Table

TABLE 4.18
POTENTIAL LAND-USE CONFLICTS IN THE PINELANDS

- Public ownership versus lost municipal tax revenues
- Land-use restrictions versus private property rights
- State and federal regulatory power versus home rule
- Extensive versus intensive land uses
- Preservation of lifestyle indigenous to the Pines versus wish for technological improvement
- Preservation of traditional lifestyles versus suburbanization
- Preservation of open space versus need for housing of longtime residents
- Preservation of open space for residents versus preservation of open space for nonresidents
- Intensive recreational use versus light recreational use
- Development of recreation fisheries versus development of commercial fisheries
- Free and unlimited public access versus access for wilderness needs and research
- Preservation of historic sites versus development for recreation
- Preservation of present landscapes versus needs for resource use and habitat restoration

SOURCE: Pinelands Commission 1980.

TABLE 4.19
ESTIMATED LAND USES IN THE PINELANDS, IN THOUSANDS OF ACRES (PINELANDS NATIONAL RESERVE = 1,082,816 TOTAL ACRES)

County	Land area in national reserve	Forest and wetland	Agricultural land	Developed land
Atlantic	243.6	201.6	16.5	25.4
Burlington	346.6	295.6	24.8	26.2
Camden	54.6	39.5	6.5	8.6
Cape May	85.6	78.7	2.3	4.6
Cumberland	55.7	52.4	1.0	2.3
Gloucester	33.2	23.5	5.9	3.8
Ocean	263.5	235.3	1.0	27.2

SOURCE: Pinelands Commission 1980.

4.22) and for different growth scenarios of development.

As the year 2000 approaches, it has become clear that the plan has not inhibited growth in the Pinelands. Rather, growth has been directed to the most suitable locations. For example, Pinelands municipalities have continued to authorize more permits on average than other municipalities in southern New Jersey and the remainder of the state (New Jersey Pinelands Commission 1998). The economic health of the region has remained strong. Unemployment in the Pinelands declined through the 1990s. In addition, population inside the Pinelands has continued to grow at a faster rate than the rest of southern New Jersey or the state (New Jersey Pinelands Commission 1998).

The Biodiversity Plan for the Camp Pendleton Region, California

The focus of the Camp Pendleton landscape planning study was natural systems—the protection of the region's biodiversity. The reason for the concern about biodiversity was the rapid human population growth in Southern California. The Camp Pendleton team began their discussion of the human community with a summary of the region's history from Spanish colonization in the 1740s, through the rich agricultural and ranching period, and into the rapid population growth following the Second World War (Steinitz et al. 1996).

The population of the Camp Pendleton study area was approximately 1.1 million at the time of the study. Regional planning agencies project that the area will grow to 1.6 million by 2010 (Steinitz et al. 1996) (Figure 4.10). The Camp Pendleton Marine Corps Base is located in the midst of this region, occupying 123,172 acres (49,867 hectares) of land that "still retains much of the landscape character of the early California days of missions and ranchos" (Steinitz et al. 1996, 18).

Instead of preparing a separate land-use map, the Camp Pendleton team combined land use, vegetation, and terrain into a single land-cover map (Figure 4.11). According to Carl Steinitz and his colleagues, "The classification of land cover is a generalization of more than 200 groupings of vegetation and land use described by the local and regional plans in the study area" (1996, 19).

The team also conducted a visual preference analysis for the Camp Pendleton area. They followed methods used by the U.S. Forest Service (1974) and Bureau of Land Management (1980) with three phases: (1) preferences, (2) exposure,

TABLE 4.20
PINELANDS AGRICULTURE

	Pinelands Area		Seven Counties		New Jersey	
Crop	**Acres (100) (× .4047 ha)**	**Income ($1,000)**	**Acres (100) (× .4047 ha)**	**Income ($1,000)**	**Acres (100) (× .4047 ha)**	**Income ($1,000)**
TOTAL	578.2	61,041.82	—	—	6,116.2*	359,590
Field crops	268.2	3,859.61	1,369	—	5,290	102,720
Corn and grain	55.3	746.18	236	5,084.8	950	19,884
Hay	58.2	478.35	210	5,190.0	1,119	23,250
Soybeans	123.4	2,484.95	715	14,527.5	2,060	42,333
Others	31.3	132.13	208	—	1,090	17,253
Ornamentals	32.9	9,863.31	—	—	—	—
Nursery	—	—	37	—	111	—
Sod	17.9	3,131.09	—	—	—	—
Trees and shrubs	9.9	2,413.98	—	—	—	—
Others	5.0	4,318.24	—	—	—	—
Fruits and berries	152.2	27,350.60	—	—	257	48,779
Apples	14.5	2,645.25	33	6,022.9	56	10,170
Blueberry	77.0	13,897.49	78	14,074.0	78	14,074
Cranberries	28.8	4,643.45	30	4,839.0	30	4,839
Peaches	27.7	5,523.79	73	14,561.2	83	16,520
Strawberries and grapes	4.2	640.62	7	1,270.5	10	1,768
Vegetables	121.6	13,477.03	—	—	711	78,762
Asparagus	1.8	172.03	11	1,103.6	19	1,789
Corn (sweet)	29.9	1,785.63	66	3,946.8	100	5,978
Peppers	8.4	914.17	39	4,128.1	60	5,709
Potatoes (white)	8.9	886.10	26	2,519.4	82	8,155
Potatoes (sweet)	17.1	2,749.47	24	3,825.2	26	4,176
Tomatoes	12.4	1,479.70	77	8,717.9	138	16,384
Others	43.0	5,489.47	—	—	286	36,562
Livestock (head)						
Cattle (dairy)	13.2	1,796.07	79	10,721.3	470	60,998
Chicken (layers)	2,251.7	2,425.97	—	6,604.2	17,160	18,488
Swine	71.3	701.16	630	5,982.4	760	6,592
Turkeys	308.8	389.15	—	—	580	762

* Total agricultural land in New Jersey is 1,058,600 acres (428,415 hectares).
SOURCE: Pinelands Commission 1980.

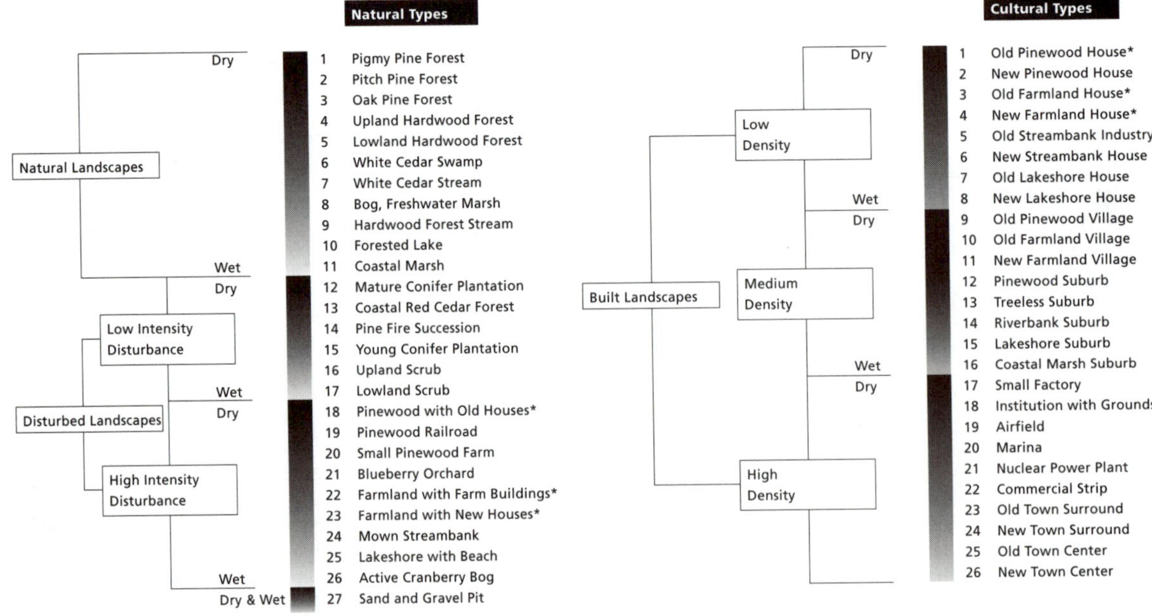

FIGURE 4.8 Pinelands visual types. *(Source: Pinelands Commission 1980)*

and (3) value (Steinitz et al. 1996). Visual preferences "were determined by using a set of 26 photographs of the study area which represent the range of land cover types in the region" (Steinitz et al. 1996, 84). Participants in the visual preference analysis ranked the photographs. The photographs were then grouped by aggregate value and mapped using GIS technology (Figure 4.12). The second step was exposure, which Steinitz and his colleagues defined as whether areas "were visible in the foreground, middleground, or background, or not visible, from all the major transportation routes" (1996, 86). These exposures were also mapped (Figure 4.13).

The third step—the assigning of values—involved combining the preference and exposure maps. The resulting map (Figure 4.14) identifies the most valuable lands to protect for visual qualities as well as those where maximum modification can occur without negative visual impact (Steinitz et al. 1996). The visual preference analysis attempted to link people to the landscape. The goal was to provide "insight into commonly held perceptions and values regarding . . . the landscape" (Steinitz et al. 1996, 84).

This recognition of the intricate interrelationship between people and landscape distinguishes the Camp Pendleton and Pinelands planning studies from more conventional efforts. Furthermore, Jon Berger and John Sinton (1985) have provided lively sketches of people from the Pine Barrens who spend their days and nights clamming, crabbing, trapping, oystering, fishing, hunting, farming cranberries and blueberries, truck farming fruits

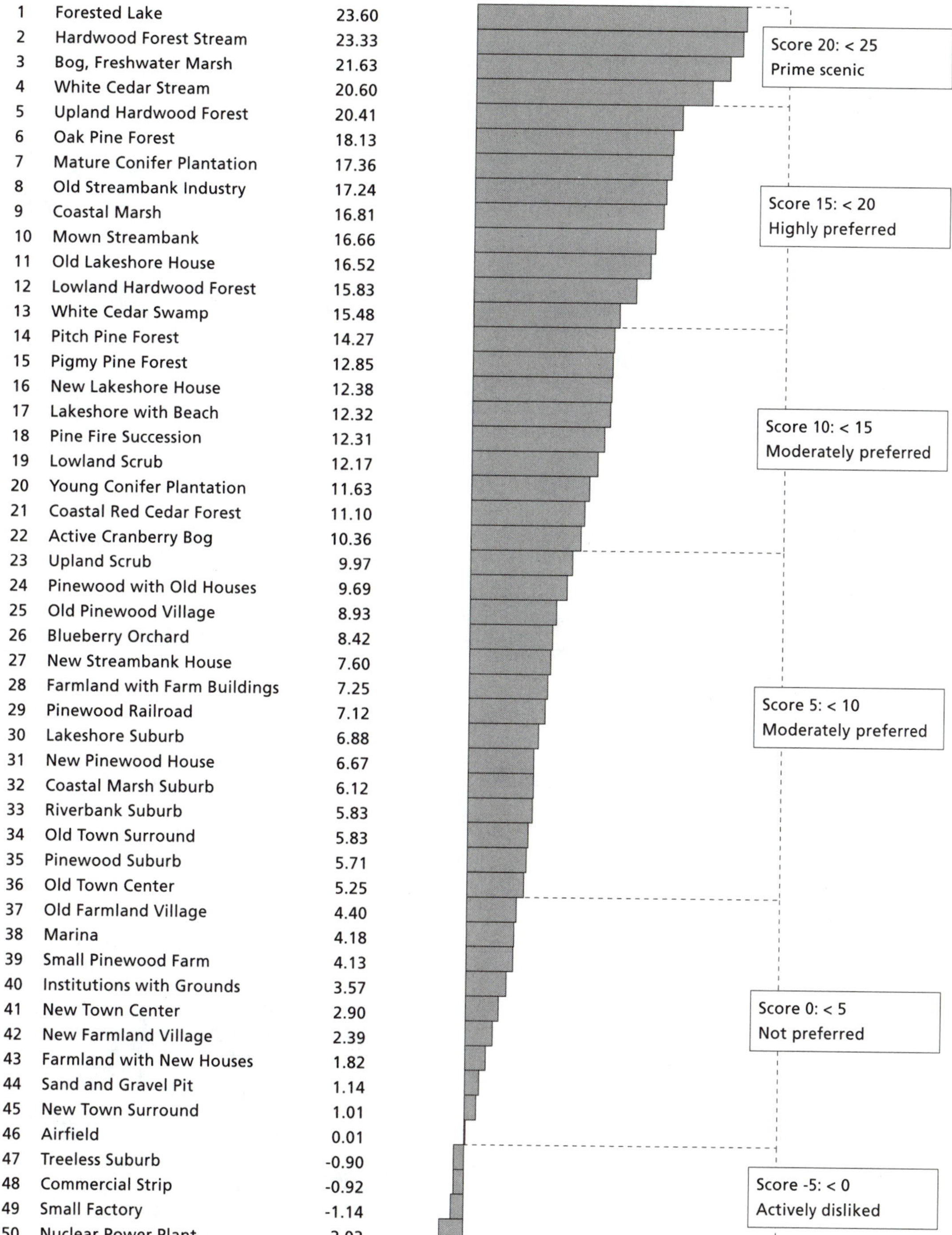

1 Forested Lake 23.60
2 Hardwood Forest Stream 23.33
3 Bog, Freshwater Marsh 21.63
4 White Cedar Stream 20.60
5 Upland Hardwood Forest 20.41
6 Oak Pine Forest 18.13
7 Mature Conifer Plantation 17.36
8 Old Streambank Industry 17.24
9 Coastal Marsh 16.81
10 Mown Streambank 16.66
11 Old Lakeshore House 16.52
12 Lowland Hardwood Forest 15.83
13 White Cedar Swamp 15.48
14 Pitch Pine Forest 14.27
15 Pigmy Pine Forest 12.85
16 New Lakeshore House 12.38
17 Lakeshore with Beach 12.32
18 Pine Fire Succession 12.31
19 Lowland Scrub 12.17
20 Young Conifer Plantation 11.63
21 Coastal Red Cedar Forest 11.10
22 Active Cranberry Bog 10.36
23 Upland Scrub 9.97
24 Pinewood with Old Houses 9.69
25 Old Pinewood Village 8.93
26 Blueberry Orchard 8.42
27 New Streambank House 7.60
28 Farmland with Farm Buildings 7.25
29 Pinewood Railroad 7.12
30 Lakeshore Suburb 6.88
31 New Pinewood House 6.67
32 Coastal Marsh Suburb 6.12
33 Riverbank Suburb 5.83
34 Old Town Surround 5.83
35 Pinewood Suburb 5.71
36 Old Town Center 5.25
37 Old Farmland Village 4.40
38 Marina 4.18
39 Small Pinewood Farm 4.13
40 Institutions with Grounds 3.57
41 New Town Center 2.90
42 New Farmland Village 2.39
43 Farmland with New Houses 1.82
44 Sand and Gravel Pit 1.14
45 New Town Surround 1.01
46 Airfield 0.01
47 Treeless Suburb -0.90
48 Commercial Strip -0.92
49 Small Factory -1.14
50 Nuclear Power Plant -2.03
Score 20: < 25
Prime scenic
Score 15: < 20
Highly preferred
Score 10: < 15
Moderately preferred
Score 5: < 10
Moderately preferred
Score 0: < 5
Not preferred
Score -5: < 0
Actively disliked

FIGURE 4.9 Final scores and order of preference of visual types. *(Source: Pinelands Commission 1980)*

TABLE 4.21
PINELANDS POPULATION AND POPULATION INCREASE, 1950–1978

	Pinelands population	Population change	Population change, %	Average Annual change, %
1950	118,400			
1950-1960		72,731	61.43	4.91
1960	191,131			
1960-1970		77,613	40.61	3.47
1970	268,744			
1970-1980		154,721	57.57	4.65
1980	423,465			
1980-1990		126,056	29.77	2.64
1990	549,521			
1990-1996		40,958	7.45	1.21
1996	590,479			

Note: $i = n\sqrt{\frac{A}{P}} - 1$ i = Average Annual Change
A = The Increased Pinelands Population
n = The Number of Years
P = The Previous Pinelands Population
SOURCE: Pinelands Commission 1997.

TABLE 4.22
HOUSEHOLD INCREASE PROJECTIONS FOR PINELANDS SECTION OF EACH COUNTY TO 2000

	1980–1990	1990–2000
Atlantic	38,700	14,600
Burlington	19,700	18,800
Camden	16,100	6,800
Cape May	4,500	2,800
Cumberland	1,300	800
Gloucester	9,000	8,700
Ocean	52,000	31,000
TOTAL	141,300	83,500

SOURCE: Pinelands Commission 1980.

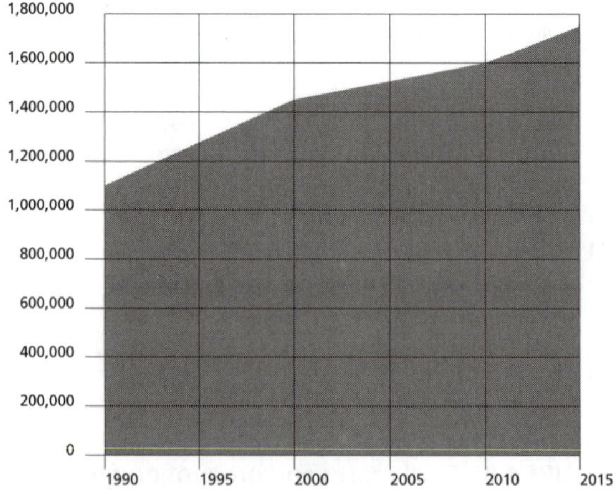

FIGURE 4.10 Population forecast for the Camp Pendleton study area. *(Source: Steinitz et al. 1996)*

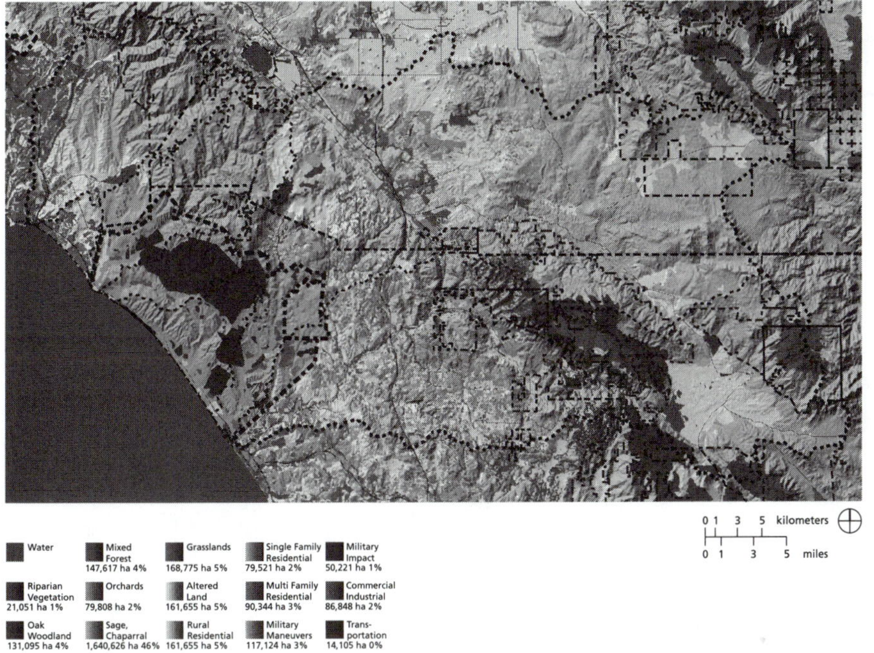

FIGURE 4.11 Land cover—land use, vegetation, and terrain. *(Source: Steinitz et al. 1996)*

FIGURE 4.12 Visual preference, Camp Pendleton study area. *(Source: Steinitz et al. 1996)*

FIGURE 4.13 Visual exposure, Camp Pendleton study area. *(Source: Steinitz et al. 1996)*

FIGURE 4.14 Visual values—combining preference and exposure maps. *(Source: Steinitz et al. 1996)*

and vegetables, and controlling the fires that are much a part of the ecosystem. Both the Pinelands and the Camp Pendleton plans include accounts of regional histories. Both planning studies also conducted detailed visual quality analyses. Such knowledge about how people live and relate their environment is too often absent from the information-collection phase of planning processes. This information is crucial for the planning process to be humanized.

5

SUITABILITY ANALYSIS

Once an ecological inventory of a place has been conducted, and some understanding of the relationships between people and environment has been achieved, it is then necessary to make more detailed studies of these interactions to present options for future use. One such type of detailed study is a *suitability analysis.* "Consult the Genius of the place in all," Alexander Pope suggested, and this is an apt definition of suitability analysis.

There are also several more recent (and rather more wordy and cumbersome) definitions. Often, *capability* and *suitability* are two words that are used interchangeably; however, there is enough subtle variation in how these terms have been adapted for the purpose of land classification that it would be useful to define each. To be *capable* is to have the ability or strength to be qualified or fitted for or to be susceptible or open to the influence or effect of. To be *suitable* is to be appropriate, fitting, or becoming (Barnhart 1953).

Various definitions for land-capability analysis have been proposed. Land-capability classification has been defined by soil scientists as a grouping of kinds of soil into special units, subclasses, and classes according to their potential uses and the treatments required for their sustained use (Brady 1974; Brady and Weil 1996). An alternate definition is evaluation based on an inherent, natural, or intrinsic ability of the resource to provide for use, which includes abilities that result from past alterations or current management practices. A third definition, suggested by the U.S. Geological Survey, relies solely on geologic and hydrologic information. According to this definition, land-capability analysis measures the ability of land to support different types of development with a given level of geologic and hydrologic costs (Laird et al. 1979, 2). A fourth definition has been developed by the U.S. Forest Service to implement the Forest and Rangeland Renewable Resources Planning Act of 1974. According to the USFS, capability is "the potential of an area of land to produce resources, supply goods and services and allow resource uses under an assumed set of management practices and at a given level of management intensity" (U.S. Congress 1979, 53984).

Land suitability may be defined as the fitness of a given tract of land for a defined use (Food and Agriculture Organization of the United Nations 1977). Differences in the degree of suitability are determined by the relationship, actual or anticipated, between benefits and the required changes associated with the use on the tract in question (Brinkman and Smyth 1973). Another definition for suitability analysis, provided by the USFS, is "the resource management practices to a particular area of land, as determined by an analysis of the economic and environmental consequences" (U.S. Congress 1979, 53985). For this chapter, suitability analysis is considered to be the process of determining the fitness, or the appropriateness, of a given tract of land for a specified use.

In this chapter, three specific suitability approaches, computer applications, and the carrying-capacity concept are reviewed. Two applications of suitability analysis are discussed as examples: Medford Township, New Jersey; and Whitman County, Washington.

APPROACHES TO SUITABILITY ANALYSIS—METHODS

Three approaches to suitability analysis that merit closer review include (1) several NRCS systems, (2) the McHarg suitability analysis method, and (3) suitability analysis methods developed in the Netherlands.

Natural Resources Conservation Service Systems

The oldest, most established system for defining the ability of soil to support agronomic uses is the U.S. Soil Conservation Service capability classification. As a result of the disastrous effects of the dust bowl era, the Soil Erosion Service was established in 1933 by the Franklin Roosevelt administration. The agency was reorganized and named the Soil Conservation Service in 1935, which in turn was renamed the Natural Resources Conservation Service in 1994. The NRCS works closely with a system of locally elected conservation district boards responsible for soil and water conservation policy in almost every county of the United States. The conservation districts receive technical assistance locally from professional NRCS conservationists.

The capability classification is one of several interpretive groupings made by the NRCS in standard soil surveys. Capability classes are based on soil types as mapped and interpreted by the NRCS. They were developed to assist farmers with agricultural management practices. While there are other systems that have also been developed to classify soils for agriculture (Donahue et al. 1977; Reganold and Singer 1978, 1979), the NRCS system is the most common one in the United States. Groupings are made according to the limitations of the soils when they are used for field crops, the risk of damage when they are used, and the manner in which they respond to management. The classification does not take into account major construction activity that would alter slope, soil depth, or other soil characteristics. Nor does it take into account reclamation projects or apply to rice, cranberries, horticultural crops, or other crops requiring special management (Davis et al. 1976).

In the capability system, all kinds of soils are grouped at three levels: the *capability class,* the *subclass,* and the *unit* (Soil Conservation Service 1975; Soil Survey Staff 1951, 1975a, 1975b). The following description of three major categories of capability classification was adopted from Klingebiel and Montgomery (1961), Singer et al. (1979), and Davis et al. (1976). *Capability classes* are the broadest groups and are designated by Roman numerals I to VIII. The numerals indicate progressively greater limitations and narrower choices for practical agricultural use, defined as follows: Class I soils have few limitations that restrict their use. Class II soils have moderate limitations that reduce the choice of plants that can be grown or require moderate conservation practices. Class III soils have severe limitations that reduce the choice of plants that can be grown, require special conservation practices, or both. Class IV soils have very severe limitations that reduce the choice of plants that can be grown, require very careful management, or both. Class V soils are not likely to erode but have other limitations that limit their use mainly to pasture or range, woodland, or wildlife habitat. Class VI soils have severe limitations that make them generally unsuited to cultivation and limit their use mainly to pasture or range, woodland, or wildlife habitat. Class VII soils have very severe limitations that make them unsuited for commercial crop production and restrict their use to recreation, wildlife habitat, water supply, or aesthetic purposes. Class VIII soils and landforms have limitations that preclude their use for commercial plant production and restrict their use to recreation, wildlife habitat, water supply, or aesthetic uses (Klingebiel and Montgomery 1961; Singer et al. 1979; Davis et al. 1976).

Capability subclasses are soil groups within one class. They are identified by adding the lowercase letters e, w, s, or c to the Roman numeral; for example, IIe. The letter e indicates that the chief limitation is risk of erosion unless close-growing plant cover is maintained. The letter w indicates that water in or on the soil interferes with plant growth or cultivation. The letter s shows that the soil is limited primarily because it is shallow, droughty, or stony; while c shows that the major limitation is that the climate is too cold or too dry. In class I there are no subclasses because there are no limitations on this class. On the other hand, subsequent classes may contain several subclasses (Singer et al. 1979; Davis et al. 1976; Broderson 1994).

Capability units are further distinctions of soil groups within the subclasses. The soils in one capability unit are sufficiently similar to be suited to the same crops and pasture plants, to require similar management, and to have similar productivity and other responses to management. Capability units are identified by the addition of an Arabic numeral to the subclass symbol; for example, IIe-2 or IIIe-3 (Singer et al. 1979; Davis et al. 1976).

In addition to capability classification for agronomic uses, soil surveys also include interpretation of limitations for such land uses as septic tanks, sewage lagoons, homesites, lawns, streets and parking lots, athletic fields, parks and play areas, campsites, sanitary landfills, and cemeteries. Soil conservationists have long stressed that the main purpose of soil survey information is for agriculture and that capability classes were developed specifically for row crops. Nevertheless, soil survey information has been increasingly utilized by planners, landscape architects, and civil engineers, because it is the most ubiquitous standard source of information about the natural environment in the United States available on the local level.

Soil surveys are seen to be useful for community and regional planning by their authors. Take, for example, this statement from the Montgomery County (Dayton), Ohio, soil survey:

> The expansion of nonfarm uses of land can remove many acres from farming in a short time. Freeways and super highways can displace up to about 50 acres per mile [20.25 hectares per mile; 31.25 acres or 12.66 hectares per kilometer]. A shopping center can easily replace 50 to 100 acres of farmland [20.25 to 40.5 hectares]. These uses tend to permanently remove land from farm use.
>
> The rapid suburban expansion has emphasized soil-related problems that builders must deal with. For example, some of the soils have severe limitations for use as septic tank disposal fields, some are shallow to hard limestone bedrock, some are underlain by a porous substratum and are droughty, some are easily eroded, and a few soils have no serious limitations. Two of the most serious concerns in community development are the limitations of the soils for septic tank disposal fields and the erosion hazard. Improperly functioning septic tank systems are a threat to health in areas where the soils have severe limitations for this use. Erosion losses in developing areas are commonly much higher than on comparable farmland, particularly during periods of construction. Erosion control practices, therefore, become very important in areas undergoing development. Specific erosion control practices for use in rural-fringe areas have been developed by the Soil Conservation Service. City officials and developers interested in these practices can obtain information about them from the office of the Montgomery Soil and Water Conservation District (Davis et al. 1976, 34–35).

Several researchers have illustrated how soil survey information can be applied to planning and resource management (Bartelli et al. 1966; Lynch 1971; McCormack 1974; Meyers et al. 1979; and Lynch and Hack 1984). Fred Miller (1978) has described how soil surveys have been criticized because of the limitations of information for urban land-use planning. According to the research of Steven Gordon and Gaybrielle Gordon (1981), soil survey information was found to be accurate for septic tank limitations but very inconsistent for homesites and roads. They warn that "this implies that planners must use these published ratings with extreme caution in making environmental and land-use planning decisions and that consultation with state and local soil experts should be sought" (Gordon and Gordon 1981, 301).

As a result of the shortcomings of the soil surveys, a dilemma is faced by conservationists and planners alike. Soil conservationists have done an excellent job mapping and classifying land in the United States and have generated the most uniformly available source of physical science information. Planners faced with tight budgets must use soil survey information because they lack the time and/or money and expertise to generate original data.

The NRCS has met the growing demand for its products with new systems to assist planners and resource managers. One such effort is the NRCS important farmland mapping program. This classification system identifies two major categories of farmland of national importance, prime and unique lands, and two other categories, farmlands of statewide and of local importance. There are national criteria for the first two categories, while the latter have criteria established on the state level (Dideriksen 1984).

The important farmland mapping program [coupled with the publication of the National Agricultural Lands Study (1981) that documented a loss in the prime cropland base of the nation] presented new problems for both planners and soil conservationists. For instance, in DeKalb County, Illinois, 97 percent of the land is prime farmland. Obviously not all this land can be preempted for agricultural use, because there are demands for other uses also. On the other hand, in Whitman County, Washington, only 2.8 percent of the land is prime. Most of the land is excluded from the prime category because of steep slopes and high erosion potential. Yet Whitman is the most productive winter white wheat county in the nation, and most of the land in the county is under cultivation. A new system was needed to weigh the agricultural capability of land against its demands for other uses. In 1981, a pilot program for such a system was launched (Wright 1981; Wright et al. 1982; Steiner et al. 1987; Steiner 1987; Steiner et al. 1994; Pease and Coughlin 1996).

Lloyd E. Wright, formerly of the NRCS Office of Land Use in Washington, D.C., along with planners and soil conservationists from 12 selected counties across the United States, was responsible for the initial design of the system, which has been refined by considerable research (Steiner et al. 1994; Pease and Coughlin 1996). The system is divided into two phases: (1) establishing an agricultural land evaluation (LE) and (2) establishing an agricultural site assessment (SA). Together the LE and SA are known as the Agricultural Land Evaluation and Site Assessment (LESA) System. For LESA, a *system* is defined as "all the factors, weights, and scales used in the evaluation of soils and other site conditions" (Pease and Coughlin 1996, 215). Two descriptions of LESA—the original 1983 version and the refined 1996 system—have been developed to help planners. The 1983 version will be explained first, followed by the 1996 modifications.

Land Evaluation Value. Agricultural *land evaluation* (LE) is a process of rating soils of a given area and placing them into ten groups ranging from the best-suited to the poorest-suited for a specific agricultural use. A relative value is determined for each group, with the best group being assigned a value of 100 and all other groups assigned a lower relative value. For LESA, a *factor* is a term used "to label a group of attributes, such as soil potential, size, compatibility, or scenic quality" (Pease and Coughlin 1996, 213). *Factor rating* then is the "number of points assigned to a factor, before weighting, on a 0–100 point scale" (Pease and Coughlin 1996, 213). The *factor scale* is the "way points are assigned to a factor on [a] 0–100 scale" (Pease and Coughlin 1996, 213). A *score,* then, is the total of all the factor ratings. The LE factors are based on soil survey information (U.S. Department of Agriculture 1983).

Land evaluation rates the quality of soil for agricultural use by incorporating four rating systems: *land-capability classification, important farmland classification, soil productivity,* and *soil potential.* NRCS recommends that one of the last two ratings (soil potential being preferred) be used in conjunction with the first two ratings. The land-use staff of NRCS has explained the method for combining these four systems in the 1983 *National Agricultural Land Evaluation and Site Assessment Handbook:*

- *Land capability classification* identifies degrees of agricultural limitations that are inherent in the soils of a given area. It enables state and regional planners to use the system for planning and program implementation at regional and state levels.
- *Soil productivity* relates the LE score to the local agricultural industry based on productivity of the

The process of land evaluation rates soils in an area from best to worst for a specific agricultural use. Farm near Triengen, Switzerland.

soils for a specified indicator crop. The use of both soil productivity and land capability classification should provide some indication of relative net income expected from each category of soils.

- *Soil potentials* for specified indicator crops are preferred in place of soil productivity in the LE system. Soil potential ratings classify soils based on a standard of performance and recognition of the costs of overcoming soil limitations, plus the cost of continuing limitations if any exist. These classes enable planners to understand the local agricultural industry.
- *Important farmland classification* enables planners to identify prime and other important farmlands at the local level. Use of the national criteria for definition of prime farmland provides a consistent basis for comparison of local farmland with farmland in other areas (Adapted from U.S. Department of Agriculture 1983).

The NRCS recommends that soils be arrayed into ten groups ranging from the best- to the worst-suited for the agricultural use considered (cropland, rangeland, forest). Each group should contain approximately 10 percent of the total planning area (U.S. Department of Agriculture 1983). The number of soils in each group may vary depending on the soil composition in the area. Three evaluation systems are used in the ranking to prevent the possibility that any one method would have an undue effect on the final outcome. For example, soil productivity may be used to establish the initial groupings. These groupings are then modified based upon the other evaluation systems. Specifically, two soils may have the same productivity rating but different land capability ratings. In this case, the soil type with the better land capability rating would be placed in a higher grouping. Similarly, prime soils (according to the important farmland classification) would be placed in a higher grouping than soils of statewide importance even though both soils may have the same productivity rating.

A relative value is determined for each agricultural grouping based on adjusted average yields. That is, a weighted-average yield is calculated for each soil type within the grouping. The weighted-average yield for each grouping is then expressed as a percentage of the highest weighted-average yield. This percentage becomes the relative value for each agricultural grouping, and the relative value is the LE value that is combined with the site assessment value (U.S. Department of Agriculture 1983). Table 5.1 gives an example of the worksheet from which the LE relative values are determined.

Site Assessment Value. Although the value from the LE system provides a good indication of the relative quality of a soil for a particular agricultural use, it does not take into account the effect of location, distance to market, adjacent land uses, zoning, and other considerations that determine land suitability. In other words, relative agricultural value is only one of many site attributes, or factors, which may be considered by planners and land-use decision makers. Consequently, NRCS has created the *site assessment* (SA) system to incorporate some of these other factors into the decision-making process.

The factors that are included in the SA system form seven groups: agricultural land use; agricultural viability factors; land-use regulations and tax concessions; options to proposed use; impact of proposed use; compatibility with, and importance to, comprehensive development plans; and urban infrastructure. The following listed factors were identified in the 1983 LESA handbook for use in site assessment procedures:

Agricultural land use

- Percentage of area in agriculture use within 1 mile
- Percentage of site farmed in 2 of the last 10 years
- Land use adjacent to site

TABLE 5.1
AGRICULTURAL LAND-EVALUATION WORKSHEET SHOWING CRITERIA FOR DELINEATING THE TEN BASIC GROUPS OF SOIL

1	2	3	4	5	6	7
Agricultural group	**Land capability**	**Important farmland determination**	**Potential or productivity**	**Percentage of total area**	**Acres**	**Relative value**
1	I	Prime	95–100	18.8	76,270	100
2	IIw	Prime	95–100	31.3	127,470	94
3	I	Prime	94	5.4	21,975	88
4	II	Prime	90–94	9.6	39,365	84
5	II	Prime	80–89	21.0	85,635	81
6	II	Prime	70–79	3.5	14,570	75
7	II	Prime	69	7.1	28,695	44
8	II/IIIw	Statewide	All	2.1	8,275	31
9	IIIe/IV/V	Statewide	All	0.9	3,410	28
10	Others	All	All	0.3	1,375	0

SOURCE: Steiner et al. 1987, adapted from U.S. Department of Agriculture 1983.

Agricultural viability factors
- Size of farm
- Agricultural support system
- Land ownership
- On-site investments (barns, storage, and conservation measures)
- Impact of this conversion on retention of other farmland and the agricultural support system
- Conservation plan

Land-use regulations and tax concessions
- Zoning for site
- Zoning for area around site
- Use of agricultural value assessment or other tax benefits
- Agricultural districts or right-to-farm legislation

Options to proposed use
- Unique siting needs for proposed use
- Suitability of site for proposed use
- Availability of less productive lands with similar attributes for proposed use
- Number of undeveloped and suitable alternative sites and need for additional land

Impact of proposed use
- Compatibility of proposed use with existing land use
- Impact on flooding
- Impact on wetlands
- Impact on historical areas
- Impact on recreation and open spaces
- Impact on cultural features
- Impact on unique vegetation

Compatibility with comprehensive development plans
- Local
- Regional
- Degree of socioeconomic importance of proposed use to the community

Urban infrastructure
- Distance to urban area
- Central water distribution system (within *x* miles)
- Central sanitary sewage system (within *x* miles)
- Investment for urban development
- Transportation

- Distance to other urban infrastructure (job centers, schools, and shopping)
- Emergency services (U.S. Department of Agriculture 1983)

Local communities may identify other factors. Any of the factors noted in the list may or may not be needed, or used, in the design of any local LESA system. Once specific factors have been chosen for the SA evaluation, each factor must be stratified into a range of possible points. The NRCS recommends that a maximum of 10 points be given for each factor. In general, the maximum points are assigned when on-site conditions are most favorable to the continuation of agriculture. For example, suppose that the factor "percentage of area in agriculture" is included in the SA evaluation. If 90 to 100 percent of the area in proximity to a site is in agricultural use, then the maximum of 10 points would be given. Alternatively, if only about one-third of the surrounding area is in agriculture, then a lower number of points (such as 4) would be given.

After points have been assigned for all factors, weights ranging from 1 to 10 can be considered for each factor. Those factors considered most important would be given the highest weights, while factors of lesser importance would be given lower weights. The weights are multiplied by the assigned points for each factor, and the resulting products are then summed. Finally, the total is converted to a scale having a maximum of 200 points. Thus, the final SA value, as recommended in the LESA handbook, can range from 0 to 200 (U.S. Department of Agriculture 1983).

Combining the LE and SA Systems. Although the LE and SA systems can be used separately, they are most useful when combined. Table 5.2 shows one method that was tested to combine these systems in a county in Washington State. For each site, the acreage of each soil unit is multiplied by its relative value (LE value). These products are summed over all units, and the sum is divided by the total acreage of the site to get an average LE value. In this example, ten SA factors were selected, with each having a maximum of 20 points. The sum of the points assigned for each factor results in the SA value, which can be a maximum of 200 points. Finally, the LE value is added to the SA value for the total LESA value. The maximum LESA value is 300. The SA system tested in this Washington county deviated from the one recommended by the NRCS in its 1983 LESA handbook. Instead of the more complicated weighting system for obtaining an SA score, a more straightforward addition approach was used.

In the example in Table 5.2, site 1 has the greatest LESA value, indicating that it is more suitable for agricultural use than site 2. Consequently, site 2 would be favored for the residential development.

In addition to being useful for judging the agricultural suitability of alternative sites, the LESA system can also be used to help decide whether a single parcel should be converted to a nonfarmland use. Local decision makers would have to specify a cutoff LESA value out of 300 points (or other maximum value). Parcels with a LESA value below the cutoff could be considered for conversion.

Modified LESA System. In the early 1990s, researchers from Arizona State University, Oregon State University, and the University of Pennsylvania studied LESA for NRCS to determine the extent of its use and its effectiveness (Steiner et al. 1994). A goal of the research was to modify and improve LESA as a result of learning from the experience of those jurisdictions which had used the systems. Two members of the team, James Pease of Oregon State University and Robert Coughlin of the University of Pennsylvania, then prepared a new LESA guidebook for NRCS (Pease and Coughlin 1996).

One contribution of the new guidebook was the clarification of terms (such as factor, factor rating, factor scale, score, and system) that were defined earlier in this chapter. Other important terms defined include ranking and weighting. *Ranking* "refers to the relative importance of a site compared to other sites" (Pease and Coughlin 1996, 11). *Weighting* involves "assigning a weight (for example, 0–1.0) to each factor in order to rec-

TABLE 5.2
HYPOTHETICAL EXAMPLE DEMONSTRATING A POSSIBLE USE OF THE COMBINED LE AND SA SYSTEMS IN A WASHINGTON STATE COUNTY

Proposed land use: single-family residential development
Site 1: 23 acres of Palouse silt loam, 7–25% slope with LE of 87
37 acres of Anders silt loam, 3–15% slope with LE of 48

Site 2: 32 acres of Cheney silt loam, 0–7% slope with LE of 80
23 acres of Staley silt loam, 7–25% slope with LE of 63

Land evaluation:

Site 1	*Site 2*
$23 \times 87 = 2{,}001$	$32 \times 80 = 2{,}560$
$37 \times 48 = \underline{1{,}776}$	$23 \times 63 = \underline{1{,}449}$
3,777	4,009

Average LE rating $= \dfrac{3{,}777}{23 + 37} = 63$ Average LE rating $= \dfrac{4{,}009}{32 + 23} = 73$

Site assessment factors	**Max. pts.**	**Site 1**	**Site 2**
1. Percentage of area in agriculture within 1 mile	20	20	10
2. Land use adjacent to site	20	20	10
3. Wasting agricultural land	20	20	15
4. Availability of nonagricultural land for proposal	20	20	15
5. Compatibility with comprehensive plan and zoning	20	17	15
6. Availability of public services	20	15	10
7. Compatibility of proposed use with surrounding use	20	20	15
8. Environmental factors	20	20	15
9. Open-space taxation	20	15	10
10. Other factors unique to the site	20	15	13
Total site assessment points	200	182	128
Average land evaluation rating	100	63	73
Total points (total of previous two lines)	300	245	201
Choice for development: Site 2			

SOURCE: Steiner et al. 1987.

ognize the relative importance of the factor in the LESA system" (Pease and Coughlin 1996, 11).

Pease and Coughlin developed a flow chart to explain how to develop a local LESA system (Figure 5.1). They suggest the formation of a local LESA committee, which may be divided into separate LE and SA committees, to choose and scale factors (Pease and Coughlin 1996). The LE factors in the modified LESA remain relatively similar to the original 1983 version, although Pease and Coughlin stress that they should be "soil-based factors" (1996, 13).

Much innovation has occurred when using the SA factors in place of the original system. Pease and Coughlin recommend three levels of site assessment:

- SA-1: Factors other than soil-based qualities measuring limitations on agricultural productivity or farm practices.
- SA-2: Factors measuring development pressure or land conversion.
- SA-3: Factors measuring other public values, such as historic or scenic values (1996, 13).

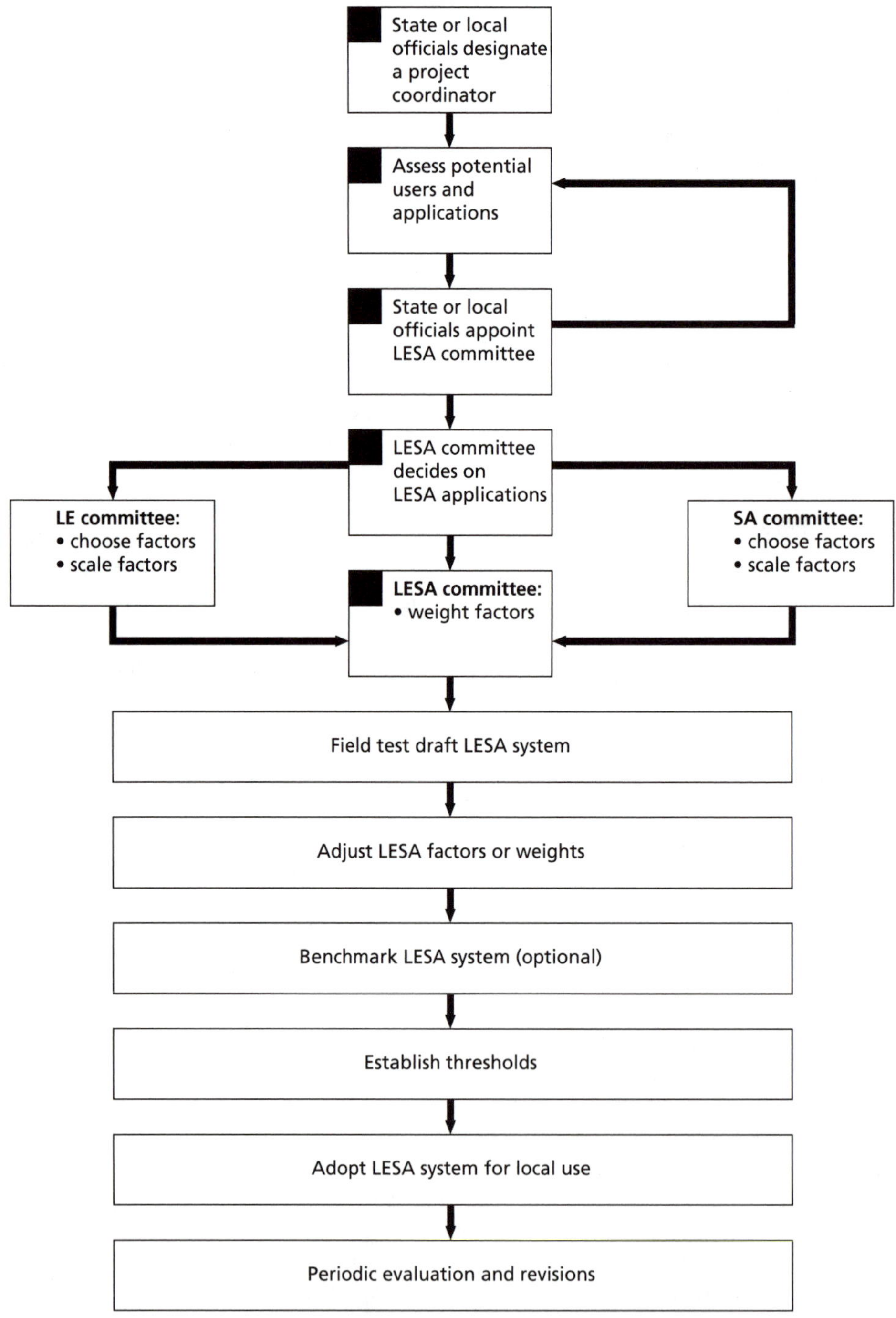

FIGURE 5.1 Flow chart for developing a local LESA system. *(Source: Adapted from Pease and Coughlin 1996)*

The modified LE and SA factors are presented in Table 5.3. A hypothetical site illustrating these factors is displayed in Figure 5.2. Pease and Coughlin note that the LESA committee will assign a relative weight to each factor (Column 3 in Table 5.4). However, they recommend the use of

> a weight range of 0 to 1.00, so that all weights add up to 1.00 for a particular factor.
>
> Once the system is set up, each site is rated for each factor on a scale from 0–100 (Column 2). Then, each factor rating is multiplied by the corresponding factor weight (Column 3) to obtain a weighted factor rating (Column 4).
>
> Weighted ratings are summed to yield the total LESA score, which will range between 0 and 100. In the example shown in Table [5.3] the total LESA score is 71.2 (Pease and Coughlin 1996, 14–15).

Pease and Coughlin recommend the use of a computer spreadsheet to calculate LESA scores and provide a model in their guidebook. They also suggest field testing the LESA system and the establishment of thresholds. Field testing involves applying draft LESA systems to several actual sites in order to adjust the factor scales and/or weights. According to Pease and Coughlin, "Thresholds are used to group sites by scores into two or more classes for decision making" (1996, 16). For example, all sites above a certain threshold may be protected for only agricultural use or all sites below a certain threshold permitted for other uses.

Pease and Coughlin (1996) identify five key design criteria for LESA systems. First, the focus of the LESA system should address the question "What are we trying to learn from the LESA score?" (Pease and Coughlin 1996, 16). Second, "Data sources for factors and their point scaling should be explicit for each factor" (Pease and Coughlin 1996, 17). Third, redundant LE and SA factors should be avoided. Fourth, the system should be reproducible, that is, in "order to obtain consistent factor ratings and LESA scores, measurable factors and clear definitions must be

TABLE 5.3
CLASSIFICATION OF TYPICAL SA FACTORS

SA-1 Factors (agricultural productivity):

- Size of site
- Compatibility of adjacent uses
- Compatibility of surrounding uses (impact on farm practices)
- Shape of site
- Percent of site in agricultural use
- Percent of site feasible to farm
- Level of on-farm investment
- Availability of agricultural support services
- Stewardship of site
- Environmental limitations on agricultural practices
- Availability and reliability of irrigation water

SA-2 Factors (development pressures impacting a site's continued agricultural use):

- Land use policy designation
- Percent of surrounding land in urban or rural development use
- Distance to public sewer
- Distance to public water
- Distance to urban feeder highway
- Distance to urban center or urban growth boundary
- Length of public road frontage of site
- Proximity to protected farmland

SA-3 Factors (other public values of a site supporting retention in agriculture):

- Open space strategic value of site (e.g., urban greenbelt)
- Educational value of site (e.g., for sustainable agriculture)
- Historic building or site
- Site of significant artifacts or relics
- Wetlands and riparian areas
- Scenic values
- Wildlife habitat
- Environmentally sensitive areas
- Floodplains protection

SOURCE: Pease and Coughlin 1996.

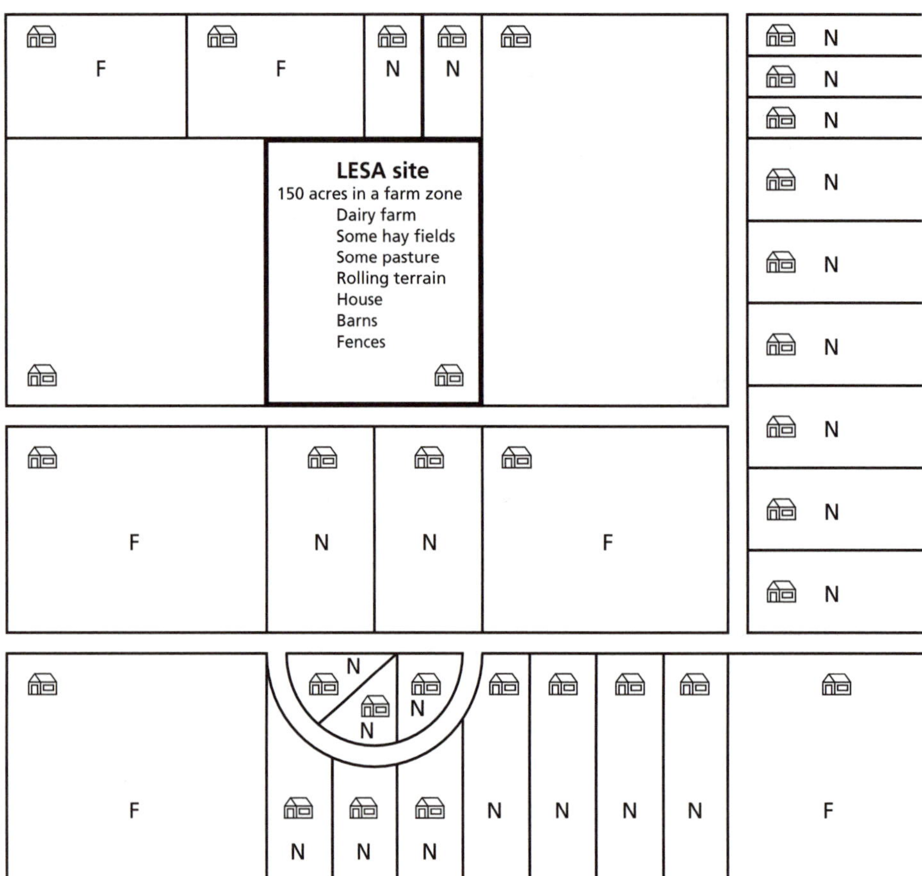

FIGURE 5.2 Illustration of a farm rated in Table 5.4. *(Source: Pease and Coughlin 1996)*

used" (Pease and Coughlin 1996, 18). Fifth, the system should be replicable, that is, different "sites with the same or similar factor characteristics should yield the same or similar factor ratings" (Pease and Coughlin 1996, 19).

The Pease and Coughlin LESA guidebook is targeted for local governments. In the years since LESA's initiation in the early 1980s, its use has spread among local and state governments. A 1991 nationwide survey identified 212 local and state governments in 31 states using LESA (Coughlin et al. 1994). In addition, its use had been extended to riparian zones (Fry et al. 1994), rural development (Bennington County Regional Commission 1994), statewide development suitability (Bowen and Ferguson 1994), housing siting in forest areas, sand and gravel mining location, and wetlands protection (Pease and Coughlin 1996).

Use of LESA at the Federal Level. LESA is also used at the national level by federal agencies. The importance of LESA was enhanced by the regulations implementing the Farmland Protection Policy Act (FPPA) of 1981. These federal rules were adopted in 1984 (U.S. Department of Agriculture 1984). The FPPA was amended and strengthened

TABLE 5.4
AN EXAMPLE OF COMPUTING A LESA SCORE

(1) Factor name	(2) Factor rating (0–100)	×	(3) Weighting (Total = 1.00)	=	(4) Weighted factor rating
Land evaluation (site with one soil):					
1. Land capability	68	×	0.30	=	20.4
2. Soil productivity	62	×	0.20	=	12.4
Subtotals			0.50		32.8
Site assessment—1 (agricultural use factors):					
3. Acreage of farm	100	×	0.15	=	15.0
4. Farm investment	80	×	0.05	=	4.0
5. Surrounding uses	60	×	0.10	=	6.0
Subtotals			0.30		25.0
Site assessment—2 (development pressure):					
6. Protection by plan or zoning	90	×	0.06	=	5.4
7. Distance to sewer	70	×	0.05	=	3.5
Subtotals			0.11		8.9
Site assessment—3 (other factors):					
8. Scenic quality	50	×	0.09	=	4.5
Subtotals			0.09		4.5
Total of factor weights	////////				
(must equal 1.00)	////////				
	////////		1.00		
Total LESA score	////////		//////		
(sum of weighted factor ratings)	////////		//////		
	////////		//////		71.2

SOURCE: Pease and Coughlin 1996.

somewhat by Congress in the passage of the Conservation Title in the Food Security Act of 1985. The FPPA requires federal agencies to identify and take into account the adverse effects of federal programs on farmland protection; to consider alternative actions, as appropriate, that could lessen such adverse effects; and to ensure that such federal programs, to the extent practical, are compatible with state, local, and private programs and policies to protect farmland (American Farmland Trust 1997; Daniels and Bowers 1997).

For the purposes of the FPPA, farmland includes land identified under the important farmland program. However, prime farmland that a state or local government has designated through planning or zoning for commercial, industrial, or residential use is excluded from the provision of the FPPA. Federal programs under this act include activities or responsibilities that involve undertaking, financing, or assisting construction or improvement projects as well as acquiring, disposing, or managing of federal lands and facilities. Some activities—such as licensing activities, the granting of permits, and national defense projects—are not subject to the act.

The NRCS has been given a prominent role in the implementation of the FPPA. In particular, the NRCS is responsible for developing the criteria that federal agencies must use in assessing the effects of their programs on farmland;

providing information to states, local governments, individuals, organizations, and other federal agencies useful in farmland protection; and providing technical assistance to states, local governments, and non-profit-making organizations wanting to develop farmland protection programs.

Regarding criteria for assessing farmland effects, the NRCS has mandated that federal agencies use LESA. The LE value is determined by the NRCS on the form (AD-1006) shown in Figure 5.3. Federal agencies must then determine the SA value and combine it with the LE value as specified in the regulations implementing the FPPA. As can be seen from Figure 5.3, the NRCS chose not to use the more complex weighting system that it had recommended for SA in its 1983 handbook. In addition, the maximum SA value that can be obtained by federal agencies is 160 from the twelve SA factors rather than the 200 maximum that the NRCS recommends in its LESA handbook. Thus, the maximum LESA value is 260 in Form AD-1006, compared to the 300 maximum in the 1983 handbook and the 100 maximum in the 1996 guidebook. In cases where a state or local government has adopted a LESA system and this system has been certified by the NRCS state conservationist, it is recommended that the federal agencies use that system to make their evaluation of the farmland conversion effects on their programs.

The McHarg, or University of Pennsylvania, Suitability Analysis Method

The seminal explanation of suitability analysis was provided by Ian McHarg (1969), based on his work with colleagues and students at the University of Pennsylvania, where he was an influential teacher. Many of his colleagues and former students have contributed to his suitability analysis method, so it may be considered the "University of Pennsylvania method."

McHarg developed his method on a solid bedrock of work in overlays by other landscape architects, but McHarg's contributions were unique and important. Landscape architects began using hand-drawn, sieve-mapping overlays in the late nineteenth century. Pennsylvania State University professor emeritus Lynn Miller (1996) credits Charles Eliot and his associates in the office of Olmsted, Olmsted, and Eliot with pioneering overlays through sun prints produced on their office windows. Both Miller and McHarg acknowledge the early contributions of Charles Eliot, an Olmsted protégé, who worked systematically with scientists to collect and map information to be used in planning and design. Warren Manning, an apprentice of both Olmsted and Eliot, used soil and vegetation information with topography and their combined relationship to land use to prepare four different maps of the town of Billerica, Massachusetts, in 1912. Manning's Billerica Plan displayed recommendations and changes in the town's circulation routes and land use (Steinitz et al. 1976; Neckar 1989; Manning 1913).

Eliot left the most explicit explanation about why and how the overlays were employed. After Eliot's death, his father Charles W. Eliot, the president of Harvard, published a biography-autobiography. *Charles Eliot, Landscape Architect* (1902) was an interpretation of his son's work. This book provides perhaps the first account of the overlay technique. The Boston Metropolitan Park work undertaken by Olmsted, Olmsted, and Eliot, with Eliot in charge, involved six months of "diligent researches" (1902, 496). Eliot used a variety of consultants, including a Massachusetts Institute of Technology professor, as well as Olmsted staff members such as Manning, to conduct surveys of the metropolitan region's geology, topography, and vegetation. These maps provided the basis for the overlay process which Eliot describes as follows:

U. S. Department of Agriculture

FARMLAND CONVERSION IMPACT RATING

PART I (To be completed by Federal agency)	Date of land evaluation request
Name of project	Federal agency involved
Proposed land use	County and state
PART II (To be completed by NRCS)	Date request received by NRCS

Does the site contain prime, unique, statewide or local important farmland? (If no, the FPPA does not apply - do not complete additional parts of this form)	Yes ☐	No ☐	Acres irrigated	Average farm size

Major crop(s)	Farmable land in govt. jurisdiction Acres: %	Amount of farmland as defined in FPPA Acres: %
Name of land evaluation system used	Name of local site assessment system	Date land evaluation returned by NRCS

PART III (To be completed by Federal agency)		Alternative site rating			
		Site A	Site B	Site C	Site D
A. Total acres to be converted directly					
B. Total acres to be converted indirectly					
C. Total acres in site					
PART IV (To be completed by NRCS) Land evaluation information					
A. Total acres prime and unique farmland					
B. Total acres statewide and local important farmland					
C. Percentage of farmland in county or local govt. unit to be converted					
D. Percentage of farmland in govt. jurisdiction with same or higher relative value					
PART V (to be completed by NRCS) Land evaluation criterion					
Relative value of farmland to be converted (scale of 0 to 100 points)					
PART VI (To be completed by Federal agency) Site assessment criteria (These are explained in 7 CFR 658.5(b))	Maximum Points				
1. Area in nonurban use					
2. Perimeter in nonurban use					
3. Percent of site being farmed					
4. Protection provided by state and local government					
5. Distance from urban built-up area					
6. Distance to urban support services					
7. Size of present farm unit compared to average					
8. Creation of nonfarmable farmland					
9. Availability of farm unit compared to average					
10. On-farm investments					
11. Effects of conversion on farm support services					
12. Compatibilty with existing agricultural use					
TOTAL SITE ASSESSMENT POINTS	160				
PART VII (To be completed by Federal agency)					
Relative value of farmland (from Part V)	100				
Total site assessment (from Part VI above or a local site assessment)	160				
TOTAL POINTS (Total of above 2 lines)	260				

Site selected	Date of selection	Was a local site assessment used? Yes ☐ No ☐

Reason for selection:

FIGURE 5.3 Farmland conversion impact rating.

> By making use of sun-prints of the recorded boundary plans, by measuring compass lines along the numerous woodpaths, and by sketching the outlines of swamps, clearings, ponds, hills, and valleys, extremely serviceable maps were soon produced. The draughting of the several sheets was done in our office. Upon one sheet of tracing-cloth were drawn the boundaries, the roads and paths, and the lettering . . . on another sheet were drawn the streams, ponds and swamps; and on a third the hill shading was roughly indicated by pen and pencil. Gray sun-prints obtained from the three sheets superimposed in the printing frame, when mounted on cloth, served very well for all purposes of study. Photo-lithographed in three colors, namely, black, blue, and brown, the same sheets will serve as guide maps for the use of the public and the illustration of reports.
>
> Equipped with these maps, we have made good progress, as before remarked, in familiarizing ourselves with the "lay of the land" (1902, 496).

After Eliot and Manning there were several studies in which the use of the overlay technique is apparent, but a theoretical explanation about the rationale for using the technique as an orderly planning method was missing. The city plan for Dusseldorf, Germany, in 1912; the Doncaster, England, regional plan in 1922 (Abercrombie and Johnson 1922); the 1929 regional plan of New York and its environment (Regional Planning Staff 1929); and the 1943 London County plan (Forshaw and Abercrombie 1943) incorporate typical characteristics of the overlay process (Steinitz et al. 1976). Thomas Adams, who directed the extensive 1929 New York regional planning study, addressed suitability in his 1934 *The Design of Residential Areas,* but mostly from an economic perspective. An academic discussion of the overlay technique did not surface until 1950 and publication of the *Town and Country Planning Textbook* containing an article by Jacqueline Tyrwhitt that dealt explicitly with the overlay technique (Steinitz et al. 1976, see also Collins et al. 2000).

In an example given by Tyrwhitt (1950), four maps (relief, hydrology, rock types, and soil drainage) were drawn on transparent papers at the same scale, and referenced to common control features. These data maps were then combined into one land characteristics map which provided a synthesis, interpretation, and a judicious blending of the first four maps (Tyrwhitt 1950, Steinitz et al. 1976). This sieve-mapping, overlay method was widely accepted and incorporated in the large-scale planning of the British new towns and other development projects after World War II (Lyle and Stutz 1983; McSheffrey 1999). At the end of the war Ian McHarg took a correspondence course offered by Tyrwhitt and others. McHarg was also involved in new town planning in the early 1950s in Scotland, so he was quite aware of the British new town program. As a result, he was introduced to the concept of overlay mapping early in his career.

George Angus Hills' plan for Ontario Province (1961) is a pioneering North American example that employed a well-documented data-overlay technique (Belknap and Furtado 1967, 1968; Naveh and Lieberman 1994; Ndubisi 1997). Hills was on the staff of the Ontario Department of Lands and Forests. His technique divides regions into consecutively smaller units of physiographic similarity based on a gradient scale of climate and landform features. Through a process of comparing each physiographic site type or homogeneous land unit to a predetermined set of general land-use categories and rankings of potential or limitation for each use or activity, the resulting units were regrouped into larger geographic patterns called landscape units and again ranked to determine their relative potentials for dominant and multiple uses. The land-use activity with the highest feasibility ranking within a landscape unit was recommended as a major use (Belknap and Furtado 1967; Collins et al. 2000). The Hills method has been influential in the development of the Canadian Land Inventory System (Coombs and Thie 1979).

The year after Hills's Ontario plan, Philip Lewis, a landscape architect at the University of Wisconsin-Madison and principal consultant to the Wisconsin Department of Resource Development, applied an overlay analysis technique to evaluate natural resources for the entire state of Wisconsin (Lewis 1964, 1969, 1996). Lewis had been recruited to Wisconsin by Gaylord Nelson to start environmental planning in the state. Lewis's work was a direct response to the growth and demand for outdoor recreation across Wisconsin. According to Forster Ndubisi, "Unlike Hills, whose work was based primarily on examining biological and physical (biophysical) systems such as landforms and soils, Lewis was concerned more with perceptual features such as vegetation and outstanding scenery" (1997, 21). Lewis stressed the importance of the patterns, both natural and cultural, within the landscape. He combined individual landscape elements of water, wetlands, vegetation, and significant topography through overlays onto a composite map depicting Wisconsin's areas of prime environmental importance (Belknap and Furtado 1967, 1968; Steinitz et al. 1976). By combining resource inventory data and soil survey data, Lewis was able to create maps that identified intrinsic (natural) patterns. Once additional resources were grouped by patterns and mapped, points were assigned to major and additional resources and totaled to identify relative priority areas. Demand for planned uses and limitations of each priority area for specific uses were then combined to assign specific uses to each priority area (Collins et al. 2000).

McHarg, Lewis, and Hills refined their approaches during the 1960s and built their work on all these earlier efforts. McHarg especially advanced previous methods significantly by linking suitability analysis with theory. He provided a theoretical basis for overlaying information. McHarg's approach focused on mapping information on both natural and human-made attributes of the study area and photographing them initially as individual transparent maps (Belknap and Furtado 1967, 1968; McHarg 1969; Gordon 1985; McHarg and Steiner 1998). The transparent prints of light and dark values were superimposed over each other to construct the necessary suitability maps for each land use. These x-ray-like composite maps illustrated intrinsic suitabilities for land-use classifications, such as conservation, urbanization, and recreation for the specific planning area. These maps were then combined with each other as overlays to produce an overall composite suitability map (McHarg 1969).

McHarg's inventory process provides one of the first examples of methodological documentation for the overlay technique (with those by Hills and Lewis). McHarg was also the first to advocate the use of the overlay technique to gain an ecological understanding of a place. He noted that "a region is understood as a biophysical and social process comprehensible through the operation of [natural] laws and time. This can be reinterpreted as having explicit opportunities and constraints for any particular human use. A survey will reveal the most fit locations and processes" (1997, 321). As a result, he was explicit about the range and sequence of mapped information to be collected. McHarg also observed that the phenomena represented by the maps were *valued* differently by various groups of people and thus could be weighted differently, depending on the circumstance.

The emergence of documentation in general literature as well as in specific projects and studies in the late 1960s and early 1970s provides an indication of the formal acceptance of the overlay technique as a means to spatially relate environmental factors and provide a composite and comprehensive view of factor and land-use relationships (see, for example, McHarg 1968; Wallace, McHarg, Roberts, and Todd 1969, 1972, 1976; Juneja 1974). Whereas Hills worked in public service for the Canadian government and Lewis was a professor, McHarg was involved in both academia and private practice. He and his colleagues at the University of Pennsylvania developed suitability analysis theory. Meanwhile, in Wallace-McHarg Associates and Wallace, McHarg, Roberts, and Todd, the technique was refined through practice. (See McHarg 1996 for a discussion of this work.)

In *Design with Nature,* McHarg explained suitability analysis in the following manner:

> In essence, the method consists of identifying the area of concern as consisting of certain processes, in land, water, and air—which represent values. These can be ranked—the most valuable land and the least, the most valuable water resources and the least, the most and least productive agricultural land, the richest wildlife habitats and those of no value, the areas of great or little scenic beauty, historic buildings and their absence, and so on (1969, 34).

Lewis Hopkins has explained this method as follows:

> The output of land suitability analysis is a set of maps, one for each land use, showing which level of suitability characterizes each parcel of land. This output requirement leads directly to two necessary components of any method: (1) a procedure for identifying parcels of land that are homogeneous and (2) a procedure for rating these parcels with respect to suitability for each land use (1977, 386–387).

A simplified illustration of how the suitability analysis procedure works is provided in Figure 5.4. Jon Berger and his colleagues (1977) have developed an outline of the method, which is summarized in Table 5.5. These seven steps are dependent on a detailed ecological inventory and analysis. Step 1 is to identify potential land uses and define the needs for each. Berger and his colleagues have suggested the use of matrices for the first and other steps. Figure 5.4 and the following matrices used for illustration were taken from an ecological inventory and land-use suitability analysis of Asotin County, Washington (Beach et al. 1978). These matrices were the working documents of a student project and so contain a few imperfections. However, they illustrate the process by which this method was thought through. Figure 5.5 illustrates the land-use needs for agricultural, recreational, residential, commercial, and industrial uses.

Step 2 covers the relationship of these land-use needs to natural factors (Figure 5.6). Next, in Step 3, specific mapped phenomena must be related to the land-use needs (Figure 5.7). Step 4 is to map the congruences of desired phenomena and formulate rules of combination to express a gradient of suitability. *Rules of combination* are the rankings used to weight the relative importance of mapped phenomena. Rules of combination assign suitabilities to sets of criteria rather than to a single criterion and are expressed "in terms of verbal logic rather than in terms of numbers and arithmetic" (Hopkins 1977, 394–395). The result of this step should be a series of maps of opportunities for various land uses.

Step 5 involves an identification of constraints between potential land uses and biophysical processes (Figure 5.8). *Constraints* are environmentally sensitive, or critical, areas that should be preempted from development because of

TABLE 5.5
STEPS IN SUITABILITY ANALYSIS

1. Identify land uses and define the needs for each use.
2. Relate land-use needs to natural factors.
3. Identify the relationship between specific mapped phenomena concerning the biophysical environment and land-use needs.
4. Map the congruences of desired phenomena and formulate rules of combination to express a gradient of suitability. This step should result in maps of land-use opportunities.
5. Identify the constraints between potential land uses and biophysical processes.
6. Overlay maps of constraints and opportunities, and through rules of combination develop a map of intrinsic suitabilities for various land uses.
7. Develop a composite map of the highest suitabilities of the various land uses.

SOURCE: Adapted from Berger et al. 1977.

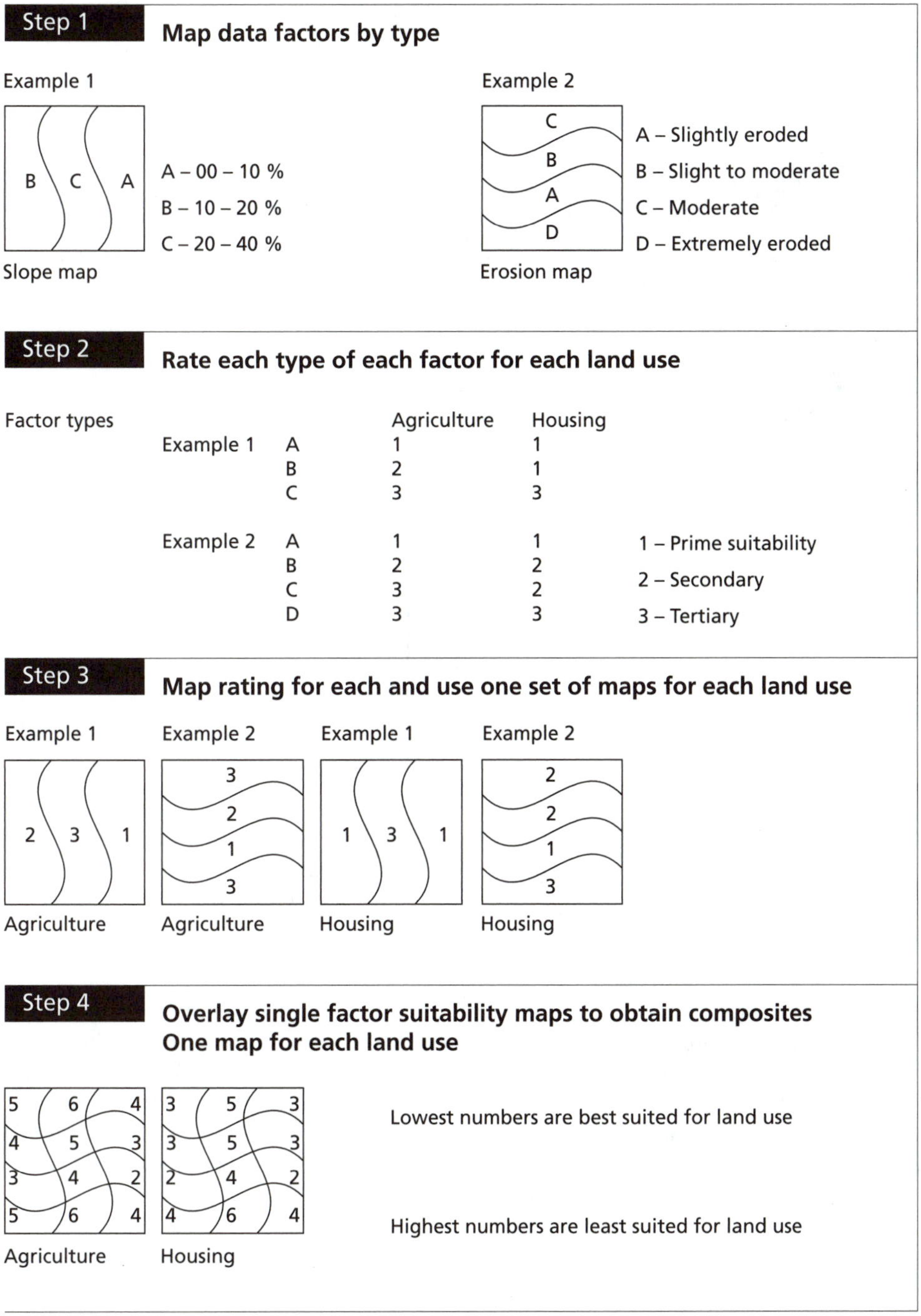

Step 1 **Map data factors by type**

Example 1

B C A

A – 00 – 10 %
B – 10 – 20 %
C – 20 – 40 %

Slope map

Example 2

C B A D

A – Slightly eroded
B – Slight to moderate
C – Moderate
D – Extremely eroded

Erosion map

Step 2 **Rate each type of each factor for each land use**

Factor types

		Agriculture	Housing
Example 1	A	1	1
	B	2	1
	C	3	3
Example 2	A	1	1
	B	2	2
	C	3	2
	D	3	3

1 – Prime suitability
2 – Secondary
3 – Tertiary

Step 3 **Map rating for each and use one set of maps for each land use**

Example 1: 2 3 1 — Agriculture

Example 2: 3 2 1 3 — Agriculture

Example 1: 1 3 1 — Housing

Example 2: 2 2 1 3 — Housing

Step 4 **Overlay single factor suitability maps to obtain composites**
One map for each land use

Agriculture: 5 6 4 / 4 5 3 / 3 4 2 / 5 6 4

Housing: 3 5 3 / 3 5 3 / 2 4 2 / 4 6 4

Lowest numbers are best suited for land use

Highest numbers are least suited for land use

FIGURE 5.4 Suitability analysis procedure.

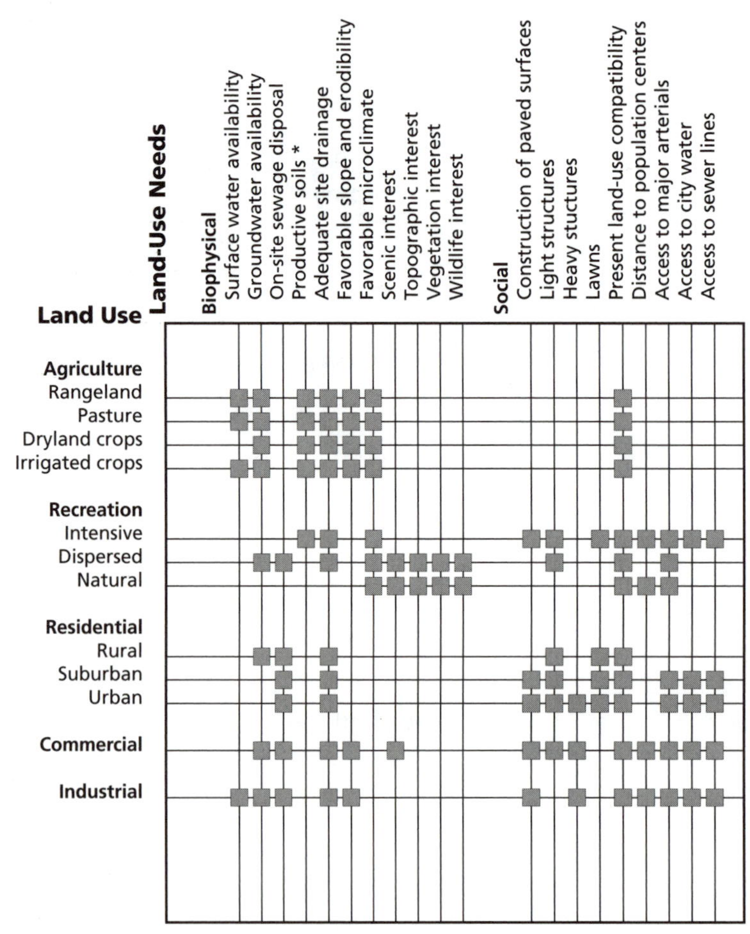

* Productive soil is defined by rock fragment content, sodium content, slick spots, and pH level.

FIGURE 5.5 Land-use needs for agricultural, recreational, residential, commercial, and industrial use in Asotin County, Washington. *(Source: Beach et al. 1978)*

physical (for instance, an earthquake hazard), biological (endangered species), or cultural (a historic site) reasons. Such areas may pose a threat to human health, safety, or welfare and/or contain rare or unique natural attributes. In Step 6 these constraints are mapped and then overlaid with those areas showing opportunities for various land uses. Finally, in Step 7 a composite map of the highest suitabilities of the various land uses is developed (Berger et al. 1977; University of Pennsylvania 1985).

One of the most attractive features of the Pennsylvania method is that it can be used for both the conservation and development of resources. One of the goals of the World Conservation Strategy (International Union for the Conservation of Nature and Natural Resources 1980) is to encourage planning that balances conservation and development. The authors of the strategy defined *conservation* as the management of human use of the biosphere to yield the greatest sustainable benefit to present generations while maintaining its potential to meet the needs and aspirations of future generations. *Development* was defined as the modification of the biosphere and the application of human, financial, living,

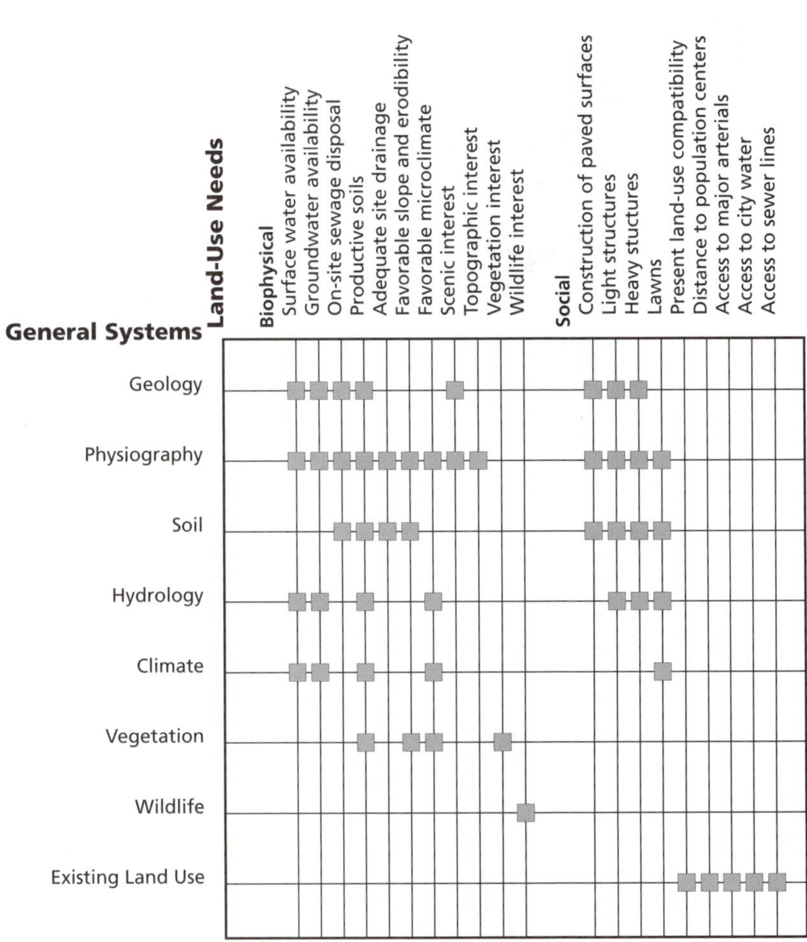

FIGURE 5.6 Relationship of land-use needs to natural factors in Asotin County, Washington. *(Source: Beach et al. 1978)*

and nonliving resources to satisfy human needs and improve the quality of human life. The Pennsylvania suitability analysis method is consistent with both definitions.

Dutch Suitability Analysis

The present Dutch landscape has resulted largely from human intervention in natural processes and represents an eloquent equilibrium between people and their environment. This balance has resulted in an elaborate system of physical planning. One component of this system is a sophisticated set of suitability analysis methods. A. P. A. Vink, a Dutch professor of physical geography and soil science at the University of Amsterdam, has made the distinction between *actual land suitability, soil suitability,* and *potential land suitability.* (See also Brinkman and Smyth 1973; Food and Agriculture Organization of the United Nations 1977; Beek 1978, for additional discussions from a Dutch perspective.) Vink's actual land suitability is analogous to McHarg's intrinsic suitability. According to Vink, *actual land suitability* is "an indication of the possibility of using the land within a particular land utilization type with-

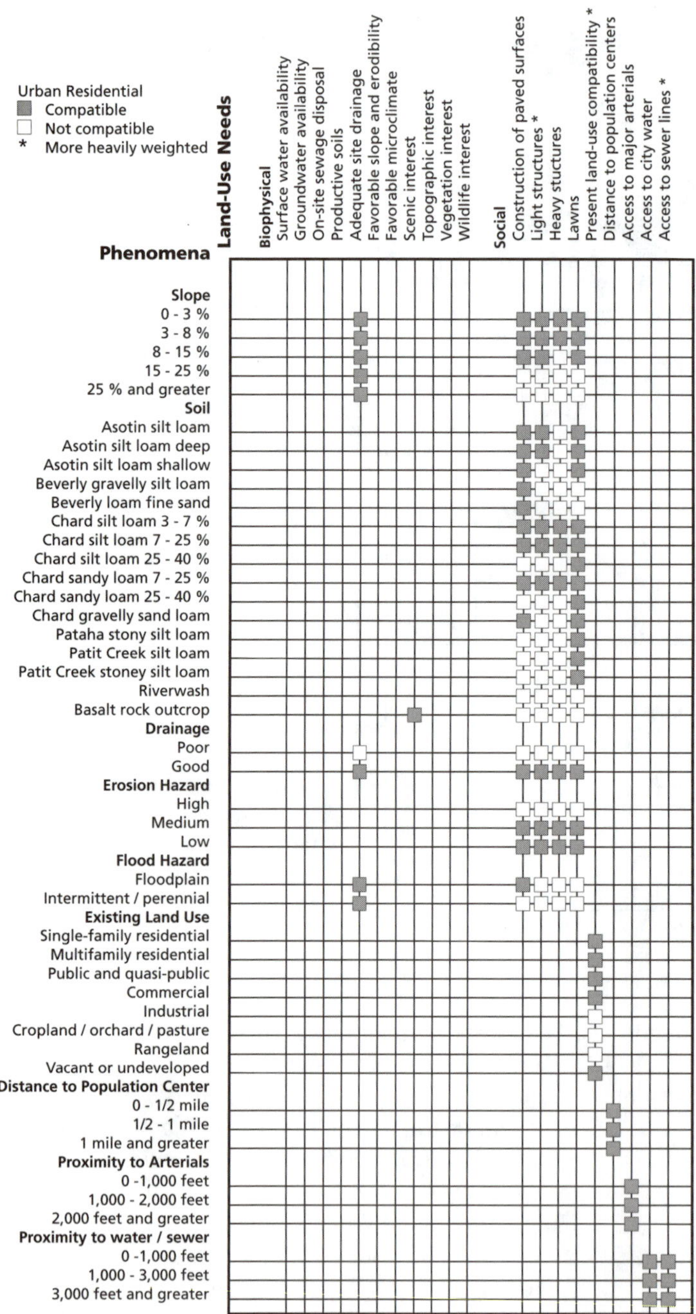

FIGURE 5.7 Relationship of mapped phenomena to land-use needs in Asotin County, Washington. *(Source: Beach et al. 1978)*

Land Uses \ Constraints	Unique geological features	Slopes greater than 25%	Problem drainage areas	High potential erosion areas	High elevation recharge areas	Shorelines and other significant waters	Hudsonian life zone	Botanically noteworthy habitats	Zoologically noteworthy habitats	Cultural and historical landmarks	Existing significant receation areas
Pasture		6		6			6 7	3	6	5 8	5 8
Rangeland		6		6			6	6	6	5 8	5 8
Cropland	7 8	2 6	6	6			6 7	3 4	3 4	5 8	5 8
Intensive recreation	7	6 8	6	6	6		6 7	3 4	3 4	5 8	
Dispersed recreation		6 8	6	6			6 7	3 4	3 4		
Natural recreation							6	6	6		
Urban residential	7 8	1 2 6 8	6	6	5 6	1 3 4 5 6	3 6 7 8	3 4	3 4	5 8	5 8
Suburban residential	7 8	1 2 6 8	6	6	5 6	1 3 4 6	3 6 7 8	3 4	3 4	5 8	5 8
Rural residential	7 8	1 2 6 8	6	6	6	1 3 6	3 6 7 8	3 4	3 4	5 8	5 8
Commercial	7 8	1 2 6 8	6	6	5 6	1 3 4 5 6	3 6 7 8	3 4	3 4	3 4	3 4
Industrial	7 8	1 2 6 8	6	6	5 6	1 3 4 5 6	3 6 7 8	3 4	3 4	3 4	3 4

Key:

1 = hazard or potential danger to human life, quality, or health
2 = hazard or potential danger to human life, quality, or health through specific human action
3 = modification of habitat and / or ground cover
4 = endangered or reducing species
5 = depletion of natural or social resources
6 = vulnerable area that requires further regulation to avoid social or environmental costs
7 = alteration of unique, scarce, or rare attribute
8 = general incompatibility with land feature or present land use

FIGURE 5.8 Identification of constraints between land uses and biophysical processes in Asotin County, Washington. *(Source: Beach et al. 1978)*

A constraint against certain uses may provide an opportunity for other uses. Central Park, New York City.

out the application of land improvements which require major capital investments" (1975, 238).

Vink defines *soil suitability* as "physical suitability of soil and climate for production of a crop or group or sequence of crops, or for other defined uses or benefits, within a specified socio-economic context but not considering economic factors specific to areas of land" (Vink 1975, 249). This would be analogous to the NRCS capability classification system. Finally, *potential land suitability* "relates the suitability of land units for the use in question at some future date after 'major improvements' have been effected where necessary, suitability being assessed in terms of expected future benefits in relation to future recurrent and minor capital expenditure" (Vink 1975, 254; Brinkman and Smyth 1973).

It is this final category, potential land suitability, that distinguishes the Dutch approaches. It has been necessary for the Dutch to reclaim wet, low-lying land in order to prosper.

Although this notion of potential suitability has particularly Dutch origins, it has broad, international implications. Some countries, like Switzerland and Japan, and certain regions, such as those encompassing Hong Kong and New York, have exceptionally high population densities and, as a result, a strong demand for future land uses. Frequently in such cases, a powerful distinction is made in planning practice between the actual and the potential suitability. The latter relies more strongly on costs for public "improvements," but does not ignore natural constraints (see, for example, Van Lier 1991).

One example of the application of potential land suitability is the polders built on the former Zuider Zee (Southern Sea) (Figure 5.9). The Zuider Zee was an extension of the North Sea into the heart of the Netherlands. According to the accounts of Roman historians, it was at one time a combination of a large inland lake and lands. As early as 1667 the Dutch speculated about damming the Zuider Zee and reclaiming it, but seventeenth-century technology was not advanced enough to tame the tempestuous inland sea of nearly 400,000 hectares (approximately 1 million acres). However, by the late nineteenth century serious plans were developed by the engineer Cornelis Lely (Ministry of Transport and Public Works no date).

The Zuider Zee reclamation plan that Cornelis Lely developed essentially was one based on the potential suitability of an area for agriculture. Soil surveys were conducted on soil samples taken from the sea. Using these surveys, Lely proposed that those areas with predominantly clay soils be made polders after the Zuider Zee was transformed into a lake and renamed IJsselmeer (Figure 5.10). The success of the Zuider Zee project is well-documented (see, for example, Steiner 1981; Van Lier and Steiner 1982; Van der Wal 1997).

Dutch planners continue to refine and apply suitability analyses techniques, especially through computer technology (see Carsjens and Van der Knaap 1996; Carsjens and Smits 1997). In the newer Dutch approaches, two elements, one more theoretical and the other more technical, are evident in suitability mapping. First, multiple criteria analyses are applied in order to weigh values among the various different, potential land

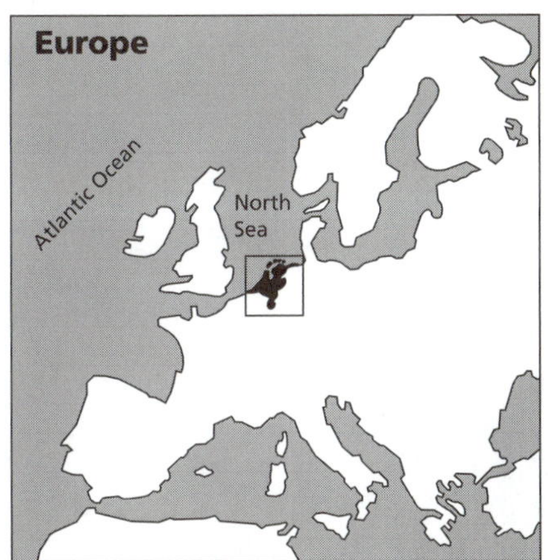

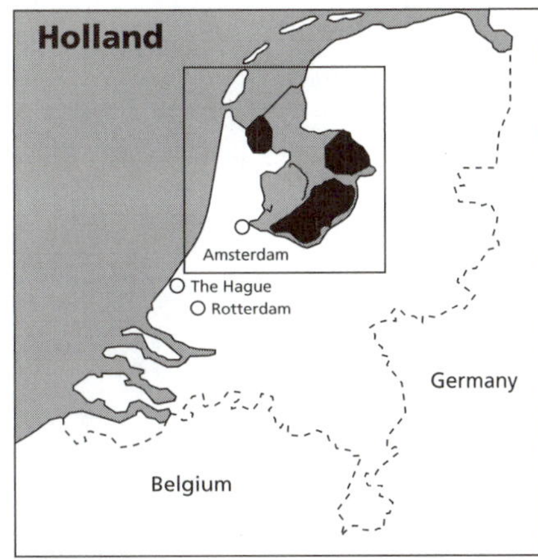

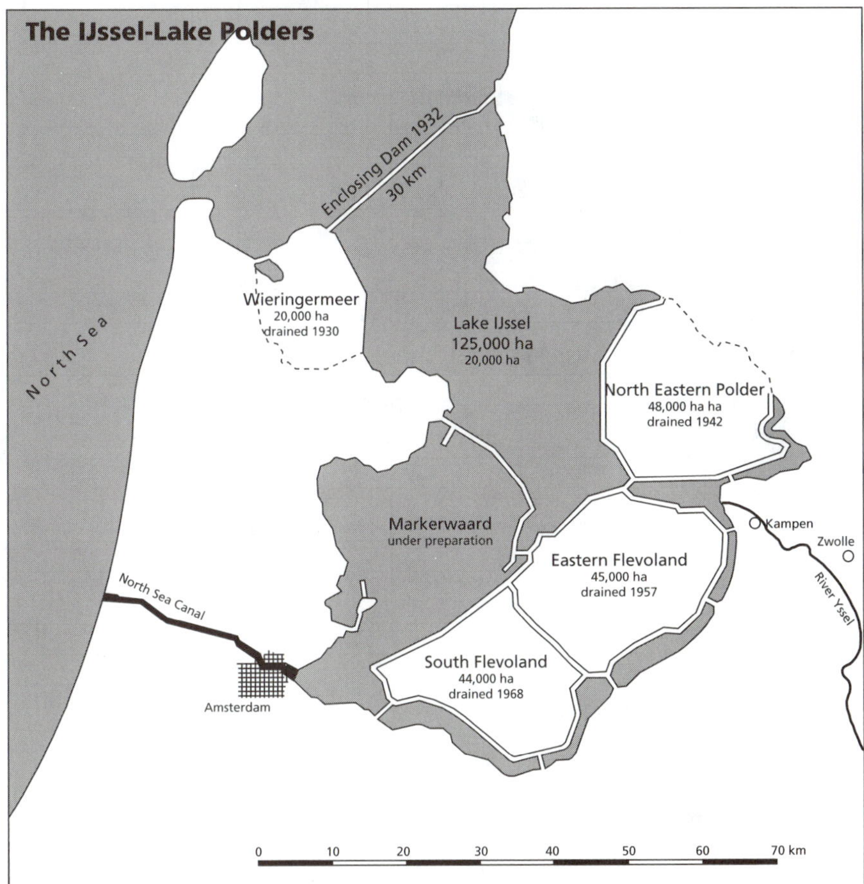

FIGURE 5.9 Location of Zuider Zee polders in the Netherlands. *(Source: IJsselmeer Polders Development Authority)*

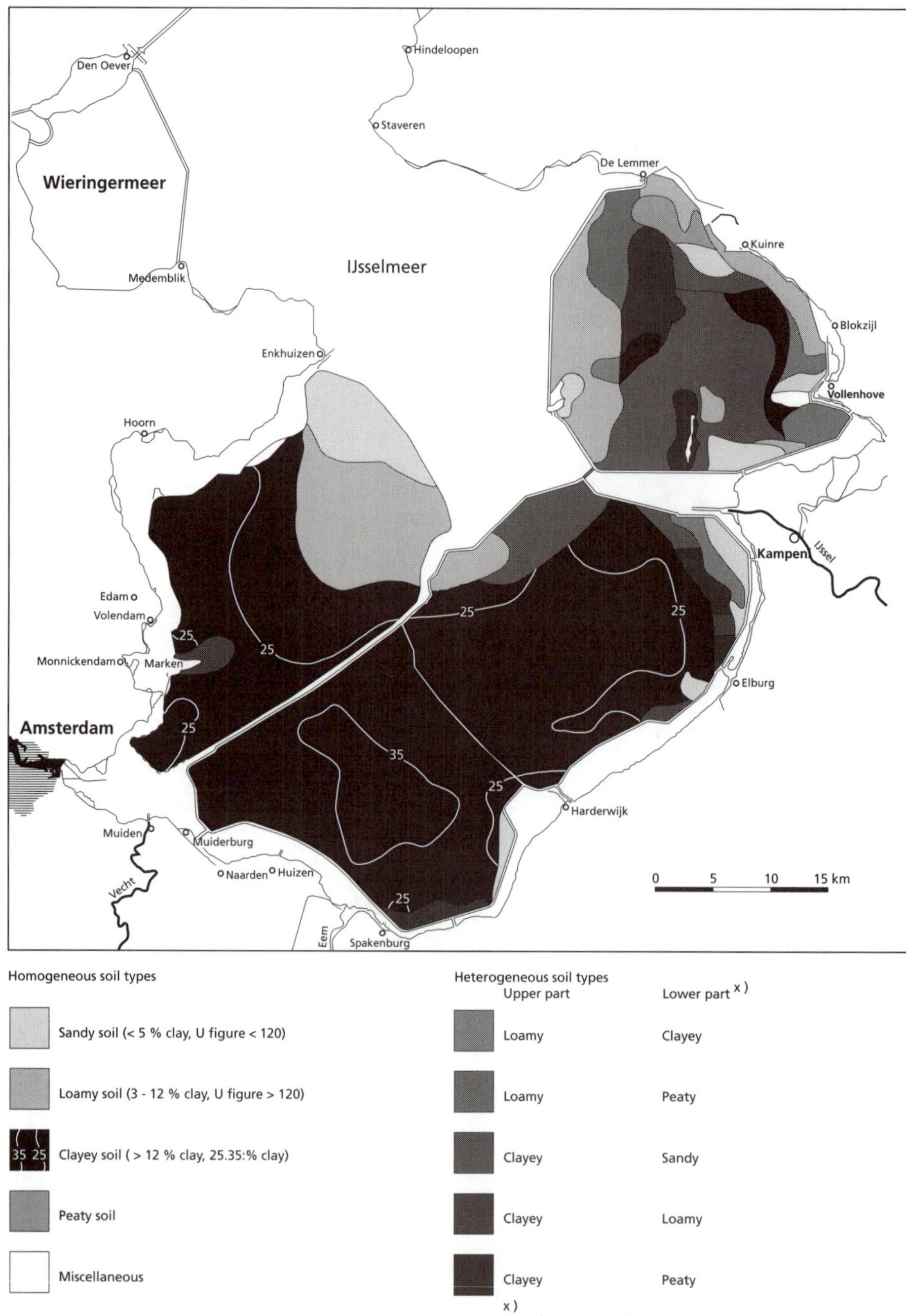

FIGURE 5.10 Location of clay soils in the former Zuider Zee. *(Source: IJsselmeer Polders Development Authority)*

uses. Second, GIS are employed in the analyses, making them more flexible and quick and easily applicable. These two elements enable Dutch planners to present a wider range of land-use possibilities, with varying suitabilities, to decision makers.

COMPUTER APPLICATIONS

Several techniques may be used to accomplish suitability analysis. Ian McHarg popularized the "overlay technique" (1969). Transparent maps with information about landscape elements are placed on top of each other to reveal areas of opportunity and constraints. This technique is used to develop the opportunities maps of Step 4, the constraints map in Step 5, the intrinsic suitability maps of Step 6, and the composite of Step 7 in Table 5.4. Bruce MacDougall (1975) criticized the accuracy of map overlays and made suggestions for improved accuracy. For instance, if there are more than three or four overlays, the map may appear opaque; there are accuracy questions raised by MacDougall (1975) and others that are especially pressing with hand-drawn maps; and there are limitations for weighting various values represented by map units. Geographic information systems computer technology has helped to overcome these limitations. Sheila Peck explains this technology as follows: "A GIS is a database for geographically referenced information. The geographic data are organized in thematic layers and linked to many other nonspatial data" (1998, 124).

Many practical difficulties exist in manually superimposing a large number of maps (Steinitz 1993; MacDougall 1975). This limitation became the focus for much planning and land-use-related research from the 1960s to the present (Collins 1996; Collins et al. 2000). The Laboratory for Computer Graphics at the Harvard University Graduate School of Design was a prominent center for the development of new, computer-based techniques and methods of land-use suitability analysis. Many early examples of georeferenced computer mapping and suitability analysis, as well as modern computer mapping theory, can be traced back to the Harvard laboratory. Perhaps the very first application of computer overlay mapping to a large geographic region came from this lab in the fall of 1966. Carl Steinitz, at that time an associate professor at Harvard's Graduate School of Design, taught a planning studio which created DELMARVA, a landscape planning study of the Delaware, Maryland, and Virginia Peninsula. While working on his dissertation, Steinitz convinced Howard Fisher, another associate professor at Harvard's Graduate School of Design, to allow him to incorporate an early, general-purpose line printer mapping program called SYMAP (for SYnagraphic MAPping), which was developed by Fisher initially at the University of Chicago in 1964, as a descriptive presentation of objects in geographic space. Steinitz and his students applied SYMAP to analyze the effect of one map factor upon another and to incorporate weighted indexes such as the capability of the area to support grain agriculture (Steinitz 1993).

Another of the more widely documented Harvard predecessors to contemporary computer-based land-use suitability was the Honey Hill study (Murray et al. 1971), named after its location in New Hampshire. In this study, Steinitz and colleagues used SYMAP to evaluate a large proposed flood-control reservoir and parkway for recreation and other land uses. The Honey Hill study offered important insight into the power of computers to combine different land-use modeling techniques to create a composite, fiscally optimal plan (Steinitz 1993). Steinitz's early work provided an important and invaluable example of the successful marriage of computers and land-use suitability, which other researchers and practitioners continued to build upon (Steinitz et al. 1994; Collins et al. 2000; Miller et al. 1998). Steinitz and his Harvard colleagues continue to refine this technology, as the Camp Pendleton Biodiversity study illustrates (see Chapters 3, 4, and 6).

A similarly pioneering contribution of more sophisticated spatial-analysis methods came through the Metropolitan Landscape Planning Model (METLAND). Researchers at the University of Massachusetts in the early 1970s, under the direction of Julius Fabos, developed METLAND (Fabos and Caswell 1977; Fabos et al. 1978). As land-use planning and data development techniques progressed, more spatial information became available from government agencies and others for land-use studies. METLAND was developed as a parametric approach to incorporate ecological, economic, and social goals in the initial indexes for land-use suitability. To accommodate this large data requirement, Fabos and his colleagues designed METLAND to manage data and to handle complex computations more efficiently. Land units were given weights, evaluated, and then combined to produce a small number of land-use plans. Each plan was then evaluated by referencing a final index of scores in dollars or noneconomic units. In order to relate and reference the data geographically, the researchers used an early computer mapping program called COMLUP, which stored land factor maps on special data storage tapes. When it was necessary to overlay these maps, the data were loaded from these tapes into the computer, and a grid cell overlay was generated. The results were mapped and presented to decision makers for final evaluation (Fabos and Caswell 1977; Fabos et al. 1978). While the process was slow and extremely lengthy compared to more modern advancements, the METLAND study identified a need for more effective data storage and manipulation techniques (Collins et al. 2000).

Modern GISs are defined as a computer-assisted technology that stores, analyzes, and displays spatial and nonspatial data and is capable of creating new data through automated overlays and spatial searches (Irish 1994; Goodchild et al. 1993; Antenucci et al. 1991; Niemann 1989; Collins 1996). Several problems with older hand-drawn, transparent overlay techniques were overcome with the development of this new technology (MacDougall 1975). A GIS can quickly and accurately provide decision makers with information in a concise map format (Collins 1996). As a result, it has become a valuable planning tool.

Numerous computer program systems have been developed that can replace the technique of overlaying information by hand. Some of these programs are intended to model only positions of environmental processes or phenomena, while others are designed as comprehensive information storage, retrieval, and evaluation systems. These systems are intended to improve efficiency and economy in information handling, especially for large or complex planning projects (Meyers 1971; Fabos and Caswell 1977; Beeman 1978; Killpack 1981; Antenucci et al. 1991; Goodchild et al. 1993).

Biophysical information for planning use can be represented in three ways: *grid cells, polygons,* and *image processing.* Figure 5.11 illustrates how mapped areas are represented with grid cells. These areas may be soil types or capa-

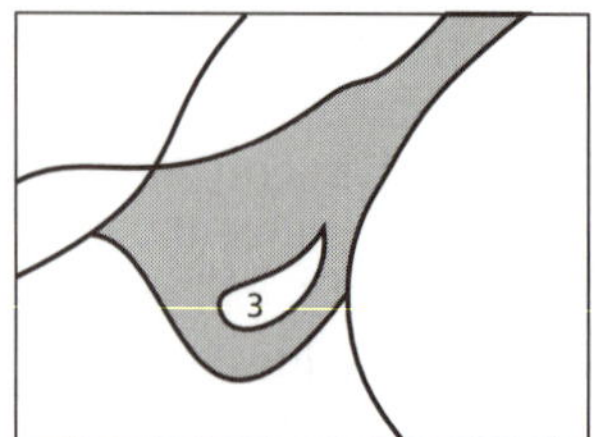

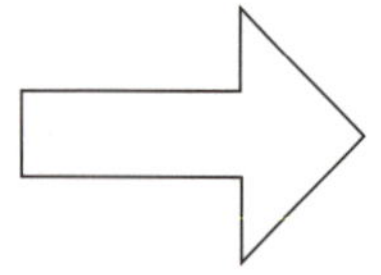

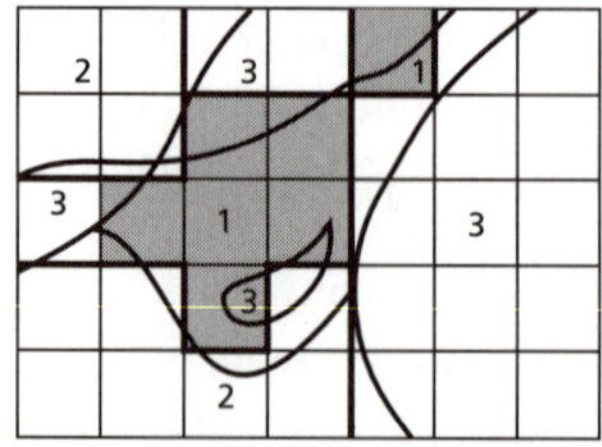

FIGURE 5.11 Mapped areas represented by grid cells. *(Source: Laird et al. 1979)*

bilities, slope angles, vegetation associations, and so on. The disadvantage of grid-cell representation is that details can be missed unless the cell size is made very small. Smaller grids necessitate more data collection. Also, the world does not fit a square or rectangular grid pattern. This forces data to be compromised in order to fit into the grid format. Mapped areas in a polygon system are represented by enclosed spaces (Figure 5.12). A polygon system can show curved lines, thus making it potentially more accurate than grid cells (Laird et al. 1979). The third approach to computer mapping is digital image processing. This is a sophisticated grid approach where the cell size is very small, similar to the cells on a television screen. Maps are created directly from photoimagery such as from satellite or airplanes. Simply put, "a digital computer processes information in discrete numerical units: digits" (Cannon and Hunt 1981, 214). Because of the level of detail that can be achieved, digital image processing overcomes many of the shortcomings inherent in the simpler grid and polygon approaches. Advancements in hardware and software technologies will continue to make computers increasingly effective tools for landscape inventory, analysis, synthesis, monitoring, and administration.

For example, Wisconsin law requires counties to prepare erosion control plans. These plans are to specify the maximum acceptable rates of erosion, identify parcels where erosion standards are not being met, identify land-use changes and management practices that would bring each area into compliance standards, specify procedures for assisting landowners and land users to control erosion, and establish priorities for controlling erosion. To achieve these goals in Dane County, an interdisciplinary team of planners and researchers from the University of Wisconsin-Madison, Dane County, the state and federal government, the Madison Area Surveyors Council, and the Wisconsin Power and Light formed the Dane County Land Records Project (Ventura 1988).

The Dane County Land Records Project developed a geographic information system that enabled the planners to collect, store, analyze, and disseminate information about the Dane County landscape. An inventory of biophysical and land-use information was undertaken. From that inventory, highly erodible lands were identified (Ventura 1988). These areas are unsuited for agriculture or need specific management practices to maintain productivity. The Dane County Land Records Project is but one example of the use of computer technology to determine land-use suitability.

Figure 5.13 is an example of suitability analyses that were conducted for the Desert View Tri-Villages Area in Arizona (Burke and Ewan 1998a). These analyses were conducted to identify the best places to locate desert preserves in the area. Individual analyses were conducted for archaeological sites, bike paths, floodplains, ownership, soils, slopes, parks, and washes. Then these analyses were combined for a final suitability for desert preserves (Burke and Ewan 1998b; Brady et al. 1998).

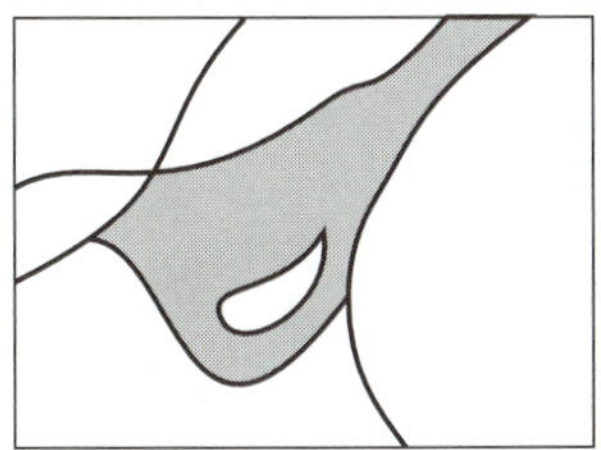
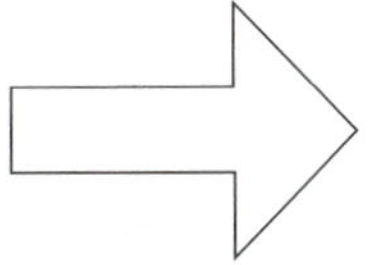
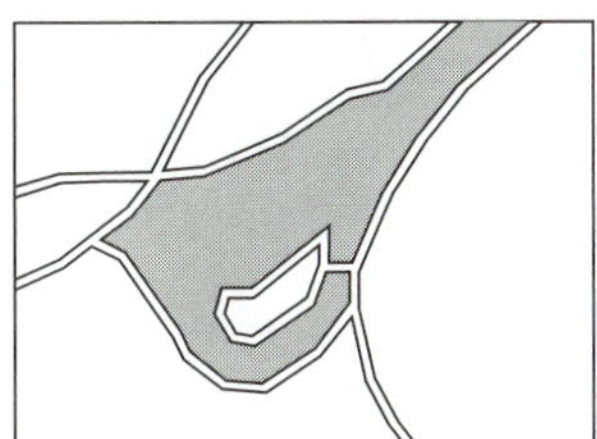

FIGURE 5.12 Mapped areas represented by polygon system. *(Source: Laird et al. 1979)*

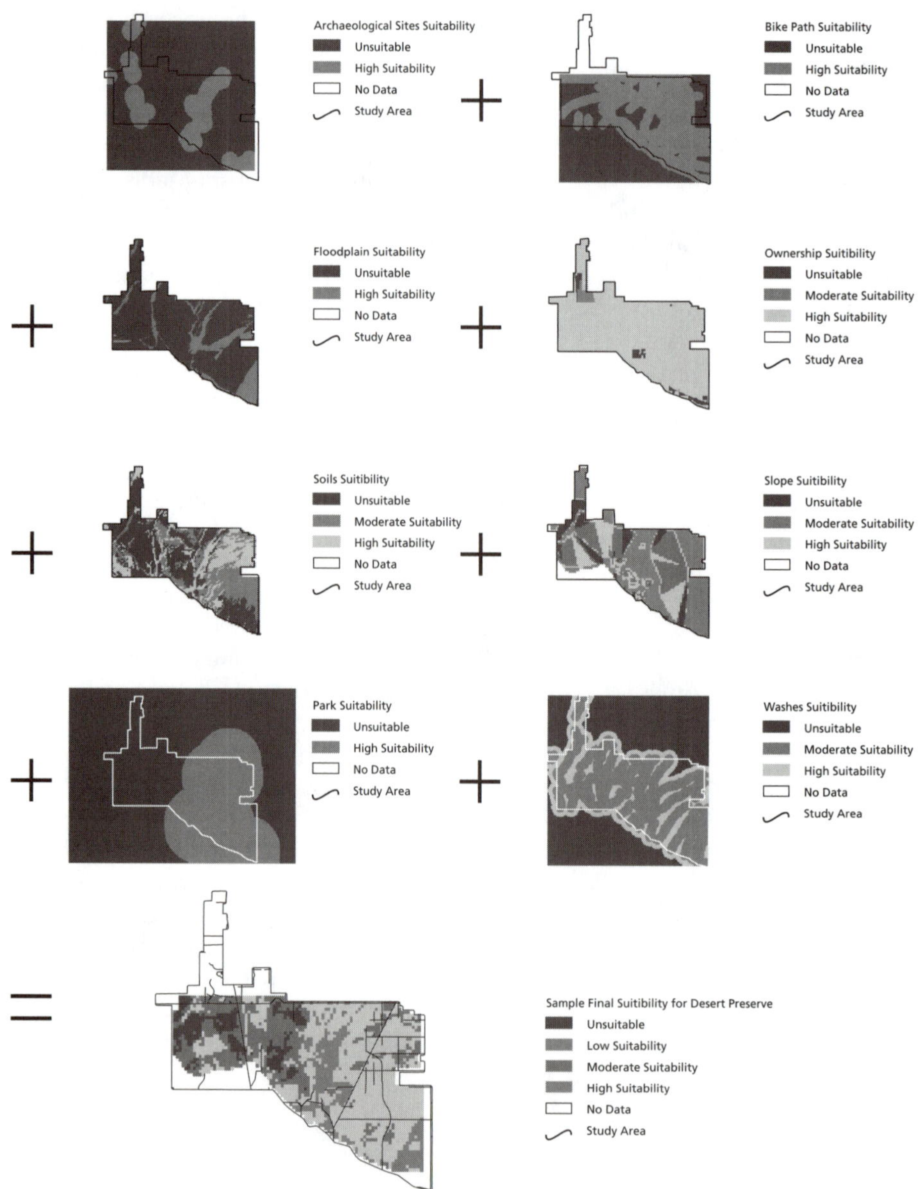

FIGURE 5.13 Suitability analysis, Desert View Tri-Villages Area. *(Source: Burke and Ewan 1998a)*

Environments are finite; users and uses can multiply and compete, or space can be provided for various uses in the most suitable locations. Park in Cremona, Italy.

THE CARRYING-CAPACITY CONCEPT

In essence, suitability analysis helps determine the carrying capacity of the planning area. William Catton, a sociologist, observed that "environments are finite; users and uses multiply and compete. Carrying capacity means the extent to which an environment can tolerate a given kind of use by a given type of user" (Catton 1983, 270).

In ecology, *carrying capacity* has been defined as the number of individuals that the resources of a habitat can support without significant deterioration. The carrying capacity concept suggests a limit of growth for populations and ecosystems, that is, "the size that can be sustained at a given time and place" (Odum 1998, 1). According to D. B. Botkin and Edward Keller, carrying capacity can be defined as "the maximum number of individuals of a species that can be sustained by an environment without decreasing the capacity of the environment to sustain that same amount in the future" (1998, 9). Young defines carrying capacity "as those numbers that can be sustained at *all* times, even when resources in an area are in the least supply" (1989, 112). In wildlife ecology, the definition used is a bit more specific: the maximum number of animals an area can support during a given period of the year. In recreation planning and management, carrying capacity has been defined as the amount of use a recreation area can sustain without deterioration of the experience provided or of the resource base. According to Schneider et al.:

> Carrying-capacity analysis, as a planning tool, studies the effects of growth—amount, type, location, quality—on the natural and man-made environments in order to identify critical thresholds beyond which public health, safety, or welfare will be threatened by serious environmental problems unless changes are made in public investment, government regulation, or human behavior (1978, 1).

Several planners, especially those in outdoor recreation management and planning, have discussed the utilization of the carrying-capacity concept (Lime and Stankey 1971; Stankey and Lime 1973; Van Lier 1973, 1980; Wagner 1974; Lime 1979; Meester and Van der Voet 1980). Planner William Rees of the University of British Columbia explains the carrying capacity as follows:

> Ecologists define "carrying capacity" as the population of a given species that can be supported indefinitely in a given habitat without permanently damaging the ecosystem upon which it depends. For human beings, carrying capacity can be interpreted as the maximum rate of resource consumption and waste discharge that can be sustained indefinitely in a given region without impairing the functional integrity and productivity of relevant ecosystems. The corresponding human population is a function of per capita rates of resource consumption and waste pro-

> duction (i.e., sustainable production divided by per capita demand) (1992, 125; see also Rees 1990a, 1990b).

Rees furthermore stated that carrying capacity for the human population "is finite and declining and should become a fundamental component of demographic and planning analysis" (1995, 346).

The outdoor recreation specialists' interest in this concept may be traced to two sources. First, they have been historically involved with forest and range ecologists, and are thus familiar with ecological terms. Second, they work within discrete boundaries where there are clear demands on and conflicts over resources. The public patronage of state and federal parks in the United States has increased dramatically since the Second World War, partly because of the interstate highway system and the increase in automobile ownership and also because of population shifts from the eastern to western states and from metropolitan to nonmetropolitan regions.

D. W. Lime and G. H. Stankey (1971) distinguished three aspects of outdoor recreational carrying capacity: *management objectives, visitor attitudes,* and *impact on biophysical resources.* The three aspects are viewed as interdependent, no single factor being necessarily more important than the others. Suitability analysis offers a framework to study in detail these three aspects.

While the concept has enjoyed relatively wide application in outdoor recreation, carrying capacity had more limited use by community and regional planning agencies until planners became more interested in sustainability. With the rise of interest in sustainability, more planners have explored the carrying capacity concept. One early exception is the Tahoe Regional Planning Agency, which adopted an environmental threshold approach based on carrying capacities. The Tahoe Regional Planning Agency defined these threshold carrying capacities as "an environmental standard necessary to maintain a significant scenic, recreational, educational, scientific, or natural value of the region or to maintain public health and safety within the region" (1982, vii).

Thomas Dickert and Andrea Tuttle of the University of California, Berkeley, advocated the use of thresholds, such as those developed by the Tahoe Regional Planning Agency, as a means to control cumulative environmental impacts. Such thresholds would be based on "an assumed acceptable amount of land-use change over time" (Dickert and Tuttle 1985, 38). They observe a problem with conventional planning in that it is often incremental, and, thus, does not address cumulative impacts. In the words of Dickert and Tuttle, "Cumulative impacts are those that result from the interactions of many incremental activities, each of which may have an insignificant effect when viewed alone, but which become cumulatively significant when seen in the aggregate" (1985, 39). They suggest an alternative approach whereby the "rate or total amount of development is managed to stay below prestated threshold levels, and halted when such thresholds are reached" (1985, 39). Such thresholds can be determined by an analysis of the suitability of resources for various uses.

An extension of carrying capacity is the *ecological footprint* concept developed by William Rees (1992, 1995, 1997; Wackernagel and Rees 1996). Rees suggests that "our shelter, energy, food, and other resource demands can be translated into estimates of the land and water areas needed to meet them" (as quoted in Beatley and Manning 1997, 8). According to Rees, an ecological footprint can be "defined as the aggregate area of land required continuously to produce the resource inputs and to assimilate the waste outputs of that population or economy wherever the land may be located" (1995, 351). Wackernagel and Rees (1996) proposed quantitative indicators to measure the impacts of an economic system on the ecological load supporting capacity of a given planning area. They consider the flows of energy and materials entering and leaving the planning area in order to assess the total resources impacted by use (see Wackernagel and Rees 1996; Rees 1995; Treu and Magoni 1998). The ecological footprint approach suggests the need for ecological inventories for places beyond the immediate planning area and for detailed studies of environmental consequences inside and outside the planning area.

Several Italian scholars have also explored the application of the carrying capacity concept to planning. Ornella Piscopo (1999) brought together much of this work in her dissertation at the University of Rome (under the mentorship of Professor Enzo Scandurra). She advocates a broader, more metaphorical interpretation and use of the concept, arguing that carrying capacity as "limit" or "threshold" is limiting. Instead Piscopo (1999) suggests that "carrying capacity can be considered as a tool for understanding the environmental conditions of a certain area." She pursued this approach through a case study of the Sarno River basin in southern Italy.

TWO APPLICATIONS OF SUITABILITY ANALYSIS

The suitability analysis for Medford Township, New Jersey, involved several of the originators of the method, including Ian McHarg and Narendra Juneja. Their ideas were extended in the late 1970s into the Pacific Northwest, in Whitman County, Washington.

The Development of Performance Requirements in Medford Township, New Jersey

The officials of Medford Township, New Jersey, sought to develop an alternative system to traditional zoning. A study exploring the use of performance requirements was undertaken for Medford by the Center for Ecological Research in Planning and Design at the University of Pennsylvania under the direction of Ian McHarg and Narendra Juneja. The performance requirements were based on the social values and natural environment of the township. (For a comprehensive description of the planning process in Medford Township, see Palmer 1981.)

Medford Township is located on the edge of the New Jersey Pinelands, within commuting distance of the Philadelphia metropolitan area (Figure 5.14). This is an area that, on the one hand, grew from the great suburban explosion of the 1950s and 1960s, but, on the other, is part of one of the few remaining natural ecosystems in the eastern United States.

After a detailed ecological inventory of the township, the planning team related the biophysical phenomena to their values to society and individuals. Juneja explained this in the following manner:

> The values assigned vary depending upon the individual's interest. For example, a farmer is concerned about sustained productivity from his land; a homeowner seeks a healthy delightful setting; and a developer searches for sites where he can build to get the most return for his money. The operative value system employed by individuals are as likely to be discrete and mutually exclusive as to be competitive and conflicting. To deal with the latter exigency and to ensure sustained health, welfare, and prosperity for all, it is important to identify those values which are common to all present and future residents of the township. This can best be accomplished by interpreting the available understanding of the extant phenomena and processes in terms which are clearly definable and about which agreement can be reached by all those affected (1974, 11).

Juneja and colleagues accomplished this by a system of matrices linked to mapped phenomena. Figure 5.15 is an example of one such matrix for vegetation. Along the horizontal axis, the values of society and individuals, as determined by the

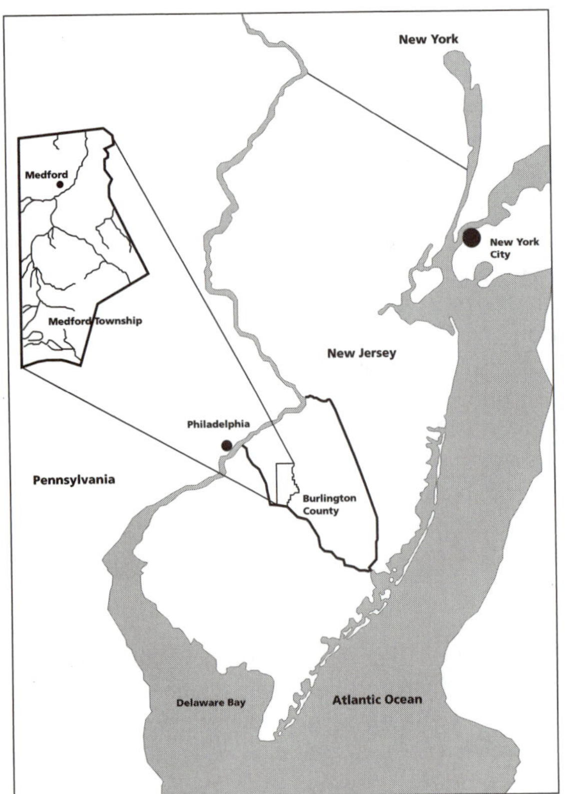

FIGURE 5.14 Location of Medford Township, New Jersey.

residents of the township, are listed. The land-cover classifications are listed as mapped on the vertical axis. Each of the categories—cropland, pasture, orchard, and so on—is explained in a technical report. The occurrence of a dot in the matrix indicates a relationship; some explanations of these relationships accompany the matrix. For instance, a dot with the number 4 indicates an ecological association of unique national value. Similar matrices were developed for geology, aquifers, microclimate, physiography, hydrology, limnology, soil types, water runoff, the depth to water table, nutrient retention, potential soil loss, recreational values of vegetation, wildlife habitats, historic sites, and scenic units (Juneja 1974).

The matrixed value-to-society relationships were used to develop constraints to various land uses. The value-to-individuals relationships were used to establish opportunities for land uses. Again, matrices and maps were used to illustrate this process. Figure 5.16 shows such a matrix listing suitability criteria for recreation and urbanization. In the translation of this information to maps, rules of combination were used. Table 5.6 lists those for recreation, while Table 5.7 is an explanation of the rules of combination for one type of urbanization (clustered suburban). Similar rules were developed for other forms of urbanization.

Suitabilities were established for forest production and agricultural production. Intrinsic suitabilities or composite suitabilities were not developed at this stage for Medford Township. Juneja and colleagues instead developed a framework for establishing performance requirements based on constraints and opportunities for specific land uses. These were proposed to then become a part of the township plan and zoning ordinance (Juneja 1974).

Locating Areas for Rural Housing in Whitman County, Washington

In July 1978, the Whitman County, Washington, Board of Commissioners adopted a revised comprehensive plan that assigned high priorities to agricultural and residential land-use issues (Whitman County Regional Planning Council 1978). The commissioners' goal was to preserve productive agricultural land and the family farm as the prime economic and social resource of the county. They believed that goal could be met by preventing land from being taken out of production by indiscriminate or excessive land-use changes.

In the case of residential land use, the commissioners' goal was to provide limited, low-density housing on unincorporated land with the lowest potential for agricultural use. This measure would attempt to satisfy those desiring a rural living envi-

	Value to society				Value to individuals: High productivity for — Extract		Agriculture					Forest		
	Inherently hazardous to human life	Hazardous to human life and health by specific human actions	Irreplaceable unique of scarce resource	Valuable resource requiring regulation to avoid social costs	Sand	Gravel	High value crops	General crops	Pasture	Fruits	Special produce	Timber	Pulp	Firewood
Cropland														
Pasture														
Orchard														
Successional meadow				8								P		P
Successional forest (inner CP)				8								●	●	●
Pine-Oak forest	1			7								●	●	●
Oak-Pine forest	1			7								●		●
Oak forest complex	1			7								●		●
Mixed deciduous forest				7							C			
Bog	1		2	11								P		
Shrub woodland	1		3	9								P	P	P
Successional forest (outer CP)	1			8								●	●	●
Pine forest	1			7								●		●
Deciduous mixed forest	1			7										●
Deciduous lowland forest	1			7										●
Floodplain forest				7/10								●		●
Cedar swamp	1		5	7/10								●		
Urban: open														
Urban: wooded														
Pine barrens	1		4	12										
Old mature specimen trees			6	13										

	Minimum on-site costs for — Foundations			Maintenance				Water supply		
	Paved surfaces	Light structures	Heavy structures	Site drainage	Paved surfaces	Lawns, playgrounds, etc.	On-site sewage disposal	Domestic use	Industrial use	Irrigation
Cropland										
Pasture										
Orchard										
Successional meadow										
Successional forest (inner CP)										
Pine-Oak forest										
Oak-Pine forest										
Oak forest complex										
Mixed deciduous forest										
Bog										
Shrub woodland										
Successional forest (outer CP)										
Pine forest										
Deciduous mixed forest										
Deciduous lowland forest										
Floodplain forest										
Cedar swamp										
Urban: open										
Urban: wooded										
Pine barrens										
Old mature specimen trees										

	Maximum desirability for — Location								Activity			
	Favorable microclimate	Topographic interest	Long views	Sense of enclosure	Water-related views	Vegetation diversity	Wildlife diversity	Historic association	Educational	Fishing	Swimming	Canoeing, boating
Cropland												
Pasture												
Orchard												
Successional meadow												
Successional forest (inner CP)												
Pine-Oak forest												
Oak-Pine forest												
Oak forest complex												
Mixed deciduous forest								●				
Bog								●	●			
Shrub woodland												
Successional forest (outer CP)												
Pine forest												
Deciduous mixed forest												
Deciduous lowland forest												
Floodplain forest												
Cedar swamp								●				
Urban: open												
Urban: wooded												
Pine barrens									●			
Old mature specimen trees								●	●			

1 Subject to forest fires endemic to the Pine Barrens ecology.
2 Scarce resource of historic value.
3 Unique herbaceous flora of educational, scientific, and recreational value.
4 Ecological association of unique national value.
5 Scarce resource of scientific and historic value.
6 Unique and scarce resource of historic and recreational value.
7 Deforestation will lead to loss of mature forest resource.
8 Other development of these areas will prevent these developing into mature forest resources.
9 Other development on these areas will preempt potential sites for growth of cedar.
10 Alteration of vegetation cover will result in disruption of stream balance and pollution.
11 Vulnerable to pollution locally and from adjacent areas.
12 Unregulated and incompatible development will degrade the unique value of this national resource.
13 Any disruption of existing conditions within the crown area will result in loss of these unique specimens.

C Cranberries only
P Potential resource

FIGURE 5.15 Matrix of vegetation values to society and individuals in Medford Township, New Jersey. *(Source: Juneja 1974)*

Development Type	Suitability factor																						
	Cost-savings for:										Maximum desirability for:												
	found-ations			main-tenance			water supply				location								activity				
Urbanization	Paved surfaces	Light structures	Heavy structures	Site drainage	Paved surfaces	Lawns, playgrounds, etc.	On-site sewage disposal	Domestic use	Industrial use	Irrigational use	Favorable microclimate	Topographic interest	Long views	Sense of enclosure	Water-related views	Vegetation diversity	Wildlife diversity	Historic association	Educational	Fishing	Swimming	Canoeing	Boating
Rural urban		▣					▣	○			▣	▣	▣	▣	▣	▣	●	●					
Suburban	○	▣		▣		▣	●	○			○	○	○	○	○	●	●	●					
Clustered suburban	▣	▣		▣	▣	○		○			○	●	●	●	●	○	○	●					
Urban	▣		▣	○	○				○				●		●			●					
Recreation																							
Intensive				▣	○	▣					○												
General				○		●					●	▣	▣	▣	▣	●	●	●	●				
Natural												▣	▣	▣	▣	▣	▣	▣	▣				
Cultural and historic																		▣	▣				
Water-related																				○	○	○	○

▣ Critical
● Optional
○ Desirable

▣ Preferred / Compatible
● Preferred / partially compatible
○ Desirable

FIGURE 5.16 Matrix of suitability criteria for recreation and urbanization in Medford Township, New Jersey. *(Source: Juneja 1974)*

ronment while protecting farmland from residential encroachment.

The commissioners realized that preserving productive agricultural land while providing limited, low-density living opportunities is not a simple process, so their revised comprehensive plan includes a number of guidelines identifying those areas suitable for rural housing. These guidelines state that areas to be considered for rural housing must be adjacent to a state or county road and also meet at least two of the following criteria:

- Land whose near-surface geology consists of basalt or alluvium or, on slopes of greater than 20 percent, crystalline rock, all as defined by Water Supply Bulletin No. 26 of the Washington Department of Ecology, *Reconnaissance of Geology and of Ground-Water Occurrence in Whitman County,* or any updated version of this document (Walters and Glancy 1969).
- Land that is not normally cultivated, used for production of forage, or used for commercial grazing of livestock.
- Distinct areas of land 15 acres [6.08 hectares] or less that are of insufficient size for farming. "Distinct" means that the area is substantially bounded by natural or man-made features that buffer this land from agricultural lands, such as wooded areas, steep canyon walls, railroads, surface water, or public roads (Whitman County Regional Planning Council 1978).

Parcel size needs to be sufficient to meet health regulations for on-site sewage disposal while pro-

TABLE 5.6
RULES OF COMBINATION FOR RECREATION IN MEDFORD TOWNSHIP, NEW JERSEY

Suitability criteria: Recreation cost savings for intensive recreation
A. Concurrence of 4 acceptable factors = prime suitability (1)
Concurrence of 3 acceptable factors = secondary suitability (2)
Concurrence of 2 acceptable factors = tertiary suitability (3)
Presence of only 1 acceptable factor = unsuitable

Factor	Acceptable Limit
Maintenance: site drainage	Somewhat poorly drained soils
Maintenance: site drainage and lawns, playgrounds, etc.	Minimum 1–3 in (2.54–7.62 cm) depth to the seasonal high-water table
Maintenance: lawns, playgrounds, etc.	Concurrence of at least two of the following: a. Moderate available soil mixture b. Fair nutrient retention c. Moderate shrink-swell potential
Maintenance: lawns, playgrounds, etc.	Maximum 100 tons/acre/year potential soil loss (100 tons/0.405 ha/year)

B. Suitability categories derived from step A are modified by the following site factors:

Factor	Location	Suitability Modified
Lack of gradient (site drainage cost)	Inner lowland; plain; Outer lowland: plain	1 becomes 2 2 becomes 3 3 becomes 4
Excessive runoff (site drainage cost)	*	1 becomes 2 2 becomes 3 3 becomes 4 4 becomes 5

Desirable locations for general, natural, and cultural-historic-educational recreation

Type	Location
Water related	Stream, artificial lakes, view of water
Scenic interest	Enclosure, regional and local prominence, terrain interest, agriculture
Vegetation and wildlife interest	Cedar swamp, bog, shrub woodland, upland successional meadow, floodplain, mixed deciduous, coniferous-deciduous mixed, pine, pine-oak, oak pine, upland successional oak, lowland successional, deciduous lowland forests, urban forested
Scenic, educational, and scientific interest	Ironstone, old mature specimen trees
Historic, cultural, and educational interest	Historic sites, land routes, water routes, and lakes

* Assumed acceptable limit is that no more than 5% of site area is required to infiltrate within 3 hours the excess runoff generated over that site during the 10-year recurrent 24-hour storm, most intense hour.
SOURCE: Adapted from Juneja 1974.

TABLE 5.7
RULES OF COMBINATION FOR CLUSTER SUBURBAN DEVELOPMENT IN MEDFORD TOWNSHIP, NEW JERSEY

Suitability criteria: Cost savings for clustered suburban
A. Concurrence of 5 acceptable factors = prime suitability (1)
Concurrence of 4 acceptable factors = secondary suitability (2)
Concurrence of 3 acceptable factors = tertiary suitability (3)
Concurrence of fewer than 3 acceptable factors = unsuitable

Factor	Acceptable Limit
Foundations: Light structure	Fair subsoil shear strength
Foundations: Paved structures	Concurrence of at least two of the following: a. Fair subsoil shear strength b. Moderate shrink-swell potential c. Moderate frost-heave susceptibility
Maintenance: Paved surfaces	Concurrence of acceptable foundation conditions for paved surfaces and maximum 100 tons/acre/ potential soil loss (100 tons/0.405 ha/year)
Maintenance: Site drainage	Somewhat poorly drained soils
Maintenance: Site drainage	Minimum 1–3 in. (2.54–7.62 cm) depth to seasonal high water table

B. Suitability categories derived from step A are modified by the following site factors:

Factor	Location	Suitability Modified
Sloping terrain (paved surfaces)	Inner lowland terrace: slope, scarp, stream dissection; inner lowland: stream dissection; inner upland: hill, slope, scarp, stream dissection; inner and outer lowland plains are also included because the saving in construction cost is negated by increased drainage cost resulting from lack of gradient	1 becomes 2 2 becomes 3 3 becomes 4
Excessive runoff (site drainage cost)	*	1 becomes 2 2 becomes 3 3 becomes 4 4 becomes 5

Desirable location
Presence of 1 desirable factor = tertiary suitability (A)

Factor	Desirable Element
Scenic interest	Regional prominence, terrain interest, view of water, field

* Assumed acceptable limit is that no more than 5% of site area is required to infiltrate within 3 hours the excess runoff generated over that site during the 10-year recurrent 24-hour storm, most intense hour.
SOURCE: Adapted from Juneja 1974.

viding adequate acreage for productive use of rural residential land. Productive uses include small numbers of livestock and large gardens. Further guidelines for rural housing include a minimum of 200 feet (61 meters) of frontage from perennial surface water passing through or along the property lines of the acreage and less than 50 percent of the acreage in a designated flood hazard area, as defined by the federal flood insurance program.

During public hearings on the plan, several local residents, including realtors and builders, questioned whether there was any land in the county that could meet these guidelines and, if so, how much? To mitigate the suspicion that these lands were inordinately scarce, a planning team was formed to investigate the potential for rural housing using these guidelines in conjunction with actual land use throughout the county.

The planning team (Steiner and Theilacker 1979) chose a 150-square-mile (388.35 kilometer^2) demonstration area adjacent to the city of Pullman for the feasibility study. The demand for rural housing is greater in this area than in other parts of the county. This area is close to the cities of Pullman, location of Washington State University, and Moscow, Idaho, location of the University of Idaho. These two cities contain most of the people in the region. Many of the faculty from the two universities seek a rural-living situation.

The planning team inventoried uncultivated "scablands" adjacent to improved county and state roads, estimating and demarcating the total area suitable for rural housing development. Scablands, as commonly defined by local farmers, are those areas not suitable for commercial cultivation.

Scientific definitions of these lands are somewhat similar. The NRCS, for example, identifies scabgrounds as those consisting of Gwin-Linvill and Gwin-Tucannon soils. These areas differ from the channel scabland identified by geologists that resulted from the Spokane, or Missoula, Flood of the Pleistocene Era.

Because the farmers' scablands definition is more readily understood by decision makers, this is the definition that was used. However, the work of scientists was not ignored. It formed the basis for the inventory process and was crucial to the selection of feasible areas.

The planning team used the principles of suitability analysis, as defined by McHarg (1969), to determine those areas feasible for rural housing. Instead of overlaying inventory information to find intrinsically suitable areas, the team overlaid information to identify areas meeting the established policy guidelines for rocky and agriculturally unproductive lands, or scablands. The team then subtracted constraint areas, leaving the areas feasible for housing (Steiner and Theilacker 1979).

The study began with an extensive inventory and mapping of the demonstration area. The team collected information at two scales: 1:2000 for the overall demonstration area and 1:100 for two more specific sites. The information collected included bedrock geology, elevation, basalt outcrops and steep slopes, soil series, surface water, wildlife habitat, transportation, property ownership, scablands, and generalized areas feasible for rural housing. The team related all this material directly to the criteria established in the comprehensive plan revision for rural housing.

The team identified scabland areas by inventorying the physical features that prevent dryland farming. Areas of basalt outcroppings and steep slopes were considered scablands, along with several soil types identified by the NRCS. These generally thin or gravelly soils, which are poor for agricultural purposes, often occur on steep slopes. Such soil types are also found in floodplains, adjacent to or deposited within basalt outcroppings.

The generalized areas feasible for rural housing were next located on maps by a process of elimination (Figure 5.17). Once the scablands were identified, conditions considered unsuitable for rural housing were addressed and such lands eliminated. These conditions included floodplain areas, valuable wildlife habitats, exposed basalt rocks, areas with slopes greater than 40 percent,

Example A

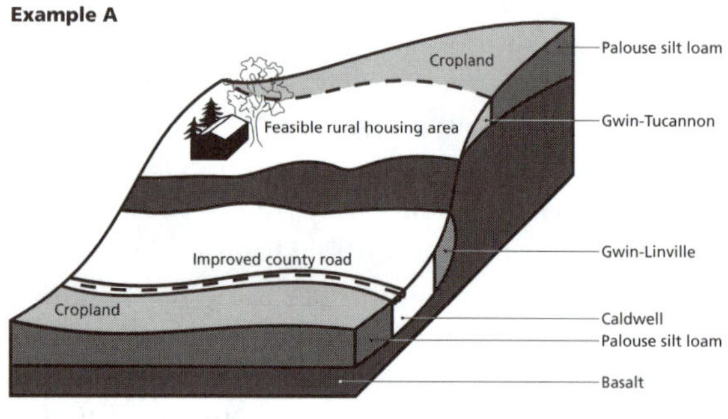

Example B

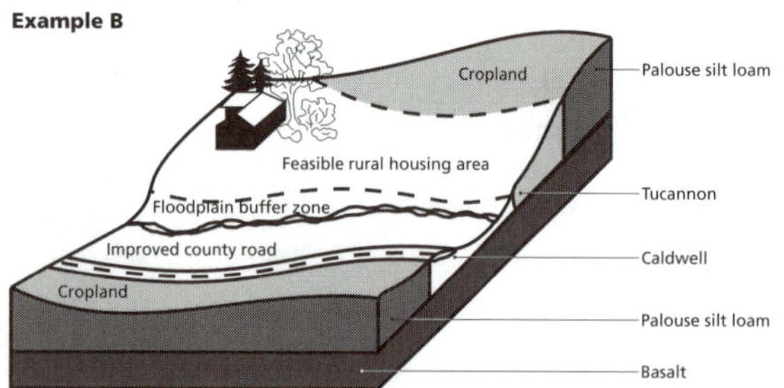

FIGURE 5.17 Generalized feasible areas for rural housing in Whitman County, Washington.

lack of frontage on improved state and county roads, and soil characteristics unsuited for structures or for on-site water supply and sewage disposal.

The planning team estimated about 12,443 acres (5,039.42 hectares) of scablands in the 150-square-mile (388.35 kilometer^2) demonstration area. In the two more specific study sites, which together totaled 76 square miles, 1,734 acres were identified with a potential for rural housing development (196.76 kilometers^2, or 702.27 hectares). These findings enabled the county commissioners to respond affirmatively to the many earlier questions about whether there was land that met the guidelines in the county comprehensive plan revision. The findings also established a procedure for identifying such land. This procedure was supplemented with a suggested environmental checklist for rural housing that can be used when developers make specific requests. The checklist helped to ensure the environmental quality sought by the commissioners by incorporating specific siting criteria into zoning and building code requirements (see Chapter 10). Since 1979, these criteria have successfully been used in Whitman County to protect good farmland, promote the siting of rural housing in suitable areas, and to concentrate urban development within the City of Pullman. (See, for example, American Farmland Trust 1977.)

The suitability analyses conducted in Whitman County and Medford Township considered a wide range of information about nature and people. This breadth distinguishes these examples from detailed studies undertaken in more conventional planning processes. Human values were considered in both examples. In Whitman County, the study was responding to values expressed in the comprehensive plan goals. Farmers' values were considered in the identification of scablands. The feelings of the community as expressed through public hearings was a major reason the study was conducted. In Medford Township, suitability criteria were developed for each land use based on values to society and to individuals. Values were important in determining rules of combination as well.

6

PLANNING OPTIONS AND CHOICES

To a large extent, every step in the planning process, like life itself, requires that choices be made. Planning may be viewed as a "process for determining appropriate future action through a sequence of choices" (Davidoff and Reiner 1962, 103). Throughout this sequence, questions arise. What goals should a community adopt? What information about biophysical and sociocultural processes of a planning area should be collected? What are the boundaries of the planning area and at what scale or in what format should information be collected and presented? In ecological planning, once detailed studies such as suitability analyses have been performed, the community will have a number of choices. The planning area may be faced with a growing population. Several specific parcels of land may be intrinsically suited for several uses—possibly agriculture, housing, and recreation. Which use should the community encourage?

The purpose of this step in the process is to attempt to answer such questions by presenting a series of options to the people of the area. Conceptual visions should be presented that link planning decisions to actions and then actions to impacts in the landscape. Such visions can be presented in a series of models or scenarios that depict the future possibilities for the planning area. Rachel Kaplan and her colleagues explain, "The purpose of providing alternatives is not to force a choice or pick a 'winner.' Rather, alternatives should provide some notions of what is feasible; they can help to communicate the range of issues that need to be considered. The final solution is likely to incorporate pieces of several alternatives" (Kaplan et al. 1998, 132).

Many techniques can assist a community in making choices among planning options. The techniques are similar to those used to identify issues and to establish planning goals, discussed in Chapter 2. A few of the more popular techniques include the charrette, task forces, citizens' advisory committees, technical advisory committees, public hearings, citizen referendum and synchronized surveys, and goals-achievement matrices. Two good examples of selecting preferences include the land-use alternatives for the Portland, Oregon, comprehensive plan; and the alternative futures for the Camp Pendleton, California, region. The Oregon case shows how options were derived from existing goals. The Camp Pendleton work displays a tie between alternative futures and biodiversity.

OPTIONAL PLANS

Suitability analyses may present a number of choices to a community. For instance, a community may have established goals both to provide for housing and to protect prime farmland. A parcel of land may be highly suited for both uses. To assist elected and appointed officials in decision making, it can be helpful to develop a number of optional landscape plans that would enable officials to see the spatial impacts of their decisions.

Two examples from the Desert View Tri-Villages Area in Arizona will be used for illustration. In the first example, Professors Rebecca Fish Ewan and Joseph Ewan led a team of landscape architects, planners, environmental scientists, and architects in an exploration of possible widths for the protection of the Cave Creek Wash. As was noted in Chapter 3, this wash is a major landscape feature in the area. In the second example, Jim Burke and Jim Coffman of the Phoenix Parks, Recreation, and Library Department developed three concepts for the creation of a Sonoran preserve in the area. They presented these concepts to village planning committees and many others. The concepts formed the basis of the Sonoran Preserve Master Plan, created by a team led by Burke and Ewan.

The Arizona State University (ASU) School of Planning and Landscape Architecture faculty began cooperating with city of Phoenix in 1994 in the Desert View Tri-Villages Area. An interdisciplinary group of environmental scientists, landscape architects, environmental planners, and architects meet monthly with city planners. This informal group, which calls itself the North Sonoran Collaborative, expanded to include state environmental management and local consultants. These meetings led to student studio projects and faculty research and other activities (including the charrette discussed later in this chapter). These meetings were held in a context of both interest in more appropriate development in the Tri-Villages as well as desert protection. Very early in the cooperation, the notion that large areas of desert should be protected was raised. At the same time, the Design Workshop (1995) and others produced a regional open space plan for the Maricopa Association of Governments that indicated that environmentally sensitive areas such as the Cave Creek Wash should be included as open spaces. Soon the mayor of Phoenix was advocating desert preservation. He was joined by the governor and legislature, which passed the Arizona Preserve Initiative, permitting certain State Trust Lands to be used as open space. But funding was limited, so the question of what lands to preserve became important to address.

A team of researchers from the ASU School of Planning and Landscape Architecture and the ASU-

West Life Sciences Department, directed by Professors Joe Ewan and Rebecca Fish Ewan, analyzed a series of options for the preservation boundaries of the Cave Creek Wash. The study was undertaken for the city of Phoenix and involved a multidisciplinary team of city staff, university faculty and students, and the state urban wildlife specialist. The disciplines involved included landscape architecture, environmental planning, ecology, recreation, and architecture. A detailed site analysis revealed four main vegetation types: (1) the main creek bed; (2) streambanks, smaller side channels, and sloped terrain; (3) cactus-dominated areas; and (4) upland areas (Ewan and Fish Ewan 1996). The team used field data to delineate three options or scenarios for possible preservation. Table 6.1 summarizes these three scenarios, which are illustrated in Figures 6.1, 6.2, and 6.3.

Ewan and Fish Ewan synthesized the extensive field data on maps and aerial photography and then organized an intense working meeting for the research team in a charrette-like format. (Charrettes are discussed in greater detail later in this chapter.) As summarized in Ewan and Fish Ewan's report:

> the group broke into subteams to consider three scenarios for preservation boundaries: one that examined maximizing the preserved area, another that looked at moderate preservation, and a third that considered a minimal area for preservation. Each subteam was given a mission statement and then asked to delineate the preservation boundary on a study map that reflected their preservation scenario, and to document specific recommendations. This information was synthesized into three boundary recommendations (Ewan et al. 1996, 4).

TABLE 6.1
PRESERVATION BOUNDARY SCENARIOS FOR THE CAVE CREEK WASH

	Vegetation Types					
Preservation Boundary Scenarios	**1**	**2**	**3**	**4**	**Damaged**	**Total**
Maximum Preservation						
Number of Acres	179	474	213	3,226	80	4,172
Percent of Total	4.3%	11.4%	5.1%	77.3%	1.9%	100%
(Includes the maximum amount of land within the Cave Creek Wash ecosystem in order to maintain the wash's natural integrity in its entirety.)						
Moderate Preservation						
Number of Acres	179	355	173	1,710	137	2,564
Percent of Total	7.0%	13.9%	6.7%	67.1%	5.3%	100%
(Includes large parcels of diverse landscape mosaics and the least costly and/or least disturbed land.)						
Minimum Preservation						
Number of Acres	179	244	89	991	38	1,541
Percent of Total	11.6%	15.8%	5.8%	64.3%	2.5%	100%
(Includes the richest and most pristine areas within the study site with minimum land acquisition.)						

SOURCE: Ewan et al. 1996.

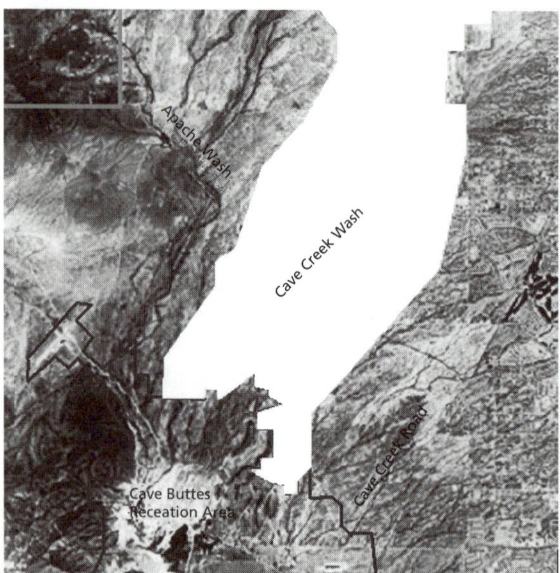

FIGURE 6.1 Cave Creek Wash, maximum preservation scenario. *(Source: Ewan et al. 1996 for the City of Phoenix Parks, Recreation, and Library Department)*

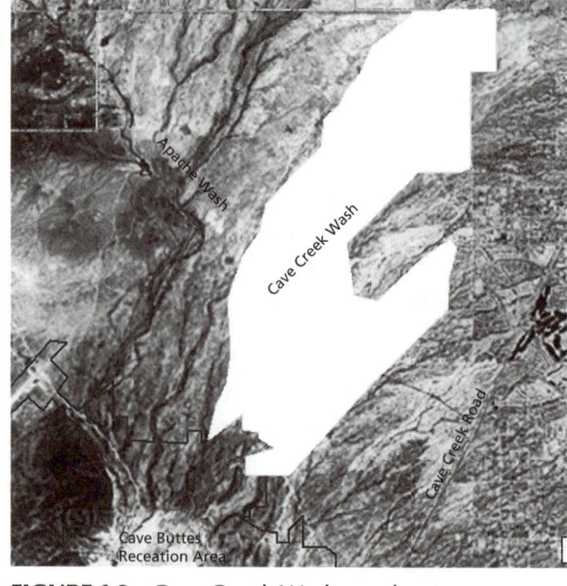

FIGURE 6.2 Cave Creek Wash, moderate preservation scenario. *(Source: Ewan et al. 1996 for the City of Phoenix Parks, Recreation, and Library Department)*

FIGURE 6.3 Cave Creek Wash, minimum preservation scenario. *(Source: Ewan et al. 1996 for the City of Phoenix Parks, Recreation, and Library Department)*

These recommendations were presented in a report to the Parks, Recreation, and Library Department and the Parks and Recreation Board, which promptly recommended the maximum preservation option to city council. The Phoenix City Council concurred and the maximum preservation option is being pursued.

The second example of alternative plan development built on the Cave Creek Wash study of Fish Ewan and Ewan. The Phoenix Parks, Recreation, and Library Department "developed three concepts for the Sonoran Preserve in 1996. The concepts illustrated options for approximately 12,000 acres [4856 hectares] in the Tri-Villages Area. These three concepts were reviewed by the public and by representatives of city, state, and federal agencies" (Burke and Ewan 1998a).

The first concept concentrated the preserve (Figure 6.4). According to the park planners, "The Concentrated Concept contains the preserve in one large contiguous parcel that maximizes habitat and

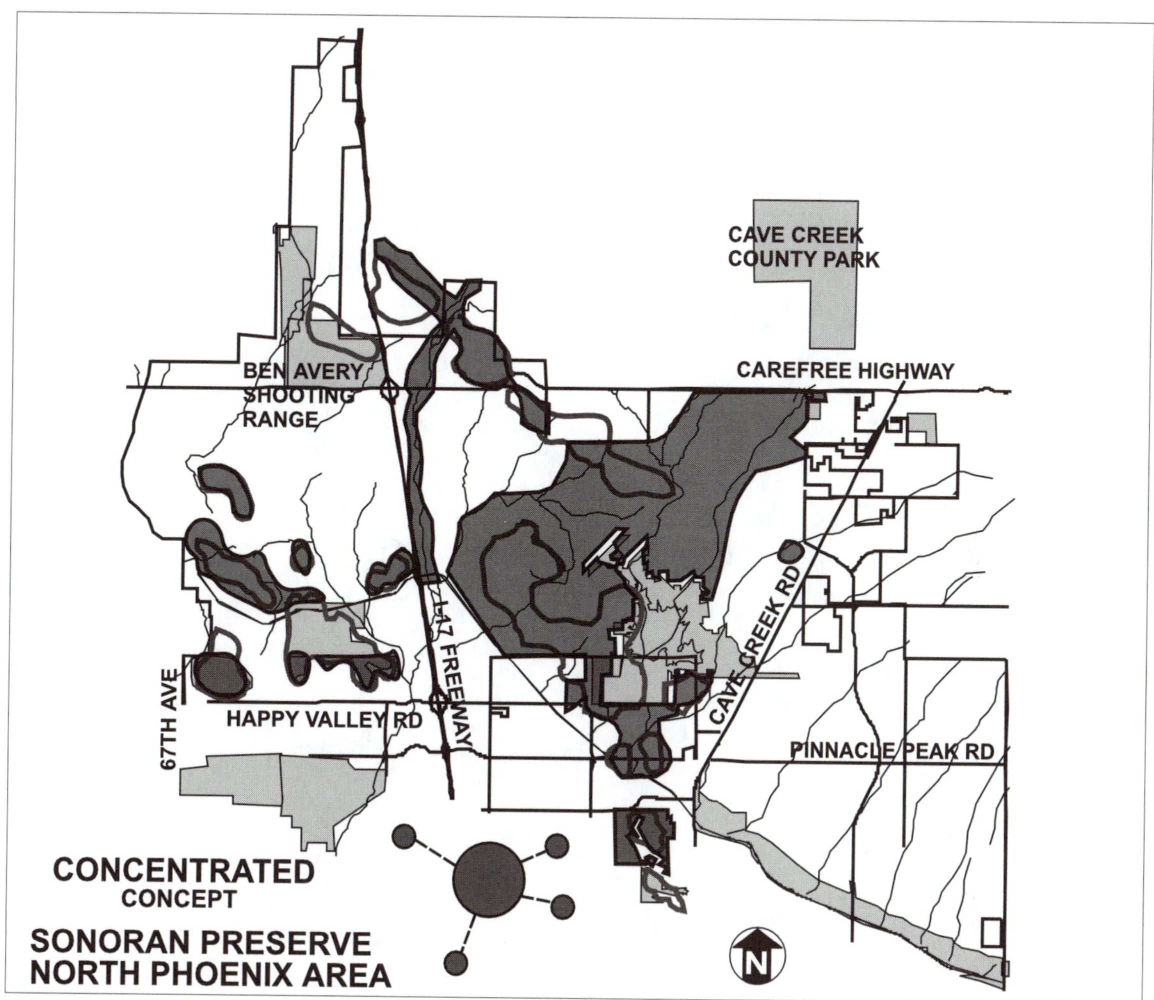

FIGURE 6.4 Concentrated preserve concept. *(Source: Burke and Ewan 1998a)*

wildlife benefits (low perimeter/area ratio)" (Burke and Ewan 1998a, 14). The preserve would function as a regional park. "This concept lessens the emphasis on recreational access and creates the greatest opportunity for isolated natural areas. The average person may have to travel longer distances to get to the preserve" (Burke and Ewan 1998a, 14).

The second option dispersed the preserve throughout the Tri-Villages Area (Figure 6.5). According to the park planners, "The Dispersed Concept integrates the preserve into developed areas allowing a great number of users access from their homes and work. This could be called a 'backyard approach,' creating a greater potential for negative impact on wildlife and habitat (highest perimeter/area ratio)" (Burke and Ewan 1998a, 14).

The third option seeks out a middle ground between the first two (Figure 6.6). According to

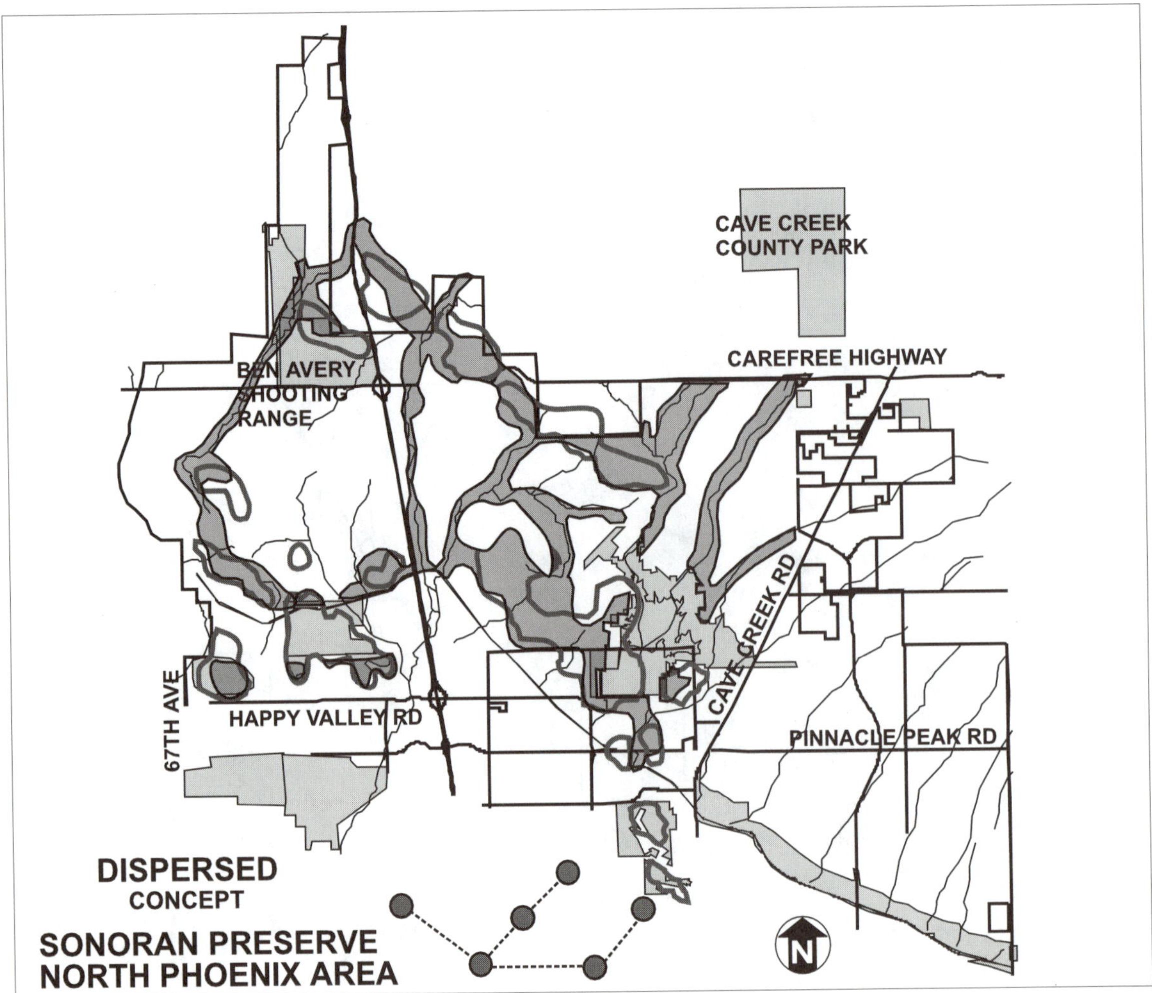

FIGURE 6.5 Dispersed preserve concept. *(Source: Burke and Ewan 1998a)*

the park planners, this Semi-Concentrated Concept "has significant areas set aside for conservation while allowing for reasonable recreation access from adjacent developments" (Burke and Ewan 1998a, 14). The option would include representative areas of all the vegetation/habitat types in the Tri-Villages Area and would have a moderate perimeter/area ratio (Burke and Ewan 1998a).

In two open houses, the public was asked to rank these three concepts. Most participants preferred the Concentrated Concept, noting that "preserving the health of the environment should be of the utmost importance" (Burke and Ewan 1998a, 15). These three concepts, as well as the Cave Creek Wash study and inventory and analysis information reviewed in previous chapters were used to develop the Sonoran Preserve Mas-

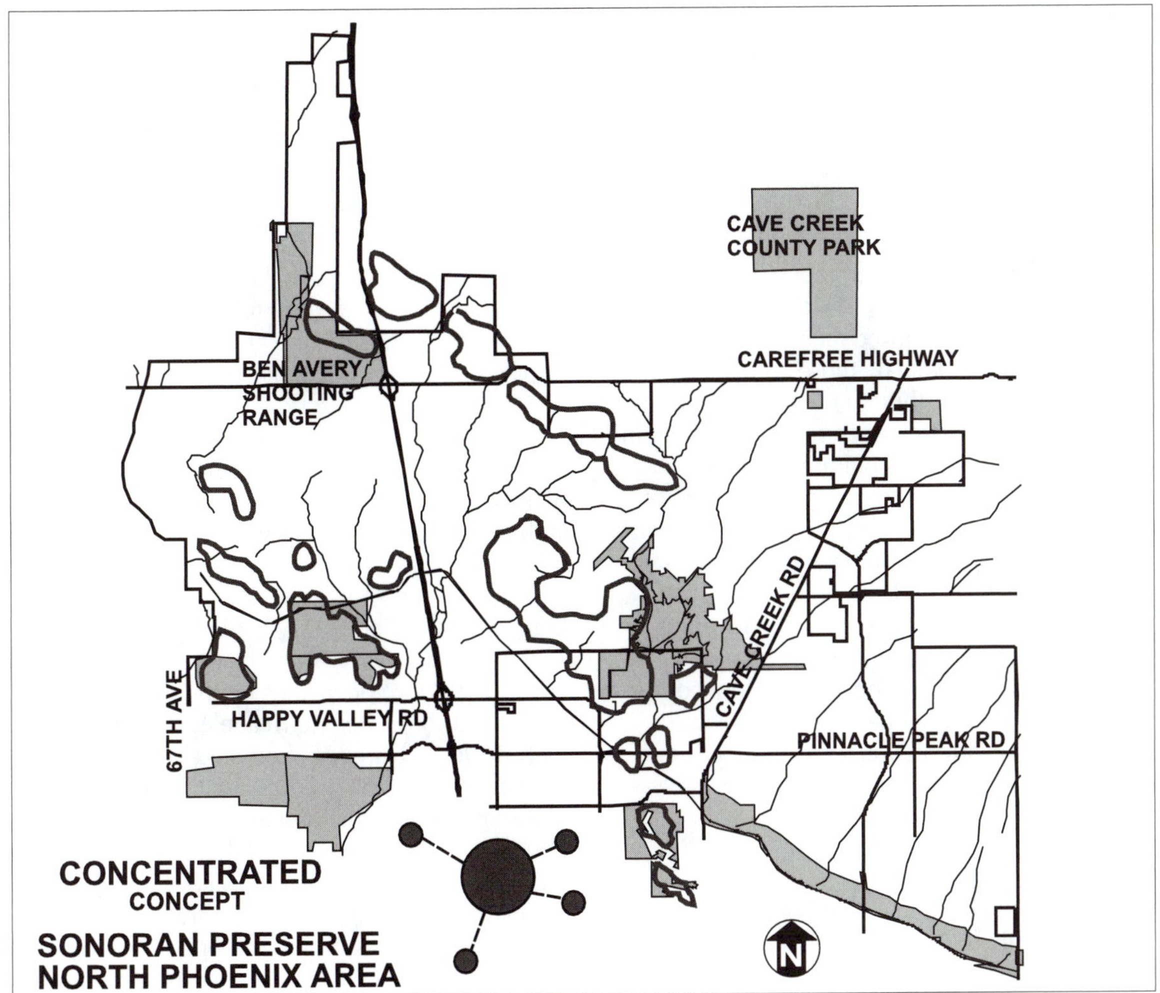

FIGURE 6.6 Semiconcentrated preserve concept. *(Source: Burke and Ewan 1998a)*

ter Plan, which will be discussed in the next chapter.

TECHNIQUES FOR SELECTING PREFERENCES

Several techniques exist to help planners develop options. Charrettes are especially helpful to help create visualizations of possible changes. As a result, the charrette process will be discussed in detail.

The Charrette

The *charrette* (from the French word for small cart) technique is derived from its original usage in the École des Beaux-Arts. The École des Beaux-Arts, the French academy of fine arts, was founded in Paris in 1617, incorporating several older art schools. The purpose was to give instruction in drawing, painting, sculpture, architecture, and engraving to a fixed number of students selected by a highly competitive examination. The training process consisted of lectures on diverse subjects, such as anatomy and history, and practice in studios under the direction of eminent master artists. Charrettes were the carts on which students of the École des Beaux-Arts carried their paintings. The paintings were criticized by those who watched the carts pass. This method of criticism was institutionalized first by the French school and later in American art, design, and planning education.

A charrette may be used to present a series of conceptual plans based on suitability analyses for various land uses. Much preparation is necessary before a session is held. Each of the plans may involve different organizations of the planning areas, with each optimizing a different use, such as agriculture, recreation, housing, nature conservation, and industry. The participants may also represent groups advocating various uses. The emphasis is placed on discussing the merits of each plan.

The Charrette Process. The charrette process can be defined as "a brief period of intense activity, if not round-the-clock work to accomplish a given task" (Riddick 1971, 1). W. L. Riddick (1971) identifies four essential ingredients for a charrette:

1. Identification of a specific community problem to study, understand, and hopefully resolve.
2. Participation of interested citizens, particularly those experiencing the problem (or its effects), who are willing to be involved in the decision-making process. This is a fundamental component of the charrette.
3. Involvement of professional experts from within and outside the community. Initially these experts listen and learn as citizens express their concerns. Later, one of the strengths of the charrette process lies in consensus building as citizens and experts brainstorm together to find solutions. Resource material is typically made available to assist in this process.
4. Commitment from the relevant power structure to put into effect the plans and recommendations of the charrette. Representatives of the power structure are to be present to hear the concerns expressed by the citizens.

Originally focusing on the design of physical structures, the charrette is now used for land-use planning in a number of countries. American architects and new urbanists Andres Duany and Elizabeth Plater-Zyberk and the U.S. Office of Education were early users of charrettes in the United States (Riddick 1971; Meyer 1994). For example, Plater-Zyberk and her colleagues used a charrette to develop visions for the redevelopment of south Florida after Hurricane Andrew in the early 1990s (Alvarez et al. no date).

Charrettes can be used during the goal-setting phase of the planning process. The City of Phoenix, however, has found that charrettes are most effective when clear goals have been set before the charrette participants are brought together. Charrettes provide an opportunity to bring together expertise to evaluate options and synthesize ideas, which is best done when the focus of the participants is clear. Additionally, support of the charrette participants is enthusiastic only when political action is considered possible. If the likelihood of immediate action on the charrette recommendations is high, it is more likely that charrette participants will be productive.

Phoenix has conducted several successful charrettes, frequently in cooperation with the ASU faculty and staff. In 1989 the city conducted the Camelback East Primary Core Urban Design Charrette, which led to a specific plan for the Camelback Road Corridor (City of Phoenix and

ASU 1989) and resulted in the plan subsequently adopted for that area of Phoenix. In 1990, the city conducted the South Central Avenue Streetscape Charrette, and in 1993 it conducted a charrette on scenic corridors in the Desert View Tri-Villages Area (City of Phoenix 1994). In 1992 the Phoenix City Zoo conducted a charrette to design animal enclosures. Other examples of charrettes in the United States include one for school design in New York City (En Charrette 1993); architecture student projects in Chicago (Paris Prize 1993); urban design and energy efficiency in downtown South Miami (D'Ambrosi and Thomas 1993); landscape architecture in San Francisco (Thompson 1993); identifying crucial city problems in York, Pennsylvania (Shumway 1973); and a series of urban designs for Seattle and the Puget Sound region (Kelbaugh 1997).

The charrette process is used frequently in Australia for land-use planning. For instance, the City of Rockdale in New South Wales conducted a one-week charrette in 1994 to formulate multiple master plans for a 43-hectare (106-acre) established industrial area of metropolitan Sydney (Meyer 1994). The Western Australia Department of Planning and Urban Development conducted a two-day charrette in March 1993 "to provide a clear picture of what an urban village would be in the [city of] Perth context" and how this could be applied in metropolitan fringe growth corridors (Adams et al. 1993, 1). In 1992, the City of Cranbourne in the outer southeastern area of metropolitan Melbourne (Victoria, Australia) conducted a charrette to plan for the growth of newly designated residential areas (Taylor 1992). A Canadian example is the Surrey Design Charrette in British Columbia (Condon 1996); a charrette for the Leidsche Rijn region near Utrecht is a Dutch example (Koekebakker 1996); and the EDAW/Pei workshop for Suzhou is a Chinese effort (Prentice 1998).

The example of a charrette for the Desert View Tri-Villages Area—the Sonoran North Land Use Character Charrette of September 1995 (McCarthy et al. 1995)—will be explored in some detail here. ASU master of environmental planning graduate student James McCarthy and Lizi McGeorge, a visiting scholar from Australia, were the main organizers of the charrette. A complete list of the participants is provided in Appendix B of this book.

Charrette Groundwork. The cooperation that led to the Sonoran North Land Use Character Charrette involved over a year of discussions between city staff and university faculty in a technical working group, as well as a series of student projects (e.g., Bagley et al. 1995) and a comprehensive inventory of environmental data sources by a student intern (Coomer 1995). These discussions and projects contributed significant background information. Concurrently, the City of Phoenix and local residents engaged in dialogue and various planning activities.

Many charrettes go on for several days, nearly 24 hours per day. The Sonoran North charrette was designed to keep the spirit of intense work, but with a less rigid three-day schedule, as shown in Table 6.2. The charrette was held at Arizona State University-West.

Introduction to Planning Area, Introduction to Participants. The core team members met Friday afternoon to tour the planning area. The tour route and stops were chosen to maximize exposure to the various landscape types, both natural and built. An overview at the Central Arizona Project canal, the southern boundary of the planning area, gave the team members an opportunity to see the developed area to the south and the abutting largely undeveloped area to the north (McCarthy et al. 1995).

The firsthand knowledge gained during the Friday afternoon tour was supplemented by a presentation from a City of Phoenix planner. He projected photographic slides and gave the charrette participants additional information concerning the present conditions of the planning area. An outside design expert was also used to place

TABLE 6.2
SONORAN NORTH LAND-USE CHARACTER CHARRETTE SCHEDULE

FRIDAY: INTRODUCTIONS	
3:00 to 7:15 pm	Tour of Planning Area
(5:30 to 6:30 pm)	Dinner
7:30 to 7:45 pm	Introduction and Welcome
7:45 to 8:30 pm	Spatial Consequences of Development
(7:15 to 9:00 pm)	Photo Exhibition
SATURDAY MORNING: PUBLIC INTERVIEWS	
8:30 to 8:40 am	Welcome and Charrette Objectives
8:40 to 9:00 am	Planning Area Overview
9:00 to 9:10 am	Introduction and Team Instructions
9:15 to 10:30 am	Core Team Interviews
10:45 to 11:30 am	Core Team Interviews
SATURDAY AFTERNOON: CORE TEAM ANALYSIS	
1:30 to 4:00 pm	Core Team Design Brainstorming
4:05 to 5:05 pm	Teams' Presentation of Initial Results
SUNDAY: CORE TEAM ANALYSIS	
10:40 to 3:30 pm	Core Team Working Sessions
3:40 to 5:30 pm	Presentation of Conclusions to Teams and Public

SOURCE: McCarthy et al. 1995.

the charrette in a larger context and provide fresh ideas. Often outside experts are used in charrettes. Especially designers from other regions or countries can bring different perspectives and encourage charrette participants to "think outside the box," that is, not to be constrained by their normal approach to their work.

One of the goals of the Sonoran North Land-Use Character Charrette was to help refine the alternate development types for the area, which were preliminarily defined before the event (Table 6.3). The focus was on the following character concepts:

- Desert preservation character
- Rural desert character
- Suburban desert character
- Growth character

The Teams. Individuals were preselected for each of four character teams to assure balanced representation by the various disciplines, which included planners, landscape architects, environmental scientists, and architects. Representatives participated from the academic, private practice, and governmental sectors. Academics included faculty at all ranks, environmental planning graduate students, and college administrators.

The core teams ranged in size from 8 to 10 members. The core teams interviewed community members. These ranged from representative residents to environmentalists to local business people to developers. Several of the community members chose to stay and observe the subsequent brainstorming and synthesis sessions. (These citizens subsequently developed a high level of ownership in the results of the charrette.)

A leader for each team was preselected. The four team leaders were professional consultants, independent from the university and city planning staffs. Although the leaders had scant experience in leading charrette teams, they were able to do so and to meet the charrette goals on schedule. This approach is consistent with the President's Council on Sustainable Development, which recommended a multidisciplinary design team approach to "design new communities and improve existing ones to use land efficiently, promote mixed-use and mixed-income development, retain public open space, and provide diverse transportation options" (President's Council on Sustainable Development 1996, 97). According to the President's Council

> These design teams should include leading experts in a broad range of fields, including architecture, transportation, land use, energy efficiency, development, and engineering. Design teams should work with state and local governments and community residents with related experience to design, develop, and make accessible to communities alternatives to sprawl development, models for regional cooperation, and sustainable building practices (President's Council on Sustainable Development 1996, 97).

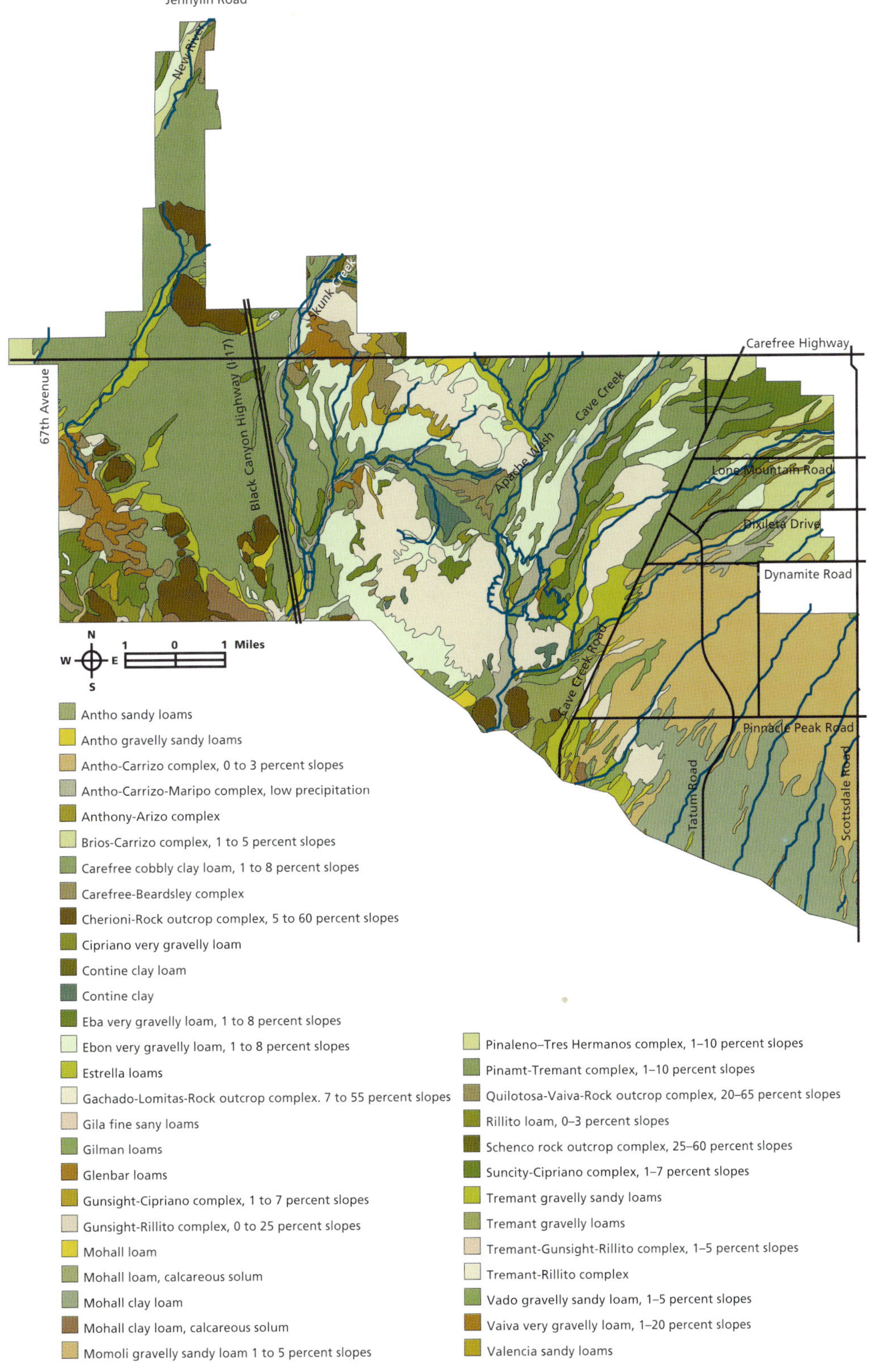

Figure 3.24 Soils, Desert View Tri-Villages Area. (Source: Brady et al. 1998)

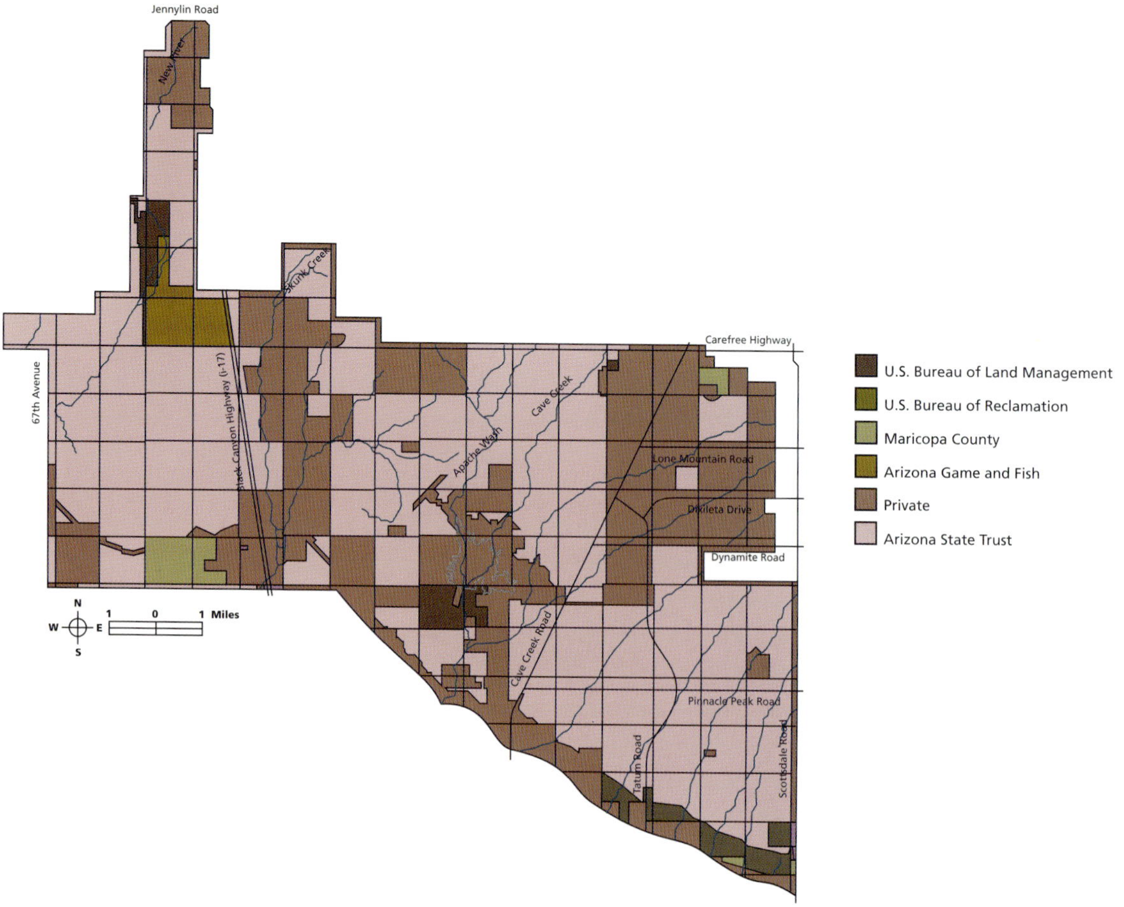

Jennylin Road
New River
Skunk Creek
Carefree Highway
67th Avenue
Black Canyon Highway (I-17)
Cave Creek
Apache Wash
Lone Mountain Road
Dixileta Drive
Dynamite Road
Cave Creek Road
Pinnacle Peak Road
Tatum Road
Scottsdale Road
N
W
E
S
1
0
1 Miles
U.S. Bureau of Land Management
U.S. Bureau of Reclamation
Maricopa County
Arizona Game and Fish
Private
Arizona State Trust

Figure 3.44 Land ownership, Desert View Tri-Villages Area. (Brady et al. 1998)

Jennylin Road
Slope 0 - 5 %
Slope 5 - 10 %
Slope > 10 %
Carefree Highway
67th Avenue
Black Canyon Highway (I-17)
Cave Creek
Apache Wash
Lone Mountain Road
Dixileta Drive
Dynamite Road
Cave Creek Road
Pinnacle Peak Road
Tatum Road
Scottsdale Road
N
W
E
S
1
0
1 Miles

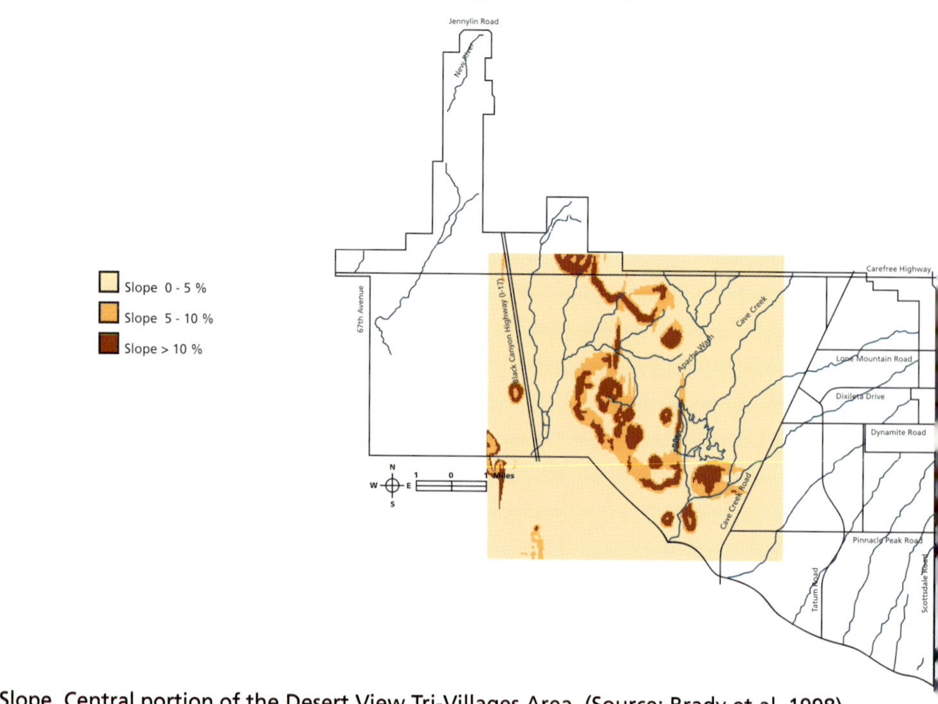

Figure 3.12 Slope, Central portion of the Desert View Tri-Villages Area. (Source: Brady et al. 1998)

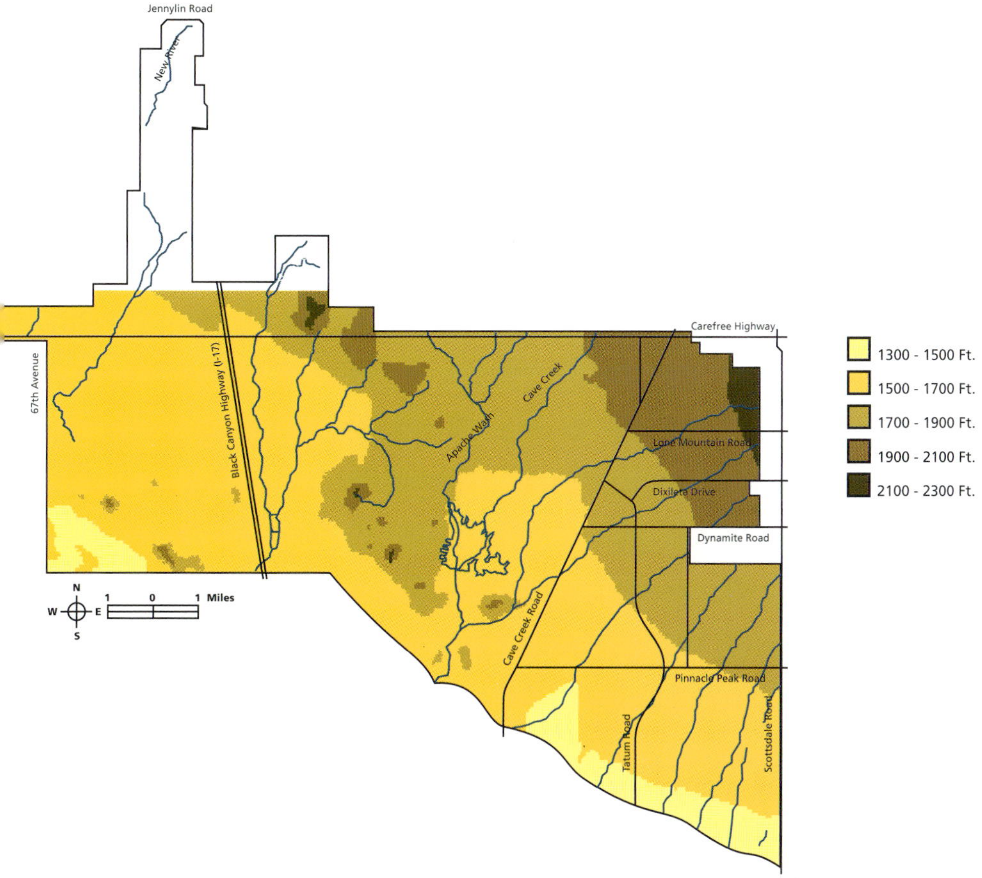

Jennylin Road
New River
Carefree Highway
67th Avenue
Black Canyon Highway (I-17)
Apache Wash
Cave Creek
Lone Mountain Road
Dixileta Drive
Dynamite Road
Cave Creek Road
Pinnacle Peak Road
Tatum Road
Scottsdale Road
1300 - 1500 Ft.
1500 - 1700 Ft.
1700 - 1900 Ft.
1900 - 2100 Ft.
2100 - 2300 Ft.
N
W
E
S
1
0
1 Miles

Figure 3.11 Elevation, Desert View Tri-Villages. (Source: Brady et al. 1998)

Basaltic rock
Granitoid rock
Metavolcanic rock
Older surficial deposit
Surficial deposit
Volcanic rock
Jennylin Road
Carefree Highway
67th Avenue
Cave Creek
Apache Wash
Lone Mountain Road
Dixileta Drive
Dynamite Road
Cave Creek Road
Pinnacle Peak Road
Tatum Road
Scottsdale Road
N
W
E
S
1
0
1 Miles

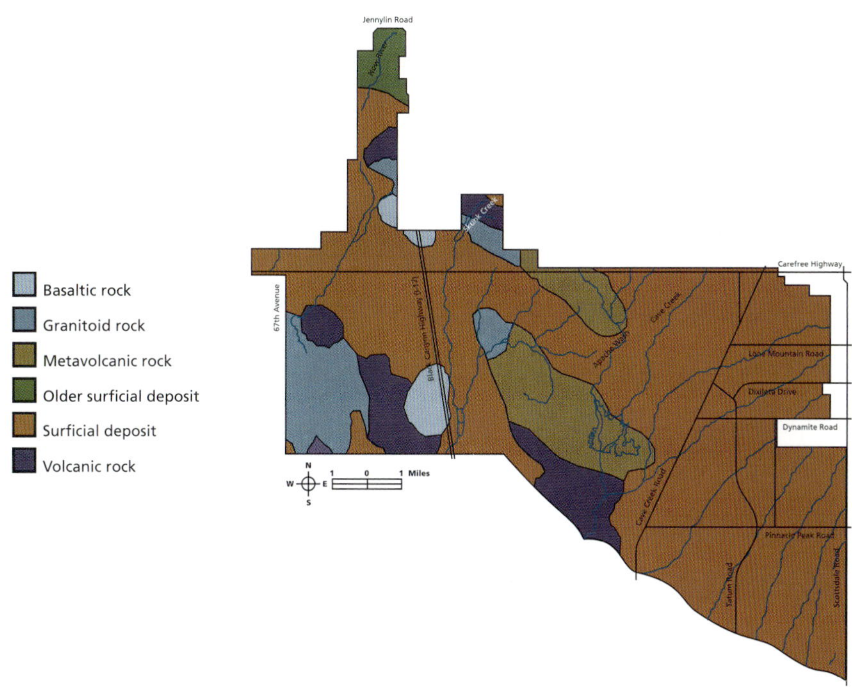

Figure 3.8 Geology, Desert View Tri-Villages. (Source: Brady et al. 1998)

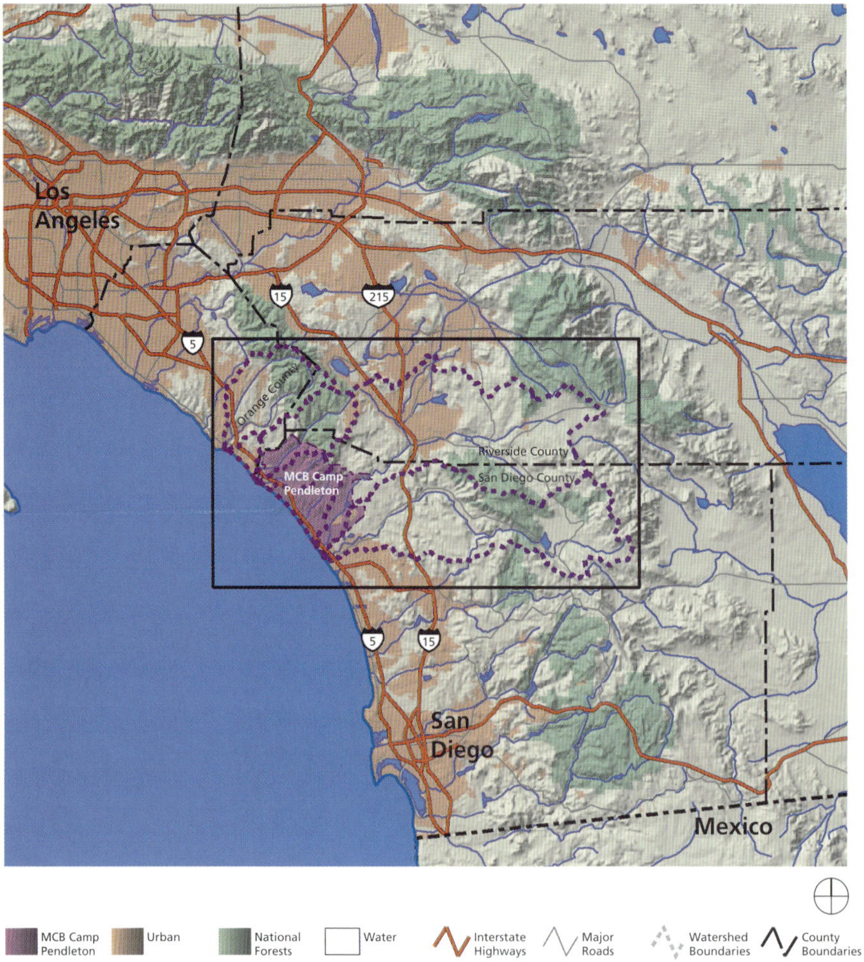

Figure 3.56 Location, Camp Pendleton region, California. (Source: Steinitz et al. 1996)

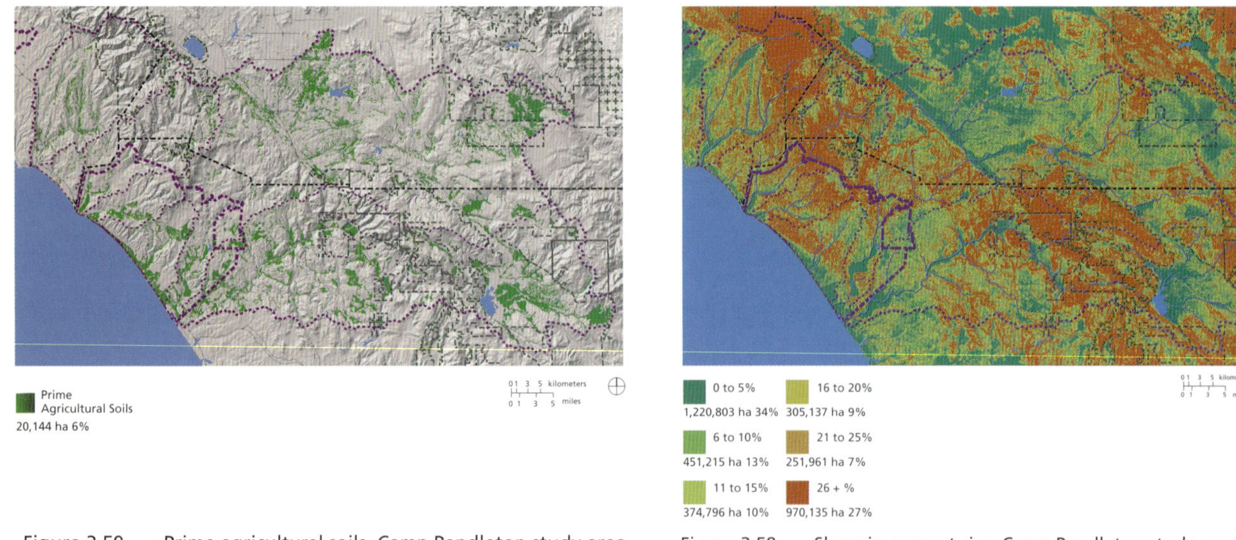

Figure 3.59 Prime agricultural soils, Camp Pendleton study area. (Source: Steinitz et al. 1996)

Figure 3.58 Slope in percent rise, Camp Pendleton study area. (Source: Steinitz et al. 1996)

TABLE 6.3
CITY OF PHOENIX PRELIMINARY LAND USE CHARACTER DESCRIPTIONS FOR THE DESERT VIEW TRI-VILLAGES AREA

Desert Preservation Character
This conceptual pattern forever preserves large enough parcels of desert to maintain an ecosystem. Patterns of desert preservation also may occur at smaller scales, perhaps relating to the other three patterns through interconnecting fingers of natural desert space, gateways, or boundary definitions. A realm of options exists for implementing this pattern, including transfer of development densities, cluster development, land trusts, fee-simple purchase, purchase of development rights, conservation easement, and dedications.

Rural Desert Character
For many people, living in the desert environment means living a rural way of life. This way of life is very much oriented to the outdoors; space and immediate access to the natural environment are important. Large open lots, single-story ranch-style homes with accessory barns or garages, little night-lighting, livestock and horses, unpaved roadways and drives, and other traits symbolize this rurality.

Presently, two differing visions exist among advocates of the Rural Desert Character Development pattern: (1) Those who desire continued equestrian privileges, thus allowing for the development of horse properties and related facilities; and (2) those who want to minimize future horse property development, instead requiring maximum building envelope standards to minimize grading and encourage the retention of undisturbed desert.

Suburban Desert Character
Based on the city's Peripheral Areas C & D Plan, the following development philosophies guide this conceptual pattern of development in the North Area:

Preserve wash corridors, mountain slopes, and native vegetation

Provide views of mountains and surrounding desert

Encourage cluster development and building envelopes

Identify scenic desert parkways

Approve plans and designs prior to site disturbance

Protect natural desert areas before development

Encourage development that is harmonious with overall environment and appearance of the area

Encourage water conservation

Growth Corridor/Core Development Character
This conceptual pattern foresees the layout of future development along major transportation corridors. Generally, this pattern recognizes that areas of activity within corridors depend on access to transportation. Two primary growth corridor/core areas exist within the area; the I-17 Corridor and the General Plan-designated Primary Core located in the vicinity of Tatum Boulevard and Cave Creek Road.

Although many linear forms of development often lack a core or center, growth corridor/core development is envisioned to have central activity nodes. The presence of a nucleus or focal point of activity within the growth corridor/core development facilitates the creation of a "sense of place."

Typically a linear type of development is synonymous with strip development, which is an undesirable type of urban form that is based primarily on automobile access and lacks the elements necessary for establishing community identity. Characteristics of the conceptual growth corridor/core pattern differ significantly from those associated with generic linear-type development.

SOURCE: McCarthy et al. 1995.

Team Instructions. Broad guidelines for the structure of the working sessions were provided. With their areas of concern defined, the teams were given a schedule which set the time periods for citizen interviews, brainstorming, and synthesis of findings. Their product, to be delivered on Sunday afternoon, was a list of overriding principles that the team thought would define their character theme. The principles were then to be expanded into more specific guidelines, and finally into a list of recommendations for further action. Additionally, the teams were requested to prepare graphic representations of the principles and guidelines for their character theme (McCarthy et al. 1995).

Citizen Interviews. After the Saturday morning introductions and instructions, the teams split up and reassembled in four separate meeting rooms. They devoted several hours to interviewing citizen and developer representatives about their concerns, experiences, and ideas. The City of Phoenix also provided reference materials such as maps and existing planning documents to stimulate discussion. The citizens' comments and ideas were documented on flip charts. Area residents, developers, realtors, neighborhood organizations, and environmental organizations were represented. Besides the invited citizens, wider public involvement was encouraged by issuing a press release to the area newspapers about the charrette (McCarthy et al. 1995). The interviews helped the teams to identify issues. For example, Table 6.4 summarizes the suburban development issues in the area.

Brainstorming and Synthesis. The interviews completed the data-gathering segment of the charrette. Next followed the brainstorming and synthesis segment, with a ground rule that any idea would be considered. After listing all the ideas and recommendations, the teams organized and synthesized the ideas to make preliminary recommendations. All charrette participants met Saturday evening to review the progress of the day. When each of the four teams presented their preliminary recommendations to the reassembled charrette group, certain themes began to emerge.

TABLE 6.4
SUBURBAN DESERT CHARACTER ISSUES

- Existing drainage regulations, which were adopted to protect natural washes and to meet flood insurance requirements, may actually result in much damage.
- Existing suburban development lacks a sense of community and has inadequate bicycle and pedestrian linkages to remote shopping and public facilities.
- New development threatens the visual quality and ecological integrity of the area.
- Current development and design review procedures are costly and unpredictable.

SOURCE: McCarthy et al. 1995.

The themes were focused and organized during the Sunday sessions. The personalities of each team were becoming clear by Sunday. For example, while most teams worked through the lunches, eating as they worked, one team thought a brief break would be more beneficial. As the deadline for the Sunday summary meeting approached, subteams emerged. Some participants concentrated on graphics, while others concentrated on the wording of principles, guidelines, and recommendations.

The original plan was to reassemble in the auditorium for the final team presentations on Sunday afternoon. But as the day progressed, it became apparent that the substantial quantity of flip charts, tracing paper overlays, and drawings that had been generated made assembling in the auditorium impractical. It was decided that meeting in the individual workrooms was more efficient, and that doing so would add a personal touch to the presentations and a sense of product ownership for each team. Thus each team made a presentation to the assembled charrette in their own room. As can be seen in Figure 6.7, the conditions were somewhat cramped, but this seemed to add to the positive atmosphere felt over the weekend (McCarthy et al. 1995).

FIGURE 6.7 Charrette presentation.

Outcomes from the Charrette. The overall charrette has had considerable influence on the planning of the Desert View Tri-Villages Area. After the actual event, representative participants met several times with the village planning committee to discuss ideas generated by the charrette. Subsequently, a report was published and distributed (McCarthy et al. 1995). The city planning staff used the findings in its effort to revise the official general plan for the area. (In Arizona, *general plan* is the legal term for a city comprehensive plan.) The technical working group also continued to meet, which generated additional faculty and student research projects. For example, the City of Phoenix funded one team to study preservation options for the Cave Creek Wash, the major wash in the area (Ewan et al. 1996); studies of four more important washes were undertaken in 1997 and 1998; another faculty, staff, and student team compiled a geographic information system database for the 110-square-mile (285 kilometer^2) area;* and a fourth faculty member studied wildlife habitat with his students.

*The City of Phoenix continues to annex land to the north. As of 1998, the planning area encompassed 130 square miles (337 kilometers^2). The initial GIS inventories focused on the 110-square-mile area but are currently expanding.

Most important, the charrette influenced city policy. How the work of Ewan and Fish Ewan impacted city policy was discussed earlier in this chapter. City planning policy changed too. On May 22, 1996, the Phoenix Planning Commission unanimously amended the city's general plan for 35 square miles (91 kilometers^2), or roughly a third of the Desert View Tri-Villages Area. The Phoenix City Council followed suit and on June 26, 1996, unanimously amended the general plan. The amendments include many ideas from the charrette (Ingley 1996; City of Phoenix 1997). A few of the new provisions include: the protection of the Cave Creek Wash in the area as an "ecological spine"; the concentration of growth near existing commercial and industrial areas and away from the most environmentally sensitive places; and the creation of three distinct community types: desert preserve, rural desert, and suburban desert. This amendment will reduce the total number of homes built in the 35-square-mile (91-kilometer^2) area by about 4 percent compared to the previous plan and concentrate where the homes will be built. Work continues on a similar amendment for the remaining two-thirds of the Desert View Tri-Villages and on the implementation of the new plan. The plan will be implemented through the creation of zoning overlays establishing development standards. Further details about implementation will be discussed in Chapter 10.

Task Forces, Citizens' Advisory Committees, and Technical Advisory Committees

Task forces, citizens' advisory committees (CACs), and technical advisory committees (TACs) were introduced in Chapter 2. A sagacious strategy is to involve the same people in determining planning preferences who established the original goals. Such involvement may be accomplished several ways. After the goals are established, task forces, CACs, or TACs may not meet until a staff com-

Task forces, citizens' advisory committees, and technical advisory committees are ways to help people discuss options and make choices.

pletes technical studies. Alternatively, these groups may assist a staff with the collection of information or may collect data themselves. If there is a period when such groups are not directly involved, then it is important to keep the participants informed about the planning activities through newsletters or other written reports.

An option may be to split the CAC or TAC into task forces after the planning goals are established. Data are next collected and each task force given the same information. It may then be the responsibility of each task force to complete a suitability analysis for one land use. The larger CAC or TAC then may reconvene in a charrette to reach a consensus about a desired composite scheme. This approach is especially useful with a technical advisory committee that has different areas of special expertise.

Citizen Referendum and Synchronized Surveys

To establish a preference among several choices, it may be helpful to return to two other techniques used to set goals: voting and surveying. If, for instance, a goal was established by an election, then a referendum may be held on proposed options to achieve that goal. An advantage of an official vote is that the selected preference might have greater popular support, which may make implementation easier.

A referendum may occur at any stage in the planning process. For instance, Oregon statewide planning laws have faced referenda four times. In 1970, prior to the legislation establishing the Land Conservation and Development Commission, a measure to repeal all state land-use laws failed by a margin of 55 to 45 percent. In 1976, an initiative sought to repeal the Land Conservation and Development Commission. It was defeated 57 to 43 percent. Another initiative was launched in 1978 and was defeated 61 to 39 percent (Pease 1984). Finally, in 1983, a final initiative to repeal several aspects of the bill was voted down. There had been a gradual increase of support for planning in Oregon at the ballot box.

An alternative to an official vote is an unofficial tally. Such a poll may be conducted through local newspapers. For instance, different plans may be published in local newspapers with relevant background data. Television can also be employed to conduct an unofficial vote. Different plans with background data can be presented on television with a poll taken afterward. Interactive cable systems greatly increase the possibilities for presenting options and for receiving indications of preferences.

Synchronized surveys proposed by Don Dillman (1977) also present possibilities to keep people involved through the planning process. Dillman believes synchronized surveys, handled correctly, may help to overcome the weakness of standard surveys described in Chapter 2. (See Figure 2.2 for an illustration of the differences between standard and synchronized surveys.) A standard model is a one-step procedure: The survey response leads directly to the policy decision, be it the establishment of goals or the selection of a preferred option. With the synchronized survey, a goal can be established with the help of a survey. Data may then be collected and options explored through another survey. A third survey then may be used to select the preferred option. This technique allows interaction between citizens and planners throughout the process.

Goals-Achievement Matrix

Often a planning team will be asked to identify the option that achieves the established goals. The goals-achievement matrix, proposed by Morris Hill (1968), is one technique that can be used to establish relationships between means and ends. Hill explained that the evaluation of various courses of action requires the determination for each option of whether the benefits outweigh the costs, measured in terms of the total array of ends. He proposed a procedure for cost-benefit accounting. Depending on the goal statements, the cost and benefits are expressed as:

1. Tangible costs and benefits expressed in monetary terms
2. Tangible costs and benefits that cannot be expressed in monetary terms but can be expressed quantitatively, usually in terms derived from the definition of the goal
3. Intangible costs and benefits (Hill 1968, 22)

This procedure is summarized in Figure 6.8. According to Hill, for each goal and for each option, costs and benefits can then be compared, aggregated when possible, and reported separately. Planners are then in a position to weigh the various courses of action against each other. Hill stressed that it is necessary to identify those sections of the public who are affected by each option. He admitted the tasks involved for such analysis are complex, but "its complexity is no excuse for abandoning the attempt" (1968, 28). Goals-achievement matrices provide a rational procedure for comparing options.

Goals-achievement options	Monetary cost benefits	Non monetary cost benefits	Intangible cost benefits
A	1.	6.	11.
B	2.	7.	12.
C	3.	8.	13.
D	4.	9.	14.
E	5.	10.	15.

1. Numbers in the matrix refer to explanations.

FIGURE 6.8 Summary goals-achievement matrix. *(Source: Adapted from Hill 1968)*

Donald Miller of the University of Washington provides an example of the use of the goals-achievement method in the evaluation of selecting neighborhoods for rehabilitation loan associations (1980). Miller evaluated different neighborhoods in the city of Everett, Washington, in terms of their relative potential for successful rehabilitation should the loan program and other public improvements be implemented. In this case consultants worked with the local planning agency, a citizens advisory committee, and the city council. According to Miller, "these groups appreciated having empirical evidence in an understandable form, were able to follow . . . the methodology, and were convinced the analysis was valid" (1980, 204).

Scenario Writing

Another technique of selecting choices is scenario writing. Larry Hirschhorn has explained that scenario writing "encompasses a broad range of approaches, assumptions, and techniques, but all share in common an attempt to describe or write a history of the future" (1980, 172). Scenarios can be developed for the various conceptual options designed to achieve planning goals.

Hirschhorn (1980) distinguishes between state scenarios and process scenarios. *State scenarios* describe what the planning area will be like at some date in the future without explaining how that situation is achieved. *Process scenarios* discuss the events that may lead to a future situation. Both can be used to explain the potential consequences of various planning options.

Hirschhorn (1980) furthermore examines four types of process scenarios. The first is the *idealization* process, whereby ideal scenarios are envisioned. The second are the *prophecy* scenarios, in which Hirschhorn notes "the prophet has a compelling vision of how the world will and must be in the future" (174). The third type is *simulation,* which Hirschhorn describes as "state driven, process based, and used for predictive purposes" (174). The final type is the *developmental* scenario, which begins "with an initial state and describes a process through which a particular social system can arrive at one or a series of end states that are not specified prior to the construction of the scenario itself" (175).

Hirschhorn makes a compelling argument for the benefits of developmental scenario writing and explains how such a scenario can be constructed in an article in the *Journal of the American Planning Association* (1980). Scenario writing presents a useful way to create a framework to discuss the consequences of various planning options by a planning commission or staff, CAC, TAC, or task force.

Public Hearings

Public hearings will probably be a legal requirement for making planning choices. As a result, planners must keep accurate accounts of the proceedings. The Institute for Participatory Management and Planning (1997) notes that the hearings proceedings consists of three parts, often called the "findings":

- A summary of the main points of the planning issue being addressed
- The range of solutions, including the recommended option
- The reactions of the various interest groups to the proposed course of action

Those who have been involved in public hearings will attest that such events are not noted for their rationality. As a result, it is essential for planners to make clear, thorough presentations of the various options available to achieve community goals. Summaries of inventories, suitability analyses, surveys, and goals-achievement matrices can be presented. It is also good to involve citizens who have participated in advisory committees and task forces, as well as expert testimony.

For example, the Yakima County, Washington, planning commission and staff worked for over a year exploring ways to slow down the conversion of prime farmland to urban uses and to direct growth near existing cities and towns. The effort had been well-publicized and involved hundreds of people. Yet, at the first public hearing where the options were presented, several individuals claimed that they had heard nothing about the program and that only a few citizens had been involved in developing the various choices.

At the second hearing the planning staff posted the numerous newspaper accounts of the program along the long hallway leading to the meeting room. All those who attended the hearing passed by this extensive account. In addition, the many people who had been involved in the process were asked to attend the hearing to testify concerning their involvement. As a result, no one raised the issue that they knew nothing about the program, and there was substantial testimony about citizen involvement. This format continued through subsequent hearings, and debate was focused on the merits of the various options available to the community to achieve its goals.

TWO EXAMPLES OF SELECTING PREFERENCES

State planning requirements lead to local action. For example, Portland, Oregon's planning has evolved from state mandates. Local and federal interests can also stimulate the design of optional plans, as is the case in the biodiversity plan for Camp Pendleton, California.

Portland, Oregon, Alternative Land-Use Plans

With the adoption of Oregon's statewide land-use planning goals in 1973, the cities and counties set about revising and updating their comprehensive plans to comply with the new requirements. Among the municipalities involved in this process was the state's largest city, Portland. The city has had comprehensive plans since early in the twentieth century, but now faced the task of adopting a new plan to be in compliance with Oregon's statewide planning goals. After detailed population, economic, and environmental studies by the city planning staff, a report entitled *The City Planner Handbook* (Portland Bureau of Planning 1977) was published. This report contained summarized background information, three alternative land-use plans, and a technical appendix. The handbook was used as a starting point for the process of selecting options for the city's future.

The focal points of *The City Planner Handbook* were the three staff-prepared land-use planning alternatives. These three options included a description of the number and types of housing units, people, and jobs each future vision might support. Each option was analyzed to assess how it addressed a list of 32 goals. The 32 goals were developed by the planning staff and related to the 15 statewide goals Portland was to meet. (Of Oregon's 19 goals, 4 are applicable to only coastal counties and municipalities, while 1 is specific for communities in the Willamette Valley.) The purpose of the Portland alternatives was to indicate the choices necessary to accomplish each goal and to seek advice from citizens (Portland Bureau of Planning 1980).

The list of goals presented a wide range of choices to Portland residents. The choices addressed neighborhood quality, city economy, housing, water and sewer systems, transportation, air and water quality, and energy conservation. Each of these choices was linked to maps that illustrated the impact of the decision on commercial, residential, agricultural and forestry, and industrial land uses in the city. Portland citizens were asked to respond by mail to the alternatives.

Community organizations, neighborhood associations, individuals, and government agencies were also asked to review and comment upon the choices presented in the handbook. Some 150 special interest groups were contacted. Meetings were held with each, including construction, business, ethnic, fraternal, health and education, legal, religious, social, service, transportation, trade, political, and union groups. In each of the city's ten districts, neighborhood associations were organized. These associations were asked by the city planning staff to review the three alternatives and to determine if an additional alternative was necessary to expand the range of choice for

Governor Tom McCall Waterfront Park, Portland, Oregon.

public discussion. The neighborhood associations were also asked to write scenarios about the implication of each alternative (Portland Bureau of Planning 1980).

There was a strong emphasis placed on neighborhood review of the options. The process of planning in Portland was used to strengthen its neighborhoods. According to a former planning commission president, Joan Smith, "If the planning process did nothing else for this city, it made many of the neighborhoods more articulate and better organized" (Sistrom 1979, 1).

From this process each planning district developed a new alternative. Evening town meetings were then held in each of the 10 districts, where testimony was heard on the scenarios developed for each option. Two citywide meetings, one during the day and one at night, were also held downtown to discuss the alternatives.

Next the city hired a consulting firm to conduct a random survey consisting of 450 in-home interviews during April and May 1978. Those interviewed were asked to evaluate each of the options. At the same time all the alternatives, including those developed by the ten planning districts, were distributed to over 33,000 people. Again citizens were asked to review each alternative and rank the list of 32 goals (Portland Bureau of Planning 1980). In a sense, this was a form of a goals-achievement matrix combined with synchronized survey.

These surveys and the testimony from the town hall meetings were analyzed and tabulated by the Center for Population Research at Portland State University. The results of this analysis were incorporated into the first draft of a comprehensive plan, called a *discussion draft.* The publication of this discussion draft initiated another round of citizen review lasting six months (Portland Bureau of Planning 1980).

During this period, over 80 neighborhood association meetings, many business and service group meetings, 2 citywide conferences, and 9 planning district town hall meetings were held, as concurrently the planning staff conducted additional surveys. Over 800 suggestions were received, of which 65 percent were used in a second draft called the *proposed comprehensive plan.* This proposed plan was taken to the city planning commission in September 1979. The planning commission held 8 public hearings during the next 2 months. At the same time, the proposed plan was distributed to neighborhood associations; civic, environmental, and business groups; and other government agencies. In addition, a total of 10,000 proposed plan maps were mailed out to groups and individuals (Portland Bureau of Planning 1980).

Responses to the mailing and testimony from the hearings were compiled in summary notebooks. These notebooks were used by the planning commission and staff to write a third draft, the *recommended comprehensive plan.* The recommended plan was submitted to the city council in January 1980. At this time nearly 14,000 recommended plans were mailed to groups and individuals. The city council then held a series of 33 more public hearings, during which time about 400 amendments were made. On August 21, 1980, the city council adopted the plan (Portland Bureau of Planning 1980).

This was a lengthy process of reviewing planning options. In the end, Portland adopted its new comprehensive plan. In 1981, the Oregon Land Conservation and Development Commission acknowledged that the plan was in compliance with the 15 statewide planning goals. Since 1981, Portland leaders have continued to respond to Oregon's evolving land-use requirements (Department of Land Conservation and Development 1996). For example, Portland must comply with Metro goals in addition to those of LCDC. Metro (the Metropolitan Service District) is a "unique type" of legislative regional planning authority (Carson 1998). Metro's jurisdiction covers 24 cities and 3 county urban areas in the Portland Metropolitan region. Its authority addresses air quality, water quality, transportation, solid waste, and the regional urban growth boundary (Carson 1998).

Light rail stations, Portland, Oregon.

Portland and Metro face a variety of planning issues. One issue faced by Portland planners is the inadequate supply of land for future growth within the urban growth boundary (Kellington 1998). A second issue concerns the cost of housing. Oregon's 4 metropolitan regions (Portland, Eugene-Springfield, Salem-Keizer, and Medford-Ashland) are among the 14 most expensive housing markets in the nation (Carson 1998). A third issue involves the quality of new development. One Portland planner quipped that between the city's wonderful downtown and the exclusive farm-use zone beyond the urban growth boundary "lies Los Angeles."

Oregon and Portland continue to attract new residents, in part because of the state's environmental amenities and its reputation for protecting those qualities. Between 1990 and 1997, Oregon's population increased by 14.1 percent, and "the cost of housing doubled" (Kellington 1998, 4). What Portland and Oregon have in place is the framework for exploring options to address the issues of growth and preservation into the future. Oregon law requires that all land-use plans must include an "evaluation of alternative courses of action and ultimate policy choices, taking into consideration social, economic, energy and environmental needs" (Department of Land Conservation and Development 1996).

The Biodiversity Plan for the Camp Pendleton Region, California

Carl Steinitz and his colleagues sought to understand the consequences of regional change. They simulated six alternative projections of development to the year 2010. To create the alternatives, the research team first analyzed the various plans of the various government entities with planning and development jurisdiction for the Camp Pendleton region. These plans projected the anticipated needs for housing, recreation, transportation, commerce, and industry. From these plans the team was able to derive the consequences of full implementation or "build out" (Steinitz et al. 1996). "Plans Build Out" represented a baseline future scenario. This scenario explored what will happen if nothing different happens. The research team noted that "it is this future scenario against which all other alternatives are compared" (Steinitz et al. 1996, 24). For each of the inventory elements, the current situation was compared with the build-out situation. For example, Figure 6.9 illustrates the landscape ecological pattern under the build-out scenario. It can be compared with Figure 3.65, which illustrates the pattern in 1990. (The oldest data used by the team were from 1990; other information was more recent, such as 1995 land-use/land-cover data.) Essentially, the build-out scenario illustrates a dramatic decline in several kinds of natural habitat and in biodiversity (Steinitz et al. 1996).

In addition to the build-out scenario, five additional alternative futures for the region were prepared by graduate students from the Harvard University Graduate School of Design. These five alternatives were described as follows:

> Alternative #1 assumes the continuation of the predominant regional trend of Spread low density rural residential and clustered single family residential development. It also assumes the weakening of some development constraints and the absence of any new conservation-oriented land acquisitions. Alternative #2, Spread with Conservation 2010, also follows the

FIGURE 6.9 Camp Pendleton, landscape ecological pattern under build-out scenario. *(Source: Steinitz et al. 1996)*

spread pattern, but implements a conservation strategy beginning in 2010. Alternative #3 follows a low density pattern but proposes Private Conservation via large-lot ownership and management of land adjacent to and within important habitat areas as a means of conserving biodiversity. Alternative #4, a Multi-Centers strategy, focuses on cluster development and new communities, and Alternative #5 concentrates most growth in one New City (Steinitz et al. 1996, 104).

The first alternative, Spread (Figure 6.10), and the final alternative, New City (Figure 6.11), are included here for comparison. The Camp Pendleton team included detailed descriptions and discussions of each in their report. They also analyzed the consequences of each and the impact on soils, hydrology, fire, landscape ecological patterns, single-species habitat potential, species richness, and visual quality (Steinitz et al. 1996). These consequences were summarized in a matrix. The team noted that all the alternatives will have serious negative consequences for the environment. However, they found that the "Private Conservation alternative, which proposes to maintain the integrity of the region's larger natural areas and their connections along the riparian network, is also the most protective of the long-

FIGURE 6.10 Camp Pendleton, land cover for spread build-out alternative. *(Source: Steinitz et al. 1996)*

term regional biodiversity" (Steinitz et al. 1996, 129).

Unlike the Portland example, the Camp Pendleton study did not involve a comprehensive public participation effort with the end goal of a plan approval. Rather, the Camp Pendleton study was a research exercise that sought to illustrate the consequences for biodiversity of various alternative futures. In this regard, it had great utility for decision makers and the public.

The Portland example employed a combination of techniques to select planning options. In Portland, public meetings, charrettes, an advisory committee, preference surveys, interviews, scenario writing, and hearings were used. Portland planners allotted ample time to discuss and select the available options. The 1980 Portland plan took four years to complete, was well-publicized with an effort to reach all people in the planning area, and was linked to state policy. Portland's program fit within Oregon statewide goals. The goal requirements in Portland have become more complex since the 1970s. Now, the city comprehensive plan must comply with Metro planning goals. Planning is an ongoing process. Alternative visions, different growth scenarios, and various planning options continue to be designed and discussed in metropolitan Portland.

FIGURE 6.11 Camp Pendleton, new city alternative. *(Source: Steinitz et al. 1996)*

As compared with more conventional planning examples, planners in Portland and in Camp Pendleton relied heavily on information about environmental resources that had been collected through inventories. The values of the people of Portland were reflected in how information about their environment would be employed to implement their plan. Landscape ecology played a central role in the Camp Pendleton study, which also used state-of-the-art GIS to illustrate why landscape planning was crucial for the future of the southern California region.

7

LANDSCAPE PLANS

Plans can take many forms. Early American plans were quite specific about the layout of cities and towns—the location of streets and the division of land—from colonial times through the nineteenth century. These early plans were *utilitarian* when used as part of a land speculation venture, or *utopian* when developed for settlement by religious sects. City planning practitioners of the late nineteenth and early twentieth centuries produced *master plans* that reflected the influence of landscape architecture, architecture, and engineering. In master plans, uses were prescribed for each place in the city or town. *Comprehensive plans* in cities and *multiple-use plans* in national forests, both advocated beginning in the early twentieth century, attempt to address competing demands for land and other resources. Beginning in the 1960s, *policy plans* became popular. Rather than specifying uses of space, policies are established for the planning area that address the goals and aspirations of its inhabitants and/or users. During the 1970s, *management plans* began to appear. Management plans present guidelines for administrators to consider when making decisions. Due to the influence of the business community, *contingency plans* and *strategic planning* became more popular in the 1980s and 1990s. Contingency plans address the uncertainty of the future and pose "what if" possibilities. A strategy is the means of deploying resources to achieve goals and objectives.

Landscape plans combine elements of all these other types of plans. Like master and comprehensive plans, they consider the physical ordering of space, a feature often not addressed in policy plans. Landscape plans also reflect policy and management strategies and should provide for contingencies. More than a land-use plan, a landscape plan recognizes the overlap and integration of land uses. Landscape plans provide a flexible framework for ordering the physical elements of a place. Such a plan is one product of the planning process. The plan provides both a documentation of the process and an image for the future of the landscape.

Federal land management agencies and some state governments have specific standards for plans, which vary in what the plans are called and what they are to contain, but include common elements. The National Park Service calls the major planning document for all parks a *general management plan.* Like other federal land resource agencies—the U.S. Forest Service and the Bureau of Land Management—the NPS combines its plan with the environmental document, either an environmental impact statement or an environmental assessment, which is required by the NEPA (see Chapter 11). Every NPS general management plan contains:

- *Purpose and need for the plan:* a discussion of planning issues, park purpose, legislative mandates, and management objectives
- *Management zoning:* prescribed land classifications to designate where various strategies for management and use will best fulfill management objectives and achieve park purposes
- *Proposal:* interrelated proposals for preservation of resources, land protection, interpretation, visitor use, carrying capacities, park operations, and a general indication of location, size, capacity, and function of physical development
- *Alternatives to the proposal:* different management approaches for dealing with issues, including no action and minimum requirements
- *Plan implementation schedule and cost estimates*
- *Description of the affected environment:* background inventory information
- *Environmental consequences:* Discussion of the proposal and alternatives (adapted from deFranceaux 1987, 15–16)

According to Cynthia deFranceaux (1987), there are several other elements that may be included in a NPS general management plan. These other components include land suitability analyses, visitor carrying-capacity analyses, a land protection component, discussion of necessary legislative actions, a transportation-access-circulation component, and wilderness studies. Although historically most national park land has been publicly owned, park planners have long had to consider inholdings and adjacent lands. Increasingly, the NPS is responsible for places that include large areas of privately owned lands. As a result, it is important for park service planners to understand traditional city and county planning. There is also much that city and county planners can learn from the long-standing planning efforts of the NPS and other federal land management agencies.

The contents of local government plans and the procedures for adopting them vary from state to state and in some cases from community to community. In some states, enabling legislation defines the minimal scope of local plans and the adoption process. In others, explicit contents for local plans and for implementation are mandated in state law. Often local governments will enact local ordinances which expand on state requirements. As with many other elements of planning, the State of Oregon has been quite clear about what constitutes a comprehensive plan.

> A comprehensive plan is a set of public decisions dealing with how the land, air, and water resources of an area are to be used or not used. These decisions are reached after considering the present and future of an area.

> Being comprehensive in scope, the plan provides for all of the resources, uses, public facilities and services in an area. It also incorporates the plans and programs of various governmental units into a single management tool for the planning area (Land Conservation and Development Commission 1980, 1)

The local comprehensive plan "guides a community's land use, conservation of natural resources, economic development, and public services" (Department of Land Conservation and Development 1996). In Oregon, land-use plans are to include an "identification of issues and problems, inventories and other factual information for each . . . goal" (Land Conservation and Development Commission 1980, 4; Department of Land Conservation and Development 1996). The guidelines for the contents of the plan are quite specific. First, they are to include the factual bases for the plan: the natural resources, their capabilities and limitations; human-made structures and utilities, their location and conditions; population and economic characteristics; and the identified roles and responsibilities. Second, the elements of the plan are to be included: the applicable statewide goals, any critical geographic area designated by the state legislature, elements that address any special needs and desires of the people, and the temporal phasing of the plan. These elements are to "fit together and relate to one another to form a consistent whole at all times" (Land Conservation and Development Commission 1980, 4; Department of Land Conservation and Development 1996).

In Oregon, plans are to be the basis for specific implementation measures (Department of Land Conservation and Development 1996). Once these findings and elements are compiled in Oregon, the plan and its implementing ordinances are to be adopted by the county or city after a public hearing. Oregon law requires that the plans be filed with the county recorder and that they be approved by the state. The state recognizes the impermanent nature of plans and requires that they be revised periodically.

Whether the planners are addressing private or public lands or both in a federal agency or for a local government, a landscape plan should include at least four key elements: (1) the formal recognition and adoption of the previous steps in the planning process; (2) a statement of policies; (3) the identification of strategies to achieve those policies; and (4) some indication of the physical realization of those policies and strategies. These components will be illustrated by using parts of two general plan amendments for the Desert View Tri-Villages Area and the Sonoran Preserve Master Plan. At the end of the chapter, the plans of the New Jersey Pinelands and Teller County, Colorado, will be used as examples.

RECOGNITION AND ADOPTION OF PLAN

A key component of the plan is the formal recognition of the findings of the previous steps of the process. The legislative body—the county commission or the city council—adopts a statement summarizing the issues facing the area. Policies are enacted that include the goals to address the problems and opportunities which have been detailed through the process. The biophysical and sociocultural elements are documented in the plan, as are the detailed studies.

Two general plan amendments have been adopted by the City of Phoenix for the Desert View Tri-Villages Area. As was noted earlier, city planners have divided the Tri-Villages into three subareas. The planning that has occurred in the area has been strongly influenced by the four character types introduced earlier; that is, *desert preservation, rural desert, suburban desert,* and *growth corridor/core development* (see Table 6.3). At the North Sonoran charrette, principles were developed for each. Table 7.1 provides the principles for suburban desert development.

The two general plan amendments recognized and adopted these character types. The first

TABLE 7.1
PRINCIPLES FOR DESERT SUBURBAN DESIGN DEVELOPED AT THE SONORAN NORTH LAND-USE CHARRETTE

Suburban desert development was defined as ranging from a maximum of ten to a minimum of two single-family dwellings per acre (10 to 1 per 0.4 hectare, or 25 to 2.5 per hectare). The principles developed by the suburban desert charrette team were:

- Although altered, elements of the desert should be retained (climate, drainage, wildlife, flora).
- The natural desert structure (plants and terrain) should be retained, or copied when disturbance is unavoidable.
- Building structures should be compatible with and responsive to the landscape and climate, including building height, color, topography, solar energy, materials, and massing.
- Large areas of land should not be bladed and desert washes should be protected.
- Opportunities should exist for a variety of housing types at a range of prices.
- A sense of community should be encouraged in the design and planning of subdivision developments.
- Recreation, education, and shopping opportunities should be provided and should also be compatible with the landscape and neighborhoods.
- Infrastructure development should have a minimum impact on the desert environment.
- View corridors to existing landscape features should be protected and enhanced in new developments.
- The golf courses should be designed *before* surrounding areas to improve integration with the natural landscape.

SOURCES: McCarthy et al. 1995; Steiner et al. 1999.

amendment—called the North Land Use Plan—applied to the eastern subarea, the portion of the Tri-Villages facing the most intense development pressure. Ray Quay, Jolene Ostler, and Al Zelinka led the city planning team for the subarea. On May 22, 1996, the Phoenix Planning Commission unanimously amended the city's general plan for 35 square miles (91 kilometers^2), or roughly all of the eastern third of the Tri-Villages. The Phoenix City Council followed suit and on June 26, 1996, also unanimously amended the general plan. These amendments include many ideas from the charrette discussed in Chapter 6 and were based on detailed environmental and social inventories (summarized in Chapters 3 and 4). A few of the new provisions include the protection of the Cave Creek Wash in the subarea as an "ecological spine"; the concentration of growth near commercial and industrial areas and away from the most environmentally sensitive places; and the creation of three distinct community types: desert preserve, rural desert, and suburban desert. This amendment dramatically changed where homes would be built in the 35-square-mile (91-kilometer^2) subarea and concentrated where they will be built while reducing the potential number of homes by only 4 percent compared to the previous plan (City of Phoenix 1996).

The plan for the eastern subarea emphasized preservation and residential development at rural and suburban densities. In contrast, the plan for the North Black Canyon Corridor, located on the western portion of the Tri-Villages, was targeted as

Desert wash in the Desert View Tri-Villages Area.

a growth corridor anchored by a new regional employment center. By permitting intense development in that corridor, the plan would allow for increased preservation of the highly valuable desert mountains and washes in the central area. The city sought to develop a "new pattern of urban growth" based on three principles:

1. The promotion of a sense of community
2. The development of a sustainable transportation system
3. The design of high quality development which both integrates with and preserves the natural desert environment (City of Phoenix 1997)

The Sonoran Preserve Master Plan was approved unanimously by the Parks and Recreation Board and then by the Phoenix City Council in January and February 1998. Jim Burke and Joe Ewan led the parks department planning team. Like the general plan amendments, the preserve plan used several key principles and built on other efforts. The three key principles were (1) to acquire a diversity of lands, (2) to preserve natural hydrological processes, and (3) to integrate a preservation ethic into the comprehensive urban form (Burke and Ewan 1998a).

The parks planners based their plan on six principles, which included:

1. Hydrologic processes should be maintained.
2. Connectivity of patches and corridors should be maintained.
3. Landscape patches should be as large as possible.
4. Unique mosaics of landforms and vegetation types should be included in the preserve.
5. Diverse mosaics should be integrated into the adjacent developed environment.
6. The preserve should be considered within the context of other significant undisturbed regional open space (Burke and Ewan 1998b, 99).

The preserve plan includes descriptions of the landscape elements of the Desert View Tri-Villages Area, making particular use of the GIS maps created at ASU. Previous and ongoing planning efforts were documented and analyzed in the plan, as they related to the preserve. The alternatives described in Chapter 6 (Figures 6.4, 6.5, and 6.6) were included. As a result, the preserve plan provided a comprehensive documentation of its purpose, principles, value, and intent.

At this stage in making a plan, several questions may be posed, such as:

- Have the findings of previous steps in the process been recognized and, if appropriate, adopted?
- Are all the issues adequately addressed?
- Have the responsible bodies reviewed and, if appropriate, modified and/or adopted the plan?

STATEMENT OF POLICIES

After the documentation and adoption of findings, plans include a statement of policies. These policies may be organized in a variety of ways. Commonly, formal goals and objectives are adopted by the appropriate legislative or administrative body. According to Edwin Verburg and Richard Coon, "goals provide statements of the condition that a plan is designed to achieve. A goal is usually not quantifiable and may not have a specific date of accomplishment. Comparatively, objectives focus on measurable results that need to be achieved" (1987, 22). A *goal* is a statement of purpose that gives direction for accomplishing the aspirations of the community, while an *objective* is a statement of the measurable and desired ends that a community will achieve to accomplish its aspirations. Often the terms *goal* and *objective* are used interchangeably, but they are different. Whatever terms are used in a plan, it is important to link broad policies with specific strategies to achieve the goals.

The Phoenix city planning staff developed six concepts for the eastern subarea of the Desert View Tri-Villages. Their intent was "to refine the existing policies" that guide development for the area. The first concept was to plan for strategic land uses; that is, to identify economic development opportunities that only come with a major travel corridor and desert preservation opportunities that only nature can provide. The second concept again emphasized the need to preserve Cave Creek Wash as an ecological spine in the desert (also addressed in greater detail in the separate parks plan). Third, the plan recognized washes as a development constraint because of their flooding and the preference to allow natural drainage over extensive engineering. The fourth concept addressed the cost effectiveness as well as the ineffectiveness of providing public infrastructure. The fifth concept was to maintain established character in the area, which was the existing community residents' desire. The final concept recognized property rights already established in the area (City of Phoenix 1996).

The North Black Canyon Corridor Plan established four goals and nine associated policy action steps, which are:

Goal 1.0 Promote the North Black Canyon Corridor as a regional employment center but not at the expense of growth within the existing city.

Policy action steps:

1.1 Design employment centers to meet market niches not provided for in adjacent village employment centers or central city employment areas.

1.2 Design employment areas that recognize the long term development cycle of employment and retail in the corridor.

Goal 2.0 Achieve a balance between employment and housing.

Policy action steps:

2.1 Regulate a jobs-to-housing ratio.

2.2 Plan for housing quality ranges to match employment income ranges.

Goal 3.0 Concentrate growth within a defined corridor.

Policy action steps:

3.1 Established a regulatory infrastructure growth line for initial development with general boundaries of I-17, Cloud Road, 19th Avenue, and Jomax Road.

3.2 Plan an efficient auto and transit circulation system.

3.3 Restructure and expand the city's infrastructure fee program for the corridor that recognizes the long term phasing of development within a corridor.

Goal 4.0 Preserve North Sonoran desert amenities and use these features to define community form and identity.

Policy action steps:

4.1 Create a North Sonoran Desert Preserve.

4.2 Provide urban desert public places that are defined by a combination of natural features and human-made features such as streets and buildings (City of Phoenix 1997).

The preserve plan established the goal of acquiring 20,000 acres [8094 hectares] within the Tri-Villages Area. This amount of land would make it the largest park in the city of Phoenix.

At this point in plan-making, it is important to ensure that clear goals and objectives are established. A common problem occurs with goals and objectives prepared by a team or a group of citizens. In order to ensure equal participation, words and phrases of all involved may be included. This may be democratic, but the result can be unintelligible. Since such goals and objectives will have significant influence, it is often helpful to let a few days pass after they are written before they are formally adopted. In the interim, the wording can be refined. Care should be given not to lose the intent of the goals and objectives, but to make them more understandable to the broadest possible public.

STRATEGIES TO ACHIEVE POLICIES

Strategies outline the approach and/or methods through which problems are solved or minimized and objectives are achieved (Verburg and Coon 1987). A *strategy* is the broadly stated means of deploying resources to achieve the community's goals and objectives. The plan should specify what actions are necessary to achieve its objectives. For each planning element, there should be clear definitions of terms so that there is no confusion, for example, between light or heavy industrial use or low-density or high-density residential use. Each strategy should contain specific actions, for instance, "the county or city shall adopt land-use ordinances to implement its policies." There should also be target dates associated with specific actions; for instance, "soil erosion shall be reduced to tolerable levels by the year 2010." Thus, strategies should be linked to *outcome measures* that are specific means of determining whether goals and objectives are being accomplished.

Strategies involve priorities, schedules, targets, and budgets. *Priorities* establish the criteria to determine the order of tasks necessary to achieve community goals. *Schedules* chart tasks and products. *Targets* involve work plans and responsibilities. The *budget* identifies the needs for staffing, equipment, consultants, and potential sources of revenue (Arizona Department of Commerce 1998).

The eastern subarea plan for the Desert View Tri-Villages identifies three strategies for implementation. First, the revised general plan for the area will guide the rezoning process. Second, desert preservation areas will be acquired through either purchasing or leasing the land. (The parks plan addresses this strategy in great detail, which is discussed later.) Third, overlay districts for the three character areas will provide performance development standards (City of Phoenix 1996). The plan for North Black Canyon Corridor also contains four strategies: adoption of a concept plan which includes basic growth management policies; the revision of the general plan map; the adoption of specific development regulations; and the production of information providing principles and guidelines for new development (City of Phoenix 1997).

The key strategies for the preserve are detailed in its acquisition plan. This plan presents "the various methods of acquiring or protecting land for the Sonoran Preserve, potential funding sources, estimated amounts of funding available, timing of funding sources and scenarios that explore the implications of different acquisition strategies" (Burke and Ewan 1998a, 34). The strategies seek to achieve the goal of acquiring 20,000 acres (8094 hectares).

The methods and techniques for acquisition and protection available to the City of Phoenix include:

- Methods of city acquisition of land
  - Fee simple purchase
  - Purchase of development rights
  - Purchase of rights-of-way/easements
  - Leases
  - Condemnation/eminent domain
  - Donations and gifts
- Governmental regulation protection techniques
  - Planned community district
  - Planned residential district
  - Hillside ordinance
  - Special overlay district
  - Design guidelines
  - Performance zoning
  - Dedications/exactions
  - Transfer of development rights

Potential funding sources available include:

- Bonds
- General purpose taxes
    - Sales
    - User
    - Property
- Infrastructure fees
- Grants
- Fund-raising program
- Government coordination
    - Land exchange
    - Preferential tax treatment
- Voluntary landowner participation/non-profits
    - Conservation easement
    - Preservation easement
    - Land trusts (Burke and Ewan 1998a, 36)

Several of these methods and techniques were discussed in detail in the Sonoran Preserve Master Plan. (Chapter 10 will address them as well.) After analyzing the possible implementation possibilities, the park planners recommended the following strategy:

> 1. Obtain city council approval of the plan and amend the Arizona Preserve Initiative . . . application to include all Arizona State Trust Lands identified in the Sonoran Preserve Plan (approximately 15,000 acres) [6071 hectares] and submit to the State Land Commissioner. Work through the public review process to defend the plan and application. Generate public support for the application and requested conservation designation.
>
> 2. If successful and the State Land Commissioner designates the targeted lands as suitable for conservation work with the Arizona State Lands Department . . . and the Planning Disposition Division to have the lands appraised and auctioned. Obtain City Council approval to acquire the designated parcels of state lands and coordinate the financing.
>
> 3. Review the proposed deeds and follow the advertising for the auction, and bid on the subject property. Right-of-way . . . and utility corridors are to be excluded from the preserve acquisition and acquired separately through other mechanisms.
>
> 4. As private parcels (approximately 5,000 acres) [2024 hectares] come into the city for General Plan Amendment or zoning review for compliance with the adopted Sonoran Preserve Plan, work with the applicant on density or development rights transfer to obtain dedication of lands identified for preservation. Acquire property through purchase or eminent domain as needed.
>
> 5. Work with land owners and other public agencies to have secondary washes preserved in place as natural drainage features, maintained by home owners associations, that can contribute to the preserve system. Amend the city flood plain, grading, and drainage ordinances as needed.
>
> 6. Develop design guidelines for development adjacent to the preserves. This will be a critical step in integrating the preserve into the lives of the future residents and allowing access for those residents who are not fortunate enough to live close to or adjacent to the preserve. Amend zoning and subdivision ordinances as needed (Burke and Ewan 1998a, 48–49).

At this point in plan-making, the strategies should be checked to ensure consistency with the goals and objectives. Again, the planners should return to the original issues and ask:

- Are they being adequately addressed by these strategies?
- Are problems being solved and opportunities being pursued?
- Is it clear that people will benefit and that environmental quality will not suffer?

LANDSCAPE PLAN MAP

The landscape plan map should attempt to physically represent information collected and decisions reached in the previous steps in the planning process. It should reflect existing land uses and land users. The plan should also consider potential land users, who can be identified through population projections. Their impact on the land can be analyzed by making development projections for various uses. Environmentally sensitive or constraint areas that present a concern because of health, safety, or welfare considerations should be mapped. Composite suitabilities should be included in the landscape plan map, as should preferred concepts or options considered for the area.

Michael Neuman notes that plans "chart collective hope" and that the "use of images of place . . . portray collective hope" (1998a, 214–215). The landscape plan map provides one such "image of place."

Figure 7.1 provides an image for the Desert View Tri-Villages Area from the perspective of the planning department. The map emphasizes both the growth corridors and the preserves. The parks landscape plan (Figure 7.2) focuses in greater detail on the preserves. Together, the planning department and parks department plans provide images for maintaining habitat corridors, promoting a density of diversity, and creating a sense of community.

PLAN ELEMENTS AND ORGANIZATION

The four key components of a landscape plan (*the recognition and adoption of the findings of the*

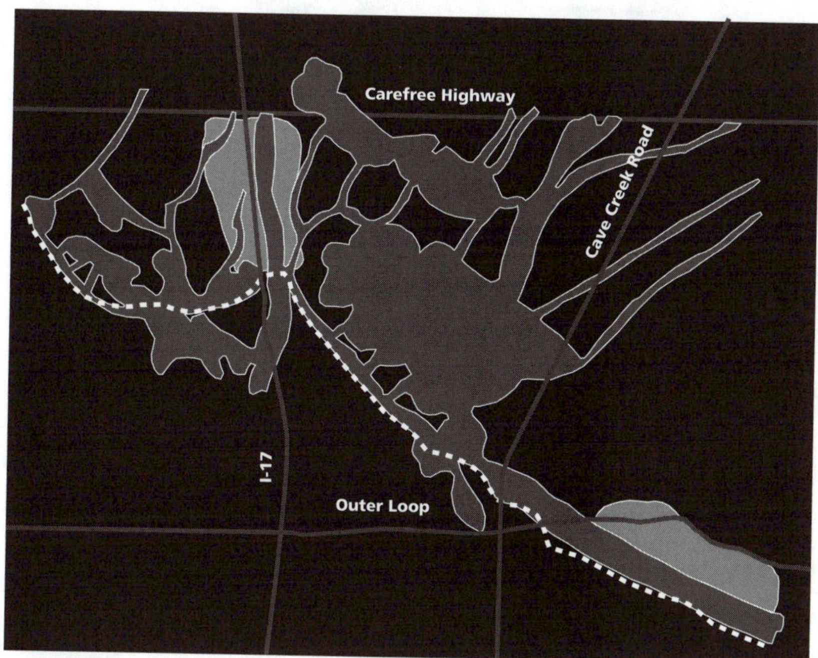

FIGURE 7.1 City of Phoenix Planning Department preservation and growth plan for Desert View Tri-Villages Area. *(Source: City of Phoenix Planning Department)*

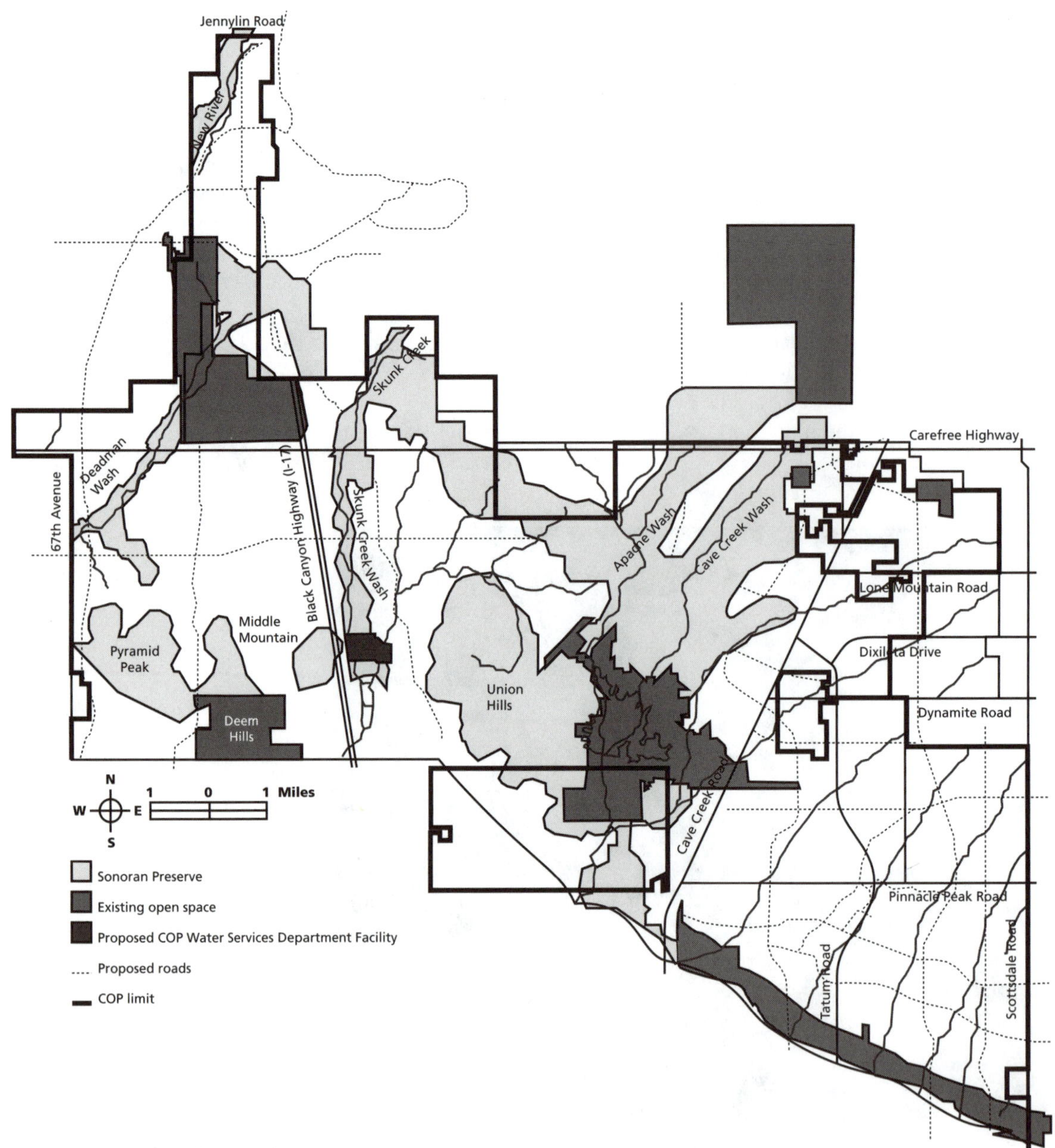

FIGURE 7.2 City of Phoenix Parks, Recreation, and Library Department plan for Desert View Tri-Villages Area. *(Source: Burke and Ewan 1998a)*

process, policy statements, strategies, and a map) can be organized as follows.

OUTLINE OF LANDSCAPE PLAN ELEMENTS

1. Summary of major recommendations
2. Recognition and adoption of findings
   a. Purpose and need of the plan
      (1) Problems and/or opportunities
      (2) Planning issue(s)
      (3) Enabling legislation
   b. Affected environment
      (1) Biophysical environment
      (2) Sociocultural environment
   c. Detailed studies
      (1) Population and development projections
      (2) Suitability analysis: opportunities and constraints for development and conservation
3. Policy statements
   a. Residential land use
      (1) Goal(s) and objective(s)
      (2) Goal rationale
   b. Commercial land use
      (1) Goal(s) and objective(s)
      (2) Goal rationale
   c. Industrial land use
      (1) Goal(s) and objective(s)
      (2) Goal rationale
   d. Agricultural land use
      (1) Goal(s) and objective(s)
      (2) Goal rationale
   e. Public facilities land use
      (1) Goal(s) and objective(s)
      (2) Goal rationale
   f. Parks and recreation
      (1) Goal(s) and objective(s)
      (2) Goal rationale
   g. Transportation
      (1) Goal(s) and objective(s)
      (2) Goal rationale
   h. Environmental quality
      (1) Goal(s) and objective(s)
      (2) Goal rationale
   i. Economic development
      (1) Goal(s) and objective(s)
      (2) Goal rationale
4. Implementation strategies
   a. Residential land use
      (1) Definitions
      (2) Implementation actions
      (3) Enforcement provisions
      (4) Compliance dates
   b. Commercial land use
      (1) Definitions
      (2) Implementation actions
      (3) Enforcement provisions
      (4) Compliance dates
   c. Industrial land use
      (1) Definitions
      (2) Implementation actions
      (3) Enforcement provisions
      (4) Compliance dates
   d. Agricultural land use
      (1) Definitions
      (2) Implementation actions
      (3) Enforcement provisions
      (4) Compliance dates
   e. Public facilities land use
      (1) Definitions
      (2) Implementation actions
      (3) Enforcement provisions
      (4) Compliance dates
   f. Parks and recreation
      (1) Definitions
      (2) Implementation actions
      (3) Enforcement provisions
      (4) Compliance dates
   g. Transportation
      (1) Definitions
      (2) Implementation actions
      (3) Enforcement provisions
      (4) Compliance dates
   h. Environmental quality
      (1) Definitions
      (2) Implementation actions
      (3) Enforcement provisions
      (4) Compliance dates

i. Economic development
   (1) Definitions
   (2) Implementation actions
   (3) Enforcement provisions
   (4) Compliance dates
5. Landscape plan map
   List of responsible individuals and parties
   Bibliography
   Glossary

Plans take time to prepare. Usually, they are collaborative undertakings involving many individuals and several agencies. The authors and participants in the process should be acknowledged. For a city- or county-level plan, the normal participants include the planning staff, the planning commission, and the city council or the county board of supervisors. Additional city or county departments and commissions, as well as consultants and citizens' groups, may also be involved.

TWO EXAMPLES OF PLANS

Michael Neuman (1998a, 1998b) asserts that plans provide valuable instruments for governance. They link aspirations to actions through prose and imagery. "Plans can be used," according to Neuman (1998a, 215), "to set agendas and resolve conflicts, because they are ideal 'single texts' that the participants in plan-making rely on to make decisions." The comprehensive plan for the New Jersey Pinelands and the growth management plan for Teller County and Woodland Park, Colorado, offer examples of collective hopes of their citizens embodied in plans.

Comprehensive Management Plan for the New Jersey Pinelands

The comprehensive management plan for the New Jersey Pinelands has been used in earlier chapters as an example of establishing planning goals (Chapter 2) and inventory and analysis (Chapters 3 and 4). The process undertaken by state, federal, and local officials resulted in an exemplary plan. (For the most up-to-date information about the plan, see the New Jersey Pinelands Commission's website: www.state.nj.us/pinelands.) The plan is divided into two parts. The first part documents the natural and human history of the Pine Barrens, describes regional growth factors, identifies ecologically critical areas, establishes goals and policies, lays out the structure for intergovernmental coordination, and establishes the financial and public participation programs. The second part contains the legal, substantive land-use programs and development standards that implement the plan. This part sets forth the procedures under which the Pinelands Commission certifies that county and local master plans and implementing ordinances are consistent with the plan (Pinelands Commission 1980). As in Oregon, all county and local plans in the Pinelands region must be consistent with the goals for the larger area.

Resource goals and policies comprise the heart of the Pinelands plan. The goals in Table 2.1 were established by the Pinelands Commission, based on its analysis and on provisions of state and federal legislation. These goals and policies also reflect the land capability of the area. The land capability map identifies those areas that are most suited for preservation, forestry, agriculture, rural development, and growth, as well as existing towns and villages and military and federal installations. From the capabilities for these uses, eight allocation areas are defined in the plan as follows:

> The *Preservation Area District* represents that area found by the New Jersey Legislature to be "especially vulnerable to the environmental degradation of surface and ground waters which would be [negatively impacted] by the improper development or use thereof"; and "which constitutes an extensive and contiguous area of land in its natural state."
>
> The *Agricultural Production Areas,* occurring in both the Preservation and Protection Areas, represent those areas that are primarily devoted to field agri-

cultural uses, and adjoining lands with soil conditions suitable for those farming activities.

The *Special Agricultural Production Areas,* occurring in the Preservation Area, represent those areas devoted to berry agricultural and native horticultural uses, and the adjoining lands utilized for watershed protection, to be designated at the option of the municipality.

The *Military and Federal Installation Area,* occurring in both the Preservation and Protection Areas, represents major federal landholdings with an established land-use pattern and providing significant benefits to the people of the Pinelands.

The *Forest Areas* of the Protection Area represent largely undisturbed forest and coastal wetland areas adjoining the Preservation Area and extending into the southern section of the Pinelands. The Commission has determined that these areas possess "the essential character of the existing Pinelands environment," which the Legislature said was the Commission's responsibility to "preserve and maintain."

The *Rural Development Areas* in the Protection Area represent those transitional areas that generally separate growth areas from the less developed, predominantly forested areas of the Pinelands. These areas are somewhat fragmented by existing development and serve a dual purpose as buffers and reserves for future development.

The *Regional Growth Areas* represent those land areas that are (1) in or adjacent to existing developed areas, (2) experiencing growth demands and pressure for development, and (3) capable of accommodating development without jeopardizing the most critical elements of the Pinelands environment.

Pinelands Towns and Villages are spatially discrete existing developed areas. Most of these settlements have cultural, historical, and commercial ties to the Pinelands environment, while others represent areas of concentrated residential, commercial, and industrial development (Pinelands Commission 1980, 195–196; New Jersey Pinelands Commission 1998).

These allocation areas formed the basis for a planning map that designated preservation and protection areas in the national reserve (Figure 7.3). The Pinelands plan is based, first, on state and federal law, then, second, on the 5 resource and use goals and the 25 related policies (Table 2.1). These goals and policies then led to the spatial description of the region and the allocation of appropriate land uses among the different areas. From this allocation, programs were developed "to ensure that activities allowed within different areas are compatible with the characteristics of particular sites" (Pinelands Commission 1980, 193).

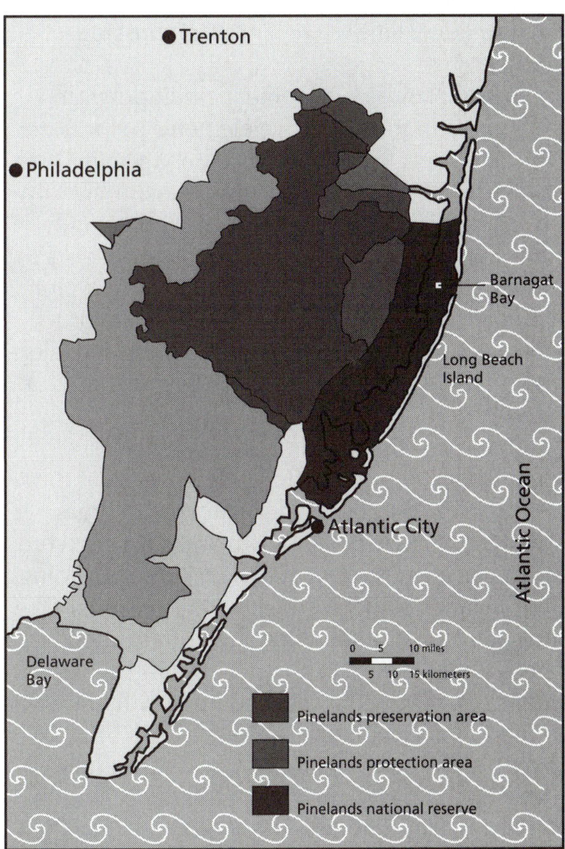

FIGURE 7.3 New Jersey Pinelands preservation and protection areas. *(Source: adapted from Pinelands Commission 1980)*

Seventeen programs (plus additional strategies) were developed for areas adjacent to the Pinelands that are important for water management or cultural viability. The 17 programs address development credits; land acquisition; surface and groundwater resources; vegetation and wildlife; wetlands; fire management; forestry; air quality; cultural resources; natural scenic resources; agriculture; waste management; resource extraction; recreation; housing; capital improvements; and data management. The most significant areas of the preserve are to be acquired with federal and state funds. As of 1998, over 65,000 acres (26,306 hectares) of environmentally important land had been purchased (New Jersey Pinelands Commission 1998).

The Pinelands development credit program is one of the more innovative elements of the plan. The Pinelands Comprehensive Management Plan establishes a land-use regulatory system that limits residential development in environmentally sensitive regions. Concurrently, the plan seeks to direct growth toward designated areas in a more compact pattern. The development credit program supplements land-use regulations. Development credits are provided to landowners in preservation and agricultural areas where residential uses are limited or prohibited. The credits can be sold by the landowners from these restricted areas to individuals in growth areas. The landowners in the growth areas use the credits to gain bonus residential densities. According to Pinelands planners, the credits "thus provide a mechanism for landowners in the [restricted] areas to participate in any increase in development values which is realized in growth areas" (Pinelands Commission 1980, 210). As of 1998, over 12,000 acres (4856 hectares) of land had been permanently deed restricted under the Pinelands development credit program (New Jersey Pinelands Commission 1998). (For more discussion about the transfer-of-development-rights concept, see Chapter 10.)

Rural landscape near Steamboat Springs, Colorado.

Teller County/City of Woodland Park, Colorado, Growth Management Plan

The City of Woodland Park in Teller County, Colorado, is located 20 miles (32 kilometers) west of Colorado Springs, which has a metropolitan population of nearly 400,000 (Figure 7.4). This proximity to Colorado Springs is a source of both opportunities and problems for Woodland Park and Teller County. The scenic Rocky Mountain location makes the city and county attractive places for growth. But the growth, in turn, has the potential to destroy the very natural and scenic qualities that attract people in the first place.

Gold mining created boomtown settlement in the late nineteenth century. With the demise of mining, the population declined until the 1960s. Teller County's population had peaked in 1900 at around 30,000* and bottomed out at 2495 in 1960 (Ansbro et al. 1988; Steiner et al. 1989). Between 1970 and 1980, the population increased 142.3 percent, to 8024. This growth has

*Although transient populations during the nineteenth-century gold rush have been reported to be as high as 160,000, the peak resident population appears to have been somewhere around 30,000 people.

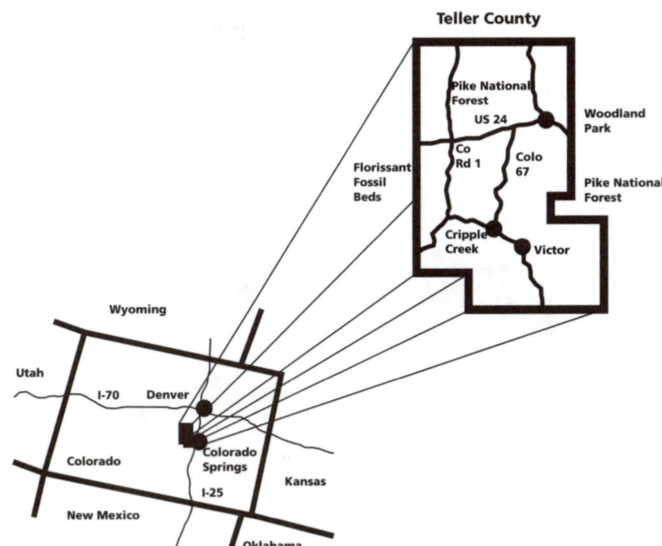

FIGURE 7.4 Location of Teller County and Woodland Park, Colorado.

continued, and the population is expected to double between 1980 and 2000. Most of these people have settled in and around Woodland Park, which has become a "bedroom community" for Colorado Springs. The majority of Woodland Park residents commute over 30 minutes to work, which emphasizes the economic linkage to Colorado Springs (U.S. Bureau of the Census 1983).

The continued growth of Teller County and Woodland Park raises several specific issues that need to be addressed by local officials and planners. A primary concern of local residents is that new development should not be a burden on taxpayers. A second important issue involves the quality of new development. It is felt that there should be policies and guidelines that ensure quality development. A third concern is that new development be timed and sequenced with the ability of local governments to provide services and facilities. These three issues have been identified by local residents through an ongoing public participation process initiated by local citizens. Once the concerns were publicly identified, there was a desire that the issues generated by growth be addressed.

As a result, planners and citizens of Woodland Park and Teller County initiated a growth management process in cooperation with the School of Architecture and Planning, University of Colorado at Denver. Through the School of Architecture and Planning, Teller County and the City of Woodland Park involved two planning studios in the development of a growth management plan. The first phase of the work involved research and data collection in the fall of 1988. Students from the planning studio inventoried and analyzed natural and social conditions of the Woodland Park growth management area as well as the whole county (Ansbro et al. 1988; Bowie et al. 1988). There were two teams of students, one working on Teller County and the second on Woodland Park. The teams collected and interpreted, in reports and on maps, information about natural resources, including the fundamental geologic, hydrologic, and bioclimatic processes that form the landscape. They also collected information about the socioeconomic and built environments of Teller County. They conducted surveys about the public attitudes concerning growth. This information was presented to county and city officials and planners to provide a basis for understanding environmentally sensitive areas and opportunities and constraints for development. Suitability analyses were conducted for several land uses at both the city and the county levels.

The second phase was undertaken during the spring of 1989. Again there were two teams of students: one each for Teller County and Woodland Park. These two teams made detailed population and development projections for the county. Essentially, because of its proximity to Colorado Springs and its scenic mountain location, the county's population has been growing and is expected to continue to grow. The students developed visions and concepts for the county and the city as well as landscape plans and development design guides. Detailed designs were completed for specific areas in the region (Bell et al. 1989). The students analyzed options to implement the growth management plan. In addition, they developed a point system for development review that recognized environmentally sensitive areas and set performance criteria for various land uses.

The plan is one that attempts to direct new growth to suitable areas and away from environmentally sensitive places. The Teller County and Woodland Park landscape plans prepared by the students influenced the growth management plan adopted by county and city officials (Petersen et al. 1989). The Teller County landscape plan (Figure 7.5) was based on the landscape patterns plus the opportunities and constraints for development that were derived from the ecological inventory and analysis. Several conceptual visions were used to formulate the plan. The concepts for Teller County were to preserve and enhance its rural and historic character, its scenic views, its economic base (including outdoor recreation and tourism), and its identity and sense of community. Additional Teller County concepts included the integration of development into the landscape, the interpretation and protection of the county's rich history, the creation of a tourism circulation system using existing roads, and the protection of environmentally sensitive areas (Bell et al. 1989).

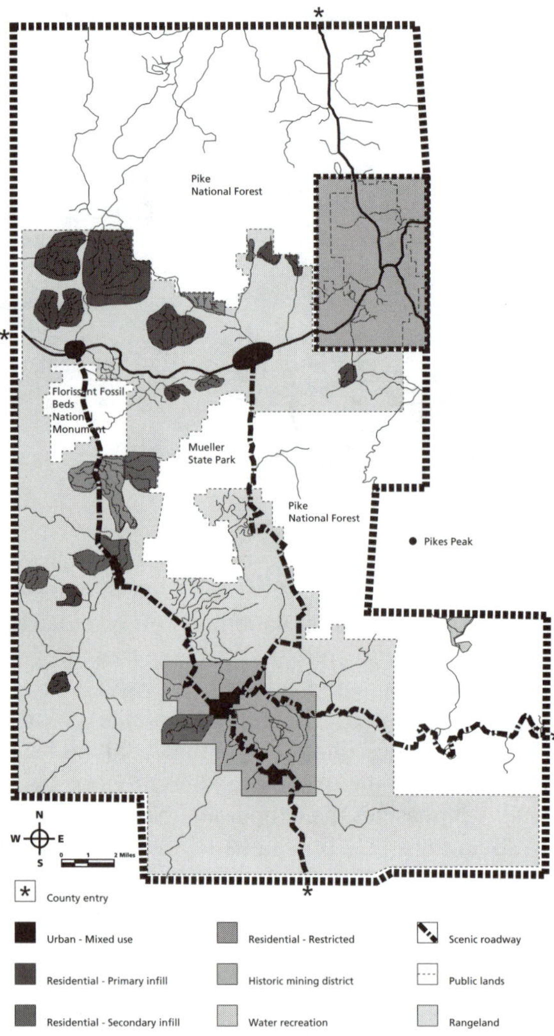

FIGURE 7.5 Teller County landscape plan. *(Source: adapted from Bell et al. 1989)*

The resulting landscape plan is an attempt to order the physical elements of the county in response to these concepts. The Teller County plan comprises the following components of land use: residential, urban, historic mining district, water recreation, scenic roadways, entryways, public lands, and rangeland (Bell et al. 1989). Three categories of future residential development indicate primary, secondary, and tertiary locations for new housing. Urban centers are represented on the plan as three unincorporated communities, two towns, and the City of Woodland Park (which was addressed in a separate landscape plan). Within these centers, the land uses involve a combination of commercial, office, industrial, recreational, and residential properties. Two of the centers—Cripple Creek and Victor—are further recognized for their historic value. The two towns are part of a historic district listed on the National Register of Historic Places (Bell et al. 1989).

Eight areas are designated in the plan for future water recreation use, currently an underutilized resource in the county. The plan also suggested the creation of a scenic tourism circulation system that would include improving the quality of entryways into the county. These scenic roadways would take advantage of the stunning visual resources in the area. Since public lands constitute almost half the county, the lands managed by the state and federal government provide an additional resource for tourism and recreation. Finally, the landscape plan designated rangeland areas that are important as open space and as a reminder of the cowboy heritage of the county (Bell et al. 1989).

In 1990, Teller County adopted its official master plan based in large part on the growth management planning process, including the landscape plans (Teller County Planning Commission 1990). After the growth management plan was prepared and the county plan adopted, the voters of Colorado approved gambling for Cripple Creek in Teller County. The growth management plan helped mitigate some of the negative impacts that resulted from the gaming industry. In addition, following adoption of the growth management plans, gold mining experienced a renewal. The plans also helped to diminish the negative consequences of the mining. The growth plan formed the basis for six regional action plans. The University of Colorado study also influenced city and town plans. These regional and municipal plans continue to direct growth in the county (Teller County Planning Commission 1995, 1998a, 1998b; City of Woodland Park 1996).

For example, the intent of the 4-Mile regional action plan "is to preserve the character and environment . . . while recognizing population growth in the area will occur (Teller County Planning Commission 1995, 1). In accordance with the growth management plan, resource protection, historical, and cultural overlays are used to protect specific and unique landscape features. The Divide regional plan recognizes "scenic and highly valued landscapes," "sensitive areas," and the "carrying capacity of land" (Teller County Planning Commission 1998a, 2–3). Meanwhile, the Florissant regional action plan identifies "critical areas," including cultural sites, natural hazard areas, and natural resource areas. Cultural sites "include areas of historic or archaeological significance," while natural hazard areas are defined to "include flood plains, steep slopes, wildlife lands, and geological hazards" (Teller County Planning Commission 1998b, 4).

The Pinelands and Teller County plans differ from conventional comprehensive plans in their recognition of landscape ecology. In the Pine Barrens, where the protective document is called a *comprehensive management plan,* critical landscape features are documented, recognized, and protected. In the Pinelands plan, the goal is established to "preserve, protect, and enhance the overall ecological values of the Pinelands." This goal is backed up both by specific policies and detailed implementation strategies. These policies and programs are concerned with soil, water, biotic, air, and human elements. The areas most suited for protection and for growth are identified both on a map and in writing. The plan seeks to achieve a balance between preservation and development.

In Teller County, landscape processes were linked to the planning process. Landscape analyses were conducted at two scales to reveal patterns. These patterns were recognized first in a set of concepts for Teller County and Woodland Park and then in landscape plans for each. The landscape plans differ from conventional land-use plans in their recognition of integrated, rather than separated, uses.

8

CONTINUING CITIZEN INVOLVEMENT AND COMMUNITY EDUCATION

Education is a lifelong process that should seek to achieve awareness, balanced perception, learning, and decision making. To accomplish these goals, individuals must develop a functional understanding of their cultural inheritance as well as the ability to contribute in a positive manner to society. Education occurs through the traditional institutions identified for that purpose, through continuing involvement in a discipline, through community programs, and, in the broadest sense, through popular culture. Community education increases both citizens' and planners' knowledge about a place.

Many planners have urged that public education and involvement efforts be integrated thoroughly into each step of the planning process. For instance, according to William Lassey:

> If planning is to be successful, a major reordering of public education, involvement, and communication processes may be necessary. Existing scientific knowledge about effective communication processes, and knowledge about human learning provide vastly

> increased potential for public understanding, appreciation, and involvement in significant societal decisions. Formal education methods for diffusing information and internalizing knowledge are archaic compared with potential learning capability of the human population. It is increasingly clear that lifelong educational processes are essential for adequate human adjustment to changing job requirements and life-styles, but effective communication of knowledge crucial to public decision making is equally important if the planet is to survive (1977, 74).

As a result, community education must be both future-oriented and ongoing. Continuing education should assist people in making linkages between their individual skills and interests and larger public issues. Without such linkages, the rules and regulations developed to protect people's health, safety, and welfare will be treated with suspicion by those whom they were meant to protect. Although community education and citizen involvement should be considered central and integral to each step in the planning process as indicated by Figure 1.1, they are placed here in the process as a reminder that even after a landscape plan has been developed, continued explanation about the plan is often necessary before it is implemented.

Rachel Kaplan and her colleagues argue that "genuine participation needs to start early and reach the diverse segments of the population" (Kaplan et al. 1998, 126). They also note that "meaningful participation requires information that is readily understood" (Kaplan et al. 1998, 128). A strategy that combines these two points would be to involve people early, then collect and synthesize the relevant information so that it may be understood, and then reengage the public. However, citizens can be involved in even the most technical steps of the planning process. For example, in the early 1970s, Ian McHarg worked with the people of Wilmington and Dover, Vermont, to compile a detailed ecological inventory and analysis of their region (McHarg 1998).

Planners, politicians, architects, landscape architects, and other community leaders have much to gain from citizen participation. A public involvement program can guarantee the success of a policy or project. It is also democratic. When viewed as part of ongoing community education, citizens and planners widen their planning knowledge as a result of participatory efforts.

Citizen involvement techniques can be classified as *information dissemination, information collection, initiative planning, reactive planning, decision making,* and *participation process support.* Community organizations, publications, and television and radio can be used in a community education program. Two examples of planning efforts that have included an educational element include the University of Wisconsin Community Development Program and the Blueprint for a Sustainable San Francisco Bay Area.

CITIZEN INVOLVEMENT

One of the major purposes of planning is to involve citizens in their government. A program should be developed that seeks to involve all citizens in each step of the planning process. There is no formula as to how to involve citizens in all phases of planning. However, the characteristics of such an open planning process are easy to identify. According to the U.S. Department of Transportation,

> Openness means that the purpose and the content of the process as well as the schedule for doing it, are described as clearly and concretely as possible—the decisions that have to be made, the information that will be used to make them, the choices which are and are not open for consideration and why, and the time when different steps are necessary and desirable (1976, 8).

Many state laws and legislation for federal land management agencies mandate such involvement. In Oregon, for instance, county and city governments, which are responsible for preparing and adopting comprehensive plans, must have a program that involves the public in an iterative way. The Oregon citizen involvement program has six components:

1. Citizen involvement
2. Communication
3. Citizen influence
4. Technical information
5. Feedback mechanisms
6. Financial support (Department of Land Conservation and Development 1996).

The guidelines for the citizen involvement component stipulate that the program should use a range of media, including television, radio, newspapers, mailings, and meetings. Oregon universities, colleges, community colleges, high schools, and grade schools are to provide information and courses about land-use planning. The program is also to include an officially recognized committee for citizen involvement. This committee is responsible for assisting the county commission or city council in the involvement effort (Land Conservation and Development Commission 1980; Department of Land Conservation and Development 1996).

Two-way communication between the governing body and the public is to be assured in Oregon cities and counties. Mechanisms such as newsletters, mailings, posters, and mail-back questionnaires are recommended. The purpose of the involvement and the communication is to give Oregon citizens direct influence in the planning process. Citizens are to be involved in data collection, plan preparation, the adoption process, implementation, evaluation, and revision (Land Conservation and Development Commission 1980; Department of Land Conservation and Development 1996).

Planners in Oregon are responsible to "assure that technical information is available in an understandable form." There is also a requirement that "feedback mechanisms" exist to "assure that citizens will receive a response" from policymakers. Finally, Oregon law requires that there be adequate financial support to ensure "funding for the citizen involvement program" (Land Conservation and Development Commission 1980, 3; Department of Land Conservation and Development 1996).

Other states have followed Oregon's lead. For example, Arizona's 1998 "Growing Smarter" law promotes citizen participation in general plan adoption and amendment. Local governments in Arizona are required "to adopt written procedures to provide effective, early and continuous public participation from all geographic, ethnic, and economic areas of the municipality" (Arizona Department of Commerce 1998, 3). These procedures must include: "(a) broad dissemination of proposals and alternatives; (b) opportunity for written comments, (c) public hearings after effective notice; (d) open discussions, communications programs and information services; and consideration of public comment" (Arizona Department of Commerce 1998, 3).

All federal land management agencies have guidelines for public participation, but the requirements vary. For instance, the intent of public participation in the National Forest System is to:

- Ensure that the U.S. Forest Service understands the needs and concerns of the public
- Inform the public of U.S. Forest Service land and resource planning activities
- Provide the public with an understanding of U.S. Forest Service programs and proposed actions
- Broaden the information base upon which land and resource management planning decisions are made
- Demonstrate that public issues and inputs are considered and evaluated in reaching planning decisions (adapted from U.S. Congress 1979)

One of the reasons why federal land management agencies have public participation programs is to comply with National Environmental Policy Act requirements and regulations (see Chapter 11). As a result of NEPA, federal land planning activities are subject to environmental impact reviews. USFS public participation efforts include keeping the news media informed of planning actions. Other activities include "requests for written comments, meetings, conferences, seminars, workshops, tours, and similar events designed to foster public review and participation" (U.S. Congress 1979, 53988). To increase information about its plans, the USFS is supposed to coordinate its planning activities among all levels of government, including other federal agencies, state and local governments, and Indian nations.

CLASSIFICATION OF CITIZEN PARTICIPATION TECHNIQUES

The U.S. Department of Transportation (1976) has classified citizen participation techniques, such as those described in Chapters 2 and 6, on the basis of their function, as follows:

One of the major purposes of an open planning process is to involve citizens in their government.

- Information dissemination
- Information collection
- Initiative planning
- Reactive planning
- Decision making
- Participation process support

Although a technique may have more than one function, the classification is based on its primary purpose. The *information dissemination* class "contains techniques which inform the public of any steps the agency is taking, any opportunities the public has to [influence] the process, and the proposed plans that have been brought forward" (U.S. Department of Transportation 1976, 18). Various community education and information programs and open meetings are examples of this technique classification.

Information collection techniques are used to identify the major issues facing a community or to assess the attitudes that community may have regarding the issues. These techniques can also be used to determine the public support for planning goals, policies, and strategies as well as to collect inventory information. Surveys, public opinion polls, Delphi, community sponsored meetings, public hearings, and participant observation are some ways information is collected (see Chapter 4).

In *initiative planning,* the responsibility for producing proposals and structuring options is assigned to the community or its representatives. Planning agencies, meanwhile, supply information and technical assistance. Advocacy planning, task forces, workshops, and charrettes are examples of initiative planning. Conversely, in *reactive planning,* it is the agency that makes the proposals and the community that reacts. Citizens' advisory committees are an example of reactive planning (U.S. Department of Transportation 1976).

Decision-making techniques are designed to help a community develop a consensus on an issue, a goal, an option, or a plan. Such techniques do not replace the responsibilities of elected or appointed officials but are intended to augment them. Referenda, which may in fact be binding, and citizen review boards are two decision-making techniques (U.S. Department of Transportation 1976).

The final classification is *participation process support techniques.* According to the Department of Transportation (1976), these methods serve to make other types of techniques more effective and to cut across all of the other categories. Citizen honoraria may be used, for instance, to compensate people for being involved in the process. Such payment may permit people to become active who would not otherwise be able to participate. But paying people to be citizens raises important ethical questions about the responsibilities of people in a democracy. Another technique is citizen training, where individuals are taught leadership and planning skills (U.S. Department of Transportation 1976).

CONTINUING COMMUNITY EDUCATION

Public participation is concerned both with involving people in the process and then continuing to inform citizens about changes and adjustments to the plan and its implementation and administration. Once a community is organized for the process, some form of that organization can continue. For example, in the New Jersey Pinelands a commission was established that is responsible for involving people in the planning process and establishing a continuing information effort. The public participation program included activities like workshops and conferences, public workshops on specific topics, personal communications and meetings, and the use of knowledgeable private individuals for guidance in research areas of interests to the Pinelands Commission (Pinelands Commission 1980). Means to keep people informed included newsletters, television, radio, and websites.

Information and Education

In addition to being a means for establishing goals and for selecting preferences, community organizations can provide information and education and can keep people involved. As reviewed in Chapters 2 and 6, there are various types of organizations that can be used in a community, including task forces, advisory committees, and neighborhood councils. Such groups might sponsor a lecture by an expert and/or the showing of a film or a slide presentation. Other meetings may take the form of a workshop where the group interacts with facilitators or with a two-way television connected with an individual or individuals or another group or groups.

Information can also be presented to communities through conferences and symposia. Community colleges, universities, or the Cooperative Extension Service may be used to help organize such gatherings. Professional and academic associations may be contacted for involvement as well. Since many members of associations are required to receive a certain number of hours of continuing education credit annually, conference organizers may want to arrange to offer credit when appropriate. The content of conferences and symposia may range from that of a general nature to very advanced. In the Pinelands, for example, conferences and workshops have been organized ranging from rather simple question-and-answer sessions to academic conferences on the ecology and culture of the Pine Barrens.

Planners are often invited to community organizations and clubs, such as those listed in Table 4.1, to make presentations. These are good opportunities to explain the planning process. Youth groups such as the Scouts and 4-H also often invite speakers to their meetings.

Many planning agencies and commissions, including the Pinelands Commission and the Oregon Department of Land Conservation and Development, maintain websites. For example, in 1998 the Pinelands Commission featured a website on

Maps and aerial photographs can help citizens understand the spatial consequences of planning actions.

"The Pine Barrens Tree Frog & Other Friends." The Pine Barrens tree frog is viewed as a symbol for the region. In addition to information about the ecology of the tree frog, artwork and photography were displayed. The commission indicated that different wildlife and vegetation species will be featured on its website (www.state.nj.us/pinelands).

The Pinelands Commission developed a continuing program based on providing information to the public, creating awareness through education, and involving people in the implementation of the plan. According to the Pinelands Commission:

> The public has to be kept informed of the Commission's activities and the purpose of the Comprehensive Management Plan. Public information efforts must reach as wide and diverse an audience as possible. Educational materials have to be provided, emphasizing the sensitive nature of the Pinelands' resources and detailing critical issues related to their protection. Points at which public involvement is most meaningful have to be highlighted, with a range of opportunities provided for both active and passive involvement. The overall program must be visible, continuous, and responsive (1980, 330).

Pinelands planners recognized that information, education, and involvement would inevitably overlap. "All information is educational in nature, and education requires involvement" (Pinelands Commission 1980, 330). Publications such as newsletters and interaction with reporters from the print and electronic media are crucial elements of the public information program in the Pinelands.

In the view of the commission, the Pinelands are "a living laboratory" for education. Similarly, any place, any landscape can be considered a classroom to study natural, physical, and cultural processes. In the Pinelands, state and regional resources have been utilized to develop curriculum material for students and teachers at both the primary and secondary school levels. Bibliographic and library resources have been created as part of the process and have been made available to teachers and researchers. With the National Park Service, interpretation programs about recreational areas and historic sites have been developed. A speakers bureau was created to match experts on various topics with community groups. In addition, the commission developed ongoing educational activities with private nonprofit and public organizations like the 4-H, the Boy and Girl Scouts, garden clubs, and environmental groups (Pinelands Commission 1980).

The Pinelands Commission attempts to keep the public involved in a number of ways. There are the meetings of the commission and its subcommittees. Advisory committees established during the planning process remain intact. The commission also maintains its liaison with county and municipal governments (Pinelands Commission 1980). Planning depends on the involvement of people. To keep people involved, planners must provide timely and accurate information and create educational opportunities. There are several media that can be utilized for information and education.

Publications

Many types of publications are helpful as educational tools: newspapers, popular magazines, extension bulletins, planning agency reports and manuals, and professional journals. Newspapers are, of course, quite interested in planning issues at stages of controversy. Often the passage or failure of a new plan or regulation can hinge on how it is reported in local newspapers and by the ebb and flow of letters to the editor. Concise press releases are helpful to brief reporters during periods of controversy. Press releases should include the name, address, and phone number of the chief contact on the planning staff as well as a succinct summary of the debate. It may also be necessary to include dates and places of meetings and hearings.

The Institute for Participatory Management and Planning identifies four ground rules for press releases:

- Always put the information in its proper context; make the meaning of any announcement clear by giving sufficient background information. Assume the reader is not familiar with the issue.
- Be concise. Send a few short, well-presented messages rather than a big, complex, combined message. You should assume that the reader has a short attention span.
- Clearly distinguish fact from opinion. While opinions—or ways of interpreting certain facts—can and should be communicated, you must be careful that you don't label them as facts.
- Avoid any and all jargon. A good rule of thumb is: use only expressions and words that your mother [or father]—who happens not to be a systems analyst—would understand (1997, V-41).

In addition to working with the press during times of controversy, journalists should be informed during less heated times. Ecological inventory information makes interesting copy for Sunday supplements or series by nature reporters. A rare plant or animal species can arouse much public interest. Popular magazines may be used in much the same way. Regional and city magazines are a good forum. *Southern Living,* for instance, has published especially good articles on planning issues such as historic preservation, energy conservation, and farmlands protection. In addition, *Southern Living* is an advocate of regional natural and cultural ecology. Articles about flora and fauna mixed with vernacular architecture and rich southern literary comment are common.

One nationwide educational organization with an extensive publication program is the Cooperative Extension Service. As its name indicates, the extension service is a cooperative organization that involves federal, state, and local governments as well as state land-grant universities. The mission of the Cooperative Extension Service is to foster the transfer of technological and scientific knowledge generated from land-grant university research to the citizens of each state and to encourage adoption of that knowledge. Although the extension service is active in urban areas, its traditional clientele is rural people. Broadly the subject matter to be addressed by the extension service is to be related to agriculture and home economics. Publications are the major device that the extension service has used to disseminate information. The Cooperative Extension Service works with both local officials and the public. While the extension service vigorously promotes the transfer of knowledge and information, it does not take positions on political issues. In several areas, the extension service has collaborated with local agencies to provide and to distribute publications about planning.

The Cooperative Extension Service prints helpful planning-related reports and bulletins in many states. Although it cannot print advocacy publications, the extension service can provide information helpful for citizens to gain a better understanding about planning issues and techniques. One noteworthy example is the Coping with Growth series published by the Western Rural Development Center, a consortium of western land-grant universities. This informative series addresses topics such as community needs assessment, population studies, fiscal and social impacts, and citizen involvement, and is available through the Western Rural Development Center, Oregon State University, Corvallis, Oregon. Similar rural development consortia of land-grant universities exist in the northeast at Pennsylvania State University, in the midwest at Iowa State University, and the south at Mississippi State University.

Non-land-grant universities also provide community service through design and outreach centers. For example, the Herberger Center for Design Excellence coordinates research and outreach activities for the ASU College of Architecture and Environmental Design. The Joint Urban Design Program, part of the Herberger Center headquartered in downtown Phoenix, leads the outreach mission. Charrettes, often in collaboration with the City of Phoenix, are one outreach activity (see Chapter 6). The Herberger Center also disseminates information through publications. Two- and four-page newsletter-like reports summarize charrette and other community events. The Herberger Center publishes longer, more technical reports as well. Most American colleges of architecture, planning, and landscape architecture have similar centers.

Increasingly, teaching, research, and service activities are becoming more intermingled at universities. This approach is consistent with Ernest Boyer's (1990) call to replace the traditional teaching-research-service triad for higher education with the scholarship of discovery, the scholarship of integration, the scholarship of application, and the scholarship of teaching.

Planning agency reports and manuals are important educational tools. Some of these reports must be technical and thus will have a limited readership; others, however, should be written for a broader audience. Manuals in plain English that explain regulatory procedures are especially helpful for real estate agents, home builders, and developers. Packets and websites explaining a community comprehensive plan, zoning ordinance, subdivision regulations, public services, cultural activities, and natural and social histories are interesting to new residents of an area.

Professional and academic journals address a narrower audience. Such publications are invaluable forums for sharing experiences. But planners should not be constricted by disciplinary territorialism. They should read—and publish in—journals of the many related disciplines. This is a way to build needed linkages among people trained or educated in various fields.

Television and Radio

Television is a ubiquitous part of American life, while radio provides an ongoing narration of public events. Commercial television and radio news are interested in controversial local issues in the same way as newspapers. Television and radio reporters can be approached in the same way as print journalists, although commercial stations will seldom explore issues in much depth during news programs. Television "magazine" and talk-show programs offer opportunities to explore issues in greater detail.

Public television and radio may even devote more time to certain issues than will their newsprint colleagues. Many planners cooperate with public broadcast journalists to develop in-depth analyses of issues and explanations of legislation. The Cooperative Extension Service frequently works with public broadcasting stations and provides background information through television and radio similar to that found in its printed bulletins and reports.

The continued extension of cable television systems offers expanded opportunities for conveying planning information. Because of the increase in the number of channels, there is a need for programming to fill the time. Planning commission meetings and hearings can be broadcast live. Interactive arrangements between individual homes and government offices can be made so that interested citizens can convey their views to elected and appointed officials. Public opinion polls and preference surveys can be conducted via television. Cable systems also offer opportunities for continuing education courses through community colleges and universities. These can be flexible short courses, or an extended series targeted at the public, elected and appointed officials, or professional planners.

TWO EXAMPLES OF EDUCATION PROGRAMS

Involvement in government is fundamental to democracy. Information about the consequences of decisions enhances the effectiveness of participation. Average citizens tend not to read government reports, including plans. As a result, the design and readability of documents can either help or hinder the planning process. The University of Wisconsin-Extension Community Economic Development Program and the Blueprint for a Sustainable Bay Area provide good examples of effective programs.

University of Wisconsin-Extension Community Economic Development Program

During the 1970s and 1980s the University of Wisconsin-Extension initiated a long-term relationship with a number of small towns in Dane County as a part of the extension service's community development program. More recently, the mission of extension service shifted, and the program is now called the Center for Community Economic Development. First, the Dane County efforts are described, followed by the more recent activities.

In each Dane County town involved with the program, a similar community development strategy was employed (Figure 8.1) and a similar format for reports was used (Figure 8.2). The county

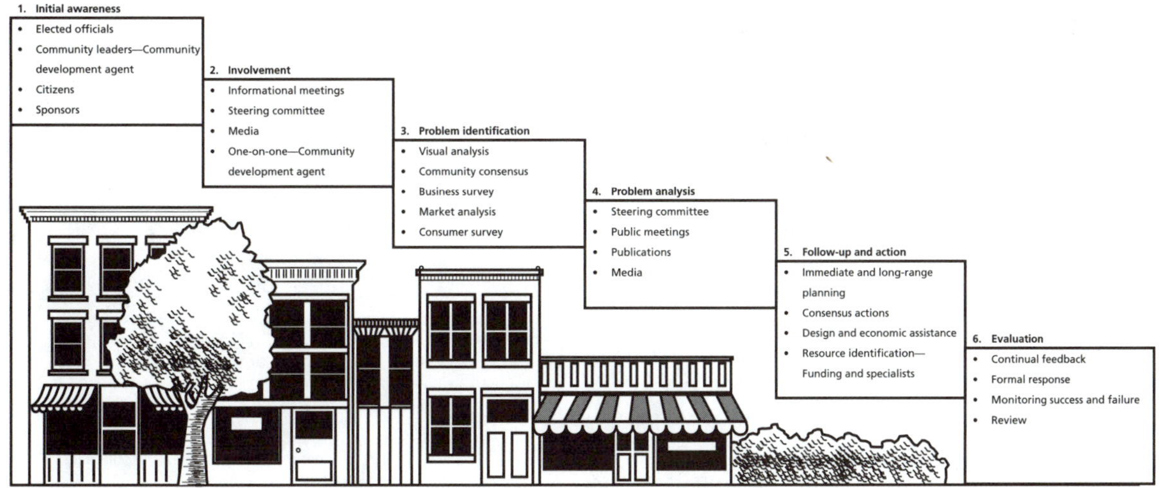

FIGURE 8.1 University of Wisconsin–Extension community development strategy. *(Source: Domack 1981)*

FIGURE 8.2 University of Wisconsin–Extension community development report format. *(Source: Domack 1981)*

extension agent coordinated with and involved various academic departments at the University of Wisconsin. These departments included city planning, economics, rural sociology, landscape architecture, and architecture. The extension service was able to bring to these small towns information that was not otherwise readily available to citizens and leaders. The extension service was then able to demonstrate to the citizens how this information could be useful (Domack 1981).

A common set of studies was undertaken in each Dane County town. These studies included a community-consensus study, a visual analysis, a trade area survey, a survey of business owners/managers and building owners, a threshold-level analysis, and a report concerning the design options for the main business district. The community-consensus study was essentially a preference survey. Three categories of people were surveyed: elected officials, nonelected community leaders, and citizens in general. These groups were asked to rank potential problems facing the community (Domack 1981).

The community-consensus survey consisted of five steps. First, a survey designed specifically for each small town was developed. Second, the people to be surveyed in the three categories were identified. The third step was to conduct the interviews, which were done by University of Wisconsin students meeting directly with the identified individuals. Table 8.1 shows how the survey included 17 general topic categories, plus other miscellaneous questions (Domack 1981).

Compiling and analyzing the survey information was the fourth step in the community-consensus study. Results were reported back

TABLE 8.1
TOPIC CATEGORIES USED IN THE UNIVERSITY OF WISCONSIN-EXTENSION COMMUNITY CONSENSUS STUDY

Topic Categories
1. Parking
2. Traffic
3. Streets and roads
4. Public transportation
5. Community growth and planning
6. Economic growth
7. Shopping for goods and services
8. Condition and appearance of downtown
9. Crime and law enforcement
10. Public utilities
11. Local government officials and city service
12. Health care
13. Education
14. Recreation and leisure-time activities
15. Local environment
16. Housing
17. Human relations
18. Other

SOURCE: Domack 1981.

through community meetings, local news media, and publications. After about 10 weeks, once the survey results were reported, the fifth step was taken. This involved again surveying the elected officials, community leaders, and the sampling of citizens to ascertain if any change may have occurred as a result or a reaction to the original survey (Domack 1981).

The downtown areas of smaller towns deteriorate slowly, in a process that is often unnoticed by local residents. The purpose of the visual analysis portion of the University of Wisconsin-Extension program was to help each community see how their town looked to outsiders. This was accomplished through an extensive photographic effort, in which between 600 and 800 slides were taken. The effort concentrated on important gathering areas such as the downtown, parks, schools, and churches. The results of the visual analysis were presented at community meetings (Domack 1981).

According to the University of Wisconsin-Extension, a *trade area* is the economic region from which community businesses draw their customers. It comprised both rural and built-up areas. In the University of Wisconsin-Extension trade area survey, a consumer questionnaire was utilized to provide local businesses with information about their current and potential customers. In this survey the following information was sought from local consumers:

- Where do they shop (what towns and shopping centers)?
- What influence does media advertising (newspapers, radio, television, and/or direct mail fliers) have on their shopping decisions?
- What are their main considerations (price, quality, and/or brand name) when they purchase a particular product?
- Where do they purchase specialized goods and services most often?
- Are existing store hours compatible with their schedules?
- What additional services and facilities do they think the community needs?
- How can government officials better serve the needs of downtown businesspeople (Domack 1981, 12)?

The survey of business owners/managers and building owners was used to determine what these people thought about potential economic development in their downtown area. The survey helped to gauge the willingness of the business community to participate in change. This survey also provided an overview about how the businesspeople viewed economic opportunities and problems in their towns (Domack 1981).

The final survey used in the extension program was the *threshold-level analysis.* This was a market survey used to determine whether a particular type of new business could be a success in the town. According to the University of Wisconsin-Extension, a *threshold* is the minimum number of people needed to support one business of a particular type. The extension service has developed thresholds through the study of 100 small Wisconsin communities. Table 8.2 illustrates threshold populations, hierarchical marginal goods, and the rank of selected central functions for central place hierarchy in Wisconsin. Figure 8.3 illustrates the relationship between community size and the number of businesses that can be supported, while Table 8.3 shows the number of people required to support various businesses in Wisconsin. Threshold-level analysis helps local businesspeople and investors create an accurate picture of the economic potential of their town (Figure 8.4) (Domack 1981).

The purpose of all these studies—the community consensus, visual analysis, trade-area survey, survey of business owners/managers and building owners, and threshold-level analysis—was to help small-town residents better understand their community, and particularly its

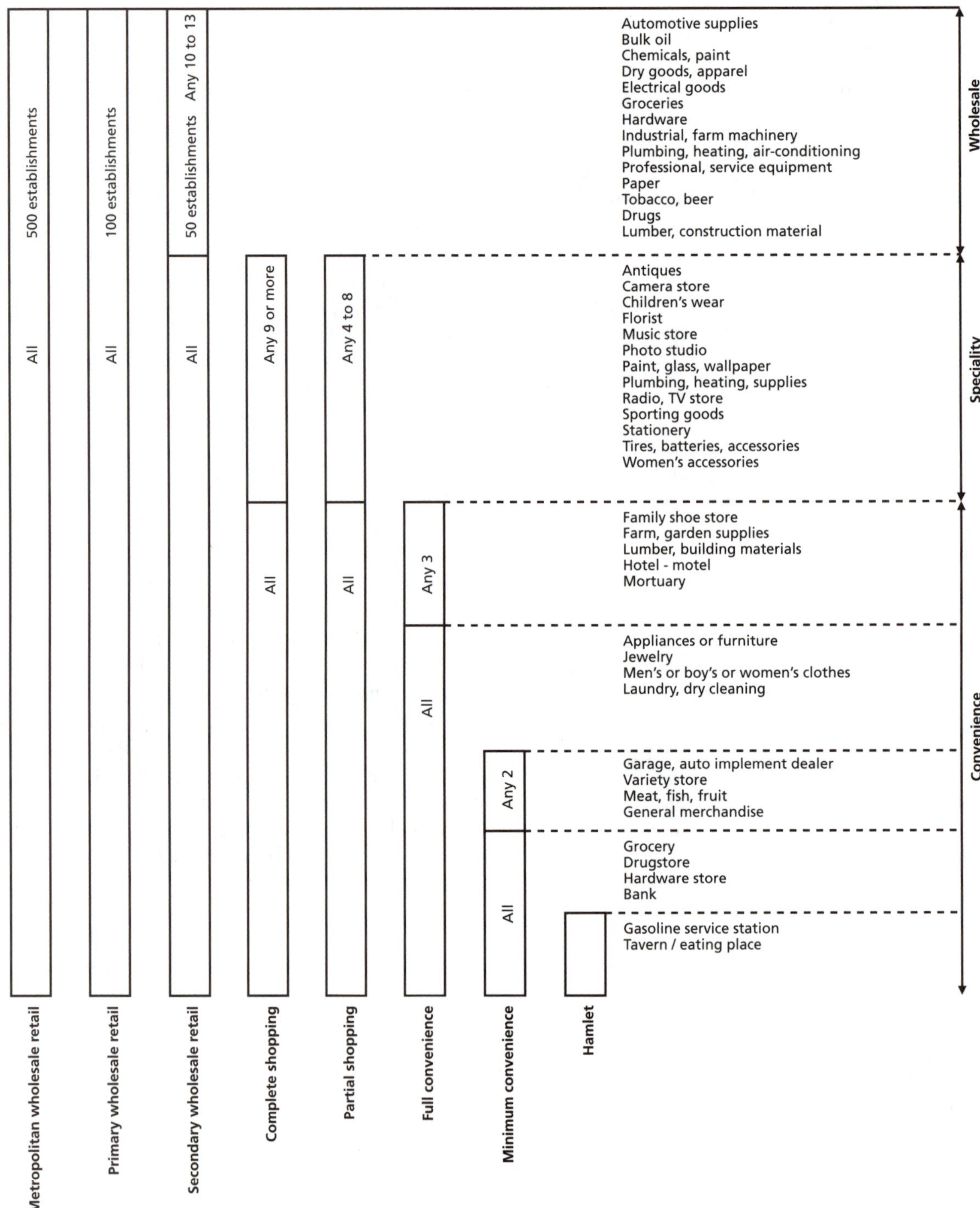

Selected business functions
Automotive supplies
Bulk oil
Chemicals, paint
Dry goods, apparel
Electrical goods
Groceries
Hardware
Industrial, farm machinery
Plumbing, heating, air-conditioning
Professional, service equipment
Paper
Tobacco, beer
Drugs
Lumber, construction material
Wholesale
Antiques
Camera store
Children's wear
Florist
Music store
Photo studio
Paint, glass, wallpaper
Plumbing, heating, supplies
Radio, TV store
Sporting goods
Stationery
Tires, batteries, accessories
Women's accessories
Speciality
Family shoe store
Farm, garden supplies
Lumber, building materials
Hotel - motel
Mortuary
Appliances or furniture
Jewelry
Men's or boy's or women's clothes
Laundry, dry cleaning
Garage, auto implement dealer
Variety store
Meat, fish, fruit
General merchandise
Grocery
Drugstore
Hardware store
Bank
Gasoline service station
Tavern / eating place
Convenience
500 establishments
All
100 establishments
All
50 establishments
Any 10 to 13
All
Any 9 or more
All
Any 4 to 8
All
Any 3
All
Any 2
All
Metropolitan wholesale retail
Primary wholesale retail
Secondary wholesale retail
Complete shopping
Partial shopping
Full convenience
Minimum convenience
Hamlet

FIGURE 8.3 Relationship between community size and the number of businesses that can be supported. *(Source: Domack 1981)*

TABLE 8.2
THRESHOLD POPULATIONS, HIERARCHICAL MARGINAL GOODS, AND RANK OF SELECTED CENTRAL FUNCTIONS FOR THE CENTRAL PLACE HIERARCHY IN WISCONSIN

Hierarchical Level	Central Functions		Mean Population
Hamlet	Taverns Grocery stores	Service stations	200
Minimum convenience	Post office Bank Elementary and secondary school Beauty shop Hardware stores Farm supplies Motor vehicle dealer Lumber and building materials Insurance agent Dentist Farm machinery and equipment Physician Barber shop Auto repair	Drugstore Auto parts and supplies Legal services Hotel or motel Bowling alley Public golf course Furniture store Bakery Women's clothing store Laundry and cleaning service Variety store Petroleum bulk station Real estate agent Liquor store	800
Full convenience	Funeral home Radio and television store Accounting, auditing, and bookkeeping services Optometrists Shoe store Movie theater	Jewelry store Florists Billiard hall Sheet-metal works Men's clothing store Photographer	2,000
Partial shopping centers	Nursing home Sporting goods and bike shops Labor unions	Fire and casualty insurance brokers Civic, social, and fraternal associations Engineering and surveying services	3,800
Complete shopping centers	Amusement and recreational services Family clothing stores Gift and novelty shop	Auto and home supply store Wholesale beer distributor	11,000
Wholesale-retail centers	Telephone office Dairy wholesalers Department stores Chiropractors Business associations Janitorial services Used car dealers (used only) Specialty repair Sports and recreation clubs Fuel oil wholesalers Boat dealers Day care centers Floor covering stores Used merchandise stores Title abstract services	Mobile home dealers Sewing, needlework, and piece goods Industrial equipment and machinery Paint, glass, and wallpaper Meat and fish markets Livestock marketing Welding repair Hospitals Radio stations Lumber, plywood, and millwork Dairy product stores Car washes Stationery stores Household appliance stores	62,000

SOURCE: Domack 1981.

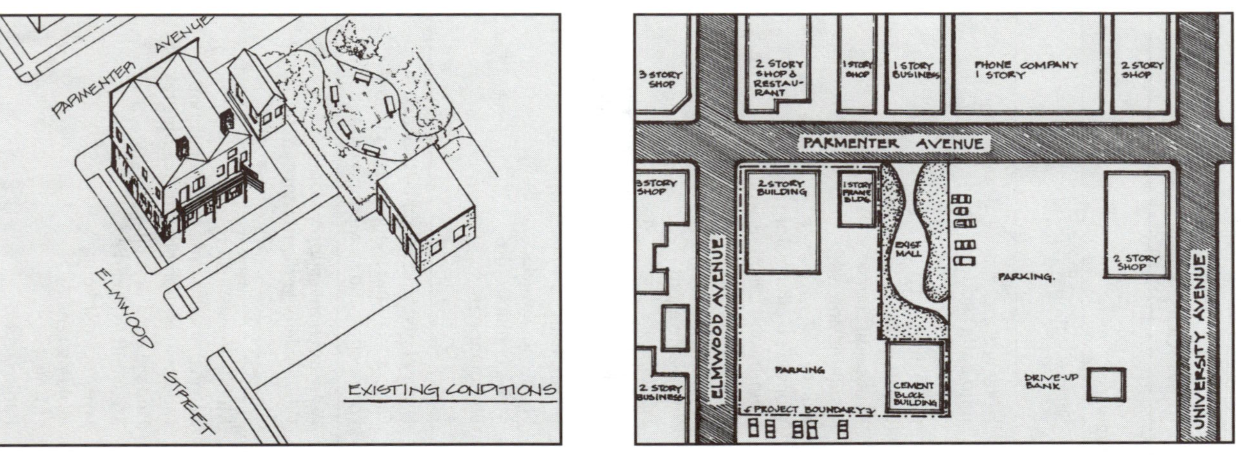
PARMENTER AVENUE
ELMWOOD STREET
EXISTING CONDITIONS
3 STORY SHOP
2 STORY SHOP & RESTAU-RANT
1 STORY SHOP
1 STORY BUSINESS
PHONE COMPANY 1 STORY
2 STORY SHOP
PARMENTER AVENUE
3 STORY SHOP
2 STORY BUILDING
1 STORY FRAME BLDG.
EXIST MALL
PARKING.
2 STORY SHOP
ELMWOOD AVENUE
UNIVERSITY AVENUE
2 STORY BUSINESS
PARKING
CEMENT BLOCK BUILDING
DRIVE-UP BANK
PROJECT BOUNDARY

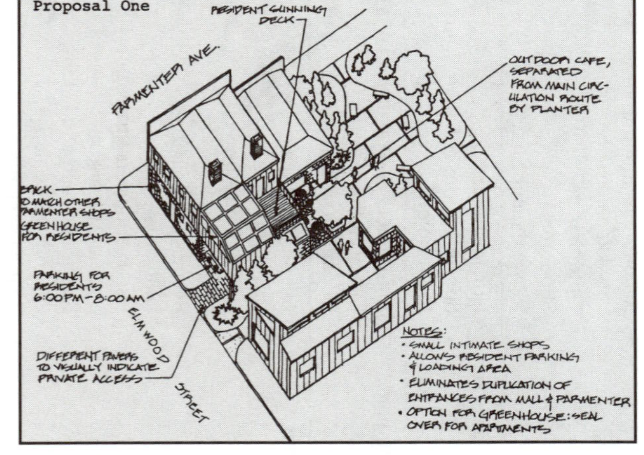
Proposal One
RESIDENT SUNNING DECK
PARMENTER AVE.
OUTDOOR CAFE, SEPARATED FROM MAIN CIRCULATION ROUTE BY PLANTER
BRICK TO MATCH OTHER PARMENTER SHOPS
GREENHOUSE FOR RESIDENTS
PARKING FOR RESIDENTS 6:00PM–8:00AM
ELMWOOD
DIFFERENT PAVERS TO VISUALLY INDICATE PRIVATE ACCESS
STREET
NOTES:
• SMALL INTIMATE SHOPS
• ALLOWS RESIDENT PARKING & LOADING AREA
• ELIMINATES DUPLICATION OF ENTRANCES FROM MALL & PARMENTER
• OPTION FOR GREENHOUSE: SEAL OVER FOR APARTMENTS

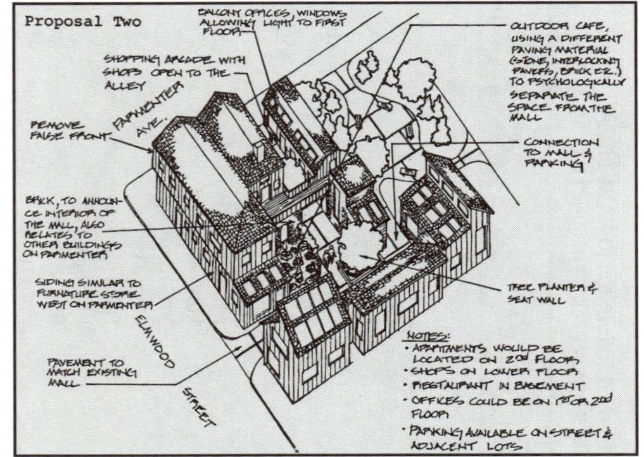
Proposal Two
BALCONY OFFICES, WINDOWS ALLOWING LIGHT TO FIRST FLOOR
SHOPPING ARCADE WITH SHOPS OPEN TO THE ALLEY
PARMENTER AVE.
REMOVE FALSE FRONT
OUTDOOR CAFE, USING A DIFFERENT PAVING MATERIAL (STONE, INTERLOCKING PAVERS, BRICK ETC.) TO PSYCHOLOGICALLY SEPARATE THE SPACE FROM THE MALL
CONNECTION TO MALL & PARKING
BRICK, TO ANNOUNCE INTERIOR OF THE MALL, ALSO RELATES TO OTHER BUILDINGS ON PARMENTER
SIDING SIMILAR TO FURNITURE STORE WEST ON PARMENTER
TREE PLANTER & SEAT WALL
PAVEMENT TO MATCH EXISTING MALL
ELMWOOD
STREET
NOTES:
• APARTMENTS WOULD BE LOCATED ON 2ND FLOOR
• SHOPS ON LOWER FLOOR
• RESTAURANT IN BASEMENT
• OFFICES COULD BE ON 1ST OR 2ND FLOOR
• PARKING AVAILABLE ON STREET & ADJACENT LOTS

FIGURE 8.4 An example of decision options resulting from a University of Wisconsin-Extension community development program. *(Source: Domack 1981)*

TABLE 8.3
POPULATIONS REQUIRED TO SUPPORT ADDITIONAL ESTABLISHMENTS OF SELECTED FUNCTIONS IN WISCONSIN

	Number of Establishments			
Function	**1**	**2**	**3**	**4**
Taverns	77	244	478	711
Food stores	92	1,104	4,697	29,119
Fuel oil dealers	164	685	1,577	2,850
Filling stations	186	459	799	1,135
Feed stores	247	4,895	28,106	97,124
Beauticians	268	851	1,673	2,702
Insurance agencies	293	666	1,077	1,514
Farm implements	309	3,426	14,004	38,025
Restaurants	316	754	1,253	1,797
Hardware stores	372	1,925	5,032	9,949
Auto repair shops	375	1,148	2,209	3,517
Motels	384	2,072	5,557	11,189
Real estate agencies	418	1,226	2,301	3,597
Auto dealers	420	1,307	2,937	4,063
Plumbers	468	2,717	7,604	15,780
Physicians	493	1,352	2,436	3,702
Lawyers	497	1,169	1,927	2,748
Radio-TV sales	521	1,815	3,765	6,316
Drive-in eating places	537	4,851	17,572	43,799
Dentists	563	1,744	3,379	5,402
Supermarkets	587	2,968	7,610	14,881
Appliance stores	607	3,709	10,691	22,659
Liquor stores	613	4,738	15,669	36,509
Barber shops	632	5,297	18,372	44,404
Furniture stores	637	4,833	15,819	36,686
Drugstores	638	4,285	13,053	28,771
Auto parts dealers	642	5,496	19,284	46,991
Laundromats	649	5,665	20,114	49,264
Women's clothing stores	678	5,471	18,544	44,133
Department stores	691	5,408	18,012	42,295
Dry cleaners	692	4,131	11,746	24,655
Shoe stores	712	7,650	30,670	82,146

SOURCE: Domack 1981.

limitations and potentials. The program integrated community education with citizen participation.

The Center for Community Economic Development was established in 1990 by coalescing the extension specialists involved in community development. As of 1999, the center had a staff of seven. The center maintains an affiliation with the University of Wisconsin Department of Urban and Regional Planning. The academic department offers a graduate degree in community development. The center helps communities throughout Wisconsin to strengthen business activities. A website describes the center's economic development programs (www.uwex.edu/ces/cced). Center staff and University of Wisconsin faculty undertake market analyses for business, identify community indicators for economic development, and various urban initiatives.

The Blueprint for a Sustainable Bay Area

In 1996, a not-for-profit nongovernmental organization called Urban Ecology published their green plan for the San Francisco Bay region. The *Blueprint for a Sustainable Bay Area* defined the region consisting of 9 counties, 100 cities (including San Francisco, Oakland, and San Jose), 7400 square miles (19,166 square kilometers), and over 6 million people (Urban Ecology 1996; see also McNally 1999). Urban Ecology's blueprint is based on principles of sustainability and focuses on four levels: the home, residential neighborhoods, urban centers, and the region as a whole. The blueprint is compiled in an attractive, easy-to-read publication with a clear organizational structure (Figure 8.5).

Urban Ecology defines seven principles for sustainable development that guide the blueprint:

1. *Choice.* Provide Bay Area residents with new choices for a prosperous life.
2. *Accessibility.* Promote development and transportation alternatives that connect the region.
3. *Nature.* Protect, restore, and integrate nature into the lives of Bay Area residents.
4. *Justice.* Work toward a Bay Area that is more socially, economically, and environmentally just.

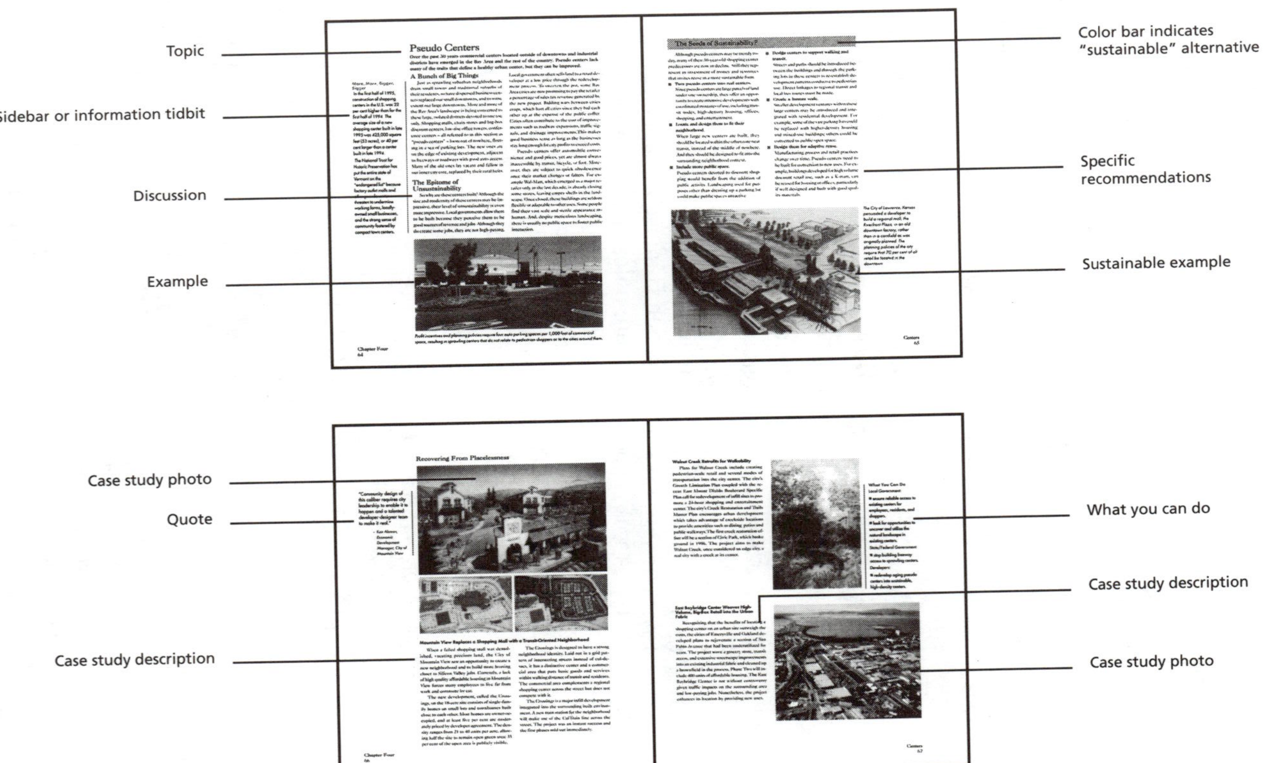

FIGURE 8.5 The blueprint for a sustainable Bay Area. *(Source: Urban Ecology 1996)*

5. *Conservation.* Encourage resource conservation and reuse as integral to the Bay Area way of life.
6. *Context.* Design with respect for the uniqueness and history of localities and the region.
7. *Community.* Enable Bay Area residents to nurture a strong sense of place, community, and responsibility (Urban Ecology 1996, 16–17).

Examples were drawn from within the Bay Area and elsewhere to illustrate these seven principles at the various scales. From these examples and the principles, the authors of the blueprint offered suggestions for achieving local and regional sustainability. For neighborhoods, these included a feeling of belonging, safety, and support; an identity; diversity close at hand; streets primarily for people; a range of public spaces; access to nature; connections to centers; self-reliance; and active self-governance (Urban Ecology 1996). They also identified indicators for assessing whether a neighborhood is in decline (Table 8.4).

"There's no such thing as a purely local community," the blueprint authors declare (Urban Ecology 1996, 69). They define the region's ecology as "a product of the interdependence of the natural systems and those made by humans" (Urban Ecology 1996, 69). Considerable attention is given to helping residents recognize the region as "a place of many pieces," then stimulating them to "think regionally." Thinking regionally involves understanding the bioregion, making use of the region's natural potential and amenities, and balancing local and regional decision making (Urban Ecology 1996).

Five suggestions are made for better planning. First, the bay and the existing greenbelt through the region need to be protected. Second, transportation systems and land uses should be connected. Third, economic connections to "a healthy natural and social environment" need to be understood. Fourth, materials, water, and energy should be used more carefully. Fifth, spending and decisions should be made more wisely (Urban Ecology 1996).

TABLE 8.4
INDICATORS FOR ASSESSING WHETHER A NEIGHBORHOOD IS IN DECLINE

Is Your Neighborhood In Decline?

The more items you can check on this list, the more likely your neighborhood is vulnerable to decline and abandonment by residents, businesses, and government. See the case studies to find out what neighborhoods in the Bay Area are doing to reverse this trend.

- ❑ You send your children to schools outside the neighborhood.
- ❑ Your children hang around the house when not in school because there's no safe local place to play or hang out.
- ❑ People can't use, enjoy, or feel safe in parks, streets, and other neighborhood places.
- ❑ There is no park in your neighborhood.
- ❑ You have to leave your neighborhood to get basic goods and services such as grocery stores, banks, and drugstores.
- ❑ The bus stop is too far to walk to, and service is infrequent or irregular.
- ❑ The sidewalks and front yards are untidy.
- ❑ Potholes aren't getting fixed.
- ❑ Police take five minutes or more to respond to emergency calls.
- ❑ Property values are declining due to crime, drugs, or a bad reputation.
- ❑ You know few of your neighbors and rarely interact with them.
- ❑ You are embarrassed to tell people where you live.

SOURCE: Urban Ecology 1996.

The devices that Urban Ecology used to illustrate the regional consequences of such planning or lack thereof included a series of three maps (Figure 8.6). These maps illustrate the bay as

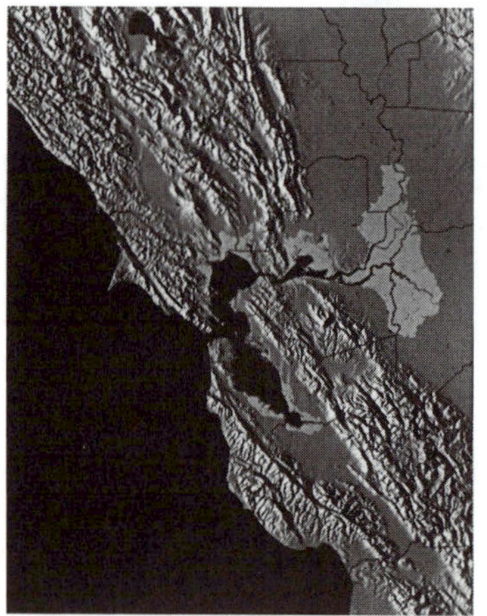

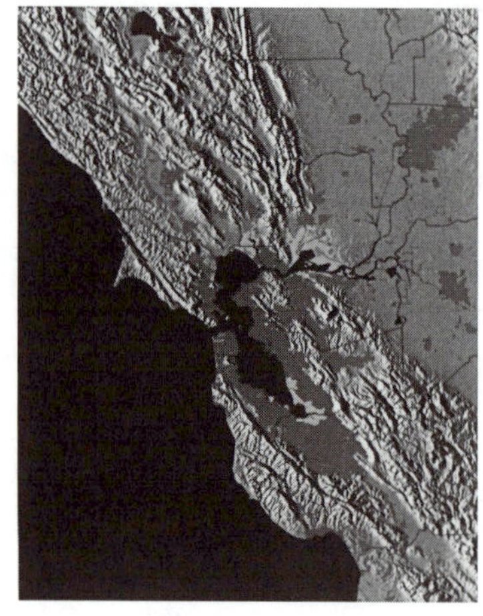

1848: The Way We Were

The Bay Area's greenspaces, bay, and estuary largely as nature made them. Green indicates the extent of marshlands. The settlements around the five California missions do not show at this scale.

1990: The Way We Are

Development has spread throughout the inner bay and leapfrogged into the greenbelt. Parts of the bay have been filled.

2010: The Way We Might Become

This is how our region will look if development is not held in check.

FIGURE 8.6 Bay Area greenspaces. *(Source: Urban Ecology 1996)*

greenspaces existed in 1848 and in 1990, as well as how it could develop without better planning in the future. An EcoAtlas of the bay, developed by the San Francisco Estuary Institute (Figure 4.1), was also used (Grossinger et al. 1999).

The blueprint was compiled as an educational resource for Bay Area residents. Its premise is that to "make sustainability happen," people need to work together. They also should understand the ecology of their region and the consequences of their actions. The blueprint makes specific recommendations for how individuals, government, business, and groups of people can work together to plan a more sustainable region.

A goal in both the Bay Area Blueprint and the Wisconsin Community Development Program was to illustrate cause-and-effect relationships. The thesis is: If people better understand such relationships, then they will support government actions based on the same understanding. The Bay Area Blueprint links these relationships to sustainability. The authors of the blueprint declare: "A sustainable Bay Area supports and improves the quality of life of all its residents and recognizes the interdependence of its people, culture, economy, [and] urbanized and natural environments. More importantly, it is a region that knows itself, demands the utmost of itself, and understands what it has to lose" (Urban Ecology 1996, 125). As with the Wisconsin effort, the authors of the blueprint envisioned an ongoing public education and involvement process. This vigorous pursuit of public education differentiates these examples from more conventional planning processes, where an educational campaign may only be mounted at one or two steps in the process.

9

TESTING PLANNING CONCEPTS THROUGH DESIGN

Design involves the conception of culturally beneficial change. Design changes elements of the physical environment as well as relationships among elements. By making specific designs based on the plan and the planning process, landscape planners can help decision makers and citizens visualize and comprehend the consequences of their policies. By carrying policies through to the arrangement of the physical environment, another dimension is added to the process. The spatial organization of a place is affected through design. Specific designs represent a synthesis of all the previous steps in the planning process. During the design step, the short-term benefits for the land user or individual citizen have to be combined with the long-term economic and ecological goals for the whole area.

According to Anne Spirn (1989, 1998), design should respond to the "deep structure" and "deep context" of the place. She defines *deep structure* as the fundamental geologic, hydrologic, and bioclimatic processes that form the landscape. *Deep context* is how these processes have interacted with culture through time to form the unique spatial characteristics of a place. Spirn's design theory is "based upon an understanding of nature and culture as comprising interwoven processes that exhibit a complex, underlying order that holds across vast scales of space and time" (1988, 108). The purpose of making designs a part of planning is to manifest an understanding of these fundamental processes and their capacity to accommodate change as well as to illuminate the underlying order so that it will be helpful in decision making. Design should make the interrelationships between natural and cultural processes and political choices less abstract. Design should make visible "natural processes and their temporal cycles," according to Spirn (1988, 108).

Designs may be presented in various formats. The design may involve individual site or land-user plans that form parts of the overall landscape plan. Examples of such specific designs are the farm and ranch conservation plans completed for individual land users by the U.S. Natural Resources Conservation Service. A design simulation may be done that compares the existing situation with various scenarios, such as one based on the landscape plan and one with no action, or one based on preservation versus another on development. There may be specific designs for new facilities to illustrate the implications of plan implementation. Such designs can be derived through charrettes or other public participatory techniques, and they may be done by landscape architects and architects. Demonstration projects can be built as prototypes to exemplify the consequences of the plan. Innovative design projects can also influence public policy. Ideas about sustainable design and the new urbanism are especially relevant to ecological planning. Two examples of specific landscape design will be presented here, one from the Connecticut River Valley in Massachusetts, and the other from the New York City region.

SITE DESIGN

Site design is concerned with the physical arrangement of the built and natural elements of a specific land parcel. A single house or group of houses, an office park, a commercial shopping center, or a combination of uses may be involved. Kevin Lynch and Gary Hack define *site planning* as "the art of arranging structures on the land and shaping the spacing between, an art linked to architecture, engineering, landscape architecture and city planning" (1984, 1). *Site design* may be viewed as the application of the planning process to a specific parcel of land. Kevin Lynch, who wrote the standard text on the topic, identified the eight stages of site planning proper as:

1. Defining the problem
2. Programming and the analysis of site and user
3. Schematic design and the preliminary cost estimate
4. Developed design and detailed costing
5. Contract documents
6. Bidding and contracting
7. Construction
8. Occupation and management (Lynch and Hack 1984, 11)

Lynch recognized this process as a standard organizing tool but one that seldom occurs in a step-by-step fashion. "Reciting these stages makes them sound logical and linear, but the recital is only conventional; the real process is looping and cyclical" (Lynch and Hack 1984, 11). Design, according to Lynch, is the "search for forms" that "deals with particular solutions" (Lynch and Hack 1984, 127). Lynch and Hack observe that "site design deals with three elements: the pattern of activity, the pattern of circulation, and the pattern of sensible form that supports them" (1984, 127).

The conventional Lynch site planning process has many strengths, but design is not part of broader planning concerns, except in its response to government restrictions, nor is the site linked to its larger context. Lynch wrote elsewhere about "the sense of the region," and Lynch and Hack mention "contextualism" in the third edition (1984) of Lynch's (1962) classic text on site planning, but the site is not viewed as part of a hierarchical organization.

One approach that does advocate a hierarchical perspective is "diagnosis and design," developed by planner John Raintree for agroforestry work in Africa and other tropical and subtropical places. It is a method for the diagnosis of land management problems and the design of solutions. Raintree bases his approach on a medical analogy, "Diagnosis should precede treatment" (1987, 4). The key features of a diagnosis and design approach, according to Raintree, are its flexibility, speed, and repetition.

In the diagnostic stage, the planner asks, "How does the system work?" (Raintree 1987, 6). Such questions inevitably lead the planner to view the site as part of a larger network of activities. The design stage then focuses on how to improve the system. Raintree's approach includes a regional reconnaissance, from which sites are selected for diagnosis and design. When conducting a diagnosis of a place, the planner conducts surveys, makes analyses, and identifies specifications for appropriate interventions. Design at the site level then represents appropriate interventions at the local level.

Agroforesters such as Raintree helped to create the foundation for sustainable design. The rise in interest in sustainability has coincided with the movement in architecture originally called *neotraditional town planning* and currently known as the *new urbanism.* The Ahwahnee principles (Table 1.4) provide helpful guidance for site design. The sustainable design evaluation checklist (Table 9.1) can also be helpful.

Timothy Beatley and Kristy Manning credit new urbanism with contributing much "to the critical dialogue and assessment of contemporary development patterns" (1997, 20). However, they argue that new urbanism "is not strongly environmental in orientation" (Beatley and Manning 1997, 21). Beatley and Manning offer ways to go beyond the new urbanism to create human places that are "restorative and regenerative" (1997, 22). Ecologically based design holds the prospect of being restorative, regenerative, and creative (Thompson and Steiner 1997).

Sketch for Rebstock Park in Frankfort, Germany by Laurie Olin. *(The Olin Partnership)*

INDIVIDUAL LAND-USER DESIGNS: FARM AND RANCH CONSERVATION PLANS

Farm and/or ranch conservation plans are an example of site-specific, land-user designs with a relatively long tradition in the United States. Farm-level conservation plans were first conceived during the 1930s to help farmers address soil erosion problems. For 50 years, these plans remained voluntary. In the early 1980s, states like Iowa and Wisconsin began to require such plans as prerequisites for certain types of financial benefits. Then, in 1985, the U.S. Congress passed conservation provisions requiring conservation plans on highly erodible land in order for landowners to remain eligible for federal agricultural programs.

TABLE 9.1
SUSTAINABLE DESIGN EVALUATION CHECKLIST

SUSTAINABLE	Completely	Partly	Neither	Partly	Completely	NOT SUSTAINABLE
Creates new permanent jobs						Reduces employment opportunities
Buildings and spaces are adaptable						Buildings and spaces are not adaptable
Provides educational opportunities						Reduced educational opportunities
Creates affordable human habitat						Destroys affordable human habitat
Reduces health risks						Increases health risks
Diminishes inequities						Increases inequities
Increases opportunities for social interaction						Reduces opportunities for social interaction
Enhances safety						Creates unsafe environments
Maximizes open space provision						Minimizes open space provision
Builds on local context						Disregards local context
Reduces stress (physical and psychological)						Increases stress
Beautiful						Destroys beauty
Diverse						Homogeneous
Remediates natural landscape						Degrades natural landscape
Creates purer air						Destroys pure air
Creates purer water						Destroys pure water
Uses rain water						Wastes rain water
Replenishes groundwater						Depletes groundwater
Produces its own food						Produces no food
Creates richer soil						Destroys rich soil
Uses solar energy						Wastes solar energy
Stores solar energy						Consumes fossil fuels
Creates silence						Destroys silence
Consumes its own wastes						Dumps waste unused
Maintains itself						Needs repair/cleaning
Matches nature's pace						Disregards nature's pace
Provides wildlife habitat						Destroys wildlife habitat
Moderates climate and weather						Intensifies climate
Increases use of renewable resources						Increases use of non-renewable resources
Uses local resources						Imports resources
Self-sufficient						Reliant on imports
Encourages walking/biking						Encourages automobile use
Encourages transit use						Encourages private automobile use
Reduces length of daily automobile trips						Increases length of daily automobile trips

SOURCE: Steiner et al. 1998, Pijawka et al. 2000.

The plans are prepared by NRCS conservationists with land users in cooperation with local conservation districts. A conservation plan involves a process parallel to the broader one being described in this book and with similarities to the approaches advocated by Lynch and Raintree. A conservation plan is a collection of information, an identification of erosion and other conservation problems, and the proposal of solutions. The planning principles, the elements of the planning process, and the data to be used in the plans are clearly outlined in the NRCS's *National Conservation Planning Manual.* The planning principles include close personal contact with farmers and ranchers, the use of interdisciplinary resource information, an open-ended planning process, and flexibility to local situations (U.S. Soil Conservation Service 1978; U.S. Natural Resources Conservation Service 1998).

According to the NRCS approach, site-level planning involves the pooled knowledge and experience of both the planner and the land user. It is stressed that there is "a direct and essential link between effective participation in planning and applying resource management systems on the land" (U.S. Soil Conservation Service 1978, 506–3). To accomplish this linkage, a process is suggested similar to the one presented in this book. The NRCS process consists of three phases and nine steps. The first phase, *collection and analysis,* includes problem and opportunity identification, the determination of objectives, the inventory of resources, and the analysis of resource data.

Phase 2 is *decision support* and involves the formulation of alternatives, the evaluation of alternatives, and the selection of alternatives. *Application and evaluation* is the focus of the final phase (U.S. Natural Resources Conservation Service 1998).

SIMULATION

Perspective drawings, artist's impressions, photography, three-dimensional models, and four-dimensional computer walk-throughs are some of the techniques that can be used to simulate the consequences of a plan. Drawings are used commonly to describe visual changes. A sequence of sketches can be used to show the existing conditions, the consequences of current trends, and the potential outcomes of various interventions (see the discussion of the Connecticut River Valley and the New York City region later in this chapter). Computers can be used to produce perspective drawings or to montage a drawing into a photograph. There are various ways to manipulate photographs to illustrate the consequences of an action, including photomontage and photoretouching. Three-dimensional models can be built that graphically display before-and-after situations. Videotape or film may be used to give people a ground-level view of those models over time (Ortolano 1984, 1997).

In its 1988 state development and redevelopment plan, the New Jersey State Planning Commission used drawings to illustrate its regional design system. The regional design system attempts to link communities into networks by redistributing "regional growth from sprawling settlement patterns into a variety of relatively compact, mixed-use communities" (New Jersey State Planning Commission 1988, 45).

The New Jersey regional design system has three components. The first part is a five-level hierarchy of central places: cities, corridor centers, towns, villages, and hamlets. Transportation corridors form the second component, and the land surrounding the central places the third part. The New Jersey State Planning Commission has developed a series of strategies and policies to direct growth to the central places and away from the surrounding areas and to manage the development of transportation corridors. Community design plans, which include site design criteria and design review procedures, are to be used by the state, counties, and municipalities. The consequences of this regional design system were illustrated with drawings simulating existing conditions (Figure 9.1), trends (Figure 9.2), and the implemented plan (Figure 9.3) (New Jersey State Planning Commission 1988).

CONCEPTUAL DESIGN FROM CHARRETTES

Charrettes are fertile sources for design ideas. The Sonoran North Land Use Character Charrette (discussed in Chapters 6 and 7) produced design ideas for four land-use character types. For example, the charrette raised as many questions as it answered about suburban desert development in the north Sonoran Desert. How much suburban development can the landscape absorb? At what point does the Sonoran Desert cease to exist? How well does native desert wildlife mix with suburban development? What species of wildlife should be retained and how? Can more water be retained on-site during storms? What is the "southwestern lifestyle?" How can a sense of community be created? What are the long-term costs to the city for providing services and maintaining the infrastructure required to accommodate suburban development? Are these costs more or less than the overall benefits? In light of the fact that inner city neighborhoods are in need of

FIGURE 9.1 Simulated existing conditions. *(Source: New Jersey State Planning Commission, Communities of Place: The Preliminary State Development and Redevelopment Plan for the State of New Jersey 1988, Vol. 2)*

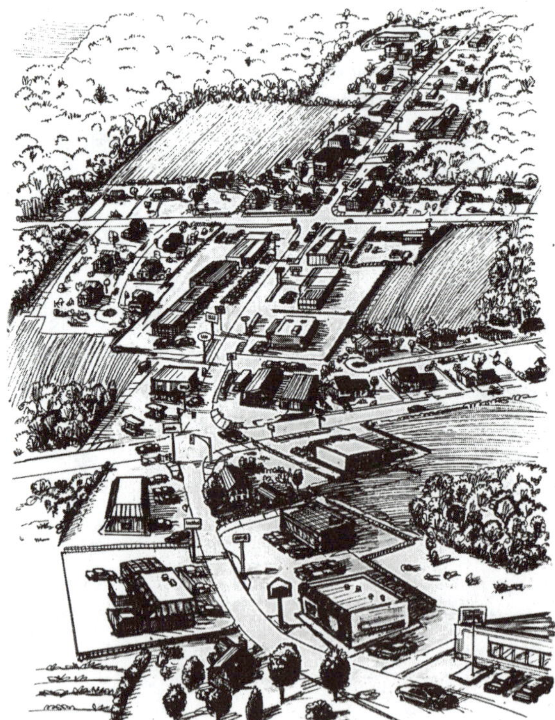

FIGURE 9.2 Simulated trends. *(Source: New Jersey State Planning Commission, Communities of Place: The Preliminary State Development and Redevelopment Plan for the State of New Jersey 1988, Vol. 2)*

FIGURE 9.3 Simulated consequences of the regional design system. *(Source: New Jersey State Planning Commission, Communities of Place: The Preliminary State Development and Redevelopment Plan for the State of New Jersey 1988, Vol. 2)*

repair and improvement, are new suburban developments a wise use of the relatively pristine Sonoran Desert? How does automobile-oriented suburban development impact traffic, noise, and air quality?

The issue of suburban development and whether it fits the landscape is often defined solely in terms of density. Lower densities are thought to cause fewer negative environmental impacts than higher densities. However, this may not always be the case—especially if the overall density of the site (gross density) is being compared with the density of development on only a portion of the site. For example, a certain number of large lots spread out over the entire site may result in a greater impact on the environment than an equal number of small lots clustered on one portion of the site. Therefore, development plans must be evaluated by weighing the impacts on the environment and not by measuring the size of the lots being proposed by the developer.

For example, Figure 9.4 illustrates an open space system based on desert washes. The idea was to use the wash structure to provide a framework for development. Figure 9.5 is a second sketch from the charrette illustrating this design in greater detail. A third charrette drawing (Figure 9.6) contrasted the current suburban pattern with a more sensitive option. The more sensitive design protected more natural areas by narrowing roads and placing buildings closer to the streets. New houses were also kept below the existing tree canopy, and only native plants were used.

The overall charrette process generated development characters for various densities. Diversity of density is advocated for the Desert View Tri-Villages Area. Desert suburban development is viewed as one density along with higher densities in the growth corridor to lower densities in rural areas and no development in the preserves. However, the character envisioned for suburban development is different than the existing patterns. A desert suburban character is suggested, one where new communities fit the Sonoran landscape.

In 1997, David Pijawka and the author received a Sustainable Development Challenge Grant from EPA.* As part of that grant, they organized two charrettes with an interdisciplinary team of ASU faculty, design and planning practitioners, and graduate students in environmental planning. Bill Kasson and John Blair played vital roles as project manager and senior research associate, respectively (Pijawka et al. 2000).

*Portions of this section were adapted from Steiner et al. 1998 and Pijawka et al. 2000.

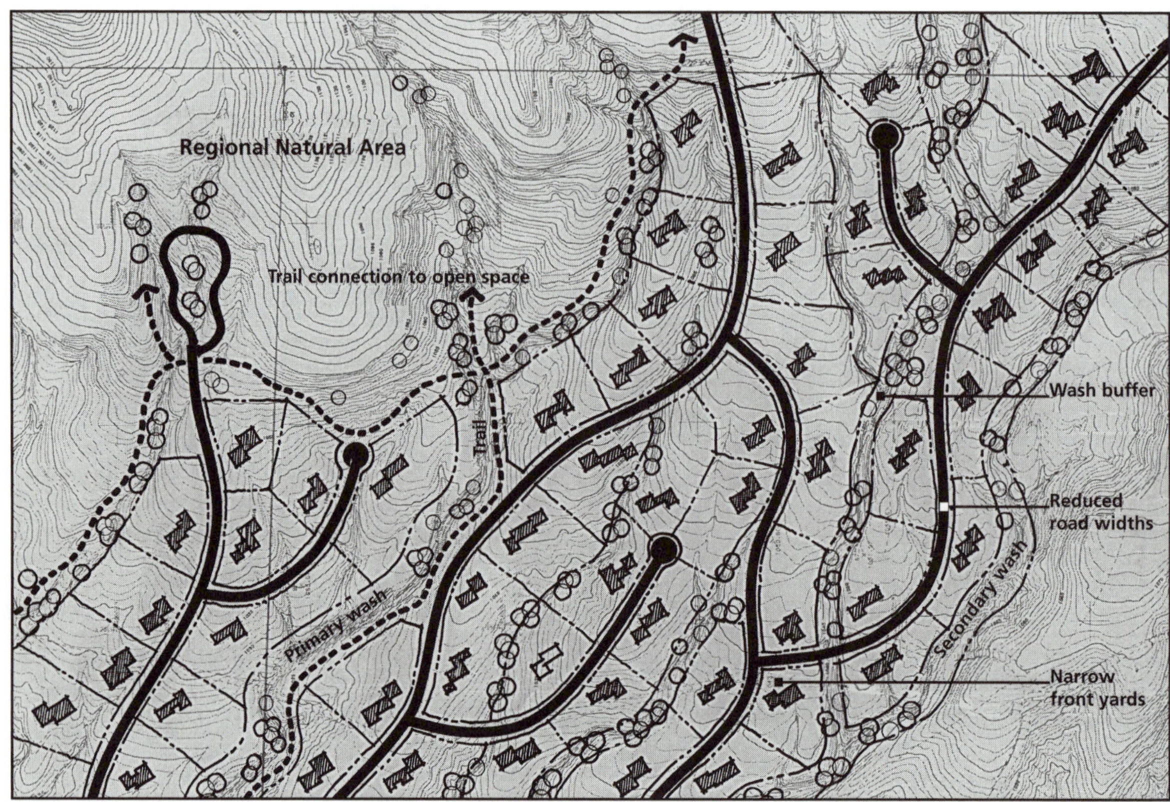

FIGURE 9.4 Open-space system based on desert washes.

La Lomita Charrette

The first charrette was held in November 1997 and addressed a 180-acre (73-hectare) vacant site near downtown Phoenix called La Lomita (Ingley 1998). The La Lomita site lies near the center of the Phoenix metropolitan area. The Arizona State Land Department owns the property and is constitutionally charged with obtaining the highest possible price for its sale or lease. The land department is also obligated to oversee the disposition of archeological resources known to exist on the site. The land was under cultivation into the 1970s and the surrounding area has long acted as the transition zone between residential uses to the north and the historic stockyards and present-day industrial uses to the south. The site is less than one mile from Phoenix Sky Harbor International Airport, is bisected by one of the region's major freeways, and is less than one-half mile (0.805 kilometer) from one of Phoenix's primary village core areas. Development of that core is anticipated in the near future (Pijawka et al. 2000).

Common Themes from the La Lomita Charrette

The participants at the charrette came up with four designs for the La Lomita site. Although each design was distinct, several similarities

FIGURE 9.5 Wash corridor as open-space system.

emerged among the four designs (Figures 9.7 and 9.8). Each scheme dedicated the northern portion of the site as residential/retail space with a fairly high density, while the southern portion—with its limited road access and proximity to the Phoenix Sky Harbor International Airport—was designated as light industrial and office space. A significant archeological site was left undeveloped and provided open space and educational opportunities. Other important themes identified by each of the groups included suggestions for building codes, community gardens, housing, and solar energy.

Building Codes. Existing city zoning and building codes are not conducive to sustainable development. For example, live/work systems, large community garden plots, mixed density, many solar options, narrow unpaved lanes, and graywater use—all characteristic of a sustainable development environment—are not permitted under the current code. One strategy for creating a sus-

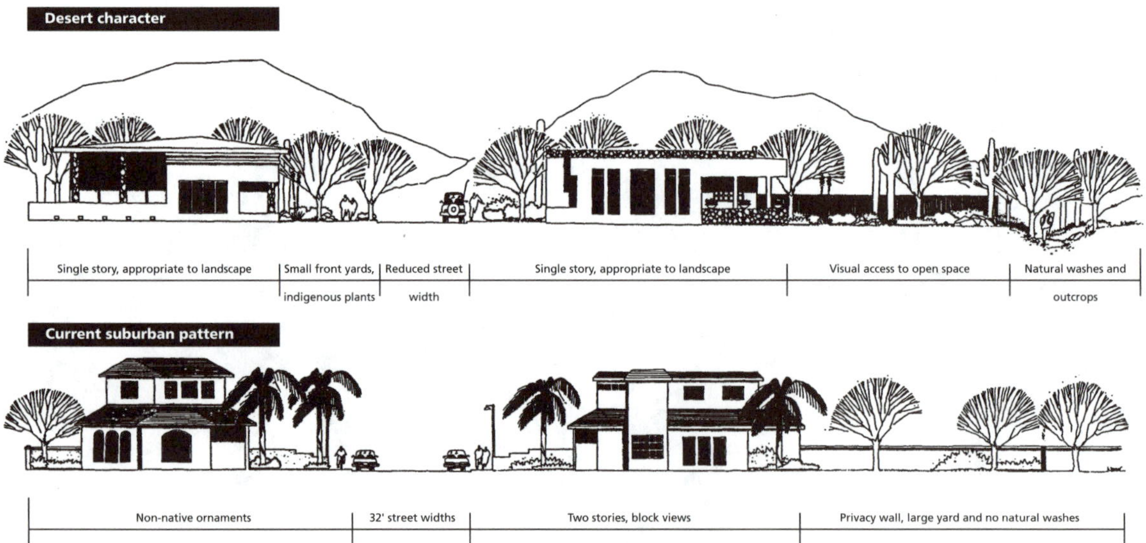

FIGURE 9.6 Comparison of current suburban pattern to one integrated with the desert.

tainable neighborhood would be to permit developers a one-time-demonstration waiver on certain codes. Such a demonstration could help city officials determine the feasibility of changing existing codes.

Community Gardens. Community gardens are active green spaces which serve many neighborhood and environmental purposes. Because they are occupied by those planting, harvesting, and maintaining the plants and the land, they are not attractive to criminals. Gardens provide a retreat for residents. They enable residents to grow their own food and use their own compost. Gardens are sustainable.

Housing Possibilities. A variety of mid- and high-density housing possibilities emerged from the charrette teams. Live/work areas were designated in each design. Multistory buildings with solar collectors and seasonal shading with appropriate plantings were explored, as were various loft, flat, and in-law arrangements. A variety of densities were recommended to eliminate a feeling of being too crowded, and to integrate a greater variety of income groups, ages, races, and genders.

Solar Energy. Solar energy presents a great natural opportunity in the Phoenix metropolitan area, like many other regions. Solar collection influences the siting of buildings. Natural day-

FIGURE 9.7 La Lomita design concept for an integrated living and working environment. *(Drawn by Bruce Kimball)*

FIGURE 9.8 La Lomita design concept for plaza and canal. *(Drawn by Bruce Kimball)*

lighting also presents opportunities for minimizing energy use (Pijawka et al. 2000).

Arroyo Vista Charrette

The second EPA sustainability charrette was conducted in February 1998 on a suburban fringe site in north Scottsdale, near the Desert View Tri-Villages Area. The 1000-acre (405-hectare) site was called Arroyo Vista. As with the Tri-Villages and La Lomita sites, a thorough ecological inventory and analysis was conducted prior to the char-

Dancing Walls Sculpture Garden in Sante Fe, New Mexico. *(Designed by Clair Reiniger; photograph by Benjamin T. Rogers)*

rette. The site was selected for contrast with the La Lomita parcel and because it is typical of the areas experiencing the most intense development pressure in the Phoenix metropolitan region.

Most of the research team and the charrette participants would have preferred that no development occur on the Arroyo Vista site. However, that was unrealistic because the site was surrounded on all sides by development and was zoned for light industrial, commercial, and residential use. The team developed a list of goals and objectives for the charrette (Table 9.2).

For each design objective in Table 9.2, the team developed ideas in advance to stimulate thought and discussion among the charrette participants. These were:

1. Ecological integrity
   Density: Either clustering or dispersion can serve to preserve/protect ecological health, depending on ecological priorities.
   Open space: Enhance the natural ecological features of the site by preserving natural drainage, washes, desert biodiversity, topographic patterns, and linkages to the regional open space system.
   Circulation: Use low impact, permeable materials for road, foot, and bike networks; avoid interrupting wildlife corridors; design with the topography; use circulation to deemphasize car reliance.
   Land use: Avoid land uses that have negative ecological impacts; implement mixed uses that allow for codependent resource use between businesses and households; employ design that aesthetically, structurally, and functionally harmonizes with the surrounding desert environment.
   Building materials: Use environmentally responsible materials and construction processes.
2. Energy
   Density: Use density to reduce trip loads within the sites, provide efficient and

TABLE 9.2
CHARRETTE GOAL AND OBJECTIVES

Goal:

To demonstrate how sustainable design contributes to better neighborhood and community living.

Objectives:

1. In the context of comprehensive neighborhood development, produce building and landscape archetypes that serve as models and prototypes for sustainable design.
2. Demonstrate how thoughtful, sensitive, and innovative design principles address issues of environmental sustainability.
3. Demonstrate the value of a highly participatory and interdisciplinary design process.
4. Integrate elements that contribute to sense of place, respond to context, and improve the quality of life that are consistent with the larger social, economic, and ecological principles of sustainable design.
5. Use the charrette results as an educational tool to inform the greater public and development community.
6. Disseminate and evaluate the charrette results to contribute to dialogue, debate, and discussion at future public forums.
7. Establish a common dialogue regarding sustainability among citizens, municipal officials, academia, and the development community.

Design Objectives:

1. *Ecological integrity:* Retain the desert ecosystem, allowing for maximum systemic cohesion wherever possible.
2. *Energy:* Reduce energy consumption per capita, by capitalizing on the natural energy resources available in the desert Southwest by using passive and active design and technology.
3. *Water use/quality:* Recognize the necessity for reduced water consumption per capita in the desert setting, as well as the maintenance/improvement of total water quality.
4. *Waste:* Minimize waste through structural, individual, household, community, and systemic output reduction.
5. *Sense of community/context:* Identify and celebrate the historical, physical, social, and natural elements that construct/inform/influence desert sites.

SOURCE: Steiner et al. 1998

affordable public transit for external trips. Density also reduces total albedo, allows for shared spaces such that residents become more interdependent and can share more resources.
Circulation: Minimize walking/transport distances between residential/commercial and public facilities; provide multiple options to automobile transportation.
Land use: Structural orientation, use of alternative energy sources, natural lighting, and shared spaces can contribute significantly to total energy reduction.

3. Water use/quality
   Density: Reduces total acreage requiring irrigation; allows potential for efficient community graywater system. Consider implementation of on-site waste water treatment/recycling plant (constructed wetlands) and groundwater replenishment.
   Open space: Permits climatic desert habitat, accesses regional viewsheds. Do not permit invasive vegetative species that may demand greater water supplies.
   Land use: Implement low-flow fixtures.
4. Waste
   Density: Allow for shared resources such as community composting/gardens/recycling; higher densities may reduce total construction waste.
   Open space: The more native and natural an area, the less waste produced.
   Circulation: Options to automobiles reduce total air pollution. Strategic neighborhood layout, with accessible central business/job node, allows for multiple tasks to be carried out efficiently, reducing driving time and pollution.
   Land use: Use local, recyclable building materials; build structures for 100+ year life cycles that are adaptive to multiple uses; incorporate businesses that utilize wastes and byproducts from one another.
5. Sense of community/context
   Density: Can facilitate social interaction, social variation, "eyes on the street," and community sufficiency.
   Open space: Public areas, common spaces, parks, and sports facilities create identity, sense of place, context, interaction, and aesthetic experiences.
   Circulation: Develop networks that foster contact and chance encounters, and that allow residents to appreciate their local surroundings.
   Land use: Reduce setbacks for greater sense of "familiarity;" build a community center; provide local jobs; design in styles that are appropriate to the desert landscape and qualities; consider street scale to generate security, enclosure, and safety (adapted from Pijawka et al. 2000).

The Arroyo Vista site is a parcel of relatively undisturbed desert land on the northeastern perimeter of greater Phoenix. Urban development from Scottsdale and Phoenix is rapidly approaching from the south and southwest. While the desert on the site is relatively pristine, in recent years the site has been surrounded on the north, west, and south sides by residential development of both suburban and low-density rural character. The site is bisected by two major desert washes and is home to typical Sonoran Desert flora and fauna (Pijawka et al. 2000). Several common themes emerged at the charrette for the Arroyo Vista site (Figures 9.9 and 9.10).

As with the La Lomita charrette, four designs were prepared. Each design sought to maintain the integrity of the wash system as a part of a unique and threatened ecosystem. Road systems avoid the washes, while trails are separated from the most sensitive areas. Most designs tried to minimize automobile use by providing alternative paths for walking and bicycling. Alternative road surfaces were advocated to match the natural albedo, enhance groundwater replenishment, and slow traffic.

FIGURE 9.9 Arroyo Vista design concept for a megastructure inspired by Paolo Soleri. *(Drawn by Bruce Kimball)*

Higher densities were concentrated in the western and northern portions of the Arroyo Vista site. Mixed-use and clustered development were used to reduce automobile reliance and achieve energy savings. Lower-density, single-family residences were located in the southern and eastern parts of the site to blend with adjacent neighborhoods. Building orientations were planned to take advantage of the area's abundant sunlight. Solar collection, natural daylighting, and shading were factors considered in developing building (Pijawka et al. 2000).

CONCEPTUAL DESIGN OF NEW FACILITIES

To illustrate the impact of the plan on the landscape, it may be helpful to design new facilities. In the Palouse region of eastern Washington and northern Idaho, the area connecting Pullman and Moscow had been recognized as a "light industrial opportunity area" in the 1978 county comprehen-

FIGURE 9.10 Arroyo Vista design concept for a transit stop. *(Drawn by Bruce Kimball)*

sive plan. Because Washington State University was located in Pullman and the University of Idaho in Moscow, there were also strong demands on the 10-mile (16.09-kilometer) corridor for transportation and recreational use. There are also established goals in the region and state for the conservation of soil and water resources as well as the protection of environmentally sensitive areas. The design of a new facility—a recreational path—was used to show how all these conflicting goals could be achieved. Planner Dennis Canty and landscape architect Christine Carlson from the National Park Service cooperated with local citizens, elected officials, and county, city, and university planners in 1986 to prepare such a design.*

The Concept Design

There were two major interests in the design of the path. The first was to provide a safe, attractive recreational link between the communities of Pullman and Moscow. The second was to conserve the natural and cultural features in the corridor area between the two communities. The concept design that follows was developed directly from these interests by Canty, Carlson, Washington State University faculty, and the local residents.

The central element of the concept is a pathway designed to meet recreation and conservation needs that physically links Pullman and Moscow and is the backbone of a broader enhancement program for the local landscape. The path is a way for the community as a whole to assume responsibility for the shape and quality of the corridor area between Pullman and Moscow.

The basic ingredients of the concept plan are design components of the path—the function, form, and character it manifests as it passes through the landscape. To be successful, any path must flow from place to place, and sometimes back again, in a continuous manner, like a stream or river. It must connect places with each other. And it must begin some place and end somewhere else; it must have a clear origin and destination and provide a strong sense of direction. These characteristics—continuity, connection, and an origin and destination—are fundamental to the development of any path. The function, form, and character of the path are the physical means by which these intrinsic requirements are met (Carlson and Canty 1986).

The Palouse path was to have a variety of functions. It was to be used for safe transportation and recreation and for fostering understanding of the intricate relationships between the natural and cultural resources of the Palouse landscape. The path was to capture the ambiance of the Palouse and present it in ways that are interesting, educational, and satisfying for all who use the Pullman-Moscow corridor.

The implementation of the concept plan is divided into two phases that develop the function, form, and character of the path. Phase 1 provides a response to the immediate need for safe travel for bicyclists and, consequently, motorists between Pullman and Moscow. It also establishes a physical and planning framework for future development of the path. Phase 2 supplements the development actions of Phase 1. It outlines options for more extensive, formalized development and for use by a broader constituency of users. The following sections review how the function, form, and character of the path are developed in each phase.

Phase 1. Important features of Phase 1 are the incorporation of the path into existing circulation patterns, the development of roadside recreation sites and conservation areas, and the promotion of safe transportation for bicyclists between Pullman and Moscow by upgrading bicycle use areas.

The emphasis in Phase 1 is on upgrading bicycle use on all established routes in the corridor area (Figure 9.11). These roads are an integrated transportation network between Pullman and

*This section has been adapted from Carlson and Canty 1986, and Carlson et al. 1989.

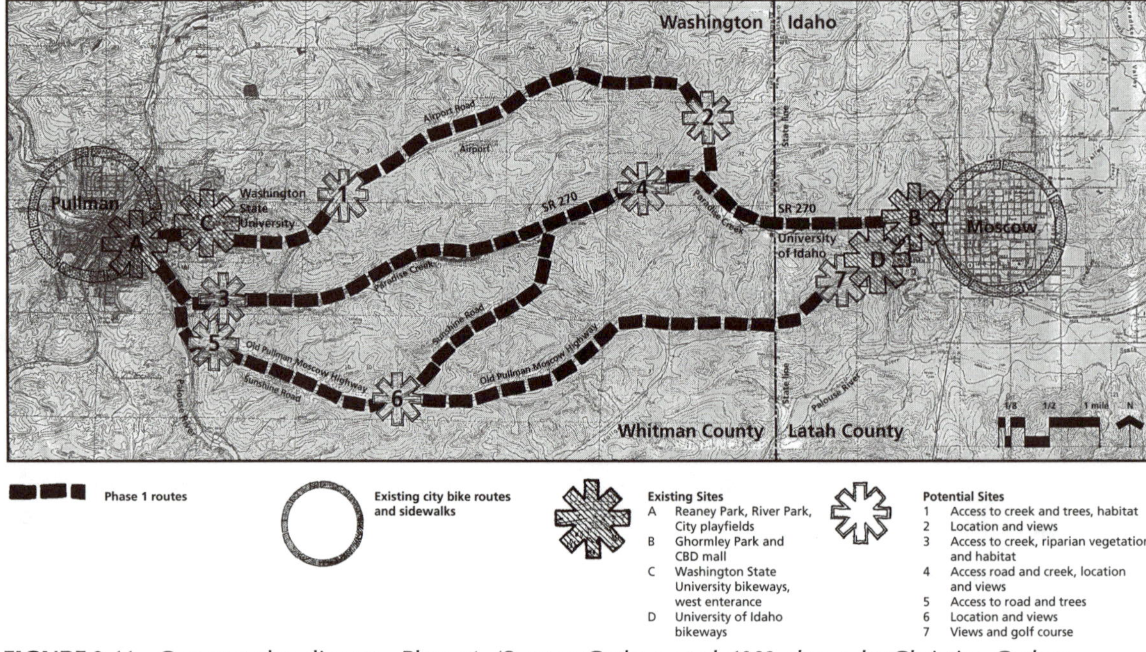

FIGURE 9.11 Concept plan diagram, Phase 1. *(Source: Carlson et al. 1989, drawn by Christine Carlson and Dennis Canty)*

Moscow that fits the landscape. In general, they wind through lowlands and stream valleys and, with the exception of state highways 270 and 8 (the Pullman-Moscow highway), are narrow and quiet. Because of the proximity and predominance of agriculture, these roads are also the primary means of experiencing the landscape. Various wildlife and plant communities populate the roadsides, and long views of distant forests and ridges are often visible from the open-road corridors. Consequently, local roads are used heavily by bicyclists, joggers, and pedestrians for recreation and commuting. However, roads are often unsafe because of narrow shoulders, visual obstructions, and consistently heavy traffic along the Pullman-Moscow highway. Improvements to road shoulders and road surfaces, formal designation of bike routes and scenic and/or recreation routes by cities, counties, and state departments of transportation, and frequent placement of signs and pavement markings will be used to ensure safe use of roads by recreationists (Figure 9.12). The cities of Pullman and Moscow and Washington State University and the University of Idaho have designated corridors that could unite the Palouse path with city parks and other facilities, schools, and the downtown business districts.

Sites 1 through 7 on Figure 9.11 indicate places for potential development as small roadside rest stops, gathering places, safe pullouts for picnicking, bike maintenance, or relaxation, and conservation areas. Each site is defined by important and interesting natural and cultural features in the corridor area, such as distinct riparian zones, access to Paradise Creek (a tributary of the Palouse River), and pleasant views of attractive farmsteads and distant ridges that can enhance the recreational and visual character of the path as it moves between Pullman and Moscow. Each site also provides recreationists with an opportunity to

FIGURE 9.12 Phase 1 bicycle standards for highway width and traffic controls. *(Source: Carlson et al. 1989, drawn by Christine Carlson)*

understand complex interrelationships that make up the landscape and the need to protect them. Site designs could combine conservation measures, such as supplemental plantings to buffer existing habitat and plant communities, with other site detailing to protect the resources while simultaneously allowing contact with them (Figure 9.13).

The Pullman-Moscow corridor will come under increasing land-use pressures in the coming years as demand for recreational, agricultural, commercial, industrial, and residential uses increases. Without a concerted effort to resolve the demands of competing users, land-use conflicts will increase, and air and water quality, wildlife habitat, and the visual character of the corridor will be degraded. The Phase 1 path provides an opportunity to establish a program of locally administered design and planning standards to separate and buffer adjacent uses. The standards could emphasize setbacks, vegetative and topographic buffers, provisions for safe vehicle access, and control of

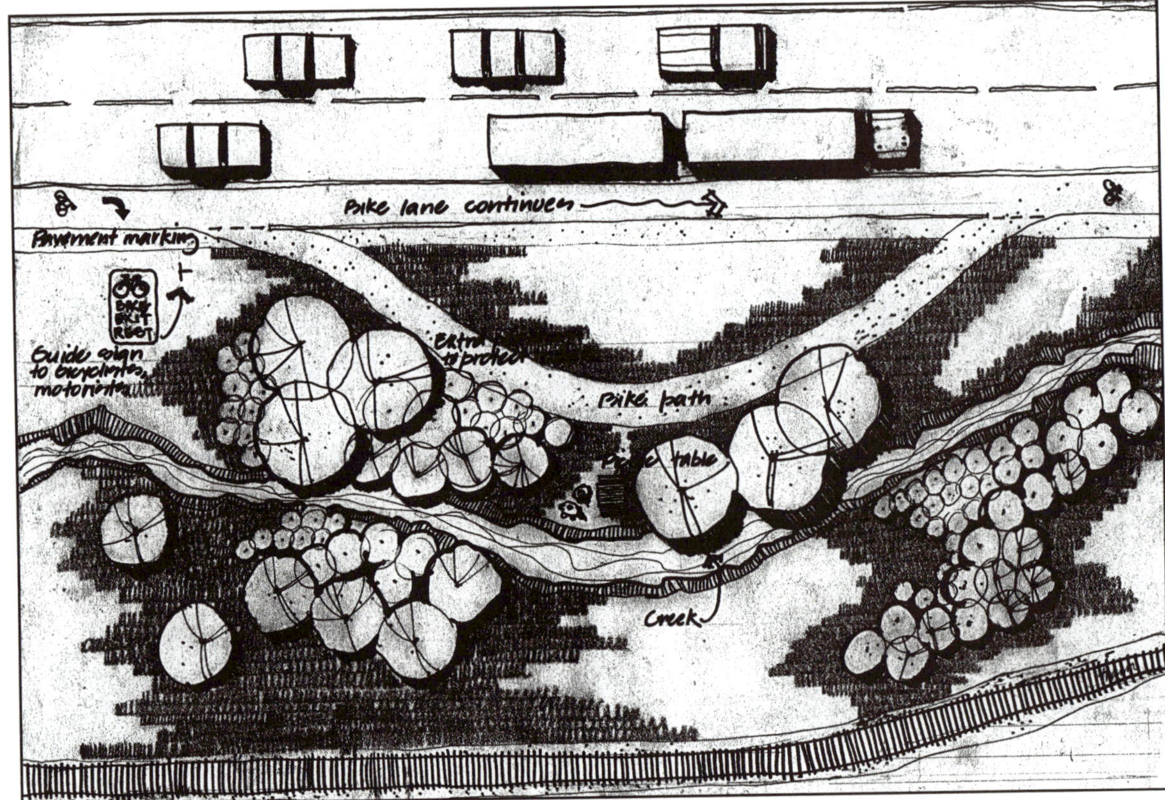

FIGURE 9.13 Typical roadside rest stop. *(Source: Carlson et al. 1989, drawn by Christine Carlson)*

noise and water contamination. With sensitive siting and the use of such standards, the continued use and development of the corridor need not be at the expense of its quality (Figure 9.14).

Phase 2. The purpose of Phase 2 is to broaden the function, form, and character of the path from a linear transportation corridor to an intensive recreation and conservation greenbelt between Pullman and Moscow. An abandoned railbed is adapted for the path. More formalized settings for recreation are developed. Along with bicyclists and joggers, walkers, hikers, motorists, and others use the path for recreation. Upon completion of Phase 2, the path will be a highly designed facility that meets all the priorities established by the local task force organized for the project.

The concept design diagram for Phase 2 (Figure 9.15) and Figures 9.16 and 9.17 present one of many options for intensive path development. Although the same sites are reserved for development in Phase 2 as in Phase 1, they take on a greater, more developed recreation function. A simple rest stop in Phase 1 might become a small streamside park in Phase 2 with picnic tables, pathways to and from the creek, and interpretive signs describing small mammal and bird habitats in the park. Sites could be expanded into county or state parks in the corridor area with highly developed facilities. As these sites are developed,

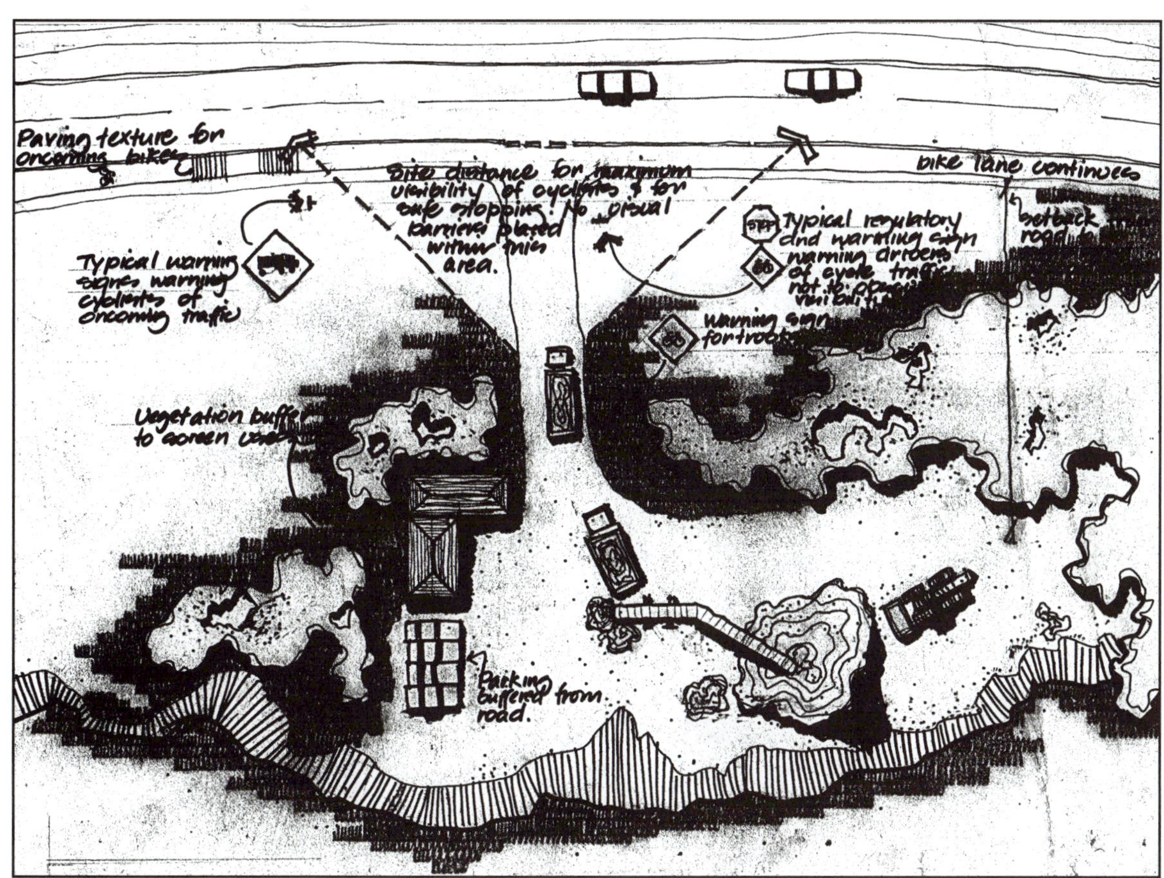

FIGURE 9.14 Typical standards for safe vehicle access, setbacks, and vegetation buffers. *(Source: Carlson et al. 1989, drawn by Christine Carlson)*

the path becomes a means of linking them together, and the sites themselves become more important components of the concept plan.

In Phase 2, the path connects a variety of park-like settings. These sites are a backdrop for recreation activities, such as interpretation of physical features or elements belonging to the cultural development of the corridor area. For example, interpretive signs could be located near riparian zones to explain the nature of their habitats and the composition of their plant communities. The site can be arranged to focus views on a historic farm or scenic landscape and can include displays describing its significance. Through its alignment, the path itself can be interpretive, directing users to important features or moving them past others.

The path moves along and off the road, connecting sites that feature access to Paradise Creek, dense clusters of willow or hawthorn, and wildlife habitats. Flexibility in path alignment and the rich resources available create many opportunities to include conservation as an important path function. The path can move people away from fragile habitats. It can buffer native plant communities and protect stream banks with

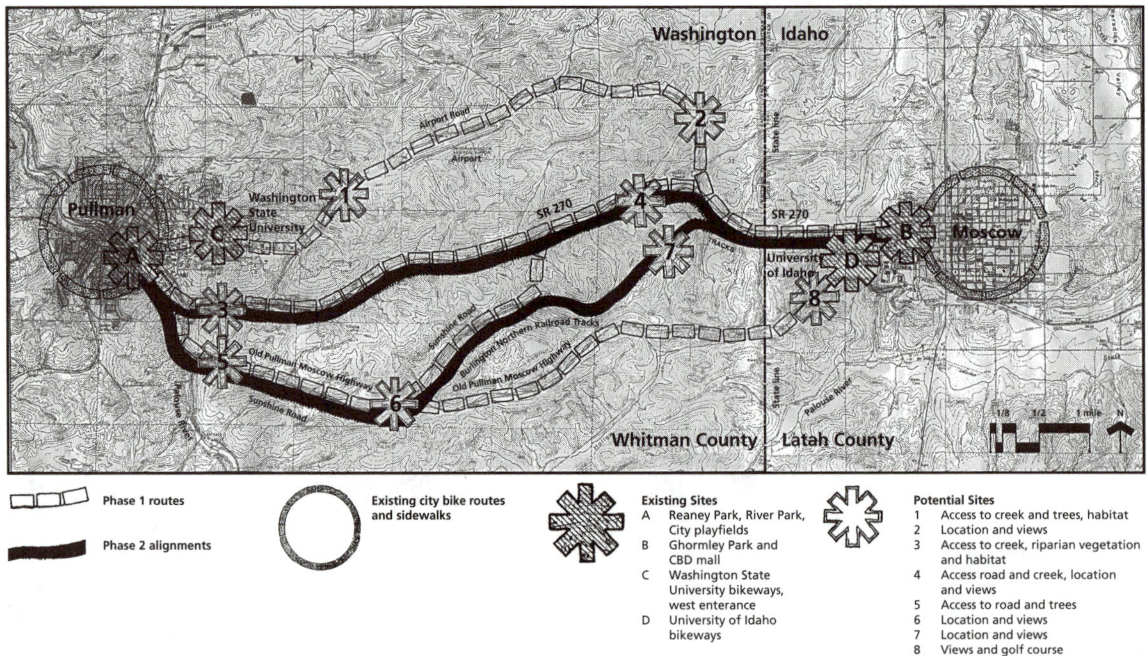

FIGURE 9.15 Concept plan diagram, Phase 2. *(Source: Carlson et al. 1989, drawn by Christine Carlson)*

design features that include special planting schemes and bank fortification measures. In conjunction with the development of interpretive features, it can educate users about the protection of the landscape.

The form of the path in Phase 2 is complex. Unlike the simple linear alignment and basic form of the Phase 1 path, the Phase 2 path alternatively follows roadways, railbeds, and features in the landscape. In shape and materials, it becomes a separate and formal feature in the corridor area. Finally, it is no longer simply a line between the two communities of Pullman and Moscow but a link between several formal gathering places along the way. The character of Phase 2 begins with the best of the natural and cultural features of the corridor area and adds an extra ingredient, that of people entering, using, and enjoying the Palouse landscape.

Summary of the Concept Design

Phase 1 of the concept design secures a safe route for commuters and recreationists between Pullman and Moscow. It establishes a recreation route through the corridor area at minimal costs, using the existing planning structure. It provides a practical means for directing changes in land uses that accommodate growth and development and preserve the visual quality and natural resources of the often politically controversial corridor area. Finally, it sets the stage for more intensive development of the pathway.

Phase 2 completes the concept plan. It supplements the development of Phase 1 with highly designed, expanded parks and recreation sites for many user groups. It changes the role of the path from that of a transportation link between Pullman and Moscow to that of a link between the

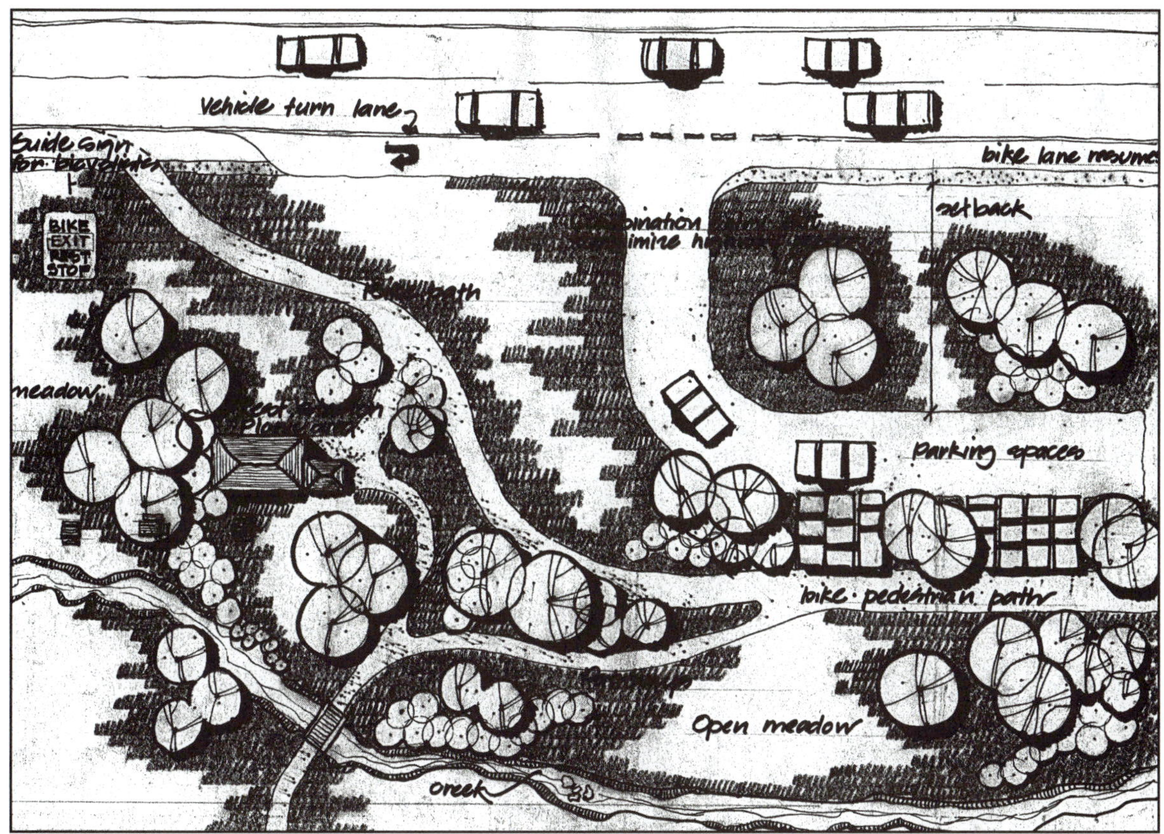

FIGURE 9.16 Phase 2 typical roadside park. *(Source: Carlson et al. 1989, drawn by Christine Carlson)*

two communities. Along with performance standards, it forms the nucleus for future land uses.

The conceptual design for the path was warmly embraced by the local community. In particular, local activist Nancy Mack and other members of the Pullman Civic Trust championed the path concept and lobbied tirelessly for its implementation. Federal law allowed for rail-to-trail conversion. Mack and her colleagues convinced the three railroad companies transiting the area to combine their service on one line, thus freeing parts of the rights of way for trail usage. A 1993 federal grant provided $900,000 toward the overall project. The City of Pullman, Whitman County, and the private sector were to come up with another $450,000. Eventually more than $525,000 was raised through donations. Significant donations were made by Carol Chipman, whose husband had been killed in an automobile accident (Caraher 1998). In the spring of 1998—some twelve years after the conceptual design and with much continued planning—the Bill Chipman Palouse Trail opened.

DEMONSTRATION PROJECTS

Conceptual designs may remain just that—paper images illustrating how the plan can be realized.

FIGURE 9.17 Conceptual sketch of Phase 2 pathway. *(Source: Carlson et al. 1989, drawn by Christine Carlson)*

FIGURE 9.18 Typical urban street design for West Colfax Avenue. *(Source: City of Lakewood 1988a, drawn by Roger Wadnal)*

Such designs may or may not actually be built. A more concrete way to show the realization of the plan is to construct a demonstration project. One of the ugliest of America's ugly commercial strips is Colfax Avenue, which passes through Aurora, Denver, and Lakewood, Colorado. As a section of U.S. Route 40, Colfax Avenue was formerly part of one of the major east-west routes in the nation. After the completion of Interstate 70, the road began a steady economic and aesthetic decline.

In 1988, in response to goals established in its comprehensive plan, the city of Lakewood adopted design guidelines for West Colfax Avenue (City of Lakewood 1988a). The guidelines included design standards for urban and suburban streets (see Figures 9.18 and 9.19). Specific guidelines were included for street trees and other plantations, sidewalks, curbs, and building setbacks. The planners also established standards for building height and scale, building design, pedestrian access, site design, signage, lighting, and parking.

Further, the city together with local business leaders undertook the West Colfax Pedestrian Improvement Demonstration Project, which involved a four-block area. The project included both public and private improvements. The city provided street trees and plantations plus improved sidewalks, curbs and gutters, pedestrian seating areas, street furniture, and lighting. Utilities were also relocated underground to reduce the visual clutter of overhead wires. Business owners improved building facades, signage, parking lots, and the general character of the site (City of Lakewood 1988b). The project was intended to demonstrate the implications of the recommendations in the design guidelines. As a result of the project, Lakewood planners were able to provide before-and-after images of Colfax Avenue (Figure 9.20). The demonstration project illustrated to business owners, citizens, and local officials the ramifications of the city goals for economic revitalization and for the redevelopment of strip commercial areas. Subsequent Colfax Avenue and Lakewood planning efforts built on these demonstration efforts (see, for example, City of Lakewood 1997). A 1993 revitalization plan for West Colfax Avenue, prepared jointly by Lakewood and Denver, incorporated many of the

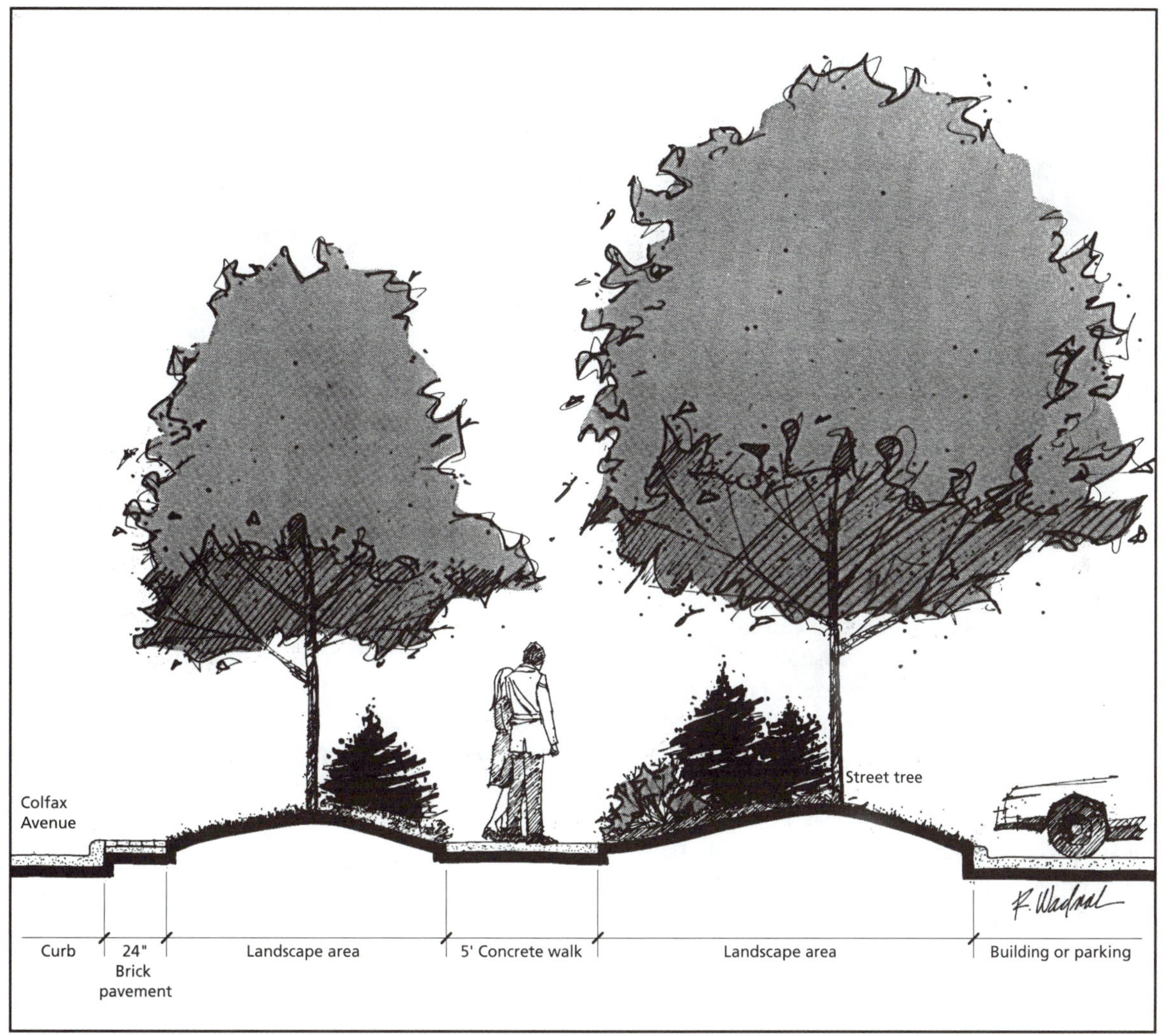

FIGURE 9.19 Typical suburban street design for West Colfax Avenue, Lakewood, Colorado. *(Source: City of Lakewood 1988a, drawn by Roger Wadnal)*

ideas from the demonstration design (City of Lakewood and City and County of Denver 1993).

In another demonstration project, in 1995 the Arizona Public Service sought to provide an example of energy efficiency, water conservation, appropriate building materials, and sustainable design. As a result, the Phoenix Environmental Showcase Home was designed by Eddie Jones of Jones Studio (Figure 9.21). As David Pijawka and Kim Shetter observed, "in addition to saving energy, water, and materials, the home is designed to create less pollution than a standard production home does, from the manufacture of the construction materials to the final walk-through and beyond" (1995, 3).

FIGURE 9.20 West Colfax pedestrian improvement demonstration project—before and after. *(Source: City of Lakewood 1988b)*

The Environmental Showcase Home was designed and built as a demonstration of sustainable design. Many people interested in principles of sustainability visit the house. In the book documenting the design and construction process, Pijawka and Shetter (1995) extended the process to the next logical step: the design of a prototypical subdivision (Figure 9.22). Architect Michael Underhill laid out the subdivision featuring appropriate solar orientation and a mix of densities.

FIGURE 9.21 Environmental Showcase Home designed by Eddie Jones. *(Source: Pijawka and Shetter 1995; photograph by Scot Zimmerman, courtesy of Arizona Public Service)*

INNOVATIVE DESIGN PROJECTS

Architects and landscape architects can provide visionary concepts that can influence the detailed designs of others. The Sonoran region of the southwestern United States and northwestern Mexico has long been a spawning ground for innovative urban visions. The Hohokam, "those who have disappeared," built a thriving, dispersed civilization in what is now Phoenix, Arizona from A.D. 300 to 1450. They "disappeared" for unknown reasons, but the remnants of their canal system provided the basis for the one that allowed the current Phoenix to rise from the ashes of the Sonoran Desert heat. Frank Lloyd Wright's vision for a Broadacre City was conceived in the Midwest prairies but hatched at Taliesin West in what is now Scottsdale, Arizona. In contrast to Wright's dispersed organicism, Paolo Soleri advocates a nation of "organic" mile-high megastructures. Soleri's prototype, Arcosanti, continues to be built in central Arizona, while to the south, near Tucson, Biosphere II presents yet another vision for future settlement.

Broadacre City represents one vision of an organic, living city, and Wright's model is strikingly similar in several respects to present-day

FIGURE 9.22 Prototype sustainable neighborhood designed by Michael Underhill. *(Source: Pijawka and Shetter 1995, courtesy of Arizona Public Service)*

Phoenix. According to Peter Rowe, in Wright's proposal "there was an insistence on regional authenticity and meaningful functional integration that we might do well to practice today, together with a regard for both buildings and land as being parts of a more general and significant landscape" (1995, 50).

Wright's erstwhile protégé Paolo Soleri has suggested an alternative urban vision in Arizona. Like Wright, Soleri suggests respect for the landscape.

He advocates a merger of architecture and ecology. But, where Wright's organic city was dispersed, Soleri's is dense and clustered (see Soleri 1987). Rather than focusing on this disparity at the moment, it is worth noting that four of Soleri's recommendations for urban form are especially appropriate for the American Southwest:

- *The Greenhouse Effect.* Greenhouse designs are used to collect solar energy.
- *The Horticultural Effect.* Trees can also be used as collectors of solar energy as well as coolers for adjacent areas.
- *The Apse Effect.* Apses can be used to take advantage of the different angles of the sun at different times of the year to provide shade or to permit sunning.
- *The Chimney Effect.* Chimneys can collect winds and provide cool air for dwellings.

The new urbanists Andres Duany and Elizabeth Plater-Zyberk (DPZ) have also designed an alternative settlement pattern for the Sonora. With architect Max Underwood, the landscape architect Christy Ten Eyck, the landscape architects of Design Workshop, and several others, DPZ designed a 30-acre (12-hectare), 383-unit manufactured home park east of Mesa, Arizona, for the innovative developer Craig Bollman. Initially called "Rosa Vista" and now called "Monte Vista," the project applies Duany and Plater-Zyberk's urban design concepts to a significant form of affordable housing (Figure 9.23).

The DPZ team designed a pedestrian circulation system for Monte Vista. They adapted southwest building design to mobile homes and made extensive use of low walls. The plan also encourages the use of native vegetation such as palo verde trees and cacti. The plan is oriented to enhance and celebrate views of surrounding mountains and sunsets.

Others have given thought to how to use environmental knowledge to inform community planning and design. A team of planners and

FIGURE 9.23 Monte Vista, Mesa, Arizona. *(Source: Duany Plater-Zyberk and Company, architects and town planners; Christy Ten Eyck, landscape architect; Craig Bollman, developer)*

designers used a McHarg overlay process with participatory planning for the Tucson Solar Village called "Civano" (Figure 9.24). The goal of the Tucson Solar Village is to develop a sustainable community. Civano will be a sustainable community for 5000 people on 820 acres (332 hectares) within the city of Tucson. To reach its goal of sustainability, specific performance targets were set for the plan, including:

- To save 75 percent of energy needs through solar design, conservation, and efficient use.
- To reduce by 90 percent the amount of landfill-destined solid waste.
- To reduce air pollution by 40 percent through a circulation system encouraging bicycle and pedestrian use.
- To provide one job in the community for every two residential units built.

Civano is a rare example of a community being planned to meet specific performance targets for sustainability. Its plan is also based on a thorough analysis of ecological processes that revealed suitabilities for various land uses. The new urbanists Stefanos Polyzoides, Elizabeth Moule, Elizabeth Plater-Zyberk, and Andres Duany are involved in

FIGURE 9.24 Perspective of Civano neighborhood. *(Source: Moule and Polyzoides Architects for the community of Civano)*

Civano's design. Their design draws on both the historical and the environmental context of the Tucson region (see Wilson et al. 1998). The Civano design fits its region. In other regions, similar models to those provided for the southwest by Polyzoides and Moule, Duany and Plater-Zyberk, and Wright and Soleri can inspire design and planning innovation.

TWO EXAMPLES OF DETAILED DESIGN

David Orr identifies several common characteristics of good design, including the "right scale, simplicity, efficient use of resources, a close fit between means and ends, durability, redundance, and resilience" (1994, 105). Good design, according to Orr, promotes: "human competence, instead of addiction and dependence, efficient and frugal use of resources, sound regional economics, and social resilience" (1994, 105). Two examples of regional designs that were integrated into planning processes follow.

Connecticut River Valley, Massachusetts

The Connecticut River Valley provides an example of "greenline" planning, an approach developed and promoted largely by the National Park Service Mid-Atlantic Regional Office in Philadelphia. A greenline park contains a mixture of public and private land, more like a European national park than the traditional American national park. Some land and structures may be acquired by the federal or state governments, but most of an area is protected through scenic easements, local zoning, and other techniques (Corbett 1983; Alesch 1987; Little 1990; Ahern 1995; Fabos and Ahern 1996). The greenline planning process involves the cooperation of local, state, and federal officials in analyzing landscape resources, establishing priorities for conservation and development, creating regulatory measures, and continuing to manage the area according to the plan (Corbett 1983).

The Connecticut River forms the border between Vermont and New Hampshire, then flows southward through Massachusetts and Connecticut before entering the Atlantic Ocean. In 1984, the Mid-Atlantic Regional Office of the NPS began work on a management plan with state agencies from Massachusetts on the 68-mile (109-kilometer) portion of the river that passes through that state. The NPS is authorized to participate with state and local agencies in such greenline efforts through Section 11 of the Wild and Scenic Rivers Act (Public Law, 90-542, as amended). The NPS planning team cooperated with the Massachusetts Department of Environmental Management and three other state agencies, the Audubon Society, the former U.S. Soil Conservation Service, the regional utilities company, and two local planning and watershed groups.

Based on the problems and opportunities facing the people of the valley, the planning team identified a number of rural resource issues that included agricultural land protection (Sutro 1984), water quality, recreation, natural resource conservation and management, soil and stream bank erosion, cultural and historic resources, and economic development. Local landowners were surveyed and township zoning ordinances analyzed (U.S. National Park Service 1985, 1986). Based on an analysis of the issues and the various options to resolve them, a number of actions were recommended to balance conservation and development.

Among the recommendations was the suggestion that state and local efforts to protect prime farmland be expedited. The Center for Rural Massachusetts of the University of Massachusetts developed this suggestion through the production of a compelling design manual for the valley (Yaro et al. 1988). A series of beautiful drawings by Kevin Wilson and Harry Dodson illustrated specific sites in the valley, contrasting conventional development with creative landscape designs. Specific suggestions were made to integrate new development into the rural landscape, review site plans for proposed development, control signs, manage development of land adjacent to rivers and lakes, protect farmland, encourage the preservation of open space, and make rural roadways attractive.

The interdisciplinary team of planners and landscape architects prepared site-specific designs that provided conceptual demonstrations of the options for the valley (Robert Yaro, Randall Arendt, Harry Dodson, and Elizabeth Brabec). Site G, for example, was the Franklin Emery farm. The existing conditions of this site—its landform, land use, land cover, utilities, and zoning—were described. The University of Massachusetts landscape planners prepared an aerial view of this site before development (Figure 9.25), a ground-level view before development (Figure 9.26), and a plan of the site before development (Figure 9.27) (Yaro et al. 1988).

The owner of the 200-acre (81-hectare) dairy farm and orchard was a tenth-generation Yankee whose ancestors had settled the land over 200 years ago. Franklin Emery had declined several offers to purchase the farm before he died in 1982. His heirs did not want to continue farming, however, and wished to sell the property for the

FIGURE 9.25 Aerial view of site before development. *(Source: Yaro et al. 1988, Center for Rural Massachusetts, University of Massachusetts, Amherst, drawn by Kevin Wilson)*

FIGURE 9.26 Ground view of site before development. *(Source: Yaro et al. 1988, Center for Rural Massachusetts, University of Massachusetts, Amherst, drawn by Kevin Wilson)*

highest possible price. Because of its proximity to a large university, conventional development of the property would result in multifamily apartment buildings. There was considerable local opposition to such apartment development because it clashed with the rural character of the town. However, multifamily housing was consistent with the local zoning regulations. The impact of this conventional development scenario was illustrated by the University of Massachusetts landscape planning team by drawing an aerial view of site G after conventional development (Figure 9.28), ground-level view after conventional development (Figure 9.29), and a plan of the site after conventional development (Figure 9.30) (Yaro et al. 1988).

To contrast the conventional scenario, the University of Massachusetts team proposed a creative development scenario. With this design, apartments would be smaller in scale, more varied, and sited in the woodland adjacent to the farmland. The design of the apartments would create a sense of privacy, easy access, and screened parking. The apartment units would have views of the farmland and a pond that would increase their value and marketability. A new road would wind through the woodland and respond to the topography. The existing eighteenth-century farmstead would be restored and sold as a single-family residence (Yaro et al. 1988).

The creative scenario involved siting the new development at the edge of the woodland. To preserve the farmland and orchard, the apartment developer would donate a conservation easement on that part of the land and rent it to a young farmer. In return for the easement, the developer would receive a substantial tax deduction. The landscape architects designed controlled access to the farmland for the new apartment dwellers by fencing and pathway alignment. The design was illustrated with an aerial view of site G after creative development (Figure 9.31), a ground-level view after creative development (Figure 9.32), and a plan view after creative development

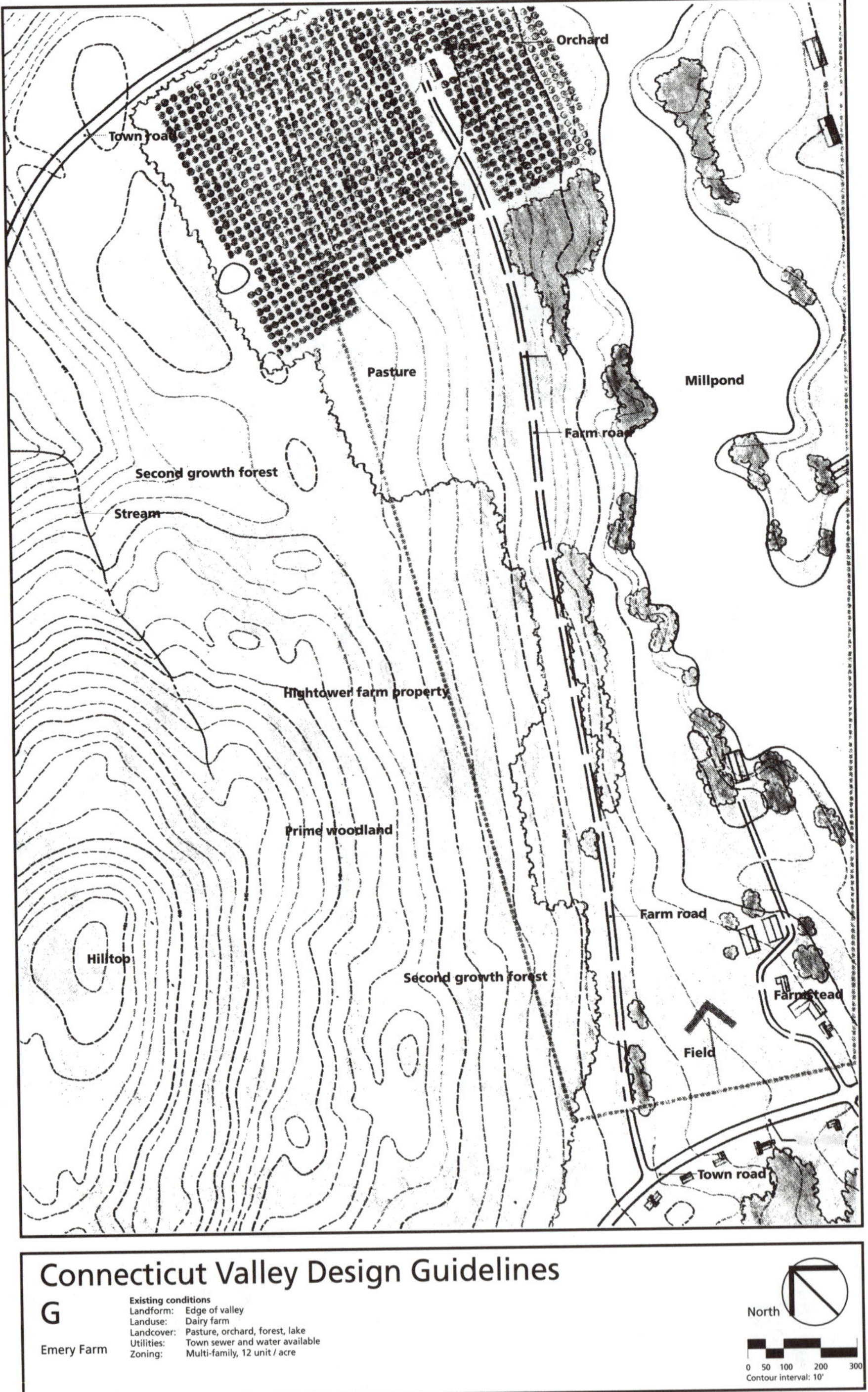

FIGURE 9.27 Plan of site before development. *(Source: Yaro et al. 1988, Center of Rural Massachusetts, University of Massachusetts, Amherst)*

FIGURE 9.28 Aerial view of site after conventional development. *(Source: Yaro et al. 1988, Center for Rural Massachusetts, University of Massachusetts, Amherst, drawn by Kevin Wilson)*

FIGURE 9.29 Ground view of site after conventional development. *(Source: Yaro et al. 1988, Center for Rural Massachusetts, University of Massachusetts, Amherst, drawn by Kevin Wilson)*

(Figure 9.33) (Yaro et al. 1988). This creative scenario for the land involved preserving the farmland and open space and clustering residential development. Thus, a design was presented that fitted the goals and plans to protect the farmland and visual quality of the Connecticut River Valley.

The Connecticut River Valley concepts have had an enduring influence locally and even nationally and internationally. Many planners and landscape architects follow the triptych visualization approach. The study influenced the commonwealth's conservation efforts. For example, the state enacted an influential purchase of development rights program. Land trusts, notably the Franklin Land Trust in the north Connecticut valley, are active locally and statewide. Most riverfront towns in the valley adopted waterfront development guidelines recommended by the University of Massachusetts team. In addition, 61 towns adopted the model open space zoning.

Although the team responsible for the Connecticut River Valley disbanded, its participants continued to pursue the approach. Randell Arendt has continued to advocate a conservation approach to design (Arendt 1996). His colleague Bob Yaro has applied similar ideas to the New York City region (see next section).

New York-New Jersey-Connecticut Metropolitan Region

In late 1989, Bob Yaro left the Center for Rural Massachusetts to become the executive director of the Regional Plan Association (RPA), based in New York City. The RPA is a not-for-profit or nongovernmental organization and is the oldest regional planning entity in the United States. Yaro led the creation of RPA's third plan for the region and used design concepts that he had pioneered with the Connecticut River plan.

The first RPA plan was completed in 1929 under the direction of Thomas Adams (Regional Planning Staff 1929). As was noted in Chapter 5,

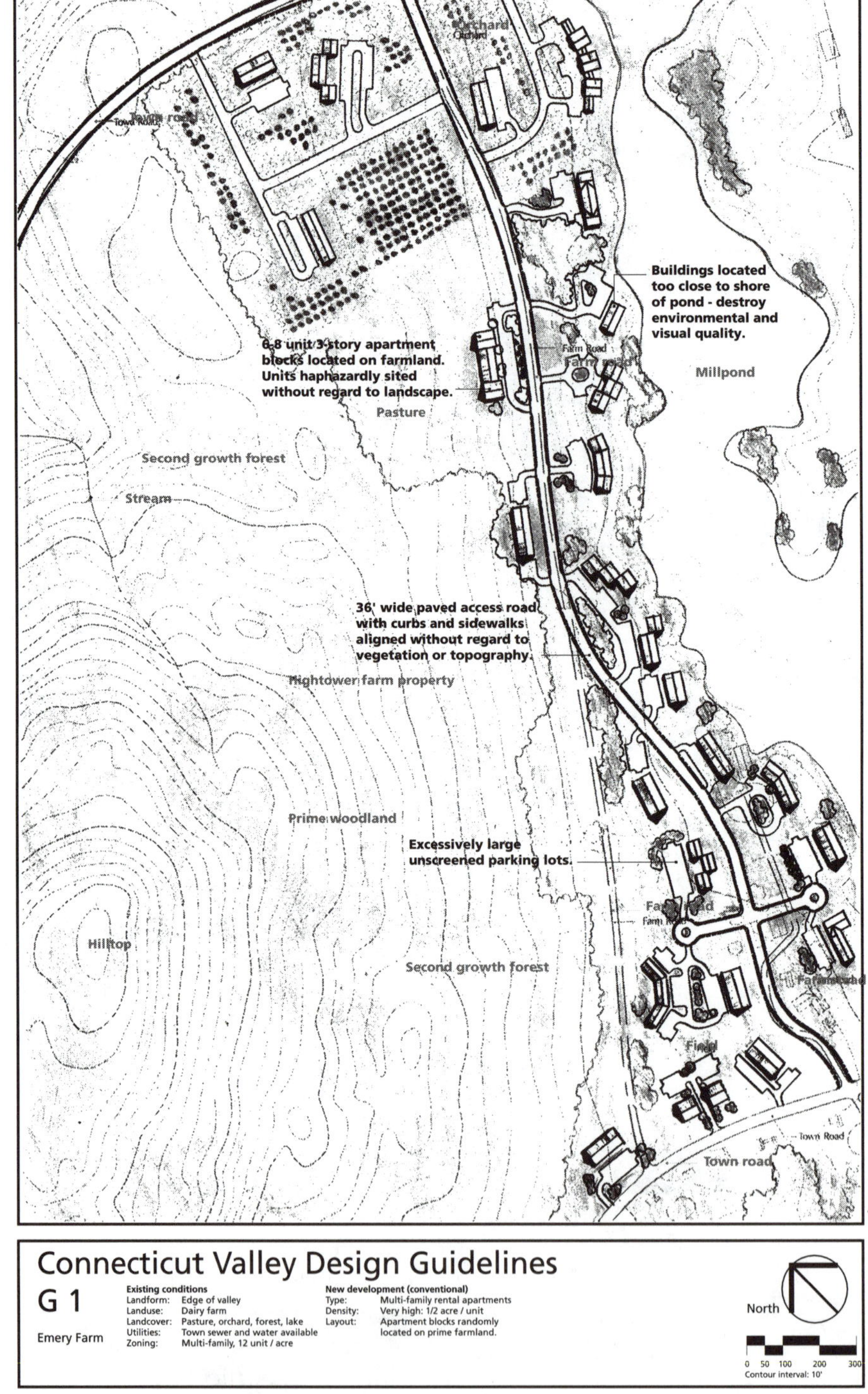

FIGURE 9.30 Plan of site after conventional development. *(Source: Yaro et al. 1988, Center for Rural Massachusetts, University of Massachusetts, Amherst)*

FIGURE 9.31 Aerial view of site after creative development. *(Source: Yaro et al. 1988, Center for Rural Massachusetts, University of Massachusetts, Amherst, drawn by Kevin Wilson)*

FIGURE 9.32 Ground-level view of site after creative development. *(Source: Yaro et al. 1988, Center for Rural Massachusetts, University of Massachusetts, Amherst, drawn by Kevin Wilson)*

the 1929 plan was an early example of the overlay technique. The second RPA plan was presented in 1968. That plan attempted to address the issues of suburban sprawl and inner-city decay. The third plan of 1996 attempts "to reconnect the regions to its basic foundations." RPA calls these interlocking foundations the "Three E's'—economy, environment, and equity" (Yaro and Hiss 1996, 6). Where these three foundations coincide positive quality of life results. The diagram that RPA developed to illustrate this point (Figure 9.34) has subsequently been used to illustrate the principles of sustainable development.

Yaro turned to his former Connecticut River Valley colleague Harry Dodson and illustrator Kevin Wilson to develop regional simulations of the future development patterns for the cities, suburbs, and countryside. As with the Connecticut River Valley, drawings were made of alternative futures. For example, Figure 9.35 illustrates a view of an exurban highway cloverleaf at present, which is compared to what it will look like with current development patterns (Figure 9.36) and how it could look if reoriented around a village center and rail station (Figure 9.37) (Yaro and Hiss 1996). Meanwhile, Figure 9.38 shows an urban industrial waterfront at present while Figure 9.39 illustrates what it could look like with creative design (Yaro and Hiss 1996).

The technique for making the drawings for the New York region differed slightly from its precedent. In the Connecticut River Valley, Dodson and Wilson had relied on slide traces. For RPA, a computer-aided design (CAD) system created perspectives which were then rendered to illustrate the scenarios. Yaro and Dodson also involved a broader group of design talent—including Jonathan Barnett, Robert Geddes, and Ray Gastil—to create the images.

Anne Spirn advocates ecological design that recognizes the deep structure of the place. The detailed designs for the Connecticut River Valley in Massachusetts and the New York City region

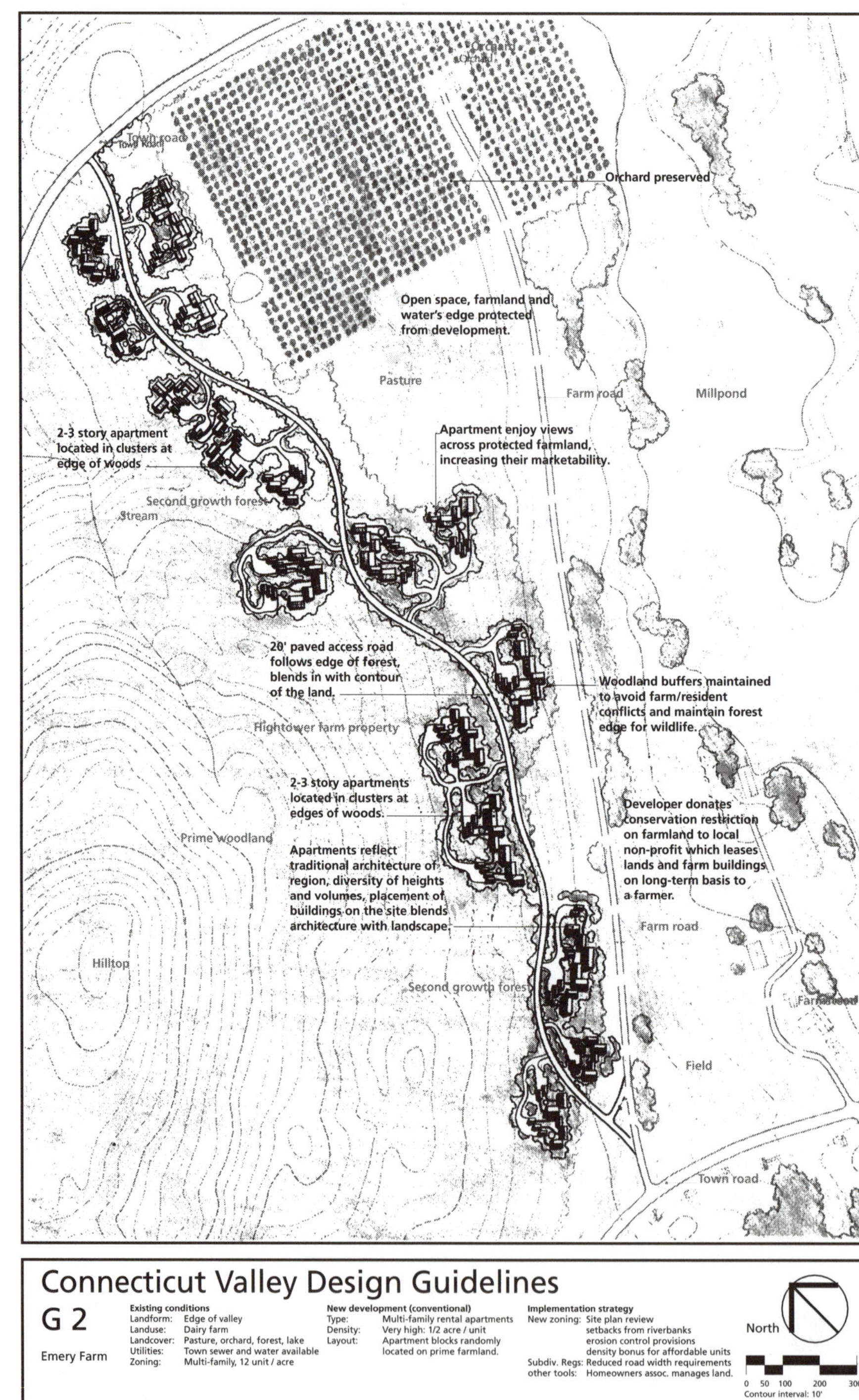
Orchard
Town road
Orchard preserved
Open space, farmland and water's edge protected from development.
Pasture
Farm road
Millpond
2-3 story apartment located in clusters at edge of woods
Apartment enjoy views across protected farmland, increasing their marketability.
Second growth forest
Stream
20' paved access road follows edge of forest, blends in with contour of the land.
Woodland buffers maintained to avoid farm/resident conflicts and maintain forest edge for wildlife.
Hightower farm property
2-3 story apartments located in clusters at edges of woods.
Developer donates conservation restriction on farmland to local non-profit which leases lands and farm buildings on long-term basis to a farmer.
Prime woodland
Apartments reflect traditional architecture of region, diversity of heights and volumes, placement of buildings on the site blends architecture with landscape.
Farm road
Hilltop
Second growth forest
Farmstead
Field
Town road
Connecticut Valley Design Guidelines
G 2
Emery Farm
Existing conditions
Landform: Edge of valley
Landuse: Dairy farm
Landcover: Pasture, orchard, forest, lake
Utilities: Town sewer and water available
Zoning: Multi-family, 12 unit / acre
New development (conventional)
Type: Multi-family rental apartments
Density: Very high: 1/2 acre / unit
Layout: Apartment blocks randomly located on prime farmland.
Implementation strategy
New zoning: Site plan review
setbacks from riverbanks
erosion control provisions
density bonus for affordable units
Subdiv. Regs: Reduced road width requirements
other tools: Homeowners assoc. manages land.
North
0 50 100 200 300
Contour interval: 10'

FIGURE 9.33 Plan of site after creative development. *(Source: Yaro et al. 1988, Center for Rural Massachusetts, University of Massachusetts, Amherst)*

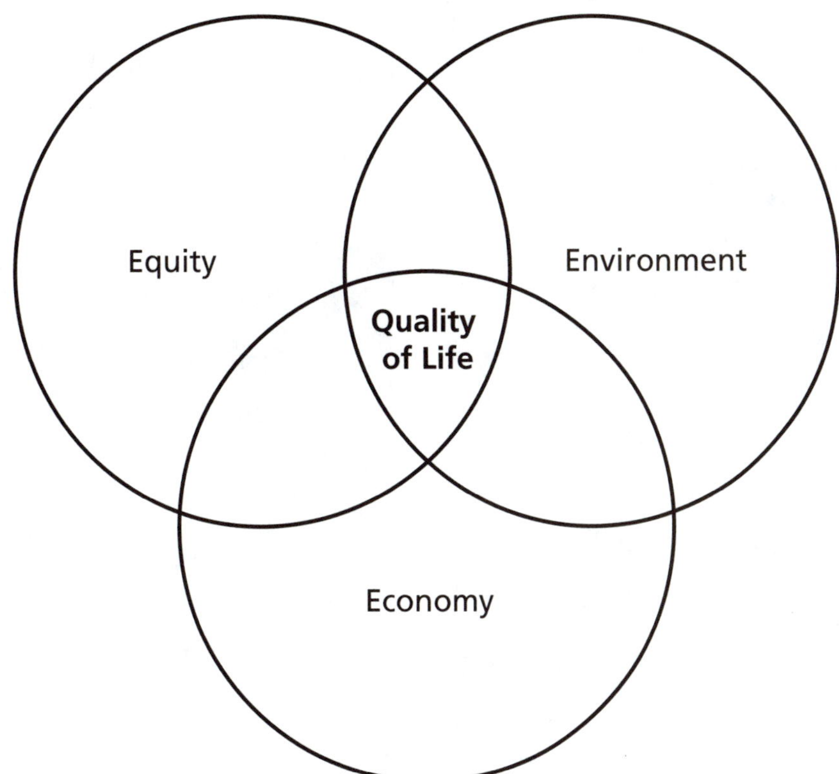

FIGURE 9.34 Three-E diagram. *(Source: Yaro and Hiss 1996)*

respond to the natural and cultural processes, the landscape patterns that give each place its identity and character. The designs differ from more conventional approaches in both their response to landscape ecology and their linkage to a broader planning process.

The Center for Rural Massachusetts design manual for the Connecticut River Valley integrated local planning efforts with those undertaken by the state and the National Park Service. The design manual included specific ways to fit development into the fabric of the landscape through creative design. Site plan review with detailed design guidelines and performance standards were suggested for the towns in the valley. Recommendations were made to control signage and to manage development on riverfronts and lakefronts and along roadways. The planning team advocated measures to protect farmland and open space. The landscape planning suggestions were illustrated through a series of designs.

The detailed designs completed in the Connecticut River Valley differ from more conventional approaches in several ways. Many conventional designs are not explicitly linked to

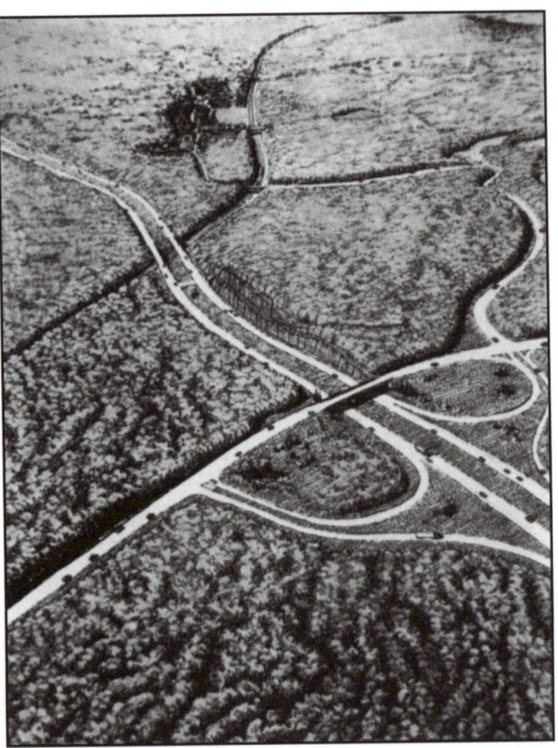

FIGURE 9.35 Exurban highway at present. *(Source: Yaro and Hiss 1996)*

FIGURE 9.36 Exurban highway with current development patterns. *(Source: Yaro and Hiss 1996)*

the planning process except to the extent they respond to government regulations. Conventional designs are often not connected to scales higher than the site level—the community and the region. The Center for Rural Massachusetts designs were undertaken as part of a comprehensive landscape planning process.

The Connecticut River Valley is mostly a rural place. The tristate New York City metropolitan region is the most densely populated area of the United States and, obviously, one of the largest cities in the world. Bob Yaro and his Regional Plan Association colleagues have used design to provide visions for the metropolitan region's future.

The Connecticut River Valley and Regional Plan Association designs seek to respond to the landscape ecology of their regions and to be appropriate to the local culture. Laurie Olin (1988, 1997) has identified several elements that are central to thoughtful contemporary landscape design. The subject matter identified by Olin (1988) as important includes ideas of order, ideas of nature, ideas about the arrangement of places, ideas that reveal something about process, and considerations about the history of places.

Ecological design intelligence can help guide future settlement. Such intelligence is defined by David Orr as "the capacity to understand the ecological context in which humans live, to recog-

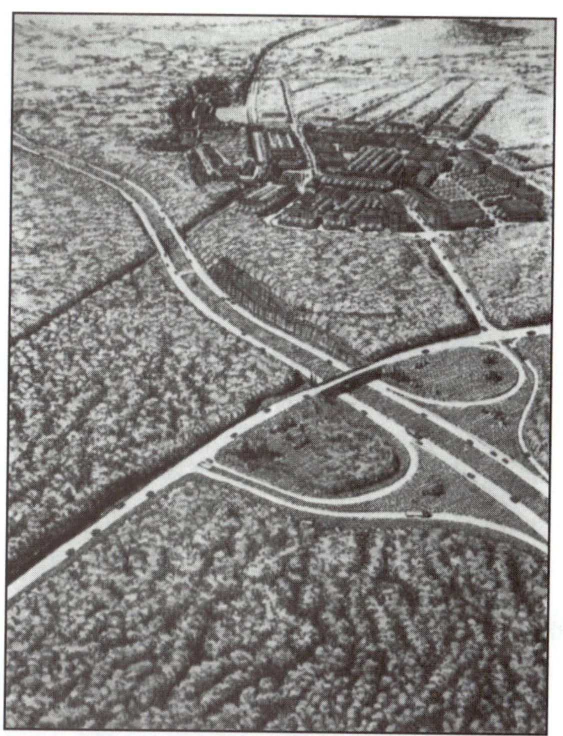

FIGURE 9.37 Exurban highway with village center design concept. *(Source: Yaro and Hiss 1996)*

FIGURE 9.38 Urban industrial waterfront at present. *(Source: Yaro and Hiss 1996)*

nize limits, and to get the scale of things right. It is the ability to calibrate human purposes and natural constraints and do so with grace and economy" (1994, 2). These ideas and considerations are evident in the designs completed for the Connecticut River Valley and the New York-New Jersey-Connecticut metropolitan region.

FIGURE 9.39 Creative design of urban industrial waterfront. *(Source: Yaro and Hiss 1996)*

10

PLAN AND DESIGN IMPLEMENTATION

Politicians, planners, lawyers, and public administrators have been quite resourceful in developing a wide array of techniques to realize plans. Once a plan has been prepared and adopted, then it is necessary to develop the means for implementation. Often the selection of an implementation strategy coincides with the selection of a preferred option, the development of a landscape plan, and/or the preparation of a detailed design. For this discussion, it is helpful to separate the steps in the planning process to illustrate the intricacies involved in each.

Local governments possess four general kinds of authority that can be used to implement plans: the power to *regulate,* the power to *condemn* and *exact,* the power to *spend,* and the power to *tax. Regulation* derives from the police powers to protect public health, safety, welfare, and morals. The most common, and perhaps least popular, regulatory technique used in the United States is zoning. Other techniques, which may be used in conjunction with zoning, include planned unit developments (PUDs), performance standards, design guidelines, critical (or environmentally sensitive) areas protection, wetland and riparian area protection, habitat conservation plans, historic preservation, subdivision regulations, and building codes. Covenants are private contracts that can be used to regulate many of the same features as zoning, design guidelines, and subdivision ordinances.

The power to require private individuals to turn over property or money is the second authority. *Condemnation* and *exactions* are examples. Condemnation involves the seizure of property through eminent domain power. Eminent domain can be used for a public purpose, such as the removal of blight. Obviously the use of such power can be controversial.

Governments may *spend* money in a variety of ways to implement plans. Governments can buy full or partial rights to a parcel of property. Governments may manage major expenditures through capital improvement programs and through the administration of public lands.

The power to *tax* is the fourth general kind of authority. Taxing can be selective—rewarding some kinds of development and penalizing others. Referenda and state caps limit the extent of local taxation.

All four powers may be used in concert. The activities and programs of agencies can be coordinated to manage growth. In addition to government activities, there are also nongovernment strategies that can be used to implement plans. For example, voluntary neighborhood or homeowners' associations can help realize plans. These nongovernmental strategies can be employed in coordination with the efforts of governments, or at deliberate variance.

Whatever means is selected to implement community goals, it is crucial to assign responsibilities, resources, and authority for the selected measure(s). One device to help organize such responsibilities is an implementation matrix. After presenting an example of this matrix, three examples of planning implementation will be described: the York County, Pennsylvania, sliding-scale zoning; the Black Hawk County, Iowa, agricultural zoning; and the Scottsdale, Arizona, environmentally sensitive lands ordinance.

POWER TO REGULATE

The government power to regulate human activity is carefully balanced against fundamental freedoms of the individual. Cities and counties derive limited regulatory power from the states, but local governments must use those powers in reasonable ways to achieve public goals without infringing on basic individual rights. Regulations involve rules and restrictions that are used to control what an individual, a family, or a business can do with its property. Such rules and restrictions may also involve how land use on one property affects neighboring areas. Regulations can direct activities from ones with negative consequences to those with positive results. Restrictions and rules help reinforce the responsibilities which accompany property ownership.

Zoning

The planning profession is a fickle friend to zoning. Since the 1960s, there has been a continual stream of criticism about zoning in the planning community. The noted historian John Reps called for a "requiem for zoning" as early as 1964. Such diverse individuals as Herbert Gans, Richard Babcock, Ada Louise Huxtable, and Andres Duany joined the chorus of criticism. Much of this criticism was justified; zoning is an imperfect device.

Because of this criticism, the curricula of many university planning programs do not address zoning in much depth. For three reasons, academic planning programs have been in error for not addressing zoning more fully in their curricula. First, the use of zoning is incredibly widespread in the United States. Although cities or counties are not required to use it as a tool, nearly all do. Second, other professions—law, civil engineering, geography, public administration, and landscape architecture—have continued to incorporate zoning into their education and practice (Platt 1996; Cullingworth 1997). Third, zoning has remained an important tool for the practice of planning. With weak comprehensive planning statutes in most states, planners must rely on case law for implementation. Zoning is used because of the strong body of case law to support it. Zoning has been upheld continually in the courts. The first zoning ordinances in the United States were adopted in California in the late nineteenth century for repugnant reasons (Hagman and Juergensmeyer 1986). The purpose was to discriminate against Chinese immigrant businesses, specifically laundries, which were considered fire risks and public nuisances. These ordinances were upheld in the California courts.

At about the same time in the eastern and Great Lakes states and cities, similar devices were being used to regulate the height and bulk of buildings. For example, early in the twentieth century, Boston enacted building height controls because of shadowing. The first comprehensive zoning ordinance, written largely by attorney Edward M. Bassett, was adopted in New York City in 1916. Because of the interest in zoning created by Bassett and other lawyers (such as Alfred Bettman, James Metzenbaum, and F. B. Williams), the U.S. Department of Commerce published the Standard Zoning Enabling Act in 1922. Zoning was found to be constitutional in 1926 as a result of the U.S. Supreme Court's landmark decision *Euclid vs. Ambler Realty Co.* (272 U.S. 365). As a result, even more local interest was generated, and states continued to adopt the standard zoning enabling act.

The power to zone is derived from the police power of government to ensure the welfare of a community. Zoning aims to reduce the negative impacts that one land use will impose on surrounding landowners or occupants (e.g., the impacts of heavy commercial traffic or loud industrial noises on nearby residences). Such negative impacts are called "externalities" by economists, although "positive" externalities are also possible.

A well-prepared zoning ordinance, based on a plan, seeks to secure the most appropriate use of land and facilitate adequate but economical provision of public improvements. The authority for local governments to adopt zoning ordinances is contained in state enabling legislation. For example, according to the Alabama enabling law, the specific purposes of zoning regulations include: to lesson congestion in the streets, to secure safety from fire and panic, to provide adequate light and air, to prevent overcrowding of the land, to avoid undue concentration of population, to facilitate the provision of public services, and to provide for the health and general welfare (Juster 1994). Ideally, and as required by law in some states, a comprehensive or general plan is a prerequisite for the preparation of a zoning ordinance.

Zoning refers to the land-use controls that limit the use to which land in an area may be put. Zoning includes variances, special-use permits, and other devices that allow regulatory flexibility. According to Robert Leary, "zoning is a means of [ensuring] that the land uses of a community are properly situated in relation to one another, providing adequate space for each type of development" (1968, 403). Zoning ordinances address five general sets of issues, according to Eric Kelly (1993) and Robert Juster (1994): *land use, the intensity of that use, the bulk and form of buildings, the size of yards and other open spaces around structures, and the density of population.*

The basic idea of zoning is to separate potentially conflicting land uses. Through such separation, property owners' investments are protected and land values are stabilized. Zoning ordinances usually include a statement of purpose, definitions, and a description of districts. Zoning districts commonly include specific uses like residential (R), agriculture (A), commercial (C), and industrial (I), as well as areas like floodplains (FP) and open space (OS). Uses are further specified by intensity like R1 (low-density residential) and R3 (high-density residential). Some rural counties have adopted similar hierarchies for agricultural land use [e.g., A1 (orchards) to A3 (pastureland)]. Each zone is regulated by specific provisions, including permitted uses, accessory uses, provisional uses, height restrictions, yard regulations, land-to-building ratio, parking requirements, fencing and screening requirements, sign requirements, and ingress and egress requirements. The districts are designated in a map which is part of the ordinance. Ideally, these zoning districts should relate to the suitability of the land for such use. Ordinances also include provisions for nonconforming uses, variances, enforcement, and penalties.

Zoning overlay districts offer a means to protect certain resources within a more traditional ordinance. A district recognizing a valuable resource, usually prime farmland, an historic place, or an environmentally sensitive area, overlays the other underlying zoning categories. Such areas then receive special protection. Specific places may also be recognized in separate zoning categories, rather than overlays. Agricultural protection zoning (APZ) provides an example (American Farmland Trust 1997; Daniels and Bowers 1997). APZ ordinances "protect the agricultural land base by limiting non-farm uses, prohibiting high-density development, requiring houses to be built on small lots and restricting subdivision of land into parcels that are too small to farm" (American Farmland Trust 1997, 317). The types of APZ include exclusive agriculture zoning, large minimum lot sizes, and area-based allowances.

Exclusive agricultural zoning "prohibits non-farm residents and most non-agricultural activities; exceptions are made for parcels of land that are not suitable for farming" (American Farmland Trust 1997, 317). Large minimum lot size APZ require a certain amount of land for every non-farm dwelling in the zone. Area-based allowance ordinances "establish a formula for the number of permitted non-farm dwellings" (American Farmland Trust 1997, 317). Such ordinances can either establish fixed area-based allowances or sliding scale area-based allowances. (See examples later in this chapter.)

There are a number of requirements that zoning ordinances must follow. They are summarized by Leary:

- While regulations may vary for different zoning districts, they must be uniform within each district for each class and kind of building.
- State legislatures and the courts have insisted that there be a reasonable basis for classifying particular areas differently from others.
- The courts have insisted that an ordinance cover the entire jurisdictional area of a city or county [or township], rather than singling out a small area for regulation and leaving the remainder unrestricted.
- The courts insist that the zoning regulations be reasonable in their application to particular properties. In other words, there should be a relationship between the physical character of an area and its zoning classification (1968, 404).

Four common criticisms of zoning are inconsistency between the zoning ordinance and planning goals and policies; the relative ease of zone changes or rezoning; the case of obtaining variances; and the vulnerability of ordinances to ephemeral political changes. From the late 1960s and through the 1970s there have been a number of gradual changes that somewhat ameliorate these past weaknesses. Three court decisions especially important in this regard include:

- *Udell vs. Haas* (21 N.Y. 2d 46, 1968), in which the New York Supreme Court in 1968 struck down zoning provisions as contrary to the comprehensive plan
- *Fasano vs. Board of County Commissioners of Washington County* (507 P. 2d 23, 1973), in which the Oregon Supreme Court in 1973 determined that zone changes must be in conformance with the local comprehensive plan
- *Baker vs. City of Milwaukie* (P. 2d 772, 1975), in which the Oregon Supreme Court in 1975 held that zoning decisions must be in accordance with the comprehensive plan (Callies 1980).

Combined with new planning legislation in several states mandating—rather than enabling—local planning, these three court decisions and many others have resulted in a resurgence of zoning and of comprehensive planning. The renaissance has been strengthened by the growing movement to protect resources such as wetlands, coasts, farmlands, and historic places. In their farmland protection work, for instance, several planners have found zoning to be more acceptable by rural people generally, and farmers specifically, than more complex, innovative land-use controls (Kartez 1980; Toner 1981; Platt 1991).

However, a strong force against land-use controls in general and often zoning in particular emerged during the 1980s and 1990s in the United States. Called the "wise use" or "property rights" movement, advocates of this view oppose almost any government action curtailing what a property owner may do with her or his land. A more conservative U.S. Supreme Court resulted because of appointments made by Presidents Ronald Reagan and George Bush. This court made decisions that reinvigorated the taking clause as a limit. The four important U.S. Supreme Court decisions in this regard include:

- *First English Evangelical Lutheran Church vs. County of Los Angeles* (107 S. Ct. 2378, 1987), in which the court found that a county moratorium on rebuilding a camp for handicapped children in the floodplain of a canyon after a flash flood was a form of temporary inverse condemnation (Platt 1996; Carson 1998).
- *Nollan vs. California Coastal Commission* (107 S. Ct. 3141, 1987), in which the court found that the California Coastal Commission could not place a restriction on a rebuilding permit, which required that the owners provide an easement for the public to use the beach in front of their home (Humbach 1989; Platt 1996; Carson 1998).
- *Lucas vs. South Carolina Coastal Council* (112 S. Ct. 2886, 1992), in which the court found that the state could not deny building permits to an owner of two ocean-front lots (Platt 1996).
- *Dolan vs. City of Tigard* (114 S. Ct. 2309, 1994), in which the U.S. Supreme Court reversed the Oregon Supreme Court and found that the city could not require a property owner to dedicate a portion of her property lying in a 100-year floodplain in order to receive a building permit to enlarge a hardware store (Platt 1996; Carson 1998).

These "conservative" decisions did *not* invalidate the authority of local governments to zone and otherwise regulate land. In addition, advocates for more control argue two points. First, in addition to "takings," government "givings" ought to be considered (Riggle 1994). Government decisions, like zoning, may restrict or take value, but they may also add value. Second, whatever property rights an individual has with his or her own land cannot be used to harm others. This good-neighborliness is at the essence of zoning; that is, uses that negatively impact one another should be separated.

The basic idea of zoning is to separate potentially conflicting land uses and to integrate supportive uses to form communities. Here is an example where uses are separated, but the new use is inappropriate and does not fit the landscape. As a result, instead of helping to build a community, the new use disrupts the traditional settlement pattern. *(USDA–Natural Resources Conservation Service)*

Three principles emerge for planners from the "property rights" cases. First, land-use controls cannot remove all of the economic value from a parcel of property. Second, the conditions or measures required for landowners must bear a *clear relation* to the public purpose on which the government bases its justification for the ordinance. Third, the amount of burden or loss imposed on the landowner must be roughly proportional to the size of the problem that the land use might cause. If a planner follows these three guidelines, zoning controls remain workable, even under the rules set by the most conservative courts.

Planned Unit Developments (PUDs)

A *planned unit development* (PUD) is comprehensively conceived and contains some mix of residential, commercial, industrial, institutional, and recreational land uses on a single tract of land. Sometimes a PUD ordinance is included as a part of zoning regulations, while at other times it is addressed under separate rules. PUD ordinances offer benefits to both developers and communities.

Under PUDs, developers are allowed greater design flexibility and greater densities, while communities are able to protect environmentally sensitive areas or enforce design standards. For instance, a tract of land may include areas with steep slopes and unique vegetation. Part of the land may be located inside a floodplain. These steep-sloped, vegetated, flood-prone places could be left in open space, allowing the developer to cluster denser housing or commercial structures in a more suitable location.

PUD ordinances usually require a developer to submit a complete development plan for review. Such a plan usually includes a combination of maps, drawings, site designs, charts, and supportive narrative material that portray the development to be achieved in the overall project. The PUD documents provide sufficiently detailed information to both illustrate and describe the intended character and configuration of the proposed development. These proposals are reviewed by the city or county staff, the planning commission, and the elected officials.

Early PUDs have had three major characteristics, according to Joseph De Chiara and Lee Koppelman (1975):

1. PUDs have usually involved areas and undertakings of a relatively large scale, encompassing at least 100 acres (40.5 hectares) and occasionally smaller, but usually larger, up to 1,000 acres (405 hectares).
2. PUDs have usually involved a mixture of land uses, building types, and densities.
3. PUDs have usually involved stage-by-stage development over a relatively long period of time (5 to 15 years) during which buildings, arrangements, and uses may have to be redesigned to meet changes in market conditions, technology, financing, or even design concepts.

Through time, PUDs have evolved. Today, PUDs tend to address smaller areas of land, often 10 to 50 acres (4.05 to 20.25 hectares).

PUDs can result in the protection of important or sensitive lands. Such lands sometimes are transferred to public ownership or to a not-for-profit conservancy organization. Frequently, homeowners' associations become responsible. Barry Cullingworth (1997) notes that such associations play an important role in managing commonly held property. Homeowners' associations also become responsible for restrictions and covenants placed on the PUD by the developer. Such restrictions can require, for example, that homeowners use only native plants on their lawns and paint their houses certain colors for compatibility. (See further discussion about covenants later in this chapter.)

Performance Standards

Like many other planning techniques, *performance standards* is a rather broad, generic term that has been defined and applied in several different ways. Basically, the term refers to criteria that are established and must be met before a certain use will be permitted. These criteria, or standards, may be a set of economic, environmental, or social factors or any combination of these factors.

Originally, performance standards were used as a means for prescribing specific conditions for observable or scientifically measurable industrial plant emissions. This system was first proposed by Dennis O'Harrow, the executive director of the American Society of Planning Officials, in his 1954 study *Planning Standards in Industrial Zoning.*

More recently, performance standards have been linked to zoning ordinances in various ways. For instance, in some areas that permit septic tanks, a number of environmental factors (such as the soil type and depth to the water table) are used to determine whether housing will be allowed. Permitting too much housing with septic tanks in many areas will result in environmental degradation that can endanger human health. However, some locations may be suitable for such housing. Performance standards identify those factors that make a site suitable or unsuitable for a specific use. Conventional *prescriptive zoning ordinances* "are based on the principle that most [land] uses are incompatible and should be separated from one another" (Juster 1994, 29). In contrast, *performance zoning* "is based on the premise that within broad limits different [land] uses can coexist with one another" (Juster 1994, 30).

In the Whitman County, Washington, zoning ordinance, performance standards were established that created minimum standards for agricultural districts, including requirements for single-family housing. The intent of this district was that agriculture be the primary use and that all other uses be sited so as to minimize their impact on, or conflict with, adjacent agricultural uses (Table 10.1).

Bucks County, Pennsylvania, developed the first system for performance zoning. This straightforward system is based on a five-step process outlined in Table 10.2 (Kendig 1977). Both the Whitman and Bucks County examples rely on accurate technical information concerning an area's resources.

TABLE 10.1
WHITMAN COUNTY ZONING ORDINANCE FOR RURAL HOUSING

Two of the following three conditions must exist:

1. The subject lot is underlain by basaltic or alluvial surface geology, or if it is underlain by crystalline surface geology, the average slope must be no less than one vertical foot in five horizontal feet. These facts must be verified by reference to the geological map contained in Water Supply Bulletin No. 26, *Reconnaisance of Geology and Ground-Water Occurrence in Whitman County, Washington,* published by the State of Washington, Department of Ecology, and dated 1969. Whenever difficulty exists in the verification of surface geological conditions from this map, reference shall also be made to the maps of detailed soil mapping units maintained by the Soil Conservation Service, which maps shall either indicate or not indicate a pattern of specific soil types which is known to be associated with basaltic, alluvial or crystalline surface geological conditions.
2. The subject lot has been cultivated, used for production of commercial forage for sale, commercial grazing of livestock for sale or subjected to any agricultural practice designed to produce a product for sale in the preceding three years.
3. The subject lot is within a distinct area of land 15 acres or less which is of sufficient size, quality and/or accessibility to be efficiently used for agricultural production for income. "Distinct" shall mean that the subject area is substantially bounded by natural or man-made features which buffer this land from agricultural lands, such as: wooded areas, steep canyon walls, railroads, surface waters or public roads.

All the following requirements must be met:

1. The subject lot must have frontage on an improved county or state road of at least 200 feet. "Improved" shall mean a gravel surface or better.
2. If perennial surface water passes through, or along any boundary of the subject lot, there must be at least 200 feet of frontage along such surface water.
3. Less than one-half of the area of the subject lot shall be in an area of special flood hazard and/or a floodway as designated on the flood hazard boundary map of the *Flood Insurance Study for Whitman County.*
4. Construction plans for structures, parking areas and private roads on the subject lot shall leave a maximum amount of existing vegetation undisturbed.
5. The area of the subject lot shall be less than the minimum area required by the Whitman County Department of Environmental Health to safely accommodate approved water supply and on-site sewage disposal systems.

SOURCE: Whitman County Regional Planning Council 1979.

TABLE 10.2
BUCKS COUNTY, PENNSYLVANIA, PERFORMANCE ZONING

STEP 1. Calculating Base Site Area

Certain portions of tracts may not be usable for the activities proposed for the site. These are subtracted from the site area to determine base site.

	Site A	Site B
1. Site area as determined by actual on-site survey.	20.6 acres	20.6 acres
2. Subtract land within ultimate right-of-way of existing roads, or utility rights-of-way or easements.	–0.6	–0.6
3. Subtract land which is not contiguous:	0	0
a. A separate parcel which does not abut or adjoin nor share common boundaries with the rest of the development.		
b. Land which is cut off from the main parcel by a road, railroad, existing land uses, or major stream so as to serve as a major barrier to common use, or so that it is isolated and unavailable for building purposes.		
4. Subtract land which in a previously approved subdivision was reserved for resource reasons such as flooding or recreation.	0	0
5. Subtract land used or zoned for another use (land which is used or to be used for commercial or industrial uses in a residential development, or land in a different zoning district than the primary use).	0	0
	20.0 acres (8.1 hectares)	20.0 acres (8.1 hectares)

STEP 2. Subtracting Resource Protection Land

		Site A		Site B	
Resource	Open space ratio	Acres of land in resource	Resource protection land (acres in resource × open space ratio)	Acres of land in resource	Resource protection land (acres in resource × open space ratio)
Floodplains	1.00	0.5	0.5	4.5	4.5
Floodplain soils	1.00				
Lakes or ponds	1.00				
Wetlands	1.00	0.2	0.2	1.5	1.5
Natural retention area	0.90				
Sleep slope (25% or more)	0.85				
Forest	0.80	1.0	0.8	2.3	1.84
Pond shore	0.80				
Lake shore	0.70				
Steep slope (15–25%)	0.70				
Steep slope (8–15%)	0.60	___	___	___	___
Total land with resource restrictions		1.7		8.3	
Total resource protection land			1.5		7.84

All land within the base site area shall be mapped and measured for the purpose of determining the amount of open space needed to protect it.

TABLE 10.2
BUCKS COUNTY, PENNSYLVANIA, PERFORMANCE ZONING *(Continued)*

STEP 3. Allowing for Recreation Land

While some of the open space required by the zoning district may be resource protection land, the intent is to provide for usable public or common open space as near to each unit as possible. Thus, there is a need for specific guidelines ensuring that a minimum amount of land not restricted by 1 or 2 above is retained for this purpose. Therefore:

		Site A	Site B
Take	Base site area	20.0 acres	20.0 acres
Subtract	Total land with resource restriction	− 1.7	− 8.3
Equals	Total unrestricted land	= 18.3	= 11.7
Multiply	Total unrestricted land by 0.2	× 0.2	× 0.2
Total	Recreation land	= 3.66 acres	= 2.34 acres

STEP 4. Determining Site Capacity

Individual site capacity is found by calculating net buildable site area. For single-family, single-family cluster, or performance subdivisions, the number of allowable dwelling units is determined by multiplying the net density by net buildable site area. The calculations are as follows:

		Site A	Site B
Take	Resource protection land	1.5 acres	7.84 acres
Add	Recreation land	+ 3.66	+ 2.34
Equals	Total open space	= 5.16	= 10.18 acres
Take	Base site area	20.0	20.0
Multiply	By open space ratio*	× 0.4	× 0.4
Equals	Minimum required open space	= 8.0 acres	= 8.0 acres
Take	Base site area	20.0 acres	20.0 acres
Subtract	Total open space or minimum required open space, whichever is greater	− 8.0	= 10.18
Equals	Net buildable site area	= 12.0 acres	= 9.82 acres

* Each zoning district has minimum open space requirements as described in its zoning regulations. In this example it is 40% (0.4).

STEP 5. Calculating Permitted Number of Dwelling Units

		Site A	Site B
Take	Net buildable site area	12.0 acres	9.82 acres
Multiply	Net density	× 2.4	× 2.4
Equals	Number of dwelling units (do not round off)	= 28.0 du/acre	= 23.568 du/acre

SOURCE: Adapted from Kendig 1977.

Kirk Wickersham (1978) and Lee Nellis (1980, 1981) have developed permit systems to implement performance standards. Permit systems do not rely on conventionally defined (residential, industrial, and agricultural) zoning districts to segregate potentially incompatible uses. Instead, these systems evaluate all development proposals on the basis of their compliance with a checklist of performance standards. The standards are derived from the planning goals and policies. Most permit system checklists include two kinds of policies: *absolute* and *relative*. Absolute policies require or prohibit certain kinds or levels of performance, while the performance of the project on the relative policies is assessed by using a point-scoring system. The total "score" of a project may be used as the basis for density bonuses that reward positive actions on the part of developers.

While permit systems do not use conventional zoning districts, they may make extensive use of mapped environmental information. They may also be implemented on a neighborhood basis, in which a different set of policies applies to each neighborhood, with the neighborhoods being defined by watershed boundaries, visual or historical character, or the presence of a local "sense" of community. The development of a permit system for a particular place usually involves extensive public participation and an emphasis on procedural simplicity. Permit systems have been successfully used in growing rural areas in the Rocky Mountains, Alaska, and the Missouri Ozarks.

Planner Lee Nellis (1994) incorporates LESA with performance standards and point systems in Idaho and other western states. For example, Nellis prepared a development code for Fremont County, Idaho. The Fremont code is the basis for a

> fixed-area allocation system that limits development of both productive farmland and naturally hazardous or sensitive sites. The owner of "productive croplands" (which are identified using the local LESA system) may develop one dwelling unit for each 40 acres [16.2 hectares] of such land, but may place that dwelling on as little as one acre [0.4047 hectare], while leaving the remaining 39 acres [15.8 hectares] in production" (Nellis 1994, 220) (Table 10.3).

An example of a point system used with zoning districts exists in Breckenridge, Colorado (Wickersham 1978; Humphreys 1985). The Breckenridge comprehensive plan sets forth the guidance of growth as the town goal to preserve historic buildings in the old mining town and to integrate new buildings. To implement the plan, a land-use guidance system was adopted which establishes 42 districts with specific standards for uses and architectural character. The guidance system is enforced through the Breckenridge Development Code, a set of policies covering a range of subjects like air and water quality, the restoration of historic artifacts, and housing (Humphreys 1985).

The Breckenridge code contains both: absolute and relative policies. Projects are analyzed by planners based on a point system to determine

TABLE 10.3
BASE RESIDENTIAL DENSITY ASSIGNMENTS BY LAND TYPE

This Is One of the Density Assignment Tables Adopted in the Fremont County Development Code. Productive Croplands Are Defined Using the Fremont County, Idaho, LESA System.

Site characteristics	Base density, one dwelling unit per
Productive croplands	40 acres
Wetlands, slopes over 30%	25 acres
Stream and lakeshore corridors, slopes of 15–30%	10 acres
Other areas	2.5 acres
Minimum lot size	1.0 acres

Notes: Where site characteristics overlap, the most restrictive density assignment shall apply. Remember that the base densities are averages, allowing the developer substantial flexibility in the actual arrangement of lots. State health regulations may prevent a development from attaining the average density or minimum lot size permitted by these regulations.
SOURCE: Adapted from Nellis 1994.

how well the proposed development meets both absolute and relative criteria. A proposed project must be approved by the town of Breckenridge when it meets all of the absolute policies or has no negative effect on those policies and when it receives a positive score for its compliance with relative policies. According to Humphreys, the point analysis "is the quantitative backbone of the development code system" (1985, 23). He noted that "over the past three years, I have watched over some 1,200 reviews, and, in that time, I have come to believe that the development code has major strengths in flexibility, comprehensiveness, and capacity for negotiation and revision" (Humphreys 1985, 24).

Similar point systems, added on top of traditional zoning regulations, have also been used to help manage growth on a competitive basis in Petaluma, California; Boulder, Colorado; and Ramapo, New York. In competitive systems added to zoning ordinances, a fixed number of permitted developments within each zone is allowed each year. Development proposals are measured against fixed standards and permitted or denied on their merits.

Design Guidelines and Controls

Design guidelines and controls establish standards for architecture and landscape architecture features of new development. Samuel Stokes and his colleagues note that design guidelines "can illustrate what acceptable development in the community should look like, and they can be published by citizens' groups or governmental bodies" (1997, 199). Design review processes can be either voluntary or required. When voluntary, the applicable standards are usually referred to as design guidelines. Mandatory review standards are called design controls. The guideline or control standards are published by the municipality or the county. A proponent for a new development or a change of a building's use must present designs illustrating how they are in compliance with the standards. Usually a design review board, comprised of local experts, is responsible for checking whether the designs are in compliance.

The standards address requirements for the site, for proposed structure(s), and often for off-site features (Shirvani 1990). Site standards usually include guidelines for parking, circulation, paving, lawns, plantings, drainage, irrigation, signs, fencing, setbacks, and building envelopes. Building standards address elements such as height, color, materials, roofing, floor-area ratios, and building footprints. The off-site elements may include views, buffers, roadways, and adjacent land uses.

Critical or Environmentally Sensitive Areas

Performance standards and design guidelines are tools to encourage as well as control development. In contrast, critical or environmentally sensitive areas protection are a way to prohibit or minimize development. Critical and environmentally sensitive areas are terms and concepts often used interchangeably. Critical areas were proposed by the American Law Institute's *Model Land Development Code,* which described them as:

- An area significantly affected by, or having an effect upon, an existing or proposed major public facility or other areas of major public investment
- An area containing or having a significant impact upon historical, natural or environmental resources of regional or statewide importance (American Law Institute 1974)

The Washington State Environmental Policy Act (SEPA) describes environmentally sensitive areas as: "[those that] could have a significant adverse environmental impact, including but not limited to, areas with unstable soils, steep slopes, unusual or unique plants or animals, wetlands, or areas which lie within flood plains" (State of Washington 1984, section 908, see also Washington Department of Ecology 1995).

Adapting the Washington State definition, environmental sensitive areas can be thus defined as places vulnerable to negative environmental impacts. These could include areas such as unstable soils, steep slopes, floodplains, wetlands, and certain plant and animal habitats. Forster Ndubisi and his colleagues define environmentally sensitive areas as "landscape elements or places which are vital to the long-term maintenance of biological diversity, soil, water, or other natural resources both on the site and the regional context. They include wildlife habitat areas, steep slopes, wetlands, and prime agricultural lands" (1995, 159).

Certain states (such as Washington) and local jurisdictions (such as Scottsdale, Arizona, and Waterloo, Ontario) require the protection of environmentally sensitive areas. The State of Washington protects environmentally sensitive areas through its state environmental policy act provisions. SEPA provisions in Washington enable city and county governments to designate areas within their jurisdictions that are environmentally sensitive. As a result of SEPA, a procedural review is required for proposed actions that may impact the environment. Some actions, however, are specifically exempt from the environmental review process. Because these actions still may have a significant impact on environmental quality, the SEPA law includes the provision allowing the local designation of environmentally sensitive areas. Within locally designated areas, proposals, programs, and actions are subject to environmental review procedures (Jennings and Reganold 1988; see also City of Everett 1994). Furthermore, the Washington Growth Management Act requires cities and counties to identify and protect critical areas. (See Kitsap County Department of Community Development 1998, for example.) These Washington provisions are consistent with the suggestions of the American Law Institute (1974) that critical area policy be adopted on the state level.

On the local level, such an area may be separated by zoning districts or overlay several zones. For example, the city of Scottsdale defines and regulates "land slopes of 15 percent or more in the mountains, unstable slopes, special features, water courses, geologic conditions, and native vegetation" as environmentally sensitive (City of Scottsdale 1991a, 4). The Regional Municipality of Waterloo in Ontario, Canada, identifies an environmentally sensitive policy area as a place demonstrating one or more of the following characteristics:

1. The occurrence of significant, rare, or endangered indigenous species within the designated area
2. The identification of plant and/or animal associations and/or landforms which are unusual or of high quality, regionally, provincially or nationally
3. The classification of the area as one that is large and undisturbed, thereby potentially affording a habitat to species that are intolerant of human disturbance
4. The classification of the area as one which is unique with limited representation in the region, or a small remnant of once-larger habitats which have virtually disappeared
5. The classification of the area as one containing an unusual diversity of plant and animal communities due to a variety of geomorphological features, soils, water, and microclimatic effects
6. The identification of the area as one which provides a linking system of undisturbed forest or other natural refuge for the movement of wildlife over a considerable distance
7. The performance of the area in serving a vital ecological function, such as maintaining the hydrological balance over a widespread area acting as a natural water storage or recharge area
8. The recognition of the area as one demonstrating any of the above qualities but suffering from a minor reduction of its uniqueness or rareness by intrusion of human activities (Smith et al. 1997)

The courts have generally taken a favorable view toward protecting critical or environmentally sensitive areas. For instance, in the classic 1972 case *Just vs. Marinette County* (56 Wisc. 2d 7), the Wisconsin Supreme Court upheld county restrictions on wetlands. According to the Wisconsin court: "[Marinette County's] ordinance that requires a wetland owner to obtain a permit before filling, draining, or dredging is constitutional, since restrictions on use of privately owned wetlands serve to protect the state's natural resources and constitute reasonable application of police power" (Wisconsin Supreme Court 1972).

In this case, wetlands were clearly identified through state policy and local ordinance. According to the Marinette County shorelines ordinance, such wetlands needed protection because "uncontrolled use of shorelines and pollution of navigable waters adversely affect public health, safety, convenience, general welfare, and impair the tax base" (Wisconsin Supreme Court 1972).

George Newman (1982) suggested a system for classifying environmentally sensitive areas adapted from those developed by the New Jersey Pinelands Commission and the Smithsonian Institution (Table 10.4). The Pinelands Commission divides environmentally sensitive areas into four categories: *ecologically critical areas, perceptually and culturally critical areas, economically critical areas, and natural hazard-critical areas.* Newman renamed economically critical areas "resource production critical areas" and developed the following definitions:

TABLE 10.4
ENVIRONMENTALLY SENSITIVE AREA CLASSIFICATION SYSTEM

Class	Subclass
Ecologically critical areas	1. Natural wildlife habitat areas 2. Natural ecological areas 3. Scientific areas
Perceptually and culturally critical areas	4. Scenic areas 5. Wilderness recreation areas 6. Historic, archaeological, and cultural areas
Resource production critical areas	7. Agricultural lands 8. Water quality areas 9. Mineral extraction areas
Natural hazard critical areas	10. Flood-prone areas 11. Fire hazard areas 12. Geologic hazard areas 13. Air pollution areas

SOURCES: Column 1 is adapted from Pinelands Commission 1980; column 2 is adapted from Center for Natural Areas, Smithsonian Institution 1974.

1. *Ecologically critical areas* contain one or more significant natural elements that could be degraded or lost as a result of uncontrolled or incompatible development. Significant elements are those that are identified as being necessary to maintain the essential character and integrity of the existing environment. They are based on the quality, the scarcity, or the role the element plays in the ecosystem. These areas can provide many amenities and services to the public and to private landowners. Maintaining the natural system helps to provide flood control, water purification, water supply, pollution abatement, wildlife habitat, and a pleasing and visually diversified landscape. Ecologically critical areas provide sites for outdoor education, scientific study, or habitat for the spawning and rearing of anadromous fish. Such areas also have psychological or philosophical value for those who gain comfort from knowing that open semiwilderness areas and rare and endangered species and habitats still exist.
2. *Perceptually and culturally critical areas* which contain one or more significant scenic, recreational, archaeological, historical, or cultural resources that could be degraded or lost as a result of uncontrolled or incompatible development. They have features such as access and proximity to water, special recreational resources, or buildings possessing significant historical or archaeological values.

3. *Resource production critical areas* provide essential products supporting either the local economy or economies of a larger scale. The significant resources can be either the essential products (e.g., agricultural crops, timber products, or sand and gravel) or the elements necessary for the production of such essential products (e.g., soil and water). These resources are primarily economically valuable; however secondary values may include recreational values or cultural or life support values associated with local communities. These resources can be renewable, like timber, or nonrenewable, like mineral resources.
4. *Natural hazard critical areas* may result in the loss of life and/or property due to incompatible development. These places include landslide, flood, earthquake, avalanche, or fire-hazard-prone areas (Adapted from the Pinelands Commission 1980; Newman 1982).

Newman suggested the use of the definitions developed by the Smithsonian Institution for use in the subclasses of his system:

1. *Natural wildlife habitat areas* are essential to the preservation of game species and rare, threatened, or endangered species. They provide food, shelter, and breeding areas and must be large enough to fulfill the species needs. Such areas include sites where animals seasonally concentrate, such as deer yards, migratory stop-over spots, aquatic spawning pools, and nesting places for birds. It is important that the area is inherently stable, which is more likely if it contains a high diversity of flora or fauna. Additionally, a greater variety of animal species is associated with a diversity of vegetation types. The uses of these areas will vary according to wildlife. Habitats of endangered species may have to be strictly protected, while recreational hunting can be permitted in areas supporting game species.
2. *Natural ecological areas* have ecosystem units that are either superlative examples of their type or locations that perform a vital function in maintaining the ecological integrity and environmental quality of a larger region. These are areas containing an unusual diversity of plant and animal communities due to a variety of geomorphological features, soils, water, and microclimate conditions. Furthermore, natural ecological areas may be an important component of the human life support system, such as flood control, water purification, water supply, pollution abatement, and oxygen regeneration. Examples include wetlands and riparian areas.
3. *Scientific areas* are of geological interest or present ecological processes warranting study. Most of these areas have been studied, and they can be identified by experts within the local scientific and academic community. Scarcity of geological or ecological features on regional, state, and national levels is an important factor.
4. *Wilderness recreation areas* are tracts of land large enough to support recreational activities such as camping, hiking, birdwatching, and canoeing. Isolated wilderness areas close to population centers are especially valuable.
5. *Scenic areas* contain natural features of sufficient aesthetic quality to warrant their preservation. Several methods have been developed for determining scenic values, but the determination of aesthetic quality remains subjective. Some methods attempt to survey the public's values of various landscapes and geological formations, while other methods review such factors as vegetative type, composition, and texture; topography; and geographic features. The scarcity and location of these areas is often an important consideration.
6. *Historic, archaeological, and cultural areas* are important to the heritage of the community, region, state, or nation. These areas may contain structures or artifacts, or they may be

associated with an historic event. The sites may be considered by archaeologists as likely to yield important information. These areas are often listed by state historical and heritage agencies or societies, although most of these organizations do not rate the sites according to their importance. Such areas may also emerge as a result of analysis in response to a threat.

7. *Agricultural lands* are used for crop or animal production or for silviculture. A reason for including these lands in the subclassification is that the private market is unable to adequately incorporate long-term or future agricultural demands so as to ensure prime lands will remain in farm use. Soils for agriculture and forest for timber production are renewable resources when properly managed. However, development of these areas may cause irreversible damage to the resources. Soil productivity (generally based on NRCS land capability or productivity ratings) and the availability of water are the factors important for crop production. The LESA system, described in Chapter 5, can be used to help identify important agricultural areas. State agriculture departments have production yield figures, and the USFS maintains a forest growth potential rating system to determine timber production areas.
8. *Water quality areas* ensure the maintenance of sources of clean water. These areas are generally aquifer recharge areas, headwaters, stream corridors, and wetlands that function as a natural filter for surface waters.
9. *Mineral extraction areas* contain sufficient quantities of high-quality minerals to warrant their protection from development that would exclude the possibility of extraction. These areas contain minerals or materials of commercial quality and quantity that may include, but are not limited to, sand, gravel, clay, peat, rock, and ores.

Water quality areas ensure the maintenance of sources of clean water.

10. *Flood prone areas* are identified on the basis of the frequency of flooding. They may be either floodplain areas adjacent to rivers or coastal areas within the hurricane zone. The U.S. Army Corps of Engineers can help to identify the frequency of flooding in these areas.
11. *Fire hazard areas* are identified by the USFS and state wildfire management agencies as being particularly susceptible to forest fires. The important factors are the type and quantity of fuel accumulation and weather.
12. *Geological hazard areas* are characterized by a high frequency of earthquakes, landslides, fault displacements, volcanic activity, subsidence, or severe erosion.
13. *Air pollution areas* require restraints on air pollution emissions due to periods of poor vertical air mixing and the subsequent entrapment of polluting substances. Topographic features and meteorological conditions are the most important factors in their identification (Center for Natural Areas, Smithsonian Institute 1974; Pinelands Commission 1980; Newman, 1982).

The identification of critical areas in the Pinelands was based on the work of the Philadelphia-based consulting firm Rogers, Golden, and Halpern. Areas for consideration as critical were nominated and ranked. Table 10.5 illustrates how mapped areas were ranked, while Table 10.6 shows the criteria used for ranking ecological critical areas in the Pinelands. Four types of environmentally sensitive areas that have received especial attention are *floodplains, wetlands, wildlife habitats, and places of historical significance.* These four types will be discussed in greater detail.

Floodplain Management

Flooding can create hazards for human safety and health. Floods can also result in significant property damage. Conversely, natural flooding cycles also benefit water quality, soil development, and wildlife habitat. The National Flood Insurance Program (NFIP) was created by Congress through the National Flood Insurance Act of 1968. The NFIP established a national policy and framework for floodplain management. The initial act has been modified and refined since 1968 by Congress. The NFIP is administered by the Federal Insurance Administration and the Mitigation Directorate which are part of the Federal Emergency Management Agency (FEMA) (Morris 1997).

The NFIP makes flood insurance available to property owners, only if their community participates in the program. Furthermore, loans for purchasing property are linked to the NFIP. As a result, there are strong incentives for communi-

TABLE 10.5
SAMPLE OF FORM USED TO RANK ECOLOGICALLY CRITICAL AREAS IN THE NEW JERSEY PINELANDS

CEDAR CREEK WATERSHED Critical Area Mapping Units	Critical Area Criteria	Linkage Corridors	Unique or Exceptional Ecosystems	Pristine Aquatic Communities	Headwaters	Nationally Endangered Animal Species	Diversity of Vegetation Types within a Given Area	Nationally Proposed or under Review Plant or Animal Species	State Endangered, Threatened, Declining, or Undetermined Plant or Animal Species	Representative Vegetation Types	Outlier, Disjunct, or Relict Species	Species at the Limits of Their Range	Restricted and Endemic Species	Breeding Areas (Nesting and Spawning)	Overwintering Concentrations	Migratory Stopover Areas	Areas of Scientific Interest and Research	Oldest, Largest, or Exceptional Specimen Trees
Cedar Creek (1)														•		•		
Cedar Creek (2)				•	•		•	•	3		•	3	•		•			
Factory Branch				•	•		•			•								
Newbolds Branch				•	•		•	•	•		•	•						
Daniels Branch			•	•	•		•	•	•	•	•	•						
Bamber Lake			•	•	•		•	•	•	•	•	•			•			
Chamberlain Branch				•	•		•		•	•	•	•			•			
Webbs Mill Branch			•	•	•		•	•	3		2	2			•		•	

Legend
· The criterion applies to the critical area.
2 Two species from the criterion are found in the critical area.
3 Three species from the criterion are found in the critical area.
SOURCE: Pinelands Commission 1980.

TABLE 10.6
RANKING CRITERIA FOR ECOLOGICALLY CRITICAL AREAS IN THE NEW JERSEY PINELANDS

	Group and Sample Size (*n*)				
Critical areas criteria	**Staff, scientists and consultants (*n* = 17)**	**Burlington County Public Meeting (*n* = 31)**	**Atlantic County Public Meeting (*n* = 22)**	**Ocean County Public Meeting (*n* = 29)**	**Average (*n* = 99)**
Pristine aquatic communities	1	1	1	2	1
Headwaters	2	2	2	1	2
Unique or exceptional ecosystems	3	3	3	3	3
Nationally endangered species	5	5	5	7–8	6
Linkage corridors	4	4	7	4	4
State endangered, threatened, declining, or undetermined species	7	9	6	5–6	5
Breeding areas (nesting or spawning)	6	6	4	5–6	5
Species proposed or under review for national list	8	12–13	10	10	11
Diversity of vegetation types within a given area	9	7	11	9	8
Outlier, disjunct, or relict species	11	16	14	15	15
Migratory stopover areas	12	8	8	12	9
Restricted and endemic species	10	11	12	14	13
Overwintering concentrations	14	10	9	11	10
Representative vegetation types	13	12–13	13	7–8	12
Species at limits of their geographic range	15	15	16	16	16
Areas of scientific interest and research	16	14	15	13	14
Oldest, largest, or exceptional tree specimens	17	17	17	17	17

SOURCE: Pinelands Commission 1980.

ties to be involved in the NFIP. Morris notes that the "NFIP strategy is to provide the benefits of federally backed flood insurance coverage in return for mitigation of flood risks through community regulation of floodplain development" (1997, 4). Participation involves the incorporation of floodplain management provisions into a city, town, or county's zoning and subdivision ordinance or by developing a separate overlay floodplain management ordinance (Morris 1997). Local ordinances must meet minimum standards for flood-damage reduction established by the NFIP. Critics of the program argue that these standards are too liberal and that more rigorous thresholds for hazards should be created. However, FEMA estimates that the NFIP regulations prevented more than $770 million in flood damage to buildings and their contents between 1978 and 1997 (Morris 1997).

FEMA introduced its Community Rating System (CRS) in 1990 to provide incentives for jurisdictions that go beyond minimum standards. For jurisdictions participating in the CRS, insurance premiums are reduced for all policy holders (Morris 1997).

Floodplain regulation is to be based on maps produced by FEMA that are called Flood Insurance Rate Maps (FIRMs). These maps are accompanied by text describing flood areas and related hazards. One-hundred-year flood boundaries are delineated on FIRMs. "A '100-year flood,' or base flood, is the flood that has a one percent or greater chance of being equaled or exceeded in any given year" (Morris 1997, 6). FIRMs also show the location of floodways and often 500-year flood boundaries. The NFIP requires that all lands within the 100-year floodplain be regulated. As a result, it is important to include FEMA, FIRM, and related data in the ecological inventories discussed in Chapter 3. Marya Morris (1997) provides an excellent detailed discussion about how flood information can be incorporated into subdivision and other local ordinances.

Wetland and Riparian Area Protection

The protection of wetlands and riparian areas has emerged as an important environmental planning issue. In the United States, several federal, state, and local laws have been enacted to protect wetlands and riparian areas. Specifically, the federal Clean Water Act (CWA) includes protection requirements in Sections 301 and 303 for state water quality standards, Section 401 for state certification of federal actions (projects, permits, and licenses), and Section 404 for dredge and fill permits. The Section 401 water quality state certification element has been called the "sleeping giant" of wetlands protection because it empowers state officials to veto or condition federally permitted or licensed activities that do not comply with state water quality standards. State officials have used this power infrequently, although considerable potential exists for stronger state and local wetlands protection efforts (World Wildlife Fund 1992).

Historically, wetlands and riparian areas were viewed differently than they are today. Throughout human history people have located their settlements near rivers and lakes for water supply and waste disposal. As a result, most cities and towns are near, or have replaced, wetlands and riparian areas. Prior to 1970, wetlands and riparian corridors were generally viewed as waste areas that had minimal value for urban uses such as housing and commerce. Because of flooding dangers, areas adjacent to rivers and streams can be dangerous places to locate homes and businesses. As a result, wetlands and riparian areas often became sites for unwanted or undesirable uses such as heavy industry and landfills. But with the growth of metropolitan regions, wetland and riparian areas have become more desirable for development. As William Reilly, the former EPA director, noted before a U.S. Senate panel, "Wetlands are where the country is going. [Population is concentrated] on the coasts; on rivers; around lakes; on flat, undeveloped, cheap and developable land. Wetlands are, and will continue to be, under stress" (Lawson 1991, 77–78).

Since 1970, there has been a change in the public perception of wetlands and riparian areas. Increasingly, these areas have become recognized for their positive values for flood protection, water quality and supply, recreation, and as wildlife and fish habitats. As a result, a few states, then the federal government, and finally several more states and localities implemented programs encouraging the protection of wetlands and riparian areas. Beginning in the late 1960s and throughout the 1970s, there was a host of such laws addressing clean water, floodplains, wild and scenic rivers, the coastal zone, endangered species, and mining reclamation (U.S. Department of Interior 1988). Beginning in 1985, the preservation of wetlands on farms was required as a prerequisite for federal agricultural subsidies. These federal laws and associated state laws are dynamic and continue to evolve (Steiner et al. 1994). The federal and state laws have prompted, and even required, local regulation.

States have adopted various protection strategies, including:

- Assumption of the CWA, Section 404 permitting program
- Involvement in implementation of a federal CWA, Section 404 permitting program
- Implementation of a CWA, Section 401 certification program
- Promulgation of narrative or numeric standards and/or use of antidegradation standards to protect wetland/riparian areas
- Other natural resource protection programs that protect riparian areas
- Establishment of voluntary or mandatory watercourse alteration or streamside forestry best management practices
- Establishment of protection mandates through executive orders
- Creation of opportunities for protection through tax incentives, easements, recognition programs, technical assistance, and education
- Protection by acquisition
- Inclusion of riparian areas and wetlands in definitions of "waters of the state" for regulatory purposes (Steiner et al. 1994)

Federal Wetlands Protection. As observed by William Want, "Most wetlands regulation has been done at the federal level and the federal program of regulation has become very complex" (1990, 1–1). Historically, federal and state governments were concerned about waterways for their navigational values, principally for defense and commerce. Water was relatively plentiful and abundant in the eastern United States. With increased knowledge about sanitation and disease in the nineteenth century, coupled with the growth of industrial cities, there began to be concern about water quality. As the people of the nation moved West, wetlands were viewed as a nuisance to be converted to productive use as water irrigation systems were developed for agriculture and urban uses. In the late 1960s, the status quo began to change as federal agencies began to protect wetlands for their ecological values (Want 1990). In 1972, with the passage of the Federal Water Pollution Control Act Amendments [the Clean Water Act (CWA)], a new era of water quality protection began that included valuing wetlands differently.

The CWA is the principal law authorizing wetlands regulation (33 USC 1251–1376). A major regulatory program is the National Pollution Discharge Elimination System (NPDES), which is administered by the EPA. Want notes, "Section 301 of the Act prohibits the discharge of any pollutant without a permit. Section 402 of the [Act] authorizes EPA [or an approved state] to issue such permits. Section 404 of the Act carves out from the general EPA permit authority a special authority for the [U.S. Army Corps of Engineers] to issue permits for the discharge of two types of pollutants: dredged material and fill material" (1990, 2–7). As a result, the EPA and Corps jointly administer the 404 program. EPA has veto authority over the issuance by the Corps of the 404 permits. However, EPA has seldom used this power. According to former EPA administrator William K. Reilly, the "Corps issues over 10,000 permits every year, and in the 18-year history of the program, EPA has vetoed only 11 projects" (1991, 193).

The main purpose of the CWA "is to restore and maintain the chemical, physical, and biological integrity of the Nation's water." In the 1987 amendments to the act, Congress established the policy "to recognize, preserve, and protect the primary responsibilities and rights of states to prevent, reduce, and eliminate pollution, to plan the development and use (including restoration, preservation, and enhancement) of land and water resources. . . ." The 1987 amendments also established the policy of state implementation of Sections 402 and 404 permit programs.

Section 401 of the CWA allows the states "to veto federally permitted or licensed activities that do not comply with state water quality standards" (Ransel and Meyers 1988, 340). The states have the responsibility for setting these standards, subject to EPA approval. Section 303 of the CWA gives states "great latitude in formulating their water quality standards" (Ransel and Meyers 1988, 344). States may establish designated water uses and water quality standards criteria sufficient to "protect the public health or welfare, enhance the quality of the water and serve the purposes of the Act" [33 USC 1313 (c)(2)(A)].

According to K. Ransel and E. Meyers, quoting partially from the CWA, "any applicant for a Federal license or permit for conducting any activity . . . which may result in any discharge to the navigable waters' [is required] to secure from the state in which the discharge originates a certification that the discharge will comply with several provisions of the CWA related to effluent discharge limitations and water quality standards" (1988, 342). Thus, a denial of Section 401 certification "operates as an absolute veto" and "the state's decision is not reviewable by the federal permitting agency or the federal courts" (Ransel and Meyers 1988, 342). As a result, Ransel and Meyers observe, "the states' most important role in the Section 401 certification process is to determine whether an applicant for a federal license or permit has demonstrated compliance with state water quality standards and, if not, to deny or 'condition' certification so that the activity will comply with those standards" (1988, 343).

General State Responses. States have responded to federal law in a variety of ways. For instance, as a result of the CWA, states "may assume responsibility for issuing [404] permits in certain waters under their jurisdiction in accordance with criteria developed by EPA" [U.S. General Accounting Office (GAO) 1988, 10]. Thus far, only Michigan and New Jersey have assumed primacy for issuing 404 permits, although several other states have considered or are considering the possibility (World Wildlife Fund 1992). Most states have obtained primacy from EPA for the Section 402 NPDES permit program.

According to D. Salvesen, "The resulting programs [of the states], no two of which are identical, vary from those that regulate a wide range of activities such as dredging and draining, to programs that provide tax incentives to protect wetlands permanently" (1990, 43). Salvesen notes that, in general, states regulate wetlands in two ways: "indirectly, as part of broad regulatory programs such as the coastal zone management program or the water quality certification provisions under Section 401 of the Clean Water Act, and directly, by enacting laws specifically to regulate activities in wetlands" (1990, 43).

Although California, Oregon, and Washington have noteworthy wetlands programs built on coastal protection laws, western states have been slow in developing overall protection policies. In 1985 J. A. Kusler noted that "no state west of the Mississippi has adopted a comprehensive wetland or riparian habitat protection program for public or private lands, unlike the coastal states which have all adopted some protection for their coastal wetlands and 11 eastern states which have adopted freshwater protection statutes" (1985, 6). Western states face a special opportunity and challenge because of the large blocks of public lands. Kusler notes that six western states have adopted floodplain regulatory laws, but "these are narrowly aimed at reducing flood losses and have no provision for vegetation" (1985, 6). Conversely, Oregon has adopted statewide planning guidelines for riverside lands and a state tax credit program, while Washington includes inland shorelines as part of its coastal zone program.

According to C. R. Griffin, "nearly half of the 50 states regulate wetlands uses to varying degrees; however, many of these states protect only coastal wetlands, with inland wetlands being largely unprotected except by federal regulations" (1989, 25). These inland areas are significant because they represent the majority of the wetlands remaining in the lower 48 states. Much of this inland wetland is closely associated, physically and biologically, with riparian areas. Griffin (1989) has identified only 13 states nationwide with comprehensive inland wetlands protection laws, while the World Wildlife Fund (1992) notes that 20 states have enacted wetlands regulatory programs.

The situation is changing both for inland wetlands and in the western states. For example, the Wyoming legislature passed the Wyoming Wetlands Act in February 1991 (WS 35-11-308 through 35-11-311). In that act, the legislature declared that

> all water, including collections of still water and waters associated with wetlands within the borders of this state are property of the state. The legislature further declares that water is one of Wyoming's most important natural resources, and the protection, development and management of Wyoming's water resources is essential for the long-term public health, safety, general welfare and economic security of Wyoming and its citizens.

Action by Wyoming and other states is important because federal agencies have not been successful in preventing the loss of wetlands. The U.S. General Accounting Office (1988) has been critical of the Army Corps of Engineers for not systematically seeking out 404 permit violators and for not conducting follow-up investigations of suspected violations. GAO researchers have found that the Corps "rarely uses available civil or criminal remedies and suspends or revokes few permits, preferring instead to seek voluntary correction of the violations observed" (U.S. General Accounting Office 1988, 3). The GAO has also observed "limited involvement" by EPA in wetlands program enforcement (Steiner et al. 1994).

Overall, there is relative consistency among all states concerning the role played in Section 404 permitting and Section 401 certification. Only Michigan and New Jersey have assumed primacy in Section 404 permitting. In all other cases, states defer to federal agencies for Section 404 permitting, but implement a 401 certification program. Fewer states (approximately half) have established narrative or numeric standards and/or use antidegradation standards for wetland or riparian areas. At least 28 states have other natural resource protection programs, including coastal zone management programs, that provide protection for wetland and/or riparian areas. Executive orders for protection are less common, occurring in only 7 states. Other nonregulatory programs such as tax incentives, easements, recognition programs, subsidies, technical assistance, education, and acquisition are used by numerous states and in a variety of ways. Most states have some form of nonregulatory program in place. Voluntary and regulatory best management practices are used in well over half the states, more relying on mandatory than on voluntary measures, with 15 using both. Thirty-six states indicated that wetlands and riparian areas are included in the definition of "waters of the state." Table 10.7 summarizes selected programs from all states (Steiner et al. 1994).

Local governments often are responsible for the implementation of these state and federal initiatives. Local governments may also initiate programs for wetland and riparian area protection. A variety of regulatory devices can be employed. Overlay zones restrict development within wetland and riparian areas and direct new growth away from such places. According to the World Wildlife Fund, "overlay zones provide a mechanism to prohibit development and limit other activities in wetlands, impose wetlands buffers, or require measures to reduce the effects of development in wetlands without affecting development outside the designated wetlands area and adjacent buffer zones" (1992, 115). Other devices available for localities include special permits or conditional uses, cluster zoning and PUDs, performance standards, and subdivision regulations (World Wildlife Fund 1992).

Habitat Conservation Plans

Habitat conservation plans (HCPs) are adopted by local governments to protect plant and animal

TABLE 10.7
SUMMARY OF STATE PROGRAMS[a]

State	Regulatory						Nonregulatory			
	Assumption of 404 programs by state	Involvement in federal 404 programs	Implementation of 401 certification	Numeric, narrative, or antidegradation standards	Other natural resource protection programs	Mandatory or voluntary best management practices	Executive order for wetland protection	Nonregulatory programs; tax incentives, easements recognition programs, subsidies, technical assistance	Wetland acquisition programs	Riparian and wetlands in definition of waters of state
Alabama	N	Y	Y	N	Y	M	N	O	N	O
Alaska	N	Y	Y	N	Y	M,V	N	T,E,S	N	N
Arizona	N	Y	Y	Y	Y	M,V	Y	E,R,TA	Y	Y
Arkansas	N	Y	Y	N	N	O	N	T,E,S	N	Y
California	N	Y	Y	N	Y	M	N	R	O	N
Colorado	N	Y	Y	N	N	O	N	R	N	N
Connecticut	N	Y	Y	N	Y	M	N	T,R,S,TA	N	Y
Delaware	N	Y	Y	O	Y	O	N	O	O	O
Florida	N	Y	Y	N	Y	M	N	R	Y	Y
Georgia	N	Y	N	O	N	M	N	E,S	Y	Y
Hawaii	N	Y	Y	Y	Y	M	N	E	Y	Y
Idaho	N	Y	Y	N	Y	M,V	N	R,S,TA	Y	Y
Illinois	N	Y	Y	Y	Y	O	N	E,S,TA	Y	Y
Indiana	N	Y	Y	Y	N	O	N	S,TA	N	O
Iowa	N	Y	Y	Y	N	O	N	T,R,S,TA	Y	O
Kansas	N	Y	Y	N	Y	M	N	E,TA	N	Y
Kentucky	N	Y	Y	N	Y	O	N	E,R,TA	Y	Y
Louisiana	N	Y	Y	N	Y	O	N	O	N	Y
Maine	N	Y	Y	N	Y	M	N	E,S,TA	N	Y
Maryland	N	Y	Y	N	Y	M,V	N	E,S,TA	Y	Y
Massachusetts	N	Y	Y	N	Y	O	N	TA	N	Y
Michigan	Y	Y	Y	Y	Y	O	N	E,TA	Y	Y
Minnesota	N	Y	Y	Y	N	O	Y	E,R,S,TA	Y	Y
Mississippi	N	Y	Y	N	Y	O	N	O	N	Y
Missouri	N	Y	Y	Y	N	M	N	E,S,TA	Y	Y
Montana	N	Y	Y	N	N	M,V	N	S,TA	Y	Y
Nebraska	N	Y	Y	Y	N	M,V	N	T,E,S,TA	Y	Y
Nevada	N	Y	Y	Y	N	M,V	N	T,E,S,TA	N	N
New Hampshire	N	Y	Y	O	Y	M,V	N	T,E,S,TA	Y	Y
New Jersey	Y	O	O	O	O	O	O	O	O	O
New Mexico	N	Y	Y	N	N	M	N	O	O	N
New York	N	Y	Y	Y	Y	O	Y	T,S	N	Y
North Carolina	N	Y	Y	N	Y	O	N	T,S	N	N
North Dakota	N	Y	Y	N	N	M,V	N	TA	N	Y
Ohio	N	Y	Y	Y	N	O	Y	E,TA	Y	Y
Oklahoma	N	Y	Y	N	N	M	N	S,TA	N	N
Oregon	N	Y	Y	N	Y	O	N	T,E,S,TA	N	Y
Pennsylvania	N	Y	Y	Y	Y	M,V	N	T,E,S,TA	N	Y
Rhode Island	N	Y	Y	N	Y	M,V	N	T,E	Y	Y
South Carolina	N	Y	Y	N	Y	M,V	N	O	N	Y
South Dakota	N	Y	Y	N	N	O	N	O	N	O
Tennessee	N	Y	Y	Y	N	M	Y	E,S,TA	Y	Y
Texas	N	Y	Y	Y	N	O	N	O	N	Y
Utah	N	O	O	O	O	O	O	O	O	O
Vermont	N	O	O	O	O	O	O	O	O	O
Virginia	N	O	O	O	O	O	O	O	O	O
Washington	N	Y	Y	Y	Y	M,V	Y	TA	Y	Y
West Virginia	N	Y	Y	Y	N	M,V	N	TA	Y	Y
Wisconsin	N	Y	Y	Y	Y	M,V	N	R,S,TA	Y	Y
Wyoming	N	Y	Y	Y	N	V	Y	TA	Y	O

[a] N = no, Y = yes, M = mandatory, V = voluntary, T = tax incentives, E = easements, R = recognition programs, S = subsidies, TA = technical assistance and education, O = no data.

SOURCE: Adapted from Steiner et al. 1994

species and to promote biodiversity. The basic concept is that a species' habitat, its home, must be protected in order for it to survive. HCPs are made in the United States under the framework created by the Endangered Species Act (ESA) of 1973 (Beatley 1994a, 1994b). The original 1973 act has been amended by Congress several times. Timothy Beatley calls the ESA "perhaps the strictest environmental protection statute in the world" (1994a, 10). Essentially, the federal government through the U.S. Fish and Wildlife Service identifies protected species and conservation standards. Once species are identified, the state and local governments negotiate HCPs with all the interested "stakeholders" and then the USFWS must approve the negotiated HCP. Although the USFWS must approve the HCP, the agency also is usually heavily involved throughout the usually very lengthy negotiation process.

Christopher Duerksen and his colleagues (1997) suggest several implementation tools that can be used in a HCP (Table 10.8). They provide

TABLE 10.8
THE SCALE/TOOL MATRIX

		Landscape-scale tools	Site-scale tools
Regulatory tools	Zoning texts and maps	X	X
	Special overlay districts	X	X
	Agricultural and open space zoning	X	
	Performance zoning		X
	Phasing of development		X
	Subdivision review standards	X	X
	Sanctuary regulations	X	
	Urban growth boundaries	X	
	Targeted growth strategies	X	
Incentive tools	Density bonuses	X	X
	Clustering		X
	Transferrable development rights	X	
	Preferential treatment	X	
Acquisition programs	Fee-simple purchase	X	X
	Sellbacks and leasebacks	X	X
	Options and rights of first refusal	X	X
	Easements and purchases of development rights	X	X
	Land dedications and impact fees	X	X
Development agreements			X
Control of public investments		X	X
Taxing and assessment districts		X	X
Private-sector initiatives	Land trusts		X
	Limited conservation development		X
	Industrial restoration showcase projects		X
Intergovernmental agreements		X	
Education, citizen involvement, and technical assistance		X	X

SOURCE: Duerksen et al. 1997.

useful, detailed descriptions of how HCPs can be incorporated with many of the implementation tools reviewed in this chapter including zoning, performance standards, and subdivision regulations (Duerksen et al. 1997). Whatever the tool or combination of measures used in a HCP, it should be based on a thorough ecological inventory and analysis of the planning area.

Sheila Peck (1998) discusses the use of habitat conservation areas (HCAs), transitional areas, and removal areas in HCPs. In the Northern Spotted Owl Conservation Plan in the Pacific Northwest, for example, the HCAs were developed "from maps depicting the range of the owls, the distribution of their old-growth habitat, locations where they now occur, and lands suitable for the establishment of HCAs" (Peck 1998, 104–105). The idea is to protect large enough habitats for rare or endangered species to enable them to thrive. *Transitional areas* are areas that possess good habitat but for some reason are not feasible to include in a preserve area. *Removal areas* have low-quality habitat or are located in places where habitat conflicts with adjacent uses. Species in *removal areas* are moved to HCAs (Peck 1998).

A federal-state program that can assist in habitat conservation planning is the Gap Analysis Program (GAP), part of the U.S. Geological Survey. GAP seeks to identify the degree to which species and natural communities are represented in protected areas. Species and habitats not adequately represented in such areas are identified as "gaps." The Cooperative Fish and Wildlife Research Units implement the GAP in partnership with universities, private business corporations, nonprofit conservation groups, state game and fisheries departments, and other governmental agencies (Zube et al. 1994).

A strength of GAP is its emphasis on partnerships. High technology satellite imagery and computer mapping information are available to state and local governments to implement habitat conservation plans. GAP is not, Noss and Cooperrider observe, "directly involved in the process of landscape design and zoning. Rather, it provides data and assessments that allow planners to conduct these activities intelligently" (1993, 5).

Historic Preservation

Places can be especially sensitive to change because of their archaeological or historical significance. As a result, many communities have adopted special districts to protect these cultural resources. Often this is accomplished by an "overlay zone," that is, a special designation in addition to the regular zoning. Historic properties within such a zone receive special protection but are subject to specific regulations.

The National Environmental Policy Act indicated that it is the responsibility of the federal government to "preserve important historic, cultural and natural aspects of our national heritage. . . ." NEPA is one of several federal laws, regulations, and executive orders designed to protect historical and archaeological sites, including the Antiquities Act of 1906; the Historic Sites, Buildings, and Antiquities Act of 1935; the National Trust Act of 1949, which established the National Trust for Historic Preservation; and the National Historic Preservation Act of 1966, as amended in 1980 and 1992 (Canter 1996). The National Historic Preservation Act provisions are especially important for planning implementation. This act states that any "federal undertaking" has to evaluate potential impacts on historic and archaeological resources. Projects involving federal funds or any federal permits are subject to this law. As a result, local road-building projects using federal highway funds, local community development block grant projects, undertakings on federal lands, and many other efforts result in a review of their impact on historic and archaeological resources.

The 1935 law established the National Register of Historic Places, which was expanded by the National Historic Preservation Act for districts, sites, buildings, structures, and objects significant in American history, architecture, archaeology, and culture (Canter 1996). The act provides funding to states for historical surveys and planning as well as for preservation, acquisition, restoration, and development projects. These programs are administered through state historic preservation officers, or SHPOs. Certified local government historic preservation programs can work with SHPOs to nominate properties to the National Register, which is administered by the U.S. Department of Interior. Once a property is listed on the National Register, it is eligible for special protection and benefits. The act only protects sites against federal actions.

Additional opportunities exist through the National Trust for Historic Preservation's Main Street Program and Your Town Workshops. Beginning in 1977, the Main Street Program has been active in 37 states and 900 communities (Stokes et al. 1997). Focused on smaller cities and towns, the program uses a four-point approach: promotion, economic restructuring, design, and organization. These are coupled with eight principles: comprehensiveness, incremental change, self-help, public-private partnerships, identifying and capitalizing on existing assets, quality, change, and action-orientation (Stokes et al. 1997). The Main Street Program can contribute much to the preservation of historic downtowns as well as their revitalization.

The National Trust initiated the Your Town Workshops in 1991 with the Faculty of Landscape Architecture at the State University of New York at Syracuse, with funding from the National Endowment for the Arts. The program brings together rural decision makers in intense three-day charrettelike workshops to explain the potential for design to improve their communities. The workshops teach decision makers how to value the assets of their communities, including their history (Hawks and Mastran 1997).

Subdivision Regulations

In contrast to performance standards and critical areas, subdivision regulations and building codes are much older forms of land-use controls. In the Old Testament there is a description of the proposals made by Ezekiel for the building of Jerusalem. The first recorded regulations on the division of land in the Western Hemisphere were the Laws of the Indies of 1573 used in Spanish colonization. According to John Reps, "in 1573, Phillip II proclaimed the Laws of the Indies to establish uniform standards and procedures for planning of towns and their surrounding lands as well as for all other details of colonial settlement" (1970, 41). The Laws of the Indies were based on older European laws dating back to the time of the Romans. Modern American subdivision regulations are, according to Philip Green,

> locally adopted laws governing the process of converting raw land into building sites. They normally accomplish this through plat approval procedures, under which a developer is not permitted to make improvements or to divide and sell [the] land until the planning commission has approved a plat (map) of the proposed design of [the] subdivision. The approval or disapproval of the commission is based upon compliance or noncompliance of the proposal set forth in the subdivision regulations. In the event that the developer attempts to record an unapproved plat in the local registry of deeds (or county record's office) or sell lots by reference to such a plat, [the developer] may be subject to various civil and criminal penalties (1968, p. 445).

There is a strong enforcement capability in such regulations, but also significant loopholes in many places. The purpose of subdivision regulations is to protect the public interest during the laying out of land and the construction of public and private improvements. Like comprehensive or general plans and zoning ordinances, local governments have the authority to enact subdivision regulations through state enabling legislation. Subdivision regulations usually have strong enforcement provisions: Deeds to subdivided land may not be recorded or registered, and consequently land may not be sold, until the planning commission forwards an approved copy of a final plat to the county clerk or auditor (Kleymeyer, no date). The required "improvements" may be in the public way, as well as on private land.

Subdivision regulations often require a six-step process:

1. A *preapplication stage,* where the developer and planning staff discuss the proposed development to determine whether all the requirements are met.
2. A *preliminary plat,* prepared by a landscape architect, registered surveyor, or engineer, is then submitted to the planning agency.
3. The planning commission and/or agency *reviews* the preliminary plat and approves or denies it.
4. Most subdivision regulations next require that the developer *construct the improvements* specified in the preliminary plat.
5. A *final plat* (which is sometimes two documents, i.e., an engineering plat and a plat of record) is submitted for approval.
6. The *approved plat* is recorded.

Like performance standards and critical areas protection, subdivision regulations are often connected to zoning ordinances. Much innovation occurred in the drafting of subdivision regulations during the 1970s as a result of the energy crisis. These innovations rely heavily on natural science information: regional climate, slope (aspect and steepness), microclimate, and vegetation. For instance, Figure 10.1 compares poor solar orientation of streets and houses in a subdivision with good solar practice.

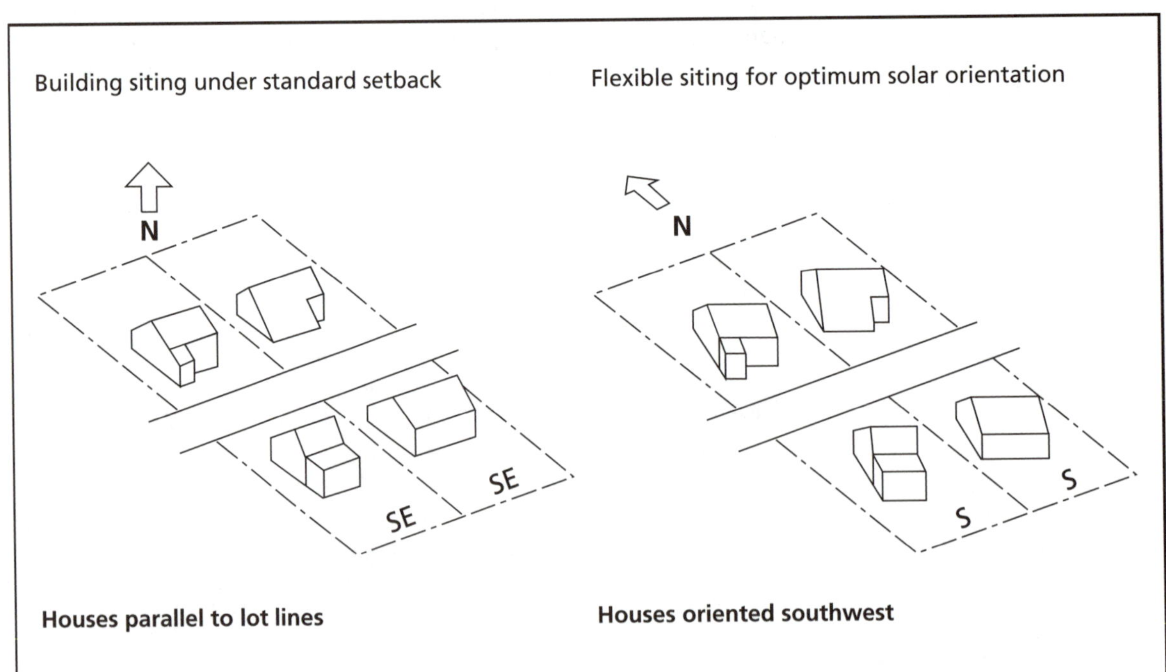

FIGURE 10.1 Poor solar orientation of streets and houses in a subdivision, compared with good solar orientation. *(Source: Jaffee and Erley, no date)*

Building Codes

Building codes have a long history. The code of the Babylonian King Hammurabi is the first written reference to building codes. The code of Hammurabi sets forth the principle of compensatory justice for damages and punishment for faulty construction. There are biblical references to building specifications that were used to construct the ark and the temple. Poor natural conditions and overcrowding in ancient Rome necessitated the development of tenement codes that were adopted in Roman new towns. There are numerous examples of codes in European cities after the Renaissance, such as those in Munich, Kiev, and London.

Building codes in North America began in Boston in 1629 and continued with English colonial activity in the middle Atlantic and southern states. After the American Revolution, height limitations were imposed on the new federal capital in Washington, D.C. The overcrowding and new building technology that resulted during the Industrial Revolution led to new codes, including the development of a national electrical code and uniform building code early in the twentieth century.

Building codes help to standardize construction practices and expedite the spread of new materials and practices. Codes specify the size and use of materials as well as help protect the safety of the public through ensuring structural soundness and fire prevention and control. Health is protected through specifications for water and sewage systems. Building codes are often used with zoning ordinances and subdivision regulations to control population density. The purpose of building and other codes is to secure the general public safety, health, and welfare through structure strength, stability, sanitation, adequate light, and ventilation. Codes also ensure safety to life and property from fire hazards incident to the construction, alteration, repair, removal, demolition, use, and occupancy of buildings or premises. As with zoning ordinances and subdivision regulations, the authority for codes is derived from state enabling legislation with local governmental adoption (Kleymeyer, no date).

The major codes include the Uniform Building Code (UBC) (Table 10.9) used in the western United States; the Council of American Building Officials (CABO) code, used in the northern United States; and the Standard Building Code (SBC), utilized in southern states. The International Conference of Building Officials (ICBO) is currently developing a new consolidated national code for the United States called the International Building Code, which will include recognition in sustainable building practices and plumbing, electrical, mechanical, fire, and (recently) solar codes. These codes are usually enforced through a permit process. Plans are approved by inspection of new construction and remodeling. Continuing inspections are made during construction by the building, fire, plumbing, electrical, or elevator inspectors as well as other specialists employed by the building or health department of the jurisdiction. Violations are noted by these inspectors and are written as "building orders" against the owners of the properties in violation. Owners are given a specified time to correct the deficiencies or face a court action. A building official checks the structure to ensure that it complies to the codes before an occupancy permit is granted. Those not making the necessary corrections are cited to court, where they may be fined or imprisoned under the terms of the codes (Kleymeyer, no date).

There is much room for creative innovation in the linkage between the natural environment, new building materials, and codes. Davis, California, is an example of a city that completely revised and updated its codes to encourage energy conservation. The revised codes take into account the climate, hydrology, and vegetation of Davis. For instance, it was hypothesized that light-colored roofing materials might serve to reflect heat in the intense summer climate of central California and therefore keep buildings cooler. Davis officials experimented with numer-

TABLE 10.9
UNIFORM BUILDING CODE (SUMMARY OF COMPONENTS)

1. Location on the lot
2. Light, ventilation, and sanitation
   a. Windows and ventilation
   b. Ceiling heights
   c. Room size
   d. Sanitation
   e. Fire warning system
3. Private garages and carports
4. Foundations, retaining walls, and drainage
5. Chimneys, fireplace, and barbecues
   a. Reinforcing and seismic anchorage
   b. Flue area
   c. Height
   d. Inlets
   e. Loads on chimney
6. Masonry chimneys
   a. Lining
   b. Wall thickness
   c. Support
   d. Clearance
   e. Factory-built chimneys
7. Fireplaces
   a. Fireplace walls
   b. Lintel
   c. Hearth
   d. Hearth extensions
   e. Combustible materials
   f. Imitation fireplaces
8. Framing
   a. Workmanship
   b. Spacing and penetration of nails
   c. Columns or posts
   d. Wood and earth separation
   e. Headers
9. Floor construction
   a. Foundation ventilation
10. Roof framing
   a. Design
11. Wall construction—wood
   a. Wall and partition framing
   b. Bracing
   c. Foundation cripple studs
   d. Fire-stops
12. Weather protection
   a. Flashing
   b. Exterior wall covering
      (1) Siding
      (2) Plywood
      (3) Shingles or shakes
      (4) Nailing
   c. Exterior plastering
13. Wall construction—masonry
   a. General
      (1) Height
      (2) Chases
      (3) Supported members
      (4) Support
      (5) Anchorage
      (6) Piers
      (7) Openings
   b. Solid masonry
      (1) Construction
      (2) Corbeling
   c. Grouted masonry
   d. Reinforced grouted masonry
   e. Hollow-unit masonry
   f. Cavity-wall masonry
   g. Stone masonry
   h. Veneered walls
14. Exits
   a. Doors
   b. Door landings
   c. Emergency exits
15. Stairs
   a. Rise and run
   b. Winders
   c. Spiral stairs
   d. Handrails
   e. Headroom
   f. Guardrails
16. Plastering and installation of wallboard lathing
   a. Application
   b. Gypsum lath
   c. Stripping
   d. Cornerite
   e. Metal plaster bases
   f. Exterior surfaces
   g. Building paper
17. Plastering
   a. Interior
   b. Exterior
18. Wallboard
   a. Gypsum wallboard
19. Softwood plywood paneling
20. Roof covering
   a. General
   b. Wood shingles
   c. Hand-split shakes
   d. Asphalt shingles
21. Valley flashing
   a. Wood shingles and wood shakes
   b. Asphalt shingles
22. Glass and glazing

ous roofing materials, found their theory substantiated, and then incorporated their findings into the building code.

Building codes can address the use of natural ventilation and natural sunlight. For example, building orientation and configuration can be related to wind flows and solar orientation. Specific design elements such as window design and surface colors can be specified in codes. Interest in sustainable development is prompting cities to enact specific environmental standards for buildings.

For example, Barcelona, Spain, has required specific environmental construction standards, such as giving priority to the use of recyclable materials. Additional building elements that Barcelona officials have mandated for developers include:

- Good orientation and natural lighting
- The incorporation of traditional systems for sun and temperature control
- Limited use of exotic timber or timber from mature forests
- Alternatives to the use of plastics
- Elimination of CFCs, HCFs, and HFCs in refrigeration systems
- Shutters on all external glass apertures in main rooms
- Predominant use of low polluting forms of energy from existing suppliers
- Treatment of flow at all water consumption points
- Collective antenna
- Double-glazing in exterior windows of main rooms

Furthermore, Barcelona officials have required that air conditioning systems be designed to reduce environmental contamination in a way that the noise level is 5 percent below established norms. Barcelona has required developers to supply information about buildings to their occupants regarding the installations and the sustainability, recycling possibility, and origin of the materials.

Covenants

Covenants are agreements, usually voluntary, that restrict what can be done with private property. Generally, for a covenant to be imposed, property has to change hands, at which time these agreements appear in the new deed. Typically, covenants are placed on a property by an owner prior to sale. Usually private parties, rather than governments, impose covenants. Covenants are usually backed up by government authority and may be called *voluntary covenants, restrictive covenants,* or *deed restrictions.* The purpose of covenants is to place additional rules, regulations and/or restrictions upon the use of land over and above, or not capable of being implemented, in the zoning ordinances, subdivision regulations, or building codes; or in the absence of such ordinances, regulations, or codes. The authority for covenants is derived from real estate laws that have been codified by the various states, based upon English common law and additionally interpreted by the state and federal courts (Kleymeyer, no date).

Often all lots within a subdivision will have covenants attached to the land title that describe and design limitations on houses or other structures such as outbuildings and fences. The same principle has been used to a limited extent to control the use of land in the larger community. For instance, a local government may choose to implement its land-use plan through covenants rather than zoning. Another example may be the use of covenants by a citizen group to implement a plan. Farmers in a watershed could agree to keep their land in agricultural production rather than convert it to urban or industrial use.

If a covenant is broken, then other landowners affected by the action can bring suit to restore the original covenant-specified condition or receive compensation for damages. Covenants specify who can bring suit, sometimes including local municipalities. Since neighbors find it very difficult to bring suit against each other, often covenants are not enforced. Therefore, the use of voluntary covenants would only be a reasonable means to control the use of land as long as the parties affected by the covenants are willing to see that they are enforced. One way covenants could be made more efficient in land-use control is for a homeowners' or watershed association to be formed, so that complaints are a result of a collective, rather than individual, action.

POWER TO CONDEMN AND TO EXACT

As previously mentioned, the government can directly purchase private property. If property is needed for a public purpose and the owner is unwilling to sell it, then it may be obtained through condemnation. The Fifth Amendment to the U.S. Constitution states "nor shall private property be taken for public use without just compensation." *Condemnation* is the process of legally appropriating property for public use. To condemn property in the United States, the public purpose must be clearly defined, and "just compensation" must be awarded the property owner. Through condemnation, the public entity acquires any property interest, including full ownership, an easement, or a lesser estate. The use of condemnation in the United States is referred to as *eminent domain.* The federal government, each state, and municipalities have the power of eminent domain within their jurisdiction (Hagman and Juergensmeyer 1986).

Christopher Duerksen and his colleagues (1997), note that "one of the most effective ways of preserving wildlife habitat is to buy it" (1997, 42) (which can occur voluntarily or through condemnation). They identify several types of acquisition programs (Table 10.8). Fee-simple purchase gives "the purchaser full title to and possession of all rights associated with the purchased property, subject only to the constraints imposed by nuisance laws and valid public regulations, including zoning and subdivision" (Duerksen et al. 1997, 42). Important lands can be purchased by park departments or private conservancies and incorporated into existing parks, open space, or preserve areas.

From a government point of view, there are obvious benefits to owning the property outright. The government has a freer reign on the possibilities for its use. A highway, hydroelectric plant, or flood-control project can be more easily constructed. Conversely, the fiscal, social, and political costs can be high. People value their property highly and resist its taking, even for a clearly defined public use. The costs of condemnation, in particular, can be high. This resistance can result in financial costs because of project delays and lawsuits. Social costs can be caused by the destruction of established neighborhoods, even if the larger community benefits. Political costs may result from the emotional and bitter struggles that accompany many projects involving condemnation. These costs may be avoided through other, voluntary forms of acquisition, such as fee-simple purchase and integration into other open space purchase programs.

Impact Fees and Land Dedications

Local governments may require developers to pay for the costs of facilities and services resulting from their projects. Such a requirement is called an *exaction.* Service costs can be related to the time required by planners and other public officials to process plan and zone changes, subdivision reviews, and permits. Affected facilities can include parks, roads, sidewalks, and schools. Such payments are called *impact fees.* The courts have required that the costs imposed must be related to those resulting from the development. In other words, local governments cannot impose additional costs for services or facilities on a developer beyond those of the project. As a result, costs need to be carefully calculated by local planners to ensure a nexus between the fees imposed and the scale of the development. (For a good discussion of the legal issues involved, see Duerksen et al. 1997). J. C. Nicholas and his colleagues (1991) provide a useful guide for calculating impact fees (Table 10.10).

TABLE 10.10
THE BASIS FOR CALCULATING IMPACT FEES

1. The cost of existing facilities
2. The means by which existing facilities have been financed
3. The extent to which new development has already contributed, through tax assessments, to the cost of providing existing excess capacity
4. The extent to which new development will, in the future, contribute to the cost of constructing currently existing facilities used by everyone in the community or by people who do not occupy the new development (by paying taxes in the future to pay off bonds used to build those facilities in the past)
5. The extent to which new development should receive credit for providing common facilities that communities have provided in the past without charge to other developments in the service area
6. Extraordinary costs incurred in serving the new development
7. The time–price differential in fair comparisons of amounts paid at different times

SOURCE: Adapted from Nicholas et al. 1991, 91.

Local governments can also require developers to dedicate land necessary to provide public services related to their projects. Such land is necessary for parks, open space, roads, and schools. According to Christopher Duerksen and his colleagues, "Land dedications are conveyances of land from a private owner, either voluntarily or to offset the anticipated impact of a proposed development. An increasing number of local governments are imposing land dedication requirements or fees in lieu of dedication as conditions for permit approvals" (1997, 46).

Impact fee and *land dedication* programs can be used to support the preservation of environmentally sensitive areas through parks and open spaces. Impact fees can be used to help implement plans by financing projects consistent with local goals in suitable locations. A danger of impact fees is that local planning agencies can become too dependent on developers to finance necessary public programs.

The use of impact fees and land dedications varies widely in the United States. The variation is related to the diversity of state laws relating to impact fee and land dedication programs. For example, Washington State's Growth Management Act requires the fastest-growing cities and counties to have comprehensive plans. Cities and counties are required to follow these plans and to identify how all the implementing programs will be financed. The growth management law also requires that zoning be brought into conformance with comprehensive plans and that the plans establish "urban growth areas" as well as the designation of important agricultural and forest lands (Kelly 1993). The City of Olympia collects impact fees for several categories of facilities, including parks and transportation. Each new residential unit in Olympia pays about $6700 in impact fees, of which about $1800 is dedicated for parks, trails, open space, and recreation (McQuary 1998, personal communication).

POWER TO SPEND

The most direct way that a government may exert its power to spend is by purchasing land fee simple. This can be an expensive option in terms of both the initial price and long-term management. Other options available include *easements* and *development rights purchases and transfers.* As previously noted, governments also have the power to gain ownership, for compensation and for a public purpose, through condemnation. Governments can implement plans through capital expenditures and through public property management.

Easements

The ancient Romans created the first easements for rural areas. The Roman easements provided a means for an owner to voluntarily share benefits derived from his private property. In contemporary terms, an *easement* is the purchase of partial rights to a piece of land. It is enacted through an agreement between two parties for the purpose of a specific use. The most common form of easement occurs when a property owner agrees to let a utility company cross the land with a service line. Easements can also be made to provide access across one property to another. The right to the limited use specified in the easement is usually purchased for a specified period of time, which can be indefinite.

Governments have purchased easements for scenic or aesthetic purposes. In this case, the seller of the easement agrees not to alter the land in a way that would change its scenic value. For example, a grove of trees may be of sufficient historic, aesthetic, or ecologic value to warrant a local, state, or federal government purchase of an easement that would prohibit the removal of the grove.

Similarly, it is possible for the government or a nonprofit organization to purchase an easement that would limit the owner's use of land in order to preserve its usefulness for conservation purposes. This limitation could apply for a specified period of time or be perpetual, and it could be paid for at a mutually agreeable price. The purchase controls and limits use of the land for a specified period, a number of years, or in perpetuity. However, the land and all its associated rights ultimately rest with the property owner. Therefore, such a conservation easement, especially if it is donated, might make the property owner eligible for certain tax benefits.

Land trusts have been active in pioneering and promoting conservation easements. Charles Eliot originated the land trust concept in the establishment of the Massachusetts' Trustees of Public Reservations in 1891. The Massachusetts effort became the model for subsequent conservation and historic preservation organization in the United States and abroad (Morgan 1991). As Keith Morgan writes, "Now known simply as the Trustees of Reservations, this private-sector, not-for-profit organization continues to acquire and maintain lands significant for their natural beauty, unique resources and cultural associates throughout the Commonwealth of Massachusetts" (1991, 6).

According to the Land Trust Exchange (now the Land Trust Alliance), in 1985 more than 500 government agencies and nonprofit organizations were using conservation easements. These easements, both purchased and donated, protect more than 1.7 million acres (688,500 hectares) of land in the United States (Emory 1985). By 1998, land trusts were protecting 3 million acres (1,214,100 hectares) more of land, or approximately 4.7 million acres (1,902,090 hectares). According to the Land Trust Alliance, there were 1213 nonprofit land trusts in the United States, Puerto Rico, and the Virgin Islands (*Planning* 1998). The amount of land protected by these groups (the 4.7 million acres) is an area larger than the states of Connecticut and Rhode Island combined. This total does not include the lands protected by national conservation organizations (*Planning* 1998).

The major public goals implemented by these easements include:

- Permanent protection of beautiful scenery visible from a public road or waterway
- Protection of pure drinking water in urban areas
- Preservation of the rural character of a town
- Maintenance of critical wildlife habitat
- Conservation of farm, forest, or grazing land (Emory 1985; see also Wright 1993)

Development Rights Purchase and Transfers

Some local and state governments separate property ownership and the rights to the development of property. One person can own the land while another can own the right to develop the same parcel of land. In essence, development rights are among those rights that can be controlled by easements.

Through the *purchase of development rights* (PDR), the property owner's development interests are relinquished to the purchaser of the development rights. The idea is to guarantee the rights associated with private property (Figure 10.2). A public government entity may purchase the development rights and hold them in trust, thereby withdrawing them from use. Or, the rights may also be donated to nonprofit organizations, who then control the use.

This land-use management concept is viewed as a means of divesting the developmental potential of the property so that it will remain in its present use (e.g., natural area, agriculture, historic building or site). PDR would be especially useful when zoning mechanisms or voluntary controls like covenants are limited either through inappropriateness or by lack of authoritative control.

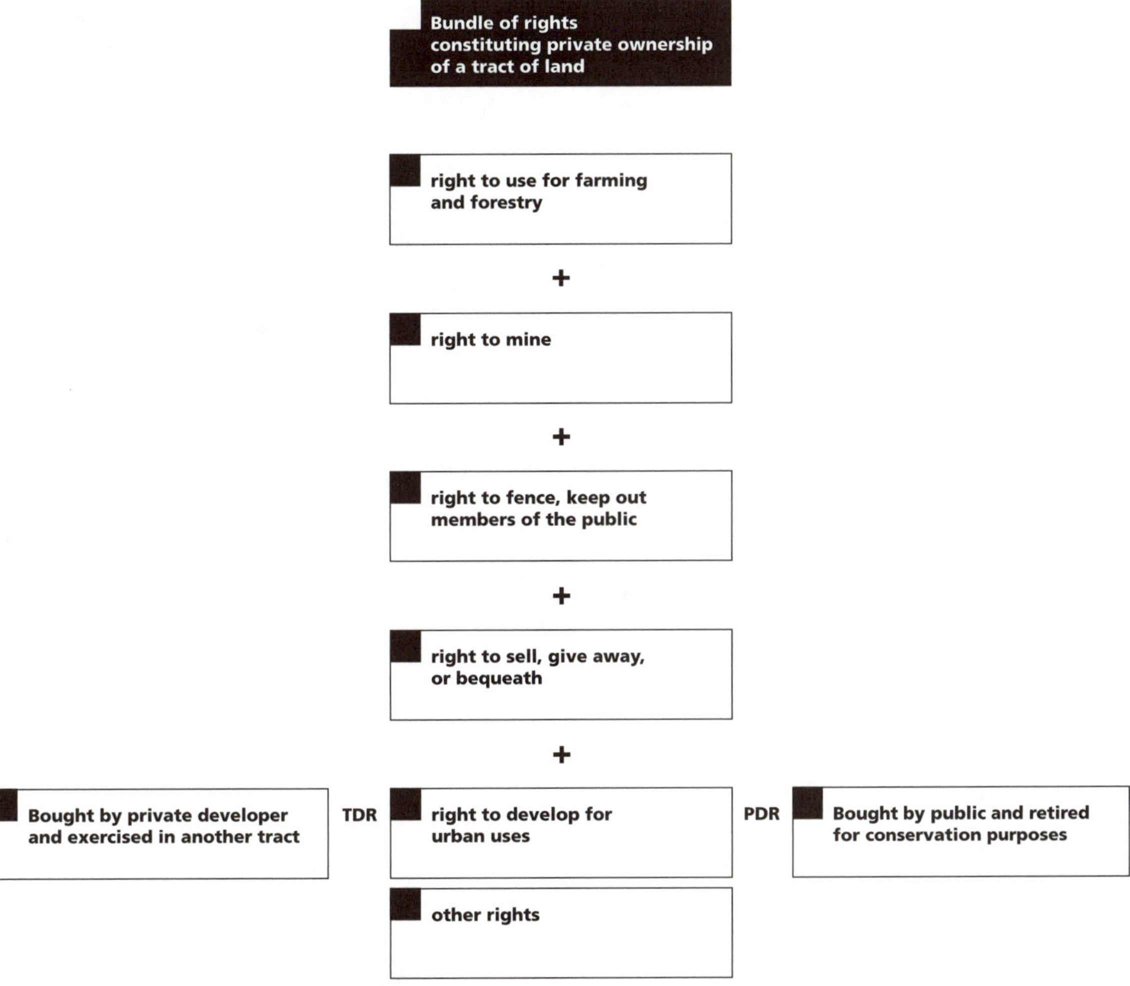

FIGURE 10.2 How the bundle of ownership rights is affected by purchase of development rights and transfer of development rights. *(Source: Adapted from Coughlin and Keene 1981)*

PDR programs exist in 18 states, and 46 states have enacted legislation to permit governments to acquire development rights to private property (Daniels and Bowers 1997). Suffolk County, New York, and King County, Washington are two examples of local governments that have adopted PDR programs. The oldest of these programs is that of Suffolk County. Suffolk County is the easternmost county on Long Island, bounded to the north, east, and south by water and to the west by Nassau County, which is adjacent to New York City (Figure 10.3). Because of this proximity to the nation's largest city, Suffolk County has been under intense development pressure for decades. Still, during the 1970s county farmers managed to produce an annual cash crop of $100 million (mostly from potatoes and cauliflower), which is the greatest cash crop of any county in New York State (Fletcher 1978).*

* In 1992, this figure had risen to over $133 million (Jones and Fedelem 1996).

To protect this threatened resource, the county has developed a program to purchase development rights on its best agricultural land. The initial legislation was approved by the Suffolk County Legislature in 1974. In September 1976, the county approved a $21 million bond issue to begin the first phase of the program—the purchase of development rights on approximately 3800 acres (1539 hectares) of farmland. In 1977, the first contracts were signed with two farmers to purchase their development rights. The ultimate goal of this program is to purchase development rights to about 12,000 to 15,000 acres (4860 to 6075 hectares) of the best farmland, or between 30 and 38 percent of the existing agricultural base at an estimated cost of $55 million (Fletcher 1978). Thus far, however, Suffolk County has fallen short of this goal. By 1996, only 7000 acres (2833 hectares) of farmland had been protected by easement (Jones and Fedelem 1996).

Economically, the farm industry remains important in Suffolk County, generating 8000 jobs and

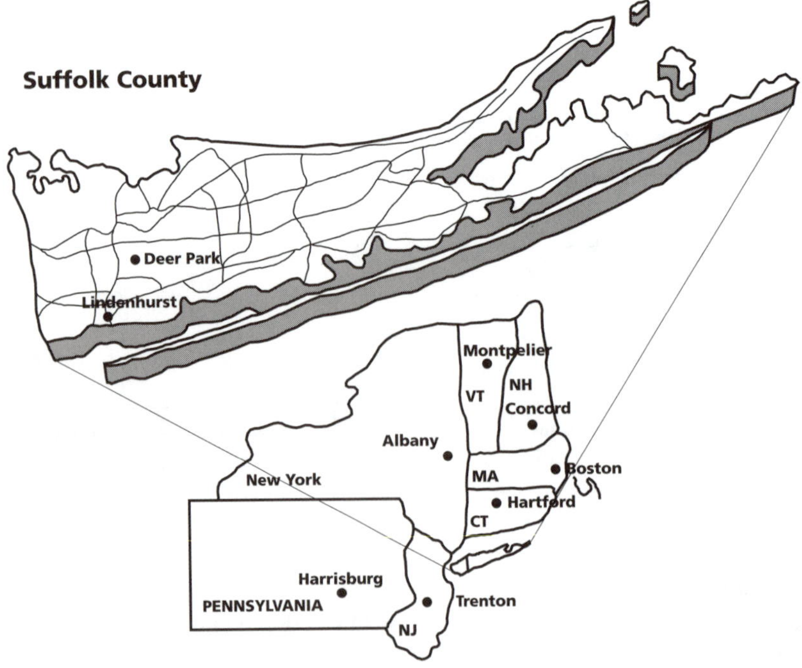

FIGURE 10.3 Location of Suffolk County, New York.

contributing a quarter of a billion dollars to the local community (Jones and Fedelem 1996). However, farmland declines continue—from 123,000 acres (49,778 hectares) in 1950 to about 31,000 acres (12,546 hectares) in 1996 (Jones and Fedelem 1996). As a result, in 1996 the county established a new goal to achieve 20,000 acres (8,694 hectares) of protected farmland (Jones and Fedelem 1996). PDR remains the principal mechanism to achieve this goal. The cost of protecting the additional 13,000 acres (5261 hectares) had risen since the 1970s, with the 1990s price tag at $100 million (Jones and Fedelem 1996). The county now had allies in this effort. Several NGOs are actively involved, and New York State supports PDR programs.

One variation on easement and development rights programs is to simply purchase the land outright, then lease it for a specified use. This is a strategy used by several public-interest trusts. A criticism used against easements or development rights and fee simple purchases is that they are expensive.

A related implementation technique is the *transfer of development rights* (TDR). This technique involves the same development rights as PDR. However, in this case the development rights are purchased to be used in another location, rather than to be retired. Development rights are sold in a *sending* or *preservation* zone to be used in a *receiving* or *development* zone. Generally, the private market is the transfer mechanism, although often transfer banks, such as in the Pinelands, are established to facilitate the process.

The TDR concept was developed to help mitigate the problem of zoning *windfalls* and *wipeouts.* For example, the rezoning of an owner's property from agricultural to urban use could cause an increase in value that could financially benefit the landowner, thus creating a windfall. However, a property owner whose land remains in an agricultural zone may be deprived of the increased value that may be derived from an urban use zone. This could cause the property owner economic hardship—a wipeout situation. The transfer of development rights attempts to distribute economic gains created by development from all property owners in an area, not just those who receive a windfall from a favorable zoning decision (Barron 1975).

One of the first examples of this concept was provided in the Wallace-McHarg Plan for the Valleys, described by Ian McHarg in *Design with Nature* (1969). Developed in 1963 for an area northwest of Baltimore, Maryland, the plan addressed the issue of how to fairly compensate owners whose land was being proposed for a less intensive use. McHarg and David Wallace proposed a syndicate to both develop and preserve the land involved. Through this scheme, the profits from land transactions and developments would be used to compensate landowners whose property was not planned for development (McHarg 1969).

TDR can be described through the following example. A county commission designates two 100-acre (40.5-hectare) parcels of land, A and B. Each parcel is zoned for residential development at one unit per acre. The commissioners later decide that parcel A should remain in its current agricultural use. As a result, to ensure the continued agricultural use, the county permits the transferring of the one unit per acre development rights to parcel B. The property owner can then use those rights to develop parcel B at one unit per ½ acre (0.203 hectare), which amounts to the original one unit per acre plus the transferred unit per acre (Figure 10.4).

Tom Daniels and Deborah Bowers indicate that successful TDR programs require four basic elements:

1. A designated preservation zone, usually called the *sending zone,* from which development is sent away or transferred
2. A designated growth area, usually called the *receiving area,* to which development rights are transferred

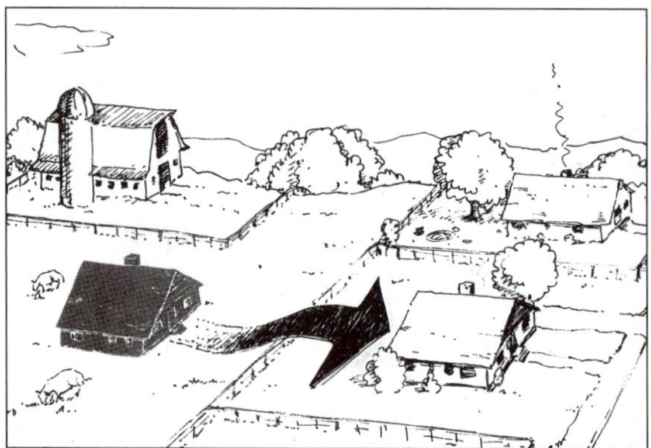

FIGURE 10.4 Illustration of the transfer of development rights concept.

3. A pool of development rights (from the sending area) that are legally severable from the land
4. A procedure by which development rights are transferred from one property to another (Daniels and Bowers 1997, 174)

As noted in Chapter 7, a TDR approach has been used to implement part of the Pinelands plan. A land-use regulatory system was established "which limits residential development in the undisturbed, environmentally sensitive parts of the Pinelands and seeks to direct growth into a more compact pattern within designated growth areas" (Pinelands Commission 1980, 210). To augment the regulatory elements of the plan, a development rights program was established. Property owners in preservation and agriculture zones receive rights, known as *development credits,* that they can sell for use in growth areas. The sales of such credits are recorded on the property deeds, which acts as a controlling and monitoring device.

Capital Improvement Programming

Capital improvements are major projects that require the expenditure of public funds over and above annual operating expenses (Meyer 1980). Some examples of such projects are airports, jails, courthouses, fire and police stations, parks, bridges, streets and roads, sidewalks, sewer and water lines, sewage treatment plants, traffic and street signs and lights, and fire hydrants. According to Frank So *capital improvement programming*

> is a multiyear scheduling of public physical improvements. The scheduling is based on studies of fiscal resources available and the choice of specific improvements to be constructed for a period of five to six years into the future. The capital improvement *budget* refers to those facilities that are programmed for the next fiscal year. A capital improvements *program* refers to the improvements that are scheduled in the succeeding four-or-five-year period. An important distinction between the capital budget and the capital improvements program is that the one-year budget may become a part of the legally adopted annual operating budget, whereas the longer-term program does not necessarily have legal significance, nor does it necessarily commit a government to a particular expenditure in a particular year (1988, 449).

A capital improvement program, then, is a means to implement plans by directing public expenditures into areas suitable for needed projects. Roads, sewers, water lines, and other structural elements of community development can be directed to those areas identified though suitability analysis.

The major steps in developing a capital improvement program include:

1. Submission of project proposals to a review team or coordinator
2. Evaluation of each project, and selection and ranking of projects for inclusion in the program
3. Financial analysis of the jurisdiction's ability to pay for the projects, and selection of the means to be used in financing them
4. Preparation of a proposed capital improvement program

5. Consideration and final approval of the program by the responsible governing body
6. Public approval of financing arrangements for individual projects
7. Annual review and revision of the program (adapted from Meyer 1980)

Advocates of "smart growth" contend that public services, especially infrastructure, should be in place before development can occur. This "concurrency" concept is used in Florida and Oregon "to promote orderly development that will not overburden a community" budget (Daniels and Bowers 1997, 51). Many communities require that specific public services be provided before new development occurs. Tom Daniels and Deborah Bowers suggest that "a community must join its land-use goals and objectives with the capital improvement program so that public facilities that are known to induce growth are available in areas where the community wants growth and kept out of those areas, such as farm and forest lands, that the community wants to protect" (1997, 51).

Public Land Management

About a third of the land in the United States is owned by federal, state, and local governments (Lewis 1980; U.S. Bureau of Land Management 1998). In the 1980s, the federal government alone administered 32 percent of the 2.3 billion acres (932 million hectares) of land in the nation (U.S. Bureau of Land Management 1988). Because of large transfers of federal land to the public sector during the 1980s and early 1990s, this amount had dropped to about 24 percent of the total area of the country by 1997 (U.S. Bureau of Land Management 1998). Most the federal land is in the western states and includes national parks, forests, resource lands, wildlife refuges, designated wildernesses, wild and scenic rivers, national trails, and military installations. All federal land management agencies are subject to environmental planning laws, notably NEPA. Agencies that are especially large and important landholders include the U.S. Forest Service, National Park Service, Bureau of Land Management, and the Department of Defense. Each federal agency has its own planning procedures. Many federal agencies use planning processes with similarities to the one described in this book. Communities can influence federal and state property management to achieve local goals.

One way that communities can influence the use of public property is by encouraging federal and state agencies to adopt plans consistent with local goals. Conversely, federal and state agencies can encourage local governments to do the same. This may require that plans be amended or modified. Cooperation can be accomplished between governments through memorandums of understanding or agreement. Military base operations and closures significantly impact local communities. Base closures during the early 1990s promoted much cooperation to manage the transition. Many former military bases have been transformed into community assets such as schools and open space. Housing has been adapted for lower income groups. Military bases are important economic assets to many communities. As a result, local planners often implement programs to ensure that other land uses do not conflict with military operations.

Central Park, New York City.

Government can also set an example through the management of its property. If a state government seeks to encourage energy conservation, then it can start with the design of its own buildings. The design of government buildings can be used to demonstrate the realization of planning policies. Governments can locate their buildings out of floodplains and other environmentally sensitive areas. Through effective property management, governments can provide models for the rest of the community.

POWER TO TAX

Taxes may be used as incentives for implementing plans. Two examples are the various tax benefits offered for farmland and often for open-space owners in all states, and the incentives given to businesses and industries to locate in certain areas. *Enterprise zones* are another means that may be considered to encourage business development.

All states have adopted some form of legislation providing tax relief for owners to keep their land in agricultural and/or open space use (Table 10.11). Richard Dunford (1984), an economist, has explained the three types of tax relief used: preferential assessment, deferred taxation, and voluntary restrictive agreements. With the *preferential assessment* system, land is taxed on its use rather than its market value. *Deferred taxation* programs provide for preferential assessment, but some or all of the property tax relief becomes due when the land is converted to a nonpermitted use. Under *voluntary restrictive agreement* programs, eligible landowners agree to restrict the use of their land for a number of years. In exchange, their property taxes are based on current-use assessments (Dunford 1984). A fourth type, *circuit breaker* tax relief credits, allows farmers to reduce part of their local tax bill (American Farmland Trust 1997). The costs of these credits are distributed to taxpayers

TABLE 10.11
STATE DIFFERENTIAL ASSESSMENT AND CIRCUIT-BREAKER TAX RELIEF LAWS

State	Type of program	Date enacted
Alabama	Deferred Taxation	1978
Alaska	Deferred Taxation	1967
Arizona	Preferential Assessment	1967
Arkansas	Preferential Assessment	1980
California	Restrictive Agreement	1965
Colorado	Preferential Assessment	1967
Connecticut	Deferred Taxation	1963
Delaware	Deferred Taxation	1968
Florida	Preferential Assessment	1959
Georgia	Deferred Taxation	1987
Hawaii 1	Deferred Taxation	1961
Hawaii 2	Deferred Taxation	1973
Idaho	Preferential Assessment	1971
Illinois	Preferential Assessment	1977
Indiana	Preferential Assessment	1961
Iowa 1	Circuit Breaker	1939
Iowa 2	Preferential Assessment	1967
Kansas	Preferential Assessment	1989
Kentucky	Deferred Taxation	1976
Louisiana	Preferential Assessment	1976
Maine	Deferred Taxation	1971
Maryland	Deferred Taxation	1956
Massachusetts	Deferred Taxation	1973
Michigan	Circuit Breaker	1974
Minnesota	Deferred Taxation	1967
Mississippi	Preferential Assessment	1980
Missouri	Preferential Assessment	1975
Montana	Preferential Assessment	1973
Nebraska	Deferred Taxation	1974
Nevada	Deferred Taxation	1975
New Hampshire 1	Restrictive Agreement	1976
New Hampshire 2	Deferred Taxation	1972
New Jersey	Deferred Taxation	1964
New Mexico	Preferential Assessment	1967
New York 1	Deferred Taxation	1971
New York 2	Circuit Breaker	1996
North Carolina	Deferred Taxation	1973
North Dakota	Preferential Assessment	1973
Ohio	Deferred Taxation	1974
Oklahoma	Preferential Assessment	1974
Oregon	Deferred Taxation	1963
Pennsylvania 1	Deferred Taxation	1966
Pennsylvania 2	Deferred Taxation	1975
Rhode Island	Deferred Taxation	1968
South Carolina	Deferred Taxation	1975
South Dakota	Preferential Assessment	1967
Tennessee	Deferred Taxation	1976
Texas	Deferred Taxation	1966
Utah	Deferred Taxation	1969
Vermont	Deferred Taxation	1977
Virginia	Deferred Taxation	1971
Washington	Deferred Taxation	1970
West Virginia	Preferential Assessment	1977
Wisconsin 1	Circuit Breaker	1977
Wisconsin 2	Deferred Taxation	1995
Wyoming	Preferential Assessment	1973

SOURCE: American Farmland Trust 1997.

statewide. The American Farmland Trust (1997) identifies Michigan, Wisconsin, and New York as states with income tax circuit breaker programs, and Iowa as a state that offers a credit against local school tax credits for agricultural land.

Numerous criticisms have been levied against such programs. The programs are often abused by speculators and developers in order to avoid taxes. Penalties under deferred taxation programs may be minor when compared to inflated land values. Also, unequal tax shifts, or perceived inequalities, can occur as a result of such programs. Yet another weakness is that with the exception of a few states there is no connection between state tax-relief programs and local planning and zoning.

Another type of tax program involves offering incentives to businesses and industries to locate in certain areas. One such type of program is *tax-increment financing.* Wisconsin has a typical program (Huddleston 1981), which permits incorporated cities and villages to create tax-increment districts to eliminate blight, rehabilitate declining areas, and promote industrial growth.

In these districts, for a period of time, all the increase in tax revenue from the property will go only to the municipality involved. The property owners will be free of tax increases from various other local taxing entities, such as school districts and the county. All of the increased revenue must be spent for public facilities in the district: roads, sidewalks, parking areas, sewers, water lines, street trees, and so on. Bonds may be sold first in order to rebuild an area to make it more attractive to investors. The dedicated revenue from the tax-increment district in turn is used to repay the bonds.

Another approach, originated by the British Conservative Party, is the *enterprise zone concept.* The underlying thesis is that the incentive for entrepreneurship must be restored in the inner city. Stuart M. Butler, a proponent of the concept, explained it in the following manner:

> Small businesses would be encouraged to start up by drastic cuts in regulation and taxes (e.g., abating property taxes, reducing Social Security taxes, and changing depreciation schedules). Mixing land uses would be facilitated by relaxing zoning. In short, a climate for enterprise would be established by cutting the cost and complexity of going into business and by allowing entrepreneurs to make do with whatever is available. No grants, no special loans, no expensive plans. It would be an exercise in *unplanning* (1981, 6).

The enterprise zone concept is based on the opinion that the costs of government inhibit small business. An alternative view is that private-sector costs such as interest on loans and fees for services (legal, insurance, health care, and so on) inhibit small businesses. An opposing concept to enterprise zones is that new businesses and industries should pay their share of the services they need—sewer, water, transportation, and so on—and that businesses and industries are responsible for the health, safety, and welfare of their neighbors. Indeed, in some communities growth impact fees are assessed on new developments for certain public services.

Empowerment zones build on the enterprise zone concept, targeting especially low-income or so-called "brownfields" areas. *Brownfield* sites are underused urban areas, generally resulting from abandoned industrial, commercial, or even agricultural uses. Many advocate that it is wiser to reuse brownfields than create new uses in so-called "greenfields." Enterprise and empowerment zones are two approaches to help implement brownfields redevelopment.

INTERAGENCY COORDINATION FOR GROWTH MANAGEMENT

Government agencies can coordinate their activities to implement plans and manage growth. To manage growth, it may be necessary to use some or all of the implementation strategies discussed thus far. A central feature in the concept of growth management in plan implementation is the coordination of various responsible groups. Often this involves different government agencies at the local, state, regional, and federal levels. Tom Daniels and Deborah Bowers describe *growth management* as the "use of regulations and incentives to influence the rate, timing, location, density, type, and style of development in the community" (1997, 315).

Ronald Canham (1979) defines *interagency coordination* as a process in which two or more organizations come together to solve a specific problem or meet a specific need. Interagency coordination implies that by working together, agencies will increase their effectiveness, resource availability, and decision-making capabilities. As a result, the agencies will more effectively assist in the resolution of a community need or problem that could not be met by any single agency acting alone. Interagency coordination is often essential to implement a plan.

Bruce Weber and Richard Beck (1979) provide an example of interagency coordination for coordinated growth management. The location, density, and site design of residential developments have a direct effect on the costs of installing public facilities and providing services, as well as varying potential impacts on the natural environment. As illustrated in Figure 10.5, proposed subdivision A would require a considerable length of sewer and water pipes across vacant land and consequently would result in higher costs to the taxpayer than subdivision B (Weber and Beck 1979).

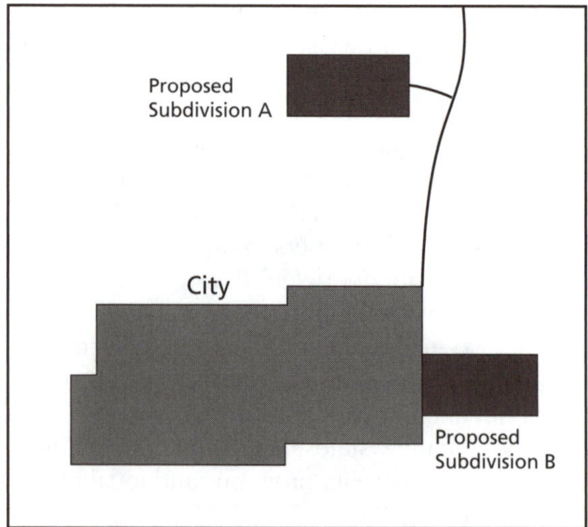

FIGURE 10.5 Comparison of distances for the extension of services to two subdivisions. *(Source: Weber and Beck 1979)*

To encourage subdivision B over subdivision A, it will be necessary for the city and the county (or possibly the township) to cooperate. The cooperation of agencies within each jurisdiction may include combinations of zoning ordinances, performance standards, capital improvement programming, and taxing programs. Interjurisdictional agreements and the establishment of spheres of influence may also be necessary.

Interjurisdictional agreements can involve growth management techniques other than zoning, budgeting, and taxing programs—for example, *service districts, annexation, moratoriums,* and *impact fees.* States like Oregon and Vermont permit local governments to divide their jurisdictions into *urban and rural service districts* with different tax rates. According to Harris, services "are not extended to a rural service district until the area is reclassified as an urban service district, at [a] higher tax rate, which takes place at the time the district is developed for commercial, industrial, or urban residential use" (Harris 1988, 469). Such a change from rural to urban use can be coupled with *annexation.* The determination of urban and rural service districts as well as the coordination of annexations require cooperation among several jurisdictions.

Moratoriums involve the prevention of the issuance of building permits until urban service capacity levels are attained or until plans and ordinances are completed (Harris 1988). *Impact fees* are imposed to require developers to pay for new public services necessary for new growth. Florida state law, for instance, requires "that growth be accommodated and that localities find ways to provide the necessary facilities and services while minimizing the negative effects of growth" (Harris 1988, 470). Impact fees can be linked to local policy related to low- and moderate-income housing, recreation facilities, or open space protection.

PROGRAM LINKAGE AND CROSS-COMPLIANCE

Certain government benefits (the "carrots") can be linked to requirements (the "sticks") for specific actions. For instance, preferential property taxation can be tied to zoning. For a landowner to receive property taxes at current use rates, like for open space or agriculture for example, a county may require that the land be zoned for open space or agricultural use. Sometimes a government, a nongovernmental organization, or private developer can link several implementation measures in a new planned community. Such a package is often referred to as *codes, covenants, and restrictions* (CC&Rs).

The U.S. government has adopted such a linkage strategy to implement soil conservation goals. As a result of the 1985 Food Security Act, landowners wishing to remain eligible for federal agricultural benefits are required to have a conservation plan, prepared by the NRCS, for highly erodible lands. The federal programs affected include price support payments, storage facility loans, crop insurance, disaster payments, and other loans and subsidies. Many farmers participate in these programs, so there is a strong incentive to comply with the requirement. The concept of cross-compliance among various programs is that private citizens should not receive windfalls or support from the government without taking actions that promote public objectives.

NONGOVERNMENTAL STRATEGIES

Implementation need not rest on the actions of government alone. Nongovernmental organizations (NGOs) can use some of the same implementation strategies that have been described in this chapter. Several national organizations—such as the National Trust for Historic Preservation, the American Farmland Trust, the National Audubon Society, The Nature Conservancy, and the Trust for Public Land—are active in land planning. Numerous local land trusts and conservancies make fee-simple purchases of land. Such groups buy and receive donated easements. They may be involved in developing or overseeing restrictive covenants. NGOs consult with citizens about the tax aspects of land use. NGOs can play an important role in community education (see Chapter 8). They can also be watchdogs, monitoring government agencies to ensure that plans are followed.

One example of a local NGO is the Brandywine Valley Association, a local group organized in 1945 in Chester County in eastern Pennsylvania. Its dues-paying members are interested in improving, conserving, and restoring the natural resources of the Brandywine River Valley. This group is a model of a locally based group with a long-term commitment to preserving its rural heritage. With a small professional staff, it urges and helps the people of Chester County unite their efforts to make the Brandywine Valley a more pleasant and profitable place in which to work and live. The Brandywine Valley Association accomplishes this goal through a variety of educational programs and through lobbying with local governments. Many such local groups are active in neighborhoods and at the community or watershed level.

The 1000 Friends of Oregon is an example of a statewide, nongovernmental organization that has been highly instrumental in planning implementation. The group was organized to ensure that local governments comply with the Oregon land-use law (see Chapters 2 and 6 as well as the case study section of the next chapter). The 1000 Friends of Oregon has been active in ensuring implementation by providing continuing citizen support for planning. The 1000 Friends of Oregon, with its dedicated, professional staff, has taken numerous cities and counties to court over noncompliance with the statewide laws. The organization has had an excellent success rate with these suits. The result is that Oregon not only has a good planning enabling act and well-defined statewide goals but a record of case law that supports plan implementation. The organization's influence transcends the state borders, as it spawned similar groups like 1000 Friends of Florida, 1000 Friends of Washington, and 1000 Friends of New Mexico.

DESERT VIEW TRI-VILLAGES IMPLEMENTATION

From the principles reviewed in Chapters 7 and 9 (see Table 7.1), a series of actions were recommended for new developments. The focus here will be on desert character overlay districts developed by Phoenix planners with the Desert View Village Planning Committee in 1998. The planners and planning committee designed three overlay districts: *desert preserve, rural desert,* and *suburban desert.* Each overlay district applied to specific areas. Provisions were made in each for previously developed property. Certain uses were specified for each district.

Desert Overlay

The desert overlay district lies adjacent to the Sonoran Desert Preserve and other previously designated park areas. Single-family detached dwellings are permitted in the desert overlay but not in the Sonoran Desert Preserve (planned by the Phoenix Parks, Recreation, and Library Department). In selected, suitable areas, attached dwelling units are allowed. Topography and other natural features determine the lot size and building envelope in the district. "The building envelope is to be surveyed and made part of the public record by recording of a Natural Area Easement with the City of Phoenix over the portion of the lot outside the building envelope with the final plat approval process" (Desert View Village Planning Committee 1998, 3).

A 25-foot (7.6-meter) setback from any property line is required in undisturbed natural desert, except for the area necessary for a driveway. Building "envelopes" are used to keep permanent undisturbed open space on private land. That is, certain activities are permitted on either side of a line around the building called its envelope. Building heights are limited to one-story or 22 feet (6.7 meter), measured to the top of the parapet or to the top of the ridge on sloping roofs. Specific guidelines regulate density, parking, access points, driveways, street widths, lighting standards, and perimeter walls and fences.

The staff planners and village planning commission designated four wash types: scenic vista wash corridors, primary washes, secondary washes, and minor washes. The scenic vista wash is a regional drainage, such as Cave Creek Wash, and must meet minimum flow requirements. Each wash type related to flood flows. Specific conservation measures for vegetation and views are required depending on the wash type.

The city requires a detailed site analysis for any proposed development in this district. The analysis is to include a current aerial photograph at the scale of 1 inch (2.54 centimeter) equals 100 feet (30.5 meters), with the following information included on overlays:

- Land contours at 2-foot [.6-meter] intervals
- Wash corridors and preliminary hydrological information ([cubic feet per second] flows, on-site and off-site, velocity)
- Identify specimen plants and significant stands of vegetation
- Identify potential view corridors
- Identify potential development areas
- Identify potential street alignments
- Identify the 100-year floodplain boundary
- Provide evidence of a record check for archeological sites if any (Desert View Village Planning Committee 1998, 6)

Clustering is encouraged for certain locations in the district to preserve undisturbed natural areas.

Design guidelines and standards apply to the desert preserve overlay district. These guidelines emphasize "developments which blend with rather than dominate the undisturbed desert environment" (Desert View Village Planning Committee 1998, 10). The guidelines link development proposals to detailed site analyses. Sites are to be designed to protect the washes and other natural features, to use materials and colors that blend with the environment, to minimize erosion, to minimize disturbance, and to consider views.

Suburban Desert Overlay

Arizona State University researchers recommended similar guidelines for suburban and rural desert development. Phoenix planners are designing new overlay districts for these characters with the village planning committee. The ideas for the suburban character follow. The city of Phoenix should require developers to submit a site analysis and a landscape plan with the rezoning application. Both written descriptions and maps should be required. The maps for site analysis should include: the regional context, existing topography, slope analysis, hydrological features of the site and its context (pre- and postdevelopment), existing vegetation, views, environmental sensitive areas, and solar orientation (McCarthy et al. 1995; Steiner et al. 1999).

The recommended landscape plan maps for the suburban desert overlay district should include postdevelopment vegetation, drainage, topography, views, and lot layout. The landscape plan should include conservation and revegetation. The site analysis and landscape plan should be prepared by a licensed landscape architect. The city should have an adequate staff of landscape architects and environmental specialists to review site analyses and landscape plans. Furthermore, the city should develop an integrated trail system which is connected to schools and community recreation facilities.

City regulations need to be modified to include and/or permit:

- Creative approaches to retaining water on site that emphasize natural hydrologic functions of the Sonoran desert ecosystems
- Design standards for southwest desert subdivision elements in the area (i.e., walls, lighting, plants, trails, signs, and retention basins)
- Alternative paving surfaces (as long as they do not produce too much noise)
- Alternative street standards (local, collector, arterials) in an effort to reduce impervious surfaces, lighting, noise, and speeds of automobiles
- New standards regarding parking (on-street and off-street) and sidewalks. Alternative zoning ordinances to allow greater flexibility regarding setbacks and site plan review standards
- Use of solar energy and building design responsive to the southwestern solar environment
- Use of reclaimed water to create wetland/riparian areas (McCarthy et al. 1995; Steiner et al. 1999)

The Phoenix overall districts depart from conventional planning implementation. Planners emphasize character over land use. Detailed design guidelines link community concerns about preservation to new forms for development based on natural process. The measures implement community goals and reflect much public involvement, especially on the part of the village planning committee.

IMPLEMENTATION MATRIX

Often a community will select more than one means to implement its goals. Because of the potential complexity and confusion in overlapping or conflicting responsibilities, it is helpful to clarify roles of involved groups. One way to assist in such organization is an implementation matrix. Such a matrix can be illustrated by the Desert View Tri-Villages example.

The City of Phoenix council adopted several goals that will shape the development of the Tri-Villages area. A sampling of these goals appears in Table 10.12. Each goal has a different imple-

TABLE 10.12
IMPLEMENTATION MATRIX

Planning Goal	Implementation measures	Primary responsibility	Secondary responsibilities	Backup power	Administrative responsibilities
Strategic growth corridors	General plan amendment Zoning revision	City planning commission	Village planning committee	City council	Planning department/ Economic development department
Suburban desert development	General plan amendment Zoning revision Design standards	City planning commission	Design review committee/ Village planning committee	City council	Planning department/ Community development department/ Development services department
Rural desert development	General plan amendment Zoning revision Design standards	City planning commission	Design review committee/ Village planning committee	City council	Planning department/ Community development department/ Development services department
Desert preservation	Preservation plan Property acquisition	Parks and recreation board	City planning commission	City council/ State lands department	Parks department

mentation measure and different, although sometimes overlapping, groups responsible for its implementation. To encourage strategic growth in the area the general plan was amended and the zoning ordinance revised. The primary responsibility for planning and zoning in Phoenix rests with the planning commission. The city is divided into several "villages," each with its own planning committee. These village planning committees advise the planning commission and city council, which has the backup power for enforcing the plan and zoning ordinance. The planning department administers the ordinance. In addition, the city economic development department will be involved in encouraging strategic growth. (The roles of planning commissions and planning agencies are discussed in more detail in Chapter 11).

The goals for suburban desert and rural desert development are handled in a manner similar to that for strategic growth. The major differences are the use of design standards as an implementation measure, participation by the design review committee in an advisory capacity, and the community development and development services departments in administration. In Phoenix, all site planning and permitting is done by the development services department in cooperation with the planning and community development departments.

Desert preservation involves different measures and responsibilities. A specific plan for the preserve was adopted and an acquisition strategy authorized. The primary responsibility for the plan rests with the parks and recreation board. The planning commission has secondary responsibility, while the city council still provides the backup power. In this case, since state lands are involved and the state legislature created the Arizona Preserve Initiative to facilitate the transfer of significant open-space lands from the state to the city, the state land department also has considerable backup power. The parks department will administer the preserve.

THREE EXAMPLES OF PLANNING IMPLEMENTATION

In the examples which follow, different issues and concerns prompted local planning. In York County, Pennsylvania, and Black Hawk County, Iowa, the loss of important agricultural land protection initiated the planning process. Farmland preservation is central to the implementation measures. In Scottsdale, Arizona, the major issue involved the preservation of environmentally sensitive lands. The Scottsdale program resulted from local initiatives as well as a state court decision.

Innovative Zoning for Agricultural Land Protection in York County, Pennsylvania, and Black Hawk County, Iowa

The concern about the conversion of agricultural land to other uses was an emergent issue during the 1970s. The National Agricultural Lands Study, an interagency project, was initiated by President Jimmy Carter in 1979 to address the issue. A conclusion of the study was that the problem was a "crisis in the making." One of the suggestions made by the participants in the study was that farmland protection was best addressed by state and local governments (National Agricultural Lands Study 1981). Two local governments that have developed innovative programs include York County, Pennsylvania, and Black Hawk County, Iowa.*

York County is located in south-central Pennsylvania, 25 miles (40 kilometers) south of Harrisburg (Figure 10.6). The county had a population of just under 313,000 people living on 911 square miles (2360 square kilometers) in 1980. The county is in one of the richest agricultural regions in the United States, yet is within a half-hour's drive to Harrisburg, an hour to Baltimore, and an hour and a half to Philadelphia.

According to planner William Conn (1984), the York County Planning Commission became concerned about the problem of declining farmland in 1975. The commission reviewed various options to reverse this trend. Among the techniques reviewed were the transfer and purchase of development rights, easements, and tax benefits. The planning commission selected zoning as the best way to protect the farmland in the county.

The majority of the county municipalities using zoning adopted a novel sliding-scale approach. As described by William Toner, under sliding-scale zoning "each landowner is entitled to a certain number of buildable lots according to the size of the parcel—permitted density varies inversely with the size of the parcel. Thus, small landowners are permitted to develop a higher percentage of their property than are large landowners" (1978, 15).

According to Toner (1978), the rationale supporting this inverse relationship between size of a parcel and permitted density is that large landholdings must be retained in agricultural use if the community is to retain its agricultural base. Officials in Peach Bottom Township of York County decided to use the sliding-scale approach in their zoning ordinance. Table 10.13 is an excerpt from

* More complete descriptions of both the York and Black Hawk County examples are provided by officials from those counties in Steiner and Theilacker (1984). See also American Farmland Trust (1997).

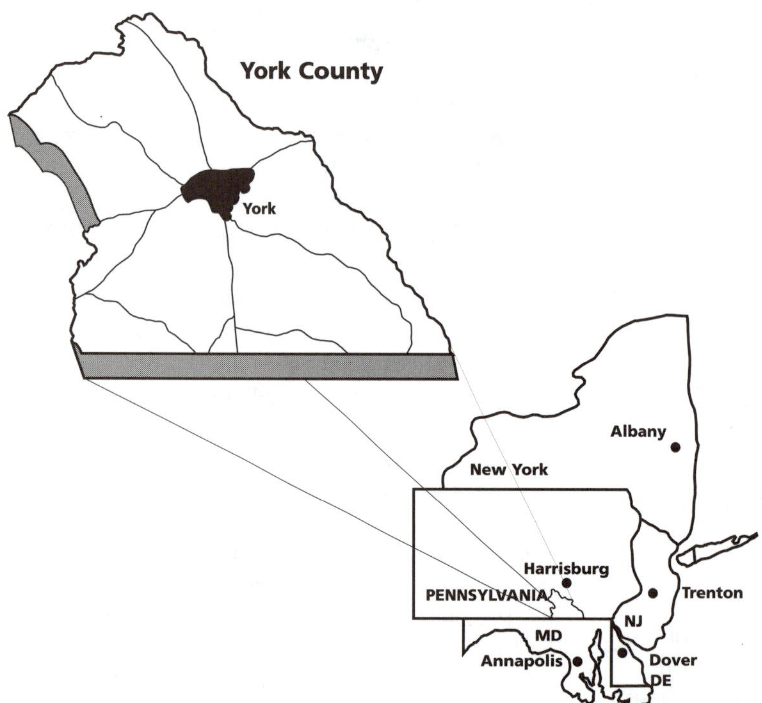

FIGURE 10.6 Location of York County, Pennsylvania.

that ordinance. Single-family housing is regulated in the township in the agricultural zone on a sliding scale through a conditional use procedure. In Peach Bottom Township, a minimum lot size of 1 acre (0.405 hectare) is permitted, and a maximum of 1 acre is also established unless it is determined that the additional land desired is either on poor soil or cannot feasibly be farmed because of size, shape, or topographical considerations (Conn 1984).

In 1988, the Pennsylvania legislature approved legislation authorizing transfer of development rights. Even before this legislation, at least one York County township (Chanceford) experimented with TDR. As of 1997, five other townships in the county (Codorus, Hopewell, Lower Chanceford, Shrewsbury, and Springfield) had TDR programs. The Lower Chanceford Township program protected the most land (200 acres, 81 hectares) (American Farmland Trust 1997). Several York townships "allow farmland owners to transfer development rights to an adjoining parcel in the same township, but the receiving sites must be located on low-quality sites" (American Farmland Trust 1997, 127).

Black Hawk County, Iowa, has taken a different approach to protect farmland than that employed by York County, but has also used zoning. The county is located in northeastern Iowa (Figure 10.7). The two largest cities in the county, Waterloo and Cedar Falls, adjoin each other and are the largest places of employment. It is a metropolitan county with over 100,000 residents (Daniels and Reed 1988). John Deere and Company has major manufacturing facilities in the metropolitan area of the two cities. Both growing cities were expanding into the fertile cornfields of Black Hawk County.

In 1971, county officials working with the Iowa Northland Regional Council of Governments

TABLE 10.13
PEACH BOTTOM TOWNSHIP SLIDING SCALE

1. There shall be permitted on each tract of land the following number of single-family dwelling units:

Size of tract of land, acres	Number of single-family dwelling units permitted
0–7	1
7–30	2
30–80	3
80–130	4
130–180	5
180–230	6
230–280	7
280–330	8
330–380	9
380–430	10
430–480	11
480–530	12
530–580	13
580–630	14
630–680	15
680–730	16
730–780	17
780–830	18
830 and over	19

2. New single-family dwelling units shall be located on lots in soil capability units IIIe-3 through VIIs-2, as classified by the *Soil Survey of York County, Pennsylvania,* Series 1959, No. 23 issued May 1963, or on lots of lands, which cannot feasibly be farmed; (*a*) due to existing features of the site such as rock outcropping, swamps, the fact that the area is heavily wooded, or the fact that the slope of the area exceeds fifteen (15) percent or (*b*) due to the fact that the size or shape of the area suitable for farming is insufficient to permit efficient use of farm machinery. Where such location is not feasible, permits shall be issued to enable dwelling units to be located on lots containing higher quality soils. However, in all cases such residential lots shall be located on the least agriculturally productive land feasible, and so as to minimize interference with agricultural production.
3. A lot on which a new dwelling is to be located shall not contain more than one (1) acre, unless it is determined from the subdivision plan submitted by the property owner that the property owner has sufficient land of the type described in paragraph 5 of this section to justify using more than one (1) acre for the location of the proposed dwelling unit, or that the physical characteristics of the land itself requires a lot size in excess of one (1) acre.
4. A property owner submitting a subdivision plan will be required to specify on his plan which lot or lots shall carry with them the right to erect or place any unused quota of dwelling units his tract may have.
5. Lots for the location of single-family dwelling units in addition to those authorized by subparagraph (1) and all the additional new dwelling units are located on lots which are located:
   a. On land in soil capability units IVe-5 through VIIs-2 as classified by the *Soil Survey of York County, Pennsylvania,* Series 1959, No. 23 issued May 1963; or
   b. On lands which cannot feasibly be farmed:
      (1) Due to the existing features of the site such as rock outcropping, rock too close to the surface to permit plowing, swamps, the fact that the area is heavily wooded, or the fact that the slope of the area exceeds fifteen (15) percent; or
      (2) Due to the fact that the size or shape of the area suitable for farming is insufficient to permit efficient use of farm machinery.

   Such additional lots must meet all the requirements of the ordinance, the Township Subdivision Ordinance and all requirements of the Pennsylvania Department of Environmental Resources.
6. The applicant shall have the burden of providing that the land he seeks to subdivide meets the criteria set forth in this section.
7. Any landowner who disagrees with the classification of his farm or any part of it by the *Soil Survey of York County, Pennsylvania,* Series 1959, No. 23 issued May 1963, may submit an engineering analysis of the soils on the portion of the farm which he seeks to have reclassified, and if the Board of Township Supervisors finds his study correct, it shall alter the township soil map to reflect the results of such analysis.

SOURCE: Conn 1984.

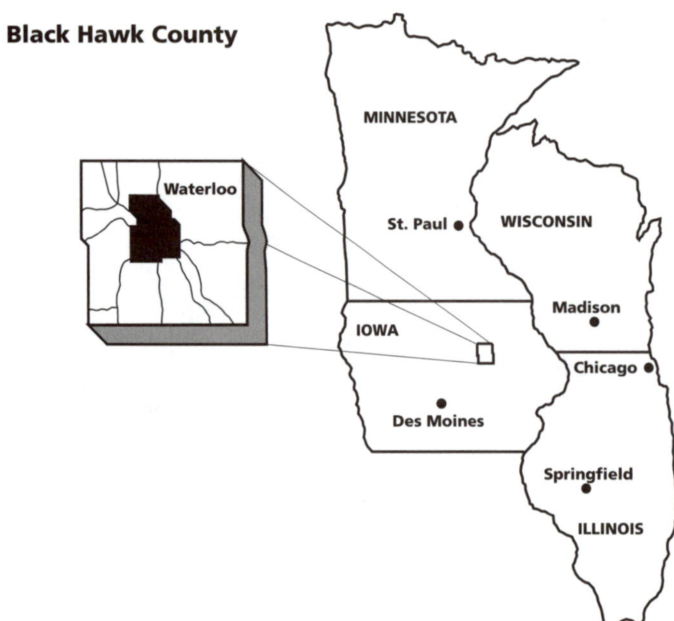

FIGURE 10.7 Location of Black Hawk County, Iowa.

began to address the issue of the conversion of farmlands. After two years of planning, the county officials decided to implement their farmland protection policy through zoning. The policy includes a clear statement of purpose: farmland protection is stated as a goal of the zoning ordinance (American Farmland Trust 1997).

The unique feature of this 1973 ordinance was a system for rating soil types for their relative long-term ability to produce corn and other crops. This system was named the Crop Suitability Rating (CSR), although it is more popularly known as the "Corn" Suitability Rating. The CSR scale ranges from 5 to 100. County officials decided those soil types receiving a ranking of 70 or better would be considered "prime"; such soils will yield an average of about 115 bushels or higher of corn per acre. Using this criteria, 68 percent of the county has prime soils. For those soils with a CSR above 70, there is a 35-acre (14.2-hectare) minimum for nonfarm uses.

Black Hawk County also addressed the issue of allowing some people the opportunity to live in the country and completed a rural living study. Planners discovered 15 soil types with a CSR of 70 and below that also had very few limitations for development. A zoning ordinance was then developed to allow rural housing on these soils, with a minimum 3-acre (1.2-hectare) lot size (Iowa Northland Regional Council of Governments 1975).

This system is working well, and the regional council has expanded its use to the other five counties in its jurisdiction. In the years since the implementation of the zoning ordinance, a major redirection in land use has occurred within Black Hawk County. As the late planner Janice Clark (one of the principal individuals responsible for the ordinance) observed: "The rate of residential development within the unincorporated areas has remained fairly steady, but this development is now occurring on soils deemed suitable for such land use, while the vast majority of land in the county remains in agricultural production" (Clark 1977, 154).

Sonia Johannsen and Larry Larsen (1984) report that from 1979 through 1981, 680 acres (275.4

hectares) were requested to be rezoned from the "A-1" Agricultural District to another district. Only 72 acres (29.2 hectares) were approved, of which only 42 acres (17 hectares) were on land that had a majority of its soils rated prime by the CSR process. The lands that were approved for rezoning had already been committed to other uses by subdivision approval or were difficult sites to farm. Johannsen and Larsen concluded that the CRS is working and that "many potential requests for rezoning of farmland have been discouraged by the county's reputation for preserving these lands" (1984, 124).

An analysis of zoning decisions between 1975 and 1985 by Tom Daniels and David Reed (1988) indicates that the administration of the Black Hawk County program has continued to improve. Relatively little farmland has been rezoned in the county "for nonfarm uses, and several proposals for nonfarm uses have been denied" (Daniels and Reed 1988, 303). According to Daniels and Reed, the "local farm economy appears stable, given the slight decline both in the number of farms and the amount of farmland. The large majority of nonfarmland transfers have occurred near urban boundaries. About one-quarter of the farmland transfers have also occurred near cities. These figures suggest urban sprawl is being fairly well contained" (1988, 303). They also observe that the best farmland in the county is in quite stable ownership and is not likely to be developed.

According to the American Farmland Trust, the Black Hawk ordinance "is strongly supported by the county's farmers, despite the fact that it restricts their ability to sell land for development" (1997, 70). The agriculture zoning ordinance in Black Hawk County "was enacted when agriculture was the dominant land use, development pressure was minimal to moderate, and the price of land in rural areas was close to its value for farming" (American Farmland Trust 1997, 71).

One unique aspect about both York and Black Hawk counties is the use of information about nature in implementation ordinances. Most zoning ordinances before the 1970s were based primarily on economic determinants. In York and Black Hawk counties, information about the physical suitability for a specific use (agriculture) and natural limitations of the land were used to implement a community goal.

Scottsdale, Arizona, Environmentally Sensitive Lands Ordinance

In 1977, the City of Scottsdale adopted its Hillside Ordinance. This overlay zone applied to approximately 24 square miles (62 kilometers^2) in the city's northeastern area. Conservation zones were designed for lands above 25 percent slopes, where development was prohibited. Only limited development was permitted in other places, and open space was protected through easements. In areas with less than 25 percent slopes, development required a special review process. Landowners were required to transfer the residential units allowed in the underlying district from the conservation zone to development zones (Burns and Onderdonk 1993). This system was similar to the TDR program in the New Jersey Pinelands.

In 1985, the Arizona Court of Appeals found that the Scottsdale required transfer of development rights was "a taking of private property without just compensation instead of a regulation permitted under the city's police power" (Burns and Onderdonk 1993, 136). As a result, the Hillside Ordinance was considered unconstitutional in Arizona, and Scottsdale planners began to search for an alternative means to implement their goal of protecting environmentally sensitive lands. A comprehensive "McHargian" ecological inventory and analysis was conducted for the northern portions of Scottsdale. A citizen advisory committee considered various options and developed an Environmentally Sensitive Lands Ordinance (ESLO), which was adopted by the city council in 1991.

The ESLO covers 134 square miles (347 kilometers^2) with an overlay zone. Scottsdale planners designed the new ordinance to meet Arizona constitutional requirements while addressing two main goals: preserving the mountains and maintaining the desert character. The ESLO defines six types of sensitive lands: land slopes, unstable slopes, special features, watercourses, geologic conditions, and native vegetation. *Land slopes* are defined by the steepness of the gradient. *Unstable slopes* are places where rocks or soils may move under certain conditions, causing risk to people or property. *Special features* are large boulder piles, highly visible peaks and ridges, natural landmarks, and historical and archaeological sites. *Watercourses* flood and possess important riparian habitat. *Geologic conditions* refer to places where rock is exposed or soil is thin and where building is expensive. *Native vegetation* refers to unique Sonoran species that contribute to the scenic beauty of the region (City of Scottsdale 1991a).

The method for achieving the first goal is based on the steepness of the land. Slope is calculated by how high the ground rises compared to the horizontal distance. The ESLO establishes four slope categories (less than 15 percent, 15 to 25 percent, 25 to 35 percent, and above 35 percent). Restrictions increase with greater slopes. Landowners have two options. The first is a voluntary density transfer. The second possibility involves very large homesites with specific design restrictions. The size of the homesites increase with the slope gradient. The design restrictions involve average 300-foot (91-meter) and 200-foot (61-meter) setbacks from peaks and ridges; the limitation of nonindigenous plants to a 20-foot (6.1-meter) maximum height; building colors that blend with the landscape; and limitations on cuts and fills (City of Scottsdale 1991b).

The second ESLO goal is to maintain the character of the desert spaces surrounding the mountains. To achieve this goal, development restrictions are imposed to protect washes, natural landmarks, and native vegetation. Scottsdale calls these restrictions natural area open spaces, which are based on slopes and landforms. The city divided its northern areas into three landform classes: hillside, upper desert, and lower desert. *Hillsides* include peaks and ridges, unstable and steep slopes, boulder features, and deep-cut washes. *Upper desert landforms* are characterized by rock outcrops, boulder fields, lush desert habitat, and deep-cut washes. The *lower deserts* have shallow washes with unpredictable, braided flows and lush vegetation (City of Scottsdale 1991b).

The city requires varying degrees of natural area open spaces for new development, based on landform. The most open space is required in the hillside landform; the least in the lower desert. The city reviews all construction plans to ensure that the required open space is met on each site. The city also encourages clustering.

Applications for development projects in areas covered by the ESLO are to be submitted to a development review board. This board is responsible for reviewing site plans for compliance with ESLO before the application is presented to the planning commission and city council public hearings. All applications need to include the following:

Base submittal requirements

- Topographic map
- Slope analysis for natural area open space and intensity calculation
- Number of proposed dwelling units and proposed density
- Map and figures showing the slopes and elevations or other data used for natural area open space calculation and the total open space
- Proposed building materials, paint colors, and landscape plants

Environmental analysis

- Soil and geology report
- Special features and viewshed report
- Survey of significant archaeological and historic sites
- Floodplain identification and analysis
- Map of areas of human "scarring"
- Identification of plant communities (City of Scottsdale 1991c)

In addition, the ESLO requires specific information in applications for single-family development; rezoning, use permits, and preliminary plat applications; and master development plans. For example, master planned developments require:

- General location map
- Size of the entire development
- Development site information
  - The size of each development site
  - The land use of each development site
  - The density of all sites
  - The zoning of each site
  - Vista and scenic corridors within the development project
- Circulation master plan
- Phasing master plan
- Open space master plan
- Parking master plan
- Drainage master plan
- Water and wastewater master plans
- Environmental design concept master plan (City of Scottsdale 1991c)

The Scottsdale ordinance represents a shift away from traditional zoning. The typical ordinance focuses on land use. The ESLO instead stresses the suitability of the land and how its constraints place limitations on possible uses. The ordinance contains detailed performance standards for land use. These standards were derived from an understanding of the landscape. As Donna Gelfand has observed, "The ESLO was a result of changing community values [toward] protection of the fragile desert environment and the unstable, erodible hillsides" (1992, 50).

The York and Black Hawk Counties and City of Scottsdale examples illustrate how planning goals are carried through to implementation. All three rely more on biophysical information than on conventional planning processes. The York County sliding-scale system utilizes information about soils, geology, surface water, and vegetation. Suitability analysis played a central role in the implementation of the Black Hawk County zoning ordinance. Both the York and Black Hawk programs were undertaken to implement goals to protect farmland.

In the City of Scottsdale, growth is managed to help protect environmentally sensitive areas. The identification of the environmentally sensitive areas evolved from a comprehensive ecological inventory and considerable public participation. The philosophy is not antigrowth or no-growth, but rather managed growth, managed in such a way as to protect the environment and valuable natural resources. Development and conservation need not be viewed as competing interests, but rather as ultimately mutually dependent. Such a perspective requires the careful balancing of interests to administer implementation measures through time.

11

ADMINISTRATION OF PLANNING PROGRAMS

Once a plan and implementing measures have been adopted by the appropriate legislative body, it is usually necessary to establish some form of ongoing administration. This may be accomplished in several ways. One way to administer a plan and its implementing measures is through the use of commissions and review boards comprising elected or appointed citizens. Such groups often require technical assistance from a professional staff.

Administration presents many challenges for planners. As planning goals are institutionalized, a greater distance grows between the excitement of creation and the routine of everyday management. The typical office is isolated from the living landscape. Yet, for the landscape to be managed effectively there must be some set of rules for management and for those who are responsible to ensure that the rules are indeed obeyed. Rules should not inhibit the creation of sustainable places. Rather, they should provide the framework for regenerative community design and place making. Flexibility is often necessary, so that plans can adjust to changing conditions, while continuing to achieve its goals.

Local governments can effectively manage many land-use programs. However, local communities must be viewed in terms of larger and more complex interacting regions. The technological potentials for the exploitation of nature and the increase in knowledge about biophysical and sociocultural processes have resulted in the necessity for continued innovation in the administration of planning programs. Many efforts need to be addressed by multiple levels of government and by partnerships between government and nongovernment organizations. To be most effective and equitable, administration must be a two-way street—managers and planners must understand the people they serve and citizens must appreciate and monitor the bureaucrats. Such communication and interaction form the basis of "results-based government."

This chapter will explore the current systems used to administer plans. The role of planning commissions, review boards, and planning staffs will be described. The impact of procedural requirements will be discussed briefly. One administrative tool is the budget. Three budgeting techniques will be described: the planning, programming, and budget system (PPBS); program strategies; and capital improvement programming (CIP). Impact statements are an approach to evaluate government programs and projects. Two examples of planning administration are presented: regional growth management planning in Portland, Oregon; and the Tucson, Arizona, WASH ordinance.

CURRENT PLANNING

Local planning commissions and agencies administer a myriad of activities. They address long-term, midrange, and current plans. The scales of such plans range from the neighborhood to the metropolitan region. Many basic urban functions are included in these plans, including utilities, drainage, circulation, and public facilities. Planning agencies and commissions address a broad range of topics including budgets, annexations, brownfields redevelopment, in fill, freeway mitigation, and historic preservation. Planning commissions, review boards, and planning staffs are thus central to the functions and forms of contemporary settlement patterns.

The Role of Planning Commissions and Review Boards

Planning commissions originated in the early twentieth century. The idea was promulgated by municipal reformers dismayed by the corruption of big-city politics. Planning commissions were proposed as independent advisory boards of honest, civic-spirited citizens. The commissions were to make recommendations to elected officials. The concept was embodied in the model Planning Enabling Act of 1928 published by the U.S. Department of Commerce and adopted by many state legislatures. Such commissions are created by ordinance by the appropriate city, special-use, county, regional, state, or federal jurisdiction. Usually planning commissions consist of five to nine members. The members are typically appointed by an elected official for a specific period of time.

Planning commissions usually have two functions. The first is advisory. They assist elected officials in establishing goals, objectives, and policy for the jurisdiction. In this capacity, they may conduct research and review options facing the planning area. Sometimes a jurisdiction may be subdivided into smaller areas, each with its own planning committee. In such cases, these committees may also conduct research and advise the planning commission. The second function of the planning commission is administrative. In cities and counties, planning commissions review subdivision proposals to assure that they conform to regulations.

Planning commissions may also hold hearings to review proposed changes in zoning ordinances and comprehensive plans. Such hearings are quasi-judicial proceedings in some states and take on a courtlike format. Planning commission findings from hearings are passed on as recommendations to elected officials. If those people proposing changes are not pleased with the decision of the elected body, then they may appeal it to the court.

The relative ease of rezoning and amending comprehensive plans has been criticized as a weak link in the American planning process. Political pressure can be used to force appointed and elected bodies to approve such changes even if they are contrary to established goals and the conclusion of scientific and technical research. Anyone who has been involved in such hearings will testify that they are a very human procedure—with the outcome often based more on the persuasive power of key individuals and emotion than on logic.

Another type of citizen body involved in planning administration is the *review board.* These are usually special-purpose groups. Examples include zoning review boards, boundary review boards, design review boards, and environmental quality councils. *Zoning review boards,* also called *boards of adjustments,* administer variances from zoning ordinances and conditional uses that may be permitted in the ordinances with special permission. *Boundary review boards* may be involved in such matters as annexations and capital improvements. *Design boards* may arbitrate aesthetic matters in a community and are often composed of architects, landscape architects, artists, and designers. *Environmental boards* review matters of environmental quality and are made up of individuals with an interest or training in the relevant sciences. Some review boards include some or all members who are elected officials or professionals rather than appointed citizens.

The Role of Planning Staffs

Many planning agencies are split into two divisions to separately handle long-range and current functions. The long-range division is responsible for research, projections, comprehensive planning, and special functions that may arise as a result of a specific issue. The current planning division is responsible for the administration of regulations. This function may be shifted to another department of government such as that responsible for public works.

The current planning staff is generally responsible for processing applications of those who want to change the use of their property or develop it for some purpose. The current planning staff often works with the property owner to ensure the application meets all the necessary requirements of the commission or review board. The staff may be responsible for presenting its findings to the commission or review board. They may also be responsible for the public notice of hearings to review such proposals. In many jurisdictions the current planning staff has the authority to process applications that meet specified requirements. In these municipalities and counties, commissions or boards review only those applications where a variance is needed.

The Phoenix planning department moved away from the current and long-range structure to a more issue and geographically based team approach. The city planning department adopted a vision to "provide excellent customer service and consistent policy advice that guides the physical, economic and social growth of Phoenix to achieve a better quality of life." The staff organization reflects this vision (Figure 11.1). The city is divided into three parts: north, south, and south with an associated team. The north area team is responsible for the Desert View Tri-Villages Area planning described throughout this book. Other teams address specific topics like growth, freeways, and research as well as current planning (hearings and zoning).

The weaknesses involved in rezoning through commissions and the sheer number of applications for zone changes have prompted some jurisdictions to make this function a staff respon-

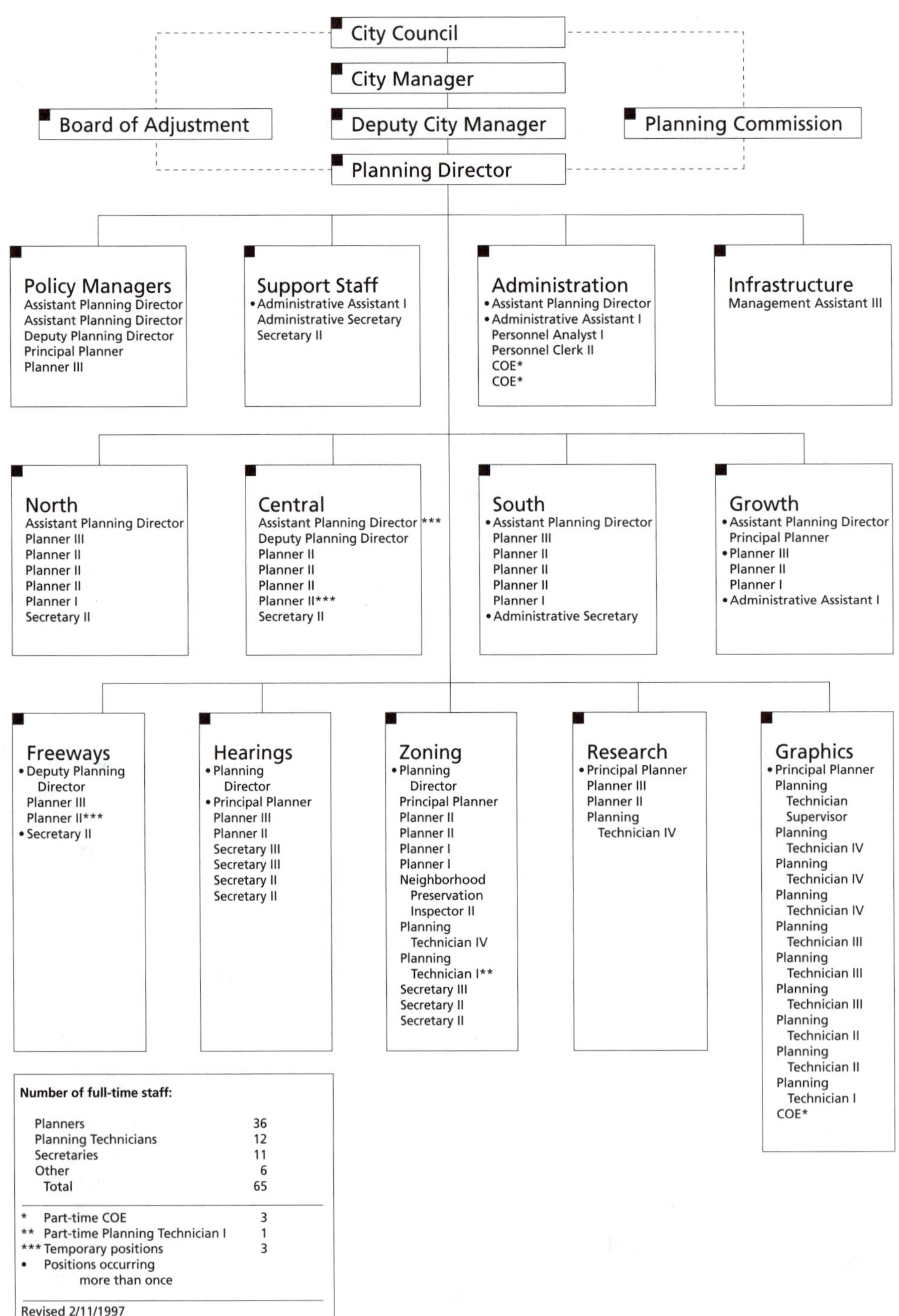

FIGURE 11.1 City of Phoenix Planning Department organization chart.

sibility. These *hearings examiners* or *zoning adjusters* have the administrative responsibility to approve zone changes on the merits of the case. Presumably, these decisions may be made in a more unbiased, professional manner than by a citizen board or commission. The rulings of hearings examiners, or zoning adjusters, are subject to appeal if the applicant or other party is not satisfied with the results.

In areas where performance standards have been adopted, it may be necessary for a team to visit sites to ensure the criteria have been met. For instance, for a proposed residential development in an agricultural area, such a team may comprise a staff planner, a soil scientist from the NRCS, an engineer, and a health officer. These individuals are responsible for making a report of their findings concerning the conformance of the site to the standards.

The Impact of Procedural Requirements

The process that individuals must go through to meet the legal requirements of a jurisdiction obviously has an impact on their personal plans for the use of property. Procedural requirements should ensure that the laws of the jurisdiction are met, yet be fair and swift to minimize unnecessary costs to individuals proposing changes.

Generally, regulatory systems have three basic elements in common. First, there is a *preapplication* stage, during which proponents of a land-use change discuss ideas with the planning staff. Second, there is a *technical staff review.* At this stage, proponents submit a formal application, often accompanied by plans and drawings. The planning staff reviews the application and makes recommendations to elected officials. Finally, there is the *official review* made by the appointed and/or elected officials or possibly by an administrator. Often proponents of a change are responsible for the costs involved in the technical and official reviews.

For those responsible for such reviews, it would be wise to remember that the word *administration* in its original Latin form meant to give help or service. Mission and vision statements for planning commissions and planning department staffs can reinforce the importance of public service. There are numerous ways that these administrators can help people through the regulatory process. One way is to minimize the number of required permits. Another is to publish the procedural requirements in a straightforward format. (Figure 11.2 is an example of the application procedure for a certificate of zoning compliance in Whitman County, Washington.) Also, the application forms should be easy for all to understand. (Figure 11.3 is an example of an application for a certificate of zoning compliance in Whitman County, Washington.) Finally, it is important for administrators to be courteous and friendly. We need to listen to those we serve (see, for example, McClendon 1992).

THE BUDGET

Planners and public administrators seek more effective ways to link policy objectives and government expenditures. Too often goals to protect environmental quality become disconnected from day-to-day decision making. Actions can be taken, often with public funds, which result in the very environmental amenities valued by the public. The budget can be administered to ensure a connection between goals and actions.

Planning, Programming, and Budget System (PPBS)

The budget is perhaps the most effective way to administer planning programs. There are numerous techniques to manage budgets. In the early 1960s, the planning, programming, and budget system (PPBS) was initiated in the U.S. Depart-

Date: ______________________

Case Number: ______________________

Purpose

Within the agricultural zoning district of Whitman County, residential land use must meet certain minimum-lot size requirements. The requirements are waived for homes proposed on lands not useful for commercial agricultural production. In their place are a number of "conditions" that must be met to qualify a site for development. Usually, a much smaller lot is possible by meeting these conditions than would normally be required.

To determine if a proposed site qualifies for the waiver, county and regional planning staff evaluate the site. If the criteria are met, a certificate is issued. The certificate entitles the recipient to secure building, sewer, and water system permits.

Application

A complete application must be filed prior to the staff's review of the request. An application will not be accepted unless it is complete in the judgment of the administrative official and the application fee paid.

A complete application shall include:

——— 1. Application for certificate of zoning compliance form.

——— 2. Environmental checklist.*

* The environmental checklist will be reviewed by the administrative official. Based upon that review, the designated "responsible official" will make a determination under the guidelines of the State Environmental Policy Act (SEPA) whether the proposed issuance of a certificate will have a significant or nonsignificant environmental impact. If it will be significant, the applicant will have to provide an environmental impact statement. At her or his option, the responsible official may convene the environmental review committee to aid in her or his determination of significance.

——— 3. Applicant's statements describing the site's compliance with the zoning ordinance requirements.

——— 4. Application fees

a. Certificate review fee $ 25.00

b. Environmental impact statement (if necessary) cost

——— 5. Site description

A description of the site giving distance from the permanent landmarks adequate in detail for staff to visit the site and determine from the description its approximate boundaries. Permanent landmarks would include roads, section markers, power poles, etc. If a legal description is available, that should be given.

——— 6. Site plan map

A site plan showing the approximate location of major site features.

——— 7. Written permission

If the applicant is not the owner of the site, he or she must provide a statement from the owner giving their permission for the staff site survey and the issuance or denial of a certificate of zoning compliance.

Note: Special help:

The administrative official will be happy to answer any questions. If in doubt about any portion of this application, please ask. Telephone Number: 397-4361.

Procedure

——— 1. Submit completed application to the administrative official.

——— 2. The administrative official provides the planning director with a completed application for her or his review.

——— 3. The planning director has 14 days to render a decision if the site shall not be granted a certificate of zoning compliance. If necessary, he or she may extend this period for an additional 14 days, and will notify the applicant of this additional review period.

During the review, the planning director will consult with health department, engineering, and Natural Resources Conservation Service personnel to aid in her or his decision.

The decision will be provided to the administrative official, who shall notify the applicant in writing of the decision.

Failure of the planning director to render a decision within the period allotted, shall constitute a denial of the request.

——— 4. If a certificate of compliance is issued, the administrative official shall notify property owners within 300 feet (91.5 m) of the proposed site that they have 20 days from the date of issuance to appeal the planning director's decision.

——— 5. If a certificate of compliance is not granted, the administrative official shall notify the applicant that they have 20 days from the postal date to appeal the decision.

——— 6. In the event of appeal, a hearing date will be set before the hearing examiner committee. The applicant and property owners within 300 feet (91.5 m) of the property will be notified of the hearing.

——— 7. If the hearing results are challenged, that must occur by legal action by any affected party in a court of competent jurisdiction within 10 days of the committee's decision.

FIGURE 11.2 Procedure for application for a certificate of zoning compliance in Whitman County, Washington.

Consistency with the Zoning Ordinance

The following is excerpted from the county's zoning ordinance and is the basis for decisions called for by this application:

1. Two of the following three conditions must exist:
   a. Land whose near-surface geology consists of basalt or alluvium, or on slopes of greater than 20%, crystalline rock, all as defined by *Water Supply Bulletin No. 26* of the Washington Department of Ecology, *Reconnaissance of Geology and of Ground-Water Occurrence in Whitman County*, or any updated version of the document. Whenever difficulty exists in the verification of surface geological conditions from this map, reference shall also be made to the maps of detailed soil mapping units maintained by the Natural Resources Conservation Service, which maps shall either indicate or not indicate a pattern of specific soil types which is known to be associated with basaltic, alluvial, or crystalline surface geological conditions. All of these facts shall be verified by on-site inspection.
   b. The subject lot has not been cultivated, used for production of commercial forage for sale, commercial grazing of livestock for sale, or subjected to any agricultural practice designed to produce for sale in the preceding three years.
   c. The subject lot is within two distinct areas of land 15 acres (4.6 m) or less which is insufficient size, quality, and/or accessibility to be efficiently used for agricultural production for income. "Distinct" shall mean that the subject area is substantially bounded by natural or human-made features which buffer this land from agricultural lands, such as: wooded areas, steep canyon walls, railroads, surface waters, or public roads.
2. All of the following requirements must be met:
   a. The subject lot must have frontage on an improved county or state road of at least 200 feet (61 m). "Improved" shall mean a gravel surface or better.
   b. If a perennial surface water passes through, or along any boundary of the subject lot, there must be at least 200 feet (61 m) of frontage along such surface water.
   c. Less than one-half of the area of the subject lot shall be in an area of special flood hazard and/or floodway as designated on the flood hazard boundary map of the *Flood Insurance Study for Whitman County*.
   d. Construction plans for structures, parking areas, and private roads on the subject lot shall leave a maximum amount of existing vegetation undisturbed.
   e. The area of the subject lot shall be no less than the minimum area required by the Whitman County Department of Environmental Health to safely accommodate water supply and on-site sewage disposal systems.

FIGURE 11.2 *(Continued)*

ment of Defense by Robert McNamara, who brought the concept with him from his experience in the automobile industry (Graham 1976; Hudson 1979; and So 1988). Otis Graham describes the system in the following way: "PPBS starts with the whole, not the parts; it forces explicit statements of assumptions; it begins with strategic goals, sets up alternative plans for their realization, qualifies costs and benefits" (1976, 172).

Frank So (1979, 1988) of the American Planning Association describes PPBS as having four distinct characteristics. These include (1) focusing on the identification of the fundamental objectives of the program, (2) the explicit identification of future-year implications, (3) the consideration of all costs, and (4) the systematic analysis of the options involved (So 1979). So is critical of PPBS. According to him, the system has proven too complicated to be administered by local officials.

Program Strategies

However, a number of more effective systems have evolved from PPBS. Frank So cites the example of the Dayton, Ohio, method, called *program strategies.* He contends that the purpose of this system "is to describe municipal services in a language elected officials and the community understand while at the same time allocating [financial] resources (local, state, and federal) in such a way as to classify expenditures on the basis of policies and programs" (1979, 126).

The Dayton budget model follows three basic processes that help provide continuity to decision-making:

1. Assess current conditions, problems, needs, strengths, and weaknesses to best prepare plans to meet those demands.
2. Develop goals, objectives, policies, and plans to determine the work program.

Date Received:
Case Number:

1. Applicant

Name:
Address:
Telephone:

Status: (lessee of property, agent, owner, prospective purchase, etc.)

2. Property Owner (if different from the applicant)

Name:
Address:
Telephone:

For purpose of this applicant, "owner" shall mean

1. The mortgagee (person buying the land with a bank loan)
2. The contract seller (person holding a contract on the land and selling it to another person)
3. Person who holds clear title to the land
4. Corporation, partnership, or estate that holds title to the land

3. Property owners within 300 feet (91.5 m) of the property to be included within the Certificate of Zoning Compliance

a. Name:
Address:
Telephone:

b. Name:
Address:
Telephone:

c. If additional parties, put information on a separate sheet of paper.

4. Description of site

This description will be used to locate the site and determine its boundaries:

a. Township Range Section

b. Major road intersection nearby is and it is miles to the site heading (north, south, east, west).

c. Provide the approximate boundaries of the site using permanent landmarks like roads, power poles, section lines, etc.

If a legal description is available of the site, it should be attached. If it describes the property adequately, the above-requested description is not necessary.

5. Site plan

A site plan should be drawn. It need not be drawn professionally, but must be legible and drawn to an appropriate scale. It will be used by staff to evaluate the site to determine if it meets the zoning ordinance criteria. It should show:

a. Boundaries with dimensions
b. Proposed home location
c. Drainfield location
d. Well location
e. Driveway location
f. Stream or creek within site
g. Areas of intended excavation
h. Vegetation that will be removed
i. Rock outcropping
j. Existing fencelines
k. Existing buildings
l. Names of property owners within 300 feet (91.5 m) on the property they own

FIGURE 11.3 Application for certificate of zoning compliance in Whitman County, Washington.

6. Statement of Zoning Ordinance Compliance

Review the requirements that must be met to achieve zoning ordinance compliance. They are found on the first page of the application instruction section. State if your proposal complies, does not comply, or is not related to the stated criteria.

Applicant ______________________ Date ______________

(To be completed if the applicant is not the owner of the property involved)

____

Owner's affidavit

State of Washington)
: ss.
County of Whitman)

I, being duly sworn, depose and say that I am the owner of property or her/his authorized agent, involved in this application, and that the foregoing statements and answers herein contained and the information herewith submitted are in all respects true and correct to the best of my knowledge and behalf; and I grant my permission to the above-named applicant to apply for a certificate of zoning compliance for the above-described property; and for county staff to examine this subject property in the cause of their work related to this application.

Subscribed and sworn to before me
this day of 2000.

Signed:
Address:
Telephone:

Notary Public in and for the
State of Washington, residing
at

FIGURE 11.3 *(Continued)*

3. Implement those plans and policies and prepare to evaluate their effectiveness and shortcomings (City of Dayton 1995).

Dayton has six program budget areas: regional center, community health and safety, leadership and social advocacy, neighborhoods, urban management, and economy (City of Dayton 1995). The *regional center program* seeks to strengthen Dayton's position as its region's center for culture, commerce, heritage, and leisure activities. The *community health and safety program* attempts to protect the lives, health, and property of all citizens by reducing drugs, violence, crime, and environmentally unsafe conditions. The *leadership and social advocacy program* focuses on public forums that benefit citizens. The *neighborhood program* fosters investment and diversity. The *urban management program* seeks to enhance Dayton's commitment to public administration. The *economy program* aims to diversity and expand the city's economic base while providing economic opportunities for all citizens (City of Dayton 1995). All six programs are linked to short-term and long-term city plans as well as capital improvement programming.

Table 11.1 lists the program strategies and 1995 resource allocations for Dayton neighborhoods. Table 11.2 summarizes the budget for urban management programs in Dayton. According to So, it "can be seen that specific objectives are presented in significant detail. This detail allows Dayton [officials] to determine, during the year, whether or not it is meeting its objectives by keeping track of the performance criteria" (1979, 127).

The administration of the program strategies method is the responsibility in Dayton of a strategy planning group comprising the city manager, the deputy city manager, the planning director, and three assistant city managers. Neighborhood citizens' advisory boards review program strategies affecting their communities. In this way, budgets receive both agency and community-level review.

Capital Improvement Programming

Capital improvement programming (CIP) was introduced in Chapter 10 as a technique to implement planning programs. Attention should be paid to the administration of CIP. Frank So (1979, 1988) outlines the following typical steps involved in CIP administration. The first step is an analysis of the fiscal resources of the community—the revenue and expenditure projections. The second step is a listing of all capital-improvement-projections-related projects in the jurisdiction. This listing is usually collected by the planning department or finance office.

The next step involves each department of the jurisdiction completing detailed project forms describing the capital improvements. Each department will rank its projects. Then a review group

TABLE 11.1
1995 CITY OF DAYTON, OHIO, NEIGHBORHOODS PROGRAM STRATEGY

Goal: To encourage desirable neighborhoods by fostering investment and diversity through a high level of responsive public services and active partnerships with neighborhood institutions, leaders and citizen groups.

Program	1994 Budget	1995 Budget	Budget % change
Partnerships	$6,541,600	$6,815,000	4.2
Housing and physical appearance	$24,930,700	$24,166,100	–3.1
Total	**$31,472,300**	**$30,981,100**	**–1.6**

The category of Neighborhoods is down slightly due to a lower level of capital projects in the area of Housing and Physical Appearance. In 1994, the funding for the FROC Pool was completed along with the Innereast Defensible Space Plan. Investments in 1995 include all HOME-funded housing projects as well as the Emergency Shelter grant.
SOURCE: City of Dayton 1995.

TABLE 11.2
1995 CITY OF DAYTON, OHIO, URBAN MANAGEMENT PROGRAM STRATEGY

Goal: To enhance the city's tradition of professional and committed city management, ensuring the effective use of the city's financial, human and capital resources.

Program	1994 Budget	1995 Budget	Budget % change
Financial management	$15,448,900	$15,157,900	–1.9
Human resource management	$8,279,900	$8,518,800	2.9
Communications and information systems	$15,601,100	$16,161,200	3.6
Infrastructure maintenance and development	$17,933,300	$19,035,500	6.1
Facility management	$8,392,300	$7,351,900	–12.4
Total	**$65,655,500**	**$66,225,300**	**0.9**

The Urban Management budget is up 0.9%. This reflects minimal growth in operating budgets combined with a reduced capital program for Facility Management. An increase in funding for Infrastructure Maintenance & Development capital projects reflects additional dollars for the 1995 asphalt resurfacing program. Also included is an expanded sanitary sewer replacement program to ensure the Valley Street sewer is repaired prior to the road reconstruction work scheduled for that area.
SOURCE: City of Dayton 1995.

discusses all the department proposals. This group includes the planning director, finance officer, the local government manager, top elected officials, and department heads. Often public hearings are held concerning the proposed expenditures. From this stage a priority ranking of the projects is achieved.

The CIP is then presented to the appropriate legislative body. After this body determines its own expenditure priorities and choices, the CIP is adopted (So 1979). Budgeting is a cyclical process, usually occurring annually. One of the strengths of CIP is that projects and programs can be linked to community goals and the ability of an area to sustain proposed capital improvements.

ENVIRONMENTAL IMPACT ASSESSMENTS

As a result of NEPA, a national policy for the environment and the Council on Environmental Quality (CEQ) were established. The central purposes of the act were:

> to declare a national policy which will encourage productive and enjoyable harmony between man and his environment; to promote efforts which will prevent or eliminate damage to the environment and biosphere and stimulate the health and welfare of man; to enrich the understanding of the ecological systems and natural resources important to the Nation and to establish a Council on Environmental Quality (U.S. Congress 1969).

The requirements for *environmental impact statements* (EISs) were established by Section 102(2) of the National Environmental Policy Act as follows:

All agencies of the federal government shall—

A. Utilize a systematic, interdisciplinary approach which will insure the integrated use of the natural and social sciences and environmental design arts in planning and in decision making which may have an impact on man's environment;
B. Identify and develop methods and procedures in consultation with the Council on Environmental Quality . . . which will insure that presently unquantified environmental amenities and values may be given appropriate consideration in decision making along with economic and technical considerations;
C. Include in every recommendation or report on proposals for legislation and other major federal actions significantly affecting the quality of the human environment, a detailed statement by the responsible official on—
   i. The environmental impact of the proposed action,
   ii. Any adverse environmental effects which cannot be avoided should the proposal be implemented,
   iii. Alternatives to the proposed action,
   iv. The relationship between local short-term uses of man's environment and the maintenance and enhancement of long-term productivity, and
   v. Any irreversible and irretrievable commitments of resources which would be involved in the proposed action should it be implemented (U.S. Congress 1969).

The purpose of an EIS is to serve as "an action-forcing device to insure that the policies and goals" defined in the National Environmental Policy Act "are infused into the ongoing programs and actions" of the federal government. The EIS is to provide "full and fair discussion of significant environmental impacts" and is to "inform decision-makers and the public of reasonable alternatives which would avoid or minimize adverse impacts or enhance the quality of the human environment." According to the Council on Environmental Quality, "An environmental impact statement is more than a disclosure document. It shall be used by Federal officials in conjunction with other relevant material to plan actions and make decisions" (1986, 791).

Often the EIS (or a less comprehensive review known as an *environmental assessment*) is prepared jointly between a federal agency and state or local governments. Since NEPA states that "major Federal actions significantly affecting the quality of the human environment" require an EIS, both federally funded projects and federal permits and licenses are subject to the law. The approval process for projects, permits, or licenses may affect how a local plan is implemented or administered. If, for instance, a county has a policy to protect farmland and environmentally sensitive lands, and a federal project is proposed, such as a dam or highway, then county officials may object during the EIS process. On the other hand, it may be county policy to provide new sources of water or transportation. In this case, the county may work with a federal agency to advocate water-supply and transportation options which would be studied through the EIS process. A developer may propose a project that requires a permit (e.g., Section 404 dredge and fill permits required through clean water legislation for wetlands). In such a case, county officials can comment during the EIS process concerning the consistency of such a proposal with local plans.

The CEQ has developed a recommended format for EISs that is similar to the ecological planning process being described in this text. The following standard format is to be used by federal agencies to prepare EISs:

- Cover sheet
- Summary
- Table of contents
- Purpose of and need for action
- Alternatives including the proposed action
- Affected environment
- Environmental consequences
- List of preparers
- List of agencies
- Index
- Appendixes

The cover sheet includes relevant information about the proposal, such as the responsible agencies, the title of the proposed action, contact people, the designation of the EIS as draft or final, an abstract, and the date by which comments must be received. The summary provides a synopsis of major conclusions, areas of controversy, and the issues to be resolved. The EIS is then to briefly specify the underlying purpose and need to which the agency is responding (Council on Environmental Quality 1986).

The heart of the EIS is the description of the alternatives including the proposed action. Planners are to rigorously "explore and objectively evaluate all reasonable alternatives." Each alternative is to be considered in detail. An "alternative of no action" is to be included in the analysis. The agency is to identify its preferred alternative or alternatives and to include appropriate mitigation measures to address environmental impacts (Council on Environmental Quality 1986).

The EIS is to describe "the environment of the area(s) to be affected or created by the alternatives under consideration." The affected environment section of an EIS is an inventory and analysis of the planning area, such as what was described in Chapters 3 and 4. The affected environment section is to be followed by detailed studies of the environmental consequences. The environmental consequences section "forms the scientific and analytic basis" for comparisons of alternatives. The consequences are to include discussions of direct effects of the alternatives and their significance; indirect effects and their significance; energy requirements and conservation potential of various alternatives; natural or depletable resource requirements and conservation potentials; urban quality, historic and cultural resources, and the design of the built environment, including reuse and conservation potentials; and means to mitigate adverse environmental impacts. This section is also to address possible conflicts between the proposed actions and the objectives of federal, regional, state, local, and Indian land-use plans, policies, and controls for the area concerned (Council on Environmental Quality 1986).

In addition to the federal environmental protection law, 27 states, the Commonwealth of Puerto Rico, and many local governments have adopted impact statement or assessment requirements. According to Leonard Ortolano (1984), 14 states use comprehensive statutory requirements, 4 have comprehensive executive or administrative orders, and 9 have special-purpose EIS requirements. For example, the Washington State Environmental Policy Act (SEPA) has four primary purposes

1. To declare a state policy which will encourage productive and enjoyable harmony between people and their environment
2. To promote efforts which will present or eliminate damage to the environment and biosphere
3. To stimulate the health and welfare of people
4. To enrich the understanding of ecological systems and natural resources important to the state and the nation (Washington Department of Ecology 1995, as listed in Chapter 43.21C Revised Code of Washington)

As many as 80 other nations also have environmental impact assessment requirements (Westman 1985; Canter 1996; Ortolano 1997). The United Nations, the World Bank, the U.S. Agency for International Development, and the aid agencies of many European nations have played important roles in encouraging developing nations to adopt environmental review procedures. As of 1992, "37 out of the 51 countries in Africa had established 'Ministries of Environment, Natural Resources, or Nature Conservations/Protection' " (Ortolano 1997, 62, citing Tolba et al. 1992, 724–725).

In 1985, the European Union (EU) approved a directive (85/337) which requires member states to undertake environmental impact assessments. European nations that previous to the EU directive did not have environmental review requirements subsequently adopted measures. For example, the 1986 Italian law that created the Ministero dell'Ambiente (Department of Environment) also accepted the EU directive. Then, in 1988, two Italian laws were enacted that defined environmental review requirements. Like environmental review procedures in the United States, Italian studies are required to assess the consequences of government actions. The Italian law includes a procedural framework, a project framework, and an environmental framework. The Netherlands, another EU member, has a similar law. The Dutch law requires that one of the possible alternatives focus on the best environmental consequences. The Dutch law also establishes an independent scientific review board to verify the accuracy of environmental impact assessment documents.

A major criticism of environmental impact review at the federal level in the United States is that essentially the process is procedural rather than substantive (Ortolano 1997). For instance, the Natural Resources Defense Council has observed:

> Environmentalists today are turning more attention toward the substantive quality of the NEPA statements which are prepared. Unfortunately, far too frequently the quality of these impact statements leaves much to be desired. For example, NEPA statements are sometimes silent on the most severe environmental effects caused by a proposed project (1977, 28).

Critics argue that NEPA has been little more than a bureaucratic exercise that requires federal agencies to complete paperwork that they subsequently file and ignore. Valerie Fogleman declared, "as NEPA is presently written, agencies that comply with its procedures by spending millions of dollars analyzing proposed actions, do not violate NEPA if they proceed with environmentally destructive actions contrary to NEPA's policies and purposes" (1990, 245).

In some states with comprehensive statutory requirements, the EIS process has become somewhat more substantive. Washington State's comprehensive SEPA contains substantive policies and goals that apply to all levels of government. A proposal may be denied under SEPA if an agency finds that:

- The proposal would likely result in significant adverse environmental impacts identified in an EIS
- Reasonable mitigation measures are insufficient to ameliorate the identified impact (see Washington Administrative Code 197-11-660)

Thus, SEPA in Washington can be used by the state and local governments to permit or deny projects. Washington State courts have held that SEPA applies to comprehensive plans, preliminary plats, and all kinds of permits. Generally, however, the EIS process in many states, like at the federal level, tends to be more procedural than substantive. In spite of these problems, environmental impact statements and environmental assessments can be an important administrative tool. Astute planning administrators can make use of EISs to justify and explain their projects to decision makers and the public. Such projects may be to implement the goals of their constituents. Conversely, during the process as state and local officials review EIS, they can comment about impact of a proposal on the programs and policies of their jurisdictions. Administrators may better gauge the impact of projects through a systematic use of environmental, economic, fiscal, and social analyses.

Environmental Impact Analysis

The CEQ has put in place a uniform EIS review with a standard terminology. These terms include the *categorical exclusion,* the *environmental assessment* and/or *environmental impact statement,* a *finding of no significant impact,* a *scoping of issues,* and *process monitoring* (Buskirk 1986; Fogleman 1990; Canter 1996). In addition to the federal agencies that adopted the procedure and terminology recommended by the CEQ, a number of states adapted the process. Washington is one such state.

The Washington Department of Ecology (DOE) paraphrases its SEPA process in part as follows (Figure 11.4): The environmental review process generally begins when someone submits a permit application to an agency or when an agency proposes some activity, policy, plan, ordinance, or

Environmental impact analysis can result in the protection of stream corridors and provide buffers between stream channels and new development. Marin County, California.

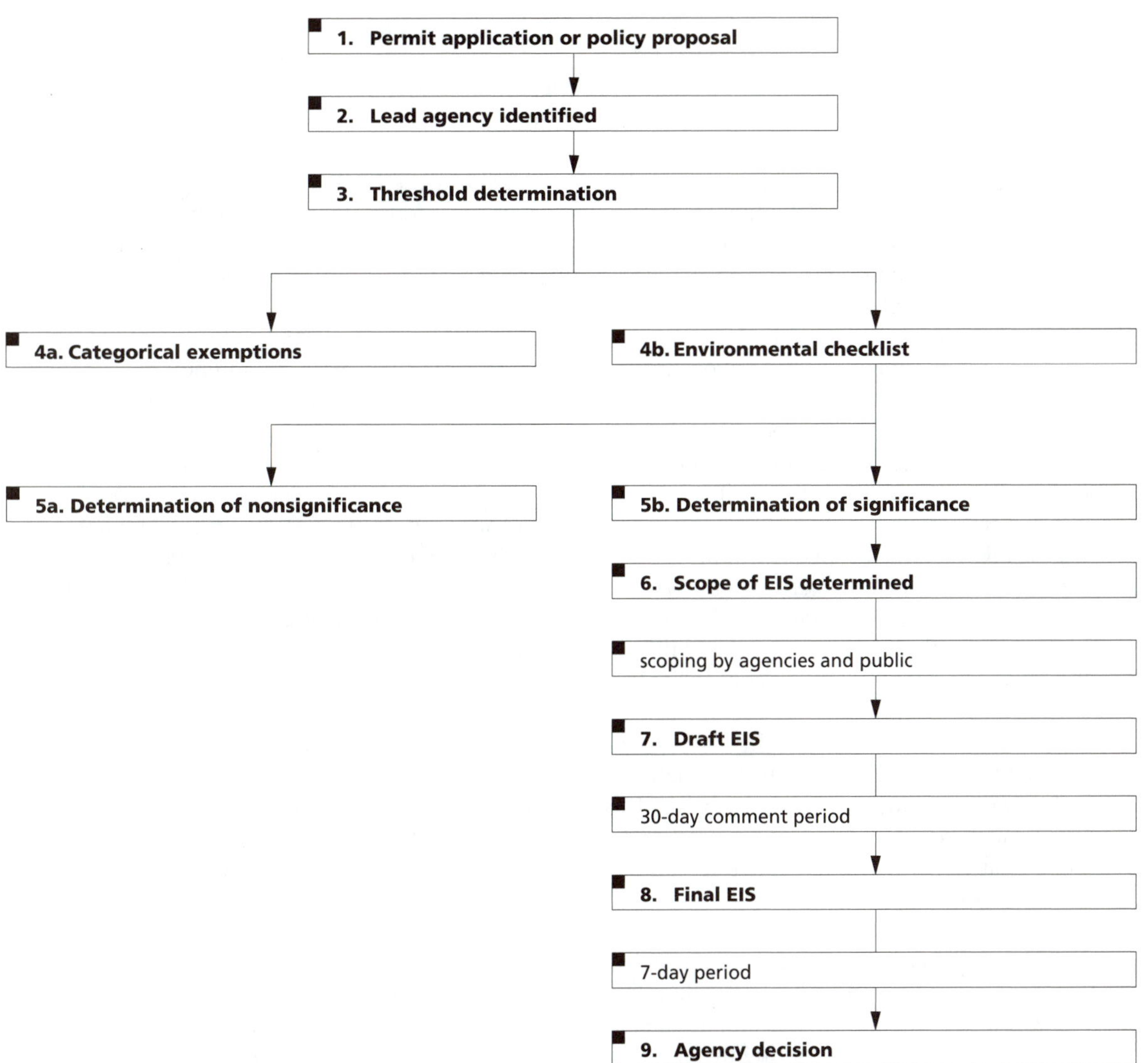

FIGURE 11.4 Process for Washington State environmental impact statement review.

regulation. Once this occurs, a *lead agency* is selected, which has the principal responsibility for implementing SEPA procedures for the specific proposal. The lead agency, which is normally the city or county where the proposal has been made, then makes a *threshold determination* to decide whether a proposal is likely to have a probable significant adverse environmental impact (Washington Department of Ecology 1984, 1995).

Some categories of actions that may have significant environmental impacts have been excluded by the Washington legislature for political reasons and thus are exempted from the process. If a proposal is not categorically exempt, then the proponent completes an *environmental checklist.* This checklist helps the lead agency identify environmental impacts that may result from the proposal and decide whether the impacts are significant. If both the proponent and lead agency agree the impacts are indeed significant, then a checklist need not be completed and an EIS is instead completed (Washington Department of Ecology 1984, 1995).

If, based on the checklist, the lead agency concludes that the proposal would not have a probable significant adverse environmental impact, then it issues a *determination of nonsignificance* and no EIS is prepared. If the opposite is found, then the lead agency issues a *determination of significance* that would require an EIS to be prepared. There is some middle ground allowed. When some environmental impacts are foreseen that can be addressed with specific mitigation measures, then a *mitigated determination of nonsignificance* can be issued. Such a document would describe mitigation measures that will be implemented (Washington Department of Ecology 1984, 1995).

If an EIS is to be prepared, then the lead agency must decide its scope, which means the range of actions, options, and impacts to be analyzed. This process is called *scoping.* The scoping process leads to a draft EIS, which is circulated to various government agencies and interested parties for a 30-day comment period. After considering the comments and revising the draft EIS accordingly, the lead agency issues a final EIS. All agencies must then wait for 7 days before acting on the permit or approval. After considering the appropriate environmental concerns and documents, along with other relevant factors, agencies may then act upon the permit or other approval required for a proposal to proceed (Washington Department of Ecology 1984).

Washington State's Growth Management Act influences SEPA administration. The Growth Management Act identifies 13 goals to be achieved through local comprehensive plans and development regulations. The law requires local jurisdictions to systematically inventory environmental resources and to rely on forecasts of future population and employment levels. Early and continuous public participation is mandated throughout the planning process. Many steps for planning dictated by the Growth Management Act are "actions" under SEPA and, as a result, require SEPA compliance (Washington Department of Ecology 1995).

As noted in Chapter 10, Washington's SEPA *permits* cities and counties to designate environmentally sensitive areas. In addition, the Growth Management Act *requires* local jurisdictions to identify critical areas and develop regulations to protect these places (Washington Department of Ecology 1995). As a result, planners in Washington can use both state environmental review and growth management laws to protect wetlands, aquifer recharge areas, fish and wildlife habitat, frequently flooded areas, and geologically hazardous places.

In Washington State the elements of the physical and human environment that must be considered in an environmental checklist and an EIS are contained in the State Environmental Policy Act and DOE guidelines. These elements are listed in Table 11.3. As can be seen, the elements are similar to those previously discussed in Chapters 3 and 4. As a result, the legal framework exists in Washington State to connect landscape inventory and analysis information to the administrative review of proposed projects and actions.

Economic Impact Analysis

Critics of impact analyses argue that nonenvironmental elements are not adequately considered. As a result, techniques for *economic, fiscal,* and *social* impact analyses have been developed and proposed. (Information about these techniques can be obtained from the website of the Western Rural Development Center at Oregon State University, www.orst.edu/dept/WRDC.) *Economic impacts* are those that affect the private sector,

TABLE 11.3
ELEMENTS OF THE PHYSICAL AND HUMAN ENVIRONMENT REQUIRED IN CHECKLISTS AND IMPACT STATEMENTS BY THE WASHINGTON STATE ENVIRONMENTAL POLICY ACT

WAC 197-11-444: Elements of the environment

1. Natural environment
   a. Earth
      (1) Geology
      (2) Soils
      (3) Topography
      (4) Unique physical features
      (5) Erosion/enlargement of land area (accretion)
   b. Air
      (1) Air quality
      (2) Odor
      (3) Climate
   c. Water
      (1) Surface water movement/quantity/quality
      (2) Runoff/absorption
      (3) Floods
      (4) Groundwater movement/quantity/quality
      (5) Public water supplies
   d. Plants and animals
      (1) Habitat for and numbers or diversity of species of plants, fish, or other wildlife
      (2) Unique species
      (3) Fish or wildlife migration routes
   e. Energy and natural resources
      (1) Amount required/rate of use/efficiency
      (2) Source/availability
      (3) Nonrenewable resources
      (4) Conservation and renewable resources
      (5) Scenic resources
2. Built environment
   a. Environmental health
      (1) Noise
      (2) Risk of explosion
      (3) Releases or potential releases to the environment affecting public health, such as toxic or hazardous materials
   b. Land and shoreline use
      (1) Relationship to existing land-use plans and to estimated population
      (2) Housing
      (3) Light and glare
      (4) Aesthetics
      (5) Recreation
      (6) Historic and cultural preservation
      (7) Agricultural crops
   c. Transportation
      (1) Transportation systems
      (2) Vehicular traffic
      (3) Waterborne, rail, and air traffic
      (4) Parking
      (5) Movement/circulation of people or goods
      (6) Traffic hazards
   d. Public services and utilities
      (1) Fire
      (2) Police
      (3) Schools
      (4) Parks or other recreational facilities
      (5) Maintenance
      (6) Communications
      (7) Water/storm water
      (8) Sewer/solid waste
      (9) Other governmental services or utilities
3. To simplify the EIS format, reduce paperwork and duplication, improve readability, and focus on the significant issues, some or all of the elements of the environment in 197-11-444 may be combined.

while *fiscal impacts* refer to those that affect the public sector. Economist Ronald Faas has noted that:

> Mining, industrial expansion, and energy facility construction affect the private sector of a community's economy. Such projects require new investment in plant facilities and lead to increased local employment, income, and sales. In addition, the new economic activity often stimulates local business. Commercial activities and residential housing expand to serve the new population (1980, 1, updated version Faas and Holland 1994).

Faas stresses that economic impacts should be considered by both private-sector managers and public administrators. He points out that promoters of a particular project often emphasize the new jobs, increased payrolls, expanded sales, and new investments. These factors can form a persua-

Canada geese on the Clearwater River, Idaho. *(Barry Kough,* The Lewiston Morning Tribune*)*

sive argument when public officials are asked to make a zoning change, grant a variance, or allow a tax concession. But these claims should not be accepted at face value; rather an objective evaluation of the economic impacts should be made.

Economists have developed techniques that can be helpful in measuring such impacts. One tool is the *economic multiplier.* Multipliers are based on the interdependency between two types of businesses in the local economy—the export (or basic) and service (or nonbasic) sectors. *Export* activities produce goods and services for *outside* the local economy, while *service* activities sell goods and services *within* the local economy. An expansion of sales in the basic sector generally has a multiplier effect on the local service sector. *Economic multipliers* may be defined then, as the numerical relationship between an original change in economic activity and the ultimate change in activity that results as the money is spent and respent through various sectors of the economy (Faas 1980, Faas and Holland 1994). This concept is illustrated in Figure 11.5. Of $1 in wages, half may be spent locally, of which half again goes to wages. As a result, the original dollar generates another $.25 of income the first time it is respent.

Several types of multipliers have been identified, including employment multipliers, income multipliers, and output multipliers. An *employment multiplier* is the total change in full-time equivalent employment (FTE) generated in the local economy for each change of one FTE in an export sector of the local economy. A *household income* (or *earnings*) *multiplier* is the total change in household income throughout the local economy from a $1 change in household income payments by an export sector. An *output* (or *business*) *multiplier* is the total change in sales generated throughout the local economy by a $1 change in export sales (Faas 1980, Faas and Holland 1994).

There are many techniques for estimating economic multipliers. Two such techniques include the *export-base approach* and the *input-output model* (see Chapter 4). The amount of income generated in the local economy for the actual dollars spent will vary. The sophistication and type of technique used will differ with the local structure

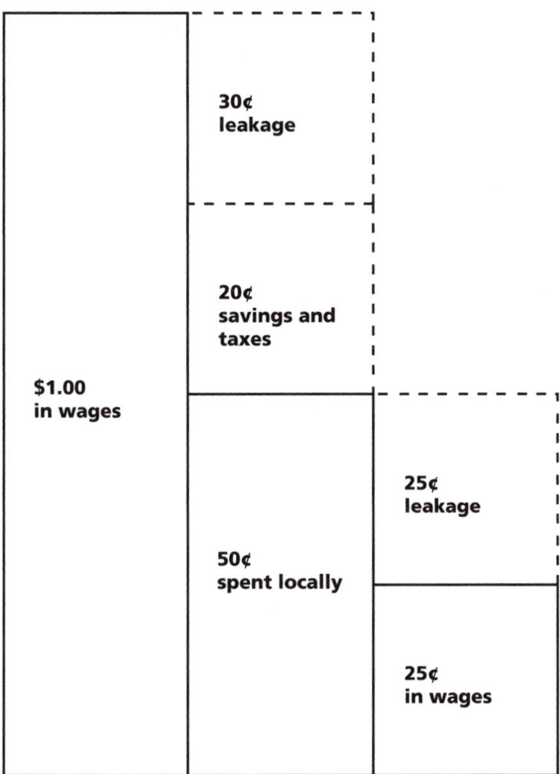

FIGURE 11.5 Economic multipliers. *(Source: Faas 1980)*

and the nature of the proposed project or program.

Fiscal Impact Analysis

Fiscal impact analysis refers to the study of the effect of proposed projects or actions on government expenditures and revenues and on taxes. Theodore R. Siegler and Neil L. Meyer (1980) presented a framework for fiscal impact analysis. They suggest starting with three key questions:

- How many people are expected to move into the community; how long will they stay; and where will they live?
- What costs will be incurred in providing expanded public services and facilities to accommodate the growing population, and when will these costs be incurred?
- What revenues will be generated by the growth, and when will the revenues be available? (Siegler and Meyer 1980, 2)

The answers to some of these questions may already exist if the community has developed an inventory and analysis of human factors. That information can then be used for the administrative review of proposed project actions. Siegler and Meyer have developed a worksheet (Table 11.4) for estimating additional operating and maintenance costs and capital costs associated with incoming population for services commonly provided by communities. *Operating and maintenance costs* may be estimated for the incoming population by examining the community budget. The total operating and maintenance costs for each service divided by the existing population represents the present per capita cost of providing each service. This per capita cost can be multiplied by the estimated size of the incoming primary (persons directly associated with the source of growth) and secondary or tertiary (workers and their families required in other sectors of the local economy to provide expanded or new services) population to provide what Siegler and Meyer term a "minimum estimate" of the total additional operating and maintenance costs associated with the new population.

Capital costs may be estimated for the incoming population in various ways. Local officials must estimate the capacity of existing facilities and then judge which facilities will require additional capital investment. By dividing the total expansion investment cost by the expected number of new residents, an investment cost for each new resident can be estimated (Siegler and Meyer 1980; see also Cooke et al. 1996). Siegler and Meyer have developed a checklist of revenue sources potentially affected by community population growth (Table 11.5). An analysis of poten-

TABLE 11.4
ESTIMATING ADDITIONAL OPERATING AND MAINTENANCE COSTS AND CAPITAL COSTS ASSOCIATED WITH INCOMING POPULATION FOR SERVICES COMMONLY PROVIDED BY COMMUNITIES

	Operating and Maintenance Costs				Capital Costs		
						Anticipated Expenditure	
Public Service	Current Costs (a)	Costs per Capita (b)	Size of Incoming Population (c)	Change in Costs (b × c)	Capacity Needed	Year	Amount
General government							
Education							
Judicial							
Law enforcement							
Fire							
Libraries							
Public works							
Roads							
Sewer							
Water							
Solid waste							
Health							
Welfare							
Other							

SOURCE: Siegler and Meyer 1980.

tial revenues can help a community determine whether the fiscal costs of growth will be borne by the proposed project or action.

The American Farmland Trust and Loudoun County, Virginia, designed a procedure for fiscal impact analysis, using county data, to estimate (1) the net public costs of new residential development and (2) whether these costs could be expected to vary significantly with the density of development. American Farmland Trust researchers pursued these objectives by (1) identifying the major categories of public costs and revenues for Loudoun County in metropolitan Washington, D.C., (2) developing a representative demographic profile of a new 1000-household residential community, (3) projecting four different density distributions for the prototype community, and (4) analyzing costs and revenues for each of the four densities (American Farmland Trust 1986).

The public costs and revenues were determined for major categories on a current annual basis, using the county budget and other published fiscal records. The researchers found that public education consumes most of the county budget (68 percent), followed by health and welfare (9 percent) and public safety (8 percent). General property taxes account for 48 percent of the county revenue, followed by state funds (31 percent) and other local taxes (9 percent) (American Farmland Trust 1986).

For the American Farmland Trust study of Loudoun County, age-specific census data for tracts in different parts of the county were examined. These data enabled the researchers to construct a prototype community, which they divided into four possible density groups

TABLE 11.5
REVENUE SOURCES POTENTIALLY AFFECTED BY COMMUNITY POPULATION GROWTH

	Current revenue (a)	Current per capita revenue (b)	Size of incoming population (c)	Change in revenue (b × c)	Date revenue will be available to spend
Local					
Real property					
Personal property tax					
Permits					
Fines					
Service fees					
User charges					
Development fees					
Hookup charges					
Prepayment of taxes					
Negotiated impact payments from development					
Other					
State					
Motor vehicle tax					
Liquor tax					
Cigarette tax					
Sales tax					
Grants-in-aid					
Severance tax					
Other					
Federal					
Revenue sharing					
Grants					
Federal *en lieu* payments					
Special programs					
Other					

SOURCE: Siegler and Meyer 1980.

Rural low density: 1 dwelling unit per 5 acres

Rural cluster: 1 dwelling unit per acre

Medium density: 2.66 dwelling units per acre

High density: 4.5 dwelling units per acre (American Farmland Trust 1986)

While researchers held the total population, age structure, and number of dwellings constant, the dwelling unit density varied. The researchers showed that the cost for public services such as education, road maintenance and construction, and water and sewer facilities was significantly greater for rural low-density, nonfarm settlement than higher-density development. In addition, "slightly higher revenues were projected from the higher-density communities" (American Farmland Trust 1986, 4). In addition, the American Farmland Trust research indicated that farms were less costly to service.

Following the Loudoun County study, the American Farmland Trust (1997) repeated the approach elsewhere and other researchers adapted the method (see, for example, Crane et al. 1996). According to the American Farmland Trust:

> It costs local government much less to serve one or two families living on a 200-acre [81-hectare] farm than it does to provide education, roads, water, sewers, and police and fire protection to 400 families living on half-acre [0.2-hectare] lots in a 200-acre [81-hectare] subdivision (1997, 149).

In more than 40 "cost of community service studies" undertaken or compiled by the American Farmland Trust, various researchers have shown "that farmland owners pay more in taxes than local governments pay to provide them with services, while homeowners receive more services than their taxes pay for" (1997, 149) (Table 11.6). Ratios on Table 11.6 display the "relationship between revenues generated by each land use category and the cost of providing municipal services to that category" (American Farmland Trust 1997, 149).

In a study for the Potawatomi Land Trust, University of Michigan researchers reported similar findings (Crane et al. 1996). Adapting the American Farmland Trust's "cost of community services" method, the Michigan researchers asked: Does development pay for itself, and has developed land contributed enough to local government to cover costs that accompany such development? The study focused on Scio Township in Washtenaw County, Michigan. The researchers concluded "that residential land did not contribute enough revenue to pay for the services that it received" (Crane et al. 1996, iv)

Cost of community services studies, such as those undertaken by the American Farmland Trust and by others who have adapted their method, can help local planners assess fiscal impacts of new development. Such fiscal impact analyses can provide justification to protect important natural resource lands, such as those used for farming, as well as environmentally sensitive lands.

Overall, the American Farmland Trust studies find "that higher net public costs are associated with lower-density residential development" (1986, 4). The Loudoun County study illustrates that fiscal impact analyses can be constructed "at the county level for a given residential development at different densities, using existing data for major categories of public costs and revenues." Furthermore, the research shows that for many densities "the ongoing public costs of new residential development will exceed the revenues from such development" (American Farmland Trust 1986, 5). Research independent of the American Farmland Trust supports the findings about the public costs of single-family housing. For example, an Oregon study determined that the cost of growth for a single-family residence was $23,013 (Carson 1998). As a result, once a plan has been adopted and its implementing measures put in place, planning administrators should carefully analyze the fiscal impacts of proposed new development, especially those that require amending the adopted plan and implementing ordinances.

Social Impact Analysis

A straightforward way of assessing social impacts of a project is to ask who suffers and who benefits as a result of the proposal? One tool to analyze who suffers and who benefits is a *matrix*. The matrices introduced in Chapter 4 may provide a starting point. For example, a western city proposes the construction of a dam and reservoir in a mountain environment to supply water. Several groups will suffer and benefit from the proposal (Table 11.7).

TABLE 11.6
SUMMARY OF COST OF COMMUNITY SERVICES STUDIES (RATIOS IN DOLLARS)

State/Town	Residential including farmhouses	Combined commercial and industrial	Farm/forest open land
Connecticut			
Durham	1:1.07	1:0.27	1:0.23
Farmington	1:1.33	1:0.32	1:0.31
Hebron	1:1.06	1:0.47	1:0.43
Litchfield	1:1.11	1:0.34	1:0.34
Pomfret	1:1.06	1:0.27	1:0.86
Maine			
Bethel	1:1.29	1:0.425	1:0.06
Maryland			
Carroll County	1:1.15	1:0.48	1:0.45
Frederick County	1:1.05	1:0.39	1:0.48
Massachusetts			
Agawam	1:1.05	1:0.44	1:0.31
Becket	1:1.02	1:0.83	1:0.72
Deerfield	1:1.16	1:0.38	1:0.29
Franklin	1:1.02	1:0.58	1:0.40
Gill	1:1.15	1:0.43	1:0.38
Leverett	1:1.15	1:0.29	1:0.25
Westford	1:1.15	1:0.53	1:0.39
Williamstown	1:1.11	1:0.40	1:0.34
Minnesota			
Farmington	1:1.02	1:0.18	1:0.48
Lake Elmo	1:1.07	1:0.20	1:0.27
Independence	1:1.04	1:0.19	1:0.47
New York			
Amenia	1:1.23	1:0.17	1:0.25
Beekman	1:1.12	1:0.18	1:0.48
Farmington	1:1.22	1:0.27	1:0.72
Dix	1:1.51	1:0.27	1:0.31
Fishkill	1:1.23	1:0.31	1:0.74
Hector	1:1.30	1:0.15	1:0.28
Kinderhook	1:1.05	1:0.21	1:0.17
Montour	1:1.50	1:0.28	1:0.29
Northeast	1:1.36	1:0.29	1:0.21
Reading	1:1.08	1:0.26	1:0.32
Red Hook	1:1.11	1:0.20	1:0.22
Ohio			
Madison Village	1:1.67	1:0.20	1:0.38
Madison Township	1:1.40	1:0.25	1:0.30
Pennsylvania			
Bethel Township	1:1.08	1:0.17	1:0.06
Carroll Township	1:1.03	1:0.03	1:0.02
Straban Township	1:1.10	1:0.11	1:0.06
Rhode Island			
Hopkinton	1:1.08	1:0.31	1:0.31
Little Compton	1:1.05	1:0.56	1:0.37
West Greenwich	1:1.46	1:0.40	1:0.46
Virginia			
Clarke County	1:1.26	1:0.21	1:0.15
Wisconsin			
Dunn	1:1.06	1:0.29	1:0.18

SOURCE: American Farmland Trust 1997, 150

TABLE 11.7
WHO SUFFERS AND WHO BENEFITS

Affected Groups	Suffers	Benefits
City users	x	x
Suburban users	x	x
Developers		x
On-site landowners	x	
Off-site landowners		x
Farmers	x	
Water conservation advocates	x	
Sportspeople	x	x
Environmentalists	x	
Consultants		x
Scientists	x	

City and suburban water users will both benefit and suffer from the proposal. They may benefit from more water but will suffer from the added costs to pay for the facility. Developers stand to benefit because new areas will be open for development once new water is available. The on-site landowners whose land will be flooded by the dam will suffer. Some off-site landowners downstream may be protected from floods and as a result benefit. But off-site farmers downstream will suffer from the decline of available water for irrigation. Water conservation advocates stand to suffer because with new water supplies there will be less of an incentive to conserve.

The stream that will be dammed is a natural trout habitat. The stream bank contains vegetation that provides wildlife habitat. As a result of the destruction of the stream and the riparian vegetation, sportspeople will suffer. New fish habitat may be created by the reservoir too, so some fishing enthusiasts may benefit. Environmentalists who appreciate the scenic beauty and natural qualities of the stream corridor will suffer. Consultants involved in the planning and design of the new dam will benefit. Scientists who conduct biological and geological research in the watershed will suffer.

Such a matrix helps clarify who stands to gain from the proposal and who will lose. Planning administrators can use such a matrix, with a written analysis, to assess social impacts. As a result, decisions can be made more fairly so that costs and benefits can be evenly distributed.

TWO EXAMPLES OF PLANNING ADMINISTRATION

Governments use administrative strategies to ensure that community goals are achieved. Increasingly, many goals relate to environmental protection and growth management. Planning administration can be viewed ecologically. The process connects various administrative activities, making the interrelationships between aspiration and action explicit.

Portland, Oregon, Regional Growth Management Planning

The process of selecting among planning options in Portland, Oregon, was discussed in Chapter 6. This process resulted because of the Oregon statewide goals reviewed in Chapter 2. A key aspect of administering plans is the ability to adapt to change. Firm plans need to be guided by flexible planners. Portland helps to illustrate how firm plans have been modified within Oregon's statewide framework. Planning in Oregon is governed by a set of mandatory statewise goals and procedures for holding local plans, ordinances, and court decisions accountable to achieving the goals (Johnson 1974; Oregon Supreme Court 1979; Portland Bureau of Planning 1980; Carson 1998, Daniels 1999). Since 1988, the most intensive test of these goals has centered on the Portland metropolitan region, the largest urban area in the state. Like other American cities, this region is coping with the problems and opportunities associated with rapid population growth. Unlike those other American cities, greater Portland has a regional government, called Metro, with the authority to guide planning and the mandate to

The Oregon statewide planning program supports the use of urban growth boundaries to control development. *(Oregon Department of Land Conservation and Development)*

achieve the statewide goals among three counties and 24 municipalities, including the city of Portland. Metro is similar to regional governments in other nations.

Oregon's land use planning goals include mandates for intensive public participation in planning, the control of urban development to protect farmland and reduce public infrastructure costs, provide affordable housing, and provide land for industry and economic development. The urban growth (commonly called "sprawl") and farmland protection goals center on a requirement that Metro and other Oregon cities have an *urban growth boundary* (UGB). Land-use changes outside the UGB are limited to farm, forest, and low-density residential zones with very limited commercial and infrastructure development. Lands inside the UGB have few such limits but are required to maintain a 20-year rolling supply of developable land available for many uses.

The Portland region has a long tradition of planning to maintain a high quality of life. These efforts have successfully maintained many natural areas within cities; small-town characteristics in many identifiable neighborhoods within cities; good mass transit; many mixed-use truly urban areas; beautiful buildings; and a safe, day-around-lively downtown center. But, with the advent of rapid economic and population growth in the region during the late 1980s and early 1990s, these qualities came under intense pressure. It fell upon Metro to continue this planning tradition and maintain these qualities with growth well into the twenty-first century (Ribe and Seltzer 1992).

The response to this challenge was the Region 2040 Planning Process, which began in 1989, produced a regional framework plan in 1994, and continues today. Metro began by seeking a consensus about the planning process and purposes. This was found through a complex, intensive set of public meetings and negotiations among the numerous jurisdictions and private interests with roles and potential veto powers in finding and successfully promulgating a regional plan. The final results were documented in the Regional Growth Goals and Objectives (RGGOs) (Metro 1991). The RGGOs document constituted an agreement about general goals and processes to maintain a comprehensive regional planning partnership, and it provided a sketchbook about the attributes that the region would seek to achieve by the year 2040. It also sought to clarify the relationship between within-jurisdiction planning efforts and the regional plan's formulation and enforcement.

Region 2040 planning began by taking stock of the region's social values, historical development patterns, resources, trends, and essential qualities that make for a uniquely livable and attractive landscape. Portland State University and the University of Oregon helped this effort (Ribe and Seltzer 1992; Abbott 1994). This basic information was then used to begin to develop alternative regional patterns for growth. The consulting firms Eco-Northwest, Walker-Macy, and others aided this task. Through many public meetings around the region, four alternative patterns were proposed. The first was a base-case describing roughly what would happen if existing growth patterns continued. One alternative emphasized densification of commercial and housing development along mass-transit-intensified corridors with modest expansion of the UGB. Another alternative called for more generalized densification of land uses focusing on town centers inside existing cities, a more intensive expansion of transportation systems, and no expansion of the UGB. A third option advocated small expansions of the existing UGB, lots of new mass transit, and the creation of new satellite cities outside current urbanized areas.

These alternatives formed the basis for a public participation and education process that developed the criteria for evaluating the future options for the region. The process included mailing a newspaper-style description of the various alternatives' virtues and trade-offs to more than half a million households, which elicited over 17,000 citizen responses. The planners also sent out more formal questionnaires and organized public meetings, workshops, newsletters, presentations to civic groups, and television and radio call-in programs. At the same time, modeling efforts sought to predict traffic, air quality, and land use consequences of the alternatives, and this information was incorporated into the public participation efforts as they progressed (Ribe and Seltzer 1992).

Public opinion was especially sought about certain issues (Metro 1994). One was average regional residential lot sizes, which seemed amenable to a slight reduction from about five dwelling units per acre to seven. Another was reducing average regional parking spaces per dwelling unit and per square foot of commercial or office space, which had some modest support, in principle, provided quality alternative transit options and improved pedestrian systems were available. The densification of existing town centers around mass transit gained general support as an alternative to UGB expansion and as a way to reduce traffic congestion. Urban growth boundary expansion garnered considerable opposition (and some support provided it was limited as much as possible and well-planned). Parks and greenspaces were desired in and near urban areas for both recreation and habitat.

The draft Region 2040 plan underwent another extensive public review process during 1994. This included a video describing the plan, which Blockbuster Video made available free of charge, and a series of before-and-after illustrations at many scales by architect Peter Calthorpe. At this stage considerable opposition to UGB expansion still remained, along with concern that growth management planning would only encourage more growth.

The final plan was adopted in December 1994 (Metro 1994). It mixed elements of all the alternatives and some new ideas from the public. It called for UGB expansion amounting to 7 percent by 2040. (This amount has since increased slightly due to new state laws and higher-than-expected growth rates.) The expansions of the UGB were carefully located to avoid prime and viable farmlands and to focus on areas already disturbed by rural residences and otherwise more suitable for development. The plan called for densified regional town centers served by improved mass transit and pedestrian systems, as well as general increases in housing densities wherever possible throughout the region and including fair shares of affordable housing in all jurisdictions. It called for expansion of the region's light rail system and more greenspaces inside and just outside urban areas.

This was a lengthy and complex process of developing regional plan options. In the end, the Portland region adopted its first unified and legally enforceable growth management plan in response to many difficult challenges. It attempts to preserve elements from the past valued by the region's residents and to create a future in ways that all the individual jurisdictions could accept and write their own plans to implement. The plan got off to a good start as voters approved bond measures for light rail and greenspaces acquisition in the two years after its adoption.

The Tucson WASH Ordinance and Environmental Resource Zone

Tucson, Arizona, has enacted two measures to protect environmentally sensitive areas within its city boundaries. Its *watercourse amenities, safety and habitat* (WASH) ordinance was adopted by city council in 1991 and is administered by the city engineer's office. The *environmental resource zone* (ERZ) is administered by the Tucson planning department.

The WASH ordinance includes specific development requirements for channels and banks of washes. The ordinance prohibits alteration without a mitigation plan. This plan is submitted to the city engineer. The ordinance details specific requirements for the mitigation plan as well as the review and approval process. The review process involves both the city planning and the city engineering departments (City of Tucson 1991).

The planning director is responsible for the review of a required plant and habitat plan as well as a required preservation and revegetation plan. The planning director has five working days either to accept the inventory and plan or to request further information. After acceptance, the director has 15 working days to approve or to reject the inventory and the plan. The decision notice is sent to both the applicant and the city engineer. The engineer is then required to incorporate these findings into the decision on a hydrology study and a mitigation plan (City of Tucson 1991).

In making the review, the planning director considers several specific standards, including the existing condition of the site; the existing character of vegetation upstream and downstream in the channel, on the banks, and 50 feet (15 meters) from the banks; the amount, type, and characteristics of the vegetation upstream and downstream of the site; linkages to open space systems; and critical and sensitive wildlife habitat (City of Tucson 1991).

The city engineer must review a required hydrology/hydraulic study and the mitigation plan. The engineer has five working days after receiving the study and the plan to accept them or request more information. After acceptance, the city engineer has 20 working days to approve or reject the study and the plan. Notice of the engineer's decision is provided to the applicant, the planning director, and all property owners within 200 feet (61 meters) of the site (City of Tucson 1991).

The city council set specific standards for the city engineer's review. These standards address drainage, erosion, flooding, utility lines and roadway improvements, consistency with the regulatory intent, and whether restoration is possible. The city defined an appeals process as well as possible variances (City of Tucson 1994). The WASH ordinance establishes clear, interrelated responsibilities between two city departments.

The ERZ is an overlay zone. It also requires coordination between the planning department and the city engineer. Encompassing broader geographic areas than the WASH ordinance, the zone intends to preserve all of the critical habitat within designated resource corridors. Applicants for projects affected by the ERZ are required to submit their plans to the planning department. The staff has five days to accept or reject the application, based on completeness (City of Tucson 1998).

The owner may be required to submit a mitigation plan if all critical riparian habitat on the site is not preserved. In such cases, the applicant must explain why the preservation of all the habitat cannot be preserved. The plan must also document the specific environmental impacts of the proposed development on existing critical habitat. The mitigation plan presents the techniques that will lessen these impacts as well as the measures to preserve and to restore other areas (City of Tucson 1998). The regulation includes diagrams to illustrate mitigation options (Figures 11.6 and 11.7)

Several lessons about program administration can be derived from Portland and Tucson. The metropolitan Portland example illustrates that administration must be based on a solid legal foundation. Furthermore, planning administration relies on a competent staff, and administrative activities should be linked to other steps in the planning process. Planning administration in Oregon is guided by specific statewide goals. Court cases have further articulated plan review and administrative procedures in Oregon. The development of such statewide goals for land-use planning has occurred relatively recently in the United States. When compared to more conventional planning processes, planning in metropolitan

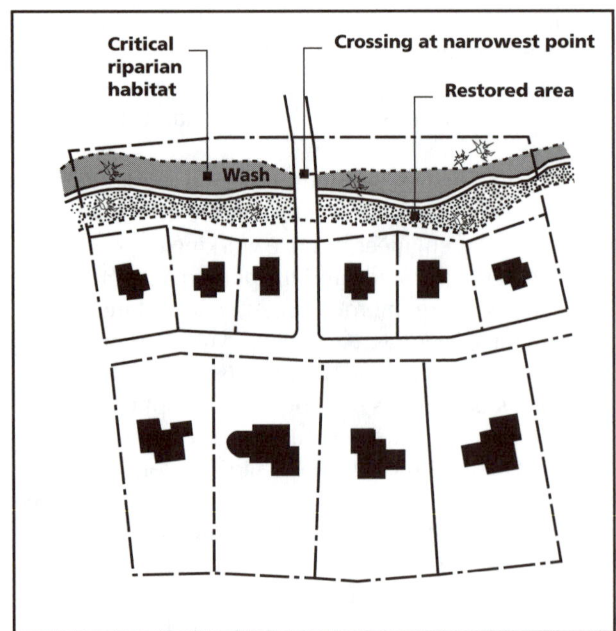

FIGURE 11.6 City of Tucson environmental resource zone mitigation options.

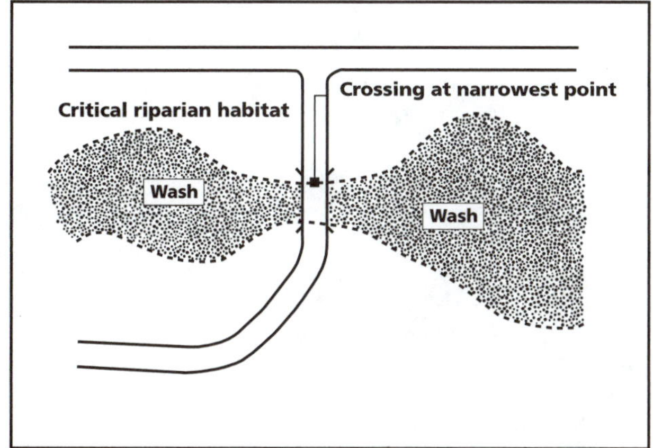

FIGURE 11.7 City of Tucson environmental resource zone riparian crossing.

Portland exhibits a greater ability to adjust to change. A sophisticated planning culture exists in Portland. Planning has broad public support. As a result plans are administered strictly, but planning adjusts to changing conditions while always seeking to improve environmental quality and enhance economic opportunities.

The Tucson example helps to illustrate the importance of the staff in planning administration. Close cooperation between the city engineer and the planning department is required in Tucson. The Tucson example illustrates a more comprehensive use of biophysical information in planning administration as compared with more conventional programs. The WASH ordinance and ERZ require considerable information about the terrain, hydrology, vegetation, and wildlife habitat of sites. The review process mandates timely decisions and a substantive consideration of the environmental consequences of proposed developments.

Part of the success of planning in metropolitan Portland and the rest of Oregon is due to the broad public understanding of its statewide goal. This is partially the result of the attention generated by the various referenda and court cases. Another reason for the visibility of planning in Oregon is the dedication of key political leaders, such as the charismatic former governor, the late Tom McCall. A third reason is that responsible officials have continually attempted to explain the law to the citizens of Oregon and to adjust their plans through time.

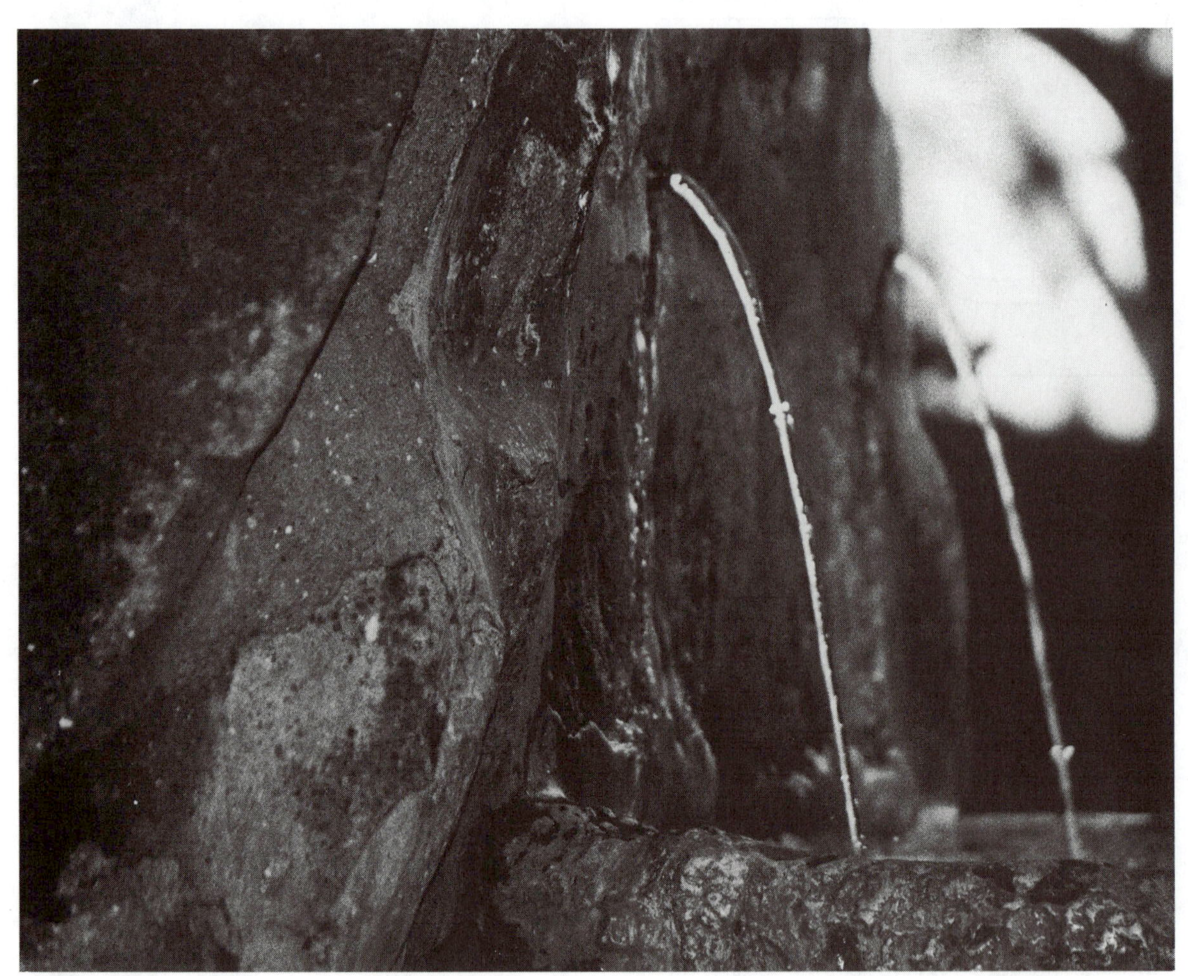

12

CONCLUSION

From within the planning community, there have been many critics of a normative, rationalist approach to planning. The normative perspective suggests a standard, model, or pattern of conduct for planners. Normative planning is where "planners subject both the ends and means of public policy to rational consideration" (Klosterman 1978, 38). Critics of this rational approach contend that it focuses on problem solving: "Take the problem, break it down into its component parts, and let's see what we can do about it" (Forester 1982, 61). They argue that "this may serve well for relatively routine, conventional, stable problems—but perhaps not for most planning and policy problems" (Forester 1982, 61).

Rationalists believe that "reason, independent of the senses, constitutes a superior source of knowledge" (Lai 1988, 19). This belief leads to a model that should be applied a priori to any situation or setting. A rationalist tradition underlies the planning profession because of its foundation in the fields of architecture, landscape architecture, engineering, and law. In addition, the very definition of the word *planning* suggests rationality.

A sustainable approach to planning also implies rationality or, at least, pragmatism. John Dewey, William James, and other pragmatists recommend that philosophy works best when eternal questions are connected to everyday practice. How best to live on earth in a sustainable, or better yet, regenerative way provides such an eternal question.

Herbert Gans was especially critical of the physical bias of planning prior to the 1960s. Yet, Gans espoused a rationalist perspective: "Planning must be and can be *rational*—rationality being achieved when planners develop plans or programs which can be proved to implement the goals that are being sought" (1968, ix). Gans was largely successful in his effort to wean planners from their architectural and site planning roots and lay the foundation for a social rationalist approach. Although Gans believes that "planning and social policy must and can be *rational,*" he also recognized that goals cannot "be rational, or rationally selected. . . . They must reflect values about which people differ—and about which they therefore have to argue so as to persuade one another or achieve a viable compromise" (Gans 1993, x).

Lewis Mumford, who was certainly critical of the architectural rationalists, was nevertheless an advocate of the spatial, physical concepts of planning. He proposed an organic approach to planning: "Organic planning does not begin with a preconceived goal: it moves from need to need, from opportunity to opportunity, in a series of adaptations that themselves become increasingly coherent and purposeful, so that they generate a complex, final design" (1961, 302).

Mumford's organic approach foreshadows a contingency view. Contingency is the condition of being subject to chance. The concept of contingency has been explored by theorists in management, organization behavior, and planning. According to Fremont Kast and James Rosenzweig:

> The contingency view seeks to understand the interrelationships within and among subsystems as well as between the organization and its environment and define patterns of relationships or configurations of variables. It emphasizes the multivariate nature of organizations and attempts to understand how organizations operate under varying conditions and specific circumstances (1974, ix).

Human organizations and their interactions with each other and their settings are complex. The postmodern condition would lead some to conclude that humans are doomed to exist in chaos. Students of chaos, however, have detected that order exists in apparently chaotic situations (Prigogine and Stengers 1984). Planners face the task of making order out of chaos; they must be able to adapt to changing conditions and to act in a contingent manner. Chaos theory emphasizes the complexity of our planet and its natural and social systems. Planning and planners should accept the fact that the world presents a complex array of possibilities. Such acceptance is fundamental in the search for a "new rationality" in planning (Verma 1998). New rationalism is not "independent of the senses," rather it is based on the need for pragmatism in a complex world. A. Budoni and S. Macchi observe, "The thought of complexity defines a 'new rationality' which negates any correspondence between science and certainty, between probability and ignorance, and opens the 'necessary' world of nature to possibility, to unpredictability, to multiple choices" (1998, 1). The "necessary world of nature" is physical and biological and social; it is ecological.

In spite of the criticisms made by Herbert Gans over three decades ago, many planners, or at least individuals who hold that title in local and even higher levels of government, are faced with situations concerning the physical ordering of the built and natural environments. Planners must address issues concerning the use of land and other natural resources. To be effective, they require a repertoire of approaches that can be applied to a variety of situations.

A revised view of planning is emerging—pragmatic, yet still optimistic and even visionary, socially conscious while engaged in the physical reordering of settlements and the protection of natural systems. Timothy Beatley (1994b) advocates a new set of principles for ethical land use. He identifies several key elements of ethical land use policy, including "environmental duties." Beatley describes these duties as an acknowledgment of "obligations to protect and conserve the natural environment, both for humans and other forms of life. Ethical obligations to the environment lie at . . . ecosystems, species and organism levels. In particular, ethical land-use policy acknowledges that *Homo sapiens* is not the only species on the planet and that nonhuman life has inherent worth as well" (1994b, 266).

William Lucy calls for a broader view of planning, based on the principle "that the field and the profession should nurture healthy people in healthy places" (1994, 305). He observes that "the relationships between people and place lie at the heart of physical design and that is why design should have a meaningful role in planning" (Lucy 1994, 313). Michael Neuman (1998a, 1998b) argues for the centrality of two elements associated with design—the plan and plan-making—in the enterprise. The essence of ecological planning and design is what many call sustainability, but clearly we must go beyond merely supporting and holding up what we have now. John Lyle advocated a regenerative approach. He noted, "Regeneration has to do with rebirth of life itself, thus hope for the future" (Lyle 1994, 11).

Even the most forward-looking proponents of a new, ecologically based planning acknowledge the necessity to learn from the experience of others (Aberley 1994; Hersperger 1994). According to Doug Aberley, "There are perceptions and processes—tools of change—that we don't have to reinvent. We simply need to learn how to use, and further adopt, what others have struggled so hard to create" (1994, 11).

While learning from the past, planners should avoid previous pitfalls. Paul Niebanck (1993) identified a schism between the "rule making" and the "place making" traditions in environmental planning. One tradition is derived from the planning discipline's association with the law as well as the social and natural sciences. The other tradition derives from the environmental design arts of architecture and landscape architecture, although several notable cultural geographers and historians contribute much to our knowledge of places. Ecological planning provides a synthesis that values both the necessities of rule making and place making.

The model for planning presented here is a cyclical yet iterative process—identification of issues; establishment of goals; inventory and analysis of the biophysical and sociocultural environments at the regional and local levels; detailed studies such as suitability analysis; determination of options; development of a plan for the landscape, continued public participation and community education; detailed design; implementation; and administration. The process is an elaboration of Patrick Geddes' survey → plan → action, to a more cyclical survey → action → plan → action → survey. Action may precede a

Central Park, New York City.

plan and even a survey, but understanding the place and creating a vision remain integral to the process. A linear approach is inadequate for most situations—after starting to implement a plan, the original goals may change or there may be new information discovered about the environment. A feedback process is necessary to reformulate and restudy issues. In many cases, this process of review may occur repeatedly. As a result, instead of having a linear planning process, in many cases one experiences a cyclic form of planning, reviewing previous stages again and again.

Such a cyclical process occurred in the Desert View Tri-Villages Area of Arizona, which has been used as an example in several sections of this book. The Tri-Villages example helps to illustrate how an ecological approach can be integrated into conventional planning processes. The Tri-Villages Area is located in the Sonoran Desert region, which covers much of Arizona, the Mexican states of Sonora, Baja Nord, and Baja Sur, plus a small part of California. The first general plan for the Tri-Villages Area was adopted in 1987, when it was called Peripheral Areas C and D by City of Phoenix planners. The Phoenix metropolitan region is one of the most rapidly growing parts of the United States. New development is progressing at a pace of over an acre (.4047 hectare) an hour.

After 1987, several events caused city officials to revise and update the general plan for the area. The concern focused on the growth and the impact of that growth on beautiful desert lands. As a result, by the early 1990s the Desert View Tri-Villages Area faced several development-related problems and opportunities. The problems included how to protect environmentally sensitive areas and where to locate new development. Every five years, there is a demand for 5000 new homes in the Tri-Villages—which, with current development patterns, will consume 2000 acres (810 hectares) of land. Meanwhile, the current residents want to maintain their rural way of life.

An overriding issue was the rising concern about the very nature of suburban sprawl in the Phoenix metropolitan region. The Phoenix, Arizona, metropolitan area is a late-twentieth-century place, largely suburban in character. Its development occurred as a result of improved automobile and air transportation as well as the invention of air-conditioning technology. Large national government subsidies for water, highway, and housing development, plus significant national military investments in the region, stimulated much growth, especially after the Second World War. Phoenix had only slightly over 65,000 residents in 1940; today it is the seventh-largest city in the United States, with a population of over 1 million. Meanwhile the metropolitan area grew from just over 186,000 people in 1940 to over 2.4 million people by 1995. According to City of Phoenix Planning Department data, the region is adding about 63,000 residents per year, who require about 23,000 new housing units (*Tempe Daily News Tribune* 1995, A9). The region's population is expected to double by 2020.

The region is a challenging place to inhabit. Frank Lloyd Wright defined the Sonoran Desert as a place "where plants exist between hell and high water." Although challenging to inhabit, the Sonoran Desert is the location of one of the fastest-growing regions in the United States. People move to this challenging place because they like it. They enjoy their backyard swimming pools and barbecues. They like the perceived safety and access to open space. They enjoy the climate. The price of homes is reasonable for lower and middle income residents. Phoenix has one of the highest percentages of home ownership of any major city in the nation. If widespread property ownership is a route to both personal freedom and democratic government, as John Locke and Thomas Jefferson believed, then the Phoenix region is the embodiment of the American dream (or perhaps the American nightmare). As Herbert Gans illustrated in his classic 1967 study of Levittown, Americans like suburban life. But suburban development poses many challenges for landscape planning, such as the loss of environmentally sensitive areas, prime farmlands, and wonderful views as well as rising fiscal and energy costs and worsening air quality.

As a result of these problems and opportunities, Phoenix city planners decided to revise the general plan for the area and with the village planning committee set some preliminary goals. Current desert rural ways of living should be maintained. Property rights should be protected. Fragile deserts should be preserved. New growth should be accommodated in the most suitable places.

The city planners turned to the Arizona State University School of Planning and Landscape Architecture for help with understanding the ecology of the area. In addition to environmental planners and landscape architects, an environmental resource program had been recently added to the school. This program included faculty and students with expertise in plant and wildlife ecology, soils science, GIS, and remote sensing. An informal technical working group was formed in 1994. The North Sonoran Collaborative consists of environmental scientists, planners, landscape architects, and architects from ASU, the City of Phoenix, consulting companies, and the State of Arizona. Initially, the collaborative met monthly for two years and more sporadically since to discuss the environment of the Desert View Tri-Villages Area and to speculate about the future. As a result of the collaboration, several ASU student projects were undertaken that studied the landscape ecology of the area and possible environmental impacts of its development.

These studies provided much of the groundwork for the examples described in Chapters 3, 4, and 5. However, planning is seldom as neat and linear as chapters in a book. The process is, and was in this case, more iterative. Initial, large-scale ecological inventories and suitability analyses were conducted, but these raised more questions and demonstrated gaps in the knowledge about the ecology of the Desert View Tri-Villages Area and the Sonoran Desert in general.

Very early in the process, strong political support developed for protecting large areas of desert in the Tri-Villages. But what areas should be protected? The Phoenix Parks, Recreation, and Library Department (PRLD) funded a detailed study of the Cave Creek Wash, headed by ASU landscape architecture professors Rebecca Fish Ewan and Joe Ewan (Ewan et al. 1996), to answer this question. Their research contributed to the proposed protection of a significant portion of the Cave Creek Wash drainage way. The work was so compelling that the PRLD decided to fund additional studies of other major washes in the area, also headed by Fish Ewan and Ewan (Ewan et al. 1998). These studies indicated a paucity of knowledge about wildlife along the washes. As a result, the PRLD funded research directed by ASU environmental scientist professor Bill Miller to study wildlife habitats.

The student inventories, suitability analyses, and other research had provided a good beginning, but a richer database was needed. As a result, the PRLD supported the development of a GIS database for the Desert View Tri-Villages Area (Brady et al. 1998). Also used as an example in Chapters 3 and 5, this effort was headed by ASU environmental scientist professor Ward Brady and involved GIS specialists Jana Fry and Mike Collins among others.

Meanwhile, the North Sonoran Collaborative developed four character concepts—desert preservation, rural desert, suburban desert, and growth—that would later serve as the organizational elements for the formation of four teams in a 1995 charrette organized by ASU and the City of Phoenix. This charrette, discussed in Chapter 6, helped to refine concepts and visions for the area. The process led to general plan revisions for the eastern portion of the Tri-Villages (adopted in 1996), the Interstate 17 corridor in the west (proposed in 1998), and the Sonoran Preserve concentrated in the center but including sites throughout the area (adopted in 1998). (See chapter 7 for discussion of these plans.)

Throughout the process, public involvement and education were extensive and ongoing. The village planning committee, the Sonoran Preserve Advisory Committee, and the planning and parks commissions were especially active. Techniques such as those introduced in Chapter 8 were employed. In addition to utilizing the charrette process, the planners organized workshops and hearings, conducted surveys, and disseminated information. The local press gave prominent coverage to many of these activities.

In spite of considerable discussion and promising ideas introduced at the 1995 charrette, design visions still need greater resolution. The Phoenix Design Review Committee revised its housing design review standards somewhat, but these changes will have little significant impact on how new neighborhoods look. Arizona State University, in conjunction with its EPA Sustainable Development grant, conducted neighborhood design charrettes in 1997 and 1998, but here, too, much of the subsequent development in the area looks the same, (although it has been directed away from the most sensitive areas). The Desert View Tri-Village Planning Committee has recommended Desert Character Overlay Districts which, if adopted by the city, will influence new development.

The Desert View Tri-Villages Area process is continuing, like many other plans introduced in this book. The Tri-Villages undertaking is relatively recent, and the author is intimately involved. As a result, an objective assessment of the process is impossible at present, although much hope exists. Some of the more established efforts introduced here have yielded impressive results. The successes of Oregon's statewide planning law and the associated renaissance of Portland are well documented (see, among many sources, Kellington 1998). The Pinelands plan has also contributed much to its region (Platt 1996). As Robert Yaro and Tony Hiss report

> . . . in comparison to surrounding southern New Jersey, residential land values in The Pinelands have increased by 10 percent. The success of this integrated conservation and development program has resulted in broad public support for The Pinelands Commission. In a 1994 poll, 79 percent of the New Jersey residents favored continued protection for The Pinelands landscape (1996, 90–91).

Landowners, many of whom are middle and lower income individuals, have seen their prop-

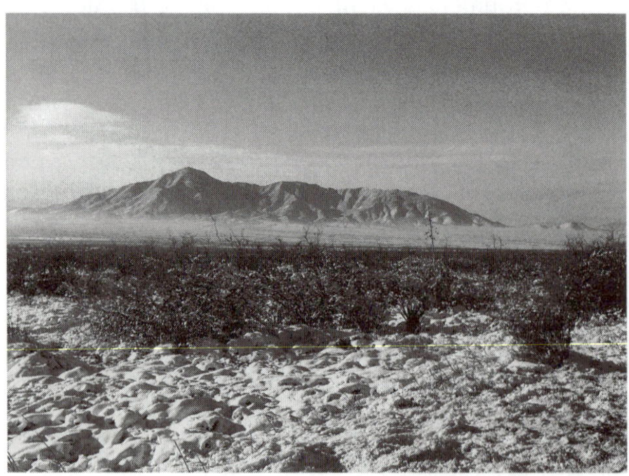

Landscape in the San Pedro River Watershed, southern Arizona (USA) and northern Sonora (Mexico).

erty values increase in the Pinelands. This fact illustrates that environmental protection need not negatively impact property rights and, indeed, can enhance them. Meanwhile, the New Jersey Pinelands Commission has made allocation for affordable housing opportunities, ensuring access to a broad range of people.

As the previous quote illustrates, the Regional Plan Association planners sought to learn from the work of others, those in the Pinelands as well as from Portland and other places. Bob Yaro and his Regional Plan Association colleagues also brought experience gained from other places, such as the Connecticut River Valley. Planning remains fundamentally an art, built from experience, applied to the specifics of the place.

The method described in this book reflects a middle-ground approach to landscape planning that is somewhere between a purely organic and a truly rational one. Ecology is central to the method, as it should be for our future. As Lynton Caldwell and Kristin Shrader-Frechette note, "Ecological literacy has not always been characteristic of modern authors [or planners and designers]. It will be an unavoidable feature of postmodern society" (1993, 5). The method presented here is not suggested as a rigid, lockstep approach that is appropriate for every situation, but rather a flexible, iterative method that can be used when a group of people identify an issue or set of issues. The method is a framework for problem solving. As the feedback arrows in Figure 1.1 indicate, there are many steps in the process where it may be adjusted or modified. Certainly, the steps may be reordered or skipped entirely depending on the situation. For instance, in some cases it may be appropriate to conduct inventories and analyses (Steps 3 and 4) before establishing goals (Step 2). In Mumford's words, the method represents "a series of adaptations."

The issue or set of issues may be viewed as symptoms of the problems and opportunities facing the planning area. In order to prescribe an appropriate intervention, the landscape planner then may make a diagnosis about the situation based on an understanding of the nature of the place.

APPENDIX A

COMPREHENSIVE VEGETATION LIST

(SOURCE: from Ewan et al. 1998)

(Alphabetized by scientific name)

Trees

Acacia greggii	Catclaw acacia
Celtis pallida	Desert hackberry
Cercidium floridum	Blue palo verde
Cercidium microphyllum	Foothill palo verde
	Little leaf palo verde
Olneya tesota	Ironwood
Prosopis velutina	Mesquite

Shrubs

Ambrosia ambrosioides	Bursage
Ambrosia artemisifolia	Common rag weed
Ambrosia deltoidea	Triangle-leaf bursage
Ambrosia eriocentra	Wooly bursage
Baccharis salicifolia	Seep willow
Baccharis sarothroides	Desert broom
Bebbia juncea	Sweet bush
Calliandra eriophylla	Fairy duster
Cassia artemisioides	Feathery or Silvery cassia
Chrysothamnus sp.	Rabbit brush
Encelia farinosa	Brittlebush
Ephedra trifuca	Mormon tea
Gutierrezia sarothrae	Snakeweed
Hymenoclea salsola	Burro brush
Krameri agrayi	White ratany
Larrea tridentata	Creosote bush
Lycium andersonii	Anderson thornbush
Lycium fremontii	Fremont thornbush
Ziziphus obtusifolia	Graythorn

Cacti

Carnegiea gigantea	Saguaro
Echincereus engelmannii	Hedgehog cactus
Ferocactus acanthodes	Barrel cactus
Mammilaria microcarpa	Fish hook cactus
	Pin cushion cactus
Opuntia acanthocarpa	Buckthorn cholla
Opuntia arbuscula	Pencil cholla
Opuntia bigelovii	Teddy bear cholla
Opuntia fulgida	Chain fruit cholla
	Jumping cholla
Opuntia imbricata	Tree cholla
Opuntia leptocaulis	Desert Christmas cactus
Opuntia phaeacantha	Prickly pear cactus

Forbs

Acourtia wrightii	Brownfoot
Amaranthus blitoides	Prostrate pigweed
Amsinckia intermedia	Fiddleneck
Astragalus nutallianus	Nutall locoweed
Boerhaavia diffusa	Spiderling
Bowlesia incana	Hairy boweslia
Brickellia coulteri	Brickell bush
Camissonia californica	Mustard evening primrose
Capsella bursa-pastoris	Shepherdspurse
Cassia covesii	Desert senna
Centaurea solstitialis	Yellow starthistle
Chaenactis stevioides	Esteve's pincushion
Chenopodium sp.	Lambsquarter
Chorizanthe brevicornu	Brittle spine flower
Chorizanthe rigida	Rigid spiny herb
Clematis drummondii	Virgin's bower
Daucus pusillus	Wild carrot
Descurainia pinnata	Yellow tansy mustard
Dichelostemma pullchellum	Blue dick

Erigeron divergens	Spreading fleabane
Eriogon umdeflexum	Buckwheat, Skeleton weed
Eriogonum inflatum	Desert trumpet
Eriophyllum lanosum	Wooly daisy
Erodium cicutarium	Filaree
Erodium texanum	Texas filaree
Eschscholtzia californica	Mexican poppy
Eucrypta micrantha	Small-flowered eucrypta
Euphorbia albomarginata	Rattlesnake weed
Euphorbia sp.	Spurge
Funastriium hirtellum	Rambling milkweed
Galium stellatum	Bedstraw
Herniaria cinerea	Burstwort
Janusia gracilis	Slender janusia
Lactuca serriola	Prickly lettuce
Lashtenia chrysostoma	Goldfields
Lesquerella gordonii	Gordon's bladderpod
Linanthus demissus	White starflower lianthus
Lotus humistratus	Hill lotus
Lotus tomentellus	Hairy lotus
Lupinus concinnus	Lupine
Malva neglecta	Common mallow
Malva parviflora	Mallow
Medicago polycarpa	Burclover
Melilotus officinalis	Yellow sweetclover
Melilotus sp.	Clover
Microseris linearifolia	Silver puffs
Monolepis nutalliawa	Poverty weed
Oenothera primiveris	Evening primrose
Orthocarpus purpurascens	Owl clover
Pectocarya recurvata	Arch-nutted comb
Phacelia distans	Wild heliotrope
Porophyllum gracile	Odora
Polygonum aviculare	Prostrate knotweed
Pterostegia drymarioides	ncn
Rafinesquia neomexicana	Desert chicory
Salsola iberica	Russian thistle Tumble weed
Salvia columbariae	Chia
Silene antirrhina	Sleepy catchfly
Sisymbrium altissimun	Tumble mustard
Sisymbrium irio	Yellow rocket
Sphaeralcea ambigua	Desert globe mallow
Sonchrus oleraceus	Annual sowthistle
Trixis californica	Trixis

Grasses

Aristida purpurea	Purple threeawn
Avena barbata	Oats
Bromus catharticus	Rescue grass
Bromus rubens	Redbrome
Cynodon dactylon	Bermuda grass
Erioneuron pulchellum	Fluff grass
Hilaria mutica	Tobosa
Hordeum arizonicum	Arizona barley
Lepidium densiflorum	Pepperweed
Phalaris caroliniana	Carolina canary grass
Poa bigelovii	Bigelow bluegrass
Vulpia octoflora	Six weeks fescue
Schismus barbatus	Mediterranean grass

APPENDIX B

LIST OF PARTICIPANTS, SONORAN NORTH LAND USE CHARACTER CHARRETTE, SEPTEMBER 22–24, 1995

Participants were divided into four charrette teams. Each group included core team members and community resource people. Charrette facilitators worked with all four teams. The participants are listed below.

CHARRETTE ORGANIZERS:
Jim McCarthy, Arizona State University School of Planning and Landscape Architecture

Lizi McGeorge, ASU School of Planning and Landscape Architecture

Frederick Steiner, ASU School of Planning and Landscape Architecture

CHARRETTE FACILITATORS:
Laurel Kimball, ASU College of Architecture and Environmental Design
Ray Quay, City of Phoenix Planning Department

ILLUSTRATORS AND ARTISTS:
Jesse Drake, Arizona Land Use Planners and Case Maker Exhibits
Tom Strich, Artist and Sculptor

Charrette Team: Desert Preservation Character

CORE TEAM MEMBERS:
Ward Brady, ASU School of Planning and Landscape Architecture

Edward Cook, ASU School of Planning and Landscape Architecture

Joe Ewan, ASU School of Planning and Landscape Architecture

Jack Gilcrest, THK Associates, Inc. (a private planning and design company)

Jim Haklik, ASU School of Planning and Landscape Architecture

Mary Kihl, ASU Herberger Center for Design Excellence, College of Architecture and Environmental Design

Tom McMahon, Arizona Game and Fish Department

Jolene Ostler, City of Phoenix Planning Department

Tom Strich, Artist and Sculptor

Randy Weaver, City of Phoenix Planning Department

COMMUNITY RESOURCES:

Bob Bacon, RJ Bacon and Associates (development company)

Christopher Estes, Sonoran North, Desert View Tri-Villages Planning Committee

Stephen Jones, Desert Foothills Land Trust

Tom Lazzelle, Sierra Club

Ralph Rooke, private citizen

Susanne Rothwell, private citizen

Don Steuter, Sierra Club

Charrette Team: Rural Desert Character

CORE TEAM MEMBERS:
Duane Blossom, The Planning Center (a private planning and design company)

Rebecca Fish Ewan, ASU School of Planning and Landscape Architecture

Lizi McGeorge, ASU School of Planning and Landscape Architecture

John Meunier, ASU College of Architecture and Environmental Design

David Pijawka, ASU Center for Environmental Studies and School of Planning and Landscape Architecture

Christy Ten Eyck, Floor and Ten Eyck (a private landscape architecture firm)

Gary Whysong, ASU School of Planning and Landscape Architecture

Al Zelinka, City of Phoenix Planning Department

COMMUNITY RESOURCES:
Dan Abrams, Abrams Realty and Management

Jean Anderson, private citizen

Faith Sussman, Desert View Tri-Villages Planning Committee

Charrette Team: Suburban Desert Character

CORE TEAM MEMBERS:
Kirsten Barré, Design Workshop, Inc. (a private planning and design company)

Dean Brennan, City of Phoenix Planning Department

Doug Green, ASU School of Planning and Landscape Architecture

John Jennings, Design Workshop, Inc. (a private planning and design company)

Jim McCarthy, ASU School of Planning and Landscape Architecture

Laurel McSherry, ASU School of Planning and Landscape Architecture

Mark Soden, Design Workshop, Inc. (a private planning and design company)

Catherine Spellman, ASU School of Architecture

Frederick Steiner, ASU School of Planning and Landscape Architecture

Joe Yarchin, Arizona Game and Fish Department

COMMUNITY RESOURCES:
Matthew Brady, Desert View Tri-Villages Planning Committee

Richard Corton, private citizen

John Miller, Los Arroyos (a development company)

Len Pritchard, PK Development (a development company)

Charrette Team: Growth Character

CORE TEAM MEMBERS:
Ann Bonnette, Goucher College, Towson, Maryland

John Brock, ASU School of Planning and Landscape Architecture

Tim Campbell, BRW (a private planning and design company)

Michael Dollin, Urban Earth Design (a private planning and design company) and ASU Joint Urban Design Program

Subhrajit Guhathakurta, ASU School of Planning and Landscape Architecture

Dave Longey, private consultant in landscape architecture and planning

Lionel March, University of California at Los Angeles, School of Arts and Architecture

Jim Mathien, City of Phoenix Planning Department

John McNamara, BRW (a private planning and design company)

COMMUNITY RESOURCES:
Curt Nelson, Continental Homes

Price Nosky, Sunbelt Holdings

GLOSSARY

The glossary was compiled from many sources. For the second edition the following publications were especially helpful:

American Farmland Trust. 1997. *Saving American farmland: what works.* Northampton, Massachusetts: American Farmland Trust.

Daniels, Tom, and Deborah Bowers. 1997. *Holding our ground: protecting America's farms and farmland.* Washington, D.C.: Island Press.

Pease, James R., and Robert E. Coughlin. 1996. *Land evaluation and site assessment: a guidebook for rating agricultural lands* (2nd ed.). Ankeny, Iowa: Soil and Water Conservation Society.

Duerksen, Christopher J., Donald L. Elliott, N. Thompson Hobbs, Erin Johnson, and James R. Miller. 1997. *Habitat protection planning: where the wild things are.* Chicago, Illinois: American Planning Association.

abiotic Those aspects dealing with nonliving matter.
adaptation A genetically determined characteristic that enhances the ability of an organism to better adjust to its surroundings.
adiabatic lapse rate A variation in temperature of a parcel of air up or down a change in elevation. This does not take into account exchanges of heat between the air parcel and the environment.
administration Execution of an organizational policy to reach predetermined objectives.
advection The transfer of an atmospheric property due to mass air motion along a gradient of the property in question; the horizontal spreading of local effects by wind.
agricultural district A legally recognized geographic area formed by one or more landowners and approved by one or more government agencies, designed to keep land in agriculture. Agricultural districts are created for fixed, renewable terms. Enrollment is voluntary; landowners receive a variety of benefits that may include eligibility for differential assessment, limits on annexation and eminent domain, protection against unreasonable government regulation and private nuisance lawsuits, and eligibility for purchase of agricultural conservation easement programs. Agricultural districts are also known as agricultural preserves, agricultural security areas, agricultural preservation districts, agricultural areas, agricultural incentive areas, agricultural development areas, and agricultural protection areas.
agricultural lands Places used for crop or animal production or for silviculture.
agricultural zoning A zoning ordinance or zoning district designed to protect farmland from incompatible nonfarm uses. There are several types of agricultural zoning, which vary according to: (1) the uses allowed in the zone (i.e., exclusive or nonexclusive farm use); (2) the minimum farm size allowed, such as a 50-acre (20.2-hectare) minimum lot size; (3) the number of nonfarm dwellings allowed, such as one building lot per 25 acres (10.1 hectares); and (4) the size of setbacks or buffer areas between farms and nonfarm properties.
air mass A widespread body of air that gains certain characteristics while set in one location. The characteristics change as it moves away.
air parcel A space of air over a certain area of land.
air pollution areas Places that require restraints on air pollution emissions due to periods of poor vertical air mixing and the subsequent entrapment of polluting substances.
albedo Reflected solar radiation factor.
alluvium The soil material deposited by running water.
analysis The examination of individual parts to find out their nature, function, and interrelationship with other parts.
annexation The incorporation of land into an existing community that results in a change in the community's

boundary. Annexation generally refers to the inclusion of newly incorporated land but can also involve the transfer of land from one municipality to another.
aquifer A water-bearing layer of permeable rock, sand, or gravel.
aspect Orientation toward some direction.
basalt A hard, fine-grained igneous rock caused by volcanism.
base map A reproducible map used to display various types of information.
biodiversity (biological diversity) The variety and abundance of all lifeforms considered at all levels of organization, from the genetic level through the species and higher levels of taxonomic organization, and including the variety of habitats, communities, landscapes, and ecosystems.
biogeochemical cycles Mineral and nutrient cycles that are important to the biological community.
biological Those aspects dealing with living matter.
biomass The amount of living matter in a given unit of the environment.
biophysical Biological and physical factors.
biosphere The portion of earth and its atmosphere that can support life.
biota All living organisms that exist in an area.
biotic community An assemblage of plants and animals living in the same community, forming a system that is mutually sustaining and interdependent and influenced by the abiotic factors of the ecosystem. A biotic community is generally characterized by the dominant vegetation.
board of adjustment An independent board created to handle conditional uses, variances, and special applications of regulations established by a zoning ordinance and to hear and act on appeals.
building code The legal requirements pertaining to the building of structures.
canopy layer The uppermost layer of forest vegetation.
capability An evaluation based on a resource's inherent, natural, or intrinsic ability to provide for use and includes that existing ability that is the result of past alterations or current management practices. Often *capability* is used interchangeably with *suitability.*
capability class An evaluation made by the U.S. Natural Resources Conservation Service concerning the agricultural management of a soil type.
capital improvement programming (CIP) The multiyear scheduling of public physical improvements. The scheduling is based on studies of fiscal resources available and the choice of specific improvements to be constructed for a period of five or six years in the future.
carnivores Organisms that feed on animal tissue.
carrying capacity (1) In ecology, the number of individuals that the resources of a habitat can support. (2) In wildlife, the maximum number of animals an area can support during a given period of the year. (3) In recreation, the amount of use a recreation area can sustain without deterioration of its quality.
circuit breaker tax relief A tax abatement program that permits eligible landowners to take some or all of the property tax they pay on farmland and farm buildings as a credit to offset their state income tax. Generally, farmers are eligible for a credit when property taxes exceed a set percentage of their income.
citizen participation The involvement of the public in the planning process.
citizens' advisory committee (CAC) A group of citizens called together by an agency to represent the ideas and attitudes of their community in advising and giving consultation to the agency.
clay Soil particles smaller than 0.002 millimeters in diameter.
climate The set of meteorological conditions characteristic of an area over a given length of time.
cluster development Grouping houses on part of a property while maintaining a large amount of open space on the remaining land. Cluster development should be seen as an open-space protection tool rather than a farmland protection tool.
cognitive mapping A process by which people acquire, code, store, recall, and decode information about the relative locations and attributes of phenomena in the everyday spatial environment.
cohort-survival method A popular method for making population projections based on fertility, mortality, and net migration.
community (1) In sociology, a variety of physical and social areas and institutions within which and with which people live. (2) In ecology, an association of interacting populations, usually determined by their interactions or by spatial occurrence.
compensating wind Wind originating above plains and flowing toward nearby mountains along a pressure gradient.
competition The use or defense of a resource by one individual which reduces the availability of that resource to other individuals.

comprehensive plan A document setting forth official governmental policy for the long-term future development of an area that considers all major determinants of growth and change—economic, political, social, and biophysical.
comprehensive planning A process for coordinating and establishing the policies set forth in a comprehensive plan.
conditional use A permitted use allowed in zoning ordinances that requires review by a board of adjustment or similar review agency.
conifer A cone-bearing plant whose needles remain on the tree all year.
conservation The management of human use of the biosphere to yield the greatest sustainable benefit to present generations while maintaining its potential to meet the needs and aspirations of future generations.
conservation easement A nonpossessory interest of a holder in real property imposing limitations or affirmative obligations the purposes of which include retaining or protecting natural, scenic, or open-space values of real property, assuring its availability for agricultural, forest, recreational, or open-space use, protecting natural resources, maintaining or enhancing air or water quality, or preserving the historical, architectural, archaeological, or cultural aspects of real property. Most are permanent; term easements impose restrictions for a limited number of years.
corn suitability rating (CSR) A numerical system for rating the productivity of farmland, used primarily in Iowa.
critical areas Places significantly affected by, or having an effect on, an existing or proposed major facility or other areas of major public investment; or containing or having a significant impact on historical, natural, or environmental resources of regional or statewide importance.
cropland Land regularly used for production of crops, except forestland and rangeland, including permanent pasture.
cross section A graphic tool that illustrates a vertical section of land.
cumulative impact assessment A comprehensive planning process whereby the rate or total amount of development is managed to stay below prestated threshold levels and is halted when such thresholds are reached.
deadwater Unflowing stream or river water.
decomposers Organisms responsible for breaking down matter.
deferred taxation A form of differential assessment that permits eligible land to be assessed at its value for agriculture. Taxes are based on how much money the land could produce in crops or livestock, instead of its speculative value for development. Deferred taxation is similar to preferential assessment, but landowners must pay some or all of the taxes that were excused if they later convert land to ineligible uses. Rollback taxes assess the difference between taxes paid under differential assessment and taxes that would have been due if the land was assessed at fair market value.
Delphi A method for systematically developing and expressing the views of a panel of experts.
design guidelines Local ordinances that establish standards for architecture and landscape architecture features of new development.
detritus Freshly dead or partially decomposed organic matter.
detritus-feeding animals Animals that ingest and break down fragments of organic matter.
detrivores Animals that obtain energy from decaying plant and animal matter.
development The modification of the biosphere and the application of human, financial, living, and nonliving resources to satisfy human needs and improve the quality of human life.
development rights Development rights entitle property owners to develop land in accordance with local land use regulations. These rights may be sold to public agencies or qualified nonprofit organizations. Sale of development rights to a government agency or land trust generally does not pass any affirmative interest in the property. Rather than the right to develop the land, the buyer acquires the responsibility to enforce the negative covenants or restrictions stipulated in the development rights agreement.
differential assessment An agricultural property tax relief program that allows eligible farmland to be assessed at its value for agriculture rather than its fair market value, which reflects "highest and best" use. The tax takes three different forms: preferential assessment, deferred taxation, and restrictive agreements. This approach is also known as current use assessment, current use valuation, farm use valuation, and use assessment.
dike Hardened lava extending in a direction other than that of the flow. Also, earthen elevated barrier erected to prevent land from uncontrolled flooding.

dominant species A species that has a controlling influence on the local environment.
downzoning A change in the zoning for a particular area that results in lower residential densities. For example, a change from a zoning ordinance that requires 10 acres (4.05 hectares) per dwelling to an ordinance that requires 40 acres (16.2 hectares) per dwelling is a downzoning.
drainage basin A part of the earth's surface that is occupied by a drainage system, which consists of a surface stream or a body of impounded surface water together with all tributary surface streams and bodies of impounded surface water.
drainage class The relative terms used to describe natural drainage as follows:

Excessive: Commonly very porous and rapidly permeable soils that have low water-holding capacity.

Somewhat excessive: Very permeable soils that are free from mottling throughout their profile.

Good: Well-drained soils that are nearly free of mottling and are commonly of intermediate texture.

Moderately good: Moderately well-drained soils that commonly have a slow permeable layer in or immediately beneath the solum. They have uniform color in the surface layers and upper subsoil and mottling in the lower subsoils and substrata.

Somewhat poor: Soils wet for significant periods but not all the time. They commonly have a slowly permeable layer in the profile, a high water table, additions through seepage, or a combination of these conditions.

Poor: Soils wet for long periods of time. They are light gray and generally are mottled from the surface downward, although mottling may be absent or nearly so in some soils.

drainage wind A wind flowing from a higher elevation to a lower elevation.
duplex A detached structure containing two dwelling units.
dwelling unit An independent living space within a structure designed and intended for occupancy by not more than one family and having its own housekeeping and kitchen facilities.
easement The purchase of partial rights in a piece of land.
ecologically critical areas Places containing one or more significant natural resources that could be degraded or lost as a result of uncontrolled or incompatible development.
ecological planning The application of ecological knowledge to community, regional, and resource planning.
ecology The reciprocal relationship of living things to one another and to their physical and biological environment.
economic Of or having to do with the management of the income and expenditures of a household, business, community, or government.
economic multiplier The numerical relationship between an original change in economic activity and the ultimate change in activity that results as the money is spent and respent through various sectors of the economy.
ecosystem The interacting system of a biological community and its nonliving surroundings.
ecotone Transitional areas between two ecological communities, generally of greater richness than either of the communities it separates.
elevation The height of land (in feet or meters) above sea level.
energy That which does or is capable of doing work.
environment The sum of all external influences that affect the life, development, and survival of an organism.
environmental impact statement (EIS) A document required of federal agencies by the National Environmental Policy Act for major projects or legislative proposals. It is used in making decisions about the positive and negative effects of the undertaking and lists alternatives. Some states and several other nations also require impact statements.
environmentally sensitive areas Places vulnerable to negative environmental impacts, such as unstable soils, steep slopes, floodplains, wetlands, and certain plant and animal habitats.
environmental thresholds The level beyond which additional stress to an ecosystem results in a marked decrease in the system's performance or an adaptive change in the system's structure or both.
eolian soils Soils deposited by the wind.
erosion The process of diminishing the land by degrees by running water, wind, ice, or other geological agents.

erosion, bank The destruction of land areas by active cutting of stream banks.
erosion, beach The retrogression of the shoreline of large lakes and coastal waters caused by wave action, shore currents, or natural causes other than subsidence.
erosion, gully The widening, deepening, and headcutting of small channels and waterways due to erosion.
erosion, rill The removal of soil by running water with formation of shallow channels that can be smoothed out completely by normal cultivation.
erosion, sheet The removal of a fairly uniform layer of soil or materials from the land surface by the action of rainfall and runoff water.
estuary A semienclosed coastal body of water that has a free connection with the open sea; it is thus strongly affected by tidal action, and within it seawater is mixed (and usually measurably diluted) with fresh water from land drainage.
evaporation The loss of water to the atmosphere from the surface of a soil or a body of water.
evapotranspiration The sum of evaporation and transpiration during a specific time period.
exotics Plants or animals introduced into a community that are not normally constituents of that community.
factor The term used to label a group of attributes, such as soil potential, size, compatibility, or scenic quality.
factor rating The number of points assigned to a factor, before weighting.
factor scale The way points are assigned to a factor.
fault A fracture line along which movements have occurred, causing the geologic units on either side to be mismatched.
fauna Animal life.
fee simple A form of land ownership that includes all property rights, including the right to develop the land.
fire hazard areas Places identified by the U.S. Forest Service and state wildfire management agencies as being particularly susceptible to forest fires.
first-order stream See stream orders.
flooding The general and temporary condition of partial or complete inundation of normal dryland areas from the overflow of streams, rivers, and other inland water or from abnormally high tidal water resulting from severe storms, hurricanes, or tsunamis. Also, any relatively high stream flow overtopping the natural or artificial banks in any reach of a stream, or a relatively high flow as measured by either gauge height or discharge quantity.
floodplain The area of land adjoining a body of water that has been or may be covered by floodwater.
flood-prone areas Places identified on the basis of the frequency of flooding.
floodway The channel of a river or other watercourse and the adjacent land areas required to carry and discharge a flood of a given magnitude.
flora Plant life.
fog Suspended liquid particles formed by condensation of vapor.
food chain The interconnected feeding relationships of various species that transfer energy from an initial source through a series of organisms.
forb Herbs other than true grasses, sedges, and rushes and nongrasslike plants having little or no woody material.
forestland Land that is at least 10 percent stocked by trees of any size, and land from which the trees have been removed to less than 10 percent stocking but that has not been developed for other use.
fragmentation The breaking up of continuous areas of habitat into smaller parcels. For example, a forest becomes fragmented when sections are cleared for agriculture or when trees are cleared to build roads.
frost pocket A hollow in the topography into which cold air will flow, thereby lowering temperatures in the bottom of the hollow.
geographic information system (GIS) A method of storing geographic information on computers to create a map or a series of maps. Geographic information can be obtained from a variety of sources, including topographical maps, soil maps, aerial and satellite photographs, and remote sensing technology. This information can then be used to create special maps for recordkeeping and decision-making purposes. GIS may be used to maintain maps of protected land or make decisions about which farmland to protect.
geologic map A graphic representation of the rock units and geologic features that are exposed on the surface of the earth.
geological hazard areas Places characterized by a high frequency of earthquake shaking, landslides, fault displacements, volcanic activity, subsidence, or severe erosion.

geology The science dealing with the study of rocks, often in an attempt to learn more about the history of the earth.
geomorphology The science dealing with the interpretation of the relief features of the surface of the earth.
givings The adding to the value of private property through a government action or actions. Givings include public investments, outright subsidies, tax breaks, and even regulations that give some land uses a competitive edge over others.
goal A concise statement of a community or organization's central aspirations in addressing a problem or an opportunity expressed in terms of a desired state or process that operating programs are designed to achieve.
grass Plant species with narrow leaves and jointed stems.
greenbelt An area of protected open space around a city or town, or an area that separates two built-up places.
ground cover Plants grown to keep soil from eroding.
groundwater Water that fills all the unblocked pores of material lying beneath the water table.
groundwater recharge areas Areas where additions are made to an aquifer by infiltration of water through the land surface.
group dynamics A generic term classifying a variety of interpersonal techniques used to foster group interaction and achievement of group goals and problem-solving techniques designed to clarify substantive issues.
growth management The use of regulations and incentives to influence the rate, timing, location, density, type, and style of development in the community.
habitat The sum of environmental conditions in a specific place that is occupied by an organism, population, or community.
hedgerow A group or row of trees and shrubs separating two grassy areas.
herb Any flowering plant that does not develop a persistent woody stem above ground, including forbs, grasses, and grasslike plants.
herbicide A chemical that controls or destroys undesirable plants.
herbivores Primary consumers or animals that obtain energy from plants.
historic, archaeological, and cultural areas Sites important to the heritage of the community, region, state, or nation.
human ecology The interdisciplinary study of human-ecosystem relationships.
humus The semistable fraction of the soil organic matter remaining after the major portion of added plant and animal residues has decomposed, usually dark-colored.
hydrograph A graph showing the volume of water that passes a point of a stream over a certain period of time.
hydrologic cycle A recurring series of events involving the circulation of water through the environment. The cycle includes precipitation, storage, and evaporation.
hydrology The science dealing with the study of groundwater and surface water and the changes that occur during the hydrologic cycle.
impact fees A growth management technique that requires a developer to pay for public services necessary for new urban development.
indicator species A species (either plant or animal) generally limited to a particular environment so that its presence will usually indicate that environment or life zone.
infiltration rate The rate of speed at which water flows into soil through small pores.
insolation Incoming solar radiation that is absorbed by the land, largely dependent on landforms and wind direction.
intrinsic suitability The inherent capability of an area to support a particular land use with the least detriment to the economy and the environment.
introduced species A species brought into an area by people; one that is not a native.
inventory The gathering of data for future use.
inversion An atmospheric condition caused by a layer of warm air preventing the rise of cool air trapped beneath it.
land evaluation and site assessment (LESA) A numerical system that measures the quality of farmland. It is generally used to select tracts of land to be protected or developed.
land trust A private, nonprofit conservation organization formed to protect natural resources such as productive farm and forest land, natural areas, historic structures, and recreational areas. Land trusts purchase and accept donations of conservation easements. They educate the public about the need to conserve land, and some provide land use and estate planning services to local governments and individual citizens.
landscape All the natural and cultural features such as settlements, fields, hills, buildings, deserts, forests, and

water bodies that distinguish one part of the surface of the earth from another part. Usually a landscape is that portion of land or territory which the eye can comprehend in a single view, including all its natural and cultural characteristics.

landscape architecture The art and science of arranging land so as to adapt it most conveniently, economically, functionally, and gracefully to any of the varied wants of people.

landscape ecology A study of the structure, function, and change in a heterogeneous land area composed of interacting ecosystems.

landscape plan A written and graphic documentation of a community's goals, the strategies to achieve those goals, and the spatial consequences of the implementation strategies.

land use The occupation of an area for a particular purpose, such as rangeland or industrial areas.

land-use need A factor that is essential or beneficial for a particular land use.

land user A person using a land resource who may or may not own title to that land.

langley A measurement of solar radiation equivalent to one calorie per square centimeter over some increment of time.

leaching The process by which nutrient chemicals or contaminants are dissolved and carried away by water or are moved into a lower layer of soil.

life cycle The stages an organism passes through during its existence.

life zone A biotic region with a distinctive flora and fauna. The region is based on climatic conditions, elevation, and other natural factors.

limestone A metamorphic rock formed from organic remains.

limnology The study of the physical, chemical, meteorological, and biological aspects of fresh water.

loam A soil mixture of sand, clay, and silt.

loess Predominately silt-sized particles that have been transported and deposited by the wind.

lot A parcel of land under one ownership, used or capable of being used under the subdivision regulations of a zoning ordinance, including both the building site and all required yards and open spaces.

matrix A graphic tool that plots two groups of interdependent factors against each other (one in rows and one in columns) to help illustrate their relationships.

meandering stream A stream that follows many S-shaped curves.

metamorphic rock A previously igneous or sedimentary rock that was exposed to conditions which entirely altered its original condition.

metropolitan statistical area (MSA) Following the 1980 U.S. Census, the term standard metropolitan statistical area (SMSA) was shortened to metropolitan statistical area (MSA). If any area has more than 1 million population and meets certain other specified requirements, then it is termed a consolidated metropolitan statistical area (CMSA), consisting of major components recognized as primary metropolitan statistical areas (PMSAs). In addition there are special New England county metropolitan areas (NECMAs) in that region of the United States. MSAs, PMSAs, and NECMAs are categorized by their population size, as follows:

Level A: Areas of 1 million or more

Level B: Areas of 250,000 to 1 million

Level C: Areas of 100,000 to 250,000

Level D: Areas of less than 100,000

Metropolitan statistical areas are defined in two ways: a city of at least 50,000 population or an urbanized area of at least 50,000 population with a total metropolitan area population of at least 100,000. MSAs are defined in terms of whole counties, except in the six New England states where they are defined in terms of cities and towns. In addition to the county containing the main city, an MSA also includes additional counties having strong economic and social ties to the central county.

microclimate The climate from the surface of the earth to a height at which the local effects of the earth can no longer be distinguished from the general climate.

migratory animals Animals that periodically pass from one region or climate to another for feeding or breeding purposes.

mineral extraction areas Places that contain minerals or materials of commercial quality and quantity that include, but are not limited to, sand, gravel, clay, peat, rock, and ores.

mission statement A brief declaration of the purpose for which a unit exists and functions. A mission statement can help define the purpose of a plan.

moratoriums The prevention of the issuance of building permits until urban service capacity levels

are attained or until plans and ordinances are completed.
morphology The study of surfaces and forms.
multifamily dwelling A building containing three or more dwelling units.
multiple use Harmonious use of land for more than one purpose, such as grazing of livestock, wildlife production, recreation, and timber production. It is not necessarily the combination that will yield the highest economic return or greatest unit output.
natural ecological areas Places with ecosystem units that are either superlative examples of their type or areas that perform a vital function in maintaining the ecological integrity and environmental quality of a larger region.
natural hazard critical areas Places in which incompatible development may result in the loss of life or property or both.
natural selection The process of survival of the fittest by which organisms that adapt to their environment survive and those that do not disappear.
natural system The biophysical factors, such as geology, soils, and wildlife.
natural wildlife habitat areas Places essential to the preservation of game species or unique, rare, or endangered species.
neighborhood planning council A locally based organization that permits citizen participation in policy decisions and in planning issues affecting their immediate geographic area.
niche An area that provides the necessary elements for the existence of a particular organism.
nominal-group workshop A citizen-participation technique based on the concept that people think most creatively while working in a group.
nonconforming use Any lawful use of activity involving a building or land occupied or in existence at the effective date of a zoning ordinance that does not conform to the principal, accessory, or conditional uses permitted in, or the density provisions of, the zoning district in which it is located.
non-point-source pollution Caused by residuals carried into streams, lakes, and estuaries by surface water as well as to groundwater zones by infiltration and percolation. These pollutants do not result from a direct release from a pipe or channel.
nutrients Elements or compounds essential to the growth and development of living things: carbon, oxygen, nitrogen, potassium, and phosphorus.
objective A clear and specific statement of planned results to be achieved within a stated time period.
oceanography The study of the sea in all its physical, chemical, geological, and biological aspects.
omnivores Animals that obtain energy from plants and other animals.
open space A relatively undeveloped green or wooded area provided usually within an urban development to minimize the feeling of congested living.
organic Referring to or derived from living organisms. In chemistry, it is any compound containing carbon.
organic matter Matter derived from living matter.
organism Any living things.
organization development A discipline involved in intervening in social networks to foster higher levels of cohesion and effectiveness.
osmosis The tendency of a fluid to pass through a permeable membrane (such as the wall of a living cell) into a less concentrated solution so as to equalize concentrations on both sides of the membrane.
parent material The unconsolidated and chemically weathered mineral or organic matter from which soils are developed.
patch A spatially separate instance of a given type of habitat.
pedology The study of soils.
pedon A three-dimensional soil sampling unit from 1 to 10 square meters, large enough so the nature of its soil horizons can be studied and the range of its properties identified.
perceptually and culturally critical areas Places containing one or more significant scenic, recreational, archaeological, historical, or cultural resources that could be degraded or lost as a result of uncontrolled or incompatible development.
perched water table condition A layer of soil separated above the saturated zone by an impermeable layer.
percolation The downward movement of water in a soil.
perennial plant A species of plant that lives longer than 2 years.
performance standards Criteria that are established and must be met before a certain use will be permitted. These criteria, or standards, may be a set of economic, environmental, or social factors or any combination of these factors.
permeability The rate at which water can move through soil.

pesticide Any substance used to control pests ranging from rats, weeds, and insects to algae and fungi.
pH A measure of the acidity or alkalinity of a material, solid, or liquid. pH is represented on a scale of 0 to 14, with 7 being a neutral state, 0 most acid, and 14 most alkaline.
photogrammetry The art or science of obtaining reliable measurements through photography.
phyllite A rock similar in composition to silt and schist.
physical In ecological planning, the abiotic elements of the environment, including geology, physiography, soils, hydrology, and climate.
physiography The science dealing with the study of physical features of the land, in particular slope and elevation.
planned unit development (PUD) A tract of land that is controlled by one entity and is planned and developed as a whole, either all at once or in programmed stages. PUDs are developed according to detailed site plans and may incorporate both residential and commercial land uses. They generally include improvements such as roads and utilities.
planning The use of scientific, technical, and other organized knowledge to provide choices for decision making as well as a process for considering and reaching consensus on a range of options.
planning commission An appointed citizen body that advises elected officials on such matters as the comprehensive plan, zoning ordinances, and subdivision regulations.
planning, programming, and budget system (PPBS) A complex annual budget system that involves the linkage of programs to the budgeting process.
planning staff The professional staff for the planning commission.
plant community An association of plants characterized by certain species occupying similar habitats.
plat A map or plan, especially of a piece of land divided into building lots.
plateau A large, flat area of land that is higher in elevation than some adjacent land.
police power The right of government to restrict an owner's use of property to protect the public health, safety, and welfare. Restrictions must be reasonable and be conducted according to due process.
policy A definite course or method of action selected by a governmental agency, institution, group, or individual from among options and in light of given conditions to guide and usually determine present and future decisions.
preferential tax policies Favorable taxation of land in exchange for an agreement to use that land for a certain use, such as agriculture, or for open spaces.
prime agricultural land Farmland that has a gentle slope and well-drained soils and requires a minimum of conservation practices. It is the easiest land to farm. Class I and II soils, as defined by the Natural Resources Conservation Service of the U.S. Department of Agriculture, are considered prime agricultural soils.
process The action of moving forward progressively from one point to another on the way to completion.
primary consumers Herbivores or animals that obtain energy from plants.
pristine Pure and untouched.
producers Organisms that can use solar energy to convert inorganic substances into organic substances.
profile A graphic tool that shows a portion of the surface of the earth and the features on this portion.
project planning Designing a solution to a specific problem such as a dam, highway, harbor, or a single building or group of buildings.
public hearing An open forum where statements become part of official records. Public hearings are often required by law.
public opinion poll (preference survey) A means of gathering information, attitudes, and opinions from a large number of people.
purchase of agricultural conservation easements (PACE) PACE programs pay farmers to keep their land available for agriculture. Landowners sell an agricultural conservation easement to a qualified government agency or private conservation organization. Landowners retain full ownership and use of their land for agricultural purposes. PACE programs do not give government agencies the right to develop land. Development rights are extinguished in exchange for compensation. PACE is also known as purchase of development rights (PDR) and as agricultural preservation restriction (APR) in Massachusetts.
purchase of development rights (PDR) The property owner's development interests are relinquished to the purchaser of the rights, who can be a government or nongovernmental entity, such as a land trust. The purchaser then can limit the development of the property to encourage agricultural, open space, or environmental uses.

putative species The species expected to occur in an area based on habitat requirements.
rain shadow An area that has decreased precipitation because it is to the leeward side of mountains.
rangeland Land in grass or other long-term forage growth of native species used primarily for grazing. It may contain shade trees or scattered timber trees with less than 10 percent canopy. It includes grassland, land in perennial forbs, sagebrush land, and brushland other than sage. The term *nonforest range* is used to differentiate the nonforest range from the forest range when both are being discussed.
receiving area Areas designated to accommodate development transferred from agricultural or natural areas through a transfer of development rights program.
recharge Process by which water is added to the zone of saturation, as recharge of an aquifer.
recharge areas See groundwater recharge areas.
recreation Any experience voluntarily engaged in largely during leisure (discretionary time) from which the individual derives satisfaction.
region (1) An uninterrupted area possessing some kind of homogeneity in its core but lacking clearly defined limits. (2) A governmental jurisdiction or designation. (3) A frame for multidisciplinary research: a demand for the integration of data from many realms of ecological reality and, therefore, an opportunity for specialists to work together on theoretical conceptions of human ecology as a synthesis.
regolith The predominantly loose surficial material overlaying bedrock. It is roughly equivalent to what engineers term *soil* and may contain or be capped by a true soil pedon, as used by soil scientists.
remote sensing The detection, identification, and analysis of objects or features through the use of imaging devices located at positions remote from the objects of investigation.
resident Animals that remain in one region or climate through the year.
residium Unconsolidated and partly weathered mineral materials accumulated by disintegration of consolidated rock in place.
resource A substance or object required by an organism for normal maintenance, growth, and reproduction. If a resource is scarce relative to demand, then it is referred to as a *limited* resource. *Nonrenewable* resources (such as space) occur in fixed amounts and can be fully utilized; *renewable* resources (such as food) are produced at a fixed rate with which the rate of exploitation attains an equilibrium.
resource production critical areas Places that provide essential products supporting either the local economy or economies of a larger scale.
restrictive agreement A type of differential assessment that requires a landowner to sign a contract to keep land in agricultural use for 10 years or more as a condition of eligibility for tax relief. If the landowner gives notice of intent to terminate the contract, assessed value of the property increases during the balance of the term to the full fair market value.
riparian Relating to a habitat on the banks of streams, rivers, and lakes.
river basin The land area drained by a river and its tributaries.
rubble A mass of broken stones and rocks, often at the base of a cliff.
runoff Water from rain, snowmelt, or irrigation that flows over the ground surface and returns to streams.
sand Soil particles between 0.05 and 2.0 millimeters in diameter.
scale The relative size of an area of interest. If the focus on relatively small areas (for example, the area around a house or a single subdivision), the focus is *fine scale*. If the focus is on a much larger area (i.e., a county or watershed), than it is a *coarse scale*.
scenic areas Places that contain natural features of sufficient aesthetic quality to warrant their preservation.
scientific areas Places of geological interest or places that present ecological processes warranting study.
score This term is used for the total of all factor ratings.
secondary consumer Carnivore or animals that obtain energy from other animals.
second-order stream See stream orders.
septic tank An enclosure in which the organic solid matter of continuously flowing wastewater is deposited and retained until it has been disintegrated by anaerobic bacteria.
service districts The division of a jurisdiction into areas based on the level of urban and rural services, with different rates of taxation.
setback A zoning provision requiring new homes to be separated from existing farms by a specified distance and vice versa.
shale A sedimentary rock formed from tightly packed clays and silts.

silt Fine soil particles between 0.05 and 0.002 millimeter in diameter that can be picked up by air or water and deposited as sediment.
single-family dwelling A detached building containing one dwelling unit.
slope The incline of the land surface, usually expressed in percentage of slope. Often slopes are expressed as follows:

0–3 percent	nearly level
3–7 percent	gently sloping
7–12 percent	moderately sloping
12–25 percent	strongly sloping
25–40 percent	steeply sloping
40–70 percent	very steeply sloping
70–100 percent and above	extremely steeply sloping

slope wind Winds flowing up or down slopes along a temperature gradient.
social Relating to human society and the interactions of the community.
sociocultural A combination of the social and the cultural characteristics of an area.
soil A natural, three-dimensional body on the surface of the earth that supports plants and has properties resulting from the integrated effect of climate and living matter acting upon parent material as conditioned by relief over periods of time.
soil association Soils of different series found in the same area.
soil catena A group of related soils that have developed from the same parent material but differ in drainage class due to different locations on a slope.
soil depth The depth of soil material that plant roots can penetrate readily to obtain water and nutrients. It is the depth to a layer that, in physical or chemical properties, differs from the overlying material to such an extent as to prevent or seriously retard the growth of roots or penetration of water. The depth classes are (1) very deep, more than 60 inches (1,500 millimeters); (2) deep, 40 to 60 inches (1,000 to 1,500 millimeters); (3) moderately deep, 20 to 40 inches (500 to 1,000 millimeters); (4) shallow, 10 to 20 inches (250 to 500 millimeters); and (5) very shallow, 1 to 10 inches (25 to 250 millimeters).
soil profile A vertical section of the soil through all its horizons and extending into the parent material.
soil series Soils from the same parent material having similar horizon characteristics.
soil texture The relative proportions of sand, silt, and clay particles in a mass of soil. The basic textural classes, in order of increasing proportion of fine particles, are shown in the following chart.

SOIL TEXTURE

General terms	Basic soil textural class names
Sandy soils	
Coarse-textured soils	Sand
Moderately coarse-textured soils	Sandy loam Fine sandy loam
Loamy soils	
Medium-textured soils	Very fine sandy loam Loam Silt loam Silt
Moderately fine textured soils	Clay loam Sandy clay loam Silty clay loam
Clayey soil	
Fine-textured soils	Sandy clay Silty clay Clay

soil types Soils within a series having the same texture.
solar radiation The energy from the sun that reaches the earth.
solum The upper and most weathered part of the soil profile; and A and B horizons.
species A group of closely related organisms potentially able to reproduce viable offspring.
species diversity The number of different species occurring in a location or under the same conditions.
sprawl Unplanned development of open land.
standard A statement that describes a condition when job is done properly. Standards show how well something should be done rather than what should be done.
strategy The approach and/or methods through which problems are solved or minimized and objectives are achieved.
stream A general term for a body of flowing water. In hydrology, the term is generally applied to the water flowing in a natural channel as distinct from a canal. More generally, as in the term *stream gauging,* it is applied to the water flowing in any natural or artificial channel.

stream, ephemeral A stream that flows only in response to precipitation.
stream, intermittent A stream that flows only part of the time or through only part of its reach.
stream orders First-order streams are primary drainageways. Second-order streams are the confluence of two first-order streams. Third-order streams are the confluence of two second-order streams, and so on.
stream, perennial A stream that flows continuously.
street The entire width between property boundary lines of every way that provides for public use for the purpose of vehicular and pedestrian traffic and the placement of utilities.
strip-cropping Growing crops in a systematic arrangement of strips or bands that serve as barriers to wind and water erosion.
structures, heavy A building of generally great weight and size, such as a mill or factory.
structures, light A building of generally, slight weight and size, such as a residence.
subdivision The division of a lot, tract, or parcel of land into two or more lots, plats, sites, or other divisions of land for the purpose, whether immediate or future, of sale or building development.
subdivision regulation The legal requirements pertaining to the subdivision of land.
subsoil The B soil horizon; the layer of soil below the layer in which grass roots normally grow.
succession The orderly progressive replacement of one community by another until a relatively stable community occupies an area.
suitability analysis The process of determining the fitness of a given tract of land for a defined use. *Suitability* is often used interchangeably with *capability.*
surface water Water that remains on the top of land, such as lakes, rivers, streams, and seas.
sustainability The maintenance of the health and productivity of ecosystems, which provide a variety of benefits over time.
sustainable development Development that meets the needs of the present without compromising the ability of future generations to meet their own needs.
swale An elongated depression in the land.
synthesis The combining of all the parts to form an interrelating whole.
taking An illegal government appropriation of private property or property rights. Traditionally, takings law has addressed physical seizures of land, but regulations that deprive landowners of certain property rights may also result in a taking in special circumstances. Courts decide whether a particular government action constitutes a taking.
task force An agency-sponsored citizen committee with a specific task and charge usually related to a single problem or subject.
technical advisory committee (TAC) A group of individuals with specific expertise, usually from various disciplines, brought together by an agency for giving advice and consultation.
temperature gradient The difference in temperature along some horizontal distance or up a vertical parcel of air.
terracing Dikes built along the contour of agricultural land to hold runoff and sediment, thus reducing erosion.
third-order streams See stream orders.
topoclimate The term used when the topographic variations of the land on microclimate are considered.
topography The physical features of a surface area, including relative elevations and the position of natural and artificial features.
town meeting The traditional New England meeting of the people of a town.
transfer of development rights (TDR) program A program that allows landowners to transfer the right to develop one parcel of land to a different parcel of land to prevent farmland conversion. TDR programs establish "sending areas" where land is to be protected by agricultural conservation easements and "receiving areas" where land may be developed at a higher density than would otherwise be allowed by local zoning. Landowners in the sending area sell development rights to landowners in the receiving area, generally through the private market. When the development rights are sold on a parcel, a conservation easement is recorded and enforced by the local government. In some cases, the local government may establish a "TDR bank" to buy and sell development rights. The development rights created by TDR programs are referred to as transferable development rights (TDRs) or transferable development credits (TDCs).
transpiration The loss of water to the atmosphere from plants.
tree A woody, perennial plant with a single main stem.
trophic levels The different levels through which energy flows from producers to consumers.

understory Herbs and shrubs that grow beneath a forest canopy.
upzoning A change in the zoning for a particular area which results in higher residential densities. For example, a change from a zoning ordinance that requires 100 acres (40.47 hectares) per dwelling to an ordinance that requires 25 acres (10.1 hectares) per dwelling is an upzoning.
urban growth boundary Line to which urban areas may grow based on population projections and physical conditions of the area.
urban morphology The study of the city as human habitat.
USGS map U.S. Department of Interior Geological Survey map.
valley wind Winds flowing up or down valleys along temperature gradients.
variance A special situation that creates a need to deviate from the established zoning ordinances and requires review by a board of adjustment or similar review agency.
vegetation Plant life: trees, shrubs, herbs, and grasses.
vegetation type A classification given to plants that are found in the same place on a landscape.
ventilation The circulation of fresh air across the land, largely dependent on landforms and wind direction.
voluntary covenants Agreements that limit what can be done with property.
wash An ephemeral stream; that is, one that flows only during or after rainstorms. Called an *arroyo* in Spanish.
water A transparent, odorless, tasteless liquid; a compound of hydrogen and oxygen (H_2O) that freezes at 32°F (0°C) and boils at 212°F (100°C). Most water is more or less in an impure state, and constitutes rain, oceans, lakes, rivers, and other such bodies. It contains 11.188 percent hydrogen and 88.812 percent oxygen by weight.
water balance The ratio of water lost from a system and brought into a system.
water quality areas Aquifer recharge areas, headwaters, stream corridors, and wetlands that function as a natural filter for surface waters.
watershed A drainage area separated from other drainage areas by a dividing ridge.
water table The upper surface of groundwater or that level below which the soil is saturated with water.
weighted factor rating This term is used to denote the factor rating after weighting.
weighting This term refers to assigning a weight (for example, 0–1.0) to each factor in order to recognize the relative importance of each factor.
wilderness recreation areas Isolated tracts of land that are large enough to support recreational activities like camping, hiking, and canoeing.
wildlife Animals that are neither human nor domesticated.
windchill The relationship between body heat loss and the cooling power of different wind and temperature combinations.
zone An area or areas of the community or county in which certain land uses are permitted and other uses are prohibited by the zoning ordinance. Common zones are residential, commercial, industrial, and agricultural.
zone change An action taken by the local governing body to change the type of zoning on one or more pieces of land. For example, a zone change or rezoning could be from A-1, agricultural, to C-2, medium-density commercial. A zone change for specific properties can happen in two ways. A property owner may ask for a zone change, which is a quasi-judicial action. Otherwise, either the planning commission or the governing body may seek a zone change through a legislative action. If a zone change is approved, the zoning map must also be amended. Some zone changes may require amending the comprehensive plan map.
zoning Land-use controls such as limiting the use to which land in each area may be put, minimum lot size, and building types.
zoning ordinance The legal document establishing the division of a municipality or other governmental unit into districts and the regulation within those districts.

ACRONYMS

ADEQ Arizona Department of Environmental Quality
AMA Active management areas
APR Agricultural preservation restriction
APZ Agricultural protection zoning
ASCS Agricultural Stabilization and Conservation Service
ASLD Arizona State Lands Department
BLM Bureau of Land Management
CABO Council of American Building Officials
CAC Citizens' Advisory Committee
CAD Computer-aided design
CAP Central Arizona Project
CC & Rs Codes, covenants, and restrictions
CEQ Council on Environmental Quality
CIP Capital improvement programming
CMSA Consolidated metropolitan statistical area
CRS Community Rating System
CSR Crop suitability rating (corn suitability rating)
CWA Clean Water Act
CZMA Coastal Zone Management Act
DEM Digital elevation model
DLCD Department of Land Conservation and Development (Oregon)
DLG Digital line graph
DOE Department of Ecology (Washington)
DPZ Duany and Plater-Zyberk
EIS Environmental impact statement
EPA Environmental Protection Agency
ERZ Environmental resource zone
ESA Endangered Species Act
ESLO Environmentally sensitive lands ordinance
EU European Union
FAA Federal Aviation Administration
FEMA Federal Emergency Management Agency
FIRM Flood Insurance Rate Map
FPPA Farmland Protection Policy Act
FTE Full-time equivalent employment
GAO U.S. General Accounting Office
GAP Gap Analysis Program
GIS Geographic information systems
GMA Groundwater Management Act
HCA Habitat conservation areas
HCP Habitat conservation plan
HSI Habitat suitability index
ICBO International Conference of Building Officials
LCDC Land Conservation and Development Commission (Oregon)
LE Land evaluation
LESA Agricultural Land Evaluation and Site Assessment System
MAG Maricopa Association of Governments (Arizona)
MLRA Major land resource area
MSA Metropolitan statistical area
NECMA New England County Metropolitan Area
NEPA National Environmental Policy Act
NFIP National Flood Insurance Program
NGO Nongovernmental organization
NOAA National Oceanic and Atmospheric Administration
NPDES National Pollution Discharge Elimination System
NPS National Park Service
NRCS Natural Resources Conservation Service
PACE Purchase of agricultural conservation easements
PCD Planned community district
PDR Purchase of development rights
PMSA Primary metropolitan statistical area
PPBS Planning, programming, and budget system
PRD Planned residential district
PRLD Phoenix Parks, Recreation, and Library Department
PUD Planned unit development
RGGO Regional Growth Goal and Objective
RPA Regional Plan Association

RUSLE Revised universal soil loss equation
SA Site assessment
SBC Standard Building Code
SCS Soil Conservation Service
SEPA State Environmental Policy Act
SHPO State historic preservation officer
SIC Standard Industrial Classification
SMSA Standard metropolitan statistical area
TAC Technical Advisory Committee
TAZ Traffic analysis zones
TDC Transferable development credit
TDM Donald Dillman's total design method
TDR Transfer of development rights
UBC Uniform Building Code
UGB Urban growth boundary
UNESCO United Nations Educational, Scientific, and Cultural Organization
USDA U.S. Department of Agriculture
USFS U.S. Forest Service
USFWS U.S. Fish and Wildlife Service
USGS U.S. Geological Survey
USLE Universal soil loss equation
WCED World Commission on Environment and Development

BIBLIOGRAPHY

Abbott, Carl. 1994. *Settlement patterns in the Portland region: a historical overview* (January) Portland, Oregon: Metro.

Abercrombie, P., and T. H. Johnson. 1922. *The Doncaster planning scheme.* London: University Press of Liverpool.

Aberley, Doug (ed.). 1994. *Futures by design: the practice of ecological planning.* Gabriola Island, British Columbia: New Society Publishers.

Adams, Rob, Bill Chandler, Wendy Morris, and Bruce Echberg. 1993. "Urban villages workshop, Western Australia style." *Urban Design Forum* 23:1.

Adams, Thomas. 1934. *The design of residential areas.* Cambridge, Massachusetts: Harvard University Press.

Ahern, Jack. 1995. "Greenways as a planning strategy." *Landscape and Urban Planning* 33:131–155.

Alesch, Richard. 1987. "Evaluating and managing cultural landscapes in the national park system." In *Aesthetics of the rural renaissance* conference proceedings. San Luis Obispo, California: California Polytechnic State University.

Alinsky, Saul D. 1946. *Reveille for radicals.* Chicago, Illinois: University of Chicago Press.

Alvarez, Leonardo, Jorge Hernández, Cathy Leff, Daniel Williams, Juan Antonio Bueno, Joseph Dillion Ford, Elizabeth Plater-Zyberk, Sonia Cháo, and Richard Weslund (eds.). No date. *The new South Dade planning charrette: from adversity to opportunity.* Coral Gables, Florida: University of Miami School of Architecture.

American Farmland Trust. 1986. *Density-related public costs.* Washington, D.C.

American Farmland Trust. 1997. *Saving American farmland: what works.* Northampton, Massachusetts: Farmland Trust.

American Law Institute. 1974. *A model land development code.* Philadelphia, Pennsylvania.

American Libraries. 1991. "Planning a Library in One Week: Architect Edward H. Healey Advocates an Innovative 'Charrette' Method for Planning a New Library." *American Libraries* 22 (4):302–304.

Anderson, James R., Ernest E. Hardy, John T. Roach, and Richard E. Witmer. 1976. *A land use and land cover classification system for use with remote sensor data* (U.S. Geological Survey Professional Paper 964).

Andres, Chris, Jodie Brown, Donna Gadbois, Matt Jennings, and Kasandra Torres. 1998. "Recovering the urban frontier: Phoenix brownfield and underutilized land study" (studio class project). Tempe, Arizona: Arizona State University School of Planning and Landscape Architecture.

Ansbro, John, Joseph Bell, Meghan Gallione, Karen Karpowich, Johnny Patta, Michael Reis, Gretchen Schalge, Maria Valdez, and David Wood. 1988. "Ecological inventory and analysis, Teller County, Colorado" (studio class project). Denver, Colorado: University of Colorado School of Architecture and Planning.

Antenucci, John C., Kay Brown, Peter L. Croswell, Michael J. Kevany, with Hugh Archer. 1991. *Geographic information systems: A guide to the technology.* New York: Van Nostrand Reinhold.

Arendt, Randall G. 1996. *Conservation design for subdivisions: a practical guide to creating open space networks.* Washington, D.C.: Island Press.

Arizona Department of Commerce. 1998. *Growing smarter legislation: a summary for cities and towns.* Phoenix, Arizona: Community Planning Program, Community Assistance Division.

Bagley, Anubhav, Ann Bonnette, Jim Haklik, Harold Housley, Jim McCarthy, and Lizi McGeorge. 1995. "Draft environmental impact statement, northeast portion of peripheral areas C and D, Phoenix, Arizona" (class project). Tempe, Arizona: Arizona State University School of Planning and Landscape Architecture.

Balling, Robert C., and Sandra W. Brazel. 1987. "Time and space characteristics of the Phoenix urban heat island." *Journal of the Arizona-Nevada Academy of Science* 21:75–81.

Barnhart, Clarence L. (ed.). 1953. *The American college dictionary.* New York: Harper & Brothers.

Barron, James C. 1975. *Transferable development rights* (E.M. 3939). Pullman, Washington: Washington State University Cooperative Extension Service.

Bartelli, L. J., A. A. Klingebiel, J. V. Baird, and M. R. Heddleston (eds.). 1966. *Soil surveys and land-use planning.* Madison, Wisconsin: Soil Science Society of America.

Beach, Richard, Don Benson, Dave Brunton, Karen L. Johnson, Julie Knowles, Joanne Michalovic, Harry George Newman, Betsy J. Tripp, and Cheryl Wunschel. 1978. *Asotin County ecological inventory and land-use suitability analysis.* Pullman, Washington: Washington State University Cooperative Extension Service.

Beatley, Timothy. 1994a. *Habitat conservation planning: endangered species and urban growth.* Austin, Texas: University of Texas Press.

Beatley, Timothy. 1994b. *Ethical land use: principles and policy of planning.* Baltimore, Maryland: Johns Hopkins University Press.

Beatley, Timothy, and Kristy Manning. 1997. *The ecology of place: planning for environment, economy, and community.* Washington, D.C.: Island Press.

Beek, K. J. 1978. *Land evaluation for agricultural development* (Publication 23). Wageningen, The Netherlands: International Institute for Land Reclamation and Improvement.

Beeman, Larry E. 1978. "Computer-assisted resource management." In *Integrated inventories of renewable natural resources: proceedings of the workshop,* H. G. Lund, V. J. LaBau, P. F. Ffolliot, and D. W. Robinson eds. pp. 375–381. Tucson, Arizona: U.S. Forest Service.

Belknap, Raymond K., and John G. Furtado. 1967. *Three approaches to environmental resource analysis.* Washington, D.C.: The Conservation Foundation.

Belknap, Raymond K., and John G. Furtado. 1968. "The natural land unit as a planning base, Hills, Lewis, McHarg methods compared." *Landscape Architecture* 58(2):145–147.

Bell, Joseph, Meghan Gallione, Gretchen Schalge, and David Wood. 1989. "Visions for the Teller County landscape" (studio class project). Denver, Colorado: University of Colorado School of Architecture and Planning.

Bennington County Regional Planning Commission. 1994. *Regional forest land evaluation and site assessment for the Taconic Mountains.* Bennington, Vermont.

Bentham, Jeremy. 1887. *Theory of legislation* (5th ed.).

Berger, Jon, Arthur Johnson, Dan Rose, and Peter Skaller. 1977. *Regional planning notebook* (course guidelines). Philadelphia, Pennsylvania: University of Pennsylvania Department of Landscape Architecture and Regional Planning.

Berger, Jonathan, and John W. Sinton. 1985. *Water, earth, and fire.* Baltimore, Maryland: Johns Hopkins University Press.

Berry, Wendell. 1972. *A continuous harmony, essays cultural and agricultural.* New York: Harcourt Brace Jovanovich.

Blumm, Michael C., and D. Bernard Zaleha. 1989. "Federal wetlands: protection under the clean water act: regulatory ambivalence, intergovernmental tension, and a call for reform." *University of Colorado Law Review* 60(4):695–772.

Bolan, Richard S. 1979. "Social planning and policy development." In *The practice of local government planning,* Frank S. So, Israel Stollman, Frank Beal, and David S. Arnold eds., pp. 521–551. Washington, D.C.: International City Management Association.

Bosselman, Fred, and David Callies. 1971. *The quiet revolution in land use control.* Washington, D.C.: U.S. Government Printing Office.

Bosselman, Fred, David Callies, and John Banta. 1973. *The taking issue.* Washington, D.C.: U.S. Government Printing Office.

Botkin, D. B., and C. E. Beveridge. 1997. "Cities as environments." *Urban Ecosystems* 1:3–19.

Botkin, D. B., and Edward A. Keller. 1998. *Environmental science: earth as a living planet* (2nd ed.). New York: John Wiley & Sons.

Boulder City Council. 1997. *Residential growth management system* (summary, February 18). Boulder, Colorado.

Bowen, Richard L., and Carol Ferguson. 1994. "Hawaii's LESA experience in a changing policy environment." In *A decade with LESA: the evolution of land evaluation and site assessment,* Frederick Steiner, James Pease, and Robert Coughlin eds., pp. 160–177. Ankeny, Iowa: Soil and Water Conservation Society.

Bowie, Robert, Cathy Chin, Jim Estus, Rita Gerou, Bruce Guerard, Jeff Hardcastle, George Hernandez,

Judith Karinen, and Susan Maxberry. 1988. "Woodland Park, Colorado: ecological inventory and analysis" (studio class project). Denver, Colorado: University of Colorado School of Architecture and Planning.

Boyer, Ernest. 1990. *Scholarship reconsidered: priorities of the professoriate.* Princeton, New Jersey: Carnegie Foundation.

Brady, Nyle C. 1974. *The nature and properties of soils* (8th ed.). New York: MacMillan.

Brady, Nyle C., and Raymond R. Weil. 1996. *The nature and property of soils* (11th ed.). Upper Saddle River, New Jersey: Prentice-Hall.

Brady, Ward, Michael Collins, Jana Fry, Jack Gilcrest, William Miller, Nancy Osborn, and Frederick Steiner. 1998. *A geographic information system application for park planning in the Desert View Tri-Villages Area, City of Phoenix.* A report for the Parks, Recreation, and Library and Information Technology Departments, City of Phoenix. Tempe, Arizona: Arizona State University School of Planning and Landscape Architecture.

Brazel, Anthony J. 1993. "The role of climatology in environment." Invited paper presentation, Indian Town Hall Annual Meeting. Tempe, Arizona: Arizona State University Department of Geography.

Brazel, Anthony J. 1998. "Surface climate and remote sensing of Scottsdale, Arizona." Tempe, Arizona: Arizona State University Department of Geography.

Briggs, Mark K. 1996. *Riparian ecosystem recovery in arid lands: strategies and references.* Tucson, Arizona: University of Arizona Press.

Brinkman, R., and A. J. Smyth (eds.). 1973. *Land evaluation for rural purposes* (Publication 17). Wageningen, The Netherlands: International Institute for Land Reclamation and Improvement.

Brinson, M. M., L. Swift, C. Plantico, and S. Barclay. 1981. "Riparian ecosystems: their ecology and status." FWS/OBS-81/17. Washington, D.C.: U.S. Fish and Wildlife Service.

Broderson, William D. 1994. *From the surface down: an introduction to soil surveys for agronomic use.* Washington, D.C.: Soil Conservation Service, U.S. Department of Agriculture.

Brown, David E. 1982. "Biotic communities of the American Southwest—United States and Mexico." *Desert Plants* 4(1–4):3–341.

Brown, S., M. M. Brinson, and A. E. Lugo. 1978. "Structure and function of riparian wetlands." In *Strategies for protection and management of floodplain wetlands and other riparian ecosystems: proceedings,* R. R. Johnson and J. F. McCormick technical coordinators, pp. 17–31. USDA, FS, GTR-WO-12. Washington, D.C.: U.S. Department of Agriculture.

Brunton, Dave, Theda Scheibner, Jill Stanton, Tom Blanchard, and Julie Knowles. 1977. "Albion ecological inventory" (class project). Pullman, Washington: Washington State University Department of Horticulture and Landscape Architecture and Program in Environmental Science and Regional Planning.

Budoni, A., and S. Macchi. 1998. "An analytical model for designing territorial sustainability: reality as a socio-technical network" (unpublished paper). Roma, Italia: Dipartimento di Architettura e Urbanistica per l'Ingegneria, Università degli Studi di Roma "La Sapienza."

Bureau of Land Management. 1980. *Visual resources program.* Washington, D.C.: U.S. Department of Interior.

Burke, James, and Joseph Ewan. 1998a. *Sonoran preserve master plan.* Phoenix, Arizona: Department of Parks, Recreation, and Library.

Burke, James, and Joseph M. Ewan. 1998b. "Sonoran desert preservation: an open space plan for the City of Phoenix, Arizona." In *1998 Annual meetings proceedings of the American Society of Landscape Architects,* pp. 98–102. Washington, D.C.: American Society of Landscape Architects.

Burns, Elizabeth K., and Dudley Onderdonk. 1993. "Urban growth and environmental protection at the local level." In *Growth management: the planning challenge of the 1990s,* Jay Stein ed., pp. 129–142. Newbury Park, California: Sage Publications.

Buskirk, E. Drannon, Jr. 1986. "Environmental impact analysis." In *The practice of state and regional planning,* Frank S. So, Irving Hand, and Bruce D. McDowell eds., pp. 238–254. Chicago, Illinois: American Planning Association.

Butler, Stuart M. 1981. "Enterprise zone theorist calls for unplanning." *Planning* 47(2):6.

Caldwell, Lynton Keith, and Kristin Shrader-Frechette. 1993. *Policy for land: law and ethics.* Lanham, Maryland: Rowman & Littlefield.

Callies, David L. 1980. "The quiet revolution revisited." *Journal of the American Planning Association* 46(2):135–144.

Calthorpe, Peter. 1993. *The next American metropolis: ecology, community and the American dream.*

Princeton, New Jersey: Princeton Architectural Press.

Calthorpe, Peter, Michael Corbett, Andres Duany, Elizabeth Plater-Zyberk, Stefanos Polyzoides, Elizabeth Moule with Judy Corbett, Peter Katz, and Steve Weissman. 1998. "The Ahwahnee Principles." In: *Creating Sustainable Places Symposium,* Audrey Brichetto Morris, ed., pp. 3–6. Tempe, Arizona: Herberger Center for Design Excellence, Arizona State University.

Camp, Philip D. 1986. *Soil survey of Aguila—Carefree Area, parts of Maricopa and Pinal Counties, Arizona.* Washington, D.C.: U.S. Government Printing Office.

Canham, Ronald R. 1979. *Interagency coordination and rapid community growth* (WREP 22). Corvallis, Oregon: Western Rural Development Center, Oregon State University.

Cannon, T. M., and B. R. Hunt. 1981. "Image processing by computer." *Scientific American* 245(4):214–225.

Canter, Larry W. 1996. *Environmental impact assessment* (2nd ed). New York: McGraw-Hill.

Caraher, Pat. 1998. "New Palouse recreation trail links university communities." *Hilltopics* (August):19.

Carlson, Christine, and Dennis Canty. 1986. *A path for the Palouse.* Seattle, Washington: National Park Service, U.S. Department of Interior.

Carlson, Christine, Dennis Canty, Frederick Steiner, and Nancy Mack. 1989. "A path for the Palouse: an example of conservation and recreation planning." *Landscape and Urban Planning* 17(1):1–19.

Carlson, Frances C. 1988. *The history of the Desert Foothills.* Scottsdale, Arizona: Encanto Press.

Carsjens, Gerrit J., and Jam F. J. M. Smits. 1997. "Topographical relationships integrated in land use allocation." *Geographic Information* 758–767.

Carsjens, Gerrit J., and Wim G. M. van der Knaap. 1996. "Multi-criteria techniques integrated in GIS applied for land use allocation problems." *Geographic Information* 575–578.

Carson, Richard H. 1998. *Paying for our growth in Oregon.* Beaverton, Oregon: New Oregon Meridan Press.

Catton, William. 1983. "Social and behavioral aspects of the carrying capacity of natural environments." In *Behavior and natural environment* (Vol. VI of Human behavior and environment), Irwin Altman and Joachim F. Wohwill eds., pp. 269–306. New York: Plenum.

Center for Natural Areas, Smithsonian Institution. 1974. *Planning conservation for statewide inventories of critical areas: a reference guide,* report 3. Washington, D.C.: U.S. Army Corps of Engineers.

Chapin, F. Stuart, and Edward J. Kaiser. 1979. *Urban land use planning.* Urbana, Illinois: University of Illinois Press.

Chronic, Halka. 1983. *Roadside geology of Arizona.* Missoula, Montana: Mountain Press.

Ciekot, Stephanie, Carol Hayden, Carlos Licón, Gary Mason, Jim McCarthy, and Jane Ploeser. 1995. "Desert View Tri-Villages, ecological inventory and analysis" (studio class project). Tempe, Arizona: Arizona State University School of Planning and Landscape Architecture.

City of Dayton. 1995. *Policy budget.* Dayton, Ohio: Office of Management and Budget.

City of Everett, 1994. *Environmental policy.* Everett, Washington.

City of Lakewood. 1988a. *West Colfax Avenue design guidelines.* Lakewood, Colorado: Planning Division.

City of Lakewood. 1988b. *West Colfax Avenue pedestrian streetscape demonstration project.* Lakewood, Colorado: Planning Division.

City of Lakewood. 1997. *Wadsworth Boulevard strategic plan.* Lakewood, Colorado: Strategic Planning Division.

City of Lakewood, and City and County of Denver. 1993. *West Colfax revitalization plan.* Lakewood, Colorado, Planning Commission and Denver, Colorado, Planning Board.

City of Phoenix. 1987. *General plan: peripheral areas C and D.* Phoenix, Arizona: Planning Department.

City of Phoenix. 1994. *Desert View Tri-Villages scenic corridor design charrette summary report.* Phoenix, Arizona.

City of Phoenix. 1995. *Phoenix growth.* Phoenix, Arizona: Planning Department.

City of Phoenix. 1996. *North land use plan* (draft). Phoenix, Arizona: Planning Department.

City of Phoenix. 1997a. *North land use plan.* Phoenix, Arizona: Planning Department.

City of Phoenix. 1997b. *North Black Canyon corridor concept plan.* Phoenix, Arizona: Planning Department.

City of Phoenix, and ASU. 1989. *Camelback east primary core urban design charrette team report.*

Tempe, Arizona: Joint ASU–City of Phoenix Urban Design Studio.

City of Scottsdale. 1991a. *ESLO users' manual.* Scottsdale, Arizona.

City of Scottsdale. 1991b. *Environmentally sensitive lands ordinance citizen's guide.* Scottsdale, Arizona.

City of Scottsdale. 1991c. *Approved environmentally sensitive lands ordinance.* Scottsdale, Arizona.

City of Tucson. 1991. "Watercourse amenities, safety, and habitat." Ordinance No. 7579. Article VIII. Tucson, Arizona.

City of Tucson. 1994. "Watercourse amenities, safety, and habitat." Ordinance No. 8303. Article VIII. Tucson, Arizona.

City of Tucson. 1998. "Overlay zones, environmental resource zone (ERZ)." Land use code, Article II. Zones, Division 8. Tucson, Arizona.

City of Woodland Park. 1996. *Master plan.* Woodland Park, Colorado.

Clark, Janice M. 1977. "Agricultural zoning in Black Hawk County, Iowa." In *Land use: tough choices in today's world,* pp. 149–154. Ankeny, Iowa: Soil Conservation Society of America.

Collins, Michael G. 1996. *An integrative approach to multi-objective greenway suitability analysis* (unpublished master of environmental planning thesis). Tempe, Arizona: Arizona State University School of Planning and Landscape Architecture.

Collins, Michael G., Frederick R. Steiner, and Michael Rushman. 2000. "Land-use suitability analysis in the United States." Tempe, Arizona: Arizona State University School of Planning and Landscape Architecture.

Condon, Patrick (ed.). 1996. *Sustainable urban landscapes: the surrey design charrette.* Vancouver, British Columbia: University of British Columbia Press.

Conn, William J. 1984. "Techniques for protecting prime agricultural land, zoning applications in York County, Pennsylvania." In *Protecting farmlands,* Frederick Steiner and John Theilacker eds., pp. 97–108. Westport, Connecticut: AVI Publishing.

Conway, Eric D., and the Maryland Space Grant Consortium. 1997. *An introduction to satellite image interpretation.* Baltimore, Maryland: Johns Hopkins University Press.

Cook, Edward, William Whitmore, and Frederick Steiner. 1991. *Verde Valley visual assessment: Verde River corridor study, Tapco to Beasley Flat.* Phoenix, Arizona: Arizona State Parks.

Cooke, Stephen, Bruce Weber, and George Goldman. 1996. *Evaluating fiscal impact studies: community guidelines* (WREP 16). Corvallis, Oregon: Western Rural Development Center, Oregon State University.

Coombs, Donald B., and J. Thie. 1979. "The Canadian land inventory system." In *Planning the uses and the management of the land,* Marvin T. Beatty, Gary W. Petersen, and Lester R. Swindale eds., pp. 909–933. Madison, Wisconsin: American Society of Agronomy, Crop Science Society of America, and Soil Science Society of America.

Coomer, Dawn. 1995. *Peripheral areas C and D resource guide.* Phoenix, Arizona: City of Phoenix Planning Department.

Cooper, D., K. Mutz, B. Van Daveren, A. Allen, and G. Jacob. 1990. *Intermountain riparian lands evaluation methodology* (draft). Washington, D.C.: U.S. Environmental Protection Agency.

Corbett, Marjorie J. (ed.). 1983. *Greenline parks.* Washington, D.C.: National Parks and Conservation Association.

Coughlin, Robert E., James R. Pease, Frederick Steiner, Lyssa Papazian, Joyce Ann Pressley, Adam Sussman, and John C. Leach. 1994. "The status of state and local LESA programs." *Journal of Soil and Water Conservation* 49(1):7–13.

Council on Environmental Quality. 1986. "Environmental impact statement." *Code of federal regulations* 40. Ch. V (7-1-86 ed.).

Cowardin, Lewis M., Virginia Carter, Francis C. Golet, and Edward T. LaRoe. 1979. *Classification of wetlands and deepwater habitats in the United States.* Washington, D.C.: U.S. Department of Interior, Fish and Wildlife Service.

Crane, Laura Priedeman, Michelle M. Manion, and Karl F. Spiecker. 1996. *A cost of community services study of Scio Township.* Ann Arbor, Michigan: Potawatomi Land Trust.

Creighton, James L. 1992. *Involving citizens in community decision making: a guidebook.* Washington, D.C.: Program for Community Problem Solving.

Cullingworth, Barry. 1997. *Planning in the USA: policies, issues and processes.* London: Routledge.

Dahl, T. E. 1990. *Wetlands losses in the United States 1780s to 1980s.* Washington, D.C.: U.S. Fish and Wildlife Service.

D'Ambrosi, C., and T. D. Thomas. 1993. "Urban design and energy efficiency in downtown South Miami:

building on the charrette process." *Environmental and Urban Issues: Florida* 20, 3.

Daniels, Tom. 1999. *When city and county collide: managing growth in the metropolitan fringe.* Washington, D.C.: Island Press.

Daniels, Tom, and Deborah Bowers. 1997. *Holding our ground: protecting America's farms and farmland.* Washington, D.C.: Island Press.

Daniels, Tom, and Arthur C. Nelson. 1986. "Is Oregon's farmland preservation program working?" *Journal of the American Planning Association 52(1):22–32.*

Daniels, Tom, and David E. Reed. 1988. "Agricultural zoning in a metropolitan county: an evaluation of the Black Hawk County, Iowa program." *Landscape and Urban Planning* 16(4):303–310.

Davidoff, Paul, and Thomas Reiner. 1962. "A choice theory of planning." *Journal of the American Institute of Planners* 28(May):103–115.

Davis, Paul E., Norbert Lerch, Larry Tornes, Joseph Steiger, Neil Smeck, Howard Andrus, John Trimmer, and George Bottrell. 1976. *Soil survey of Montgomery County, Ohio.* Washington, D.C.: Soil Conservation Service, U.S. Department of Agriculture.

De Chiara, Joseph, and Lee Koppelman. 1975. *Urban planning and design criteria.* New York: Van Nostrand Reinhold.

deFranceaux, Cynthia. 1987. "National Park Service planning." *Trends* 24(2):13–19.

DeGrove, John M. 1984. *Land, growth and politics.* Chicago: Planners Press.

DeGrove, John M., 1992. *The new state frontier for land-use policy: planning and growth management in the States.* Cambridge: Massachusetts: Lincoln Institute of Land Policy.

DeGrove, John M., 1998. "State responses to urban growth: lessons for Arizona." In *Growth in Arizona: the machine in the garden,* John Stuart Hall, N. Joseph Cayer, and Nancy Welch eds., pp. 85–94. Tempe, Arizona: Morrison Institute for Public Policy, Arizona State University.

Delbecq, André L., Andrew H. Van de Ven, and David H. Gustafson. 1975. *Group techniques for program planning, a guide to nominal group and Delphi processes.* Glenview, Illinois: Scott, Foresman.

Department of Land Conservation and Development. 1996. *Oregon's statewide planning goals & guidelines.* Salem, Oregon.

Desert View Village Planning Committee. 1998. *Desert character overall districts, desert preserve overlay sub-districts A & B.* Phoenix, Arizona: Planning Department.

Design Workshop. 1995. *Desert spaces: an open space plan for the Maricopa Association of Governments.* Phoenix, Arizona: Maricopa Association of Governments.

De Vellis, Robert F. 1991. *Scale development: theory and application.* Newbury Park, California: Sage.

Dickert, Thomas, and Robert B. Olshansky. 1986. "Evaluating erosion susceptibility for land-use planning in coastal watersheds." *Coastal Zone Management* 13(3/4):309–333.

Dickert, Thomas and Andrea E. Tuttle. 1985. "Cumulative impact assessment in environmental planning, a coastal wetland watershed example." *Environmental Impact Assessment Review* 5:37–64.

Dideriksen, Raymond I. 1984. "SCS important farmlands mapping program." In *Protecting farmlands,* Frederick Steiner and John Theilacker eds., pp. 233–240. Westport, Connecticut: AVI Publishing.

Dillman, Don A. 1977. "Preference surveys and policy decision: our new tools need not be used in the same old ways." *Journal of the Community Development Society* 8(1):30–43.

Dillman, Don A. 1978. *Mail and telephone surveys, the total design method.* New York: Wiley-Interscience.

Domack, Dennis. 1981. *The art of community development.* Madison, Wisconsin: University of Wisconsin-Extension.

Donahue, Roy, Raymond W. Miller, and John C. Schickluna. 1977. *Soils: an introduction to soils and plant growth.* Englewood Cliffs, New Jersey: Prentice-Hall.

Doornkamp, John C. 1982. "The physical basis for planning in the Third World, IV: regional planning." *Third World Planning Review* 4(2):111–118.

Duane, Timothy P. 1996. "Human settlement, 1850–2040." In *Sierra Nevada ecosystem project: final report to Congress, Vol. II: Assessments and scientific basis for management options,* pp. 235–360. Davis, California: University of California Centers for Water and Wildland Resources.

Duchhart, Ingrid. 1989. *Manual on environment and urban development.* Nairobi, Kenya: Ministry of Local Government and Physical Planning.

Duerksen, Christopher J., Donald L. Elliot, N. Thompson Hobbs, Erin Johnson, and James R. Miller. 1997.

Habitat protection planning: where the wild things are. Chicago, Illinois: American Planning Association.

Dunford, Richard W. 1984. "Property tax relief programs to preserve farmlands." In *Protecting farmlands.* Frederick Steiner and John Theilacker eds., pp. 183–194. Westport, Connecticut: AVI Publishing.

Dunne, Thomas, and Luna B. Leopold. 1978. *Water in environmental planning.* New York: W. H. Freeman.

Easter, William K., John A. Dixon, and Maynard M. Hufschmidt (eds.). 1986. *Watershed resource management.* Boulder, Colorado: Westview Press.

Easterbrook, Don J. 1999. *Surface processes and landforms* (2nd ed.). Upper Saddle River, New Jersey: Prentice-Hall.

Eber, Ronald. 1984. "Oregon's agricultural land protection program." In *Protecting farmlands,* Frederick R. Steiner and John E. Theilacker eds., pp. 161–171. Westport, Connecticut: AVI Publishing Company.

Eber, Ronald. 1999. (Telephone interview, 13 January.) Salem, Oregon: Department of Land Conservation and Development.

Eliot, Charles. 1902. *Charles Eliot, landscape architect.* Boston, Massachusetts: Houghton, Mifflin.

Emory, Benjamin R. 1985. "Report on 1985 national survey of government and non-profit easement programs: executive summary." *Land Trusts' Exchange* 4(3):2.

En Charrette Exhibition of Selected Projects from the School of Architecture, University of Illinois at Urbana-Champaign. 1993. *Reflections* 9, 58.

Environmental Reporter. 1990. "Federal wetland conservation policy may collide with constitutional rights." 21(19):377–378.

Erickson, Donna L. 1995. "Rural land-use and land-cover change: implications for local planning in the River Raisin watershed (USA)." *Land Use Policy* 12:223–236.

Ewan, Joseph, Rebecca Fish Ewan, John Brock, Matthew Bucchin, Jill Cohen, Nancy Osborne, and Laura Sychowski. 1998. *North Phoenix wash vegetation study.* Tempe, Arizona: Herberger Center for Design Excellence, Arizona State University.

Ewan, Joseph, Rebecca Fish Ewan, Timothy Craig, and Sam Scheiner. 1996. *Cave Creek wash preservation boundary study.* Tempe and Phoenix, Arizona: School of Planning and Landscape Architecture of Arizona State University-Main, and Life Sciences Department of Arizona State University-West.

Faas, Ronald C. 1980. *What does the impact statement say about economic impacts?* (WREP 31). Corvallis, Oregon: Western Rural Development Center, Oregon State University.

Faas, Ronald C., and Dave Holland. 1994. *Economic impacts: what an impact statement says* (WREP 31). Corvallis, Oregon: Western Rural Development Center, Oregon State University.

Fabos, Julius Gy., 1979. *Planning the total landscape.* Boulder, Colorado: Westview Press.

Fabos, Julius Gy., and Jack Ahern (eds.). 1996. *Greenways: the beginnings of an international movement.* Amsterdam, The Netherlands: Elsevier.

Fabos, Julius Gy., and Stephanie J. Caswell. 1977. *Composite landscape assessment: assessment procedures for special resources hazards, and development suitability.* Research Bulletin Number 637. Amherst, Massachusetts: Massachusetts Agricultural Experiment Station, University of Massachusetts.

Fabos, Julius Gy, C. M. Green, and S. A. Joyner. 1978. *The METLAND landscape planning process: composite landscape assessment. Alternative plan formulation and plan evaluation. Part 3, metropolitan landscape planning model.* Amherst, Massachusetts: Massachusetts Agricultural Experimental Station.

Falini, Paola E. 1997. "Il territorio storico di Assisi: 'una descrizione di sfondo' per il nuovo PRG." *Rassegina di Architettura and Urbanistica* 80:140–156.

Falini, Paola E., Cristina Grifoni, and Annarita Lomoro. 1980. "Conservation planning for the countryside: a preliminary report of an experimental study of the Terni Basin (Italy)." *Landscape Planning* 7:345–367.

Fletcher, W. Wendell. 1978. *Agricultural land retention: an analysis of the issue. A study of recent state and local farmland retention programs and discussion of proposed federal legislation.* Washington, D.C.: Congressional Research Service, Library of Congress.

Fogleman, Valerie M. 1990. *Guide to the National Environmental Policy Act: interpretations, applications, and compliance.* New York: Quorum Books.

Food and Agriculture Organization of the United Nations. 1977. *A framework for land evaluation* (Publication 22). Wageningen, The Netherlands: International Institute for Land Reclamation and Improvement.

Forester, John. 1982. "Understanding planning practice: an empirical, practical, and normative account."

Journal of Planning Education and Research 1(2):59–71.

Forman, Richard T. T. 1995. *Land mosaics: the ecology of landscapes and regions.* Cambridge, England: Cambridge University Press.

Forman, Richard T. T., and Michel Godron. 1986. *Landscape ecology.* New York: John Wiley & Sons.

Forshaw, J. H., and Patrick Abercrombie. 1943. *County of London plan.* London: MacMillan.

Fowler, Floyd J. 1993. *Survey research methods* (2nd ed.). Newbury Park, California: Sage.

Fox, Jeff. 1987. "Two roles for natural scientists in the management of tropical watersheds: examples from Nepal and Indonesia." *Environmental Professional* 9:59–66.

Friedmann, John. 1973. *Retracking America.* Garden City, New York: Anchor Press/Doubleday.

Fry, Jana, Frederick Steiner, and Douglas Green. 1994. "Riparian evaluation and site assessment in Arizona." *Landscape and urban planning* 28(2–3):179–199.

Gans, Herbert J. 1967. *The Levittowners.* New York: Random House.

Gans, Herbert J., 1968. *People and plans.* New York: Basic Books.

Gans, Herbert J., 1993. *People, plans, and policies.* New York: Columbia University Press.

Gelfand, Donna Issac. 1992. "Citizen participation in environmental decisionmaking: a study of two Arizona cities" (unpublished master of environmental planning thesis). Tempe, Arizona: Arizona State University Department of Planning.

Gibson, Lay James. 1975. "Local impact analysis: an Arizona case study." *Arizona Research* 24(1):1–10.

Gil, Efraim, and Enid Lucchesi. 1979. "Citizen participation in planning." In *The practice of local government planning,* Frank S. So, Israel Stollman, Frank Beal, and David S. Arnold eds., pp. 552–575. Washington, D.C.: International City Management Association.

Glikson, Artur. 1971. *The ecological basis of planning.* The Hague, The Netherlands: Matinus Nijhoff.

Gober, Patricia. 1998. "The demographics of urban growth in Phoenix." In *Growth in Arizona: the machine in the garden,* John Stuart Hall, N. Joseph Cayer, and Nancy Welch eds. Tempe, Arizona: Morrison Institute, Arizona State University.

Golley, Frank B. 1998. *A primer for environmental literacy.* New Haven, Connecticut: Yale University Press.

Goodchild, Michael F., Bradley Parks, and Louis Steyaert (eds.). 1993. *Environmental modeling with GIS.* New York: Oxford University Press.

Gordon, Steven I. 1985. *Computer models in environmental planning.* New York: Van Nostrand Reinhold.

Gordon, Steven I., and Gaybrielle E. Gordon. 1981. "The accuracy of soil survey information for urban land-use planning." *Journal of the American Planning Association* 47(3):301–312.

Gore, Al. 1992. *Earth in the balance: ecology and the human spirit.* New York: Houghton Mifflin Company.

Gosselink, J. G., and E. Maltby. 1990. "Wetland losses and gains." In *Wetlands, a threatened landscape,* M. Williams ed., pp. 296–322. Oxford, U.K.: Basil Blackwell.

Graf, William L. (ed.). 1987. *Geomorphic systems of North America.* Boulder, Colorado: Geological Society of America.

Graham, Otis L., Jr. 1976. *Toward a planned society.* London: Oxford University Press.

Grant, Jill, Patricia Manuel, and Darrell Joudrey. 1996. "A framework for planning sustainable residential landscapes." *Journal of the American Planning Association* 62(3):331–344.

Green, Philip P., Jr. 1968. "Land subdivision." In *Principles and practice of urban planning,* William I. Goodman and Eric C. Freund, eds. pp. 443–484. Washington, D.C.: International City Manager's Association.

Griffin, C. R. 1989. "Protection of wildlife habitat by state wetland regulations: the Massachusetts initiative." In *Transactions 54th North American wildlife and natural resource conference,* R. E. McCabe, ed. pp. 22–31. Washington, D.C.: Wildlife Management Institute.

Grossinger, R. M., J. N. Collins, E. Brewster, and Z. Der. 1999. "Where did today come from? (And where is it headed?): an example of historical ecology research from the San Francisco Estuary, California." Richmond, California: San Francisco Estuary Institute.

Grossinger, R. M., Zoltan Der, and Elise Brewster. 1998. "Bay area historical project" (unpublished summary). Richmond, California: San Francisco Estuary Institute.

Hagman, Donald G., and Julian Conrad Juergensmeyer. 1986. *Urban planning and land development control law* (2nd ed). St. Paul, Minnesota: West.

Hall, Peter. 1975. *Urban and regional planning.* New York: Halsted Press/John Wiley & Sons.

Harris, Dianne Chandler. 1988. "Growth management reconsidered." *Journal of Planning Literature* 3(4):466–482.

Hart, John Fraser. 1998. *The rural landscape.* Baltimore: Johns Hopkins University Press.

Hartman, George W. 1977. *Soil survey of Maricopa County: central part.* Washington, D.C.: U.S. Government Printing Office.

Hawks, Richard, and Shelley Mastran. 1997. *Your town: designing its future.* Washington, D.C., and Syracuse, New York: National Trust for Historic Preservation, and State University of New York at Syracuse.

Hendricks, David M. 1985. *Arizona soils.* Tucson, Arizona: University of Arizona College of Agriculture.

Hersperger, Anna M. 1994. "Landscape ecology and its potential application to planning." *Journal of Planning Literature* 9(1):14–29.

Higashi, Irvin, Nancy Hopkins, Rick Nishi, Jani Raymond, and Susan Vogt. 1978. "Parvin ecological study" (class project). Pullman, Washington: Department of Horticulture and Landscape Architecture and Program in Environmental Science and Regional Planning, Washington State University.

Hightower, Henry C. 1968. "Population studies." In *Principles and practice of urban planning,* William I. Goodman and Eric C. Freund eds. pp. 51–75. Washington, D.C.: International City Manager's Association.

Hill, Morris. 1968. "A goals-achievement matrix for evaluating alternative plans." *Journal of the American Institute of Planners* 34(1):19–29.

Hills, G. A. 1961. *The ecological basis for land-use planning* (Research Report No. 46). Toronto, Ontario: Ontario Department of Lands and Forests.

Hirschhorn, Larry. 1980. "Scenario writing: a developmental approach." *Journal of the American Planning Association* 46(2):172–183.

Hirschman, Joan. 1988. "Bird habitat design for people: a landscape ecological approach" (unpublished master of landscape architecture thesis). Denver, Colorado: University of Colorado Program in Landscape Architecture and Urban Design.

Holdridge, L. R. 1967. *Life zone ecology.* San Jose, Costa Rica: Tropical Science Center.

Holland, R. F. 1986. *Preliminary descriptions of the terrestrial natural communities of California.* Sacramento, California: State of California Department of Fish and Game.

Hopkins, Lewis D. 1977. "Methods for generating land suitability maps: a comparative evaluation." *Journal of the American Institute of Planners* 43(4):386–400.

Hough, Michael. 1995. *Cities and natural processes.* London and New York: Routledge.

Huddleston, Jack. 1981. "Tax increment financing in Wisconsin." *Planning* 47(11):14–17.

Hudson, Barclay M. 1979. "Comparison of current planning theories: counterparts and contradictions." *Journal of the American Planning Association* 45(4):387–398.

Humbach, John A. 1989. "Law and a new land ethic." *Minnesota Law Review* 74:339–370.

Humphreys, John A. 1985. "Breckenridge, point systems: keeping score." *Planning* 51(10):23–25.

Hunt, Charles. 1967. *Physiography of the United States.* San Francisco, California: W. H. Freeman.

Iacofano, Daniel S. 1990. *Public involvement as an organizational development process. A proactive theory for environmental planning program management.* New York: Garland.

Ingley, Kathleen. 1996. "A 'community vision' for Phoenix would protect northern desert areas." *Arizona Republic* May 20:A1.

Ingley, Kathleen, 1998. "Designs on the desert." *Planning* 64(2, February):18–21.

Institute for Participatory Management and Planning. 1997. *Citizen participation handbook for public officials and other professionals serving the public* (10th ed.). Monterey, California.

Institute for Participatory Planning. 1978. *Citizen participation handbook.* Laramie, Wyoming.

International Union for the Conservation of Nature and Natural Resources. 1980. *World conservation strategy* (published in cooperation with the United Nations Environment Programme and The World Wildlife Fund). Gland, Switzerland.

Iowa Northland Regional Council of Governments. 1975. *County living study.* Waterloo, Iowa: Black Hawk County.

Irish, Gary. 1994. *GIS overview: Joint Legislative Budget Committee, December 1, 1994.* Phoenix, Arizona: Arizona Land Resources Information System.

Jackson, Joanne Barnes, and Frederick R. Steiner. 1985. "Human ecology for land-use planning." *Urban Ecology* 9:177–194.

Jacobs, Allan B. 1985. *Looking at cities.* Cambridge, Massachusetts: Harvard University Press.

Jacobs, Allan B. 1993. *Great streets.* Cambridge, Massachusetts: MIT Press.

Jagillo, Keith J. 1987. "Structural evolution of the Phoenix Basin, Arizona" (unpublished master of science thesis). Tempe, Arizona: Arizona State University Department of Geology.

Jennings, Michael D., and John P. Reganold. 1988. "Policy and reality of environmentally sensitive areas in Whitman County, Washington, USA." *Environmental Management* 12(3):369–380.

Johannsen, Sonia A., and Larry C. Larsen. 1984. "Corn suitability ratings: a method of rating soils for identifying and preserving prime agricultural land in Black Hawk County, Iowa." In *Protecting farmland,* Frederick Steiner and John Theilacker eds., pp. 109–127. Westport, Connecticut: AVI Publishing.

Johnson, Arthur H. 1981. "Guest editorial: human ecological planning—methods and studies." *Landscape Planning* 8:107–108.

Johnson, Arthur H., Jonathan Berger, and Ian L. McHarg. 1979. "A case study in ecological planning: the Woodlands, Texas." In *Planning the uses and management of land,* Marvin T. Beatty, Gary W. Petersen, and Lester D. Swindale eds., pp. 935–955. Madison, Wisconsin: American Society of Agronomy, Crop Science Society of America, and Soil Science Society of America.

Johnson, Lee. 1974. *Attorney General's opinion on Fasano v. Board of County Commissioners of Washington County.* Salem, Oregon: State of Oregon. Department of Justice.

Jones, Stephen M., and Roy Fedelem. 1996. *Agricultural and farmland protection plan.* Hauppauge, New York: Suffolk County Planning Department.

Juneja, Narenda. 1974. *Medford: performance requirements for the maintenance of social values represented by the natural environment of Medford Township, New Jersey.* Philadelphia, Pennsylvania: Department of Landscape Architecture and Regional Planning, Center for Ecological Research in Planning and Design, University of Pennsylvania.

Juster, Robert J. 1994. *Municipal planning in Alabama.* Auburn, Alabama: The Alabama Planning Institute.

Kaiser, Edward J., David R. Godschalk, and F. Stuart Chapin. 1995. *Urban land use planning* (4th ed). Urbana, Illinois: University of Illinois Press.

Kaplan, Rachel, Stephen Kaplan, and Robert L. Ryan. 1998. *With people in mind.* Washington, D.C.: Island Press.

Kartez, Jack D. 1980. "A zoning administrator's view of farmland zoning." *Journal of Soil and Water Conservation* 35(6):265–266.

Kartez, Jack D. 1981. "Community economic base analysis" (mimeograph). Pullman, Washington: Washington State University Program in Environmental Science and Regional Planning.

Kast, Fremont E., and James E. Rosenzweig. 1979. *Organization and management: a systems and contingency approach* (3rd ed.). New York: McGraw-Hill.

Kelbaugh, Douglas. 1997. *Common place: toward neighborhood and regional design.* Seattle, Washington: University of Washington Press.

Kellington, Wendie. 1998. "Oregon's land use program comes of age: the next 25 years." *Land Use Law & Zoning Digest* 50(10):3–6.

Kelly, Eric Damian. 1993. *Managing community growth: policies, techniques and impacts.* Westport, Connecticut: Praeger.

Kendig, Lane. 1977. "Carrying capacity: how it can work for you." *Environmental comment* (December):4–6.

Killpack, Charles. 1981. "Computer mapping, spatial analysis, and landscape architecture." *Landscape Journal* 1(1):41–48.

Kitsap County Department of Community Development. 1998. *Kitsap County critical areas ordinance.* Port Orchard, Washington.

Kleymeyer, John E. No date. "Some aspects of land-use control" (class notes). Cincinnati, Ohio: University of Cincinnati Department of Community Planning.

Klingebiel, A. A., and P. H. Montgomery. 1961. *Land capability classification* (Agricultural Handbook No. 210). Washington, D.C.: Soil Conservation Service, U.S. Department of Agriculture.

Klosterman, Richard E. 1978. "Foundations for normative planning." *Journal of the American Institute of Planners* 44(1):37–46.

Koekebakker, Olof. 1996. *Charrettes voor Leidsche Rijn Utrecht.* Rotterdam, The Netherlands: NA; Uitgevers.

Kreske, Diori L. 1996. *Environmental impact statements: a practical guide for agencies, citizens, and consultants.* New York: John Wiley & Sons.

Krueger, Richard. 1988. *Focus groups: a practical guide for applied research.* Newbury Park, California: Sage Publications.

Kusler, J. A. 1985. "A call for action: protection of riparian habitat in the arid and semi-arid west." In *Ripar-*

ian ecosystems and their management: reconciling their uses, R. R. Johnson, C. D. Ziebell, D. R. Patton, P. F. Ffollion, and R. N. Hamre eds., pp. 6–8. Tucson, Arizona: U.S. Forest Service.

Kusler, J. A., and Teresa Opheim. 1996. *Our national wetland heritage: a protection guide* (2nd ed). Washington, D.C.: American Law Institute.

Lai, Richard Tseng-yu. 1988. *Law in urban design and planning.* New York: Van Nostrand Reinhold.

Laird, Raymond T., Jeanne B. Perkins, David A. Bainbridge, James B. Baker, Robert T. Boyd, Daniel Huntsman, Paul E. Staub, and Melvin B. Zucker. 1979. *Quantitative land-capability analysis* (U.S. Geological Survey Professional Paper 945).

Land Conservation and Development Commission (LCDC). 1980. *Statewide planning goals and guidelines.* Salem, Oregon.

Laslett, Peter (ed.). 1988. *John Locke: two treatises of government* (student ed.). Cambridge, England: Cambridge University Press.

Lassey, William R. 1977. *Planning in rural environments.* New York: McGraw-Hill.

Lawson, S. 1991. Under stress. *Landscape Architecture* 81(10):76–78.

Le Compte, Margaret D., and Judith Preissle. 1993. *Ethnography and quality design in educational research.* San Diego, California: Academic Press.

Leach, John Craig. 1992. "Planners and the public: a communication gap" (unpublished master of environmental planning thesis). Tempe, Arizona: Arizona State University School of Planning and Landscape Architecture.

Leary, Robert M. 1968. "Zoning." In *Principles and practice of urban planning,* William I. Goodman and Eric C. Freund eds., pp. 403–442. Washington, D.C.: International City Manager's Association.

Leopold, Aldo. 1933. "The conservation ethic." *The Journal of Forestry* 31(6):634–643.

Leopold, Aldo. 1949. *A sand county almanac and sketches here and there.* New York: Oxford.

Leslie, M., and E. H. Clark. II. 1990. "Perspectives on wetland loss and alterations." In *Issues in wetlands protection: background papers prepared for national wetlands policy forum,* G. Bingham, E. H. Clark II, L. V. Laygood, and M. Leslie eds., pp. 1–21. Washington, D.C.: The Conservation Foundation.

Lewis, James A. 1980. *Landownership in the United States,* 1978. Washington, D.C.: U.S. Department of Agriculture.

Lewis, Philip H. 1964. "Quality corridors in Wisconsin." *Landscape Architecture Quarterly* 54(2):100–107.

Lewis, Philip H. 1969. "The inland water tree." *American Institute of Architects Journal* 51(6):59–63.

Lewis, Philip H. 1996. *Tomorrow by design.* New York: John Wiley & Sons.

van Lier, H. N. 1973. *Determination of planning capacity and layout criteria of outdoor recreation projects.* Wageningen, The Netherlands: Centre for Agricultural Publishing and Documentation.

van Lier, H. N. 1980. "Outdoor recreation in the Netherlands. II. A system to determine the planning capacity of outdoor recreation projects having varying daily attendance." *Landscape Planning* 7(4):329–343.

van Lier, H. N. 1991. *Meervoudig grondgebruik. Deel A: problemen, processen, effecten en oplossingen (Multiple land use planning. Part A: problems, processes, effects and solutions).* Wageningen, The Netherlands: Wageningen Agriculture University.

van Lier, H. N., and Frederick Steiner. 1982. "A review of the Zuiderzee reclamation works: an example of Dutch physical planning." *Landscape Planning* 9(1):35–59.

Lilieholm, Robert J., and Jeff Romm. 1992. "Pinelands national reserve: an intergovernmental approach to nature preservation." *Environmental Management* 16(3):335–343.

Lime, D. W. 1979. "Carrying capacity." *Trends in Rivers and Trails* 16:37–40.

Lime, D. W., and G. H. Stankey. 1971. "Carrying capacity: maintaining outdoor recreation quality." In *Forest recreation symposium proceedings,* pp. 174–184. Upper Darby, Pennsylvania: Northeast Forest Experiment Station.

Linstone, H. A., and M. Turoff (eds.). 1975. *The Delphi method: techniques and applications.* Reading, Massachusetts: Addison-Wesley Publishing Company.

Little, Charles E. 1990. *Greenways for America.* Baltimore, Maryland: Johns Hopkins University Press.

Little, Lynne A. 1975. "Geology and land use investigation in the Pinnacle Peak Area" (unpublished master of science thesis). Tempe, Arizona: Arizona State University Department of Geology.

Litton, R. Burton, Jr. 1968. *Forest landscape description and inventories—a basis for land planning and design.* Berkeley, California: Pacific Southwest Forest and Range Experiment Station, U.S. Forest Service.

Littrell, David. 1976. *The theory and practice of community development.* Columbia, Missouri: Extension Division, University of Missouri.

Local Government Commission. 1991. *The Ahwahnee principles.* Sacramento, California.

Loe, Robert C. de. 1995. "Exploring complex policy questions using the policy Delphi: a multiround, interactive survey method." *Applied Geography* 15(1):53–68.

Long, John. 1981. *Population deconcentration in the United States.* Washington, D.C.: U.S. Government Printing Office.

Lougeay, Ray, Anthony Brazel, and Mark Hubble. 1996. "Monitoring interurban temperature patterns and associated land cover in Phoenix, Arizona using landset thermal data." *Geocarto International* 11(4):79–90.

Lovejoy, Derek (ed.). 1973. *Land use and landscape planning.* New York: Barnes & Noble.

Lovelock, J. E. 1979. *Gaia.* Oxford, U.K.: Oxford University Press.

Lowe, Charles H., and David E. Brown. 1994. "Introduction." In *Biotic communities: southwestern United States and northwestern Mexico,* David E. Brown ed., pp. 8–16. Salt Lake City: University of Utah Press.

Lowe, C. H. (ed.). 1964. *The vertebrates of Arizona.* Tucson, Arizona: University of Arizona Press.

Lowrance, Richard, Paul F. Hendrix, and Eugene P. Odum. 1986. "A hierarchical approach to sustainable agriculture." *American Journal of Alternative Agriculture* 1(4):169–173.

Lucy, William H. 1994. "If planning includes too much, maybe it should include more." *Journal of the American Planning Association* 60(3):305–318.

Lyle, John Tillman. 1994. *Regenerative design for sustainable development.* New York: John Wiley & Sons.

Lyle, John Tillman, and Frederick Stutz. 1983. "Computerized land use suitability mapping." In *Geographic information systems for resource management: a compendium,* W. J. Ripple ed. Falls Church, Virginia: American Society for Photogrammetry and Remote Sensing and American Congress on Surveying and Mapping.

Lynch, Kevin. 1960. *The image of the city.* Cambridge, Massachusetts: MIT Press.

Lynch, Kevin. 1962. *Site planning.* Cambridge, Massachusetts: MIT Press.

Lynch, Kevin. 1971. *Site planning* (2nd ed.). Cambridge, Massachusetts: MIT Press.

Lynch, Kevin., and Gary Hack. 1984. *Site planning* (3rd ed.). Cambridge, Massachusetts: MIT Press.

MacDougall, E. Bruce. 1975. "The accuracy of map overlays." *Landscape Planning* 2:23–30.

MacKaye, Benton. 1940. "Regional planning and ecology." *Ecological Monographs* 10(3):349–353.

MacNair, Ray H. 1981. "Citizen participation as a balanced exchange: an analysis and strategy." *Journal of the Community Development Society* 12(1):1–19.

Manning, Warren. 1913. "The Billerica town plan." *Landscape Architecture* 3:108–118.

Marsh, William M. 1983. *Landscape Planning.* Reading: Massachusetts: Addison-Wesley.

Marsh, William M. 1998. *Landscape planning: environmental applications* (3rd ed.). New York: John Wiley & Sons.

Mason, Robert J. 1986. "Environmental conflict and accommodation: an evaluation of regional land use management in the New Jersey Pinelands" (Ph.D. dissertation). New Brunswick, New Jersey: Graduate Program in Geography, Rutgers, The State University of New Jersey.

McCarthy, James, Kim Shetter, and Frederick Steiner (eds.). 1995. *Findings of the North Sonoran land use character charrette.* Tempe, Arizona: Herberger Center for Design Excellence and School of Planning and Landscape Architecture, Arizona State University.

McClendon, Bruce W. 1992. *Customer service in local government.* Chicago, Illinois: APA Planners Press.

McCormack, D. E. 1974. "Soil potentials: a positive approach to urban planning." *Journal of Soil and Water Conservation* 29:258–262.

McCormick, J. F. 1978. "A summary of the national riparian symposium: a proposal for a national riparian program." In *Strategies for protection and management of floodplain wetlands and other riparian ecosystems: proceedings,* R. R. Johnson and J. F. McCormick, technical coordinators USDA, FS, GTR-WO-12, pp. 362–363. Washington, D.C.: U.S. Department of Agriculture.

McCracken, Grant. 1988. *The long interview.* Newbury, California: Sage Publications.

McDowell, Bruce D. 1986. "Approaches to planning." In *The practice of state and regional planning,* Frank S. So, Irving Hand, and Bruce D. McDowell eds., pp. 3–22. Chicago, Illinois: American Planning Association.

McHarg, Ian L. 1968. "A comprehensive highway route-section method." *Highway Research Record* 246:1–15.

McHarg, Ian L. 1969. *Design with nature.* Garden City, New York: Doubleday/The Natural History Press. (1992. 2nd ed.) New York: John Wiley & Sons.

McHarg, Ian L. 1981. "Human ecological planning at Pennsylvania." *Landscape Planning* 8:109–120.

McHarg, Ian L. 1996. *A quest for life.* New York: John Wiley & Sons.

McHarg, Ian L. 1997a. "Ecology and design." In *Ecological design and planning,* George F. Thompson and Frederick Steiner eds. pp. 321–332. New York: John Wiley & Sons.

McHarg, Ian L. 1997b. "Natural factors in planning." *Journal of Soil and Water Conservation* 52(1):13–17.

McHarg, Ian L. and Frederick R. Steiner (eds.). 1998. *To heal the earth: selected writings of Ian L. McHarg.* Washington, D.C.: Island Press.

McKenzie, Ricki. 1979. *The Pinelands scenic study* (summary report). Philadelphia, Pennsylvania: U.S. Department of Interior.

McLean, Mary L., and Kenneth P. Voytek. 1992. *Understanding your economy: using analysis to guide local strategic planning.* Chicago, Illinois: American Planning Association Planners Press.

McNally, Marcia. 1999. "A regional blueprint for sustainability." *Places* 12(2):26–29.

McQuary, Julie. 1998. City of Olympia parks planner (personal communication). Olympia, Washington.

McSheffrey, Gerald. 1999. *Planning Derry, planning and politics in Northern Ireland.* Liverpool, England: Liverpool University Press.

Meeks, G., Jr., and I. C. Runyon. 1990. *Wetlands protection and the states.* Denver, Colorado: National Conference of State Legislatures.

Meester, R., and J. L. M. van der Voet. 1980. *Carrying capacity, goal or result of a policy concerning water-based recreation areas.* Wageningen, The Netherlands: Agricultural University Department of Land and Water Use.

Meinig, D. W. 1979. "Introduction." In *The interpretation of ordinary landscapes,* D. W. Meinig ed., pp. 1–7. New York: Oxford University.

Metro. 1991. *Regional urban growth goals and objectives* (September). Portland, Oregon.

Metro. 1994a. *Region 2040 public involvement report* (August). Portland, Oregon.

Metro. 1994b. *Region 2040 growth concept* (December). Portland, Oregon.

Meyer, B. 1994. "The North Arncliffe town planning charrette." *New Planner* 17:1,6,7.

Meyer, Neil L. 1980. *Programming capital improvements* (WREP 30). Corvallis, Oregon: Western Rural Development Center, Oregon State University.

Meyers, Charles R., Jr. 1971. *Regional modeling abstracts* (3 volumes). Oak Ridge, Tennessee: Oak Ridge National Laboratory.

Meyers, Charles R., Michael Kennedy, and R. Neil Sampson. 1979. "Information systems for land-use planning." In *Planning the uses and management of land,* Marvin T. Beatty, Gary W. Petersen, and Lester D. Swindale eds. pp. 889–907. Madison, Wisconsin: American Society of Agronomy, Crop Science of America, and Soil Science Society of America.

Miller, Donald. 1980. "Project location analysis using the goals achievement method of evaluation." *Journal of the American Planning Association* 46(2):195–208.

Miller, Fred P. 1978. "Soil survey under pressure: the Maryland experience." *Journal of Soil and Water Conservation* 33(3):104–111.

Miller, Lynn. 1996. Personal communication. (Professor Emeritus from Pennsylvania State University at a 20 March 1996 Arizona State University presentation.)

Miller, William, Michael G. Collins, Frederick R. Steiner, and Edward Cook. 1998. "An approach for greenway suitability analysis." *Landscape and Urban Planning* 42:91–105.

Ministry of Transport and Public Works. No date. *Room at last.* Lelystad, The Netherlands: IJsselmeerpolders Development Authority.

Monroe, S. 1991. "Arizona riparian area initiative" (paper). Ankeny, Iowa: Soil and Water Conservation Society.

Moore, Terry. 1988. "Planning without preliminaries." *Journal of the American Planning Association* 54(4):525–528.

Morgan, Keith M. 1991. "Charles Eliot, 1859–1897, held in trust: Charles Eliot's vision for the New England landscape." In *National Association for Olmsted Parks workbook series.* (vol. 1, biography, pp. 1–12). Bethesda, Maryland: National Association for Olmsted Parks.

Morisawa, Marie. 1968. *Streams.* New York: McGraw-Hill.

Morrell, Terri A. 1989. "Small social spaces in the Netherlands" (paper). Denver, Colorado: University of Colorado School of Architecture and Planning.

Morris, Marya. 1997. "Subdivision design in flood hazard areas" (Planning Advisory Service Report Number 473). Chicago, Illinois: American Planning Association.

Moudon, Anne Vernez. 1997. "Urban morphology as an emerging interdisciplinary field." *Urban Morphology* 1:3–10.

Mumford, Lewis. 1944. *The condition of man.* New York: Harcourt, Brace and Company.

Mumford, Lewis. 1961. *The city in history: its origins, its transformations and its prospects.* New York: Harcourt, Brace, and World.

Muratori, S. 1959. "Studi per una operante storia urbana di Venezia." *Palladio* IX:97–209.

Muratori, S., R. Bollati, S. Bollati, and G. Marinucci. 1963. *Studi per una operante storia urbana di Roma.* Roma, Italia: Consiglio Nazionale della Riceche.

Murray, Timothy, Peter Rogers, David Sinton, Carl Steinitz, Richard Toth, and Douglas Way. 1971. *Honey Hill: a systems analysis for planning the multiple use of controlled water areas* (2 vols). Report nos. AD 736 343 and AD 736 344. Springfield, Virginia: National Technical Information Service.

National Agricultural Lands Study. 1981. *Final report.* Washington, D.C.: U.S. Department of Agriculture and Council on Environmental Quality.

National Commission on the Environment. 1993. *Choosing a sustainable future.* Washington, D.C.: Island Press.

Nations, Dale, and Edmund Stump. 1981. *The geology of Arizona.* Dubuque, Iowa: Kendall/Hunt.

Natural Resources Defense Council. 1977. *Land use controls in the United States,* Elaine Moss ed. New York: The Dial Press/James Wade.

Naveh, Zev, and Arthur S. Lieberman. 1994. *Landscape ecology: theory and applications* (2nd ed.). New York: Springer-Verlag.

Ndubisi, Forster. 1997. "Landscape ecological planning." In *Ecological design and planning,* George F. Thompson and Frederick R. Steiner eds., pp. 9–44. New York: John Wiley & Sons.

Ndubisi, Forster, Terry De Meo, and Niels D. Ditto. 1995. "Environmentally sensitive areas: a template for developing greenway corridors." *Landscape and Urban Planning* 33:159–177.

Neckar, Lance. 1989. "Developing landscape architecture for the twentieth century: the career of Warren Manning." *Landscape Journal* 8(2):78–91.

Needham, Roger D., and Robert C. de Loë. 1990. "The policy Delphi: purpose, structure, and application." *The Canadian Geographer/Le Géographe Canadien* 34(2):133–142.

Nellis, Lee. 1980. "Planning with rural values." *Journal of Soil and Water Conservation* 35(2):67–71.

Nellis, Lee. 1981. "The bottom line: implementation of regional landscape planning through effective citizen participation and an innovative legal and administrative technique." In *Regional landscape planning,* Julius Gy. Fabos ed., pp. 72–80. Washington, D.C.: American Society of Landscape Architects.

Nellis, Lee. 1994. "Linking LESA systems to local land use planning." In *A decade with LESA: the evolution of land evaluation and site assessment,* Frederick R. Steiner, James R. Pease, and Robert E. Coughlin eds., pp. 208–222. Ankeny, Iowa: Soil and Water Conservation Society.

Nelson, Arthur C. 1992. "Characterizing exurbia." *Journal of Planning Literature* 6(4):350–368.

Nelson, Arthur C., and James B. Duncan. 1995. *Growth management principles and practices.* Chicago, Illinois: American Planning Association.

Neuman, Michael. 1998a. "Does planning need the plan?" *Journal of the American Planning Association* 64(2):208–220.

Neuman, Michael. 1998b. "Planning, governing, and the image of the city." *Journal of Planning Education and Research* 18(1):61–71.

New Jersey Pinelands Commission. 1998. *A summary of the New Jersey Pinelands comprehensive management plan.* New Lisbon, New Jersey.

New Jersey State Planning Commission. 1988. *The preliminary state development and redevelopment plan for the State of New Jersey* (vol. 2.). Trenton, New Jersey.

Newman, Harry George, III. 1982. "An environmentally sensitive area planning model for local government in the State of Washington" (unpublished master of regional planning thesis). Pullman, Washington: Program in Environmental Science and Regional Planning, Washington State University.

Nicholas, J. C., A. C. Nelson, and J. C. Juergensmeyer. 1991. *A practitioner's guide to development impact fees.* Chicago, Illinois: Planners' Press.

Niebanck, Paul. 1993. "The shape of environmental planning education." *Environment and Planning B: Planning and Design* 20:511–518.

Niemann, Bernard J. 1989. "Improved analytical functionality: modernizing land administration, planning, management, and policy analysis." In *Multipurpose land information systems: the guidebook* (2 vols.), P. M. Brown and D. D. Moyer eds., pp. 11–13. Washington, D.C.: The Federal Geodetic Control Committee.

Noss, Reed, and Allen Cooperrider. 1993. "GAP analysis as applied conservation biology." *GAP analysis bulletin* 3(Winter/Spring):3–5.

Novikoff, A. B. 1945. "The concept of integrative levels and biology." *Science* 101:209–215.

Odum, Eugene P. 1971. *Fundamentals of ecology.* Philadelphia, Pennsylvania: W. B. Saunders.

Odum, Eugene P. 1978. "Ecological importance of the riparian zone." In *Strategies for protection and management of floodplain wetlands and other riparian ecosystems: proceedings,* R. R. Johnson and J. F. McCormick, technical coordinators, pp. 2–4. USDA, FS, GTR-WO-12. Washington, D.C.: U.S. Department of Agriculture.

Odum, Eugene P. 1998. *Ecological vignettes: ecological approaches to dealing with human predicaments.* Amsterdam, The Netherlands: Harwood Academic Publishers.

O'Harrow, Dennis. 1954. *Performance standards for industrial zoning.* Columbus, Ohio: National Industrial Zoning Committee.

Ohmart, R. D., and B. W. Anderson. 1986. "Riparian habitat." In *Inventorying and monitoring of wildlife habitat,* B. S. Cooperider ed., pp. 164–199. Denver, Colorado: U.S. Bureau of Land Management.

Olin, Laurie. 1988. "Form, meaning, and expression in landscape architecture." *Landscape Journal* 7(2):149–168.

Olin, Laurie. 1997. "Landscape design and nature." In *Ecological design and planning,* George R. Thompson and Frederick R. Steiner eds., pp. 109–139. New York: John Wiley & Sons.

Opie, John. 1998. *Nature's nation: an environmental history of the United States.* Fort Worth, Texas: Harcourt Brace & Company.

Oregon Supreme Court. 1979. *Neuburger v. City of Portland* (288 Or. 155,603 P.2d 771). Salem, Oregon.

Orr, David W. 1994. *Earth in mind: on education, environment, and the human prospect.* Washington, D.C.: Island Press.

Ortolano, Leonard. 1984. *Environmental planning and decision making.* New York: John Wiley & Sons.

Ortolano, Leonard. 1997. *Environmental regulation and impact assessment.* New York: John Wiley & Sons.

Palazzo, Danillo. 1997. *Sulle spalle di giganti. Le matrici della pianificazione ambientale negli Stati Uniti.* Milano, Italy: FrancoAngeli/DST.

Palmer, Arthur E. 1981. *Toward Eden.* Winterville, North Carolina: Creative Resource Systems.

Paris Prize. 1993. "Syracuse student wins fellowship in the final charrette, Richard Lucas' design for a New York middle school, 1993." *Competitions* 3, 2.

Patton, Carl V., and David S. Sawicki. 1993. *Basic methods of policy analysis and planning* (2nd ed.). Englewood Cliffs, New Jersey: Prentice Hall.

Pearthree, Philip A. 1991. "Geologic insights into flood hazards in Piedmont Areas of Arizona." *Arizona Geology* 21(4):1–5.

Pease, James R. 1984. "Oregon's land conservation and development program." In *Planning for the conservation and development of land resources,* Frederick R. Steiner and Hubert N. van Lier eds., pp. 253–271. Amsterdam, The Netherlands: Elsevier Scientific Publishing.

Pease, James R., and Robert E. Coughlin. 1996. *Land evaluation and site assessment: a guidebook for rating agricultural lands* (2nd ed.). Ankeny, Iowa: Soil and Water Conservation Society.

Peck, Sheila. 1998. *Planning for biodiversity.* Washington, D.C.: Island Press.

Petersen, Kip, Terri Morrell, and Larry Larsen. 1989. Growth management plan, Teller County, Colorado. Cripple Creek and Woodland Park, Colorado: Teller County Planning Department and City of Woodland Park Planning Department.

Pielke, R. A., and R. Avissar. 1990. "Influence of landscape structure on local and regional climate." *Landscape Ecology* 4(2/3):133–155.

Pijawka, K. David, and Kim Shetter. 1995. *The environment comes home.* Tempe, Arizona: Herberger Center for Design Excellence, Arizona State University.

Pijawka, K. David, Frederick Steiner, William Kasson, John Blair, and Bruce Kimball. 2000. *Sustainable neighborhood design.* Tempe, Arizona: Arizona State University School of Planning and Landscape Architecture.

Pinelands Commission. 1980. *New Jersey Pinelands comprehensive management plan.* New Lisbon, New Jersey: State of New Jersey.

Pinelands Commission. 1998. *Long-term economic monitoring program, executive summary to 1998 annual report.* New Lisbon, New Jersey: New Jersey Pinelands Commission.

Piscopo, Ornella. 1999. "L'Uso del concetto della carrying capacity per il progetto della città sostenibile" (Ph.D. dissertation). Rome, Italy: Dipartimento di Architettura e Urbanistica per l'Ingegneria, Università degli Studi di Roma "La Sapienza."

Planning. 1998. "Land trusts and partners add to protected inventory." *Planning* 64(11, November):23–24.

Platt, Rutherford H. 1991. *Land use and society: geography, law and public policy.* Washington, D.C.: Island Press.

Platt, Rutherford H. 1996. *Land use and society: geography, law, and public policy* (2nd ed.). Washington, D.C.: Island Press.

Portland Bureau of Planning. 1977. *The city planner handbook* (November). Portland, Oregon.

Portland Bureau of Planning. 1980a. *Citizen involvement* (September). (Comprehensive Plan Support Document No. 9 of 11 documents.)

Portland Bureau of Planning. 1980b. *Plan review and administration.* Portland, Oregon.

Powell, John Wesley. 1879. *Report on the arid lands of the arid region of the United States.* Washington, D.C.: U.S. Government Printing Office.

Prentice, Helaine Kaplan. 1998. *Suzhou, shaping an ancient city for the New China: an EDAW/Pei workshop.* Washington, D.C.: Spacemaker Press.

President's Council on Sustainable Development. 1996. *Sustainable America: a new consensus for prosperity, opportunity, and a healthy environment for the future.* Washington, D.C.: U.S. Government Printing Office.

Prigogine, Ilya, and Isabelle Stengers. 1984. *Order out of chaos.* New York: Bantam Books.

Quinby, Peter A. 1988. "The contribution of ecological science to the development of landscape ecology: a brief history." *Landscape Research* 13(3):9–11.

Raintree, John. 1987. *D. & D. users manual.* Nairobi, Kenya: International Council for Research in Agroforestry.

Ransel, K., and E. Meyers. 1988. "State water quality certification and wetland protection: a call to awaken the sleeping giant." *Virginia Journal of Natural Resources Law* 7(2):339–379.

Rees, William E. 1990a. "Sustainable development and the biosphere: concepts and principles." *Teilhard Studies* No. 23 (Spring/Summer). Chambersburg, Pennsylvania: Anima Books.

Rees, William E. 1990b. "The ecology of sustainable development." *The Ecologist* 20(1):18–23.

Rees, William E. 1992. "Ecological footprints and appropriated carrying capacity: what urban economics leaves out." *Environment and Urbanization* 4(2):121–130.

Rees, William E. 1995. "Achieving sustainability: reform or transformation?" *Journal of Planning Literature* 9(4):343–361.

Rees, William E. 1997. "Is 'Sustainable City' an oxymoron?" *Local Environment* 2(3):303–310.

Reganold, John P., and Michael J. Singer. 1978. *Defining prime agricultural land in California.* Environmental Quality Series No. 29. Davis, California: University of California Institute of Government Affairs.

Reganold, John F., and Michael J. Singer. 1979. "Defining prime farmland by three land classification systems." *Journal of Soil and Water Conservation* 34(4):172–176.

Regional Planning Staff. 1929. *The graphic regional plan, regional plan of New York and its environs* (vol. 1). New York: Regional Planning Staff.

Reilly, W. K. 1991. "A new way with wetlands." *Journal of Soil and Water Conservation* 46(3):192–194.

Renard, K. G., and G. R. Foster. 1983. "Soil conservation: principles of erosion by water." In *Dryland agriculture,* H. E. Dregne and W. O. Willis eds., pp. 155–176. Madison, Wisconsin: American Society of Agronomy, Crop Science Society of America, and Soil Science Society of America.

Renard, K. G., G. R. Foster, G. A. Weeies, D. K. McCool, and D. C. Yoder. 1997. *Predicting soil erosion by water: a guide to conservation planning with the revised universal soil loss equation (RUSLE)* (Agricultural Handbook No. 703). Washington, D.C.: U.S. Department of Agriculture.

Reps, John W. 1964. "Pomeroy memorial lecture: requiem for zoning." In *Planning 1964,* pp. 56–67. Chicago: The American Society of Planning Officials.

Reps, John W., 1970. *Town planning in frontier America.* (Paperback ed.; original copyright 1969.) Princeton, New Jersey: Princeton University Press.

Reynolds, Stephen J. No date. *Geologic map of Arizona.* Tempe, Arizona: Arizona State University Department of Geology.

Ribe, Robert G., and Ethan Seltzer. 1992. *Ten essentials for a quality regional landscape: a guidebook for maintaining and enhancing greater Portland's special sense of place* (December). Portland, Oregon: Metro.

Ricklefs, Robert E. 1973. *Ecology.* Newton, Massachusetts: Chiron Press.

Riddick, W. L. 1971. *Charrette processes.* York, Pennsylvania: George Shumway.

Riggle, James D. 1994. "LESA and the Illinois farmland preservation act." In *A decade with LESA: the evolution of land evaluation and site assessment,* Frederick R. Steiner, James R. Pease, and Robert E. Coughlin eds., pp. 180–193. Ankeny, Iowa: Soil and Water Conservation Society.

Roberts, John C. 1979. "Principles of land use planning." In *Planning the uses and management of land,* Marvin T. Beatty, Gary W. Petersen, and Lester D. Swindale eds., pp. 47–63. Madison, Wisconsin: American Society of Agronomy, Crop Science Society of America, and Soil Science Society of America.

Rogers, Golden, and Halpern, Inc. 1986. *Reforestation in the Pacific Islands.* Washington, D.C.: U.S. Peace Corps.

Rowe, Peter G. 1995. "Broadacre city and contemporary metropolitan development." In *Frank Lloyd Wright: the Phoenix papers,* K. Paul Zygas and Linda Nelson Johnson eds., pp. 48–64. Tempe, Arizona: Herberger Center for Design Excellence, Arizona State University.

Safina, Carl. 1998. *Song for the blue ocean: encounters along the world's coasts and beneath the seas.* New York: Henry Holt.

Salvesen, D. 1990. *Wetlands, mitigating and regulating developmental impacts.* Washington, D.C.: ULI, The Urban Land Institute.

Sarkissian, Wendy. 1994. "Community participation in theory and practice." In *Casebook: community participation in practice,* Wendy Sarkissian and Kelvin Walsh eds., pp. 1–32. Murdoch, Australia: The Institute for Science and Technology Policy, Murdoch University.

Satterlund, Donald R., and Paul W. Adams. 1992. *Wildland watershed management* (2nd ed.). New York: John Wiley & Sons.

Satterlund, Donald R., and Joseph E. Means. 1979. *Solar radiation in the Pacific Northwest* (Bulletin 874). Pullman, Washington: Washington State University College of Agriculture Research Center.

Scandurra, Enzo, and Alberto Budoni. 1997. "For a critical revision of the concept of sustainable development: ten years after the Brundtland report." Paper presented to the 20th Annual Meeting, 30 May-1 June, Northeast Regional Science Association, Boston, Massachusetts.

Scandurra, Enzo, and Silva Macchi (eds.). 1995. *Ambiente e pianificazione: lessico per le scienze urbane e territoriali.* Rome, Italy: Etas Libri.

Schauman, Sally. 1986. "Countryside landscape visual assessment." In *Foundations for visual project analysis,* R. C. Smardon, J. F. Palmer, and J. P. Felleman eds., pp. 103–114. New York: John Wiley & Sons.

Schauman, Sally. 1988a. "Scenic value of countryside landscapes to local residents: a Whatcom County, Washington case study." *Landscape Journal* 7(1):40–46.

Schauman, Sally. 1988b. "Countryside scenic assessment: tools and an application." *Landscape and Urban Planning* 15:227–229.

Schmandt, Michael Joseph. 1995. "Postmodernism and the southwest urban landscape" (Ph.D. dissertation). Tempe, Arizona: Arizona State University Department of Geography.

Schneider, Devon M., David R. Goldchalk, and Norman Axler. 1978. *The carrying capacity concept as a planning tool.* PAS Report No. 338. Chicago, Illinois: American Planning Association.

Sellers, William D., Richard H. Hill, and Margaret Sanderson-Rae. 1985. *Arizona climate: the first hundred years.* Tucson, Arizona: University of Arizona.

Seltzer, Ethan. 1998. (Correspondence, December 2). Portland, Oregon: Portland State University.

Shirvani, Hamid. 1990. *Beyond public architecture.* New York: Van Nostrand Reinhold.

Shumway, G. 1973. *Charrette at York, Pennsylvania.* York, Pennsylvania: George Shumway.

Siegler, Theodore R., and Neil L. Meyer. 1980. *Assessing fiscal impact of rural growth* (WREP 29). Corvallis, Oregon: Western Rural Development Center, Oregon State University.

Singer, Michael J., Kenneth K. Tanji, and J. Herbert Snyder. 1979. "Planning uses of cultivated cropland and pastureland." In *Planning the uses and management of land,* Marvin T. Beatty, Gary W. Petersen, and Lester D. Swindale eds., pp. 225–271. Madison, Wisconsin: American Society of Agronomy, Crop Science Society of America, Soil Science of America.

Sistrom, Peter. 1979. "The comp plan goes political." *Willamette Week* 26 November, 6(3):1, 5.

Skidmore, E. L. 1994. "Wind erosion." In: *Soil erosion research methods* (2nd ed.), R. Lal ed., pp. 265–293. Ankeny, Iowa: Soil and Water Conservation Society.

Slater, T. R. (ed.). 1990. *The built form of western cities.* Leicester, England: Leicester University Press.

Slocombe, D. Scott. 1998a. "Lessons from experience with ecosystem-based management." *Landscape and Urban Planning* 40:31–39.

Slocombe, D. Scott. 1998b. "Defining goals and criteria for ecosystem-based management." *Environmental Management* 22(4):483–493.

Smith, Daniel S., and Paul Cawood Helmund (eds.). 1993. *Ecology of greenways: design and function of linear conservation areas.* Minneapolis, Minnesota: University of Minnesota Press.

Smith, Paul Jr. 1992. "The poetics of landscape: on the aesthetic experience of the ephemeral qualities of the landscape" (unpublished master of landscape architecture thesis). Berkeley, California: University of California Department of Landscape Architecture.

Smith, Tony, Brian Trushinski, Jim Willis, and Gord Lemon. 1997. *The Laurel Creek watershed study.* Waterloo, Ontario: Grand River Conservation Authority, and City of Waterloo.

So, Frank S. 1979. "Finance and budgeting." In *The practice of local government planning,* Frank S. So, Israel Stollman, Frank Beal, and David S. Arnold eds., pp. 115–149. Washington, D.C.: International City Management Association.

So, Frank S. 1988. "Financing and budgeting." In *The practice of local government planning* (2nd ed.), Frank S. So and Judith Getzels eds., pp. 435–471. Washington, D.C.: International City Management Association.

Soesilo, Andy J., and K. David Pijawka. 1998. "Hazardous waste planning." In *Encyclopedia of environmental analysis and remediation,* Robert A. Meyers ed., pp. 2072–2090. New York: John Wiley & Sons.

Soil Conservation Service. 1975. *National soils handbook.* Washington, D.C.: U.S. Department of Agriculture.

Soil Survey Staff. 1951, 1975a. *Soil survey manual* USDA Handbook 18. Washington, D.C.: U.S. Department of Agriculture.

Soil Survey Staff. 1975b. *Soil taxonomy—a basic system of soil classification for making and interpreting soil surveys.* USDA Agricultural Handbook 436. Washington, D.C.: U.S. Department of Agriculture.

Soleri, Paolo. 1987. *Arcosanti: an urban laboratory?* (2nd ed.). Santa Monica, California: VTI Press.

Spirn, Anne Whiston. 1984. *The granite garden.* New York: Basic Books.

Spirn, Anne Whiston. 1988. "The poetics of city and nature: towards a new aesthetic for urban design." *Landscape Journal* 7(2):108–126.

Spirn, Anne Whiston. 1989. " 'Deep structure:' on process, pattern, form, and design in the urban landscape." In *Linking landscape structure to ecosystem process,* conference abstracts. Fort Collins, Colorado: Colorado State University.

Spirn, Anne Whiston. 1998. *The language of landscape.* New Haven, Connecticut: Yale University Press.

Stankey, George H., and David W. Lime. 1973. *Recreational carrying capacity: an annotated bibliography.* General Technical Report INT-3. Ogden, Utah: Intermountain Forest and Range Experiment Station, U.S. Forest Service.

State of Washington. 1984. *State environmental policy act rules.* Olympia, Washington: Department of Ecology.

Steiner, Frederick. 1981. "Farmland protection in the Netherlands." *Journal of Soil and Water Conservation* 36(2):71–76.

Steiner, Frederick. 1983. "Resource suitability: methods for analyses." *Environmental Management* 7(5):401–420.

Steiner, Frederick. 1987. "Agricultural land evaluation and site assessment: an introduction." *Environmental Management* 11(3):375–377.

Steiner, Frederick, Richard Dunford, and Nancy Dosdall. 1987. "The use of the land evaluation and site assessment system in the United States." *Landscape and Urban Planning* 14(3):183–199.

Steiner, Frederick, and Laurel McSherry. 2000. "Teaching plan-making." In *AICP's collegiate handbook for planners,* Bruce W. McClendon and Anthony

Catanese eds. Chicago, Illinois: American Institute of Certified Planners. (Forthcoming.)

Steiner, Frederick, Laurel McSherry, Dean Brennan, Mark Soden, Joe Yarkin, Douglas Green, James McCarthy, Catherine Spellman, John Jennings, and Kirsten Barré. 1999. "Concepts for alternative suburban planning in the Northern Phoenix Area." *Journal of the American Planning Association* 65(2):207–222.

Steiner, Frederick, James R. Pease, and Robert E. Coughlin (eds.). 1994. *A decade with LESA: the evolution of land evaluation and site assessment.* Ankeny, Iowa: Soil and Water Conservation Society.

Steiner, Frederick, Scott Pieart, Edward Cook, Jacqueline Rich, and Virginia Coltman. 1994. "State wetlands and riparian area protection programs." *Environmental Management* 18(2):183–201.

Steiner, Frederick, David Pijawka, and Bill Kasson. 1998. *Sustainable neighborhood design for the desert southwest* (Final report for the U.S. Environmental Protection Agency). Tempe, Arizona: Arizona State University School of Planning and Landscape Architecture.

Steiner, Frederick, and John Theilacker. 1979. "Locating feasible areas for rural housing in Whitman County, Washington." *Journal of Soil and Water Conservation* 34(6):283–285.

Steiner, Frederick, and John Theilacker (eds.). 1984. *Protecting farmland.* Westport, Connecticut: AVI Publishing.

Steiner, Frederick, David C. Wood, and Robert Bowie. 1989. "The use of ecological planning information for growth management planning: the Teller County/Woodland Park, Colorado case study" (paper). Denver, Colorado: University of Colorado School of Architecture and Planning.

Steinitz, Carl. 1988. "When visual quality and ecological integrity are mutually supportive or in conflict (and what to do about it): a case study based on (still-in-progress) research in Acadia National Park." Paper presented at the Third Annual Landscape Ecology Symposium. Albuquerque, New Mexico.

Steinitz, Carl. 1990. "A framework for the theory applicable to the education of landscape architects (and other environmental design professionals)." *Landscape Journal* 9(2):136–143.

Steinitz, Carl. 1993a. "A framework for theory and practice in landscape planning." *GIS Europe* (July):42–45.

Steinitz, Carl. 1993b. "GIS: a personal historical perspective." *GIS Europe* 46:38–46.

Steinitz, Carl, Michael Binford, Paul Cote, Thomas Edwards, Jr., Steven Ervin, Richard T. T. Forman, Craig Johnson, Ross Kiester, David Mouat, Douglas Olson, Allan Shearer, Richard Toth, and Robin Wills. 1996. *Biodiversity and landscape planning: alternative futures for the region of Camp Pendleton, California.* Cambridge, Massachusetts: Harvard University Graduate School of Design.

Steinitz, Carl, Doug Olson, Allan Shearer, Irene Fairley, and Susan McNally (eds.). 1994. *Alternative futures for Monroe County, Pennsylvania.* Cambridge, Massachusetts: Harvard University Graduate School of Design.

Steinitz, Carl, Paul Parker, and Lawrie Jordan. 1976. "Hand drawn overlays: their history and prospective uses." *Landscape Architecture* 9:444–455.

Stokes, Samuel N., A. Elizabeth Watson, Genevieve P. Keller, and J. Timothy Keller. 1989. *Saving America's countryside.* Baltimore, Maryland: Johns Hopkins University Press.

Stokes, Samuel N., A. Elizabeth Watson, and Shelley Mastran. 1997. *Saving America's countryside: a guide to rural conservation* (2d ed.). Baltimore, Maryland: Johns Hopkins University Press.

Strahler, A. N. 1957. "Quantitative analysis of watershed geomorphology." *Transactions of the American Geophysical Union* 38:913–920.

Sudman, Seymour, and Norman M. Bradburn. 1983. *Asking questions, a practical guide to questionnaire design.* San Francisco, California: Jossey-Bass.

Suplee, Curt. 1998. "Earth's plants imperiled." *International Herald Tribune* (9 April):1 and 4.

Survey Research Center. 1976. *Interviewer's manual* (revised ed.). Ann Arbor, Michigan: Institute for Social Research, University of Michigan.

Sutro, Suzanne. 1984. *Farmland protection strategies for the Connecticut River Valley of Massachusetts.* Philadelphia, Pennsylvania: Mid-Atlantic Regional Office, U.S. National Park Service.

Tahoe Regional Planning Agency. 1982. *Environmental impact statement for the establishment of environmental threshold carrying capacities.* South Lake Tahoe, California.

Tarjuelo, J. M., and J. A. de Juan. 1999. "Crop water management." In *CIGR-handbook, Vol. 1: Land and water engineering,* H. N. van Lier, L. Santos Pereira, and Frederick Steiner eds. St. Joseph, Michigan: American Society of Agricultural Engineers.

Tarlet, Jean. 1985. *La planification écologique: méthodes et techniques.* Paris: Economica.

Tarlet, Jean. 1997. *Intégration des données de l'environnement naturel dans l'aménagement et la gestion de l'espace par la méthode de planification écologique.* Aix Marseille, France: Université de Provence.

Taylor, S. 1992. Editorial. *Australian Planning* August:1–2.

Teller County Planning Commission. 1990. *Growth management plan, Teller County, Colorado.* Cripple Creek, Colorado.

Teller County Planning Commission. 1995. *4-Mile regional action plan.* Cripple Creek, Colorado.

Teller County Planning Commission. 1998a. *Divide regional plan.* Divide, Colorado: Divide Planning Committee.

Teller County Planning Commission. 1998b. *Florissant regional action plan* (draft). Cripple Creek, Colorado: Florissant Planning Committee.

Tempe Daily News Tribune. 1995. Points and viewpoints. December 3:A9.

Thayer, Robert L., Jr. 1994. *Gray world, green heart: technology, nature, and the sustainable landscape.* New York: John Wiley & Sons.

Thompson, George F., and Frederick Steiner (eds.). 1997. *Ecological design and planning.* New York: John Wiley & Sons.

Thompson, J. W. 1993. "A sketching charrette is held in San Francisco." *Landscape Architecture* 83(5):48–56.

Thornbury, William D. 1969. *Principles of geomorphology* (2nd ed.). New York: John Wiley & Sons.

Tiner, R. W. 1984. *Wetlands of the United States: current states and recent trends.* Washington, D.C.: U.S. Fish and Wildlife Service.

Tolba, M. K., O. A. El-Kholy, E. El-Hinnawi, M. W. Holdgate, D. F. McMichael, and R. E. Munn (eds.). 1992. *The world environment 1972–1992.* London: Chapman & Hall.

Toner, William. 1978. *Saving farms and farmlands: a community guide* (PAS Report No. 333). Chicago, Illinois: American Planning Association.

Toner, William. 1981. *Zoning to protect farming: a citizens' guidebook* (National agricultural lands study). Washington, D.C.: U.S. Government Printing Office.

Trancik, Roger. 1986. *Finding lost space.* New York: Van Nostrand Reinhold.

Treu, Maria Christina, and Marcello Magoni. 1998. "The environmental sustainability index in the plan for the Cremona area." In: *Creating Sustainable Places,* Audrey Brichetto Morris ed., pp. 21–27. Tempe, Arizona: Herberger Center for Design Excellence, Arizona State University.

Tuan, Yi-Fu. 1974. *Topophilia: a study of environmental perception attitudes, and values.* Englewood Cliffs, New Jersey: Prentice-Hall.

Turner, Raymond M., and David E. Brown. 1994. "Sonoran desertscrub." In *Biotic communities: southwestern United States and northwestern Mexico,* David E. Brown ed., pp. 190–203. Salt Lake City, Utah: University of Utah Press.

Turoff, M. 1970. "The design of policy Delphi." *Technological Forecasting and Technical Change* 2:149–171.

Turoff, M. 1975. "The policy Delphi." In *The Delphi method: techniques and applications,* H. A. Linstone and M. Turoff eds., pp. 84–100. Reading, Massachusetts: Addison-Wesley Publishing Company.

Tyrwhitt, Jacqueline. 1950. "Surveys for planning." In *Town and country planning textbook.* London: Architectural Press.

U.S. Army Corps of Engineers. 1976. *Final environmental impact statement: New River and Phoenix city streams, Maricopa County, Arizona.* Los Angeles, California.

U.S. Bureau of the Census. 1950, 1960, 1970, 1980, 1990. *U.S. census of the population.* Washington, D.C.: U.S. Department of Commerce, U.S. Government Printing Office.

U.S. Bureau of the Census. 1983. *1980 Census of population, volume 1, characteristics of the population, chapter C, general social and economic characteristics, part 7, Colorado.* Washington, D.C.: U.S. Department of Commerce.

U.S. Bureau of Land Management. 1988. *Public land statistics 1987.* Washington, D.C.: U.S. Department of Interior.

U.S. Bureau of Land Management. 1998. *Public land statistics 1997.* Washington, D.C.: U.S. Department of Interior.

U.S. Congress. 1969. *National environmental policy act of 1968* (Public Law 91-190).

U.S. Congress. 1979. "National forest system land and resource management planning." *Federal Register* 44(181):53983–53999.

U.S. Department of Agriculture. 1983. *National land evaluation and site assessment handbook.* Washington, D.C.: Soil Conservation Service.

U.S. Department of Agriculture. 1984. "Farmland protection policy, final rule." *Federal Register* 49(130):27716–27727.

U.S. Department of the Interior. 1988. "A report to Congress by the Secretary of Interior. The impact of federal programs on wetlands." *The lower Mississippi alluvial plain and prairie pothole region, Vol. I.* Washington, D.C.: U.S. Government Printing Office.

U.S. Department of Transportation. 1976a. *Effective citizen participation in transportation planning. Volume II, a catalog of techniques.* Washington, D.C.: Socio-Economic Studies Division, Federal Highway Administration.

U.S. Department of Transportation. 1976b. *Effective citizen participation in transportation planning, volume 1, community involvement processes.* Washington, D.C.: Socio-Economic Studies Division, Federal Highway Administration.

U.S. General Accounting Office. 1988. *Wetlands, the Corps of Engineers' administration of the Section 404 program.* Washington, D.C.: U.S. Government Printing Office.

U.S. Environmental Protection Agency. 1988. *America's wetlands: our vital link between land and water.* Washington, D.C.: Office of Wetlands Protection, Office of Water.

U.S. Fish and Wildlife Service. 1981. *Standards for the development of habitat suitability index models.* Washington, D.C.: Division of Ecological Services.

U.S. Forest Service. 1973. *National forest landscape management Vol. 1, Agricultural Handbook Number 434.* Washington, D.C.: U.S. Government Printing Office.

U.S. Forest Service. 1974. *National forest landscape management Vol. 2, Agricultural Handbook Number 462.* Washington, D.C.: U.S. Government Printing Office.

U.S. National Park Service. 1985. *Connecticut Valley action program, landowner survey report.* Philadelphia: Mid-Atlantic Regional Office.

U.S. National Park Service. 1986. *Zoning review for the Connecticut River Valley of Massachusetts.* Philadelphia: Mid-Atlantic Regional Office.

U.S. Natural Resources Conservation Service. 1998. *National planning procedures handbook (amendment 2).* Washington, D.C.: U.S. Department of Agriculture.

U.S. Soil Conservation Service. 1978. *National conservation planning manual.* Washington, D.C.: U.S. Department of Agriculture.

University of Pennsylvania. 1985. *Landscape architecture and regional planning 501 course primer.* Philadelphia, Pennsylvania: Department of Landscape Architecture and Regional Planning.

Urban Ecology, Inc. 1996. *Blueprint for a sustainable Bay Area.* Oakland, California.

Van der Ryn, Sim, and Stuart Cowan. 1996. *Ecological design.* Washington, D.C.: Island Press.

van der Wal, Coenraad. 1997. *In Praise of the ordinary.* Rotterdam, The Netherlands 010 Publishers.

Ventura, Steve. 1988. *Dane county soil erosion control plan.* Dane County, Wisconsin.

Verburg, Edwin A., and Richard A. Coon. 1987. "Planning in the U.S. Fish and Wildlife Service." *Trends* 24(2):20–26.

Verma, Niraj. 1998. *Similarities, connections, and systems: the search for a new rationality for planning and management.* Lanham, Maryland: Lexington Books.

Vink, A. P. A. 1975. *Land use in advancing agriculture.* New York: Springer-Verlag.

Vroom, M. J., J. B. Struik, and M. W. M. van der Toorn. 1980. *Landscape planning in coastal areas* (Annex-B). Wageningen, The Netherlands: Agricultural University Department of Landscape Architecture.

Waananen, A. O., J. T. Limerinos, W. J. Kockelman, W. E. Spangle, and M. L. Blair. 1977. *Flood-prone areas and land-use planning–selected from the San Francisco bay region* (U.S. Geological Survey Professional Paper 942).

Wackernagel, Mathis, and William Rees. 1996. *Our ecological footprint: reducing human impact on the earth.* Gabriola Island, British Columbia: New Society Publishers.

Wagner, J. Alan. 1974. "Recreational carrying capacity reconsidered." *Journal of Forestry* 72(5):274–278.

Wallace, McHarg, Roberts, and Todd. 1969. *Ecological study for Twin Cities Metropolitan Region, Minnesota.* Prepared for Metropolitan Council of the Twin Cities Area. Philadelphia, Pennsylvania: National Technical Information Series, U.S. Department of Commerce.

Wallace, McHarg, Roberts, and Todd. 1972. *An ecological planning study for Wilmington and Dover, Vermont.* Brattleboro, Vermont: Windham Regional Planning and Development Commission and the Vermont State Planning Office.

Wallace, McHarg, Roberts, and Todd. 1976. *Lake Austin growth management plan.* Austin, Texas: Department of Planning, City of Austin.

Walters, Kenneth, and P. A. Glancy. 1969. *Reconnaissance of geology and ground-water occurrence in Whitman County, Washington.* Water Supply Bulletin No. 26. Olympia, Washington: Washington Department of Water Resources.

Want, W. L. 1990. *Law of wetlands regulation* (also 1992 revised edition). New York: Clark Boardman Company.

Wardwell, John M., and C. Jack Gilchrist. 1980. "The distribution of population and energy in nonmetropolitan areas: confluence and divergence." *Social Science Quarterly* 61(3 and 4):567–580.

Washington Department of Ecology. 1984. *State environmental policy act (SEPA) handbook.* Olympia, Washington.

Washington Department of Ecology. 1995. *State environmental policy act (SEPA) handbook.* Olympia, Washington.

Weber, Bruce, and Richard Beck. 1979. *Minimizing public costs of residential growth* (WREP 17). Corvallis, Oregon: Western Rural Development Center, Oregon State University.

West, James. 1978. "Walworth County case study—an addendum." In *Farmland preservation planning,* Peter W. Amato ed., pp. 101–105. Madison: University of Wisconsin-Extension.

Westman, Walter E. 1985. *Ecology, impact assessment, and environmental planning.* New York: John Wiley & Sons.

Whitehand, J. W. R. (ed.). 1981. *The urban landscape: historical development and management.* London: Academic Press.

Whitman County Regional Planning Council. 1978. *Whitman County comprehensive plan.* Colfax, Washington.

Whitmore, William A. 1993. "Verde River visual assessment: a study of methods" (unpublished master of environmental planning thesis). Tempe, Arizona: Arizona State University Department of Planning.

Whitmore, William A., Edward Cook, and Frederick Steiner. 1995. "Public involvement in visual assessment: the Verde River corridor study." *Landscape Journal* 14(1):26–45.

Wickersham, Kirk, Jr. 1978. "Reform of discretionary land-use decision-making: point systems and beyond." *Zoning and Planning Law Report* 1(9):65–71.

Wilkinson, Charles F., and H. Michael Anderson. 1985. "Land and resource planning in national forests." *Oregon Law Review* 64(1 & 2):1–373.

Williams, M. 1990. "Understanding wetlands." In *Wetlands, a threatened landscape,* M. Williams ed., pp. 1–41. Oxford, U.K.: Basil Blackwell.

Wilson, Alex, Jennifer L. Uncapher, Lisa McManigal, L. Hunter Lovins, Maureen Cureton, and William D. Browning. 1998. *Green development: integrating ecology and real estate.* New York: John Wiley & Sons.

Wischmeier, W. H., and D. D. Smith. 1965. *Predicting rainfall—erosion losses from cropland east of the Rocky Mountains: guide for selection of practices for soil and water conservation* (Agricultural Handbook No. 282). Washington, D.C.: U.S. Department of Agriculture.

Wischmeier, W. H., and D. D. Smith. 1978. *Predicting rainfall—erosion losses: a guide to conservation planning* (Agricultural Handbook No. 537). Washington, D.C.: U.S. Department of Agriculture.

Wisconsin Supreme Court. 1972. *Just vs. Marinette County* (4 ERC 1842).

World Commission on Environment and Development (WCED). 1987. *Our common future.* Oxford, UK: Oxford University Press.

World Wildlife Fund. 1992. *Statewide wetlands strategies: a guide to protecting and managing the resource.* Washington, D.C.: Island Press.

Wright, John B. 1993. *Rocky Mountain Divide: selling and saving the West.* Austin, Texas: University of Texas Press.

Wright, Lloyd. 1981. "Agricultural land evaluation and assessment systems: pilot program" (unpublished briefing paper). Washington, D.C.: Soil Conservation Service, U.S. Department of Agriculture.

Wright, Lloyd, Steve Aradas, Ron Darden, Sue Pfluger, and Warren Zitzmann. 1982. "Farmland: want to protect?" *Planning* 48(7):20–21.

Xiang, Wei-Ning. 1996. "GIS-based riparian buffer analysis: injecting geographic information into landscape planning." *Landscape and Urban Planning* 34:1–10.

Yaro, Robert D., Randall G. Arendt, Harry L. Dodson, and Elizabeth A. Brabec. 1988. *Dealing with change in the Connecticut River Valley: a design manual for conservation and development.* Amherst, Massachusetts: Center for Rural Massachusetts, University of Massachusetts.

Yaro, Robert D., and Tony Hiss. 1996. *A region at risk: the third regional plan for the New York–New Jersey–Connecticut metropolitan area.* Washington, D.C.: Island Press.

Young, Gerald L. 1974. "Human ecology as an interdisciplinary concept: a critical inquiry." *Advances in Ecological Research* 8:1–105.

Young, Gerald L. 1976. "Environmental law: perspectives from human ecology." *Environmental Law* 6(2):289–307.

Young, Gerald L. 1978. *Human ecology as an interdisciplinary domain: an epitesmological bibliography.* Monticello, Illinois: Vance Bibliographies.

Young, Gerald L. 1989. "A conceptual framework for an interdisciplinary human ecology." *Acta Oecologiae Hominis* 1:1–136.

Young, Gerald L. (ed.). 1983. *Origins of human ecology.* Stroudsburg, Pennsylvania: Hutchinson Ross Publishing.

Young, Gerald L., Frederick Steiner, Kenneth Brooks, and Kenneth Struckmeyer. 1983. "Determining the regional context for landscape planning." *Landscape Planning* 10(4):269–296.

Zube, Ervin H. 1980. *Environmental evaluation.* Monterey, California: Brooks/Cole.

Zube, Ervin H., Gary Hartshorn, Peter Kareiva, Lloyd Loope, Thomas Loveland, James W. Merchant, Maurice Nyquist, James Quinn, Terry L. Root, Frederick Steiner, and John Terborg. 1994. *Peer review panel report of the national GAP analysis program from the national biological survey.* Moscow, Idaho: National Biological Survey.

Zube, Ervin H., James L. Sell, and Jonathan G. Taylor. 1982. "Landscape perception: research, application and theory." *Landscape Planning* 9:1–33.

INDEX

ABOUT THE AUTHOR

Frederick Steiner directs the School of Planning and Landscape Architecture at Arizona State University. As a professional planner, he has participated in a number of community and regional plans, in Arizona, Colorado, Washington, Rhode Island, and elsewhere. In 1997, he received a grant from the U.S. Environmental Protection Agency's Sustainable Development Program with David Pijawka. He was the 1998 Rome Prize Fellow in Historic Preservation and Conservation at the American Academy in Rome and was a 1980 Fulbright research scholar in The Netherlands. The author of many professional papers and books in addition to the first edition of this book, he holds B.S., M.C.P., M.R.P., M.A., and Ph.D. degrees in planning and design from the University of Cincinnati and the University of Pennsylvania.